# THE DICTIONARY OF
# WORLD POLITICS

# THE DICTIONARY OF WORLD POLITICS

## A Reference Guide to
## Concepts, Ideas and Institutions

Graham Evans

and

Jeffrey Newnham

*University of Wales, Swansea*

## SIMON & SCHUSTER

*A Paramount Communications Company*

New York    London    Toronto    Sydney    Tokyo    Singapore

First published in the UK in 1990 by
Harvester Wheatsheaf
66 Wood Lane End, Hemel Hempstead
Hertfordshire HP2 4RG
A division of
Simon & Schuster International Group

and in the USA by
Academic Reference Division
Simon & Schuster
15 Columbus Circle
New York, NY10023
A Paramount Communications Company

Printed and bound in Great Britain at
The University Press, Cambridge

---

*Library of Congress Cataloging-in-Publication Data*

---

Evans, Graham.
  The dictionary of world politics: a reference guide
to concepts, ideas, and institutions/Graham Evans
and Jeffrey Newnham.
    p.    cm.
  ISBN 0-13-210527-6
  1. Political science—Dictionaries. I. Newnham,
Jeffrey.
II. Title.
JA61.E85 1990
320′.03—dc20                                    90-46772
                                                    CIP

---

1  2  3  4  5   94  93  92  91  90

To the memory of Agnes, Tom and David Evans,
who would have enjoyed it
(GE)

To my mother, and to the memory of my father
(JDN)

The earth is not so old, after all, and never it seems, has it been in so interesting a state.

Robert Musil, *The Man Without Qualities*, quoted in Merle, M. (1987), *The Sociology of International Relations*, p. 5.

# CONTENTS

# PREFACE

I first became aware of the need for a comprehensive dictionary of world politics when I began to study the subject at the postgraduate level in the late 1960s and early 1970s. At that time it was emerging as a fairly discrete entity in Europe but more especially in the United States where it had successfully established itself as something other than a mere sub-branch of the study of politics. However, despite a general orientation in the academic community in favour of regarding it as a separate discipline it was still an 'unruly flock of activities' with no overarching consensus about what was to be studied or how. It seemed to me then, as it does with even greater force now, that the eclectic nature of the discipline, along with its seemingly unlimited range and scope, cried out for a single-volume study devoted to the clarification of what might be termed its key concepts and major institutions. Although the history of academic inquiry into world politics is a relatively recent one, its proliferation in the second half of the twentieth century, inspired by social scientific borrowing, has given rise to a somewhat bewildering variety of methodologies, theories, frameworks for analysis, hypotheses, concepts, ideas and allusions. Such growth presents a daunting prospect even to the most industrious and diligent student. At the very least, acquiring just a rudimentary grasp of the structures and processes of world politics, whether it be from the standpoint of the scholar or the practitioner, requires some acquaintance with politics, history, law, philosophy, economics, sociology, psychology and anthropology as well as a knowledge of languages and cultures other than one's own, and perhaps a smattering of mathematics thrown in for good measure.

Clearly, the need for such a volume was self-evident. By the same token, the reason for its absence from the library shelves was obvious. Unless each entry is framed out to individual experts in a number of stipulated areas, it is difficult to imagine any one scholar possessing the necessary background to be able to offer a comprehensive and sophisticated guide – both to the state of the discipline itself and to the range of activities it purports to explain and describe.

To avoid the confines of the one-scholar approach, and mindful of the probable extravagance of the many, my colleague Jeffrey Newnham was invited to join the enterprise in the hope that such a pooling of resources would produce both economies of production and breadth of perspective. Coming from a background more sympathetic to the social scientific approach, he could leave me free to deal with the classical or traditional aspects of the work. Attacking it from two directions would not only reflect the eclecticism of the subject but hopefully strengthen the end product. In support of the dictum that the whole is more than the sum of the parts, a number of entries were more avowedly collaborative. At all times we endeavoured to present, albeit from our different perspectives, a consistency of style and content which would achieve a maximum amount of convergence and a minimum of dissonance.

# PREFACE

Entry length varies considerably and this is a function not merely of the importance of particular items but also of the availability of material connected to them: the general rule being that some items, important though they may be to the subject, are essentially non-contentious or are adequately covered elsewhere in easily digested forms. Our overall purpose was not just to write a book about world politics. We also wanted to make a contribution to it. The entries therefore are not mere explication, they do represent distinct points of view.

The selection of entries was governed by two main considerations: first those ideas, concepts and institutions which we considered essential to any understanding of world politics (e.g. power, hegemony, diplomacy) and second those which, although important, are likely to be found only in specialized texts or journals (e.g. trilateralism, unit veto or heartland). Inevitably, selection of items for inclusion or exclusion is to some extent discretionary. In many ways, the enterprise is comparable to the compilation of an anthology of poetry – some of the 'greats' must go in, but some leeway is given for personal (if not idiosyncratic) choice. As far as possible, we avoided entries on individuals except where their names were associated with particular ideas or policies (e.g. Hobbesian or Truman doctrine). Some events get in because of their continued relevance (e.g. Vietnam War or Camp David accords) but in general these have been avoided. The book does not claim to provide an exhaustive compendium of references, but we do hope that we have presented an intelligible guide through the maze of complex issues and phenomena which make world politics such a fascinating, often tragic, dimension of social behaviour.

Linkage is an important feature of any dictionary (perhaps even more so in one dealing with foreign policy issues) and accordingly the work has a cross-reference facility. The items in small capitals in the text are those which might be usefully followed up to gain a more extensive explanation, or to indicate the family of ideas to which the particular entry belongs. For example, the entry on REALISM contains references to THUCYDIDES, HOBBESIAN, the STATE, the STATE-SYSTEM, POWER, SELF-HELP, SOVEREIGNTY, NATIONAL INTEREST, BALANCE OF POWER, INTERNATIONAL LAW, ORGANIZATION, EQUALITY, HIGH POLITICS, GREAT POWERS and ANARCHY – all of which, singly or together, should provide the reader with a comprehensive overview of the item in question. At the end of the book a select bibliography has been provided, both to give guidance for further study and to acknowledge sources.

Graham Evans
Swansea, December 1989

# ACKNOWLEDGEMENTS

The authors particularly wish to thank Professor Jack Spence for his advice and encouragement throughout the project, Professor Paul Wilkinson for his pertinent comments upon an earlier draft, Professor Neil Harding for casting a critical eye over the 'A's during the gestation stage and Professor George Boyce for being there. In addition the following have helped, directly or indirectly, in producing this volume: Valerie Davies, Phyllis Hancock, Sharon Hansard, Pat Yates, Rosamund Bryar, Ian Jeffries and James McNamara. Clare Grist, Commissioning Editor for Harvester Wheatsheaf, would without doubt make a good diplomat if she ever left publishing! The Library staff at University College, Swansea were unfailingly helpful and courteous – thanks, in particular, to Paul Reynolds and Hazel Pember of the Inter-Library Loan section. Graham Evans would especially like to thank Val, Anwen and Pero who endured with good humour and fortitude the often painful lulls between thought, word, Tipp-Ex and processor. Jeff Newnham notes that during the production of the volume all his children have left the family home but promises not to make any connections with his scholarship.

# The Dictionary of
# World Politics

# A

**ABM**

Anti-ballistic missile. This is a system of interceptor missiles and accompanying RADARS which would seek to defend designated targets against incoming offensive missiles. Until the STRATEGIC DEFENSE INITIATIVE of the 1980s, it was always assumed that an ABM system could most effectively be deployed as a 'point' defence of 'hard' targets (e.g. missile silos). However, the systems first mooted in the 1960s were susceptible to various countermeasures, in particular, pre-emptive attacks on their radars. Furthermore, the development of multiple independently targeted re-entry vehicles (MIRVs) meant that any system could potentially be saturated by incoming missiles and confused by decoys all carried on one 'bus'. The originally envisaged ABM systems would have intercepted incoming missiles relatively late in their midcourse phase, thus creating the paradox that high altitude defensive detonations would severely degrade the environment of the defender.

The shortcomings of these earlier systems led to the ABM Treaty of 1972. This limited ABM deployment to two sites: one to protect the capital, the other an intercontinental ballistic missile (ICBM) site. In 1974 a further PROTOCOL was agreed limiting ABM deployment to one site. The US system was dismantled in 1975 although the Soviet Union continues to deploy the Galosh system around Moscow.

The TECHNOLOGY of space-based defence, developed during the 1980s, implies that some offensive missiles could be destroyed before re-entry into the earth's atmosphere. The significance of the type of system discussed above would therefore be reduced.

**Absolutism**

Political term usually associated with domestic politics and usually denoting a system of government which is not limited by internal institutions or laws. Many European STATES in the seventeenth and eighteenth centuries displayed this feature. In the twentieth century 'absolutism' has given way to 'totalitarianism' (though the two are not synonymous: the latter refers to total control of all aspects of society while the former refers strictly to the possession of power). In INTERNATIONAL POLITICS the term is used in two ways:

1. as above, referring to political systems extant in the post-Westphalian European STATE-SYSTEM.
2. as a metaphor to give strength to the BILLIARD BALL concept of the NATION-STATE which assumes 'absolute' internal cohesion and a single unified DECISION-MAKING structure.

Most modern writers shun the term because of its inaccurate description of the character of the nation-state and its intrinsic vagueness.

**Accidental war**

The term may appropriately be used in two senses. First, where WAR occurs literally by 'accident'; thus through some technical malfunction an act of violence occurs which nobody intended. A variation of this might be where, through insubordination or incompetence, an individual or group commits an act of violence, against the intentions of the political leadership, which leads to WAR.

Secondly, accidental war may occur because one or a number of parties in conflict misread the situation and initiate violence. 'Accident' in this second sense may be seen as a function of MISPERCEPTION rather than technical failure or failure in the chain of command. This misperception is particularly likely in periods of CRISIS where time pressure is a situational factor which often accounts for considerable psychological stress among political leaders and their senior advisors. Historians and political scientists have identified the European crisis of the summer of 1914 as exemplifying many of the characteristics of accidental war in both senses used here.

The advent of NUCLEAR WEAPONS has greatly increased concern about preventing accidental war. ARMS CONTROL theories and measures have been directed to reduce the incentives to attack and to seek to reassure adversaries, particularly in times of crisis, that they can manage the situation without recourse to war. Attention has also concentrated upon the PROLIFERATION of nuclear weapons and the likelihood that this will increase the dangers of accidental war.
*See also*: CRISIS MANAGEMENT; PRE-EMPTION

## Accommodation

Term much beloved of CRISIS MANAGEMENT theorists and practitioners of negotiational DIPLOMACY. It refers to the process whereby ACTORS in CONFLICT agree to recognize some of the others' claims while not sacrificing their basic interests. The source of conflict is not removed but the AGGRESSION it often generates is presumed to be. It assumes that international conflict is not ZERO–SUM, where the gain of one party is automatically the loss of the other. It also assumes that total HARMONY OF INTEREST does not prevail. Thus, it can be described as a half-way house (place of 'accommodation') between confrontation and harmony. The term is normally used in association with 'interests' and as such is not without sophistry.

## Accuracy

A term used in strategic analysis. The ability to hit a desired target at any required distance is obviously a function of any weapon TECHNOLOGY. The development of AIR WARFARE and NUCLEAR WEAPONS in the twentieth century substantially increased the importance of this variable. Accuracy is now expressed in terms of Circular Error Probable and is widely applied, as a comprehensive measure, on all surface-to-surface missiles. Combined with the yield or size of the warhead, therefore, it is possible to compute the lethality of any such system. Other factors being equal, the more accurate the missile and the greater the yield the more damage it can inflict. Again technology has increased the accuracy factor of missiles to such an extent that operational planners are now able to consider COUNTERFORCE options in a way that was not feasible in the third quarter of the century.

## ACP

African, Caribbean and Pacific. This is EUROPEAN COMMUNITY shorthand for those STATES in the THIRD WORLD which have negotiated a special AID and trade REGIME with the states of the Community. The TREATIES drawn up to establish this regime were signed at YAOUNDÉ and LOMÉ, respectively. Currently these relations are governed by the third Lomé Convention signed in December 1984. On this occasion the ACP states numbered sixty-six. It should be noted that many of the more significant states of the Third World in Latin America and Asia are not covered by this regime. In the future, regional groupings such as the Association of South East Asian Nations (ASEAN) might provide preferable vehicles for negotiation between Western Europe and the Third World.

## Acquiescence

Term used in INTERNATIONAL LAW to indicate recognition of territorial claims. Acquiescence itself is not a mode of acquisition, but it can strengthen a claim if it is accompanied by a degree of control over the territory in question.

## Action–reaction

The term which describes a relationship where two ACTORS are stimulated to respond to what the other is doing in an immediate reactive way. The term has been widely applied to CONFLICT analysis, particularly by GAME THEORISTS and scholars influenced by behavioural psychology. Students of ARMS RACES, such as Lewis Fry Richardson, have applied action–reaction ideas to this phenomenon. According to the Richardson process, therefore, STATE A reacts to State B's increase in military CAPABILITY by increasing its own expenditure. State B perceives this as justifying its own initiative but, at the same time feeling that A's reaction has reduced its margin of safety, B further increases its own arms budget. Richardson's work on action–reaction in arms races is set out in *Arms and Insecurity* (1960). Like many models, Richardson processes represent highly simplified versions of the real world and few would want to attempt to support the proposition that arms races cause WARS.

Nonetheless, arms races frequently precede hostilities and may, in themselves, contribute to the tension and hostility associated with violent conflict.

Action–reaction ideas have also been applied to DECISION-MAKING. The influence here has been particularly felt from behavioural psychology. Sometimes the term input–output is used rather than action–reaction. In this approach decision-making is conducted by a system. The system reacts to its environment, which includes other decision-making systems. Thus an action–reaction pattern can be again stipulated. The application of action–reaction models to decision-making in WORLD POLITICS was widely established in the third quarter of the century as a productive and plausible way of conceiving the activity.

## Act of war

Literally, any act which is incompatible with a state of PEACE. Under customary INTERNATIONAL LAW states had the right to resort to WAR whenever they deemed it necessary. The principal restraint upon this behaviour was thus the laws of warfare. Distinction must immediately be made between the laws covering the conduct of war – *jus in bello* – and the laws governing the resort to conflict – *JUS AD BELLUM*. The idea of an act of war, therefore, properly comes under *jus ad bellum*.

Before the establishment of universal international institutions in the twentieth century, there was a good deal of auto-interpretation attached to this concept. In practice states could decide for themselves what constituted an act of war. Once war had been declared between the parties then notice was served upon the whole state system that relations had changed from peace to war. A complicating factor in this was the ALLIANCE. States entering alliances took upon themselves obligations to fight each other's wars. If the alliance was to function properly the parties needed to know what constituted an act of war against themselves whereby the alliance would become operational. This is referred to as the *casus foederis*.

The current century has seen important changes in the laws of war, both 'ad bellum' and 'in bello'. Treaty law, such as that set out in the UNITED NATIONS CHARTER, now draws a clear distinction between the legal and illegal use of FORCE. The presumption is now made that force can only be used in SELF-DEFENCE. In the absence of more effective means of CONFLICT RESOLUTION, states still resort to force. The twentieth century has required its statesmen to be more imaginative in seeking justification for doing so than in the past. At the same time use of less direct modes of AGGRESSION, such as GUERRILLA WARFARE, have made it more difficult to apply the laws of war. External INTERVENTION in civil wars has become widespread in the twentieth century. Some of the most intractable regional conflicts – such as the ARAB–ISRAELI CONFLICT – originated as communal differences. In sum, just as international lawyers have attempted to establish new criteria for the use of force, other developments have increased uncertainties.

*See also*: AGGRESSION, BELLIGERENCY.

## Actor

Any entity which plays an identifiable role in INTERNATIONAL RELATIONS may be termed an actor. The Pope, the SECRETARY GENERAL of the UN, British Petroleum, Botswana and the IMF are thus all actors. The term is now widely used by both scholars and practitioners in international relations as it is a way of avoiding the obvious limitations of the word STATE. Although it lacks precision it does possess scope and flexibility. Its use also conveys the variety of personalities, organizations and institutions that play a role at present. Some authors have argued that, in effect, the system can be conceived of as a MIXED ACTOR model because the relative significance of the state has been reduced. More precise distinctions between actors can be made by introducing additional criteria. Such criteria might include the tasks performed by actors and the constituency affected by this task performance. Some commentators suggest that actors should be judged according to their degree of AUTONOMY rather than the legalistic concept of SOVEREIGNTY.

*See also*: PLURALISM.

## Adjudication

A method of settling disputes by referring them to an established court, as such it ought not to be confused with ARBITRATION. The basis of adjudication is that the adjudicator applies INTERNATIONAL LAW to settle the dispute. The creation of the WORLD COURT in the present century has meant that the means for international adjudication now exist on a permanent basis. In 1920 the PERMANENT COURT OF INTERNATIONAL JUSTICE was established by the LEAGUE OF NATIONS and between 1922 and 1940 it made thirty-three judgements and gave twenty-seven advisory opinions. In 1945 the INTERNATIONAL COURT OF JUSTICE (ICJ) was established as its successor. The main difficulties both courts have experienced are the limitations upon their jurisdiction. Parties can only submit a case for adjudication by express consent, although there is an optional clause in the statute of the ICJ (see Article 36). Moreover, only STATES may be party to cases before the Court (Article 34). This has had the effect that important non-state ACTORS, including individuals, cannot directly initiate litigation.

It must be recognized that many disputes are simply not justiciable. International actors find that other modes of CONFLICT settlement allow greater flexibility for bargaining and compromise and do not imply the same loss of control over the outcome that is inherent in adjudication. Also, international law tends to have a STATUS QUO orientation. REVISIONIST states thus tend to find that the use of adjudication does not allow sufficient scope for peaceful change. This must be said notwithstanding the ability of the World Court to apply principles *EX AEQUO ET BONO* if the parties agree (see Article 38).

Although the World Court represents the most significant attempt yet to apply the rule of law in international disputes instead of the more traditional modes of settlement (WAR, DIPLOMACY, ARBITRATION), it is severely hampered in its operation by the absence of the principle of compulsory jurisdiction. International adjudication is always dependent on the consent of states, and this is rarely given on matters of vital importance. The doctrine of SOVEREIGNTY is therefore seen by many as an insuperable barrier to the development of the international judicial system. Compulsory jurisdiction is not on the horizon and the international judicial process has played no significant part in the major issues of WORLD POLITICS since 1946 (e.g. the COLD WAR, the anti-colonial revolution, the NORTH–SOUTH division, or the regulation of NUCLEAR WEAPONS).

## Administered territory

Refers to the 'Mandates system' established in Article XXII of the Covenant of the LEAGUE OF NATIONS usually credited to Jan Smuts but actually first proposed by G. L. Beer, a member of Woodrow Wilson's staff at Paris in 1919. It involved control and administration, though not SOVEREIGNTY, over former COLONIAL possessions of Germany (in Africa and the Pacific) and Turkey (in the Near and Middle East) and was largely a US-inspired attempt to avoid the traditional IMPERIAL relationship. Administration of these territories was ceded to certain 'responsible' STATES in 'sacred trust' to the League. Thus South Africa, by mandate in 1920, was given administrative responsibility for the former German South-West Africa (now Namibia). The principles

of trusteeship, tutelage, guardianship and ultimately international supervision and control were envisaged but the international supervisionary dimension, as instanced by the case of Namibia, has proved a particularly difficult matter to enforce. The system was clearly a compromise between outright ANNEXATION of these territories and direct international administration. The struggle between the old REALIST and the newer IDEALIST approaches can be seen in the language of the Article dealing in this matter: it was designed to foster and develop territories 'which are inhabited by people not yet able to stand by themselves under the strenuous conditions of the modern world' (Article XXII). The term 'stand by themselves' is clearly a reference to the principle of SELF-DETERMINATION, the intention being that the mandatory state held administrative authority until such time (to be determined by the League) that these territories and their populations became sufficiently sophisticated to manage self-rule and achieve full legal title. To this end three classes of mandate were introduced depending on the degree of development attained and a Permanent Mandates Commission was established to oversee the process. With the creation of the UN the mandates system and administered territory was transmuted into the system. Most of the former territories have now achieved full INDEPENDENCE (including Israel, Jordan, LEBANON, Syria and Iraq) with the notable and continuing exception of Namibia. The latter, which represents the last unresolved legacy of the First World War, is now set, under UN supervision, to achieve independence in 1990.

Despite its obvious faults and despite what today might appear to be its paternalistic overtones it should be noted that the mandates system was 'the world's first experiment in the international control of dependent territories' (F. S. Northedge, *The League of Nations*, 1976). In this way, it contributed much to the downfall of the COLONIAL system that had hitherto dominated INTERNATIONAL RELATIONS.

## Afghanistan

Under the BREZHNEV DOCTRINE, which claimed rights of INTERVENTION on the part of the Soviet Union in 'threatened' socialist STATES, Afghanistan was invaded by Russian troops in December 1979. Ostensibly the intervention was by invitation but Western observers speculated that the move was inspired by traditional Soviet expansionism involving access to the Persian Gulf oilfields and a warm water port. The fact that Afghanistan is LANDLOCKED weighed lightly in this GEOPOLITICAL analysis. The invasion was widely condemned in the West and by NON-ALIGNED states and heralded a re-evaluation of the process of DETENTE. The war that ensued between the Soviet Union and the Afghan partisans (the Mujaheddin) proved extremely costly and is often referred to as 'Russia's VIETNAM'. It has been estimated that since 1979 a total of 1.24 million people have died, including over 13,000 Soviet personnel. In 1985, the new Soviet leader Mikhail Gorbachev signalled his intention to withdraw. In 1988 this was confirmed at peace talks in Geneva when the Soviet Union timetabled a complete withdrawal by 15 February, 1989.

The Afghanistan invasion, which involved over 80,000 Soviet army and air force personnel, was the first large-scale military expedition by the Soviet Union outside the WARSAW PACT area since the Second World War. Although overall it must be regarded as an abject failure, the military lessons learnt will improve the fighting CAPABILITY of the Red Army. In the first place, a new generation of Soviet officers has gained practical battlefield experience. Secondly, a review of military tactics (similar to the one undertaken by the Americans after Vietnam) will undoubtedly give greater flexibility to the Soviet military machine to enable it to fight a highly mobile unconventional WAR against a largely unseen enemy. Western observers have pointed out that during the initial stages of the war, Soviet tactics had changed little since the 1940s, i.e. concentrations of massed mechanized units making occasional highly vulnerable forays into the Afghanistan countryside. In particular, greater use of AIR POWER, both in terms of troop transport and of ground support, is likely to feature in future Soviet military planning. In addition, an enhanced role for the Soviet special forces ('Spetsnaz') is widely predicted since these units were most effective in employing COUNTER-INSURGENCY methods. In the third place, Afghanistan provided a testing ground for new Soviet weaponry and by all accounts these weapons performed well.

While the Soviet withdrawal was generally welcomed by the international community and while it provided evidence of Gorbachev's 'new thinking' on Soviet FOREIGN POLICY, the net costs to Afghanistan are incalculable. Outside intervention has ceased, but internal strife remains.

## Aggression

This word has a number of distinct meanings. It is used in INTERNATIONAL LAW and INTERNATIONAL ORGANIZATION as a concept and a form of proscribed behaviour. It has been widely studied by social scientists, in particular by psychologists and social psychologists. It is a term used in political discourse and debate, usually in a perjorative and condemnatory way. Consideration of the term will largely concentrate upon the first two contexts suggested above.

1. In law, the term aggression has been used to distinguish between JUST and unjust WARS and between legal and illegal FORCE.

Broadly it refers to an illegal, unjustified, improper or immoral attack or INTERVENTION by one STATE, or its agents, upon another. As such, it is 'offensive' rather than 'defensive', although the notion of a pre-emptive strike can blur even this broad distinction. It is usual to distinguish between 'direct' aggression (e.g. Japan's attack on PEARL HARBOR in 1941) and 'indirect' aggression (e.g. the American U2 spy-flights over the Soviet Union between

1955–60). Again, in common international usage it may not be limited to overt or covert military acts as in the examples above, but may take the form of economic measures employed by states against others (e.g. BLOCKADES or BOYCOTTS).

The difficulty of definition and the manifest lack of a common international standard has not inhibited its employment as a central concept in theories of peaceful change. In so far as international law has attempted to regulate the behaviour of states and establish universally agreed methods of promoting NATIONAL INTERESTS, efforts have been made from the beginning of the STATE-SYSTEM to label and consequently forbid 'aggression'. Medieval theories of the JUST WAR can be seen as faltering, though oblique steps in this direction. In a sense, international law has always concerned itself with this issue, but it was in the aftermath of the First World War that more self-conscious efforts were made by the international community to pinpoint and thus eliminate its occurrence. The Covenant of the LEAGUE OF NATIONS, with its emphasis on the doctrine of COLLECTIVE SECURITY was premised on the belief that (a) aggression could be easily identified and (b) that the rest of the international community could, in concert, rise up against its perpetrators. Neither assumption held and it is commonly argued that the League floundered, at least in part, because of its inability to deal with this problem. The omission of definition of aggression from the Charter of the UN, and the allocation of the task of determining its occurrence to the SECURITY COUNCIL was a tacit recognition by the framers of the need for political REALISM in the new organization. 'Acts of aggression' were what the Security Council decided them to be; thus the invasion of South Korea by the North in June 1950 was, in the absence of the Soviet representative, deemed to fall into this category.

Apart from these international institutions, the most thorough attempt at definition was made in 1933 by Litvinov, the Soviet foreign minister in the Convention for the Definition of Aggression. In this view, the phenomenon occurs when any of the following take place: (a) a declaration of WAR is made against another state; (b) an armed invasion of another's territory, without a declaration of war; (c) an attack without a declaration of war, on the territory, naval vessels or aircraft of another state; (d) a naval blockade of the ports or coast of another state; (e) aid to invading armed bands within another state and a refusal to take all possible measures on its own territory to deprive the armed bands of aid and protection. There has been no definition as specific as this since 1933. It became more obscure during the COLD WAR from 1946 onwards, when the term itself was caught up in the ideological rivalry between the United States and the Soviet Union.

Thus, apart from its general legal definition (a resort to war or measures or armed coercion undertaken in violations of TREATY obligations), the term defies stricter delineation. Indeed, the term and the phenomena it describes is endemic in the anarchical system, the main feature of which is a jealously guarded and permissive interpretation of the doctrine of SOVEREIGNTY. Attempts to define and hence limit its occurrence are inevitably bound up with the degree of cohesion the international community achieves.

2. The SOCIAL SCIENCE APPROACH to aggression may be divided, in broad terms, into those who favour an instinct theory of aggression and those who favour a learning theory of aggression. Instinct theory argues that man is innately aggressive, whereas learning theory argues that aggression is a response to various situations that individuals encounter from early childhood. All the social sciences and applied studies, such as criminology, have taken an interest in the concept, its definition, causes and manifestations. Social science, moreover, would distinguish between aggression as an attitude, or predisposition, and aggression as overt behaviour. Thus someone feeling

aggressive might not express it overtly, or might displace or project that aggression into a substitute object.

At the turn of the century Freud argued for a drive towards death – *thanatos* – as an intrinsic part of human nature. Consequentially, aggression was an instinct. This powerful, but probably erroneous, idea took hold of popular thinking about aggression thereafter. Apart from the need to treat the concept of an instinct with great caution, most social scientists reject neo-Freudian approaches to aggression. Important research published in the 1930s in the United States suggested that aggression might be regarded as a function of the amount of FRUSTRATION experienced by an individual. The rather dogmatic position of the early social scientists on frustration–aggression has been modified of late with researchers preferring to regard frustration as an instigator of aggression. More recently, social scientists have built upon these ideas to suggest that much aggression is learned as a result of socialization. Aggression is thus seen as instrumental rather than instinctive. Most social systems tend to encourage assertive and competitive behaviour while ritualized forms of aggression – for example in competitive sports – are rewarded both in material wealth and social status.

It is difficult to extrapolate from the individual behaviour motivations to the types of violence within and between societies that can broadly be called social CONFLICT. Moreover, studies of combat soldiers have suggested that obedience to authority and/ or feelings of solidarity with fellow soldiers are stronger motives than aggression in explaining why people are willing to kill on the battlefield. Modern TECHNOLOGY has made killing more efficient and more remote; it has also separated the political decision to go to war from the battlefield decision to kill and be killed. Moreover, the study of DECISION-MAKING in INTERNATIONAL POLITICS would tend to suggest that the actual decision to go to war cannot be properly explained via aggression

theories. Other psychological states of mind may be equally significant and important cultural, social and environmental factors cannot be ignored.

## AIC

Advanced Industrial Countries. UN abbreviation for North America, Western Europe, Japan and Australasia. These STATES are often referred to simply as the NORTH in documents such as the BRANDT REPORT, 1980.

## Aid

The transfer of goods and services between international ACTORS on a concessionary basis. Aid is an extremely generalized term. It covers both grants and loans, both BILATERAL and MULTILATERAL, both governmental and private. It excludes, specifically, commercial transactions where the donor makes no concessions. Aid may be given without strings or it may be tied in some way by the donor so that the recipient is restricted in the way the aid is utilized. Aid may be given for humanitarian reasons or it may have the most overt political connotations. Aid may be given to alleviate some short-term problem or it may be part of a long-term strategy for DEVELOPMENT or redevelopment.

Aid relationships, in all the contexts discussed above, have been a growing feature of WORLD POLITICS in the twentieth century. Notwithstanding the developing impact of non-STATE actors the greatest amounts of aid are still disbursed on a government-to-government basis. The United States, the most powerful economic state actor in the post-1945 system, has also been the largest donor. The first major aid programme was the European Recovery Programme (ERP). The obvious success of the ERP, or MARSHALL PLAN, encouraged the United States to attempt the same policies *vis-à-vis* the THIRD WORLD. The magnitude and scope of the problems facing any donor are totally different as between Western Europe and the Third World. State-to-state aid reached its peak in the early 1960s and has declined since. There are a number of factors behind this decline. Politically, donor states have found that aid is an expensive and inefficient instrument of FOREIGN POLICY. A sudden change of REGIME in a recipient state may mean the loss of political influence and, with it, of economic resources. Economically, aid has simply not achieved the self-sustained growth in the recipient countries originally anticipated. Political leaders and ATTENTIVE PUBLICS now tend to argue that regime change is required if the Third World is to avoid a series of major economic CRISES before the end of the century.

## Airlift

Used in two senses. In general terms as a noun to describe any significant movement of men and/or materials by air. More specifically it refers to the events of the first BERLIN CRISIS of 1948–9.

## Air power

One of the most important developments in twentieth century TECHNOLOGY has been that of heavier-than-air flight. The potential use of such power, particularly in situations of warfare and violence, was rapidly made apparent by events such as the First World WAR. The requisite base for the development of air power is an industrialized economy, skilled labour force and active research and DEVELOPMENT facilities. In practice only a small number of STATES have these facilities. Thus the development of air power has meant that a small number of states have reserved to themselves the ability to develop the necessary equipment. This equipment can, and often is, supplied to others via the ARMS TRADE. The development of air power has therefore led to a situation where some states are much more powerful than others and where the major-

ity of states are consumers rather than producers of these CAPABILITIES. The development has also had profound effects upon the conduct of war, most obviously that conducted in the air.

## Air warfare

The significance of the development of AIR POWER for the conduct of WAR was first expressed in dramatic form by novelists such as Jules Verne and H. G. Wells. Tangible evidence of these prognostications was given by the developments during the First World War where manned aircraft were used for surveillance, interception and bombing. During the inter-war years strategists such as Giulo Douhet and William Mitchell began to argue for AIR POWER as the most important instrument in future warfare. Douhet, in particular, argued that in future wars 'command of the air' should be achieved by offensive bombing of enemy targets, military and civilian, from the outset. He also suggested that civilian morale would be quickly destroyed by such a strategy. Proponents of this view took comfort from what were seen to be the lessons of the Spanish Civil War (1936–9). In the event, the experience of the Second World War showed more mixed results. Bombing was very inaccurate until the latter stages of that CONFLICT. Moreover, both the United Kingdom and Germany showed considerable defensive ability and ingenuity. The main changes produced by the Second World War were technological and scientific, in particular the development of the ATOM BOMB and surface-to-surface missiles. It was these changes, as much as anything else, which appeared to vindicate Douhet and the cult of the offensive. Traditional distinctions between the 'front line' and the 'home front' appeared to have collapsed. The use of fission bombs against Japanese targets seemed to justify these conclusions.

The main distinction that can be made in air warfare is between offensive and defensive operations. Offensive warfare is either tactical or strategic. Tactical warfare implies that forces are used in conjunction with or in support for land and sea operations. Strategic warfare implies that forces follow a more or less independent role. The latter type has been more controversial. It tends to collapse the distinction between military and civilian targets referred to above and its cost-effectiveness has sometimes been questioned. Defensive warfare may be active or passive. Active defences would include interceptor aircraft and surface-to-air missiles plus accompanying RADARS. Defensive measures would include shelters, evacuation procedures and so on. Air warfare is technologically very dependent upon research and development of types of weapons. As some of the examples used above show, these developments have been both rapid and radical.

## ALCM

An air-launched cruise missile. The launching platform for the CRUISE MISSILE in this mode would be a bomber or fighter bomber, or even a modified passenger aircraft. The TECHNOLOGY of the ALCM is essentially the same as that for the ground-launched cruise missile (GLCM) and the sea-launched cruise missile (SLMC). Like these, the ALCM is in principle a dual-capable system, that is to say, it can carry either CONVENTIONAL or nuclear warheads. The range of the missile would be affected by the choice, however.

## Alien

A person usually resident in one STATE but owing allegiance to another. In INTERNATIONAL LAW it is inseparable from the concept of sovereign territorial jurisdiction, the assumption being that people legally belong to particular states (i.e. nationals). Some IDEALIST writers, wishing to break down national boundaries and reduce the authority of the sovereign state, regard the idea of aliens as atavistic and reactionary, preferring internationalism as the focus for loyalty and allegiance (see: Kant's Perpetual Peace).

Protection of aliens is a controversial issue in international law and it illustrates the divergent approaches to INTERNATIONAL RELATIONS by developed and developing states. DEVELOPED (usually Western, capitalist) states argue that foreign nationals are protected by an 'international minimum standard' which must be upheld regardless of how the host state treats its own nationals. Developing (and also COMMUNIST) states maintain, on the other hand, that the 'national treatment standard' is sufficient. The issue is political rather than legal in the sense that developing states, resenting economic penetration and DEPENDENCY, lay stress on absolute SOVEREIGNTY and complete INDEPENDENCE, whereas the developed states, wishing to protect their investment and property, argue for a more expansive interpretation of these concepts. The most glaring and dramatic breach of the 'international minimum standard' in recent times was Uganda's expulsion of Asians in 1972.

## Alliance

A formal agreement between two or more STATES to collaborate together on perceived mutual security issues. At a minimum this collaboration will cover mutual obligations upon the outbreak of war. Allies will stipulate in TREATY form the conditions under which a military response will be required. Collaboration often extends beyond this minimum. Joint military exercises, staff training and weapons procurement may all be regarded as proper activities to come under the rubric of the alliance. Allies may feel the need to support each other diplomatically in the conduct of their FOREIGN POLICIES. As with any DIPLOMACY, alliances may be secret or open, BILATERAL or MULTILATERAL.

The alliance was a key variable in the BALANCE OF POWER. Many scholars feel that this system reached its height during the nineteenth century. That century also contains instances of the guarantee. The guarantee bears a family resemblance to the alliance, the difference being that in the guarantee obligations are not reciprocal. Thus a more powerful state will guarantee the integrity of a smaller state against third party attacks. The guarantor will not expect a guarantee in return under this arrangement.

The twentieth century has seen alliances develop more complex institutional characteristics than ever before. NATO is a good example. In addition to coordinating DEFENCE policy, NATO also attempts to coordinate policy on ARMS CONTROL, weapons procurement and defence TECHNOLOGY. The institutional structure is divided between civil and military and there is a permanent secretariat headed by a civilian SECRETARY-GENERAL who is invariably a politician of some standing within the alliance member states.

### Alternative world futures

The study of what the world system, including the world political system, may look like in the future. Despite the implication of prophecy in the nomenclature there is a methodology. It consists of extrapolating certain trends, identified at present, into the future on the basis of certain working assumptions. The term FUTUROLOGY is often used to describe the methodology and the area of study.

The study has grown apace in the last quarter of the twentieth century. This is a reflection of growing concern about a number of global issues such as population growth, environmental degradation, consumption of non-renewable resources and so on. This concern was originally expressed in the 1970s when private institutions such as the Club of Rome began to publish pessimistic projections about the future. The most distinguished of these documents was *The Limits to Growth* (1972). Other groups such as the Hudson Institute were more optimistic. In 1980 the

US government published its *Global 2000 Report*. This suggested that a major shift in POLICY-MAKING was required if the pessimists were to be confounded.

Growing interest in Alternative World Futures has formed part of the PLURALIST perspective on WORLD POLITICS. This views the problems for the planet as only amenable to solutions which escape from the straightjacket of traditional STATE-CENTRED politics.

### Ambassador

A diplomatic representative or agent of one sovereign STATE usually resident in another. As INTERNATIONAL RELATIONS implies a system of communications between states, the idea of an ambassador came to be its principle enabling vehicle. Although the practice is usually associated with the development of the European STATE-SYSTEM, references to it can be found in ancient China and India where Kautilya's *Arthashastra* is a striking example of early articulated diplomatic practice and statescraft. However, in neither of these ancient state-systems is there evidence of an ambassadorial system involving permanent embassies, missions or legations. The prevailing practice, as elsewhere in the ancient world, was the use of heralds or envoys (really, messengers) or else temporary plenipotentiaries (agents who were authorized to work out agreements).

The modern practice of resident ambassadors began to appear in Europe in the fourteenth and fifteenth centuries, probably first in Venice and Milan. The idea of DIPLOMATIC IMMUNITY was inseparable from residency and formed the basis of modern INTERNATIONAL LAW. The inviolability of the ambassador's person (and later that of his staff) was a necessary feature of this system and immunity is still regarded as the bedrock of diplomatic practice. Even its recent dramatic violation in Teheran (1979) when American Embassy staff were held hostage by government forces does not disprove the universal acceptance of the notion of immunity. Iran was, almost without exception in the international community, strongly condemned for this clear breach of the basic rules of diplomatic communication. However, whether the principle of immunity can be extended to cover aspects other than personal safety and private diplomatic affairs (e.g. parking offences or drug trafficking) is less widely accepted and subject to much current debate.

The development of the resident ambassadorial system became fully self-conscious at the Congress of Vienna (1815) which, as well as recognizing the existence of a *corps diplomatique*, strictly defined categories of representation and issued a PROTOCOL determining the functions and order of precedence of diplomatic missions. This protocol is still in use today: it underlines the importance of immunity and establishes that the doyen or spokesman of the *corps diplomatique* is either the papal representative or, more usually, the longest accredited serving ambassador regardless of the status or POWER of the country he (or she) represents. Vienna thus established the ambassadorial system as a vital institution in INTERNATIONAL RELATIONS, and one that has continued largely unchanged to the present day. In 1961 the Vienna Convention on Diplomatic Relations underlined and endorsed the achievement of the Congress.

Some writers on DIPLOMACY have questioned the continued need for an ambassadorial system. The argument is that modern technology, especially in the field of communications, as well as the decline of the traditional NATION-STATE, has destroyed the very foundation of the institution. However, although many governments are concerned to prune the resources available to the diplomatic service and direct its functions more towards TRADE and commerce rather than traditional matters of high policy, it is extremely unlikely that so useful a system will disappear. The old BILATERAL diplomatic pattern may well be undergoing significant change, especially with the increasing collectivization of international life, but the need for diplomatic machinery and representation, whether this be BILATERAL or multilateral, will remain for as long as the international state-system lasts. One is bound up with the other.

*See also*: DIPLOMACY; DIPLOMATIC IMMUNITIES AND PRIVILEGES

## Amnesty

Refers to a decision to set aside prosecution or punishment for certain types of offenders (usually political). It is similar to a pardon but without the connotations of forgiveness that this usually carries. Amnesties can be general or specific, complete or partial. The term is widely used in relation to PRISONERS OF WAR and prisoners of conscience. Amnesty International is a non-government organization devoted to overseeing, on a world-wide basis, cases where individuals or groups are punished for their political or religious views.

## Anarchy

A crucial concept in the theory of WORLD POLITICS. Its literal meaning is 'absence of government', but it is often (wrongly) used as a synonym for disorder, confusion and chaos. Thus, in traditional international theory, anarchy and order are not necessarily mutually exclusive. Anarchy in its literal sense is widely regarded as the central feature of relations between STATES and as such defines the context in which they take place. Indeed, the lack of a common government or a universally recognized common external authority is what distinguishes the international from the domestic realm of politics and law. The notions of SOVEREIGNTY and INDEPENDENCE in this way are either a consequence of, or a reason for, this condition.

The study of international theory is often presented in terms of a dialogue or a debate between those who accept the fact of anarchy and argue that this does not necessarily preclude order, society or community, and those who argue that anarchy is incompatible with these goals and that progress towards them is only possible once anarchy is ended and government prevails. For the first group of theorists the DOMESTIC ANALOGY (arguing from the experience of individuals within the state to the experience of states themselves) is invalid. INTERNATIONAL RELATIONS involves a special kind of political activity which is in fact sustained and fostered by anarchy, not destroyed by it. The second group views the domestic analogy as crucial and argues that the conditions of a peaceful and orderly world require that governmental institutions be established beyond and above the state. Only then will a genuine INTERNATIONAL SOCIETY be effected. Political philosophers most closely identified with these views are Hobbes (especially Chapter XIII of the *Leviathan*) and Kant (*Perceptual Peace*).

The whole issue of anarchy versus government is endemic in Western thinking about international relations and according to Hedley Bull (1977), a plausible account of the history of the discipline can be given in terms of it. Specifically, the term 'international anarchy' was first popularized by Dickinson (1916) who argued that anarchy, and the fear it engendered in states, was responsible for WAR in general, and the First World War in particular. Most contemporary theorists now regard the debate as somewhat sterile and simplistic and tend to view international relations in terms of an admixture of the two extremes. The obsession with issues of POWER and national security which the debate engendered has, to a large extent, been replaced by focus on the politics of INTERDEPENDENCE and transnational relations where the emphasis is on the process of bargaining and regulation rather than on varieties of dominance and order.

# ANC

African National Congress, founded in 1912 with the aims of improving the political, social and economic conditions of blacks in South Africa. Originally an organization committed to non-violence and redressing grievances through constitutional means, believing that the key to progress was the gaining of full equality initially for the Black middle classes. Its gradualist opposition to segregationism received an irreversible setback in 1948 with the election of the Nationalist Party to power. From 1949 to 1960, the ANC shifted its policy from a reformist stance to a revolutionary one. The names associated with this major change in political strategy are Anton Lembede, Walter Sisulu, Albert Luthuli, Oliver Tambo and Nelson Mandela, who became the main spokesman for the ANC in this crucial period of confrontation. After the Sharpeville affair of 21 March 1960 (where sixty-nine Africans were killed by police) the ANC was outlawed, and it subsequently went underground. Nelson Mandela (born 1918) was arrested and sentenced to life imprisonment in 1963. In his absence, Oliver Tambo assumed the leadership of the ANC from exile in Lusaka and London. The ANC is now committed to an armed struggle against APARTHEID, from within and from without.

The organization has undergone three distinct developmental phases: from 1912 to 1948 when it was reformist in character, from 1948 to 1960 when it became radical and revolutionary and from the early 1960s to the present day when the aim was the violent and complete overthrow of the South African state. As Mandela eloquently put it at his trial defending the use of force '... the hard facts were that fifty years of non-violence had brought the African people nothing but more and more repressive legislation, and fewer and fewer rights.'

It is not just in this third phase that the organization has had an international dimension – as early as 1913 a delegation was sent to London and in 1919 the ANC was present at VERSAILLES. But it is since being outlawed in South Africa that it has figured predominantly in the diplomatic councils of the FRONT-LINE STATES and others opposed to the continued existence of apartheid in South Africa.

In late 1989 a fourth evolutionary phase began to emerge: the negotiational. The election to the state presidency of F. W. de Klerk and his promise of a 'new dispensation' in South Africa has opened up the possibility of a negotiated settlement between the ANC and the Nationalist government. The apparently endless succession of CRISES in South Africa since the Soweto riots of 1976 have elevated the ANC from its position as a fairly minor irritant on the fringes of South African politics to an almost universally recognized government in exile.

Its strength now lies in its status as a national movement rather than the more limited role of a political party or military force. The extent of COMMUNIST influence on the ANC has tended to dominate assessments of the movement, particularly within South Africa itself. Indeed, hitherto the Nationalist government has actively promoted this facile identification of the *swart gevaar* (black danger) with the *rooi gevaar* (red danger). However, this is difficult to establish and most commentators would agree that the ANC is a complicated ideological package united by the common aim of opposing White domination and establishing a majoritarian system in a unitary state. There are divisions within the organization, especially concerning the nature of the 'armed struggle', the precise economic and social interpretation of the Freedom Charter and most notably on the political character of post-apartheid South Africa. Thus far, these differences have not fragmented the movement and the objective remains the practical, REALPOLITIK one of forcing Pretoria to the negotiating table. Tactically, this has meant upping the price whites have to pay to maintain power and privilege. Whether the ANC's old guard under the tutelage of Nelson Mandela and Oliver Tambo can sustain this posture in the face of increasing radicalism from the townships remains to be seen.

## Annexation

A mode of acquiring territory which belonged to another STATE, or to no one. It is usually a UNILATERAL act, but the acquiescence of the former possessor is presumed. It involves the extension of full SOVEREIGNTY by the new owner and the exercise of exclusive jurisdiction and control in the area. It differs from military occupation though annexation may arise from this. The ANSCHLUSS of 1938 when Austria became part of the German Reich is an example of annexation.

## Anschluss

Literally means union. In WORLD POLITICS it refers to the unification of Germany and Austria in 1938 (which was expressly forbidden by the Treaty of VERSAILLES). As a consequence, Austria became a province of the German Reich from 1938 to 1945.

## Antarctica treaty

TREATY concluded in 1959 between Argentina, Australia, Belgium, Chile, France, Japan, New Zealand, Norway, South Africa, the United Kingdom, the United States and the Soviet Union. The treaty came into force in 1961 and is subject to review after thirty years. Its purpose was to prevent a scramble for territory south of 60 degrees south latitude and to place the continent outside traditional COLD WAR rivalries. All signatories agreed to hold in abeyance territorial disputes and claims. It provides for freedom of movement and scientific exploration throughout Antarctica and it established a mutual inspection system to discourage militarization of the region (including nuclear explosion and the dumping of radioactive wastes). The treaty is significant in WORLD POLITICS as it marked the first DISARMAMENT agreement involving the United States and the Soviet Union. Hopes that this would lead to similar agreements covering other areas of strategic importance (e.g. the Arctic) have so far come to nothing. *See also*: NUCLEAR FREE ZONES.

## Anzus

Security TREATY concluded between Australia, New Zealand and the United States at San Francisco on 1 September 1951. Under the terms of the treaty each signatory recognized that an armed attack on one of the others in 'the Pacific area' would be 'dangerous to its own peace and safety'. The conclusion of this pact in 1951 marked a significant turning point in the defence postures of Australia, New Zealand and the United Kingdom (which is not a signatory and was excluded from participation). Australia and New Zealand redefined their security priorities and turned to the United States as the protecting power, which in fact had assumed this role since the fall of Singapore (1942). Under the terms of the ANZUS pact, an Australia–New Zealand Army Corps (ANZAC) fought in VIETNAM. Between 1965–73 469 were killed. Recently, serious tensions have appeared in the ALLIANCE due to the New Zealand Labour government's commitment to a nuclear-free Pacific and as a consequence its future as a genuine TRILATERAL pact must now be in doubt.

## Apartheid

Afrikaans word meaning 'apart-hood' or 'separateness'. It refers particularly to policies of racial segregation practised by the Republic of South Africa since the coming to power of the Nationalist Party in 1948. The population of South Africa is officially divided into four main racial groups: White, Coloured, Asian and Blacks, with the Whites forming 14.7 per cent of the total population (which is over 32 million by official estimates), Coloured 8.7 per cent, Asians 2.7 per cent and Blacks 73.8 per cent. The policies of apartheid involve legislation controlling virtually all aspects of social, political and economic life involving these racial groups: places of residence, property, movement, social and recreational amenities, schools, universities, rights of association and, of course, the franchise.

Although it is sometimes officially denied, apartheid has the effect, if not the intention, of granting a virtual monopoly of political POWER to the Whites. The Constitution of the Republic was amended in 1984 to give some political representation to the Coloured and Asian populations. Africans, though, are excluded from political participation in South Africa on the grounds that, under the logic of apartheid, they have their own separate 'homelands' (Transkei 1976, Bophuthatswana 1977, Venda 1979 and Ciskei 1981). These homelands, which the South African government regard as the historic residences of indigenous Africans, are alleged to be separate sovereign states by Pretoria, but the international community has never recognized them as such.

Other Afrikaans words and concepts frequently associated with apartheid and inseparable from it in the political context are *baaskap* (meaning boss-rule or White dominance), *verligte* (meaning enlightened or reformist especially in relation to 'petty apartheid') and *verkrampte* (meaning rigid and conservative adherence to policies of complete separate racial development). The general character of South African political life could be described in terms of a tension or interplay between the forces of *verligte* and of *verkrampte*, with the latter often achieving dominance, especially in the areas of law and order.

Apartheid is unique to South Africa. Since the transformation of Rhodesia into Zimbabwe (1980), the Republic is now the one glaring example of a political system dedicated to White dominance in a continent which has all but completely shaken off the vestiges of European COLONIAL rule. The black REVOLUTION which has characterized African politics in the second half of the twentieth century cannot be seen as complete by the majority of Africans until and unless the racial domination by the Whites in South Africa is ended. South Africa therefore is in theory, if not in practice, a besieged STATE. It is besieged from within and from without.

Before 1948 the South African political system was unexceptional and did not have any significant implications for its general position in WORLD POLITICS. Traditionally its importance to the outside world lay in its geographical position on the shortest route from Europe to Asia. This was the reason first for Dutch colonization (1652) and then for British (1795). Subsequent discoveries of gold, gems and diamonds as well as andalusite, chrome ore, vanadium, platinum, coal, iron ore and uranium, all in significant and recoverable quantities, made South Africa a powerful, developed industrial state existing prominently and self-consciously in a very poorly developed continent. South Africa is, without doubt, the SUPERPOWER of the region.

Until 1948, South Africa was not singled out for special consideration by the international community. Indeed, South Africa had in 1939 entered the WAR against Nazi Germany and in the immediate post-war years it was widely assumed that with its vast mineral wealth and its prime strategic location straddling the south Atlantic and the Indian Oceans, it would be a valuable and valued member of the Western, non-COMMUNIST grouping in the international system. The election of the Afrikaner Nationalist Party and the rigid application of its policy of apartheid in 1948, changed, probably for ever, South Africa's place in world affairs. The policy of apartheid and the perpetuation of White dominance which it involves is generally and almost universally recognized as morally repugnant and indefensible. The question that now dominates most political analyses of South Africa is: how long can South Africa and apartheid survive?

Since 1948 various forms of coercion ranging from partial economic, diplomatic and sporting BOYCOTTS to full-scale expulsions from INTERNATIONAL ORGANIZATIONS, have been the standard responses of the majority of states in the international community (a community, incidentally, which is well known for its tolerance of deviant behaviour). The UN in particular has played a prominent part in the general outlawry of South Africa. Almost annually since 1948, the GENERAL ASSEMBLY of the UN has passed resolutions condemning and criticizing the policy of apartheid and the government of South Africa (both of which are now seen to be synonymous). In 1962 the UN asked member states to break off diplomatic and economic relations with South Africa and created a permanent Special Committee on Apartheid to review racial developments with the Republic. In 1973 the General Assembly formed an International Convention on the Suppression and Punishment of the Crime of Apartheid and declared it to be 'a crime against humanity', and by 1980 fifty-eight states had agreed to be bound by the terms of this convention. Indeed, it could be argued that a constant theme of UN General Assembly politics and of THIRD WORLD rhetoric has been the continuous and continuing condemnation of apartheid. It has become one of the moral absolutes of the age. The high-water mark of this movement occurred in 1977 when the SECURITY COUNCIL of the UN, which because of the veto power enjoyed by its members had previously confined itself to condemnatory statements, implemented a mandatory arms embargo on South Africa. This was an historic step, not just in relation to the general Great Power disapproval of the Pretoria government's policies, but also because it was the first time that the Security Council had undertaken such action against a member state under Chapter 7 of the UN CHARTER.

Apart from the UN, international reaction to apartheid, and hence South Africa, can be summarized as follows:

1. The West (especially the United Kingdom and the United States): publicly to endorse opposition to apartheid, privately to engage in constructive efforts to encourage *verligte* and to preserve economic investments, always mindful of the strategic importance of the Cape and of South Africa's mineral wealth. The American policy of CONSTRUCTIVE ENGAGEMENT is designed to

preserve regional stability, to encourage reform and to maintain Western influence.

2. The East (especially the Soviet Union and China): to encourage national LIBERATION movements, to DESTABILIZE the region, to play upon the ambiguities of Western policies so as to embarrass the West, and eventually to dislodge and replace its influence in the region.

3. The Black Neighbours or FRONT-LINE STATES (primarily Zimbabwe, Mozambique, Zambia, Angola, Tanzania): to complete the anti-colonial, anti-White revolution, while not sacrificing domestic economic development and growth. South Africa is the economic giant of the region, and all its Black neighbours to some extent are economically dependent on it. Lesotho, Swaziland and Botswana have near total dependence, while Zimbabwe, Mozambique, Tanzania and Zambia have varying but significant degrees of DEPENDENCE.

4. The COMMONWEALTH: although South Africa withdrew from the Commonwealth when the Republic was inaugurated on 31 May 1961, it has always been prominent in the world campaign against apartheid. In 1985, at their summit at Nassau in the Bahamas, it appointed the Commonwealth Group of Eminent Persons to investigate conditions inside South Africa and to seek ways of establishing there a genuine non-racial democracy. Their report of 1986 recommended among other initiatives that South Africa's major trading partners should apply economic pressures on a continuing and incremental basis in order to bring about reform. Thus far, the intransigence of the UK government has seriously damaged the collective impact of the Commonwealth's recommendations.

In sum, apartheid is one of the most awkward and awesome concepts in the vocabulary of twentieth-century world politics. In view of the strength and determination of the White tribes of South Africa, it may continue to be so in the twenty-first century, although in the late 1980s there are signs that the *verkrampte* version of apartheid will not survive in undiluted form. The election to the Presidency of F. W. de Klerk in September 1989 and his promise of a new 'dispensation' in South African politics has given rise to cautious optimism that Pretoria may now be emerging from its forty-year-old self-imposed laager. The unbanning of the ANC and other anti-apartheid organizations, the release of Nelson Mandela, the lifting of curbs on the media and the apparent willingness of the government to enter into negotiations concerning the social, economic and political character of the post-apartheid state, suggest that the days of the world's only surviving pigmentocracy may be numbered. However, it is clear that South Africa's status in world politics, in particular its reintegration into the regional and global community of states, is a direct function of the present REGIME's determination to wade across the entire length of this particular Rubicon and not merely halt somewhere in the middle.

**Appeasement**
Commonly used to describe the Munich settlement (1938) which effected the dismemberment of Czechoslovakia and gave Germany virtual command of Eastern Europe. The term has acquired derogatory overtones both in common parlance and historical scholarship as it supposedly symbolizes the sacrifice of principle (the sovereign INDEPENDENCE of a SMALL STATE) for expedience (placating a dictator and buying time). In the post-WAR period such was the opprobrium associated with it, especially in the United Kingdom and the United States, that it became synonymous with weakness and cowardice. It was therefore used to justify policies of uncompromising firmness and rigidity in for example, Korea (1951), Suez (1956) and VIETNAM (1954–75).

However, this contemporary connotation is not reflected in traditional theories of

INTERNATIONAL POLITICS, especially those associated with the REALIST school, where appeasement, properly conducted, is regarded as an integral part of the BALANCE OF POWER process, the purpose of which is to maintain order and reduce the incidence of great POWER conflict. In this connection it is akin to ACCOMMODATION where quarter is given to facilitate peaceful change. Even so, it is largely a matter between GREAT POWERS and may often involve a total disregard for the vital interests of smaller states.

## Arab–Israeli conflict

One of the most intractable conflicts in twentieth century MACROPOLITICS. The conflict originated as a communal dispute and then spread to take in neighbouring STATES and four of the permanent members of the UN SECURITY COUNCIL. The location of the dispute is the territory historically known as Palestine. The land is the focus of three monotheistic religions: Judaism, Christianity and ISLAM. Politically it was controlled as part of the Ottoman Empire until the end of the First World War. A LEAGUE OF NATIONS MANDATE was granted to the British to administer Palestine during the time now known as the inter-WAR period. Under the aegis of this, and in line with the Balfour Declaration of 1917, Jewish immigration into Palestine began on a scale and with a determination never seen before. The Jews were emboldened by a nationalist, socialist IDEOLOGY known as Zionism and they soon created communal tension with the majority population, who were Arab peoples. NATIONALISM was an attitude increasingly manifested on the Arab side in Palestine as well as the Zionist side so the conflict had a strong ideological dimension for both parties.

A necessary consequence of the mandate system was that the issue of Palestine became an international one. This tendency has continued, and increased in scope, since 1945. On the Zionist side, the United States has proved the most generous and signifi-

cant supporter. On the Palestinian Arab side, neighbouring Arab states, through the ARAB LEAGUE and the Soviet Union since the middle of the century, have similarly provided assistance of all types. The UN, as successor to the League, has continued to assist the internationalization tendency. The Organization has, on occasions, taken important policy initiatives on the issue. In 1947 a partition plan for Palestine was proposed by a UN special commission. In 1956 an emergency PEACEKEEPING force was sent to Egypt by the UN. In 1967 and again in 1973 important declaratory resolutions were passed by the Security Council. The UN has consistently favoured a policy of establishing an international REGIME for Jerusalem owing to its religious significance for the three faiths.

DE FACTO partition of Palestine took place in 1948 with the establishment of the State of Israel. The majority of the old mandate territory came under the control of the new State; however, the state of Transjordan made significant territorial gains on the West Bank of the river. With these developments a new dimension was added to the problem when the majority of the Arab inhabitants of Palestine became REFUGEES. The cause of the refugee problem has become one of the issues of the conflict since 1948. Certainly, the invasion of the Arab League armies, immediately independence was declared, served to exacerbate a deteriorating communal situation. Conversely, the protagonists who served to benefit from an Arab exodus, at least territorially, were the Zionist forces. The Arab refugees from Palestine were settled in the neighbouring Arab states. In many instances little attempt was made to integrate them with the indigenous population. As a result, the Palestinians became susceptible to two political consequences in the years after 1948. First, there was a natural carry-over of the inter-War nationalism into the post-1948 situation. This led in time to the establishment of a number of nationalist organizations which collectively came under the umbrella of the PLO. Secondly, the politicization of the refugee question and the presence of large numbers of these people in other Arab lands spilled over into the domestic politics of the host states. This was very apparent during the LEBANESE civil war which commenced in the mid-1970s.

Violence between the state of Israel and its neighbours has fitted into two types. First, short, highly intense outbreaks of CONVENTIONAL warfare usually characterized by mobility and rapidly changing fortunes. The wars of 1956, 1967 and 1973 fit into this pattern; secondly, the War of Independence 1948, the War of Attrition 1970–3 and the Israeli INTERVENTIONS in the Lebanese CIVIL WAR since 1978. Here the characteristics of the warfare have been more protracted and in the case of the Lebanon costly, controversial and indecisive. Moreover, the effect of this circle of violence has left Israel currently in possession of Arab territories on the West Bank and the Golan Heights. Israel has also incorporated the city of Jerusalem into its state structure notwithstanding UN policy to the contrary.

Given the nature and intensity of the conflict, third party mediation attempts have been regularly made. Probably the first concentrated attempt at settlement was made during the mandate period when the British set up the Peel Royal Commission. This reported in favour of partition of Palestine. All subsequent mediation attempts up to 1948 were also based upon the concept of partition. With the establishment of the Israeli state, and the circle of violence referred to above, mediation has often taken the form of short-term palliatives – cease-fire agreements, TRUCE supervision, exchange of prisoners and so on. A long-term solution has been more difficult to find. Two principal mediators have been the UN and the United States. The former was initially favoured for its impartiality and ability to reflect a more global perspective. Some would argue that developments of late in the Organization have shown it to be partial to the Arab position. Conversely the United States, as Israel's staunchest ally, is seen as being able to exert leverage on that state. The most intractable issue remains the Palestinian Arabs and it is widely accepted that some form of SELF-DETERMINATION will be required to achieve an amelioration of that people's plight.

*See also*: ARAB LEAGUE: CAMP DAVID; ISLAM; LEBANON.

## Arab League

This is an international governmental institution (IGO). As the name implies it is confined to the Arab STATES of North Africa and the Middle East. The formation of the Arab League was announced at a meeting of foreign ministers at Alexandria in September 1944. Formal agreement was reached in March 1945 between Egypt, Iraq, Transjordan (now Jordan), LEBANON, Saudi Arabia, Syria and Yemen. Each member state is represented on the Council while day to day business is handled by a secretariat, headed by a SECRETARY-GENERAL. The purposes of the League are to increase cooperation between member states in military, diplomatic, economic and cultural fields. Although it is therefore recognizable as a multi-purpose institution it is best known as the vehicle whereby the Arab States maintain a united front *vis-à-vis* the ARAB–ISRAELI CONFLICT. Over the years since its inception the members have signally failed to achieve this goal. This culminated in Egypt signing a separate peace TREATY with Israel under the CAMP DAVID ACCORDS in 1979. As a result the headquarters were moved from Cairo to Tunis and Egypt left the League. On the issue of economic relations developments have been more harmonious. The assertion of the considerable oil power of the Arab states in 1973–4 through OPEC and the establishment of trading BLOCS such as the Gulf Cooperation Council show that the increased wealth of the region has facilitated more cooperation.

## Arbitration

A method of CONFLICT SETTLEMENT involving third-party INTERVENTION. Arbitration is a favoured method of settlement in domestic labour–management conflicts, at least in the advanced industrial countries (AICS). The basis of an arbitration award is that the parties to the conflict agree to submit their differences to the third party to make a binding decision to settle the dispute. The arbitrator may apply known rules, precedents and laws in seeking a settlement and the arbitration award may be reinforced by sanctions to secure compliance. It is possible, and desirable, for the parties to agree to these rules, at least implicitly, in advance. This means that existing rules and practices can be abandoned in favour of any agreed-upon set of principles. Thus arbitration is more flexible than ADJUDICATION because the latter process tends to rigorously eschew innovation and to reflect a STATUS QUO frame of reference.

In INTERNATIONAL RELATIONS arbitration as a form of settlement has always had powerful advocates but, apart from a short period in the late nineteenth and early twentieth centuries, it has been little used. Anglo–American DIPLOMACY provides the best examples in the modern world. The Jay TREATY of 1794 inaugurated arbitration as method of settlement between the two STATES. The most famous case is that of the Alabama Arbitration of 1872. Scholars are generally agreed that this settlement in favour of the United States was prompted by the desire of both parties to improve their relations rather than by any philosophical commitment to the arbitration process.

Many IDEALISTS regarded the development of arbitration as essential if WAR was to be eradicated from WORLD POLITICS. The two HAGUE CONFERENCES (1899 and 1907) failed to achieve agreement on compulsory arbitration but succeeded in creating the Permanent Court of Arbitration. This was, in point of fact, neither permanent nor a court. It was a list of persons from which the parties to a conflict could select a name. Arbitration has not had the success or impact that the nineteenth and twentieth century idealists believed. Essentially the consensus that is required to make arbitration work has been absent, Moreover, although it is marginally more flexible than adjudication, arbitration appears not to be favoured in the present system as a means of settlement. The growth of international regional institutions in the contemporary system must be accounted a major force in reducing the potential for arbitration as a third party mode.

## Armistice

The cessation or suspension of hostilities pending a PEACE settlement. It is not a peace TREATY and as such does not legally terminate the state of WAR, but clearly affords an opportunity to do so. It is BILATERAL not UNILATERAL and can be distinguished from a TRUCE by the fact that the latter usually refers to a temporary and specific declaration by belligerents with or without confirmation by the highest authorities. Sometimes, when a peace treaty proves impossible because of the intractable nature of the conflict, an armistice becomes DE FACTO the STATUS QUO. This was the case with the 1949 armistice agreements between Israel and the Arabs until the CAMP DAVID ACCORDS.

## Arms control

The exercise of restraint in the acquisition, deployment and use of military CAPABILITIES. Furthermore, the term also covers any measure that enables statesmen to conduct themselves in a more restrained way, for example by developing techniques of CRISIS MANAGEMENT. One of the most important underlying assumptions of arms control is that weapons are a continuing and persistent feature of WORLD POLITICS and that DETERRENCE policies are a valuable and positive means of coercive DIPLOMACY. Thus ideologically the arms control theorist differs, in principle, from the advocate of DISARMAMENT. While the latter may eventually look to a world without weapons, or at least a world where weapons and the threat of the use of force are substantially removed, the arms controller is quite willing to work within the existing structure. Both approaches are agreed, however, that an uncontrolled ARMS RACE will upset the system to the detriment of all.

## Arms race

Literally a competitive building-up of armaments by at least two ACTORS in CONFLICT. The basic process in the arms race is the ACTION–REACTION pattern. In CYBERNETICS the arms race is an example of positive FEEDBACK. Such races have often preceded WARS and outbreaks of violence. The outbreak of the First World War was preceded by a naval race between the United Kingdom and Imperial Germany. Sometimes, in persistent, chronic periods of CRISES an arms race will be a more or less continuous feature. The ARAB–ISRAELI CONFLICT is an example of this.

Arms races can appear to generate a dynamic of their own, particularly in a system experiencing rapid technological innovation. The race between the SUPERPOWERS since 1945 has had a tendency to create this kind of dynamic. When this happens other tendencies take over and the dynamic is no longer simply the arms levels of the perceived opponents. Vested interests, in particular the military and industrial establishments, find that the continuation of a high level of arms expenditure and the prerequisite research is to their advantage. In such circumstances the pure model of the arms race must be modified to take account of these other factors.

The relationship between the pure type of arms race and war is tentative. An arms race is neither a necessary nor sufficient condition for the outbreak of war. Moreover theories which borrow heavily from ideas about DETERRENCE usually assume that a certain level of arms is necessary to prevent war. In these formulations it is the balance between the two sides that is crucial rather than the absolute level of arms. According to this view it is imbalance in the arms race that is more likely to cause a breakdown of the system into war. This process is closely related to the concept of the BALANCE OF POWER.

It should be noted that two separate arms races can interact, as for example, the Arab–Israeli conflict and the superpowers referred to above.

## Arms sales/trade

The ability of man as a tool-maker has been recognized by students of the past, including the primeval past. This ability has, similarly, been used to make weapons. Once an economic system evinces a division of labour, specialist manufacture becomes possible. In this way production of weapons, their sale and the system known as TRADE has developed. The development of industrialized modes of production, first in Europe, has meant that much more is at stake in the creation, maintenance and growth of the arms trade. The market for arms is an important source of wealth creation for a small number of STATES. In the contemporary system the major inputs to the arms trade come from the United States, the Soviet Union, France and the United Kingdom. The reason for this is that as the costs of research and development have increased so production has concentrated in a few rich countries. Considerable political control is exercised over the trade by the main suppliers. This is achieved either by direct state ownership and control of enterprise or by a system of licensing. It should be noted that the suppliers can and often will offer concessionary terms if they wish to break into a market or feel that some other supplier is about to do so.

The existence and growth of the arms trade has long been criticized by international institutions such as the UN, the

PEACE MOVEMENT and distinguished individuals. One result of these efforts has been that independently compiled statistics about the arms trade have been drawn up. The first institution to do this was the LEAGUE OF NATIONS. Since 1945 the UN has been particularly concerned to restrict the arms trade with states such as South Africa because of its APARTHEID policy. As more and more states have joined the system increasing concern has been expressed about the amount of scarce resources THIRD WORLD STATES spend on the arms trade. Like proposals for general and complete DISARMAMENT, proposals for stopping or reducing the arms trade are, in principle, frequently advanced. Tangible results have proved much more difficult.

## Army

A military establishment which primarily functions to fight on land. The use of armies as the primary military instrument of policy goes back to classical antiquity. During the modern period important developments have been the notion of the standing army and the rise of NATIONALISM. The first was suggestive of the idea that armies should continue to exist in times of peace, thereby creating a military establishment. Nationalism imbued people with the idea that they might fight each other for motives that were not based upon financial reward or legal obligation. The development of industrialization has meant that the techniques of mass production and mechanization can be utilized to equip armies with a continuous flow of sophisticated weapons. In the contemporary world system armies are largely created and controlled by STATES. Exceptions to this might be the use of armies by international institutions such as the UN in COLLECTIVE SECURITY and PEACEKEEPING operations. The development of techniques of GUERRILLA WARFARE raises the difficult definitional issue of whether irregular forces can constitute an army.

## ASAT

An anti-satellite weapon(s). The ability of satellites to provide information about the world system is well established. The military dimension of this facility is considerable. Through satellite TECHNOLOGY, statesmen and their advisors can look, listen and respond to information about their adversaries and their allies. As such satellites are an important target for offensive operations. Both the SUPERPOWERS have been working on ASAT technology since the 1960s. The Soviet Union introduced a weapon in 1968. The United States under the Strategic Defense Initiative (SDI) has developed an interceptor rocket which is carried aboard an aircraft. Both these weapons are non-nuclear. The ARMS CONTROL implications of the development of ASAT are considerable. It has been argued that satellites provide valuable information which assists CRISIS MANAGEMENT. The introduction of offensive CAPABILITIES via ASAT may seriously reduce this facility and increase the pressure upon statesmen to launch pre-emptive attacks during periods of great tension.

## ASEAN

Association of South East Asian Nations, formed in 1967 as a result of the Bangkok Declaration issued on 8 August by the Foreign Ministers of Indonesia, Malaysia, the Philippines, Singapore and Thailand. ASEAN is an International Governmental Organization (IGO) aimed at increasing economic and political cooperation between its members and developing closer ties with external parties, particularly in the field of international economic relations. The original agreements were strengthened at the Bali summit of ASEAN heads of government held in February 1976. A secretariat was established and agreement was reached on a preferential trading arrangement between the five states. Attempts have been made to coordinate FOREIGN POLICY aims and objectives over regional issues such as Kampuchea. Globally

ASEAN is part of the NON-ALIGNED MOVE-MENT and the GROUP OF 77. Its main trading links with the advanced industrial countries (AICS) are with Japan. It is seeking to diversify this pattern and, in particular, to develop trade with the EUROPEAN COMMUNITY.

## Association

General meaning is the formation of a society of sorts, and is often used in WORLD POLITICS to distinguish between the (loose) ties between STATES and the (firm) ties between individuals within the state. The phrase 'association of states' is sufficiently anaemic to enable the writer to avoid complications inherent in the phrase INTERNATIONAL SOCIETY. More specifically, in world politics the term has carried IMPERIAL or COLONIAL overtones, especially in France. The principle of association was devised by colonial administrators and theorists in Paris (1910) to meet the practical problems created by the paradox of French IMPERIALISM existing side by side with French democratic republicanism. The French, unlike the more pragmatic British, have always felt uneasy about colonial possessions. As Europe's foremost democratic republic created out of a passion for universal liberty, equality and fraternity, it was clearly morally wrong to regard colonies as subordinate entities. Logically, overseas possessions, if they exist at all, must be fully assimilated into metropolitan France. As a practical expedient, though, assimilation gave way to association (which in effect meant subordinate status) and this attempted compromise became the orthodoxy practised by and preached to French colonial administration in the *ecole coloniale* in Paris until the Second World War.

In the United Kingdom, the concept of 'associated status' was used in 1967 specifically to cater for former colonies which desired limited INDEPENDENCE from the United Kingdom but were economically unable or unwilling to stand alone.

## Assured destruction

A term used in nuclear strategy. It has two meanings. As a CAPABILITY it refers to the technical potential to launch attacks against an adversary which lead to large-scale destruction of people and property. Before the advent of AIR POWER and NUCLEAR WEAPONS such destruction was only possible via a land invasion. Such constraints no longer operate. The capability required to achieve assured destruction is normally referred to as a SECOND STRIKE capability.

As a policy it is an example of what is termed COUNTER-CITY targeting. It is particularly associated with the conduct of US defence policy in the 1960s and with the former Secretary of Defense Robert McNamara. The United States has moved steadily away from assured destruction as a policy since the 1970s, preferring to look for allegedly greater flexibility under various COUNTERFORCE options.
*See also*: MAD.

## ASW

Anti-submarine warfare. Systems which can detect and destroy enemy submarines. The importance of this TECHNOLOGY has increased with the developments that have taken place in submarine-launched ballistic missiles (SLBMs) and nuclear powered ballistic missile submarines (SSBNs). Submarines become much more visible once they actually begin to fire their missiles.

## Asylum

Literally a sanctuary or place of refuge. It refers to a quasi-legal process where one STATE grants protection to a national or nationals of another. In INTERNATIONAL LAW it can be challenged by request for EXTRADITION. Indeed, it is sometimes said that asylum ends where extradition begins, but in the absence of a specific TREATY, there is no legal duty to extradite. Rights of asylum belong to states not to individuals, although

Article 14 of the Universal Declaration of HUMAN RIGHTS (1948) does give individuals a right of political asylum. But as the Declaration took the form of a resolution of the GENERAL ASSEMBLY, it is not legally (though it may be morally) binding on states.

## Atlantic Alliance
*See*: NATO

## Atlantic Charter
Often regarded as the genesis of the UN. In fact it was a BILATERAL declaration of WAR aims issued in 1941 by F. D. Roosevelt and Winston Churchill on board a warship in mid-Atlantic. The keynote of the Charter was the notion of 'The Four Freedoms' (freedom from fear and want, freedom of speech and religion) which to them was the basis of the Allied cause. Other principles associated with it are: SELF-DETER-MINATION, freely elected government, economic collaboration, freedom of the seas, renunciation of the use of FORCE in disputes and the post-war establishment of a permanent system of global security. These, of course, were in direct contrast to the IDEOLOGY of the AXIS powers.

## Atom bomb
Using a process known as fission it is possible to produce explosive devices which have much greater power than CONVENTIONAL methods. URANIUM 235, a natural mineral, is highly unstable and it is possible to produce a chain reaction using this mineral whereby all the fissionable material is affected at once. It is this chain reaction which generates the explosive power of the uranium bomb. Uranium 235 is also used to produce PLUTONIUM 239. Both these substances can be used to produce bombs.

The ability to produce explosive devices using a controlled chain reaction was known to physicists before the outbreak of the Second World War. The outbreak of the WAR and the knowledge that Nazi Germany could develop a bomb added a new dimension to research. In 1941 the United States began work on the MANHATTAN PROJECT to build, test and if necessary use an atomic bomb in the context of the war. No weapons were produced in time for use or demonstration against Germany but, controversially, two bombs were dropped on Japanese cities. Uranium was used in the bomb dropped upon HIROSHIMA and plutonium in the bomb dropped on NAGASAKI.

The fission process is also used for civilian purposes in the generation of electricity. Here, of course, the process is slowed down and controlled. The spread of nuclear reactors and the production thereby of plutonium has meant that PROLIFERATION of NUCLEAR WEAPONS is technically hard to control. In 1974 India tested an atomic bomb produced by material diverted from a civilian energy programme.

## Attentive public
A concept used in public opinion analysis. It refers to that proportion of the people in mass society who hold articulate, informed and coherent attitudes about public policy issues. It excludes, at the top, those who actually make, or participate in making, policy. On the other hand, it excludes those at the bottom, the mass public, who do not hold consistent and coherent views about policy. The concept lacks precision. However, a rough and ready idea can be obtained of the size of the attentive public in advanced industrial countries (AICs) by quantifying the readership of what is known as the 'quality' press (e.g. the London *Times*, the *New York Times*, *Die Welt*, *Le Monde*, etc). This is only approximate because sales and readership do not necessarily coincide. The size of the attentive public also varies as between domestic and FOREIGN POLICY issues. In general, on the latter membership is smaller.

The idea of the attentive public is particularly crucial to the PLURALIST approach to INTERNATIONAL RELATIONS. Writers in this mode argue that interest groups and political parties have an important influence upon POLICY-MAKING. Although these organizations do not actually or formally take the decisions they do contribute to the milieu in which DECISION-MAKING occurs. They also serve as reservoirs from which the political leadership is recruited. It is through these channels that the mass public is often mobilized and made more aware of international issues. The attentive public plays an important linkage function in this pyramid, therefore.

## Attrition

Literally means 'wearing out'. It usually refers to the strategy adopted by the Allies in the First World WAR who turned from an initial policy of annihilation (utter and rapid destruction of the enemy's forces) to one of attrition. Wars of attrition are usually long-drawn-out affairs, and place the entire range of the STATE's resources at the disposal of the military. The most recent example of a war of attrition is the Iran–Iraq war of 1980–9, which displayed all the features referred to above almost to the point of total exhaustion on both sides.

## Autarky

Literally, the absence of TRADE and therefore self-sufficiency. The term is most often used in international economics. However, because of the close relationship between economics and politics in the world system, it has relevance to both. Complete autarky is impossible. From the earliest times human communities have exchanged goods and services. As social systems have become more complex, and in particular as economic systems have experienced industrialization, the costs of autarky have become more manifest. Classical nineteenth

century economic LIBERALISM, heavily influenced by the theories of Ricardo, rejected autarky as inefficient and argued for the absolute and comparative advantages of international trade. As these theories became accepted a REGIME based on these ideas became established. International payments were handled through a GOLD STANDARD while London became the commercial conduit for the system. Scholars would now describe this nineteenth century system as one of INTER-DEPENDENCE. The events of the early decades of the twentieth century, in particular the First World War and the rise of FASCISM and COMMUNISM destroyed this system. The United Kingdom was no longer able to function as the pivot of the system. In Europe political leaderships came to POWER determined to use economic relations as an instrument of policy. As a result a new drive to increase autarky was evident in Germany and the Soviet Union. In Asia, Japan rejected autarky for a policy known as co-prosperity. The attempts by Anglo–American diplomats to restore a form of LIBERALISM at BRETTON WOODS checked the drift away from FREE TRADE liberalism for a time. Recently developments in the world system have suggested moves back towards greater self-sufficiency where possible. The EC has instituted an agricultural policy which has created a largely self-sufficient market within its member STATES. As suggested above, pure autarky is an ideal type against which the policies of international ACTORS can be measured.
*See also*: MERCANTILISM.

## Authority

Person or institution which legitimizes acts or commands; as such it must be differentiated from POWER which indicates capacity rather than right. It is the lack of a common and accepted authority which is said to distinguish international from domestic politics and law. Consequently, some writers argue that because of its absence INTERNATIONAL

LAW is not law properly so-called, and INTERNATIONAL POLITICS is politics only by courtesy of name. IDEALISTS in international thought frequently argue, pursuing the DOMESTIC ANALOGY, that the solution to continuing and continual international conflict is the creation of a universal authority to regulate relations, establish a properly constituted legal order and to settle disputes. The LEAGUE OF NATIONS and the UN are sometimes (though wrongly) seen as early prototypes. Other theorists argue that the absence of universal authority, particularly since the decline of the Holy Roman Empire, is a source of strength, not weakness, in INTERNATIONAL RELATIONS since it reinforces the arguments for the SOVEREIGNTY, liberty and INDEPENDENCE of the STATE.

## Autonomy

Literal meaning is self-government. As such the term is associated with the idea of SOVEREIGNTY and INDEPENDENCE. In traditional international theory all STATES are assumed to be autonomous, that is, not subject to external authority whether this is spiritual (e.g. the Church) or temporal (e.g. Holy Roman Empire). The TREATIES of WESTPHALIA, 1648, are supposed to mark the beginning of the autonomy of the STATE and hence the anarchic nature of the INTERNATIONAL SYSTEM. Many commentators argue that very few, if any, states are autonomous in the true sense, and all display DEPENDENCE or penetration to some degree. As a result the concept has now taken on a much more relativistic implication. Autonomy is now regarded, particularly by PLURALIST writers, as a matter of degree rather than absolute. Thus it is no longer used as a substitute for sovereignty but as an alternative criterion. ACTORS in WORLD POLITICS are now seen as exercising relative autonomy within the constraints referred to above. So while the idea of sovereignty excludes all but states, the idea of auto-nomy includes any potential actor which is not wholly controlled by another.

## AWACS

Airborne Warning and Control System. The need for a 'look down' surveillance CAPABILITY is met by providing an airborne RADAR platform from where it is possible to detect aircraft and CRUISE MISSILES at the preliminary stages of their take-off/launch procedure. AWACS should thus assist in reducing the likelihood of the air defences of any STATE or ALLIANCE using it from being surprised by an attack.

## Axis

Refers specifically to the German–Italian pact of 1936 in which both STATES pledged to oppose republicanism in Spain and COMMUNISM in general. It was underlined by the mutual defence TREATY signed in 1939 ('Pact of Steel') and later extended to include Japan (1940). It has GEOPOLITICAL and strategic overtones (the Berlin–Rome–Tokyo axis) and its use rather than the more conventional word ALLIANCE was intended to signify a pivotal centre in WORLD POLITICS around which other states might cluster. It was first used in this connection by Mussolini to illustrate the common Nazi-FASCIST approach to INTERNATIONAL POLITICS.

## Azania

Probable name for the Republic of South Africa, if and when black majority rule is achieved. The name achieved semi-official status in 1979 with the formation of the Azanian Peoples Organization (AZAPO). 'Azania' is the word the Pan-Africanist Congress (PAC) uses for South Africa and it now appears to have wide currency among black opposition groups.

# B

### Bacteriological weapons
*See*: CHEMICAL AND BIOLOGICAL WARFARE (CBW)

### Baghdad pact
A largely UK-inspired and US-backed complex of TREATY arrangements formed in 1955 between Britain, Iraq, Iran, Pakistan and Turkey, the principle purpose being to form a northern tier barrier between the Soviet Union and the Middle East. Originally envisaged as a comprehensive regional defence organization which would include all members of the ARAB LEAGUE it soon fell prey to the political fragmentation which has become a common feature of Middle Eastern politics. Egypt in particular was hostile to the pact and in 1958 formed a rival federation (the United Arab Republic) with Syria. After a change of REGIME Iraq left the pact in 1958 and it was reshaped as the Central Treaty Organization (CENTO), the headquarters moving from Baghdad to Ankara. This in turn was seriously damaged in 1979 with the withdrawal of Iran and Pakistan. Although the United States did not sign the Pact or join any of its central organizations it did provide military and economic AID to the signatories. Viewing it as a vital link in the American strategic doctrine of CONTAINMENT the Soviet Union (for whom containment meant ENCIRCLEMENT) saw it as part of their Middle Eastern policy to nullify the effects of the Pact and to encourage anti-Western nationalist sentiments in the region.

### Balanced forces
A term used in strategic analysis, and specifically in ARMS CONTROL and DISARMAMENT negotiations. The phrase has two meanings. First, it is used to suggest 'matching', where forces can be measured tank for tank, aircraft for aircraft and so on. Secondly, it can be used to mean 'equivalence'. Here the parties may recognize the need to offset superiority in one dimension and inferiority in another in order to achieve an overall 'balance'. Whether the term 'balanced forces' is used in the first or the second sense, it can be difficult to achieve as a policy goal. Additionally, concentrating upon numerical factors can obscure the point that comparing force levels is not simply or primarily an exercise in quantification. Less tangible factors such as the morale and training of the manpower, the loyalty and commitment of the officers and other ranks and the technical skill to maintain equipment in good order may be equally significant.

### Balance of payments
A term used in international economics. It is used to refer to balance of all economic transactions between a STATE and the rest of the system. The main elements in these transactions are visible TRADE, investment and transactions between the monetary authorities within the state and those in the rest of the system, for example the IMF. Equilibrium in the balance of payments literally means that credits plus debits are at zero. This is a normative rather than an

empirical statement and thus states may find themselves in the short-term in disequilibrium. Long-term or fundamental disequilibrium is much more serious. States with a continual balance of payments surplus, such as Japan, and those in constant deficit, such as many THIRD WORLD non-oil producers will come under pressure from other ACTORS to take remedial measures. The rise in oil prices in the 1970s placed many states in fundamental disequilibrium and this issue has been discussed in such publications as the BRANDT REPORTS. There is clearly a significant overlap area between politics and economics in the INTERNATIONAL SYSTEM and the repercussions of the balance of payments position of many states is regarded as crucial for the continued working of a viable system of trade and payments.

## Balance of power

A pervasive and indispensable concept which is part of the stock-in-trade of both students and practitioners of DIPLOMACY. Indeed, it is regarded by some scholars as the nearest thing we have to a political theory of INTERNATIONAL RELATIONS. However, its meaning is by no means clear and it is open to a number of different interpretations. Martin Wight, for example, distinguishes nine different meanings of the term:

1. An even distribution of POWER.
2. The principle that power should be evenly distributed.
3. The existing distribution of power. Hence, any possible distribution of power.
4. The principle of equal aggrandizement of the Great Powers at the expense of the weak.
5. The principle that one side ought to have a margin of strength in order to avert the danger of power becoming unevenly distributed.
6. (When governed by the verb 'to hold') A special role in maintaining an even distribution of power.

7. (When governed by the verb 'to hold') A special advantage in the existing distribution of power.
8. Predominance.
9. An inherent tendency of INTERNATIONAL POLITICS to produce an even distribution of power.

Given this wide variety of meaning, it is helpful to distinguish between balance of power as a policy (a deliberate attempt to prevent predominance) and as a system of international politics (where the pattern of interaction between STATES tends to limit or curb the quest for HEGEMONY and results in general equilibrium). British FOREIGN POLICY in relation to Europe from the sixteenth century to the early twentieth century is an example of the former, while the European STATE-SYSTEM itself, from 1648 to 1789 and from 1815 to 1914, is an example of the latter. The break in this chronological sequence is the period of the rise of French radicalism and its refusal to be bound by notions of balance. In 1815 France, after a period of Napoleonic expansion, was restored to her former territorial limits and the balancing system was institutionalized. The Congress of VIENNA and the CONCERT SYSTEM it spawned throughout the nineteenth century represents the most articulate and self-conscious expression of balance in international history. Thus the most widely accepted meaning of the term is where it refers to the process whereby no one state, or group of states, gains predominance so that in Vattel's words 'it can lay down the law to others'. It is associated particularly with INDEPENDENCE, its main function being to preserve intact the multiplicity of states and to oppose empire in particular, and change in general. Order and stability are prized values rather than considerations of justice or fair play.

### History
The idea of balance is inseparable from the mechanics of INTERNATIONAL POLITICS and the practice was familiar to the ancient Greeks. THUCYDIDES' *History of the Peloponnesian*

*War*, although not specifically acknowledging the concept, is widely regarded as a classic account of its occurrence, albeit in BIPOLAR form, revolving around the relationship between Athens and Sparta in the 5th century BC. However, although the process undoubtedly occurred in the ancient world (in Europe, in China and in India) it was not until the Renaissance that it was self-consciously recognized as one of the basic formulas of political life. The Italian CITY-STATE system of the fourteenth and fifteenth centuries, which besides being fairly self-contained had a number of distinct and independent locations of power (Florence, Milan, Naples, Venice and the Vatican), was a lively arena of diplomatic forces where the principle was able to develop. Surprisingly, it was not MACHIAVELLI who first elaborated the idea (despite his obsessive concern with POWER POLITICS), but his contemporary, Guicciardini, in *History of Italy* (1537). This is generally regarded as the first systematic analytical treatment of the theme. The first explicit reference to it in TREATY form was in the TREATY of Utrecht (1713), where the idea of maintaining the balance of power was regarded as essential for the peace of Europe.

Balance of power both as policy and system is inseparable from the diplomatic history of the modern world and a plausible account of international politics up until 1914 can be given in terms of it. The LEAGUE OF NATIONS was a specific attempt to replace it: the principle of COLLECTIVE SECURITY which was at the heart of the organization was designed to obviate the need for balance. Many REALISTS argue that its absence in the inter-war period resulted directly in the Second World War. Since 1945 the international political system is not so readily explained in terms of the concept and notions of BIPOLARITY and MULTIPOLARITY have replaced it. However, echoes of it are still common in the language of DIPLOMACY, especially BALANCE OF TERROR. Most scholars would agree that changes in the nature of POWER (especially the development of nuclear weapons) and changes in the character of the basic ACTORS in WORLD POLITICS (especially the growth of non-state actors) has led to a general disregard of the concept as an explanatory device. It is now more often used as a journalistic metaphor rather than as a theory of international behaviour.

*Theoretical implications*
Balance of power, according to Hedley Bull, has fulfilled three positive functions in the modern STATE-SYSTEM:

1. It has prevented the system from being transformed by conquest into a universal empire.
2. Local balances of power have served to protect the INDEPENDENCE of states in particular areas from absorption by a preponderant power.
3. It has provided the conditions in which other institutions on which the international order depends might develop, e.g. diplomacy, WAR, INTERNATIONAL LAW, GREAT POWER management.

Bull's analysis is perceptive but it should be noted that in relation to the first function, empire and balance have existed side by side in state policy and although the whole system was not transformed into a universal empire, parts of it were. Thus European IMPERIALISM took place during the same period that balance of power was the orthodox power management technique. In relation to the second function some states have lost their INDEPENDENCE as a result of it, e.g. the partition of Poland in the eighteenth century and Czechoslovakia in 1939. With regard to the third function, although it has provided the conditions for mitigating general ANARCHY, war is a central feature of the system, its function being either to restore the balance or to rearrange it. Thus ACTION–REACTION, challenge–response, REVISIONIST/STATUS QUO, dissatisfied/satisfied, are key ideas associated with the operation of the system. It clearly presupposes some shared beliefs among the participants, especially concerning the nature, role and LEGITIMACY of the state,

31

yet the system is inherently unstable. A simple balance involving two states (a BIPOLAR system) is likely to be more unstable than a complex balance (a MULTIPOLAR system). This is because a sudden technological change which dramatically increases the power of one of the poles (e.g. the success of the Soviet Sputnik in 1957 and its perception in the United States) can, unless immediately corrected, destroy the equilibrium. Multipolar systems, because of the possibility of shifting combinations, can more readily cope with these occurrences. Indeed, flexibility of alignment and diplomatic MOBILITY are important characteristics; under such a system states must be able to change sides regardless of ideological affinity (The Nazi–Soviet pact of 1939 is a classic example). The corollary is also true; states must be willing to abandon an erstwhile ally when conditions change. A further point to note is that the system, because it involves constant calculation of power and interest, is likely to produce an international hierarchy where states are categorized into at least three divisions: GREAT POWERS, MIDDLE POWERS and SMALL POWERS. EQUALITY therefore exists only in a formal legal sense. All states are equal, but some are more equal than others. The balance of power era has been described as the golden age of diplomacy and it is not difficult to see why. Although war is essential to it, the wars that did occur tended to be fought with limited means for limited ends. The delinquent state which had upset the balance was allowed to re-enter the system and replay the game (e.g. France after defeat in the Napoleonic Wars, 1815). It was premised on a recognition of common interests and it permitted the development of international law on the basis of RECIPROCITY – one of its most important ground-rules being NON-INTERFERENCE in the domestic affairs of other states. Obviously, it was bound up with the conditions that created it, and in the second half of the twentieth century (despite attempts by neo-realists to prove otherwise) these conditions have all but disappeared.

But whatever else might be said of it, balance of power as a method of CONFLICT MANAGEMENT was the first, and some would say, the most sophisticated, attempt to provide a practical political solution to the problem of coexistence in a decentralized international system, so much so that it became synonymous with the very idea of international relations.

*See also*: COLLECTIVE SECURITY; REALISM

**Balance of terror**

The term refers to a situation where two ACTORS can credibly threaten each other with destruction. This CAPABILITY need not be total but should certainly be unacceptable to the parties concerned. Moreover, for the balance to be stable, neither side should be able to avoid the consequences of destruction by, for example, striking first and without warning. The situation described as a balance of terror would normally apply to STATES and has been taken specifically to refer to the relationship of NUCLEAR DETERRENCE between the SUPERPOWERS and their allies. In principle, however, a balance of terror situation could be held to apply between non-state actors such as TERRORIST groups. Moreover, to the extent that terror is a state of mind, any punishment threat can induce such an outcome. Schelling has argued that the balance of terror is simply a modern version of an old idea, 'the exchange of hostages'. In terms of its etymology the balance of terror is clearly derived from the BALANCE OF POWER. Snyder argues that 'the balance of terror is primarily a deterrent balance rather than a defensive balance'. In other words, as argued above terror is induced by the threat of punishment which is expressed in an offensive mode.

It is not possible to separate balance of terror as a system from balance of terror as a policy. Pursuit of the latter necessarily involves existence of the former. The attainment by both the United States and the Soviet Union of ASSURED DESTRUCTION capabilities and the conclusion of SALT I appeared to show that balance of terror had been stabilized, but developments since the mid-1970s seem to show that this suggestion was too simplistic. Trends toward WAR fighting strategies, the new interest in ballistic missile defence (BMD), appear to show that the balance in indeed 'delicate' and that it cannot be readily assumed.

## Balkanization

Term used by historians and diplomats to describe the deliberate fragmentation of a region into a number of independent and mutually hostile centres of POWER; the purpose being the prevention of a unified concerted threat to the imposer. First used to describe late nineteenth century Russian policy towards the Balkan states, but now used with increasing frequency to describe the DE-STABILIZATION policies of South Africa on its territorial borders. A diplomatic variation on the old theme of 'divide and rule'.

## Ballistic missile

A missile that follows a trajectory largely determined by the force of gravity. A ballistic missile will consist of a booster, a guidance system and a warhead. Once the initial boost phase has terminated gravity acts to return the missile to earth. The booster may be jettisoned early in flight. Ballistic missiles are now the main means of delivery whereby armed forces can launch NUCLEAR WEAPONS at their opponents.

## Bandung Conference

Held at Bandung (Indonesia) in April 1955. This conference is generally regarded as the first demonstration of the growing diplomatic significance of the THIRD WORLD. The conference grew out of the Columbo Conference of 1954. The majority of the twenty-nine participants at Bandung were Asian states. Bandung provided a platform for leaders such as Nehru (India) and Sukarno (Indonesia) to give voice to the new DIPLOMACY of positive NEUTRALISM or NON-ALIGNMENT. It also enabled the new revolutionary leaders in states such as China and Egypt to associate themselves with these ideas. The Bandung states were particularly reacting against the perception that the United States was following a policy of extending the COLD WAR ALLIANCES into the area, the establishment of the South East Asia Treaty Organization (SEATO) in 1954 being the best example.

The Bandung Conference restated the five principles of peaceful coexistence first set out in the Sino–Indian agreement on Tibet in 1954. These principles were (a) mutual respect for each others' territorial integrity and SOVEREIGNTY; (b) non-aggression; (c) NON-INTERFERENCE in each others' internal affairs; (d) EQUALITY and mutual benefits and (e) peaceful coexistence.

The spirit of cooperation among these non-aligned states developed rapidly throughout the rest of the decade. With the growing independence of the African continent and the emergence of Tito's Yugoslavia as a new influence, the movement became more genuinely global. By the time of the BELGRADE CONFERENCE the non-aligned movement had become a significant trend in WORLD POLITICS.

## Bank for International Settlements

This institution is a central bankers bank. It functions to assist the financial institutions of its member STATES to iron out short-term fluctuations in their currency positions. These operations are conducted through the central banks of the member states. Members are also enabled to resist speculative attacks upon their currencies. The current membership list shows that the bank can be regarded as part of the FIRST WORLD of the advanced industrial countries (AICS): the United States, Canada, Japan, France,

West Germany, Italy, the United Kingdom, Belgium, Netherlands, Switzerland and Sweden.

The bank originated in the 1930s in the wake of the Young Plan on German reparations. It was then hoped that it might help to assist in the development of international TRADE within Europe in order to generate wealth to fund reparations. With the rapid revival of the European economies in the aftermath of the MARSHALL PLAN, the bank staged an impressive resuscitation.

### Banking system

There is no centralized banking system in WORLD POLITICS that is isomorphic with banking systems in the advanced industrial countries (AICS). On a number of occasions such an initiative has been proposed; for example, after 1945 the UK economist J. M. Keynes proposed the establishment of a world clearing bank. Instead the system that has been established under the IMF has some of the characteristics of a banking system. Private commercial banks operate in world politics and can be regarded as TRANSNATIONAL ACTORS. Since the early 1970s these private banks have recycled funds into the system by making loans to STATES to assist their development or their external balances. A small number of states are heavily in DEBT as a result of this policy by the private banking system.

### Bantustan

Name given to the 'homelands', alleged by the South African government to be the historic places of residence of indigenous Blacks. As such, it is an essential part of the apparatus of APARTHEID. The Bantu Homelands Citizenship Act of 1970 provides that every black in the Republic shall be the citizen of a homeland irrespective of whether he was born there or indeed has ever been there. Ten such homelands were desig-

nated, forming in total about 14 per cent of the land area of the Republic, albeit the poorest parts. Some homelands have been declared independent states by South Africa – (Transkei 1976, Bophuthatswana 1977, Venda 1979, and Ciskei 1981) – but these are not recognized as such by the international community. The six others have different levels of self-government. Under apartheid, Black political rights are located in the homelands, not in the Republic.

### Barter

A system whereby goods and services are exchanged for other goods and services. By its very nature barter arrangements are BILATERAL. The commodities selected and the terms of exchange will be determined by the parties.

### Baruch Plan

A plan for the international control of atomic energy proposed by the US delegate to the UN Atomic Energy Commission, Bernard Baruch, in June 1946. The key to the Baruch Plan was the establishment of an international institution which would have control over all nuclear production and the right of access to national territories for the purposes of VERIFICATION and INSPECTION. Once this internationalization process had been achieved the United States would cease production of its own weapons. The Soviet Union rejected the Plan on the grounds that their own SOVEREIGNTY would be compromised and that it would freeze the development of NUCLEAR WEAPONS in the United States' favour. The Soviet counterproposal included the suggestion that any control commission should be subject to the final control of the UN SECURITY COUNCIL, where the VETO could be used. They also proposed that existing stocks of weapons – which were held by the United States – should be destroyed initially. It must be noted that the seemingly well intentioned proposals of the two principal STATES contained sections which the other could not easily accept without seeming to weaken their own position *vis-à-vis* the opposition.

## Bases
Traditionally these refer to points of military supply and troop concentration and are located at strategic points dictated by the perception of likely threat. Increasingly, the term is associated with ALLIANCE politics where some of the forces and material of one STATE are located on the territory of another, usually by agreement. Thus, most West European NATO member states host American bases. The degree of acquiescence in this can and does vary both in relation to the shared perception of threat and in relation to the ideological cohesion of the ALLIANCE. In this connection, it is as well to remember that the difference between 'host' and 'hostage' is often a matter of political will.

## Bay of Pigs
An ill-fated venture by the Kennedy administration in April 1961 to land a force of Cuban exiles, trained by the Central Intelligence Agency (CIA), at an inlet in southern Cuba (Cochinos Bay). The purpose of the invasion was to encourage a general anti-Castro rising and thus restore Cuba to the orbit of American influence and control. Within forty-eight hours of landing, the invaders were captured by the Cuban army. President Kennedy was forced to admit responsibility, and the invaders were subsequently ransomed by the United States, with $10 million in medical supplies given to Cuba. It has been argued that this fiasco encouraged Khrushchev to believe that Kennedy would not dare to respond forcefully to the placing of Soviet NUCLEAR MISSILES on Cuban soil in 1962.
*See also*: CUBAN MISSILE CRISIS

## Behaviouralism
*See*: SOCIAL SCIENCE APPROACH

## Belgrade conferences
Two conferences consisting of NON-ALIGNED and unaligned STATES were held in Belgrade in 1961 and 1969, at the instigation of President Tito of Yugoslavia. The aims of both were: (a) to assert a positive influence on WORLD POLITICS; (b) to reassert the principles of non-alignment solidarity; and (c) to call for the end of COLONIAL rule throughout the world.

The significance of the Belgrade conferences were that, building on the achievements of BANDUNG the non-aligned states began to focus GREAT POWER attention on the quest for a NEW INTERNATIONAL ECONOMIC ORDER (NIEO).

## Belligerency
A term in INTERNATIONAL LAW which indicates when an armed dispute reaches the point at which the participants are accorded the status of belligerents. Recognition of such a condition and status involves certain legal consequences. It means, for example, that the participants are bound by the international legal rules of WAR, so that provisions such as those relating to NEUTRALITY and PRISONERS OF WAR become operative. RECOGNITION itself is a political matter rather than a legal one and not surprisingly international law lacks precision and clarity on some issues associated with it. Sometimes, for example, the status of belligerency is distinguished from that of INSURGENCY, the latter referring to a mid-way stage between mere law-breaking and full belligerency. But since the issues involved are political rather than strictly legal, modern behavioural practice tends to obliterate this distinction. Insurgency is more properly regarded as a provisional or intermediate classification pending a more definite recognition of status, which in turn may depend on the outcome of the conflict.

## Benelux

An economic union between Belgium, Luxembourg and the Netherlands forged in 1948 to provide initially a common customs TARIFF. A fuller economic union of the three came into operation on 1 November 1960 which provides for common commercial and trading relations with other STATES as well as common and coordinated policies on investments, agriculture and various other fiscal and social matters. Benelux, which has a secretariat in Brussels, exists within the larger framework of the EC and is widely regarded by the three participating states as enhancing their bargaining position *vis-à-vis* the larger European member states, such as France, West Germany and the United Kingdom.

## Berlin crises

This former capital of Weimar Germany was the stage for two of the major CRISES of the post-war period. The first occurred in 1948–9 and is often referred to as the AIRLIFT, because of the use made of AIR POWER by the United Kingdom and the United States to fly supplies into the city in defiance of a BLOCKADE instituted by the Soviet Union. The second crisis ran from 1958–62 and is associated in the popular mind with the building of the Berlin Wall in the summer of 1961.

Berlin, like Germany itself, was divided into occupation zones as a result of the defeat of the AXIS powers in the Second World War. Berlin was actually located deep in the Soviet zone after 1945. The three Western allies were given access routes by road, rail and air corridors into their sectors of the city one month after the German surrender. This complex of rights and obligations was crucially dependent upon the continuation of inter-allied cooperation if it was to function effectively. When the post-war relationship between the Soviet Union and its Allies began to degenerate into the COLD WAR the fragile arrangements in Berlin, and indeed the whole German ques-

tion, became key issue areas between the protagonists. On the Western side the United States and their UK allies began to pursue a coordinated policy in and towards Germany. In particular these two STATES began to take steps to establish a greater degree of AUTONOMY for their zones (which were unified into the so-called Bizone in July 1946). The impression was certainly created, thereby, that a long-term goal for Anglo–American policy at this time was an independent West German state. The year following the Bizone decision was the landmark year of such decisions as the TRUMAN DOCTRINE and the MARSHALL PLAN. In early 1948 France, the United Kingdom, the United States and the BENELUX states decided at a conference in London to establish political activity in West Germany and to make Marshall AID available to the nascent state.

The proximate cause of the subsequent Berlin crisis of 1948–9 was the series of decisions reached by the London conference. The Soviet view was that such decisions violated the principle that policy on the future of Germany required Four-Power agreement. On 1 April 1948 the Soviet Union began to impose restrictions on the movement of military supplies through their zone into Berlin. In June 1948 the three Western states announced a currency reform for their zones – but not for Berlin – and the Soviet response was to institute further restrictions on movements into Berlin. When these currency reforms were extended to the Western sectors of Berlin later in June 1948 the Soviet authorities responded with a full BLOCKADE of all land-based access routes into the former capital of Germany. The crisis had now escalated to the maximum point of confrontation.

The response from the West to these moves was to institute an airlift of supplies into Berlin. France took no part in this operation and the US Air Force and the RAF divided the responsibility between themselves roughly in proportion of two to one. Indeed, throughout the crisis the British government actively supported US tactics and goals. The airlift response of the summer of 1948 was a paradigm example of BRINKMANSHIP, because while it physically avoided the blockade, tactically it left the next move to the adversary. Initially, the Soviet authorities were sceptical that the airlift would work. They had little experience of the successful use of such measures in warfare and, although Western air power had a formidable reputation, the Soviets would have been more influenced by their own experiences than by others' reputations. In the event, the Soviet Union miscalculated badly. The airlift was expanded in scope during the summer and autumn of 1948, and continued to operate throughout the winter of 1948–9 with increasing efficiency. As time went on and the measures taken, initially with some improvisation, became more effective, the onus was switched to the Soviet Union to make the next move. In fact the airlift was never challenged militarily by the Soviets and eventually they called off the blockade in May 1949. As a 'trial of strength', Berlin was much less coercive than CUBA. The original airlift response had been a compromise between doing nothing to help Berlin, which would have meant in effect abandoning the city and forcing an armed convoy through the blockade. As a bargaining move it was seen both as a compromise between the two extremes and as a means of buying time for a negotiated solution to be worked out. Because the crisis was terminated without formal negotiations, the possibility was left open that the issue could emerge again in the future.

Structurally, the first Berlin crisis produced a hardening of the divisions of Europe after 1945. When the War ended the situation was still fluid and uncertain. By 1949 a separate West German state had been established and NATO had been founded with full US participation. In the autumn of 1949 the German Democratic Republic was established in the Soviet zone and the post-war division of Germany had become a formality. Unlike the Cuba crisis,

Berlin led to an increase in tension and hostility between the two sides in the Cold War.

Berlin again became a crisis point in SUPERPOWER relations in November 1958, when the Soviet leader Khrushchev announced against a six-month time limit that the Soviet Union wanted to negotiate a more permanent settlement to the German question. His proposals included recognition of what might be termed the 'two Germanies' solution and the internationalization of Berlin. The two German states would be internationally recognized as neutrals and the territories of these two states would become part of a NUCLEAR-FREE ZONE. The six-month time limit that Khrushchev stipulated was that, failing agreement among the powers, the Soviet Union would sign a separate peace TREATY with the DDR (as the USA had done with the Japanese). Khrushchev's threat implied that the Western powers would have to deal at least on a DE FACTO basis with the DDR in order to maintain their regular access to the city of West Berlin. The United States' counter-proposals included resuscitating the idea of reunification of Germany with the idea that the Soviet Union would withdraw its forces from the DDR. These proposals also envisaged the holding of free elections in both parts of Germany prior to unification.

At the time that these proposals and counters were being actively discussed between the two sides, the situation was complicated on the Soviet side by increasing evidence that the economic stability of the DDR was being constantly undermined by the exodus of population to the West via the open border with West Berlin. Accordingly, the Soviet leadership came under increasing pressure from the DDR to support moves to close the borders to stop this haemorrhage of its population. With the approval of the Soviet Union and the other WARSAW PACT states the DDR closed the border between the two Berlins in August 1961. Eventually this closure became a permanent physical barrier – the Berlin Wall –

and the second Berlin crisis reached its turning point.

Western reaction to the closing of the Berlin crossing routes by the DDR in August 1961 was initially very restrained. The main concern was to avoid giving any cause to incite dissident elements in East Berlin, or indeed in the DDR in general, to take to the streets in mass protest at the action of the authorities there. Only when it became clear that a potentially damaging loss of confidence was occurring among the population of West Berlin did the United States take steps to increase the size of its garrison there and to send the vice-president and General Clay, the hero (in West Berlin) of the airlift crisis of 1948–9, to Berlin to boost morale. For the DDR the outcome of closing the frontier was highly beneficial both in the short term and in terms of longer-run goals of economic development. The United States used the crisis to attempt to advance plans for changes in NATO strategy towards FLEXIBLE RESPONSE. In June 1964 the Soviet Union signed a separate peace TREATY with the DDR.


## Biafra

The name given to the Nigerian secessionist movement which declared an independent state of Biafra in the eastern region on 30 May 1967. Nigeria had become independent from Britain in 1960 under a federal, republican constitution. Like many African STATES, Nigeria is a complex of ethnic groupings and tribal loyalties, the three most significant of these being the Hausa (in the north) the Ibo (in the east) and the Yoruba (in the west). The creation of Biafra in what might be termed 'Iboland' may appropriately be regarded as an example of ethnic NATIONALISM.

The events of May 1967 were a culmination of a series of moves and countermoves among the main ethnic power centres in Nigeria. These began in January 1966 when the army staged a COUP against the civilian leadership which had governed Nigeria since INDEPENDENCE. The army leader General Ironsi announced that the federation was being ended and that Nigeria would become a unitary state. There followed an indecisive and unsettling period wherein centripetal and centrifugal forces competed and conflicted in a POWER struggle which lead to a second coup in July 1966. It seemed clear that this second coup was directed against the Ibo because a sustained pogrom was directed against these peoples throughout the summer of 1966. Ibo leaders became convinced that a centrifugal rather than centripetal outcome was preferable, at least in terms of their perceived ethnic interests.

When an attempt at MEDIATION was made by the government of Ghana in January 1967 the Ibo's demands were for a much looser confederal arrangement rather than the unitary solution proposed by Ironsi (himself an Ibo) in 1966. A complete constitutional impasse resulted when the representatives of the Federal Military Government counter-proposed a much stronger federal solution. In reality, these constitutional differences were manifestations of more fundamental latent ethnic differences between the parties.

The declaration of Biafra marked the end of the constitutional phase of the conflict and the beginning of more organized and violent civil strife. The African states were diplomatically split by the Biafran CRISIS. The majority supported the Federal Government but a number of states, of which Tanzania was probably the most influential, recognized Biafra. The Organization of African Unity (OAU) itself attempted mediation on a number of occasions, without success. Outside INTERVENTION in the military AID role was provided by the United Kingdom and the Soviet Union (in support of the Federal Government) and by France (in support of Biafra). The outcome of the WAR was a long and bitter campaign which was eventually won by the Federal forces.

The Biafran example shows how fragile the system of political participation is in multi-ethnic states, particularly in the

THIRD WORLD. It also shows how BOUND-ARIES drawn up, in this case by COLONIAL powers, can become sacrosanct. State preservation would appear to be a core value of much contemporary significance in the THIRD WORLD if this instance is at all valid.

## Bilateral

Literally refers to matters affecting two parties, in contrast to unilateral (one party) and multilateral (many parties). It is normally used in international affairs to indicate joint policies adopted by STATES, especially but not exclusively in matters of TRADE, DEFENCE and DIPLOMACY.

Economic or trade bilateralism is employed to facilitate easier commerce as well as to establish closer political relations between the parties. The Soviet Union, in particular, has favoured this pattern of activity both with its Eastern European allies and with respect to foreign AID. The Western world, in contrast, has tended to view bilateralism as divisive and discriminatory. The General Agreement on Tariffs and Trade (GATT) was signed in 1947 to expand multilateralism and to mitigate the effects of narrow bilateralism in international commerce.

In defence matters, bilateralism usually refers to a TREATY, or agreement between two states involving degrees of military support in event of an attack or threat from a third state. In this sense, pacts can be specific and active or general and consultative. In either case, bilateralism serves to guarantee the STATUS QUO. Most major states in the INTERNATIONAL SYSTEM have defence postures which combine bilateral and multilateral security pacts. The United States since the inception of the TRUMAN DOCTRINE and the quest for containment in 1947 is a good example.

Bilateral diplomacy refers to traditional modes of dialogue between two states in contrast to the more modern practice of multilateral or collective diplomacy. Diplomacy based on bilateralism has been widely criticized. In particular, many commentators have felt it to be inadequate because it failed two prevent two world WARS. The LEAGUE OF NATIONS and the UN were seen as specific attempts to create multilateral collective diplomatic institutions to supplement the existing bilateral system.

## Billiard ball model
*See*: STATE-CENTRISM

## Biological weapons
*See*: CHEMICAL AND BIOLOGICAL WARFARE (CBW)

## Bipartisanship

Refers to traditions of cooperation or collaboration between different parties and institutions in the formulation and conduct of FOREIGN POLICY, especially in the United States where the doctrine of separation of powers is thought to inhibit unity. Bipartisanship is therefore a response to the concern felt by many commentators on democratic politics (de Toqueville, 1835, being foremost among them), that the price for extensive discussion and participation in domestic matters could be paralysis or sterility in external affairs. In this sense it is a practical political variation on the old adage that 'politics stops at the water's edge'.

## Bipolar

A concept associated particularly with the COLD WAR period when the structure of the international political system was imagined to revolve around two poles – the Soviet Union and the United States. The system was said to be organized in terms of POWER, REGIMES and IDEOLOGIES which coalesced around two huge blocs, each of which was dominated by the interests and perceptions of the two SUPERPOWERS. The model includes a crude notion of balance (really equilibrium), though it is a mistake to confuse bipolarity with the system of BALANCE OF POWER, which some theorists have tended to do. The simplicity of the model (which may or may not have corresponded with the real world it purported to describe) was often alleviated by characterizing it as either rigid or loose. Bipolarity existed in contrast to MULTIPOLARITY or POLYCENTRISM where the system is dominated by a number of POWER centres, independent loci of DECISION-MAKING and interests which are not directly or even necessarily related to superpower equilibrium. Thus, it is often argued that INTERNATIONAL RELATIONS were bipolar in the 1950s and that this gave way in the 1960s to multipolarity and polycentrism. This shift is said to have occurred in accordance with the degree of cohesion/fragmentation among and within the power blocs.

Bipolarity is associated with ZERO–SUM perceptions of policy revolving around the military balance (i.e. my gain is your loss), whereas multipolar models focus attention on patterns of interaction where the outcome is not so dramatic or one-dimensional and goes well beyond traditionally defined security concerns. One way of highlighting this may be to say that bipolarity is concerned almost exclusively with East/West issues as the basis for INTERNATIONAL ORDER, whereas multipolar approaches see a much wider and richer range of issues including the NORTH–SOUTH debate, as critical points of reference on the map of WORLD POLITICS.

### Black consciousness

Mass movement of young blacks formed in the late 1960s by, among others, Steve Biko, who was later to die in a South African jail (1977). After the imprisonment of Mandela in 1964 black activist opposition groups began a new phase in the struggle against APARTHEID. The idea behind black consciousness was that blacks should break away entirely from traditional attitudes to the liberation struggle and in particular should disassociate themselves from the paternalism and smugness which many of them saw as characterizing white LIBERAL groups in South Africa. It aimed to encourage a new spirit of black self-reliance and dignity by emphasizing the exclusive nature of the plight of blacks in the Republic. The movement has its counterpart in the United States, where it originated predominantly in the urban areas, but it is in South Africa that it has had its most dramatic impact. *See also*: ANC; APARTHEID

### Blitzkrieg

German strategic term evolved during the inter-WAR years, denoting a series of short, rapid engagements against isolated targets. These 'lightning wars' were carried out by aerial assaults from dive-bombers combined with mass formations of tanks to give maximum mobility and surprise. The strategy was adopted by Hitler and his general staff to avoid a long-drawn-out war of ATTRITION against Russia and the British Empire, which Germany was bound to lose given the likelihood of eventual American entry into the fray. Swift, highly mechanized thrusts by the German forces directed specifically at isolated enemies would, it was hoped, permit rapid victory without alerting the international community to any grand design.

Blitzkrieg had diplomatic, economic and psychological dimensions as well as the purely military ones. In DIPLOMACY it required Germany to discourage the formation of military ALLIANCES in Europe, and in particular to prevent a Franco–Russian combination. The Nazi–Soviet pact of 1939 was the culmination of this quest. On the economic level, blitzkrieg avoided the need for total mobilization of the domestic German economy and if successful would bring access to new sources of raw materials. In psychological terms, its purpose was to bludgeon or stun the enemy into SURRENDER or submission before any real or protracted resistance could be offered. The brilliant success of these tactics against Poland in 1939 persuaded Hitler to bring forward his planned offensive against France and the Low Countries in 1940. Ironically, the outstanding successes of blitzkrieg in its initial operations may have contributed to the eventual downfall of the Third Reich. In the post-war world the Israelis used blitzkrieg tactics in their campaigns of 1956, 1967 and 1973, but the term is normally associated with the German tradition of attempting to avoid a European war on two FRONTS.

## Bloc

French word originally used in the domestic context to describe combinations or groupings of parties in support of, and later in opposition to, government. Now in common use in WORLD POLITICS describing a combination of STATES supporting particular military, economic or political interests, e.g. the Western bloc, the sterling bloc, the COMMUNIST bloc. It is used extensively in studies of voting behaviour in the GENERAL ASSEMBLY of the UN where collective and recurring patterns have been identified, e.g. the THIRD WORLD bloc and the African bloc. The term is often used synonymously with coalition and ALLIANCE though in the case of the latter it does not have the same legal standing since it does not require a TREATY commitment or a common and specific declaration of policy.

## Blockade

Action designed to prevent access to, or egress from, enemy territory. It usually takes the form of a land blockade or a naval blockade but air forces could also be involved. Commonly, it is employed during a state of BELLIGERENCY where its aim is to deny resources and food to enemy forces and/or civilian populations. It can also be employed in peacetime ('pacific blockade') where it falls short of an act of WAR and is a REPRISAL for the commission of an illegal act. In both, INTERNATIONAL LAW confers rights and duties to imposer, target and neutrals. For example, in wartime blockades NEUTRALS must be given advance warning and a reasonable time in which to comply with the conditions imposed. Pacific blockades are now generally seen as an aspect of reprisals and may be instituted by the UN SECURITY COUNCIL but are forbidden to individual STATES. In this context, the legality of the QUARANTINE imposed by the United States on Cuba in 1962 to prevent Soviet missiles reaching the island is questionable. Similarly 'paper blockades' are forbidden by international law, which requires that sufficient force is used to made a blockade effective. In this case, neutrals are not required to respect the wishes of the imposer. To 'run a blockade' is to attempt to evade it and if unsuccessful is likely to result in seizure or confiscation of goods or cargoes.

Blockade has always played a part in inter-state conflict, especially so in modern times because of the high degree of economic INTERDEPENDENCE. To be effective blockades ought to involve overwhelming local FORCE superiority plus an identifiable degree of VULNERABILITY on the part of the target. Thus Britain, for whom naval forces and strategy were an essential part of FOREIGN POLICY, frequently favoured this technique. It was employed, for example, during the Napoleonic Wars against France, and in the twentieth-century wars against Germany. An example, albeit unsuccessful, of a land blockade is the Soviet attempt to seal off BERLIN in 1948–9.

## BMD

An abbreviation of Ballistic Missile Defence. This is an umbrella term that covers a number of CAPABILITIES, deployments and strategies. Thus a BMD can be either endoatmospheric or exoatmospheric. A BMD can be either a point defence or an area defence. Interest in BMD has increased of late with the publically declared commitment towards a space-based system known in the United States as the Strategic Defense Initiative (SDI). Earlier attempts by the SUPERPOWERS to develop a BMD in the 1960s led to the Anti-Ballistic Missile (ABM) TREATY.

## Bogota Charter

The Ninth International Conference of American States meeting at Bogota, Colombia between 30 March 1948 and 2 May 1948 produced the charter for the ORGANIZATION OF AMERICAN STATES. Conference DIPLOMACY had been a favoured instrument for consultation and communication on a pan-American basis since the first meeting held in Washington in 1896. By the time the Bogota conference was convened the UN was already a going concern and the American document is clearly influenced by the CHARTER OF THE UN. The latter had, of course, fully anticipated the likelihood of such regional arrangements as the OAS in the provisions of Article 52.

At Bogota the Latin American STATES sought to obtain a commitment from the United States to an expanded programme of economic assistance along the lines of the MARSHALL PLAN. Secretary of State Marshall made it quite clear, however, that the United States had no such intentions at the time and preferred to see development AID proceeding on a private rather than public basis. The United States was more concerned to establish the commitment of the hemisphere states to COLLECTIVE SECURITY issues at this time.

## Boundary

This term is used in a number of contexts in WORLD POLITICS. In its legal usage a boundary represents an absolute change of legal status. Thus a legal boundary may be regarded as a demarcation line between one legal competence and another. In this sense the term is consonant with the sovereign STATE-SYSTEM. A boundary is a limit upon the territorial jurisdiction of states. Within the boundary the STATE is sovereign, outside it is not. In practice this dichotomy has always been hard to sustain. The exercise of effective control requires the ability and willingness to do so. Dominant states in a system would often effect boundary changes in their favour through a policy of ANNEXATION. Boundary changes and adjustments were regarded as appropriate means for expressing the policies of leading states in the BALANCE OF POWER. Through the principle of RECOGNITION states would either indicate their assent or opposition to boundary changes. While non-recognition does not prevent a state from exercising effective control, it does indicate that the control is DE FACTO, not DE JURE.

GEOPOLITICAL usage has identified a number of categories of boundary. The best known is probably the 'natural' boundary. What geographers have in mind here are significant physical features such as a mountain chain, a river system or a waterway. Excessive determinism should certainly be avoided in this usage. A river may divide or unite. A mountain chain may locate natural resources which require cooperative relations for purposes of exploitation. Geographers have also delimited 'natural' boundaries where the limits are based upon ethnic identity. 'Contractual' boundaries are based upon legal norms (see above) while 'geometric' boundaries reflect lines of longitude and latitude. Finally, 'power–political' boundaries reflect the roles of dominant states and may be seen as akin to the balance of power usage (see above).

The BEHAVIOURAL approach, and in particular SYSTEMS THEORISTS, have taken a transactions approach to the question of boundaries. Thus Burton has argued for a conceptualization of the subject 'without reference to political boundaries, and indeed, without reference to any physical boundaries.' Likewise, Deutsch has argued that boundaries mark 'relative discontinuities' in human relations. Recent scholarship on the concept of REGIMES has also tended to argue against the legal and geographical concept of boundary. Regimes operate under transnational criteria and therefore transcend the more traditional view of the boundary. Whatever the theoretical and heuristic merits of this approach, there can be no doubt that the idea of boundary, as traditionally understood, is still a potent force in world politics. The politics of Africa, for example, would be impossible to comprehend without an appreciation of the power–political boundary-making of European IMPERIALISM which established the contours of the present state-system in that continent.

## Boycott

Originally practised in Ireland in 1880 and named after its first target, it involves a systematic refusal to enter into social, economic, political or military relations with a particular STATE or group of states in order to punish or bring about compliant behaviour. It is most commonly used in international economic relations, where goods and services produced by a particular target would be boycotted. It can be primary, where the imposer adopts policies directly aimed at the target, or secondary, where the imposer penalizes those maintaining contact or patronage with the target. In addition it can be general, a wholesale boycott of goods and services, or specific, confined to one particular item or class of goods. It is increasingly used in WORLD POLITICS in all the above senses by states and non-state ACTORS alike although it appears to have no specific RECOGNITION in INTERNATIONAL LAW besides the strictures covering embargoes or SANCTIONS. The target with the highest profile in recent

international history has been, and still is, the Republic of South Africa.

## Brandt Reports

The Independent Commission on International Development Issues met for two years from December 1977 to December 1979 under the chairmanship of the former West German Chancellor, Willy Brandt. Its terms of reference were to consider the past, present and future for economic development as an ISSUE AREA in WORLD POLITICS. Their report entitled *North–South: A Programme for Survival* was published in 1980. Three years later the Commission produced an update, *Common Crisis*, because it was felt that in the interim many of the problems identified in the first report had worsened.

The two Brandt Reports are striking testimony to the view that crucial areas of problem-solving in world politics can be tackled by a greater commitment to cooperation and the acceptance that INTERDEPENDENCE holds the key to the future. At the same time the Reports are essentially a restatement of arguments and attitudes that had been prominent for decades in the development literature. As such the Reports are an urgent manifesto to governments, particularly in the advanced industrial countries (AICS) and to ATTENTIVE PUBLICS in those areas. Ideologically, the Brandt approach can be regarded as an example of economic LIBERALISM, although in this particular instance the liberalism is tempered to take account of the differential needs of the THIRD WORLD STATES. This modified liberalism has been termed 'compensatory' or 'International Keynesianism' by writers on this subject area.

## Bretton Woods

A series of multilateral agreements on international economic relations were reached at Bretton Woods (United States) in July

1944 under the aegis of the embryo UN. Forty-four STATES agreed to a Final Act establishing an IMF and an International Bank for Reconstruction and Development (IBRD). The proposals that were discussed at Bretton Woods were the outcome of a series of BILATERAL NEGOTIATIONS conducted between the United States and the United Kingdom over the previous two years. The IBRD was described by the London *Economist* in 1945 as 'a much simpler project which has attracted neither much discussion nor much hostility ...'. The IMF, on the other hand, was from its inception more controversial. The two STATES concerned with these preliminaries, the United States and the United Kingdom, had rather divergent ideas about the future monetary REGIME. These differences were made public in, respectively, the White Plan, originating in the US Treasury, and the Keynes Plan, originating in the UK Treasury. White envisaged a Stabilization Fund made up entirely of contributions from member states. Keynes envisaged a Clearing Union based on the overdraft principle and employing a new unit of account – the 'bancor'. Whereas the total available liquidity remained constant under White – so that drawing rights equalled liabilities – in the Keynes scheme additional liquidity could be pumped into the system to enable debtor states to overdraw. Conversely, creditor states would provide the main collateral in this arrangement.

The Anglo–American differences over the putative IMF are sometimes presented as the conservative versus the radical views of the future. It should be noted, however, that both schemes tended to reflect the perceived NATIONAL INTERESTS of the parties advocating them. In the event, the US bargaining position was more credible and the Bretton Woods conference produced a fund which bore a close family resemblance to the White Plan.

The term 'Bretton Woods system' is often used to refer to these two institutions and to the regimes thereby established. Both have changed considerably since their inception. Accordingly, the reference to 'Bretton Woods' is of historical, rather than contemporary, validity.

## Brezhnev doctrine

In the aftermath of the Soviet invasion of Czechoslovakia, Leonid Brezhnev, in a speech to the Fifth Congress of the Polish COMMUNIST Party in Warsaw on 12 November 1968, proclaimed a new and more sinister Soviet version of the limits of sovereign INDEPENDENCE within the Communist BLOC. He asserted that the 'socialist community as a whole' had a right of INTERVENTION in the territory of any one of its members whenever forces hostile to socialism threatened its ideological alignment. The doctrine is significant in that it appears to run counter to previously accepted legal norms concerning SOVEREIGNTY. Under this doctrine, the unity of the communist bloc as a whole takes precedence over the liberty of particular states. It was subsequently replaced by the GORBACHEV DOCTRINE.

The doctrine had unsettling effects both on the process of DETENTE with the West and, more importantly, on members of the Eastern bloc itself since it clearly implied that the ostensibly anti-Western military orientation of the WARSAW PACT was not exclusively so. The ALLIANCE could be, and was, used against a signatory member. Outside the pact area, the doctrine was used to justify the Soviet invasion of AFGHANISTAN in 1979.

## Brinkmanship

Brinkmanship is a strategy adopted during a CRISIS to coerce one's adversary into making a conciliatory move. The essence of the strategy is to manipulate the shared risks of violence – which it is assumed that neither party wants – to get the other to 'back down'. Thomas Schelling (1966) discusses brinkmanship in some detail and more recently Richard Ned Lebow (1981) has added impressively to the literature on the subject in his 1981 book on the international crisis.

Diplomatically, the US Secretary of State J. F. Dulles popularized the idea during the Eisenhower Administration of the 1950s. The most famous example of the use of this idiom, certainly by American statesmen, came during the CUBAN MISSILE CRISIS of 1962 when the J. F. Kennedy Administration succeeded in their commitment to the removal of perceived offensive missiles from the island of Cuba.

Brinkmanship is clearly a high-risk strategy which depends for its successful outcome on the mutual recognition of parties that WAR would be clearly the worst outcome. GAME THEORISTS claim a certain isomorphism with the mixed motive game of 'Chicken', wherein similar manipulative strategies are involved.

## Buffer state

A GEOPOLITICAL term most often associated with BALANCE OF POWER. It refers to small or weak STATES which exist on the borders of powerful states and which, from the security standpoint of the latter, serve as intermediate 'cushions' or 'crush zones'. Before the advent of AIR POWER buffer states were seen as an insurance against direct and, more importantly, surprise hostilities between GREAT POWERS. The continued INDEPENDENT existence of these states thus precariously depended on the current state of play regarding both the local and general balance of power. While not satellite states their freedom of action was a direct function of the security needs of their powerful neighbours. For example, the states of central Europe, and especially Poland, were widely regarded during the inter-war years as buffers between Germany and the Soviet Union. In the same way, AFGHANISTAN and Thailand were the crush zones that could absorb and delay Russian and French penetration into British India in the late nineteenth century.

# C

## C³I

This refers to command, control, communications and INTELLIGENCE (usually rendered as 'see-cubed-eye'). The growing commitment in the United States to ideas about COUNTERFORCE and NUCLEAR WAR fighting have directed the attention of strategists to the need to maintain an effective system of DECISION-MAKING in circumstances that are totally novel. In the language of analysis these decision systems are referred to as the National Command Authorities (NCA). WAR fighting strategies are, therefore, based upon the assumption that these NCAs would continue to function effectively during a nuclear war: giving commands, receiving reports and, possibly, engaging in DIPLOMACY with the adversary in order to secure a termination of hostilities.

Empirical studies of decision-making in CRISIS situations do not leave an optimistic picture of how well the NCA would function in a nuclear war. Since great psychological stress is a well documented factor in all acute crises, the level of stress created by the totally unfamiliar environment of a nuclear war could well be intolerable. Even if the political leadership could handle the stress level, the NCA might simply not function at a sufficient level of technical competence for the demands of nuclear warfare. It is towards these kinds of problems that the C³I literature addresses itself.
*See also*: NUCLEAR DECAPITATION

## Calvo doctrine

Carlos Calvo, an Argentinian jurist, challenged, in 1868, the accepted doctrine of the legitimacy of state-INTERVENTION in another STATE'S internal affairs to protect the rights of ALIENS. The Calvo Clause (which is a common feature of public contracts between Latin American governments and aliens) asserts that aliens have no claim to preferential treatment and that in this regard all sovereign states must be treated as equals. The MONROE DOCTRINE, while denying interventionist rights to Europeans, tacitly reserved them for the United States. The Calvo doctrine, along with that advanced by fellow Argentinian Luis Drago in 1903, was an attempt to limit the scope of Monroe and to reassert the rights of absolute SOVEREIGNTY. It was subsequently embodied in a section of Article 1 of the Second HAGUE CONVENTION of 1907.

## Camp David accords

Historic agreement reached between Israel and Egypt in 1978 through the GOOD OFFICES of the United States and named after the presidential mountain retreat in Maryland. The accords were published as two documents – the 'Framework for Peace in the Middle East' and the 'Framework for Conclusion of a Peace Treaty Between Egypt and Israel'. The first document, as its title implies, was a general statement of agreed principles relating mainly to self-government for the Palestinians, the second referred specifically to Israeli occupation of Sinai. This dual approach was deliberate and was designed to link a BILATERAL

Israeli–Egyptian agreement to a broader ARAB–ISRAELI settlement and thus avoid the accusation that Egypt was selling out the Palestinians in order to achieve a separate peace. In all, five major agreements were reached and under the terms of them Israel was to withdraw from the territory conquered in the 1967 WAR in a series of timed and monitored stages. The essence of the deal was an exchange of land for the promise of peace. Israel promised to evacuate settlements in Sinai while Egypt recognized the Jewish state. In addition, Israel was committed to negotiate on the issue of Palestinian AUTONOMY, but pending a final settlement, still retained the Gaza Strip.

The process became known as 'step-by-step' DIPLOMACY whereby the overall settlement was divided into discrete segments, each of which had to be satisfactorily resolved before the next phase was activated. This approach was regarded as preferable to a more comprehensive settlement of all the outstanding issues in the Arab–Israeli conflict, not least because the latter would require a single SUMMIT conference that would have inevitably involved the Soviet Union. None of the parties involved, not least the United States, wanted to enhance the Soviet role in the Middle East, nor did they wish to widen the Arab participation which such a conference would necessarily invoke.

Although at the time Camp David was hailed as a dramatic breakthrough in Middle Eastern politics and as a triumph of US mediatory diplomacy, the net results were disappointing. Egypt, in particular, became isolated in the Arab world and led by Syria (and backed by the Soviet Union) a 'rejectionist' front soon surfaced. In addition, Egypt lost its status as host to the ARAB LEAGUE headquarters. Carter's diplomatic DEMARCHE, like his enhanced reputation, was destined to be short-lived.

## Capability

A term used in the analysis of POWER. It refers to an attribute or possession of AC-TORS. Traditionally capability analysis concentrated upon observable factors such as military or economic possessions rather than intangibles. This has been modified of late and both tangible and intangible attributes (such as morale, diplomatic skill) are recognized as relevant. Capability analysis has also been traditionally thought of in relative rather than absolute terms. One actor was held to possess more attributes than others and therefore to be potentially more powerful. Although such analyses frequently ignored the problem of converting capability into power relationships, they were instructive and heuristic. Stratification systems based upon identifying 'great', 'super' or 'small' actors were the product of such speculation.

Capability is a necessary condition for power relationships to exist. The link between the two is mediated by the factors of DOMAIN and SCOPE. It is now generally agreed that discussions on the capabilities of actors, without specifying the domain and scope within which such attributes are exercised, is meaningless. Converting capability into POWER relations thus constitutes an empirical test, however rudimentary, of the utility of the attribute.

## Carter doctrine

Refers to President Carter's January 1980 State of the Union Address where he declared that 'any attempt by an outside force to gain control of the Persian Gulf region will be regarded as an assault on the vital interests of the United States of America and such an assault will be repelled by any means necessary, including military force.' The statement was in direct response to developments in Iran in 1979 (the fall of the Shah and his replacement by the Ayatollah Khomeini) and the Soviet invasion of AFGHANISTAN in the same year. These two events were perceived to threaten US vital interests in the Gulf region – access to oil and strategic advantage being the key motivations. Under the Carter doctrine the

United States publicly declared its resolve to defend the Gulf and in so doing removed any doubt about its intentions following the ambiguity of the NIXON DOCTRINE and the mood of NON-INTERVENTIONISM following the debacle in VIETNAM. The major policy initiative generated by the doctrine was the creation of a Rapid Deployment Joint Task Force geared for instant dispatch to the area in case of attack. It also involved renewed US efforts at securing BASES or basing rights from which such a task force could be deployed. President Carter and his national security adviser, Zbigniew Brzezinski, regarded the Soviet invasion in particular as a grave threat to regional security. Afghanistan was perceived to be a stepping-stone to Soviet HEGEMONY in the Gulf. The twin advantages of access to warm water ports and control over a major portion of the world's oil supplies were seen as historic impulses of Soviet FOREIGN POLICY, which the Soviets were determined to realize. The language of the Carter doctrine is redolent of the MONROE DOCTRINE while its content, with its implicit belief in the DOMINO THEORY, is clearly a variant of President Truman's policy of CONTAINMENT. Its overall significance was that despite President Carter's projection of his administration's determination to restore a moral dimension to US foreign policy (especially concerning HUMAN RIGHTS), the underlying REALPOLITIK of American globalism remained undiminished.

## Caudillismo

A phenomenon associated mainly with Latin American politics, which refers to political loyalty to individuals (the 'caudillo') rather than to ideas, IDEOLOGIES or issues. Inherited from Spanish and Portuguese IMPERIAL policies, this personalization of politics often bypasses the formal trappings of government. The term is sometimes used interchangeably with *personalismo*, which again refers to loyalty to a 'boss' figure.

Two outstanding examples are Juan Peron in Argentina and Fulgencio Batista in Cuba.

## CENTO

An acronym for the Central Treaty Organization.
*See*: BAGHDAD PACT

## Chargé d'affaires

DIPLOMATIC term meaning the head of a diplomatic mission (*Chargé d'affaires en titre*) attached to a Minister for FOREIGN AFFAIRS. As an interim appointment, or in the absence of the head of mission, a *chargé d'affaires ad interim* would be appointed.

## Chemical and biological warfare (CBW)

Chemical weapons fall into three broad categories; poison gases, incapacitants and anti-plant agents. Similarly biological weapons are of three types: viruses, rickettsiae and bacteria. Both classes of esoteric weapons have been the subject of significant attempts to establish an international legal REGIME. Thus, the 1925 Geneva PROTOCOL outlaws the 'use in war of asphyxiating, poisonous or other gases, and all analogous liquids materials and devices'. The Protocol is generally regarded as having two weaknesses. First, it is not actually illegal to possess such weapons, only to use them. Secondly, a number of STATES entered specific reservations at the time that they would only feel bound by the TREATY so long as others were bound, and if in any future conflict their adversaries used such weapons, then they reserved the right to reciprocate in kind. In essence, therefore, those states who reserved their commitment to the regime were merely pledging not to be the first to use such weapons.

The regime on biological weapons is more comprehensive. Since 1975 it has been illegal to develop, produce, stockpile and transfer these weapons.

## Choke points

Strategic and GEOPOLITICAL term used in naval DIPLOMACY referring to international straits or narrows, control of which could hamper warship or commercial transit. In 1982 the UN Convention on the Law of the Sea recognized the right of transit passage through 116 specified international straits, although some strait STATES (e.g. Spain and Morocco in relation to the Strait of Gibraltar) attempted to restrict the rights of movement upon, over and under these waterways to the legal REGIME covering INNOCENT PASSAGE. This would have given these contiguous states discretionary control over traffic flow.
*See also*: LAW OF THE SEA

## City-state

An independent unit of political organization which flourished in three periods of international history: in the ancient Near East, in classical Greece and in medieval and Renaissance Europe. In INTERNATIONAL RELATIONS it is particularly associated with ancient Greece from the Dark Ages to the Hellenistic period, and with medieval Italy. The Greek city-state, or *polis*, was equivalent to a small STATE or civic republic centred around an urban development but also drawing in the surrounding rural areas. Indications as to size vary, but scholars have estimated that the population of Athens at the height of its glory was between 40,000 and 140,000. Territorial extent also varied; Athens covered approximately one thousand square miles while at the other extreme the island of Ceos covered ten by six miles and was itself divided into four city-states. Citizens of these states generally knew each other personally, were acquainted with their leaders and identified with the *polis* itself rather

than with Greece or Italy as a whole. The city-state was virtually self-contained and conducted its own foreign and defence policies. They often formed leagues, ALLIANCES and federations for mutual advantage and bilateral TREATIES were also quite common. Greeks, for example, formed such collective groupings after 499 BC to resist the advancing Persians. Policies could also be IMPERIALISTIC and because of their size, these empires were usually sea-based. The most famous conflict between city-states in the ancient world was that between Athens and Sparta, the Peloponnesian Wars (432–04 BC). Indeed, its principle chronicler, THUCYDIDES is still regarded as an important point of departure in the classical study of international relations. The city-states of medieval and Renaissance Italy – Milan, Venice, Genoa and Florence – were similar in outlook and organization and their external relations are often cited as sinister case-studies in the more cynical dimensions of the politics of REALISM (*see*, for example: MACHIAVELLI's *Prince* and *Discourses*).

## Civil war

Civil war is protracted internal violence aimed at securing control of the political and legal apparatus of a STATE. Because it is protracted, it is possible to distinguish a civil WAR from a COUP D'ÉTAT. Because it is internal it is possible to distinguish a civil war from external INTERVENTION. Because it involves protracted violence it is possible to distinguish civil war from a communal CONFLICT.

In the analysis of civil wars it is generally possible to distinguish two sides: incumbents and INSURGENTS. In such circumstances other members of the society will find that they have to define their attitude to the CONFLICT. If they become drawn into supporting one side or the other then the war would be said to have 'polarized' the whole society. Degrees of participation in the war will obviously differ between individuals and groups in the society. For some, participation may be restricted to passive support for one side or the other. For others, the war may draw them into political and military activities.

The stipulation of civil war above may be regarded as the norm from which a number of deviations are possible. Three may particularly be noted. Civil wars that arise as a result of attempts being made to end COLONIALISM; civil wars that result from the desire by part of a state to break away; civil wars that result from the desire of states that have been separated to achieve reunion.

The desire by colonial peoples and territories for INDEPENDENCE is one of the most significant trends in the nineteenth and twentieth centuries. Colonial wars can become civil wars whenever a significant body of opinion within the polity wants to continue with the existing colonial REGIME. This would most obviously be the case where large numbers of settlers had arrived in the territory during colonial control. These people might perceive that they had a vested interest in the maintenance of the STATUS QUO, fearing that the anti-colonial insurgents might adversely alter political, legal and economic arrangements. This instance is a departure from the norm because these colonial civil wars have three parties – incumbents, insurgents and settlers – rather than the usual two.

Civil wars that arise from secessionist tendencies and civil wars that arise from IRREDENTIST tendencies may usefully be regarded as being opposite sides of the same coin. Secessionist civil wars are particularly associated with ethnic NATIONALISM and the desire of ethnically homogeneous peoples to greater self-determination. An example of this type of civil war would be BIAFRA. Civil wars that are prompted by the desire for reunion are, again, nationalistic in character, although in this instance the ethnic factor may not be so evident.

The role of third parties, external to the territory of the state, can be crucial in determining the outcome of civil wars. Most obviously third parties can provide assistance to incumbents or insurgents in a variety of ways. Diplomatic assistance – for example, by allowing insurgents to establish a government in exile – is both practical and symbolic. Economic assistance can help parties to finance the war. Finally, military assistance can provide the CAPABILITY required to prosecute the violence. Such assistance is clearly a form of INTERVENTION, but this behaviour pattern can be taken much further if the third party actively engages its own forces in the war. Such interventions can be decisive, as the case of the Indian intervention in the Pakistan–Bangladesh civil war in 1971 shows.

There are a number of structural factors in the contemporary world political system which serve to exacerbate the incidence and severity of civil wars. First, the state membership of the system has increased substantially since 1945. This simply gives more opportunities for civil wars to occur than in the past. Secondly, many states, particularly those located in the THIRD WORLD are inherently unstable. Thirdly, the differential possession of capability, as between the states at the top of the HIERARCHY and those at the bottom, increases the proclivities for intervention. Clearly a civil war is not a necessary condition for intervention but it may be a sufficient one. Fourthly, notwithstanding its CHARTER, provisions in favour of the territorial integrity of states (see in particular Article 2:4) the UN has failed to develop sufficient efficacy in its own instruments to prevent intervention in civil wars by third parties. Finally, the growth of transnational TERRORISM has increased the extent to which private ARMIES can feed off a civil war situation to further their own interests.

## Clausewitzian doctrine

Karl von Clausewitz (1780–1831) was a Prussian officer who is widely regarded, even in the nuclear age, as the greatest ever writer on military theory and WAR. He is best known for propagating the thesis that the political and social circumstances out of which conflicts arise should also determine their conduct. This is popularly, but inaccurately, rendered in the aphorism 'war is the continuation of policy by other means'; that is, that war is indistinguishable from political and social structures and should therefore be conceived in terms of them. The essence of the Clausewitzian doctrine is contained in this passage from *On War* (1968, p. 89):

> As a total phenomenon its dominant tendencies always make war a remarkable trinity – composed of primordial violence, hatred and enmity, which are to be regarded as a blind natural force; of the play of chance and probability, within which the creative spirit is free to roam; and of its element of subordination, as an instrument of policy, which makes it subject to reason alone. The first of these aspects mainly concerns the people; the second, the commander and his army; the third, the government. . . . A theory that ignores any one of them or seeks to fix an arbitrary relationship between them would conflict with reality to such an extent that for this reason alone it would be totally useless.

This insight, despite the bourgeois, militarist background from which it came, was taken up by Marx, Engels, Lenin and Trotsky and subsequently influenced the military thinking of an entire generation of Soviet leaders. In the West, however, Clausewitzian doctrines were regarded as excessively militaristic, typically Teutonic and casually cynical. However, with the growth of STRATEGIC STUDIES, especially in the United States, there has been a reappraisal of his contribution and although Clausewitz largely ignored the economic, technological, maritime and aerial aspects of warfare, his understanding of its essential socio–political character and the early distinction he drew between LIMITED and TOTAL warfare together form the conceptual basis of modern strategic thought, so

much so that it could be said that in the age of nuclear DETERRENCE 'policy' is now 'the continuation of war by other means'.

## COCOM
Coordinating Committee for Multilateral Export Controls. Established in 1949, this was an economic and commercial instrument of COLD WAR politics. Its rationale was to deny access to members of the WARSAW PACT to Western TECHNOLOGY which could, directly or indirectly, be used for military purposes. It has been in place for over forty years and has been a key factor in economic warfare as practised by the West. The list of items covered, according to one commentator, is of a size 'roughly equivalent to the New York telephone directory' and many argue that since it is dominated by items of marginal significance, for example categories of machine tools which are easily available elsewhere, its overall usefulness is doubtful. The onset of DETENTE and the opening up of Eastern Europe late in 1989 has cast further doubt on its overall utility. Whether the United States will abandon or radically restructure this instrument in the light of the democratization of many Warsaw Pact members remains to be seen. Until the overall strategic equation undergoes a radical change it is unlikely, at least in the areas of telecommunication and high TECHNOLOGY, to disappear altogether.

## Coercion
Coercion is a form of POWER relationship. Like all such relationships it depends first upon the possession of a CAPABILITY that can be converted into policy instruments for making threats. When considering coercive behaviour in the abstract most people think first of military capabilities and the making of punitive threats. Coercion is thus related to ideas about DETERRENCE. However, economic instruments of policy

can also be highly coercive. ECONOMIC SANCTIONS, particularly since they seek to deprive a target ACTOR of scarce goods and services, should properly be included in the repertoire of coercive strategies.

Since costs are involved, both in making threats and in carrying them out, an actor seeking to impose its will upon a re-calcitrant target will often hope that the mere threat of coercion is enough to secure compliance. If this proves not to be the case, the imposer has to face the difficult decision of making up its mind whether to carry through with the threat or not. Such decisions will often hinge upon consider-ations of CREDIBILITY and reputation.

### Cold War

A term coined by American journalist H. B. Swope and popularized by Walter Lippman, used to describe the state of tension, hostility and rivalry that developed between the Western (non-communist) and Eastern (COMMUNIST) BLOCS after the Second World War. It indicates a condition of 'neither peace nor war' which contains most of the structural features of traditional GREAT POWER rivalries yet stops short of actual armed engagements. CONFLICT was waged through IDEOLOGICAL means, economic rivalry, ARMS RACES, PROPAGANDA, diplo-matic outbursts, threats of FORCE and the use of client STATES to promote each side's cause. Its most dangerous and virulent phase was in the 1950s and early 1960s. After the CUBAN MISSILE CRISIS of 1962, which brought the United States and the Soviet Union to the brink of an all-out 'hot' war, the intensity of the conflict slowly abated until the 1972 summit meeting between Brezhnev and Nixon, where both leaders publicly denounced it and inaugurated a period of DETENTE. However, it was not for-mally ended until the Malta summit meeting between President Bush and Mikhail Gor-bachev on 3 December 1989 when both leaders publicly acknowledged that the Cold War era was now consigned to history.

There has been much scholarly debate on the origins of the Cold War, particularly from the US side. It is usual to identify three schools of thought on this issue: the tradi-tionalists, the revisionists and the post-revisionists. The traditionalists argue that the responsibility for the Cold War lies with the Soviet Union. Post-war Soviet ex-pansion into Eastern Europe coupled with the communist aim of world REVOLUTION meant that the United States had to re-spond despite its preference for passive FOREIGN POLICIES and despite its emphasis on international cooperation within INTER-NATIONAL ORGANIZATIONS. It was not until 1947 with the inauguration of the TRUMAN DOCTRINE and the MARSHALL PLAN that the United States finally accepted the need actively to confront the Soviet Union. The revisionists place the respon-sibility on the United States. They argue that even before the war had ended the United States (and to a lesser extent, the United Kingdom) had determined to limit the influence of the Soviet Union. The use of ATOMIC WEAPONS against Japan, as well as employing various forms of global eco-nomic inducements, clearly indicates that the United States had decided long before 1947 that US policy was geared to the future destruction of communism and the Soviet Union. On this view Soviet policies in Eastern Europe were purely defensive, a response to US ENCIRCLEMENT. The post-revisionists argue that the Cold War can best be understood in terms of a synthesis between the two schools. They reject the thesis that Soviet policies in Eastern Europe were defensive reflexes and they also reject the notion that it was not until 1947 that the United States entered the fray. Again they reject the idea, common to both tradi-tionalists and revisionists, that had one side or the other adopted different post-war policies then the Cold War need never have occurred. In this sense the Cold War is best explained as a logical outcome of the Second World War. Germany and Japan had been destroyed, the United Kingdom and France were reduced to decidedly secondary status and the old European empires in Africa and Asia were on the point of collapse, therefore the Soviet Union and the United States were the only two powers capable of influencing the way the post-war world would be constructed. Given that both profoundly disagreed in terms of their respective images of a future world order, conflict was inevitable.

Clearly, the debate as to origins can be seen as part of the Cold War itself and should be viewed in that context. Whether or not its occurrence was implicit in post-war WORLD POLITICS, none doubt the pathological psychology of the cold warriors which produced their respective policies. This is best summed up in the words of Thomas HOBBES, written three hundred years before the Cold War phenomenon was 'discovered' by US and Soviet commentators: 'For Warre, consisteth not in Battell onely, or in the act of fighting; but in a tract of time, wherein the will to contend by Battell is sufficiently known.' (*Leviathan*, Ch. 13)

### Collective security

Like the LEAGUE OF NATIONS with which it is most closely identified, the concept of collective security is an important innovation of twentieth century WORLD POLITICS. It asserts that the SECURITY DILEMMA of STATES can best be overcome not through national SELF-HELP and BALANCE OF POWER but through the institution of communal commitments whereby each state undertakes to join in common actions against those who threaten the territorial integrity or political INDEPENDENCE of others. Its major premise is the musketeer oath of 'all for one and one for all'. The idea of a common DEFENCE is not a new one; it is a familiar theme in international history from at least the ancient Greeks onwards and elements of it feature prominently in the writings of reformers and radicals such as Pierre Dubois (1306), the duc de Sully (1638), Kant (1795) and Bentham (1789).

But it was not until the First World War and the collapse of the notion that the international ANARCHY was tolerable that the collective security ideal gained momentum. Accordingly, the idea of a universal, permanent and collective commitment to oppose AGGRESSION and to guarantee security was enshrined in the Covenant of the League of Nations (Article 10), and reappeared in a modified form in the UNITED NATIONS CHARTER (Chapter VII). Its efficacy depended on each state, regardless of its particular or immediate interests, being prepared to pledge to act against law breakers, the assumption being that in this way it would always be possible to organize a preponderant coalition of like-minded states against an indeterminate aggressor. Thus DETERRENCE, as well as punishment and restoration of order, was part of its rationale. The abject failure of the League to provide communal security (Manchuria 1931, Ethiopia 1935, the Rhineland 1936, Austria 1938, Czechoslovakia 1939 and Finland 1940) is a reminder, even in the face of the world's first institutionalized attempt at PEACEKEEPING, of the perverse persistence of individual rather than common perspectives in the formulation and conduct of FOREIGN POLICY. The UN has not fared much better in this regard – the KOREAN WAR (1950–3) being the only (and somewhat fraudulent) major example of the international organization operating according to these principles. The onset of the COLD WAR rendered any idea of collective global responsibility for maintaining peace fanciful, and the UN has generally confined itself to the more limited role of peacekeeping operations.

Among the reasons for the failure of collective security are the following:

1. The persistence of national SOVEREIGNTY and the immediacy of the NATIONAL INTEREST.
2. The inability/unwillingness to create an international armed force of sufficient strength to deter and oppose recalcitrant states.

3. The failure to define AGGRESSION.

4. The lack of universality of membership.

5. Its tendency to freeze the STATUS QUO and the lack of procedural mechanisms for ensuring peaceful change.

6. The persistence of the JUST WAR and the increase in WARS OF NATIONAL LIBERATION.

7. The assumption that all states are equally interested in peace.

8. The paradox of waging WAR to prevent war.

In addition, the logic of collective security assumes a degree of cohesion and cultural unity in the INTERNATIONAL SYSTEM which, if present, would obviate the need for it in the first place. The term is now more commonly associated with regional alliance systems (e.g. NATO and the WARSAW PACT) but this is a debasement and perhaps reflects the fact that the original objective may be unobtainable.


## Colonialism

This is a variety of IMPERIALISM. It involves the settlement of foreign territories, the maintenance of rule over a subordinate population and the separation of the ruling group from the subject population. The relationship between the 'mother country' and the colony is usually exploitive. The earliest colonies (e.g. ancient Greek settlements in the Mediterranean or British settlements in North America) involved emigration into what were considered to be politically empty spaces and were not thought to be overtly racist, but the more modern variety usually entails this dimension. Characteristic features thus involve political and legal domination by an ALIEN minority, economic exploitation and DEPENDENCY and racial and cultural inequality. Unlike imperialism, which can involve complete assimilation, colonialism involves more or less strict separation from the metropolitan centre, the reason being

that colonies exist to serve the needs of the colonizing power and as such occupy a subordinate and servile role. Historically, the phenomenon is associated with Europe and the major colonial powers from the fifteenth to the nineteenth centuries were Portugal, Spain, Holland, Britain and France. These were joined in the late nineteenth and early twentieth century by Belgium, Germany, Italy, the United States, Japan and the Soviet Union. The unwilling targets for these competing penetrative drives were the Americas, Africa, Asia and Australasia.

Colonialism, and its antithesis anti-colonialism, have been major forces in shaping the political and economic character of the modern world. Until the nineteenth century, the practice was so common in international affairs that it generated little opposition. It was seen to be an inevitable consequence of GREAT POWER politics. With the rise of LIBERALISM, NATIONALISM and especially with the MARXIST/LENINIST critique of conventional social economic and political mores, the concept and the practices associated with it increasingly came to be regarded as illegitimate. Indeed, the very success of the anti-colonial movement was directly dependent on doctrines and IDEOLOGIES developed by the colonial powers themselves.

The incorporation of the ideas of SELF-DETERMINATION, SOVEREIGNTY, INDEPENDENCE and formal EQUALITY into the major institutions of the international community has ensured the demise of the colonial ideal. In the LEAGUE OF NATIONS the ADMINISTERED TERRITORY and mandates system reflected the general disquiet about the practice although it did not outlaw it completely. The UN, on the other hand, has always been at the forefront of the anti-colonial movement and the GENERAL ASSEMBLY in particular has been the single most important ACTOR in effecting its near universal rejection. It is a moot point whether the colonization process had beneficial effects on the targeted areas, but such is the approbrium associated with it now that it finds few contemporary supporters.

An important legacy of colonization, especially in Africa, is the contentious BOUNDARY issue which frequently bedevils African politics. The boundaries established by the colonial powers rarely, if ever, reflected indigenous racial, tribal and cultural patterns.

Clearly, the concept is not a precise one but its essence involves unequal rights, separation and deliberate exploitation. These themes are echoed in the term 'neo-colonialism' which refers to the continued domination of post-colonial independent STATES by the DEVELOPED world. Reliance on foreign investment capital, technical skills and training, manufactured goods and markets are viewed by many developing states as deliberately engineered by-products of colonialism. Thus, AID is in no sense humanitarian or altruistic. It is either belated repayment for past exploitation or else is a partially concealed attempt by the donor at obtaining political concessions. In either case, uneven development persists. Another variant is the term 'internal colonialism' which refers to cases where an economically dominant segment of a state treats a peripheral REGION as a subordinate and dependent entity. The Asian peoples of the Soviet Union, for example, are commonly regarded as victims of this practice. Again, conditions within South Africa display many of the features associated with the concept and its political system is often referred to as 'colonialism of a special type'.

## Comecon/CMEA

Council of Mutual Economic Assistance established by the Soviet Union in 1949 to integrate the economies of Eastern Europe. Along with the WARSAW PACT this regional organization is the East European equivalent of NATO and the European Economic Community (EC). Founder members are Bulgaria, Czechoslovakia, East Germany, Hungary, Mongolia, Poland, Rumania and the Soviet Union. Albania

ceased active membership in 1961. Cuba joined in 1972 followed by VIETNAM in 1978. Initially, Comecon was founded by Stalin in response to post-WAR American military and economic initiatives in Western Europe and as a means of exerting economic pressure on Yugoslavia. Structurally, it is headed by a Council which is the main DECISION-MAKING body. A permanent Executive Committee implements policy decisions and a number of subsidiary standing commissions carry out day to day operations in the various commodity areas. The secretariat is based in Moscow and is responsible to the Council. Although the Council is nominally the governing body, matters of basic policy are not within its remit. In reality Comecon has operated as a SUPRANATIONAL planning agency for the Soviet Union. The economic objectives are politically directed from the centre and involve specialization in production in member countries. Since the early 1960s the basis of East European planning has been to concentrate industrial production in East Germany and Czechoslovakia. Growing POLYCENTRISM led some members, particularly Rumania and Bulgaria, to question the (primary agricultural) roles assigned to them by central planning.

Full economic integration has not been achieved, nor has regional self-sufficiency. Apart from the economic objectives, Comecon also functions as an instrument of Soviet objectives outside Eastern Europe, especially in the THIRD WORLD.

Events of 1989 in Eastern Europe, particularly the demise of COMMUNISM and the declared unwillingness of the Soviet Union to intervene in the internal affairs of Eastern BLOC members (in accordance with the GORBACHEV DOCTRINE), have led to serious doubts about the future viability of Comecon. Czechoslovakia, in particular, but also Hungary, Bulgaria, Poland, and Rumania have suggested that an untransformed Comecon would prevent these increasingly pluralist states from restructuring their FOREIGN TRADE and currency policies. The apparent willingness of the EUROPEAN

COMMUNITY to develop a so-called 'association approach', whereby Eastern states would be offered cooperation pacts in return for an increased commitment to the values of liberal DEMOCRACY, has led many commentators to question the continued relevance of the organization. Comecon has clearly lost its original *raison d'être* and is unlikely to persist in its present form.

## Comintern

*See*: COMMUNISM

## Common market

The common market is a form of interstate INTEGRATION. The key to the market is the CUSTOMS UNION. It is also the building block, because the theory of the common market is that, once the customs union is successfully implemented, it will create needs for further integration. In particular, the free movement of two factors of production, labour and capital, are prerequisites for the common market if it is to expand dynamically upon this basis. As a result a free common market for goods and services will be established. Rules governing competition within the market will be required and a common fiscal system would be progressively instituted. In particular, harmonization of sales taxes are essential in a common market. In order to facilitate the free movement of labour, HARMONIZATION of social welfare policies would be required.

In the continuum of economic integration, the common market is the median position between the CUSTOMS UNION and full economic union. The TRADE implications of the common market are exactly the same as the customs union, so the tendency of supervisory institutions such as the General Agreement on Tariffs and Trade (GATT) has been to concentrate their attention upon the latter. Common markets are more the concern of integration theorists and in particular of the functionalist approach (*see* FUNCTIONALISM). Historically, common markets have been a feature of STATE building. Thus in nineteenth century Europe the development of a common market in Germany followed upon the establishment of the *zollverein*.

The economic history of the United States is also a good example of the positive gains from the formation of a common market. In both these nineteenth century instances protective TARIFFS were used to shelter the nascent market.

The EUROPEAN COMMUNITY (EC) is a common market with strong tendencies towards full economic union. It is clear from even the most cursory reading of the Rome TREATY that the founding states intended to go beyond the customs union stage from the outset. Moves are now in hand to convert the 'common' into the 'single' market in the Community.

## Commonwealth

A voluntary ASSOCIATION of fifty STATES, all of which were once parts of the British Empire. It is an unstructured grouping of states with no formal commitments but it does have a secretariat. The British monarch is nominally Head of the Commonwealth although some members, for example, India, are republics and no longer accept the monarchical principle. Where this principle is accepted (e.g. Canada) the sovereign is represented by the Governor General whose appointment is a matter for the host state alone. This office is the last vestige of British IMPERIAL authority. The origins of the Commonwealth can be traced back to 1867 when Canada was given Dominion status, followed by Australia in 1900 and New Zealand in 1907. British imperial authority was further relaxed at the imperial conference of 1926 when the United Kingdom and the Dominions were defined as autonomous. In 1931 the Statute of Westminster reinforced the principle of AUTONOMY and the notion of the British Empire was replaced in official usage by the British Commonwealth of Nations. By 1948 the terms 'British' and 'Dominion' were dropped and the modern Commonwealth with its emphasis on voluntarism and equality of membership emerged. In 1949 the Irish Republic withdrew, as did South Africa in 1961. In 1987, after an internal COUP, the membership status of Fiji is uncertain.

The following states are now Commonwealth members (dates of independence given in brackets):

*Africa*: Botswana (1966), Gambia (1965), Ghana (1957), Kenya (1963), Lesotho (1966), Malawi (1964), Mauritius (1968), Namibia (1989), Nigeria (1960), Seychelles (1976), Sierra Leone (1961), Swaziland (1968), Tanzania (1961), Uganda (1962), Zambia (1964), Zimbabwe (1980).

*Asia*: Bangladesh (1972), Brunei (1984), India (1947), Malaysia (1957), Maldives (1965), Pakistan (1947), Singapore (1965), Sri Lanka (1948).

*Caribbean and Americas*: Antigua (1981), Bahamas (1973), Barbados (1966), Belize (1981), Canada, Dominica (1978). Grenada (1974), Guyana (1966), Jamaica (1962), St Christopher and Nevis (1983), St Lucia (1979), St Vincent (1979), Trinidad (1962).

*Europe*: Britain, Cyprus (1961), Malta (1964).

*Pacific*: Australia, Kiribati (1979), Nauru (1968), New Zealand, Papua New Guinea (1975), Solomons (1978), Tonga (1970), Tuvalu (1978), Vanuatu (1980), Western Samoa (1962).

Membership requires the unanimous agreement of all participating states and although no formal law-making body exists, meetings are held every two years and decisions are taken by consensus.

Given the absence of any clear overall common ethnic, cultural, political, social or economic bonds, it is hardly surprizing that consensus is often very difficult to achieve. Issues which periodically threaten Commonwealth unity are relations with South Africa and the NORTH–SOUTH divide. In 1971 the Singapore meeting issued a Declaration of Commonwealth Principles which focused on the need to remove racial prejudice and to remove the wide disparities of wealth that exist both within and outside the association. In 1973 the issue of British membership of the EEC (EC) and its implications for Commonwealth TRADE preferences dominated proceedings. In 1977 members agreed to restrict sporting contact with REGIMES that practised APARTHEID. This Gleneagles Agreement is not legally binding on members but has become a powerful moral weapon in the continuing battle against racialism in South Africa. Since then constant pressure has been exerted on member states, such as the United Kingdom, which are perceived to be lukewarm on the question of ECONOMIC SANCTIONS against South Africa. In 1985 at Nassau members appointed a Commonwealth Group of Eminent Persons (seven in all) whose task was to promote a political dialogue with South Africa aimed at replacing apartheid by popular government. The issue of a NEW INTERNATIONAL ECONOMIC ORDER is perhaps as intractable as apartheid but many observers feel that the Commonwealth, because it does contain DEVELOPED and highly industrialized states, can give practical leads on questions such as the debt problem which other THIRD WORLD associations would find difficult to do.

The Commonwealth is a unique political creation. Its origins are partly historical and partly the result of conscious choice. It exists, and continues to exist, despite sometimes deep divisions, because it serves particular needs. No state is forced to join and each one makes its own calculations as to the benefits of membership. Since the creation of a Commonwealth Secretariat in 1965 it has functioned more or less as an administering unit and has instigated a wide variety of cooperative committees dealing with, for example, education, agriculture and health. The Commonwealth is not a POWER BLOC in the usual sense, but remains an important channel for consultation and cooperation between widely different states with little in common except perhaps a desire to remain together.

## ımunal conflict

ıflicts within communities – STATES, NATIONS, ethnic groups – are commonplace in WORLD POLITICS. However, if a communal conflict becomes chronic and persistent its dynamic can lead to CIVIL WAR and even external INTERVENTION. Empirical evidence seems to suggest that certain changes take place within the conflict process which leads to these developments. The conflict changes from being about interests to being about values. That is to say, rather than disagreeing about what they want, the parties disagree about what they stand for. As a result new, more ideologically defined issues come to the forefront. These issues will be presented in a biased, one-sided context and, as a result, the CONFLICT will become more violent and antagonistic. Once a cycle of violence and counter-violence has begun a communal conflict is close to becoming chronic and persistent. Individual acts of heroism or TERRORISM become mythologized into the folk history of the conflict. The process of polarization has now set in and clear physical lines of demarcation become evident between the communities. Often the physical movement of peoples will spontaneously occur as separate communities attempt to draw BOUNDARIES between each other. A new style of LEADERSHIP will emerge to symbolize the polarization that is now evident to all. The new leadership will, moreover, have an investment in the continuation of the conflict. Communication will break down between the now separate communities and, if the conflict persists over several generations, a form of 'autistic hostility' will become evident. Stereotypes of the other group will be reinforced behind the communications barrier and individuals will be socialized into a culture of group hostility and suspicion.

Some of the most intractable and violent conflicts in contemporary world politics began as communal conflicts which then escalated horizontally as outside parties were drawn in as allies and protectors. The ARAB–ISRAELI CONFLICT is a paradigm example of this process.

## Communism

A political IDEOLOGY aimed at the common ownership of land and capital and the elimination of the coercive POWER of the STATE. According to its principal exponent, Karl Marx, it must be distinguished from socialism, which is characterized as a transitional stage between capitalism and full communism when the state has 'withered away'. In this categorization, communist states are properly socialist states, since the apparatus of the state are still in place. In WORLD POLITICS the significance of the ideology from a theoretical perspective is the prominent place it assigns to IMPERIALISM as the fundamental cause of persistent international conflict. Indeed, the equation, capitalism = imperialism = WAR could be seen to constitute the communist theory of INTERNATIONAL RELATIONS.

In practice international communism has been a major force in world politics since the Bolshevik REVOLUTION in the Soviet Union in 1917, yet ever since the publication of the *Communist Manifesto* in 1848 by Marx and Engels its ideals have had a profound impact on international affairs. The central aim has been the creation of a unified international workers' movement ('proletarian internationalism') to overcome and defeat the capitalist world market. Revolution has always been central to its thesis. The creation of the 'internationals' in the late nineteenth and early twentieth century was an attempt at its practical realization. The first International was the International Working Men's Association and this lasted from 1864–76, the Second (or Socialist) International lasted from 1889–1914 and the Third International, or

COMINTERN. lasted from 1919–43. The aim of these 'internationals' was the creation of a global network of communist parties united by the ideal of overthrowing the existing capitalist INTERNATIONAL SYSTEM. After 1919, under Lenin and later Stalin, the movement was dominated by Moscow and was regarded as a global extension of Soviet domestic and FOREIGN POLICY. The Second World War and its aftermath wrought significant changes in perspectives; in particular, the focus began to move away from Western Europe to Eastern Europe, Asia and Africa. By 1948 those countries within the Allied-recognized Soviet SPHERE OF INFLUENCE – Poland, Hungary, Rumania, Bulgaria, Czechoslovakia, East Germany, Yugoslavia and Albania – had all formally become communist. By 1949, China, North Korea and North Vietnam brought Asia into the communist orbit. Increasingly, during the post-war period efforts were directed at creating communist or pro-communist REGIMES in other parts of the underdeveloped world, especially in Africa and Latin America. Hopes that international communism would develop into a coherent unified alternative world system, however, were dashed by increasing POLYCENTRISM (represented by the defection of Albania and Yugoslavia in Europe and by the Sino–Soviet split in Asia), and by the persistence of radical NATIONALISM in Africa and Latin America. During the 1950s a shift occurred in Soviet strategy. Khrushchev publicly declared that war between capitalist and communist states was not inevitable, and that there could be 'different roads to socialism'. The dominant position was still held by Moscow, but the idea of a union of Moscow-led communist states was replaced by the concept of a world socialist system which could be and indeed was, PLURALIST in character. Since then, and particularly under Gorbachev, the communist BLOC has developed into a looser ASSOCIATION where the aim is coexistence and not domination or the overthrow of the existing world STATE-SYSTEM. In the post-war world the main INTERNATIONAL ORGANIZATIONS associated with international communism have been the WARSAW TREATY ORGANIZATION, and COMECON or CEMA (Council of Mutual Economic Assistance), which was established in 1949 to integrate the economies of Eastern Europe under Soviet direction and control. Both these organizations were formed in direct response to American military and economic initiatives in Western Europe (NATO and the MARSHALL PLAN).

In the communist view of INTERNATIONAL RELATIONS the primary units of analysis are class and the relations of production, therefore the notion of STATE and the state-system are strictly speaking expendable. However, international communism showed a remarkable degree of flexibility in this regard and communist states, after theoretical REVISIONISM of original doctrines, indicated a willingness to operate within, rather than against, the traditional institutions of the post-WESTPHALIAN world.

Although at present the effects of the GORBACHEV DOCTRINE have not yet fully manifested themselves, few analysts doubt that communism, in its original guise, is something of a spent force in world politics. Even in China, the events preceding the Tiananmen Square Massacre of June 1989 clearly demonstrate that the new freedom set in motion through the policies of *glasnost* (openness) and *perestroika* (restructuring) will be difficult to contain within the traditional ideological mould. The transformation in political thinking, begun by Gorbachev, has led to a general reaffirmation of the intimate relationship between political freedom and economic prosperity. This in turn has set in motion pressures which are likely to destroy not only the theoretical underpinning of communism, but also the structure of the international SUBSYSTEM it created.

*See*: MARXISM/LENINISM

## Compellence
*See*: DETERRENCE

## Complex interdependence

A term used by Keohane and Nye in their 1977 book. Unlike the concept of INTER-DEPENDENCE, complex interdependence was clearly intended as an ideal type. In particular, the two authors sought to compare and contrast this model with REALISM as a competing paradigm of WORLD POLITICS. Three central assumptions of realism are challenged simultaneously: STATES are not necessarily coherent units nor are they always the dominant ACTORS, FORCE itself may now be an ineffective instrument of policy and the traditional HIERARCHY of issues where military/security matters take precedence over economic and social ones is now largely anachronistic. 'Complex interdependence' is the term used to reflect this new portrayal of reality. As an explanatory model of world politics it assumes multiple channels of contact between societies, an absence of hierarchy among issues and the disutility of military POWER or at best, a minor role for the use of force. Thus it gives rise to 'distinctive political processes, which translate power sources into power as control of outcomes' – among which are LINKAGE strategies, agenda control and coalition building.

The pioneering work of Keohane and Nye has been of crucial importance in the development of alternative, PLURALISTIC perspectives to that of power and security. By focusing attention on interdependence and TRANSNATIONAL relations, they have presented a vision of world politics in which actors, environments, structures, processes and outcomes are far less certain and more complex than the rather unitary and static insights offered by traditional realism. However, as the authors are at pains to point out, this approach does not make claim to exclusivity – it is a *competing* paradigm and does not altogether dispense with the earlier orthodoxy.

## Comprehensive test-ban treaty (CTB)

Moves to ban the testing of NUCLEAR WEAPONS, particularly HYDROGEN weapons, date from the early 1950s. For many years it was felt that a ban on testing in all environments, which is what a CTB involves, was impossible without a significant amount of on-site INSPECTION. The burden of scientific opinion now appears to reject this necessity. Problems with the realization of a CTB accordingly appear to be political and strategic rather than scientific and technical. These can be reduced to two propositions: first, that periodic testing of nuclear warheads is required in order to maintain confidence in their utility – this is the so-called 'shelf-life' argument. Secondly, some testing of new warheads is bound to be required whenever one of the nuclear weapon states wishes to introduce new delivery systems into their arsenals.

A CTB has been advocated by those individuals and interests within the existing nuclear states wanting to see the nuclear non-proliferation REGIME strengthened. In particular those sections of the Treaty on the Non-Proliferation of Nuclear Weapons (NPT) which require the existing nuclear states to pursue meaningful arms control regarding VERTICAL PROLIFERATION would be enhanced by a CTB TREATY. In the long run the goal of a workable CTB agreement is likely to be a matter of politics rather than seismology.

## Compromise

A form of CONFLICT SETTLEMENT involving mutual – although not necessarily balanced – concessions by parties who are engaged in NEGOTIATIONS. Before a compromise settlement can be reached the parties must agree in principle that they will settle their differences in this manner. Having made this commitment they can then commence the substantive bargaining aimed at achieving a sufficient modification of the other's position to make a settlement possible. Each party will normally have a clear perception of how far they are willing to go to make concessions and this may be termed the maximum concession point.

If a conflict is lengthy or persistent, parties may change their maximum concession points as they feel their overall position has strengthened or weakened. Sometimes parties will reject a particular compromise at the start of a conflict which they will be happy to accept at a later stage when they see how costly the conflict has become. Again the bargaining process may of itself alter the perceptions that parties have of their maximum concession points.

Third-party MEDIATION is often necessary to effect a compromise. The mediator may suggest a settlement within the maximum concession points of the parties. The mediator may offer to supervize the implementation of the settlement. Mediation is likely to be more successful between parties pursuing 'mixed motive' strategies, that is to say, by parties willing to see their relations with each other in cooperative terms. Provided that the parties can trust each other to keep their commitments, compromise settlements can produce positive FEED-BACK and lead to a general improvement in relations. Parties will then come to expect that future conflicts will be settled by compromise rather than by confrontation.

## Concert system

The concert system arose out of the deliberations at the Congress of VIENNA in 1815. It refers to the *ad hoc* system of conferences held by the major powers to regulate diplomatic CRISES in Europe between 1815 and 1854. Although it had no formal institutional structure its purpose was overtly managerial – to control, through mutual consultation, the BALANCE OF POWER in post-Napoleonic Europe. The settlement at Vienna and the concept of CONFERENCE DIPLOMACY which it inaugurated, remained the basis for international conduct throughout the nineteenth century, even though the Concert system as such was ended by the Crimean War. In this sense, it was the world's first deliberately contrived security REGIME. The second and third attempts at recreating and managing the INTERNATIONAL ORDER, in 1919–20 and again in 1945–6, owed much to the pioneering efforts of the group of 1815. The Concert met sporadically throughout the nineteenth century with the specific purpose of settling contentious issues that threatened European GREAT POWER stability. The unity of purpose it achieved was impressive and some commentators have called it a 'revolution in diplomatic history'. A number of factors contributed to its 'successful' operation (in the sense that there were no wars between the great powers for forty years)

1. There was a reasonably even distribution of POWER at the end of the Napoleonic War. Members of this great power club (Britain, Russia, Austria, Prussia, France, later joined by Italy and Turkey) were perceived to be roughly equal in military CAPABILITY and diplomatic importance.

2. There was a common realization that the politics of untutored balance of power led to great power confrontation, therefore a concerted action was needed to avert the danger.

3. Great power collaboration in bringing down Napoleonic France had the SPILL-OVER effect of maintaining a unified FRONT after the period of conflict was over. Emphasis on great power unity reinforced the conception of the European great powers as a special group with special responsibilities and privileges.

4. Meetings were confined to the great powers themselves. Sometimes lesser states were consulted, but never on the basis of EQUALITY. (This practice of according special status to the great powers was to reappear in both the LEAGUE OF NATIONS and the UN).

5. It did not challenge the ultimate SOVEREIGNTY of STATES. The unanimity rule was preferred, so that if vital NATIONAL INTERESTS were affected the system remained inactive.

6. It was not a vehicle for reform; its purpose was to manage and maintain the STATUS QUO.

7. It did not seek to eradicate conflict, simply to manage it.

8. Despite great ideological differences between the powers – the three Eastern powers were conservative and counter-revolutionary, and the Western states were more liberal in outlook – they all shared assumptions about the need to keep 'the public law of Europe' and to establish a responsible code of international behaviour.

For all these reasons, the concert system was an innovation in diplomatic relations. The balance of power was now tutored, guided and controlled and it was generally understood that the great powers had the right and the responsibility to impose their collective will on the European STATES-SYSTEM. However, it was not an unqualified success and in this connection it is important to distinguish the 'Congress era' from the Concert system. The Congress era was characterized by an attempt by the more conservative states (in particular the HOLY ALLIANCE between Prussia and Austria) to intervene, by force of arms if necessary, in the internal affairs of states to prevent a resurgence of radicalism, NATIONALISM and LIBERALISM. This interventionist stance led to bitter disputes among the powers and Britain formally withdrew from it in 1820 following demands for active Congress INTERVENTION in Greece and Spain. British Foreign Secretary George Canning did not view the Congress (or indeed the concert) system in this way. He said it was '. . . never intended as a union . . . for the superintendence of the internal affairs of other states.' With the death of the Tsar in 1825 the Congress system collapsed, although the Concert system of management through consultation survived. The Concert system succeeded because it was a loose ASSOCIATION of states sharing the same general common purpose, whereas the Congress system collapsed because it was much more specific and ideological in orientation.

## Conciliation

A form of third party INTERVENTION in CONFLICT situations. In the case of conciliation, the third party activity is non-partisan, neutral and mediatory. The primary aim of conciliation is to restore communication between the parties and to assist them to reach a better understanding of each others' position. In theory, the parties may decide that this greater clarity confirms their original hostility and suspicion and, accordingly, continue to oppose each others' interests and values. If a conflict has a long history of mistrust, conciliation may begin with the two parties refusing to discuss their DEFINITION OF THE SITUATION in the presence of the other. A stage of 'talking out' the conflict may be required before conciliation can even attempt resolution.

Any solution to the conflict which emerges from these procedures will have to be self-supporting. That is to say, the parties will come to see that a solution to their differences is available to them via the conciliation process without feeling that in any way the solution has been imposed. In this respect conciliation is one of the least intrusive modes of CONFLICT RESOLUTION.

## Concordat

A diplomatic term which refers in general to an agreement between church and STATE and in particular to agreements between states and the Holy See at the VATICAN.

## Condominium

Sovereign control over a dependent territory by two or more outside STATES. In this sense it is a form of joint IMPERIALISM where jurisdiction within the territory resides in arrangements made between the external states. It resembles co-ownership in municipal law and existed in the Sudan (between the United Kingdom and France) and in the New Hebrides islands in the Pacific (again the United Kingdom and

France). It is a comparatively rare form of political and legal control and it should be distinguished from military occupation. Thus, the joint control undertaken by the Allied states over post-Second World War Germany would not properly be called a condominium. The term has also been used to describe ALTERNATIVE WORLD FUTURES where the two dominant SUPERPOWERS jointly, and by agreement, preside over the INTERNATIONAL SYSTEM itself. However, this usage is as fanciful as the situation it purports to describe.

## Conference diplomacy

A characteristic feature of twentieth century WORLD POLITICS, mainly as a result of the creation of permanent INTERNATIONAL ORGANIZATIONS, has been the extraordinary growth of MULTILATERAL DIPLOMACY, especially in the guise of large-scale international conferences. Although not unknown in the past (the TREATIES of WESTPHALIA in 1648 and the Congress of VIENNA in 1815 being good examples), diplomacy by conference, whether permanent or *ad hoc*, is now standard practice. Indeed, the UN can be regarded as a permanent standing international diplomatic conference, and there are also regional varieties, such as the EUROPEAN COMMUNITY or the Nordic Union. A phenomenon associated with it is what some refer to as 'parliamentary diplomacy' (a term associated with the US statesman, Dean Rusk), which refers to the creation of regional or interest groupings on matters which do not adversely affect the NATIONAL INTEREST. These voting groups are formed according to a variety of criteria – political and cultural affinity, stage of economic development, geographic location, ideological like-mindedness and treaty links. Among the more prominent are the African group and the FRONT-LINE STATES, the EC, the Arab states, the Group of '77, the Socialist group and the Western group. All these seek to construct more or less permanent majorities within the con-ferences so that particular policies are adopted or particular officers sympathetic to their interests are elected to the constituent committees and agencies. (The withdrawal of US participation in Unesco was on the grounds that this organization had been 'captured' by groups hostile to American interests.) Conference diplomacy has been regarded by IDEALISTS from Woodrow Wilson onwards as part of the general solution to the problem of international anarchy, whereas some REALISTS believe that it may actually exacerbate it.

## Conference on Security and Cooperation in Europe (CSCE)

*See*: HELSINKI ACCORD

## Conflict

Conflict is a social condition that arises when two or more actors pursue mutually exclusive or mutually incompatible goals. In WORLD POLITICS conflict behaviour can be observed in WAR – both as a threatened activity and as a reality – and in bargaining behaviour short of the violent idiom. Conflict attitudes are evinced by elites, attentive and mass publics through such psychological dispositions as hostility and tension. Conflict can serve macropolitically positive functions. In particular, it can unify or at least consolidate group cohesion and enhance the position of a LEADERSHIP. It is probably chimerical to think that conflict can be eradicated. Strategies of DETERRENCE and POWER balancing are traditional forms of CONFLICT MANAGEMENT, whilst CONFLICT SETTLEMENT initiatives may be associative or dissociative. Third party actors like the UNITED NATIONS can play an important role in these cases. Finally CONFLICT RESOLUTION requires the dysfunctional effects of conflict to be emphasized rather than the functional.

*See also*: ARMS RACE; CIVIL WAR; COUP D'ÉTAT; GAME THEORY; INSURGENCY; PACIFISM; REVOLUTION; and TERRORISM)

## Conflict management

A term used to describe any situation where a CONFLICT continues but where its worst excesses are avoided or mitigated. Conflict management would, in particular, seek to avoid or terminate violence between parties. Conflict management is normally achieved by strategies of mutual, general DETERRENCE. Traditionally conceived, the BALANCE OF POWER was a system of conflict management based upon these ideas. A situation of neither WAR nor PEACE under a REGIME of mutual and general deterrence can continue for relatively long periods of time. Normally relations between the putative adversaries will show signs of improving or deteriorating as the case may be. If deterioration spills over into violence then management can be restored through palliatives such as cease-fire and TRUCE agreements. PEACEMAKING should properly be regarded as the function of CONFLICT SETTLEMENT and CONFLICT RESOLUTION rather than management.

## Conflict research

Conflict research is a field of academic inquiry within WORLD POLITICS. Its most basic premise is that CONFLICT is a basic systemic process which is shared with other systems of behaviour. Conflict research is a SOCIAL SCIENCE APPROACH which seeks to borrow ideas and methods from other disciplines and apply them to the field of study. Its theories, concepts and approaches have been applied at every LEVEL OF ANALYSIS and it is in the broadest sense eclectic. Unlike either STRATEGIC STUDIES or PEACE RESEARCH, conflict research seeks to avoid making basic a priori, philosophical commitments either in favour of or against WAR and other forms of violence. Structurally it tends to take a mixed actor, PLURALIST viewpoint avoiding the STATE-CENTRIC bias of strategic studies. In this respect at least it has close affinities with peace research. Indeed, in individual cases it is not always easy to see where conflict research ends and peace research begins.

Thus the WORLD SOCIETY paradigm is usually held by its adherents to be an instance of conflict research whilst its critics suspect that its tendency sometimes to import values into its study makes it closer to peace research.

## Conflict resolution

A somewhat esoteric form of CONFLICT termination. In order to achieve resolution the parties come to redefine their relationships in such a way as to perceive either that they can realize their goals without conflict or that they can redefine their relationship so that their goals no longer conflict. Unlike CONFLICT SETTLEMENT techniques, resolution tends to rely heavily upon academic, rather than diplomatic, modes of termination. Resolution techniques borrow heavily from sociology and social psychology and, in particular, from small group experimental studies. Resolution approaches to conflict have been strongly championed by 'controlled communication' advocates such as J. W. Burton. Experimental studies have particularly concentrated upon COMMUNAL CONFLICT situations where strong barriers often exist towards face-to-face communications and where it is held these techniques can be particularly effective. Although highly imaginative and provocative, conflict resolution is probably destined to remain an ideal type in the lexicon of conflict termination against which actual DIPLOMACY can be measured.

## Conflict settlement

A portmanteau term for the ending or termination of CONFLICT. A conflict may be settled by one side prevailing over the other. Winning as a form of conflict settlement implies conquest, defeat and submission. Historically this has been the most significant form of settlement. There is evidence, both impressionistic and quantitative, that this is currently changing and that settlements short of outright victory are becoming more prevalent. Settlement of this latter type implies a willingness by parties to COMPROMISE. In a small number of instances ADJUDICATION and ARBITRATION may be used as techniques for settling differences.

See also: CONFLICT MANAGEMENT; CONFLICT RESOLUTION

## Constructive engagement

Term used to describe US policy towards Southern Africa from 1980 onwards. The term was coined by Chester Crocker, assistant secretary of state for African affairs, and refers to US attempts to reform the South African system by working within it and honouring its rules. A form of 'quiet' DIPLOMACY which seeks to encourage White-led change in the region, focusing especially on Namibia and the withdrawal of Cuban troops from Angola. Although Southern Africa is high on its FOREIGN POLICY agenda the United States in reality has never had much political leverage in the region and UNILATERAL efforts without the active assistance of the Soviet Union were always likely to fail. The contradictions implicit in US policy (wanting an end to APARTHEID while simultaneously maintaining a pro-Western REGIME) which were evident in the very selective sanctions imposed against South Africa by the Anti-Apartheid Act of 1986, meant that the United States was not seen as an honest broker by all parties involved. In 1988–9, as a result of Gorbachev's new Soviet initiatives in Southern Africa, agreement has been reached at least in principle on LINKAGE of the Namibian INDEPENDENCE issue with the phased withdrawal of Cuban troops.

## Containment

An ambiguous concept, supposedly the guiding principle of post-war US FOREIGN POLICY. Originally advocated by diplomat George Kennan (see X) when he declared in 1947 that the basis of US foreign policy should involve 'long-term, patient but firm and vigilant containment of Russian expansionist tendencies'. Implicit in Kennan's argument was the notion that Soviet foreign policy was motivated by MARXIST/LENINIST assumptions concerning world REVOLUTION and the destruction of capitalism, and necessitated therefore a carefully constructed policy of COUNTERFORCE at its perimeters. The underlying aim of such a policy was to keep the Soviet Union within the lines of military demarcation established at the end of the Second World War. As such, containment could be seen as accommodationist rather than overtly aggressive, as some revisionist COLD WAR analysts have suggested. Instrumentally, containment merged with the TRUMAN DOCTRINE and the MARSHALL PLAN and its main ingredients were the creation of military ALLIANCES (in Western Europe, Latin America, the Middle East and the Far East), economic AID and covert forms of political and economic warfare both within and without the Soviet SPHERE OF INFLUENCE. As interpreted by the Truman and Eisenhower administrations containment also involved counter-revolutionary notions of liberation of those areas under communist control or threat. Thus, the KOREAN and VIETNAMESE WARS are often presented in terms of this framework. However, Kennan in his *Memoirs* (1967) has objected to this orthodox interpretation of the doctrine associated with his name and in particular argued that his early formulation of containment did not imply either the militarization of US foreign policy or the globalist dimensions it so quickly assumed. In a somewhat belated rearguard defence, Kennan argued that his original intention was to suggest the 'political containment of a political threat' and not active containment of the Soviet Union by military means. He also objected to the apparently unlimited capacity of US power which it assumed, to the extension of US vital interests beyond Western Europe and the Western Hemisphere and especially to the distorted image it carried about the nature of the communist threat:

> If I was the author in 1947 of a 'doctrine' of containment, it was a doctrine which lost much of its rationale with the death of Stalin and with the development of the Soviet–Chinese conflict. I emphatically deny any efforts to involve that doctrine today in situations to which it has, and can have, no proper relevance. (1967)

Although some commentators argue that containment (albeit in a looser form) is still the bottom line of US foreign policy, most analysts agree that DETENTE, POLYCENTRISM, the Sino–Soviet split, the US RAPPROCHEMENT with China, the settlement in South East Asia as well as the various ARMS CONTROL agreements, have watered it down to such an extent that the term is no longer helpful in understanding the philosophical or ideological framework out of which US foreign policy emerges. None can doubt, though, the near pathological commitment to the doctrine by US DECISION MAKERS in the early post-war period. Whether this was the cause of the COLD WAR or the result of it is now a matter of historical rather than political dispute.

## Contraband

Categories of WAR materials which, under INTERNATIONAL LAW, may be seized by one BELLIGERENT when supplied by a neutral to another. However, the exact definition of 'war materials' has always been a contentious matter and interpretations have tended to be expansive. Thus, the category of 'conditional contraband' refers to seized material which may have been destined for innocent peacetime use but which has been deemed by a belligerent as useful to the war effort. In the age of TOTAL WARFARE, the distinctions between permissible and non-permissible goods has further collapsed with the result that during the two twentieth-century world wars relations between belligerents and neutrals were often strained. Lack of clear unequivocal legal guidance has inevitably resulted in a good deal of auto-interpretation on this issue.

## Contras

Disaffected right wing opponents of the Sandinista National Liberation Front (FSLN) government in Nicaragua. Originally formed mainly of members of former President Samoza's National Guard, the Contras were first overtly, then from 1983 covertly, supported by the United States, when President Reagan, under the aegis of the MONROE DOCTRINE, publicly declared his support and his intention of opposing the spread of Marxism in Central America. Subsequently the US Congress terminated funds for the rebels who had appalling records of HUMAN RIGHTS violations. Lack of widespread popular appeal combined with the lack of an integrated command structure has hampered the movement's ability to undermine the elected government. However, despite a notable lack of military success, the Contras have featured prominently in contemporary American politics. The 'Irangate' scandal which involved the transfer to the Contras of 30 million dollars profit from the sale of arms to Iran, raised widespread doubts about the extent of Presidential control over FOREIGN POLICY initiatives. In November 1986 President Reagan ordered a review of the National Security Council, partly to contain the political damage to his administration and partly to tighten up the chain of command. The President's admission that he was not 'fully informed' of these activities has led many commentators to question the internal coherence of the US foreign policy DECISION-MAKING structure.

*See also*: REAGAN DOCTRINE

## Conventional

An adjective meaning 'normal' or

'traditional', its application to the analysis of INTERNATIONAL POLITICS and FOREIGN POLICY is appropriate wherever the analyst wishes to draw a distinction between what has happened in the past and what is happening in the present or is envisaged for the future. The adjective is particularly apposite in circumstances where change has occurred and some point of comparison with the past is required.

Thus, *conventional weapon* is a distinction frequently used in strategic analysis to draw a distinction between NUCLEAR WEAPONS, CHEMICAL AND BIOLOGICAL WEAPONS and the traditional or 'conventional' weapons used for centuries in warfare. The advent of nuclear weapons has certainly not reduced the scope for conventional weapons. Indeed, the reverse may well be true, namely that the drawbacks and difficulties of actually using nuclear weapons has enhanced the importance of the 'threshold' between nuclear and conventional. The US desire that NATO should move towards FLEXIBLE RESPONSE after 1962 was in part prompted by these perceptions.

Similarly, a distinction can be made between conventional and unconventional warfare. The latter is often thought of as GUERRILLA WARFARE which is regarded as 'unconventional' because of the types of forces and tactics employed rather than the types of weapons.

## Conventions on the rules of warfare

Rules relating to conduct during armed CONFLICT were, until the mid-nineteenth century, part of customary INTERNATIONAL LAW. Since then there have been a number of attempts to codify the rules of warfare in a succession of MULTILATERAL international conventions. These are commonly referred to as 'the law of Geneva' and the 'law of the Hague'. The law of Geneva dealt mainly with the rights and protection of those who took no direct part in the fighting and the law of the HAGUE was con-

cerned with the rights and duties of the actual BELLIGERENTS. The GENEVA conventions took place as follows: 1864 and 1907 (humane treatment of the wounded and sick in battle), 1929 (wounded and sick plus treatment of PRISONERS OF WAR), 1949 (wounded, sick and shipwrecked, prisoners of war and protection of civilians in wartime); 1977 (additional PROTOCOLS dealing with more extensive non-combatant protection and with problems arising from internal wars). By 1986 there were over 160 parties to these Geneva Conventions (including non-state ACTORS such as the Palestine Liberation Organization (PLO), the Pan African Congress and the South West Africa People's Organization (SWAPO)). As well as these codified rules, which of course lack effective sanctions, belligerents, whether or not they are party to the conventions, are bound by customary international humanitarian law which forbids unnecessary cruelty or wanton behaviour. From 1864 onwards, these conventions have been associated with the activities of the INTERNATIONAL RED CROSS movement (initially known as the International Committee for aid to wounded soldiers) which was founded in Switzerland in 1863, and which in 1949 formally extended its brief to protect civilians caught up in armed conflict.

## Convergence theory

The idea that the logic of industrial and TECHNOLOGICAL growth in advanced STATES leads to convergent patterns of political, economic and social structures regardless of formal ideological or historical differences. Propagated by prominent theorists such as Raymond Aron and J. K. Galbraith, the theory holds that the imperatives of technological growth and the technical and managerial requirements of the post-industrial state compel societies to adopt common or core practices with regard especially to the economic sector. Thus, convergence envisages COMMUNIST states beginning to relax rigid state control and develop measures or individual enterprise and managerial autonomy. Similarly, capitalist states will develop policies of social welfare and planning. The underlying idea is that as convergence proceeds, ideological differences diminish. Thus, DETENTE, peaceful COEXISTENCE, *glasnost* and *perestroika* are all evidence of the vitality of this thesis and of the technological determinism which underlies it. Critics have pointed out, however, that despite being at similar stages of technological and economic growth, there is no absolute necessity for convergence. Different types of political system can, and do, coexist at similar stages of economic development, without evolving common forms of social organization. In WORLD POLITICS the idea could be seen as a variant of the traditional REALIST view that despite formal ideological differences, GREAT POWERS are likely to behave in much the same way regarding the problems of national security and the protection of interests.

### Council of Europe

The Statute of the Council signed in May 1949 by ten STATES (Belgium, Denmark, France, Ireland, Italy, Luxemburg, the Netherlands, Norway, Sweden and the United Kingdom) was dedicated in its preamble to 'a closer unity between all like-minded countries of Europe'. Notwithstanding such references to 'unity' the Council is an INTERNATIONAL ORGANIZATION with no SUPRANATIONAL pretensions or ambitions. Indeed, the same preamble refers only to the need for 'closer association' between the member states. Article I of the Statute explicitly precludes the Council from considering matters relating to national DEFENCE. There were two reasons for this very explicit exclusion: the recently signed North Atlantic Treaty meant that the NATO ALLIANCE was intended to deal with these matters and the presence of neutral states such as Ireland and Sweden in the Council precluded any reference to military issues.

Membership is open, under Article III to all states accepting the principles of the rule of law, fundamental freedoms and HUMAN RIGHTS. A subsequent PROTOCOL to the TREATY of London pledged the signatories to the holding of free elections at reasonable intervals by secret ballot. This requirement has created difficulties for the Council membership since 1949 and member states have often departed from this provision. Thus the continued membership of Greece was in question between December 1969 and November 1974.

The strong inclination of the Council towards the maintenance and improvement of human rights causes was reinforced in November 1950 when the members concluded the European Convention for the Protection of Human Rights and Fundamental Freedoms. The Convention created a Commission and a Court of Human Rights. The work of this Court has made a substantial contribution to the development of general principles of INTERNATIONAL LAW on human rights since its inception.

Membership of the council currently stands at twenty-one states. In addition to the original ten founder members, the following are currently members of the Council: Austria, Cyprus, Federal Republic of Germany, Greece, Iceland, Liechtenstein, Malta, Portugal, Spain, Switzerland and Turkey. The principal organs of the Council are the Committee of Ministers and the Consultative Assembly. Each state is entitled to one representative on the Committee of Ministers. Representation on the Assembly is weighted pro rata in favour of the larger and more populous states.

### Countercity (sometimes rendered Countervalue)

A term used in strategic analysis. It refers to the strategy of attacking civilian targets, such as cities, which are held to be the most valued (hence the reference to 'value' above). Attacking such targets is certainly contrary to one of the most prevalent traditions in strategy, namely that the rationale for using military FORCE is to destroy the military forces of the adversary. The ability to engage counterforce targets has increased markedly with the advent of NUCLEAR WEAPONS and AIR POWER. Enormous destruction can now be caused to these areas by nuclear attacks. Indeed, so confident were some POLICY-MAKERS that these effects could be achieved that the term ASSURED DESTRUCTION was coined to encapsulate this potential.

Nuclear DETERRENCE theory has not always dealt kindly with countercity target selection. If deterrence fails then attacking cities looks extremely gratuitous. Moreover if your adversary has the CAPABILITY and the intention to attack yours in return then it looks suicidal. The implication that cities are hostages to enemies' contingencies has led some to back away from countercity towards COUNTERFORCE ideas.

## Counterforce

A term used in strategic analysis. It has two distinct meanings. First, strategists may speak of a counterforce CAPABILITY. This refers to the ability to attack and destroy sufficient numbers of adversaries' forces to prevent their launching them at the homeland, or at those of one's allies. A counterforce capability therefore gives its possessor the opportunity and the incentive to launch a FIRST STRIKE against the adversary to disarm the opposition before they can attack with their own forces. Increases in the accuracy of weapons, both CONVENTIONAL and NUCLEAR, in recent years have increased the availability of counterforce capabilities.

The term is also used as a strategy. The possession of the capability, discussed above, becomes the necessary condition for the strategy. Thus, a STATE would target a potential enemy's forces in advance of hos-

tilities and carry through a series of disarming attacks once WAR had commenced. A counterforce strategy is often thought of as being more flexible than its alternative COUNTERCITY. Attacking cities bears the hallmarks of a 'last resort' frame of mind. This reasoning has been particularly influential in the analysis of NUCLEAR DETERRENCE failures. In such situations, so it is reasoned, counterforce leaves more alternatives for hard-pressed DECISION-MAKERS.

Counterforce targeting has recently received a boost from the NUCLEAR WINTER thesis. According to this theory avoiding cities when engaged in a nuclear exchange will reduce the amount of debris drawn into the atmosphere. Crossing the threshold at which the winter is triggered is less likely in a limited counterforce exchange.

## Counter-insurgency

A type of irregular warfare which seeks to demoralize and defeat insurgencies by employing the same tactics in reverse to neutralize the planning of the insurgents. In particular counter-insurgency seeks to separate the GUERRILLA bands from the local population by winning the latter away from the former. This is sometimes referred to in the US idiom as 'hearts-and-minds' campaigns. Working out from secure BASE areas, the counter-insurgents then attempt to extend their security zones into disputed and INSURGENT territories. This 'pacification' programme is essential if an acceptable level of civil order is to be secured. Counter-insurgency requires recognition that certain political, economic and social reforms need to be effected to remove popular grievances. This last prerequisite is often the hardest to achieve, as the US experience in attempting to build up an autonomous South Vietnam during their INTERVENTION in the VIETNAM Wars shows. Notwithstanding this experience, successful counter-insurgency WARS were fought in the Philippines and Malaya after 1945.

## Countervailing

A term used in strategic analysis. Countervailing is a COUNTERFORCE strategy for fighting a NUCLEAR WAR. Formally its inception point is July 1980 when President Carter of the United States signed Presidential Directive 59. In essence the doctrine requires the political and military leadership of the United States to implement programmes and initiate strategies that would give them the facility to respond to perceived AGGRESSION at a variety of levels. Proponents of the strategy argue that if NUCLEAR DETERRENCE breaks down the US LEADERSHIP must have available options that can be reasonably implemented. A COUNTERCITY attack against the homeland of the adversary is not such an option given the PARITY condition between the sides.

Presidential Directive 59 was the culmination of eighteen years of debate within the strategic community of the United States. This debate was initiated in 1962 when Secretary of Defense Robert McNamara delivered a seminal address to the University of Michigan, Ann Arbor. For some years after, the United States moved away from countervailing ideas towards ASSURED DESTRUCTION but in the Nixon–Ford years moves were made to introduce greater flexibility should deterrence break down. The collapse of the DETENTE policy with the Soviet Union in the Carter Presidency (1977–81) gave an edge and urgency to the doctrinal statement but Presidential Directive 59 should be set within a certain tradition of American strategic thinking.

The assumptions of the countervailing doctrine are a mixture of optimism and pessimism. Thus it is assumed that once the nuclear threshold has been crossed the outcome can be controlled. On the other hand it is assumed that deterrence is a difficult relationship to maintain and that it is prudent to assume that it is not a policy for all seasons. While countervailing is clearly a WAR fighting strategy it is not a war winning one. 'Countervailing' can be restated as 'prevailing' without affecting the main assumptions of the doctrine. The enuncia-

tion of countervailing closes the gap between what is termed declaratory policy and the actual war planning contained in documents like the Single Integrated Operational Plan (SIOP). The officially available published record shows that the United States has never confined itself to a purely punishment response to its nuclear adversary but has instead intended throughout the period to engage in DAMAGE LIMITATION instead.

## Coup d'état

Literally, this refers to a sudden and decisive stroke of government policy. Popular usage now associates the term with a sudden and unconstitutional change of government or REGIME. As such the coup is part of the repertoire of radical and revolutionary movements, although it is not only the revolutionary who stages or attempts coups. Conversely it is not necessary to stage a coup to have a REVOLUTION. The link between the coup as an instrument and the revolution as a means of change is neither necessary nor sufficient.

As an instrument of change the coup may most clearly be contrasted with the mass uprising. In the former situation the perpetrators will be a small group of conspirators who will seize their opportunity to remove the incumbents by moving with great dispatch and determination to apprehend the LEADERSHIP, restrict their movements and take control of the main arteries of state POWER. They may use great violence to effect these changes or they may be achieved in a 'bloodless' fashion. A crucial determinant of these outcomes will be the extent to which the incumbent leadership is defended. For this reason the military institutions of the STATE will play an important role in deciding the level of violence required to achieve a successful coup. If the military themselves stage the coup this will usually settle the issue, at least in the short term, because their ability to provide sufficient coercive POWER will carry the day. If the coup leaders cannot be assured of the support or assistance of the military they may have to face their opposition afterwards. In this situation a coup attempt that is resisted by some or all of the armed forces can lead to CIVIL WAR. The civil strife in Indonesia in 1965 followed an abortive coup attempt that was opposed by the army and the BIAFRA CIVIL WAR followed hard upon two coups in Nigeria in 1966. Trotsky's dictum that a coup can succeed without the ARMY but that it cannot succeed against the army seems instructive here.

A high propensity to use the coup instrument as a means of political change is currently demonstrated in the THIRD WORLD. All the constituent continents – Latin America, Africa and Asia – have shown this propensity. Almost without exception such coups have been openly staged or supported by the military institutions in these states. Indeed, sometimes lengthy periods of military rule follow these INTERVENTIONS. Sometimes the military reverts to barracks fairly quickly but not before purging the political leadership.

Under the legal principle of RECOGNITION other states have to face the decision to grant or withhold this facility. Given the unconstitutional nature of the change, withholding immediate recognition might seem the more appropriate course of action. On the other hand, if the new leadership is clearly in effective control there may be little point in prevarication. Often these decisions will be influenced by political and diplomatic considerations as much as by legal ones.

## Credibility

A noun meaning literally that a statement 'or an action shows the true intentions of the ACTOR. Such inferences are by their nature subjective. Credibility is likely to be contingent upon the reputation of the actor and upon the circumstances in which the action takes place, or is likely to take place. Given these conditions, it is argued that certain actions or statements are inherently credible and that others are not. Moreover, it is generally agreed that there is a grey area of uncertainty where credibility is equivalent to dubiety. This dilemma, at the very heart of the concept, has been of particular concern to theorists of DETERRENCE. The advent of weapons of mass destruction has greatly increased the cost calculations that arise when statesmen and others make deterrent threats that cover these contingencies. Deterrence is, moreover, not a one-way street and, accordingly, threats are met with counter-threats. Credibility is not immune from this ACTION–REACTION dynamic. Credibility now becomes a relative concept. What might appear credible to threaten an unarmed opponent with, looks very dubious against an adversary equally as capable as oneself.

Credibility has, thus, become a benchmark against which deterrent policies are evaluated. MASSIVE RETALIATION was criticized for lacking credibility. Many see the issue of credibility as central to the idea of extended deterrence. The uncertainty dilemma referred to above has divided strategic analysis. Some see uncertainty as reinforcing deterrence because the adversary will not know exactly when, where or how the deterrer will act. Others argue that such uncertainties will cause deterrence theory to break down at the margin and this may be the situation where it is most needed. In statistical language, credibility is a matter of probability not proof.

## Crisis

A crisis is a perceived turning point in relationships between ACTORS or between actors and their environment. Thus the CUBAN MISSILE CRISIS was a potential turning point in strategic relations between the United States and the Soviet Union. The placement of 'offensive' missiles in Cuba threatened to change both the global strategic balance and the local strategic balance against the interests of the United States.

One of the unanticipated consequences of the crisis was that relationships between the SUPERPOWERS moved into a DETENTE phase for a brief period afterwards. The DEBT CRISIS was a perceived turning point in relations between certain Latin American states and their creditors in the FIRST WORLD. Again unanticipated consequences of the moves to buy time for the debtors may lead to further turning points in relations. Issues arising from the deterioration of the global ECOLOGICAL system may be perceived as crises in the sense suggested above. The ongoing destruction of the earth's ozone layer is clearly a turning point in man's relationship with his environment.

Contemporary literature on crises in INTERNATIONAL POLITICS and FOREIGN POLICY has shown a burgeoning output of late. Two broad approaches may be discerned and distinguished. The first approaches the subject from the DECISION-MAKING perspective. Clearly, there are good intuitive reasons for concentration here. In an acute international crisis, if the decision-makers get it wrong then events may rapidly escalate out of control and lead to violence, or lead to the exacerbation of violence that has already started. The second approach to crises takes a situational/structural perspective looking at crises as interaction sequences between international actors. A good deal of formal modelling – derived from GAME THEORY – has been productively applied here. This approach also sensitizes the study of crises to the environmental constraints and opportunities that different system structures might have for the occurrence and duration of the phenomena.

Decision-making approaches to crisis begin with the insight that the POLICY-MAKERS perceive that the consequence of their actions – even if they do nothing – will involve them in significant risk taking. Crisis decision-making is thus conceptually separate from 'normal' decision-making, where perceptions that high risks are part of the DEFINITION OF THE SITUATION are absent. Because of the high risk factor, crisis decision-making is recognized as being highly stressful. As stress increases in a crisis other factors may be consequentially affected. Decision-makers may experience pressure to act quickly, they may feel that their search for alternatives is limited. Physiologically, stress may produce exhaustion, emotionalism and poor performance. There is general agreement that while a certain amount of stress is likely to increase efficiency in the decision-making system, too much will lead to a degeneration in performance and the other physiological effects already noted.

During a crisis situation the size of the decision-making group will usually narrow. Group solidarity and cohesion may increase and while this may be conducive to better performance, it can lead to GROUPTHINK. The group *qua* group will have to cope with a substantial increase in the amount of information coming into the system from the environment. Information processing via these communication channels will intensify and in order to relieve this overload, and to save time, *ad hoc* channels may be used. During the Cuban missile crisis, message flows between the US and the Soviet leaderships increased substantially during the days after the announcement of the QUARANTINE.

Hermann (1969), who has probably contributed more than any other analyst to the decision-making approach to crises, argues for three defining characteristics. First, the crisis situation threatens core values in the decision system. Secondly, the decision situation is highly time dependent. Thirdly, the occurrence of the crisis comes as a surprise to the decision system. The first two traits have been covered in the discussion above. Surprise as a trait is perhaps more controversial. Diplomatic and strategic surprise bear a close family resemblance to crisis, but to require surprise as a necessary definition of crisis precludes the possibility that at least one party to the crisis will knowingly initiate the situation in order to force concessions from the other. Since perception of high risk has already been stipulated as a defining characteristic of crisis, it is a small step for one party to manipulate this risk to achieve its own ends. This is normally thought of as BRINKMANSHIP. As Lebow (1981) has argued following an empirical examination of twenty-six crises, 'more than half can be described as brinkmanship'. Brinkmanship aims to force concessions from the other side, or at a minimum, a TRADE-OFF between the adversaries. It seems fairly clear that the first BERLIN CRISIS was, from the Soviet perception, an instance of brinkmanship, with the looked for trade-offs being some significant retreat by the West from its initiative to establish a separate West German state.

Unlike the decision-making approach, the situational/structural perspective rests its analysis upon the basic assumption that CONFLICT is a systemic process and that, as a result, crises will occur almost naturally. One of the most influential recent texts on crises defines the phenomenon as arising 'in severe conflict, short of war, but involving the perception of a dangerously high probability of war' (Snyder and Diesing, 1977). Some writers, indeed, following Schelling's (1966) argument that most WARS are a form of bargaining behaviour, would want to argue that 'short of war' is too restrictive. Crises are then seen as generically linked to coercive barraging between putative adversaries. LINKAGE between the mainstream decision-making literature and this bargaining view of crises is provided by the literature on CRISIS MANAGEMENT.

Situational/structural approaches to crises include also the holistic type of analysis of the system into BIPOLAR or MULTIPOLAR configurations. Waltz (1964), the leading modern advocate of bipolarity, argues that crises are a symptom that the system is working. Conflict is endemic, so too is change, therefore crises cannot be avoided. Given this line of reasoning, Waltz concludes that 'the absence of crises is more worrisome than their recurrence'. In the bipolar system the assumption is that the leading states will show interventionist tendencies in all crisis situations. This INTERVENTION need not always be competitive, but when it is a crisis may result. Thus in 1973 during the Yom Kippur War in the ARAB–ISRAELI CONFLICT competitive intervention by the SUPERPOWERS produced the 'alert' crisis.

Advocates of the multipolar structure also see conflict, and therefore crises, as endemic. Here the existence of more leading STATE actors in the system means that even if two of them conflict, a number of third party roles are still available to the other powers. Indeed in a crisis situation in a multipolar system between two of the leading states, the behaviour of the remaining polar actors may be crucial. If they commit themselves to one side or the other then third party mediation may be impossible and if this happens then, as in July 1914, the system collapses into a bipolar confrontation.

The advent of NUCLEAR WEAPONS as a systemic variable has affected the occurrence and outcome of crises at this LEVEL OF ANALYSIS. Since it was clear from the outset of this discussion that high risk was a situational characteristic of crises, it would seem to follow that nuclear weapons have served to exacerbate the perception of risk even more. This is particularly pertinent for those states actually possessing them. Again PROLIFERATION, at least in HORIZONTAL directions, will further increase risks during crises. In GAME THEORY analysis the nuclear crisis is analogous to the Chicken game where the costs of both parties choosing to reject cooperation are very high indeed.

### Crisis management

Crisis management is the attempt to control events during a CRISIS to prevent significant and systematic violence from occurring. The decision problem facing the would-be 'crisis manager' is to find a balance between being tough and being tender, between using COERCION and offering concessions, between

AGGRESSION and ACCOMMODATION. Too much coercion can lead to violence which may get out of control and take on a dynamic of its own. Too much accommodation can lead to SURRENDER and to 'peace at any price'. For the DIPLOMAT the essence of crisis management is to know when to give ground and when to stand firm.

The balance between coercion and accommodation will differ over time. A typical crisis pattern is for coercion to mark the early stages so that a rapid and marked escalation occurs. Accommodation becomes more evident as the dangers of uncontrolled violence increase. Concessions may be made on a more or less reciprocal basis or, more usually, one side or the other will clearly and unambiguously make the first conciliatory gesture. Accommodation may spill over into the post-crisis phase so that the former adversaries, recognizing the tensions in their relationship, consciously move towards a more cooperative mode thereafter.

During the coercive stage, the aim of using this strategy is to manipulate the risk of WAR – which from a rational ACTOR perspective, it is assumed neither side wants – to force concessions and get the opponent to give ground. Snyder (Hermann, 1972) has suggested that the key risk to avoid is miscalculation. This may occur for a variety of reasons: poor communication, MISPERCEPTION, over-estimating one's own CAPABILITIES or under-estimating those of the adversary. For whatever cause, violence that nobody wants or expects can occur if key DECISION-MAKERS miscalculate during this coercive stage. The concept of GROUP-THINK is perhaps the most relevant exposition for the situation where a group of decision-makers apparently suspend rationality and become swept along in a group dynamic which proves to have disastrous consequences.

Again, manipulation of risk can go wrong because subordinates further down the chain of command act in an independent and unauthorized fashion. It is inevitable that during a crisis situation it will be neces-sary to issue rules of engagement to military leaders. Equally diplomats and envoys may find themselves operating at the edge of, or even outside, their instructions. In such situations individual decision-making 'on the spot' can be crucial to a particular outcome. It is against this potential scenario that efforts to improve c³I facilities have assumed so much significance.

Following on from the works published by Schelling in the 1960s, effective coercion of one's opponents is held to involve the commitment strategy. Commitment is convincing your opponent that you mean what you say; in short, that your intentions are credible. One favoured method is to make a commitment to stand firm, leaving the next move to the adversary. The Soviet move to blockade BERLIN during the 1948–9 crisis and the US BLOCKADE (or QUARANTINE) of Cuba in the 1962 crisis would both be instances here of the commitment strategy. Again a commitment may be verbal. For example, it may take the form of a TREATY of guarantee or collective SELF-DEFENCE, or it may be a vague and generalized statement to the effect that, 'we will not stand idly by . . .' or 'we will not hesitate to make difficult decisions . . .'. Often the most effective form of coercive commitment will be to combine the physical and the verbal.

The dilemma with the act of commitment is inherent in its strength. It 'burns one's bridges'. It reduces flexibility. As a result of an over-enthusiastic pursuit of victory at all costs, the chances of reaching a compromise will be lost. Since the defining characteristic of crisis management is to balance coercion and accommodation, then victory at all costs is not really sought. For this reason it has been suggested that a commitment that leaves some flexibility is to be preferred. It might be better to issue warnings rather than to make specific threats but herein the risk of having one's bluff called may have to be faced.

Escalation is a probable outcome of the strategy of commitment. The term escalation often implies beginning with fairly modest commitments and increasing the risks thereafter in order to slowly coerce the adversary into compromise, for fear that the alternative will take the parties higher up the escalation ladder. Thus in escalation the commitment strategy is double-edged. There is an explicit commitment to a particular option and an implicit commitment to further, more risky, options if the initial options do not work. Thus, in the case of the Cuban missiles it could be argued that the quarantine implied an air strike or invasion as the next significant move if the quarantine itself failed to work.

Accommodation is the antithesis of much of the above discussion. Accommodation is a way of settling the crisis – so management implies settlement – without totally capitulating to the wishes and aims of the other parties. The immediate difficulty with offering concessions is that they may be perceived as a sign of weakness which will encourage the opponent to stand out for more. The dynamic in accommodation is therefore de-escalation. If concessions become mutual it may be possible for the adversaries to reciprocate concessions. Thus a significant improvement in their relationships may result from crisis management.

Most crises are settled by one side making a differentially greater concession than the other. Sometimes, as in Cuba, the winner will make a face-saving gesture to the adversary in order to make it easier to accept the outcome or to make it easier to sell the outcome to others.

Crisis management, then, involves finding a balance between coercion and accommodation. This is a common problem in DIPLOMACY. Should one be a HAWK or a DOVE on a particular ISSUE AREA? In this sense crisis management is rightly seen as a form of diplomacy. It is diplomacy in a coercive mode, certainly. It is not routine diplomacy, but rather it is the HIGH POLITICS of the formal office holders.

### Cruise missile

A cruise missile is, in effect, a small pilotless aircraft. The original TECHNOLOGY was developed during the Second World War when Germany produced the V-1 'flying bomb'. Significant improvements were made to this technology in two respects during the years following 1945. First, it became possible to produce small, very economical jet engines, using either the turbo-jet or the turbo-fan principle. Secondly, significant developments in missile guidance techniques made it possible to 'read' the terrain over which the missile was flying and compare this information with that stored on computer. This guidance facility is particularly crucial if the cruise missile is intended for strategic purposes because, given a flight time of up to six hours, course corrections will be essential.

Cruise missiles can carry either NUCLEAR or CONVENTIONAL warheads. It is, moreover, not possible to distinguish the type of warhead from the external appearance of the missile. This has potentially daunting implications for ARMS CONTROL because counting missiles is of little value in establishing their nuclear/conventional status. This facility is referred to as 'dual CAPABILITY'.

Cruise missile development has proceeded apace since these new technologies became available. This has been particularly evident in the USA. Production and deployment has taken place in respect of air, ground and sea-launch systems. It is plausible to argue that these developments rival the advances in multiple warheads in their significance.

### Cuban missile crisis

The proximate cause of the Cuban missile crisis of October 1962 was the placement on that island, less than one hundred miles off the coast of Florida, of some sixty medium range ballistic missiles (MRBMS) and intermediate range ballistic missiles (IRBMS) by the Soviet Union. The deployment of NUCLEAR WEAPONS in the Caribbean by its adversary provoked the United

States to take prompt and coercive counter-measures and the ensuing CRISIS was extremely acute. The so-called 'eyeball to eyeball' confrontation ran the risk of ending in a nuclear exchange. In its aftermath the events influenced a literature on CRISIS MANAGEMENT and the confrontation has been one of the most widely studied examples of the genre.

Although the eventual US reaction was highly coercive, there was an INTELLIGENCE time lag between the introduction of the missiles and their discovery by the United States. Routine shipping intelligence had shown that arms were being sent to Cuba but the US assumption was that these were purely defensive. Until their DEFINITION OF THE SITUATION changed in October, therefore, the United States was acting on the assumption that the Soviet Union would not introduce offensive military CAPABILITIES into the hemisphere. US leaders sought to reinforce by verbal indications that such a move would be unacceptable.

The realization after 14 October that the United States had failed to deter the Soviets from such precipitate action came as a salutary shock to the Kennedy Administration. Once the intelligence picture was revealed to the leadership, the Executive Committee of the National Security Council (Excom) met in secret session for almost a week to consider what response the United States should make. Subsequently this long period of deliberation was held to be a significant and successful feature of US DIPLOMACY. Eventually it was decided to institute a naval blockade of Cuba, but owing to the legal dubiety of this move the BLOCKADE was termed a QUARANTINE. Although rapidly seen to be successful, it did nothing to remove the missiles. Once these became operational and once an air defence of the sites had been coordinated, the relative capabilities would alter against the United States. The crisis escalated to a very high level of tension as the United States began to raise the stakes by implying that direct action would be taken against Cuba. This proved to be effective and by the end of the first week of the quarantine the Soviet Union had made a conciliatory offer to which the United States was able to respond. The missiles were to be removed in exchange for a US pledge not to invade the island.

In terms of crisis DECISION-MAKING the Cuban case study has been instructive. Although the United States was surprised by the missile placement, the time pressure during the days prior to the quarantine announcement was handled to give the United States the opportunity to consider a range of alternatives across the spectrum of diplomacy from verbal protests to an invasion of the island. From six initial options, two evolved for more detailed consideration: an AIR STRIKE and a naval blockade. In terms of the biases of the Excom, the quarantine was a COMPROMISE behind which most shades of opinion could rally. Central political control was maintained throughout the crisis and considerable imaginative statesmanship was shown during the second week when communication flows between the adversaries produced the final compromise.

In strategic terms, the crisis occurred at a time when the United States enjoyed a favourable balance of nuclear capabilities over its adversary. The MISSILE GAP was clearly in the United States' favour – indeed some had speculated that a possible Soviet intention behind the placement of the missiles had been to attempt to close this gap – and both sides were aware of this. Additionally, the United States had CONVENTIONAL superiority in the Caribbean and Atlantic which left them with further coercive options if the quarantine failed to dislodge the 'offensive' missiles. In bargaining terms the quarantine left the next move to the opponent but its weakness, as already noted, was its indirect approach to the precipitant issue of the Soviet missiles, To compensate for this the United States had to threaten further escalation during the second week to secure Soviet compliance.

In structural terms, Cuba was a BIPOLAR confrontation situation. The Cuban role was clearly secondary to that of the Soviet Union in the crisis bargaining. US allies in Europe were informed of the US moves but not consulted in advance of them. The MONROE DOCTRINE was invoked to gain support within the hemisphere, while the UN provided GOOD OFFICES, a valuable communications channel and a very public forum for some rhetorical flourishes by both sides. In the aftermath of the crisis relations between the two protagonists improved considerably and tangible evidence of this was shown in 1963 when a number of ARMS CONTROL agreements were concluded between them.

## Customs union

The customs union is a form of interstate INTEGRATION. In this arrangement state ACTORS agree to abolish TARIFFS between themselves while they maintain a tariff REGIME against third parties. The establishment of the common external tariff (cet) against the rest of the system gives the customs union a discriminatory characteristic. Conversely, the establishment of the union between the member states gives it a FREE TRADE characteristic. Customs union arrangements are normally phased in over a number of agreed stages. This process is known as HARMONIZATION.

Economic opinion is rather divided about the efficacy of customs unions. On one hand, by encouraging free trade, they reward efficiency. On the other hand, by encouraging PROTECTIONISM, they reward inefficiency, particularly at the margin. The move towards internal free trade within the arrangement also creates a larger domestic market for goods and services behind the tariff wall. Again, this can lead to greater efficiency if, but only if, the economies of the constituent parts of the union are highly competitive. In these circumstances production will become located in the most efficient units. This balance sheet analysis of the customs union is often referred to as the balance between trade creation and trade diversion.

The TREATY of Rome, which established the European Economic Community (EEC) in January 1958, is a paradigm example of the customs union in reality. In this case the economic arguments for the move were somewhat subsumed by the political justifications for integration. Certainly both tendencies pointed in the same direction but it would probably be valid to conclude that in the case of the EUROPEAN COMMUNITY (EC) idea politics dictated economic decisions rather than vice versa.

When the General Agreement on Tariffs and Trade (GATT) was drawn up in Geneva in 1947 the parties took particular note of the customs union system of integration. Article XXIV of GATT makes provisions for such arrangements. The intention of the parties to the Agreement was that they were establishing a set of criteria against which actual instances could be judged. The nub of the problem was the cet. If the establishment of the cet involves the members of the union in raising some or all of their tariffs then under Article XXIV such moves are not permitted. In effect GATT has the task under the articles of its agreement of deciding whether a customs union is 'inward looking' (i.e. moving away from free trade) or 'outward looking' (i.e. moving towards free trade). Unfortunately economic science is unable to pronounce on these matters with unambiguous precision and the vacuum tends to be filled with special pleading that particular instances are permissible under the rules.

*See also*: COMMON MARKET; FREE TRADE AREA

## Cybernetics

The study of communication systems and how organizations function via communication. The seminal work of cybernetics and its application to politics was done by Karl Deutsch in the 1960s. The concept of FEEDBACK was taken from cybernetics by students of policy analysis thereafter.

# D

### Damage limitation

A term used in STRATEGIC STUDIES. Its use appears in two contexts: as a principle and as a posture. In the first sense, damage limitation is shorthand for the maxim that states that the main function of the military CAPABILITY of the STATE is to deny the forces of the enemy their opportunities to cause destruction by relentlessly seeking them out and destroying them thereafter. In a more passive sense, damage limitation refers to the range of measures taken by a state to deny the enemy his gains. A whole range of active and passive DEFENCE measures are regarded as appropriate under this latter heading.

In the nuclear missile age, states following the principle of damage limitation must be able and willing to launch COUNTER-FORCE attacks on the enemy, even in the first instance. Damage limitation can shade off into a FIRST STRIKE policy if the principle is to be fully and effectively implemented.

As a posture, damage limitation requires the state to have forces in being and contingency plans to hand to effect such principles. Strategic and tactical air forces and surface-to-surface BALLISTIC MISSILES would normally be the essential force infrastructure, while planning for damage limitation requires a considerable amount of reliable INTELLIGENCE about the adversaries' FORCE levels and their location. As a posture, damage limitation also requires political and military leaders to conceptualize NUCLEAR WAR as a feasible and even relatively stable state of affairs. The sort of nuclear strikes envisaged under a damage limitation posture can be viewed as the antithesis of those envisaged under mutual assured destruction (MAD), therefore.

Damage limitation – in both its contexts – has been increasingly influential in US strategic thinking since the realization of their increasing VULNERABILITY dawned upon leaders and informed publics in the United States in the late 1950s. Robert McNamara's Ann Arbor commencement address in 1962 is generally accepted as one of the earliest and most closely reasoned arguments in favour of damage limitation, in both contexts. In the intervening years the refinements of the TECHNOLOGY of the offence has increased the feasibility of a successful disarming strike.

Since the same principles and postures are available to the Soviet Union, damage limitation has become part of the DEFINITION OF THE SITUATION as far as the SUPERPOWER strategic relationship is concerned. In any event it may be noted that there is more than a grain of ETHNOCENTRISM in the inclination to view one's own commitment to damage limitation as prudent but the adversaries' as provocative.

### Debt crisis

Problems arising from the foreign indebtedness of STATES have been periodic features in WORLD POLITICS for the last two centuries. In this respect the current CRISIS is nothing new, although there are features in the situation which are at least unique to the post-war global system. Clearly indebtedness in states, as in individuals, is only critical if the debtor cannot generate enough income to service the debt payments. This was precisely the problem which confronted a number of Latin American states in 1982 and which continues to the present day. In essence, therefore, the debt crisis has been caused because a small number of middle-income Latin American states found that the ratio of their debts to their EXPORT earnings was so unfavourable that they could no longer meet their commitments.

Economic development, as a goal of state policy, has been a defining characteristic of the THIRD WORLD since 1945. External funding for development had usually been supplied on a government-to-government basis or, alternatively, through international institutions like the UN and its several agencies. Private commercial funding of THIRD WORLD development had not been a feature of this process until the 1970s. The steep rise in oil prices as a result of the OPEC initiatives of 1973–4 meant that significant capital movements took place into the coffers of the OPEC states. The decision to allow these 'petrodollars' to be recycled through the FIRST WORLD banking system meant that significant amounts of liquidity were available for lending on to would-be borrowers. Much of this private bank lending after 1973–4 was directed to the middle income states in Latin America.

Borrowing on the scale embarked upon by the Latin American countries after 1973–4 was contingent upon a number of factors, first that their export earnings would remain sufficiently buoyant enabling them to earn enough income to service their debts. This was, further, contingent upon the TERMS OF TRADE remaining favourable and upon the advanced industrial countries (AICs) being willing to accept their products into their domestic markets. Adverse movements in the terms of trade and/or a severe recession in the AICs leading to IMPORT restrictions would seriously damage the chances of the debtor states earning sufficient for debt service. Secondly, their high borrowing strategy depended upon interest

rates remaining at post-1974 levels and not significantly altering upwards in the future. Unfortunately for the debtors all these factors conspired to work against them in the period after the second 'oil shock' of 1979. Trying to apportion blame for the subsequent CRISIS, which came to a head in 1982 when Mexico announced that it was unable to meet its foreign debt payments, is of little value. The response of the IMF was immediate if predictable. Given their approach to the issue of conditionality for IMF lending, well established already, it came as no surprise that the Fund insisted that the debtor states should take steps to adjust their internal economic activity through deflationary policies. Adjustment to the debt burden is often forced onto those members of society that can least afford to see a reduction in economic activity taking place. Higher levels of unemployment, zero growth of wages and salaries in real terms, reductions in public expenditure targets, increases in wealth disparities within the debtor societies; these are the consequences of making internal adjustments to the debt crisis. For the foreseeable future Latin America will be a net exporter of capital to its creditors as a result of the policies of the post-1973–4 period.

## Decision-makers

Those who make decisions on behalf of international ACTORS. Despite the circularity of the definition, identifying who are actually the decision-makers in particular instances is often a difficult task. In the limiting case where the actor is an individual – for instance, the SECRETARY-GENERAL of the UNITED NATIONS – then the distinction is collapsed. In those many more frequent situations where the actor is a collectivity, a plausible starting point would be the documentation setting out the original purposes and functions of the actor – such as the constitution or custom of the STATE. This may be described as identifying the formal office holders as the decision-makers.

Growing awareness of the significance of groups in decision-making leads to a different and more complicated RECOGNITION. In pluralist systems the role of political parties and interest groups cannot be discounted. In some systems the military may play a key role. In those systems where decision-making is bureaucratized it may be necessary to look at particular departments of state. In the final analysis, the answer to the question, 'who are the decision-makers?' will vary according to context and content of policy.

## Decolonization

The process whereby European control of overseas territories and peoples was ended. This culminated in the movement towards INDEPENDENCE within these areas. A substantial increase in the number of STATES within the INTERNATIONAL SYSTEM resulted and terms such as the THIRD WORLD became increasingly used as collective expressions for these new ACTORS. It should be noted that the correlation between being a former colony and being a Third World state is not perfect.

The principal states involved in the process of decolonization were located in Europe. Two merit special identification: the United Kingdom and France. In the case of the former, decolonization led to the creation of the COMMONWEALTH, which in its early years was significantly underpinned by economic ties, in particular the preferential TARIFF system of Imperial Preference and the Sterling Area. The French decolonization experience was more traumatic than that of the United Kingdom, particularly in Algeria and VIETNAM. Unlike their near neighbours, the French were briefly attracted to the idea of assimilation rather than independence, and it was only when the Fourth Republic collapsed in 1958 that the issue was finally settled in favour of decolonization.

It should not be thought that policies of INTERVENTION in the affairs of overseas territories and peoples ended with decolonization. While formal political control may have ceased, more informal methods of INTERVENTION and penetration have proliferated. It should be noted that the last vestiges of colonial control have created significant FOREIGN POLICY ISSUE AREAS for the United Kingdom in respect of the FALKLANDS, Gibraltar and Hong Kong.

## de facto/de jure

Terms used in INTERNATIONAL LAW and DIPLOMACY usually in association with RECOGNITION. *De facto* normally refers to provisional recognition that a particular government exercises factual SOVEREIGNTY, whereas *de jure* implies recognition of both factual and legal sovereignty. The *de facto* variety thus implies doubt either about the long term viability of a REGIME or else of its LEGITIMACY. *De jure* implies complete diplomatic acceptance of the new STATE or government. For example, the United Kingdom recognized the Soviet government *de facto* in 1921 and *de jure* in 1924. Clearly, political calculations play a major part in distinguishing the two categories, but it should be noted that *de facto* usually applies to governments rather than states – a STATE may for all practical purposes be *de jure* while its government for political reasons may be considered *de facto*. The guiding principle is usually whether or not a government exercises effective control over the territory of the state in question, but ideological issues can, and do, intrude. During the COLD WAR, for example, selective use or non-use of these recognition categories became important discretionary instruments for registering approval or disapproval. Thus, from 1949 to 1979 the United States refused *de jure* recognition of COMMUNIST China.

*De facto* recognition is not necessarily a precondition of *de jure* recognition although in practice this has tended to be the case. The differences between them are not just a matter of degree or of political preference since *de jure* recognition entails the establishment of normal diplomatic relations whereas *de facto* does not of itself include the exchange of diplomatic relations. In addition, *de jure* can be 'express' (involving the immediate exchange of diplomatic notes) or 'tacit' (involving the declared intention at some future date to do so). Neither categories are final, although withdrawal of *de facto* recognition is easier than *de jure*.

## Defence

A relative rather than an absolute term used to describe the ability and willingness of international ACTORS – usually STATES and ALLIANCES – to resist attacks from other actors. Like DETERRENCE, a term which is in some usages closely related to defence, the latter is not exclusive to WORLD POLITICS. It is, for example, a key concept in most legal systems, the right of parties to a 'defence' being crucial to both civil and criminal proceedings. Indeed, the ability and willingness to defend oneself is a common feature of all social systems which recognize that CONFLICT is a persistent and enduring process.

In world politics the need for actors to defend themselves has often been positively correlated with the idea that the system is one of ANARCHY. The greater the anarchy, the greater the need for defence. The emergence of the state as the dominant actor in world politics from the seventeenth century onwards increased the significance of defence as a goal of state policy. Defending the territorialty of the state was held to be the first requirment. Thereafter certain assets – symbolic as well as instrumental – such as the state capital, might assume more importance than others. Because defence CAPABILITIES are not distributed evenly between state actors, some states were better able to defend themselves than others. The latter would be forced to seek alliances and guarantee TREATIES if they were to avoid the unenviable fate of being 'pawns' in the system.

An important parameter in the defence of any actor is likely to be the available TECHNOLOGY. The balance of advantage between the defender and the attacker is affected by the technological variable. In the contemporary system it is hard to resist the conclusion that AIR POWER, BALLISTIC MISSILES and NUCLEAR WEAPONS have made the task of the defence almost insuperable. Nuclear strategy has recognized the inevitable with the idea of ASSURED DESTRUCTION and its corollary of mutual assured destruction (MAD). According to this view, not only is the search for defence chimerical, it is also mistaken as the essence of the strategy is that population centres should be left undefended. In the literature this is often referred to as the 'hostage cities' consequence of MAD. The somewhat convoluted logic of MAD is not without its critics and both the SUPERPOWERS have clearly moved away from this somewhat negative attitude to defence of late. The renewal of interest in ballistic missile defence (BMD) is one example of this reexamination.

The twentieth century attempts at international institution-building via the LEAGUE OF NATIONS and the UN can be seen in this context as attempts to replace the idea of defence with the idea of COLLECTIVE SECURITY. In its pure form, collective security was certainly seen as a way out of the competitive ally-seeking and alliance-building DIPLOMACY of previous eras. However, the drafters of the MULTILATERAL TREATIES which established these institutions were careful to reserve to the state membership the 'inherent' right of individual and collective SELF-DEFENCE.

As an ISSUE AREA in a state's FOREIGN POLICY, defence questions will again be positively correlated with the extent to which conflict, and the expectation of violent conflict, are matters of great concern to the state leaders and ATTENTIVE PUBLICS. In contemporary terms, defence is an immediate and pressing issue for the government and people of Israel to an extent not evident for the government and people of

Ireland. To the extent that world politics has moved into a more pluralist context with COMPLEX INTERDEPENDENCE characterizing important relationships, defence questions will assume less importance in the foreign policy DEFINITION OF THE SITUATION. Deutsch (1957), in his studies of INTEGRATION, has suggested that whole groups of states can now be identified in the system whose regional relationships are not fundamentally and constantly being defined in terms of the most stringent and pressing defence–security contexts. If this is an important trend for the future then defence matters may assume a relatively reduced profile in the foreign policy concerns of states.

*See also*: MILITARY–INDUSTRIAL COMPLEX

## Definition of the situation

A term that has been originally attributed to the US sociologist Thomas (1958), and widely applied since by both sociologists and social psychologists. It refers to the processes of social PERCEPTION whereby individuals and groups 'construct' their reality in all its manifestations. This view, that individuals and groups respond and react to situations as they perceive them, and not as they really are, has led policy analysts to speak of a psychological environment in which policy is made. This approach is encapsulated in the phrase – again from Thomas – that 'if men define situations as real, they are real in their consequences'.

Since the processes of perception involve selecting certain cues and ignoring others, policy analysts have suggested that this insight may help others to understand how apparent 'mistakes' can be made in POLICY-MAKING. What might be seen objectively as an 'error' becomes more understandable if the definition of the situation that produced the policy is first investigated. Some of the most critical and costly 'errors', such as the US failure to anticipate the attack on PEARL HARBOR in 1941, notwithstanding their access to Japanese INTELLIGENCE, are susceptible to this explanation.

The concept of the definition of the situation is equally applicable to the analysis of mass public perceptions as to those of the LEADERSHIP. Indeed, any analysis that seeks to describe and explain how people view world events must take a position that is congruent with the definition of the situation idea. It remains an empirical question as to the content of that definition, of course.

## Démarche

A DIPLOMATIC term referring to a fresh initiative adopted by one side following an impasse in BILATERAL NEGOTIATION. A démarche does not usually involve any significant alteration to the NATIONAL INTEREST and it may have been part of the overall diplomatic strategy in the first place. It has the advantage of indicating a willingness on the part of one side to find an acceptable solution to the problem.

## Demilitarization

A policy whereby military forces are prohibited from an area. The prohibition will normally be absolute. If any forces remain they would be expected to confine themselves to non-provocative DEFENCE measures, typically associated with UN PEACE-KEEPING. Demilitarization may follow upon a withdrawal of forces or it might apply to an area where military FORCE has not been introduced. Demilitarization might occur as part of a peace TREATY or TRUCE agreement and, therefore, some VERIFICATION and observation of the situation would be built into the arrangement. Finally, if the demilitarization agreement was coterminous with the territory of a STATE, it would be expected that the FOREIGN POLICY of that state would be of a neutral or NON-ALIGNED orientation therafter.

*See*: DISENGAGEMENT.

## Demontage

Diplomatic term used in connection with WAR REPARATIONS. It refers to the dismantling of factories, industrial plant and other installations connected to the war potential of the offending STATE and their subsequent transfer to the state or states receiving reparations. It is sometimes demanded simply as a war prize by the victors but more usually it is regarded as a necessary precautionary measure against possible future hostile action by the defeated state. Thus, at the Potsdam conference of 1945 the Allies demanded the demontage or destruction of post-war Germany's war potential in all four zones of occupation.

## Dependence

Dependence is the opposite of INDEPENDENCE. It refers to a lack of AUTONOMY and control over outcomes. Dependence stems from the simple yet crucial factor of reliance. It can be demonstrated hypothetically by saying that if ACTOR A relies upon Actor B for the provision of some goods and services then A may be said to be dependent upon B. Reliance of this type is a commonplace in WORLD POLITICS and where it is clearly *mutual* – so that in our example B also relies upon A for goods and services – it is possible to speak of INTERDEPENDENCE rather than dependence. Interdependence may thus be seen as a median position between independence on one hand and dependence on the other. Thus the same developments in world politics that can be identified as leading to greater interdependence can also lead to greater dependence, since both are moves away from the same starting point: independence and AUTONOMY.

Dependence can be identified in the following contexts: military, economic and technological. Military dependence is perhaps the oldest form of reliance in world politics and is still one of the most pervasive. The establishment of ALLIANCES and the provision of military AID are the key attributes of dependence here. Economic dependence is, in the contemporary system, the most pervasive but also the most ambiguous. This ambiguity has led some writers to the view that economically dependent relationships currently constitute a POWER structure called DEPENDENCY. Others have resisted this line of argument preferring to adapt FREE TRADE ideas to contemporary circumstances and to suggest that economic dependence is a welcome and necessary feature of an expanding world economy. Technological dependence is the least unequivocal and the most obvious. Unlike military and economic dependence it is also readily susceptible to quantitative VERIFICATION, a simple but effective indicator of this type of dependence being the holdings of internationally registered patents. These clearly show that TECHNOLOGY, particularly 'state of the art' is very unevenly distributed around the system, a small number of DEVELOPED STATES and MULTINATIONAL COMPANIES being crucial suppliers of technology.

## Dependency

Sometimes rendered as 'dependencia', the term refers to a POWER structure of complex dependence between international ACTORS. According to this view relations of dependence, in the plural, become so reinforcing that the development of the dependent state becomes distorted. This asymmetry will be located in the economic system initially and the distortions may seriously hamper and impair economic development as a result. The dependency will also be marked in TECHNOLOGY where the STATE may find itself importing costly and inappropriate technologies. Dependency may become evident in military issues if the dependent STATE has internal and/or external enemies.

Dependency is both an attempt to analyse a particularly unequal power structure and a prescription for avoiding such a situation in the future. In this latter use dependency may be considered an IDEOLOGY.

Latin American political economists and sociologists have been particularly associated with this ideological approach. It might appropriately be termed a 'socialist' analysis, and its intellectual genealogy includes the study of IMPERIALISM.

## Dependent state

Originally, a dependent state was a synonym for a protectorate, that is to say, a STATE which has surrendered significant areas of its jurisdiction to an external ACTOR in return for protection. A common division of responsibility under this arrangement would be for DEFENCE and external affairs to be handled by the protecting state, and for domestic matters to remain under the control of the dependent state. Third parties would assent to this through the mechanism of RECOGNITION.

The term now has an entirely different meaning. A dependent state is one that is identified as being in a DEPENDENCE relationship with another actor or actors. The sort of legal approval implied by the mechanism of recognition no longer applies in the contemporary usage.

## Dependent territory

The term by which colonial states now refer to their remaining colonies. The twentieth century has witnessed the almost total elimination of colonial rule, and the residual holdings are normally referred to by this form of words. Sometimes, as in the case of the FALKLANDS/MALVINAS, the dependent territory can be the subject of considerable CONFLICT between STATES. In principle, colonial states stand ready to grant INDEPENDENCE to these territories, if such a demand is expressed. The perverse outcome of a territory opting to remain under colonial control is not unknown, notwithstanding the prevailing climate of opinion in institutions such as the UN that ending COLONIALISM is now de rigueur.

## Deportation

The enforced removal of an ALIEN from one STATE to another usually as a consequence of a perceived offence to the host state. However, in INTERNATIONAL LAW no reasons for deportation have to be given. Thus, in the United Kingdom the Aliens Order of 1953 empowers the Home Secretary to deport an alien if he 'deems it to be conducive to the public good' (Article 20, 2, b). Given the principle of RECIPROCITY this means that a decision to deport is all but uncontestable. M. Akenhurst (1970) quotes the case of a UK woman lecturer being deported from Malawi in 1969 for wearing a miniskirt at a party. At the airport, having prudently changed into an ankle-length dress, she told reporters that she was 'simply delighted' to be leaving! In fact, most challenges do not focus on the decision to deport, but on the conditions under which the deportee has been held. Extended periods in prison, torture, humiliation and ridicule are not unusual preliminaries to deportation.

Under the rules of NATIONALITY, when a national of one state is deported from another the 'home' state is obliged to receive him, unless he is willing to go to another state which accepts him. Since states have such wide powers in relation to deportation, it is often used as a substitute for EXTRADITION, especially in cases where no formal BILATERAL extradition treaty exists. Sometimes the term is used in relation to the enforced expulsion of DIPLOMATS, but here the process is different. The receiving state, usually on the advice of its Foreign Ministry, simply declares the offending diplomat PERSONA NON GRATA. Tit-for-tat expulsions of this kind were an integral part of COLD WAR politics.

## Destabilization

In FOREIGN POLICY analysis this refers to HEGEMONIAL attempts to promote fundamental change in a target STATE's policies without resort to overt armed CONFLICT.

As such it involves a combination of military, diplomatic, economic, social and ideological instruments. The primary objective though, is a political one. This may involve attempting to secure structural movements in an opponent's stance even to the extent of aiming for REGIME change. The intention to destabilize is not, as is commonly thought, to cause fringe irritation or discomfort; rather, it is to bring about major changes in behaviour or PERCEPTION in the target state. It commonly takes a covert form and characteristically involves targeting an opponent's vulnerable points, e.g. food or water supplies, energy sources, transportation systems and support for internal dissident groups. The overall aim would be to cause serious hardship to the indigenous population to the extent that the target state becomes compliant.

The term is most often used in connection with South Africa's policies in relation to neighbouring states, in particular Zimbabwe, Mozambique, Angola, Zambia Botswana, Lesotho and Swaziland. Pretoria's object is to keep these states economically dependent and thus severely limit their ability to damage the Republic. South Africa's policies led directly to the formation of the Southern African Development Coordination Conference (SADCC) in 1980, the main objective of which was to decouple the REGION from the grip of destabilization. Destabilization is an integral part of South Africa's 'Total Strategy' and although successful in regional terms, it has had damaging international repercussions. A perverse effect of destabilization may, in the long run, be greater INDEPENDENCE and freedom of action for the targeted states. The risk of the rebound effect makes the option of destabilization a matter of extremely delicate political calculation.

*See also*: APARTHEID; FRONT-LINE STATES; INTERVENTION

## D'Estaing doctrine

Term which refers to a FOREIGN POLICY initiative expressed by French President Giscard D'Estaing in December 1974 when he described that the main principles upon which France's world posture rested were *mondialisme et conciliation* (GLOBALISM and reconciliation). The general philosophy was that France would move away from the narrow NATIONALISM that had sometimes seemed to characterize its foreign policy (especially under De Gaulle) and would capitalize on its independent stance to offer itself as a mediator in major international disputes. Thus, through the GOOD OFFICES of France, diplomatic dialogue between the North Vietnamese and the United States began in Paris in 1970.

## Détente

A diplomatic term meaning a relaxation or a slackening of tension in the previously strained relations between STATES. In diplomatic history the term is particularly associated with the CONCERT system established in post-1815 Europe. Again, the period following the Locarno TREATIES of 1925 and resulting in the KELLOGG-BRIAND Pact of Paris in 1928 (which sought to outlaw WAR between states) is often described in these terms. However, the term is now most often used in connection with a perceived easing of relations between the United States and the Soviet Union which began, from most accounts, in the early 1960s. In this way it is sometimes used, not altogether correctly, as a synonym for RAPPROCHEMENT and PEACEFUL COEXISTENCE. Détente is sometimes referred to as the antithesis of the COLD WAR, but may also be viewed as just a stage in its development – a shift from the doctrinaire confrontational policies of the 1950s to the more flexible DIPLOMACY of the 1960s and 1970s. At any rate it is useful to distinguish between détente as a policy a state may pursue (e.g. the Nixon/Kissinger initiatives of 1972 and 1973) and détente as a condition or a process (e.g. post-1962 East–West relations). It should also be noted that détente is not restricted to GREAT POWER MULTILATERAL relationships alone. BILATERAL détentes between lesser states are also a significant feature of contemporary WORLD POLITICS. West Germany's policy of OSTPOLITIK and UK efforts in the early 1960s to play the part of 'honest broker' can be viewed in this context.

Although no formal TREATY established the recent period of détente, commentators usually cite the CUBAN MISSILE CRISIS of 1962 as the beginning of the process and the Soviet invasion of AFGHANISTAN in 1979 as its most fragile point. Indeed, for many the events of 1979–80 (Afghanistan and the election of President Reagan) signalled the end of détente and the beginning of the 'New Cold War'. Looking at it as a historical process, though, many analysts disagree as to exactly when it began and when and if it ended. Some scholars date it from as early as the Eisenhower administration and the death of Stalin (1953), others give Kennedy and Khrushchev the honour of its inauguration and yet others fix its inception with the Nixon/Kissinger overtures to China in 1972. However, most agree that it refers to a structural change in post-war SUPERPOWER relations and that it set in train a number of significant points of dialogue between them, including the HELSINKI ACCORDS (1975) and the Strategic Arms Limitation Talks (SALT).

Détente does not mean that conflicts have been resolved or that either side accepts the ideological principles of the other. Rather it should be seen as a response to changed perceptions of the INTERNATIONAL SYSTEM – an awareness of the possibility of mutual destruction, the emergence of new clusters of POWER and perhaps the promptings of domestic economic priorities – all of these played their parts in fostering improved public relations between the SUPERPOWERS. Critics of détente, especially in the Reagan administration, have argued that far from being a mutually understood halfway point between extreme hostility and overt amicability (ENTENTE), détente is little short of APPEASEMENT, which has served to strengthen the East at the expense of the West. This, however, is a distortion of the term.

## Deterrence

Deterrence is a conditional commitment to retaliate, or to exact retribution, if another party fails to behave in a desired, compliant manner. Deterrence is thus about relationships between individuals and groups. Indeed, it can be said to cover an extremely broad set of social relations from child-rearing through penal systems to WORLD POLITICS. It is possible to identify this relationship in its simplest two-person version by speaking of an Imposer and a Target. Hence the Imposer seeks to deter the Target from behaving in an unacceptable fashion by threatening punishment.

Deterrence concentrates exclusively upon negative SANCTIONS, or threats, and upon preventing undesirable behaviour. It is therefore more usual to find that deterrence is mostly prevalent and significant in relationships of antipathy rather than in relationships of harmony. Imposers are more likely to make threats in situations which they find uncongenial and *vis-à-vis* Targets whose behaviour, and even presence, they wish to oppose. In this way deterrence is a special instance of the POWER relationship – those situations of social opposition characterized by the use of sanctions. Deterrence is unequivocally about negative sanctions, moreover.

Since deterrence is based upon ideas about threat systems and conditional commitments to carry out punishment it has proved particularly congenial to the STRATEGIC STUDIES fraternity within the REALIST tradition. The advent of NUCLEAR WEAPONS after 1945 provided a new challenge to these scholars because it seemed to many that making, and potentially activating nuclear threats, had special problems both for the analyst and for the POLICY-MAKER. The inherent difficulty with this class of threats is that they lack CREDIBILITY. Faced with the knowledge that the opponent possesses nuclear weapons, the nuclear threat is a conditional commitment that the Imposer has no incentive to carry out, rationally, since he will gain nothing from its activation. If the Imposer is placed in the position of actually having to fulfill the threat then its purpose is lost and carrying it out is valueless. Paradoxically, this need not be the case if the Target can be persuaded that the threat is not idle, that the Imposer will not hesitate to activate it. In short, the more certain the contingent fulfilment, the less likely the actual fulfilment will need to be activated.

As suggested above, the problem of making this contingent threat sufficiently powerful is referred to as the problem of credibility. Credibility is the process whereby threats are made operational. First, operationlizing the threat requires that it be communicated – as unambiguously as possible. Secondly, the threat must actually deprive the Target of scarce values which he would otherwise wish to retain. The Target must value that which will be sacrificed, if they disobey, higher than any values that will be foregone if they comply. This is why it is difficult to coerce a Target who feels that he has nothing to lose. In these situations deterrence may break down and the Imposer will be faced with the prospect of activating his threat in order to retain his credibility – and not to be seen to be bluffing. This problem is referred to in the literature as the EX POST EX ANTE situation, namely, that a threat may look quite plausible before it is carried out, yet may look totally implausible afterwards. Opponents of mutual assured destruction (MAD) hold that this strategy looks much less credible in the light of this distinction.

The *ex post ex ante* issue is approached in a somewhat different way by Schelling in his 1966 volume. Using the distinction between deterrence and compellence, he seeks to separate situations where the Imposer is seeking to prevent a behaviour sequence (deterrence) from situations where the Im-

poser is seeking to redress a situation afterwards (compellence). Schelling argues that achieving a relationship of effective compellence may be more difficult because the behaviour sequence is already under way and the Imposer is, in effect, seeking to 'put the clock back' by requiring the Target to change what he is already doing.

Credibility, thirdly, requires the Imposer to possess the requisite military CAPABILITY to make and carry out threats. In his book, Glenn Snyder (1961) distinguishes two types of deterrence situations that are dependent upon different capabilities and therefore different intentions. Snyder's distinction is between deterrence by denial and deterrence by punishment. Denial deterrence works by contesting the control of territory and populations traditionally associated with any territorial DEFENCE. Prior to the development of NUCLEAR WEAPONS both denial and punishment functions would have been fulfilled with the same capability. However, the development of long-range AIR POWER, BALLISTIC MISSILES and fission and fusion weapons has meant that any STATE possessing this capability may be able to inflict great punishment upon an adversary without having the capability of denying the opponent any significant gains. In this argument deterrence and defence become alternatives, if not opposites.

With MAD the uncoupling of deterrence from defence was completed. MAD could not threaten to deny the enemy his would-be gains, so instead it threatens punishment in the form of genocide. One result of the uncoupling of deterrence and defence has been that confusion has arisen about the role of different weapons systems. From the viewpoint of defence an anti-ballistic missile (ABM) can be justified if it allows the possessor to thereby limit damage to his territory. From the viewpoint of deterrence an ABM system may seem to be destabilizing because it reduces VULNERABILITY, which is a prerequisite for MAD.

Deterrence theory raises acute questions about the circumstances in which threats can be effective means of controlling behaviour and, conversely, conditions when they may be self-defeating. There is considerable evidence for a very qualified view of deterrence assumptions. First, a threat is often perceived by a Target as motivated by the desire to injure rather than by the needs of SELF-DEFENCE. Secondly, a threat may be seen as an attempt to restrain legitimate behaviour which the Target feels entitled to engage in. Thirdly, the threat may not deter aggressive behaviour but rather deflect it onto substitute objects. Fourthly, a threat by creating stress within a DECISON-MAKING group may vitiate the rational behaviour pattern that is such a necessary prerequisite for deterrence to work. Behaviour, particularly under stress, may be counterproductive as far as deterrence is concerned. Accurate communication may be made more difficult. Stress can greatly increase the likelihood that certain values will be misperceived and that issues may be seen as matters of principle about which no concessions can be made. Jervis's (1976) discussion of the spiral theory in his work on PERCEPTION and MISPERCEPTION suggests that hostility can be self-defeating in certain circumstances and reinforces the queries raised above about this influential, but flawed, theory of social control.

## Developed state

A STATE which has achieved self-sustained economic growth over a sufficient period of time to show development in primary, secondary and tertiary sectors of industry and to have achieved thereby a consistent improvement in living standards for the population as a whole. The advanced industrial countries (AICs) are generally held to be the paradigm developed states.

It is the case that the kinds of changes associated with developed status have only been available to peoples and states over the last two hundred years. As a result of a series of initiatives taken originally in Western Europe it became possible through the processes of industrialization and mecha-

nization to create wealth in a relatively benign fashion. This process is often referred to as the 'industrial revolution'. Originally, the leading example of a developed state was Great Britain but this position was lost to the United States towards the end of the last century. There is some reason to suppose that the United States is similarly losing its status as the leading developed state and that Japan is currently the most dynamic example of the genre.

*See*: FIRST WORLD; YEN POWER

## Diplomacy

The word is often used, incorrectly, as a synonym for FOREIGN POLICY. Whereas the latter can be described as the substance, aims and attitudes of a STATE's relations with others, diplomacy is one of the instruments employed to put these into effect. It is concerned with dialogue and NEGOTIATION and in this sense is not merely an instrument of state, it is also an institution of the STATE-SYSTEM itself. Since the emergence of the state-system in Europe in the fifteenth century an organized and fairly coherent system of permanent relations has developed among the ACTORS and, even when these relations have been interrupted by armed conflict, diplomacy has still been the principal means of communication. Indeed, although it is common to separate the diplomatic and the military means at a state's disposal, actual practice has tended to blur the distinction. As Frederick the Great once remarked, 'diplomacy without force is like music without instruments'. So diplomacy as an instrument and as an institution is an essential part of the whole rationale of WORLD POLITICS.

The main function if diplomacy is negotiation – which broadly means discussions designed to identify common interests and areas of CONFLICT between the parties. To establish the conditions under which negotiations can take place a number of other tasks are undertaken. The first is representation. The emissary, or AMBASSADOR, is one of the earliest political roles established in human society, but it was not until the fifteenth century in the Italian CITY-STATES that the concept of a permanent representative mission (or legation) was formalized. During the Renaissance period a systematic and largely professional diplomatic service was established with the purpose of obtaining information, interpreting policies and trends, safeguarding military and political interests and promoting commerce and TRADE links. Certainly the promotion of trade has always been a central part of the activity of diplomacy and is not, as some allege, a comparatively recent innovation. The Venetian diplomatic service was initially a commercial venture and there is much evidence that the spur to organized diplomacy on a permanent and spatially static basis was just as much economic as political or military. A second function of diplomacy besides representation of a state's interests is to formulate and identify these goals and objectives. Preparing policy guidelines and initiatives for their political masters to accept or reject is usually the task of a Foreign Ministry, rather than an ambassador on location, although their views will obviously be influential. Another function, in the larger sense, is the overall management of orderly relations as well as being the means whereby change is effected. Finally, diplomacy is concerned with establishing and renewing the rules and procedures which regulate the INTER-NATIONAL SYSTEM. In this last sense, diplomacy is the enabling vehicle for the operation of INTERNATIONAL LAW and IN-TERNATIONAL ORGANIZATIONS.

The rules which established a common and coherent diplomatic system were developed in piecemeal fashion from the fifteenth to the twentieth centuries. The EXTRATERRITORIALITY rule was established during the period of Louis XIV, the notion of the *corps diplomatique* emerged in the eighteenth century, and the Congress of VIENNA in 1815 can be credited with laying down the procedures for precedence and with promoting the doctrine of the for-mal EQUALITY of states. In the twentieth century the Vienna conventions of 1961, 1963 and 1969 have codified international law relating to Diplomatic Relations, Consular Relations and the Law of Treaties, thus tightening up and giving new impetus to past and future practice. Most states now recognize and implement these developments. The near universal acceptance of diplomacy and its trappings has not, however, had as smooth a ride as the foregoing might suggest. It has come under attack from all aspects of the ideological spectrum in recent times. The Soviet Union rejected it in 1917 as did China from 1949 to the early 1970s, the United States, especially under Woodrow Wilson, expressed qualms about it, the new states esablished during the 1950s and 1960s as a result of the anti-colonial REVOLUTION were very uneasy about it and of course Iran and ISLAMIC fundamentalism is its most bitter contemporary opponent. Nevertheless, after an initial period of formal ideological rejection most states, including all of the above, have been drawn into the system, mainly because there exist no alternatives to it. Changes have occurred both in the conduct of diplomacy and in the personnel associated with it. Most commentators point to the following developments which occured as a result of the increasing complexity of inter-state relations: the intrusion of ideological conflict and the opening up of diplomatic dialogue; the change of emphasis from BILATERAL to MULTILATERAL dealings; the decline in the DECISION-MAKING power of the ambassador; the advent of personal diplomacy; the increased use of experts and specialists; the involvement of ministries not normally associated with foreign affairs; the increased number of TREATIES; the growth in importance of the media and the expansion of the international community and of non-state actors. This enhancement and enlargement of the SCOPE of modern diplomacy and the widening of its agenda has resulted in a change of emphasis (more on economic issues than on traditional HIGH

POLITICS), rather than on any major change in function. This remains in essence the same as it has always been; namely, to manage and conduct orderly relations in a multi-state, politically fragmented INTERNATIONAL SYSTEM.

*See also:* CONFERENCE DIPLOMACY; DOLLAR DIPLOMACY; DIPLOMATIC IMMUNITIES AND PRIVILEGES

## Diplomatic immunities and privileges

The reciprocal granting of certain immunities and privileges to diplomatic agents is grounded in the concept of SOVEREIGNTY and mutual respect for the political INDEPENDENCE and territorial integrity of STATES. In this sense diplomatic immunity implies both an exemption from rules associated with DOMESTIC JURISDICTION and also an affirmation of them. Rules relating to the special status of diplomats are common to all STATE-SYSTEMS and are among the earliest manifestations of INTERNATIONAL LAW. Communication between independent units would have been all but impossible without rules establishing the sacrosanct nature of the emissary or herald. With the development of resident embassies, permanent missions and legations during the late Renaissance period in Europe, this was extended to cover location as well as personnel. It should be noted, however, that diplomatic immunities and privileges are granted not to particular persons but to the states or organizations on whose behalf they act. Customary rules associated with exemptions were codified at the Congress of VIENNA in 1815 and more extensively at the Vienna Convention on Diplomatic Relations of 1961. (Incidentally, in both cases the word 'privileges' is preferred to 'immunities'.) The following areas are covered: the inviolability of premises and property, the personal inviolability of diplomatic officers, freedom of communication and transportation, inviolability of records, archives, documents and correspondence, customs privileges (e.g. the 'diplomatic bag'), exemption from taxation and various jurisdictional privileges. Most of these exemptions also apply to representatives of states to INTERNATIONAL ORGANIZATIONS. Representation to the UN and its Specialized Agencies is covered by the rules established by the General Convention on the Privileges and Immunities of the UN of 1946 and these are premised on an agreement between the United States as the host country and the organization itself.

The functional necessity of diplomatic privileges and immunities as a general rule for the efficient conduct of INTERNATIONAL RELATIONS is almost universally recognized. However, this does not mean that immunities are absolute or cannot be waived by the sending state or withdrawn by the receiving state (PERSONA NON GRATA). In general, violation of these rules is considered a serious international dereliction. The near universal condemnation of the Iranian imprisonment of US diplomats for use as hostages in 1979–81, and the widespread public outcry at the US raid on the Nicaraguan ambassador's residence in Panama in 1989, is testimony to this. Indeed, with regard to the latter, President Bush's remark that it was a 'screw-up' clearly implies that the violation was contrary to accepted practice.

## Disarmament

Disarmament is both a process and an end state. As a process it envolves the reduction, removal or elimination of identified weapon systems. As an end state it involves the establishment of a disarmed world and the prevention of rearmament thereafter. Disarmament may be regional or global. It may be UNILATERAL, BILATERAL, or MULTILATERAL. It may be partial or complete. It may be limited to certain weapon systems or general to all classes. In this way it may be seen that general and complete disarmament is the most comprehensive of these schemes.

In the modern STATE-CENTRED system

disarmament has usually followed defeat in war. A defeated STATE will temporarily be disarmed by the victor(s). Often, a subsequent peace TREATY or TRUCE will confirm this outcome. The vanquished may be prohibited from acquiring certain kinds or certain amounts of stipulated weapons. Negotiated agreements between nominal equals, without the test of strength of WAR, require a different approach and produce a different outcome. These agreements require the parties to recognize that coopertion is to be preferred to the continuation of the ARMS RACE. In such bargaining situations the tendency is to proceed by a strategy of INCREMENTALISM and to work from areas of agreement towards partial or limited measures. This approach shades off into ARMS CONTROL in many instances and potential confusion is not assisted by the tendency among politicians and diplomats to run these two ideas together.

The arms race, and the appropriate attitude to take towards it, is really what separates the proponents of general and complete disarmament from the proponents of arms control. Whereas arms controllers accept that weapon systems have a function and role in WORLD POLITICS, general and complete disarmers hold that the dynamics of the arms race exacerbates tensions and leads to violence, in short, that the arms race is a cause of conflict and violence, rather than merely a symptom.

Disarmament is not automatically tension-reducing. There are powerful incentives to 'cheat' on the other party during the process. Indeed, the further disarmament proceeds, the greater these incentives become. The ultimate paradox of the disarmament process is that in an effort to eliminate the tensions caused by the arms race, disarmament creates tensions itself.

As an end state, a disarmed world would require considerable centralized management to avoid these contradictions. State sponsored disarmament clearly implies the internationalization of military FORCE. If this outcome is ever achieved, two issues will immediately arise: what military CAPABILITIES will the international force require, and what policy goals will the new institution follow in order to maintain disarmament and prevent competitive rearmament? These are complex and difficult questions, but they indicate the kinds of problems that will arise if the process ever reaches the end state.

It should be noted that states do, on occasions, engage in disarmament negotiations in order to achieve what might be called 'side benefits'. These might include a desire to understand the other side's point of view, in many instances. However, more cynical motives can sometimes be identified. States will talk about disarmament in order to score PROPAGANDA points by manoeuvring the opposition into positions where they can be made to appear intransigent and insincere about the issue.

### Disengagement
The process whereby DEMILITARIZATION of a territory is accompanied by its political reorganization, disengagement is a special instance of the broader concept of demilitarization. In the 1950s it was a popular and widely canvassed policy which sought to address the issue of reunifying the two parts of Germany.

### Dollar diplomacy
Phrase particularly associated with the FOREIGN POLICY of President Taft (1909–13) and now commonly used to describe US efforts to secure their objectives through financial and economic instruments of control. Initially the target area was Central and Latin America, but the policy was extended to China and the Far East, as well as post-Second World War Europe (the MARSHALL PLAN). The assumptions behind it were that extensive US investments would create economic progress, political stability and compliance in areas that the United States considered strategically important. It

also, of course, had the benefit of furthering the interests of US business. Dollar diplomacy does not rule out the option of military or political INTERVENTION. In fact, the establishment of extensive financial commitments abroad might make it more likely in periods of instability and upheaval. This is especially true of the Panama Canal, the completion of which coincided with the origin of the phrase. Other notable examples are Guatemala (1954), Cuba (1961) and the Dominican Republic (1965). This policy, along with its successor 'missionary diplomacy' – the term given to Woodrow Wilson's missionary zeal in attempting to export democracy – has led to considerable 'Yankee-phobia' in Latin America which the GOOD NEIGHBOR policies of the 1930s were designed to dispel. Apart from the case of Western Europe, most analysts believe that dollar diplomacy and its variants (e.g. 'Coca-Cola IMPERIALISM') have failed in their general objectives and that the premise on which they are based – what's good for the United States is good for the rest of the world – may be an unsound one in the formulation and conduct of foreign policy.

## Domain

An ACTOR'S domain is a measure of the number of other actors in WORLD POLITICS over which it can effectively exert INFLUENCE at any one time. The concept is used in the analysis of POWER relationships. Its utility is considerable because it enables the analyst to look at power relations as a dynamic rather than a static set of occurrences. The term is usually used in conjunction with SCOPE and, accordingly, its explanatory value is enhanced further.

## Domestic analogy

A concept, beloved of traditionalists in international theory, whereby the domestic, political, legal and social experience is applied to inter-state affairs. Most commonly used by adherents of the HOBBESIAN view in which order is achieved in the state of nature by the creation of a Leviathan, or 'a common power' to regulate individual behaviour. The thesis is that INTERNATIONAL RELATIONS can only benefit by reproducing the institutions of domestic society. Since 'absence of government' is a defining feature of the former, its provision as per the domestic analogy ought to be a major goal of international theory and practice. The domestic analogy has always been suspect – even Hobbes himself seems to have resisted it – since the conditions of order among STATES are not generally regarded as similar to those among individuals. The best of the recent explorations of this idea and its consequences is Hedley Bull's *Anarchical Society*.

## Domestic jurisdiction

A logical consequence of SOVEREIGNTY whereby a STATE rules supreme within its own territorial frontiers. This duty of NON-INTERVENTION within the domestic jurisdiction of states means that in regard to certain issues, the international legal REGIME is not deemed valid. Article 2 (7) of the UN CHARTER provides that 'Nothing contained in the present Charter shall authorize the United Nations to intervene in matters which are essentially within the domestic jurisdiction of any state or shall require the members to submit such matters to settlement under the present Charter.' This article is one of the most controversial in the Charter and its application one of considerable dispute. In INTERNATIONAL LAW, domestic jurisdiction refers to those matters where a state's discretion is not limited by obligations imposed by international law unless the state itself agrees. However, the concept is a relative one and the influence of international law is beginning to make inroads in areas hitherto regarded as exclusive to the state and also in areas where internal regulation may have international repercussions. Thus, matters which are not generally regarded as falling within domestic jurisdiction are a breach of international law, an infringement of the interests of other states, a threat to international PEACE, violations of HUMAN RIGHTS and questions of SELF-DETERMINATION. The range of activities now considered to be within the competence of international law has grown considerably, especially in relation to the latter two categories, as the Republic of South Africa has had cause to note over the issues of APARTHEID and Namibia.

## Domino theory

An analogy with the way in which a row of dominoes falls sequentially until none remain standing, the domino theory was particularly popular with DECISION-MAKERS in the United States in the 1950s and 1960s, although some would still want to defend its cogency today. The cause of the collapsing dominoes, according to this view, was transnational COMMUNISM which, it was held, had a propensity to expand across state FRONTIERS consuming all before it. After 1949 proponents of the theory looked particularly to the People's Republic of China in this regard. The ideas and precepts of PEOPLE'S WAR were believed to be widely applicable to many parts of the THIRD WORLD. Communists had to some extent been contributors to this view themselves because they were wont to emphasize the extent to which revolutionary experience and example can be exported to and acquired by others, particulary when environmental or 'objective' conditions appear to favour it.

President Eisenhower's press conference of 7 April 1954 is usually instanced as one of the earliest and most influential statements of the theory, although some UK commentators have wanted to claim that the theory is descended from UK origins. The genesis of the theory is, however, less significant than its subsequent impact and in this regard no reputable scholar would

deny that, as a DEFINITION OF THE SITUATION, the theory is the progeny of US perceptions of post-war communism. In essence, what Eisenhower said in 1954 was that the stakes in Indo-China also included the future of the neighbouring states. However, the idea of 'neighbourhood' was interpreted to cover much of the REGION, and in this way he spoke of a 'sequence of events' linking Indo-China, Burma, Thailand, Malaya and Indonesia. Subsequently, Eisenhower extended his 'falling dominoes' ideas to Central America and the so-called 'offshore islands' of Quemoy and Matsu.

VIETNAM in particular, and Indo-China in general, are central to the domino theory thereafter. There is considerable documentary evidence now to hand to substantiate the conclusions that both Kennedy and Johnson subscribed to the theory. Indeed documentation such as the Pentagon Papers suggests that a similar PERCEPTION was held by many Cabinet members in those two Administrations. A notable and interesting exception is the Central Intelligence Agency (CIA) which queried the theory in June 1964 when specifically requested by Johnson to give an opinion on its relevance.

The Presidency of Richard Nixon, and crucially the promulgation of the NIXON DOCTRINE signified the waning of the theory as central to the definition of the situation, the event that appeared to query the worst case outcomes predicted by the theory being the failure of the Indonesian Communists to prevail during the period of intense civil strife in 1965.

Since Nixon, US leaders have been much more willing to accept that Asian REGIONALISM can provide a counter-balance to hegemonial INTERVENTION, from whatever source. The domino theory can still influence US perceptions whenever they contemplate WORLD POLITICS in areas that appear to be highly unstable, particularly if the presence of communists can be detected. Currently, Central America seems to be a favoured setting for these perceptions.

Intellectually domino thinking can be roundly criticized for its often crude and unstructured generalizations about political systems that are quite different. Its failure to apportion sufficient weight to the IDEOLOGY of NATIONALISM as an alleviation or antidote to transnational communism is almost certainly its greatest error. However, consideration of the impact that the domino theory had upon three successive US Administrations in the ISSUE AREA of Vietnam is a valuable reminder of the manner by which the images that DECISION-MAKERS hold can influence their definition of the situation and, thereby, their policy-making.

**Donor fatigue**
A term used in the analysis of FOREIGN AID, particularly by advanced industrial countries (AICS). The term refers to the development of an adverse and critical climate of informed public opinion about the principles and purposes of AID programes. This re-evaluation has been occasioned by the seeming failure of such aid efforts to realize the expectations of the donors that foreign assistance to the THIRD WORLD has had the same positive impact, both economic and political, as was achieved by the European Recovery Programme. The disappointing economic performance of many recipient STATES, added to their dogged refusal to allow the donors to buy their political allegiance, is the proximate cause of this eroding support. Other latent factors that have contributed to this re-evaluation include: the adverse economic climate in the AICs during the 1970s and 1980s, particularly the growth of unemployment and the problems of controlling inflation; and the development of a more critical market orientated political economy which tends to denigrate the applicability and relevance of what are seen as collectivist planning ideas.

**Doomsday Machine**
The agile and provocative mind of the strategist and FUTUROLOGIST, Hermann Kahn, conjured up the idea of the Doomsday Machine in his work *On Thermonuclear War* (1960). Having identified three types of deterrent situations facing a NUCLEAR POWER such as the United States, Kahn argued that, in what he termed 'type one DETERRENCE', that is to say, deterring a direct attack on the homeland of the United States, the Doomsday Machine was the near-perfect answer. In brief, the machine, which he postulated could destroy all human life on the planet, would be automatically activated once sensors had detected that NUCLEAR WEAPONS had landed on the United States. Kahn argued that if a deterrent threat was a near-certainty and if a deterrent threat posed overwhelming and unacceptable damage when carried out, then no rational DECISION-MAKER would risk the consequences by challenging the deterrer.

An exegesis of the Kahn argument is probably less important than recognition of the facet of deterrence theory that the Doomsday Machine idea highlights. In particular, by emphasizing the near-certainty of the response, Kahn answers those who have argued that deterrence would fail when it was most needed because the threatener would be 'self-deterred' by the enormity of the threat.
*See*: DETERRENCE.

**Double veto**
The VETO or unanimity rule that obtains in the UN SECURITY COUNCIL has been interpreted since the Charter Conference at San Francisco in 1945 as applying to the preliminary question of whether a matter before the Council is procedural (where the veto does not apply) or substantive. In effect, then, any of those STATES with the veto can use this facility on the initial issue as well as the consequent and substantive one. Hence the term double veto.
*See also*: SECURITY COUNCIL; VETO

## Dove

A colloquial term used in the analysis of INTERNATIONAL POLITICS and FOREIGN POLICY. A 'dove' is a personality type who favours certain approaches to dealing with other ACTORS and rejects other approaches. Generally speaking, doves are held to favour DIPLOMACY that seeks ACCOMMODATION (CONCILIATION) and CONFLICT RESOLUTION. Conversely doves oppose using excessive COERCION, see the ARMS RACE as highly dangerous and even view DETERRENCE rather critically. On the last point, doves tend to favour policies of minimum deterrence and seem to prefer COUNTERCITY ASSURED DESTRUCTION ideas to COUNTERFORCE warfighting. Doves often set much store by INTERNATIONAL ORGANIZATIONS such as the UN and their intrinsic belief in international cooperation is reflected in this supportive view. The dove or dovish personality is often used as a relative point of reference and contrast with the HAWK, who is supposed to be the antithesis of everything the dove stands for. Both terms are often used rhetorically.

## Dual nationality

Simultaneous citizenship of more than one STATE. In INTERNATIONAL LAW citizenship is either acquired *jus sanguinis* (law of blood) or *jus solis* (law of the soil) or else by the legal process of naturalization (which usually involves a minimum period of residence). Thus dual nationality can occur when a person is born in one STATE (*jus solis*) of parents belonging to another (*jus sanguinis*). It can also occur through nationalization where the original state does not accept rights of renunciation of allegiance. When this occurs, as for example it has among the English-speaking peoples of South Africa, tensions can arise over the question of an individual's duty to perform military service. This is usually, though not always, resolved in favour of

the state possessing *de facto* jurisdiction. Dual nationality is a mixed blessing. Although it confers on the individual the rights, benefits and protection of more than one state, it also involves a dual set of duties which may often conflict with one another.

## Dumbarton Oaks conference

A meeting held in Georgetown, Washington, DC, between August and October 1944 to discuss the nature and functions of the UN organization. The main participants were the United States, the Soviet Union, the United Kingdom and later China. The purpose was to hammer out agreement on the framework for post-war cooperation and to establish an effective SECURITY COMMUNITY which would supercede the somewhat ineffectual LEAGUE OF NATIONS. The preliminary draft of Proposals, with some modifications, became the UN CHARTER at the San Francisco Conference in 1945. Between these conferences, the YALTA meeting in February 1945 between Roosevelt, Churchill and Stalin confirmed the main outline of the proposals and underlined the need for GREAT POWER dominance of the new organization. The conference was virtually unanimous on the reasons for the failure of the League of Nations and injected a spirit of REALISM into their proposals for the new world organization; PEACEKEEPING responsibilities were given to the SECURITY COUNCIL where the great powers were to have permanent representation and the right of VETO. It was widely assumed by the representatives at the Conference that disagreement over the post-war political settlement could be amicably settled in the Security Council, without having to revert to the traditional practises of POWER POLITICS and regional ALLIANCE systems. Because of the two-tier structure, which emphasized great power management of operations, it was fondly believed that bypassing the organization on issues of international importance would be discouraged and that the dangers of reverting to UNILATERAL and BILATERAL polices that characterized the inter-war years would be averted.

### Dumping

Dumping is exporting goods at artificially low prices. It may be engaged in to reduce surpluses and/or to drive rivals out of the market. How low a price has to be to qualify as dumping is often a matter for political judgement since the term has a certain pejorative connotation. Most international economists would be happy with the idea that selling goods below what they would fetch on the domestic market, allowing for transport costs, is dumping.

Dumping can provoke retaliation, in the form of anti-dumping duties, from target ACTORS. Indeed the General Agreement on Tariffs and Trade (GATT), which condemns the activity under Article 6, allows STATES to take anti-dumping retaliation. Dumping can also provoke responses from third parties who feel that their market share is being unfairly damaged as a result. It would be a mistake to assume that nobody benefits from dumping, however. In addition to the self-evident interests of the actor which is actually engaged in the dumping, consumers in the target might well benefit from receiving goods at a price and/or quality which is welcomed. The EC Common Agricultural Policy has produced considerable surplus produce over the years which has been 'dumped' on markets outside the TARIFF wall. This has often provoked critical reactions from third parties, who feel that their agricultural exports have been damaged unfairly as a result.

# E

## Ecological war

Sometimes referred to as meteorological or geographical WAR it refers to the waging of war through tampering with the earth's ecosystem and environment. The danger of artificial (human) interference in the form of inducement of oceanic floods, earthquakes, expansion of the polar caps, changes in wind direction or sea currents as well as interference with ozone layers was recognized by the UN Disarmament Conference at Geneva in 1976 as potentially catastrophic and is a constant item on the agendas of ecopolitical and green movements.

## Ecology/ecopolitics

In the context of WORLD POLITICS ecology refers to the relationship between human beings and their biological and physical environment. In particular, it refers to the challenge posed by a combination of world population growth and technological developments which threaten the balance of the world's life-sustaining ecosystems. Ecopolitics, which stresses the interrelatedness of political and ecological matters, is a comparatively recent ISSUE AREA and owes much to the pioneering work of Harold and Margaret Sprout who in 1971 introduced an important and new dimension into the study of INTERNATIONAL RELATIONS with their acclaimed *Towards a Politics of the Planet Earth*.

TRADITIONAL perspectives in world politics have been obsessed with issues of PEACE, security and economic well-being embedded within the classical framework of the NATION-STATE and the STATE-SYSTEM. Ecological issues, such as food and resource scarcities, environmental degradation, climatic changes or technological developments relating to the oceans, the sea bed, the atmosphere and outer space, were generally only considered in relation to the bearing they had on the primary issues of national security and economic DEVELOPMENT. Since they were considered to be marginal or at best, long term in this context, the man/environment issue was relegated to the outer fringes of the subject. In any case, since ecological issues were indifferent to BOUNDARIES and are intrinsically TRANSNATIONAL, they were effectively beyond the range of traditional STATE-CENTRIC world politics, where self-interest and SELF-HELP are primary and, perhaps, necessary values. There is now, however, a growing body of concern about the impact of such issues as the disposal of chemical and nuclear toxic waste, deforestation, acid rain, soil erosion and POLLUTION which has slowly but perceptibly raised the ecological perspective to a higher level on the agenda of contemporary world politics. This is partly due to the fact that these matters now impinge on traditional areas of high policy (resource scarcity in, for example, oil could generate international conflict, as could a NUCLEAR ACCIDENT), but it is also partly to do with increasing awareness that species survival may in the final analysis depend on multilateral political cooperation to ensure the durability of the earth's 'carrying' capacity. Nation-states, renowned as they are for egoism and introspection, cannot unilaterally address these problems. Ecopolitics therefore focuses on the symbiotic relationship among political communities themselves and between them and their environment. In so doing, it has provided a new DEFINI-TION OF THE SITUATION.

A term commonly associated with eco-politics is global 'commons' which refers to natural resources such as the oceans, the sea bed, radio waves, the atmosphere and outer space which were previously re-garded as part of the common heritage of mankind and are not, as yet, subject to rigid control by international legal REGIME. Advances in TECHNOLOGY render these common resources vulnerable to individual exploitation. The 'tragedy of the global commons', a concept popularized by Gar-rett Hardin in 1968, envisages a scenario in which intensive, unrestricted unilateral harvesting of resources could eventually lead to resource destruction on a hitherto unimagined scale. Traditional perspectives involving notions of voluntary restraint are inadequate since the problem of the 'free rider' is always present. Ecopolitics there-fore envisages the need for strict communal regulations of the commons based on shared values such as conservation, con-trolled production and equity. Implicit in the approach is a conviction that ecological issues cannot be resolved on a unilateral basis. Whether or not the international community is willing to abandon age-old preferences and multilaterally develop the embryonic legal infrastructure to enable these problems to be resolved is a matter of considerable debate and not a little hope.
*See also*: GREEN MOVEMENT; MARITIME LAW

## Economic liberalism

A theory of political economy, economic liberalism is particularly associated with the writings of Adam Smith and the school of thinkers of the nineteenth century free market persuasion. Internally, the political implications of economic liberalism were that as far as possible government should confine itself to a minimum of tasks and roles within society. Externally, this theory of minimum government stipulated that the primary task of STATE authorities was to protect the state from external threat. As an international theory economic liberalism was particularly associated with the ad-vocacy of FREE TRADE and what would now be called COMPLEX INTERDEPENDENCE. Free traders believed that such a system of relations would remove important eco-nomic causes of conflict from the system and that this was an additional reason – above and beyond its economic rationale – for favouring it.

The failure of newly emerging economic powers such as Imperial Germany and the United States to adopt unequivocal free trade principles and policies threw the as-sumptions of classical economic liberals into confusion during the last decades of the nineteenth century. Not for the last time, PROTECTIONISM adopted by key ACTORS in the system was to represent a challenge to the LIBERAL orthodoxy. Grad-ually liberals began to realize that they would have to reverse the relationship between free trade and international co-operation. If free trade did not lead to inter-national cooperation then perhaps inter-national cooperation could establish free trade. This revision of the relationship was achieved in the post-1945 BRETTON WOODS agreements and the signing of the sub-sequent General Agreement on Tariffs and Trade (GATT). If the years after the repeal of the Corn Laws in 1846 were the 'golden age' of liberalism then the years after Bret-ton Woods ran a close second.

At the same time as the free trade order was under challenge from the newly emerg-ing economic powers of Germany and the United States, the principles of liberalism were being directly challenged by writers within the tradition. Hobson was accusing liberalism of being deflected into IMPERIAL-ISM while Hobhouse was trying to syn-thesize traditional liberal commitments to liberty with socialist commitments to equality. This compensatory or Keynesian liberalism emerged full-blown in the twentieth century as a genuine heterodoxy within the tradition. Internally these heterodox liberals argued that the state would have to intervene more significantly and regularly in the economic and social life of the nation in order to prevent significant inequalities from persisting. Left to market forces, it was argued, such readjustment would not occur. Externally the heterodox liberals still looked to greater international cooperation but believed that, again, this must be directed to reducing inequalities as much as increasing liberties.

The rise of the THIRD WORLD in the post-1945 system has presented the compensatory version of liberalism with the perfect ISSUE AREA to apply its ideas. The two BRANDT REPORTS have rightly been identified as typical of this genre. According to this view the FIRST WORLD states should be prepared to do much more for the LEAST DEVELOPED COUNTRIES (LDCs) by manually overriding the automatic tendencies of the liberal order. Many of the demands being currently made under the aegis of the NEW INTERNATIONAL ECONOMIC ORDER (NIEO) and via institutions like the United Nations Conference on Trade and Development (UNCTAD) are favourably received by compensatory liberals. Stabilization of commodity prices – which is anathema to classical liberals – in order to guarantee the LDC's continuity of income, is just one of the types of proposals currently being acted upon the influence of THIRD WORLD pressure and compensatory liberal sympathies.

## Economic sanctions

A form of economic statecraft which involves the use of economic CAPABILITY by an ACTOR or group of actors (the Imposer) in a deliberately coercive manner to pursue certain policy goals. The Imposer will identify a certain actor or group of actors (the Target) against which the sanctions will be directed. The essence of the sanctions attempt is to get the Target to behave in a more compliant way. The means used to secure this compliance will involve denying the Target access to certain goods and services that are controlled by the Imposer. Although in principle sanctions can be either positive or negative, CONVENTIONAL usage of the word in this context is always negative. Thus, when reference is made to economic sanctions, such punitive measures as the embargo, the BOYCOTT, the withdrawal of MOST-FAVOURED-NATION (MFN) status, are envisaged. Reducing TARIFFS to bribe or reward a Target, although logically sanctions, are not intended to be covered by this definition. Similarly, sanctions can be distinguished from economic warfare where the instruments are similarly negative but the policy goals are different. In economic warfare, the Imposer seeks to deliberately weaken the economy of the Target, either as a temporary or permanent measure. Such measures are usually pursued as part of a general policy of making WAR against the Target in the military idiom.

Economic sanctions may be directed at the whole Target or at some section of society within the Target. Collective sanctions directed at the Target *per se*, to the extent that they are effective, will punish everybody, weak and strong, guilty and innocent. Indeed it is often the case that collective sanctions hurt those who are least able to withstand the costs. Alternatively, sanctions can be directed at particular groups within the society. These would normally be economic groups and, in particular, corporations, businesses and firms. The usual form such individually aimed sanctions take will be to institute a blacklist. This will identify businesses that the Imposer wishes to punish. Such firms may be subject to boycott action, to confiscation of their property and to prosecution of their employees.

Sanctions may be unilateral – applied by one actor against another – bilateral –

applied by two – or MULTILATERAL. The more actors involved in the sanctions policy, the greater its chances of actually causing the Target some deprivation. However, the more actors involved in the sanctions policy, the more difficult it is to establish and maintain a common front against the Target. In particular, the attraction of defecting from multilateralism can be considerable. The defector may, thereby, steal a march on its trading rivals by replacing them in the markets of the Target. In general terms the role of what might be termed the third party – in contradistinction to the Target and Imposer – is crucial if economic sanctions are to stand any chance of success. If an Imposer cannot secure the cooperation of third parties then a policy of economic sanctions can be self-defeating and very expensive. For example, the UN policy of economic sanctions against Rhodesia (now Zimbabwe) between 1966–79 was seriously flawed by the fact that Rhodesia's second largest trading partner – South Africa – actively worked to undermine the policy. The Union was assisted in this 'busting of sanctions' by certain multinational corporations (MNCs), notably Anglo–American oil companies.

Economic analysis would suggest that, notwithstanding the role of third parties, sanctions are likely to be more or less effective depending upon a number of variables. First, the Imposer should be in a monopoly or a monopsony position *vis-à-vis* the Target. Moreover, the Target should not be able to overcome the monopoly by IMPORT substitution, nor the monopsony by finding new EXPORT markets. The Target may then be said to be highly vulnerable to economic sanctions. Secondly, the goods and services denied to the Target should supply key sectors of its economy. It is for this reason that oil has been considered a 'strategic commodity' in the sanctions context. The impact that trade dependence upon such a key commodity can have was demonstrated during the 1973–4 DIPLOMACY of the OPEC and the OAPEC states. Thirdly, the Imposer should be able to avoid self-inflicted eco-

nomic costs arising from sanctions. In addition to the third party issue discussed above, self-inflicted costs will be reduced by substitution. If substitute markets can be found for embargoed exports and substitute goods found for boycotted imports, the costs will be reduced.

Monitoring, supervision and enforcement actions will all be required to implement a sanctions policy. Such activities will require third party cooperation and this will normally involve regional or global institutions. In extremis military force may be needed to enforce control over third parties and typically this will involve a BLOCKADE of the territorial FRONTIERS of the Target state. If the Target is an island or if the Target can be isolated politically then enforcement procedures should be facilitated. The international institution will serve to legitimize as well as to enforce sanctions. Parties breaking sanctions are, in effect, defying the express purpose of the majority of the membership. As such they may be Targets for punitive sanctions themselves.

The logic of the aforesaid arguments would seem to be that economic sanctions will work best if they are universal and general. This logic points to the need to institutionalize sanctions through organizations such as the LEAGUE OF NATIONS and the UN. Thus under Article 16 of the League Covenant the member states were clearly committed to confront international wrong-doing with economic sanctions. If anything, the powers of the UN under Chapter 7 are even more extensive than those of the League and, again, in Article 41 of the Charter economic sanctions are specifically stipulated. Both these twentieth century institutions faced their most important test cases on their sanctions provisions in Africa: the League over the Ethiopian case and the UN over the Rhodesian case. In the light of the analysis already offered, the failure of the League to include oil exports on the embargo list was a serious omission from the repertoire of coercive instruments. Moreover the Suez Canal was never closed to Italian shipping and finally sanctions were not implemented until one month after the decision had been taken by the League Council to take measures under Article 16. The fact that both the United States and Germany were outside the League and that these states were not bound by League DECISION-MAKING weakened the ability of the institution to bring all putative third parties into the sanctions exercise. The use of economic sanctions by the League in 1935–6 has passed into conventional wisdom as an exercise in failure which cost both the institution and the policy dearly in terms of CREDIBILITY.

The use of sanctions by the UN against the recalcitrant Rhodesian REGIME after their Unilateral Declaration of Independence (UDI) in November 1965 constitutes the greatest challenge, to date, to the institution's capabilities. The UN did not in fact impose mandatory sanctions until December 1966, more than one year after the UDI. In the interim the UK and the COMMONWEALTH had imposed voluntary sanctions. Indeed, when it became clear in September 1965 that the voluntary policy was not working, the United Kingdom came under pressure from the Commonwealth to tighten the sanctions policy. The United Kingdom had already sought UN approval for the so-called 'Beira patrol' so the imposition of mandatory sanctions by Resolution 232 of the Security Council was a legal continuation of the same policy. Sanctions were further tightened in the spring of 1968 when Security Council Resolution 253 supposedly closed a number of loopholes. As the diplomatic record now clearly shows, a determined and successful exercise had been mounted from the outset to circumvent sanctions. To this end the role of the South African government was crucial. The eventual collapse of white domination in Rhodesia owed much more to the efforts of the black INSURGENCY movement than to UN sanctions.

Although the nature and context of the compliance sought from Italy in the 1930s and Rhodesia after 1965 by the League and the UN was quite different – one was attempting to stop an invasion from outside the territory of the victim, the other was trying to end a rebellion inside the territory of an illegal regime – the end results were equally poor for the track record of multilateral economic sanctions. Both instances show how sanctions depend upon the active cooperation of third parties. Both show that if this cooperation is absent implementation of sanctions will require the international institution to take more coercive measures of enforcement.

Psychologically, sanctions are a form of collective punishment. As such they may unite sections of a Target society in adversity and produce a dogged determination to 'tough it out'. There is no doubt that the effects of UN sanctions against Rhodesia were to hurt the African population more than the minority whites, an argument that opponents of sanctions against South Africa have used in various international bodies to resist demands that the international community should institute a policy of economic sanctions to end APARTHEID. There is no reason to suppose that such an exercise would be any more efficacious than the examples already discussed above.

## Economic statecraft

Economic statecraft is defined by David Baldwin in his 1985 book as 'influence attempts relying primarily on resources which have a reasonable semblance of a market price in terms of money' (pp. 13–14). In other words, economic statecraft is any political act which utilizes economic instruments to achieve compliant behaviour from a Target actor. In Baldwin's discussion the usage is synonymous with the idea of the POWER relationship because the economic instruments envisaged may be divided into positive and/or negative sanctions. Thus both economic AID and ECONOMIC SANCTIONS – the two most prevalent instruments – would both be subsumed under

Baldwin's definition as instances of economic statecraft.

Economic statecraft may appropriately be regarded as an umbrella term covering all instances where international ACTORS use economic instruments for political ends. It may be usefully seen as a replacement term for such stipulations as 'economic warfare' because it covers all contingencies in one portmanteau idea.

## Eisenhower doctrine

This US policy intitiative was a direct consequence of the Suez affair of 1956 when, on the insistence of the United States, the United Kingdom and France were forced to withdraw their troops from Egypt. Fearful of a POWER vacuum developing in the oil-rich Middle East, and perhaps having second thoughts about their role during Suez, a Congressional Joint Resolution in 1957 proclaimed the Eisenhower doctrine which authorized the President to assist any STATE in the Middle East which was judged to be threatened by COMMUNIST aggression. Although allegedly directed against the spread of 'international communism', this doctrine was a specific attempt to limit the expansionist ambitions of President Nasser's Egypt. Under the terms of the resolution, US forces and/or economic assistance could be sent to the region under the Mutual Security Programme. Accordingly, in July 1958 Anglo–American troops intervened to assist the pro-Western REGIMES in Jordan and Lebanon, and subsequent commitments were made to Turkey, Iran and Pakistan. The Eisenhower doctrine was thus a declaration that the Middle East was to be regarded as an area of vital interest to the United States.

## Elite

A broad based term used to identify a minority out of a total population. In ordinary usage the term often connotes superiority. Further precision can be obtained by adding the prefixes political', 'economic', 'cultural'. Indeed in most social systems found in the FIRST WORLD observers would expect to find a plurality of elites along these bases. In the above sense, an elite is simply a descriptive term for individuals and groups found at the top of a particular HIERARCHY.

The term is also used in a more prescriptive sense. Here the suggestion is that such minorities are a natural and positive outcome. It is possible in this usage to talk of 'elitism' having in mind an IDEOLOGY or value system which assumes that by nature or by nurture the majority in a population are unsuited and unqualified for elite status. However, elitism does recognize that exceptions will occur to this rule and that a 'counter-elite' may arise to challenge the existing elite structure. Whatever the outcome, elitists would still want to insist that in the end the system will resume its hierarchical structure.

Elite theories and the ideology of elitism originated with political sociology. However, the idea of an elite has been applied with considerable ingenuity to the study of POLICY-MAKING and the related issue of the role of PUBLIC OPINION on FOREIGN POLICY issues. The early seminal work in this field was Almond's (1966). Without wholly subscribing to the ideology of elitism, he did clearly distinguish a hierarchy based upon a division of labour and a division of influence. This hierarchy depended upon a four-fold division. At the bottom Almond placed the majority, the mass of the population. Distinguished from the mass was the ATTENTIVE PUBLIC. Above these two stratas Almond locates the policy elites and, finally, at the top what might be termed the formal office holders.

Public opinion polling, which has become increasingly accurate over the last half century, provides the empirical confirmation of the view that the mass of the population, in all systems, lacks either the knowledge of the inclination to exert continuing and consistent influence over the policy process. The idea of 'MOOD' has been developed to identify the manner and content of public attitudes towards foreign policy. Within the fairly permissive parameters set by public moods, the stratas above the mass of the population operate. The attentive public then, by default, becomes the audience in front of which the elites make and justify their policy.

The actual foreign policy elite is divided between formal office holders and organized interests (what Almond calls 'the policy elites'). The formal office holders will hold authority positions within the system and will be those persons officially designated to act on behalf of the STATE. Surrounding them will be a bureaucracy of departments centred around foreign ministries but including a number of other departments of STATE. The relationship between the formal office holders and their bureaucracies on one hand and organized interests on the other will differ from system to system. In general terms, whereas the formal office holders are by definition members of the elite, in the case of interest groups only the leaders will be classed as unambiguously within the elite structure. In systems where the formal office holders, their senior bureaucrats and the interest group elites are drawn from the same background the term 'establishment' is sometimes used to describe this broader arrangement. The growth in the number of state ACTORS in WORLD POLITICS since 1945 has stimulated new interest in elite theories of policy-making. In many respects the structural analysis of THIRD WORLD states seems to reflect classical elitist characteristics and structures. The actual composition of the elite in Third World states is, of course, a matter for empirical inquiry in particular cases. In all instances, however, a Western education seems a definite advantage – if not prerequisite – for recruitment into the elite. In many areas of the Third World traditional elites have capitalized on these educational opportunities to maintain their influence into the current period of national SELF-DETERMINATION. This tendency has

been particularly notable in Latin America. In other parts of the Third World, elite recruitment reflects a more heterogeneous catchment area. In all instances, however, the findings confirm the validity of the elite approach to the structure of policy making.

## Encirclement

German GEOPOLITICAL idea that refers to policies aimed at systematically surrounding a target STATE with hostile or potentially hostile powers. Originally used in this way by German Chancellor Bulow in 1906 to castigate the ALLIANCES and ENTENTE agreements between the United Kingdom, France and Tsarist Russia which he believed constituted a deliberately engineered diplomatic encirclement of Germany. For many diplomatic historians, the encirclement thesis was a contributory factor in developments leading to the First World War. The idea was revived after the Bolshevik Revolution in 1917 when the Soviet Union was perceived by its leaders to be surrounded on all sides by hostile capitalist states whose major FOREIGN POLICY goal was the political, economic and military destruction of the new state. So pervasive was the concept in early Soviet IDEOLOGY that it had profound effects not only on its foreign policy but also on social, cultural, economic and political developments within the Soviet Union. Indeed, the Stalin/Trotsky debate can be explained, at least partially, in terms of it. For Trotsky, the rational response to encirclement was international socialism and the global promotion of REVOLUTION throughout the capitalist world. For Lenin, and later Stalin, the answer was 'socialism in one country'; encouraging rapid development and MODERNIZATION within the state to provide an impermeable base from which to resist external INTERVENTION. The victory of Stalinism resulted in encirclement being used to justify the ruthless policies of repression and enforced industrialization in the Soviet Union between the wars. The Nazi–Soviet pact of

1939 was regarded in this context as an opportunistic diplomatic coup designed to break at least one link in the encirclement chain. After the war, with the successful revolution in China in 1949 and the establishment of COMMUNIST REGIMES in eastern Europe, Stalin declared that the days of encirclement were officially over. However, the US policy of CONTAINMENT revived a watered-down version of it during the critical years of the COLD WAR. The difference now, however, was that the Soviet Union perceived herself to have a protective ring of BUFFER states between its HEARTLAND and its strategic periphery. In subsequent years, encirclement has given way to peaceful COEXISTENCE and DÉTENTE.

## Enclave
Territory of one STATE surrounded by the territory of another. Thus, Walvis Bay in south west Africa is part of the domestic sovereign jurisdiction of the Republic of South Africa despite being surrounded by Namibia. Similarly, West Berlin is an enclave hemmed in by East Germany, as is the thirty-two square mile Republic of San Marino, in this case surrounded by Italy.

## END
Acronym for European Nuclear Disarmament. Formed in 1980 it is a multilateral interest group which campaigns for a non-nuclear and demilitarized Europe. Mainly composed of West Europeans, the movement has had some success in attracting support in East Germany, Hungary and Poland. Its direct impact on policy making has been minimal, although the GREEN MOVEMENT with which it is associated has undoubtedly created a climate of opinion (especially in West Germany) which appears receptive to some of its proposals. However, the claim by its supporters that the INF TREATY of 1982 was a direct consequence of END campaigning is, to say the least, an exaggeration.

## English school of international relations
This refers to the supposed existence of a distinct academic tradition of writing on INTERNATIONAL RELATIONS, which originated at the London School of Economics and Political Science in the 1950s. According to Roy E. Jones, who first identified the school (in a largely iconoclastic article in the *Review of International Studies* (1981)) its founder members were C. A. W. Manning and Martin Wright but others associated with it include Hedley Bull, F. S. Northedge, Michael Donelan, Alan James, R. J. Vincent and James Mayall. Although there is some disagreement and confusion surrounding the term, especially concerning the epithet 'English', it is now generally accepted that these writers and others constitute a distinct group whose unifying element is the concept of INTERNATIONAL SOCIETY. The approach is holistic in the sense that it displays a vision of international society where the whole is greater than the sum of its parts, i.e. the sovereign STATES that compose it. In this sense, it is sometimes referred to as the 'international society approach' and its central thesis is that state behaviour cannot properly be explained without reference to the rules, customs, norms, values and institutions that constitute international society as a whole. WORLD POLITICS is conceived as a distinct and perhaps discrete entity and the principal object of inquiry is to examine the nature of this society and its ability to deliver a measure of orderliness and freedom within a predominantly decentralized and fragmented STATE-SYSTEM. The approach can be viewed as a variant of the REALIST perspective, especially in its rejection of UTOPIAN schemes for restructuring the international system and its insistence on the necessary juxtaposition of the concepts of state SOVEREIGNTY and international society. On the methodological level, it lies firmly in the classical or TRADITIONAL mode and is dismissive of the BEHAVIOURAL or scientific approach which it sometimes identifies, somewhat pejoratively, as the 'American school of scientific politics'.

## Entente

Diplomatic term referring to a specific or non-specific 'understanding' between two or more STATES and which is distinct from a formal TREATY or ALLIANCE. The phrase *entente cordiale* was first used by French premier M. Guizot in 1843 to denote a RAP-PROCHEMENT between the United Kingdom and France in relation to matters affecting the general European BALANCE OF POWER. A specific entente was signed in 1904 which alarmed Germany and was regarded by some historians as placing unnecessary constraints on the United Kingdom's free-dom of manoeuvre in the event of a Franco–German conflict. Ententes, though, however 'cordiale' they may appear, usu-ally fall short of detailed commitment on the part of either side.

## Equality of states

One of the primary values of the modern international STATE-SYSTEM is the sovereign equality of STATES. Since the establishment of the WESTPHALIAN system the formal re-cognition of equality was intimately bound up with the notions of SOVEREIGNTY, INDE-PENDENCE and RECIPROCITY. It is enshrined in Article 2 of the CHARTER OF THE UN which asserts that 'the Organization is based on the principle of the sovereign equality of all its Members'. However, de-spite institutional recognition, the role of equality in INTERNATIONAL LAW and poli-tics is not at all clear. There is frequently confusion between its descriptive and nor-mative aspects. This confusion is magnified by the obviously hierarchical nature of the multistate system, which assigns particular status and responsibilities to the GREAT POWERS.

The condition of sovereign equality means that an ACTOR can claim the privil-eges, opportunities and diplomatic status that derive from statehood. The assertion that all states are equal does not suggest that all states are the same. Indeed, some commentators allege that equality is not a fact but an ideal; that the INTERNATIONAL COMMUNITY adopted for convenience a Platonic form of equality which, like sov-ereignty from which it derives, is a matter of degree rather than absolute. E. H. Carr put it this way: 'The constant intrusion, or potential intrusion, of power renders mean-ingless any conception of equality between members of the international community'. This observation still forms the basis of most discussions of equality, or the lack of it, in WORLD POLITICS.

Traditional thinking has it that ine-quality is endemic in a system where dif-ferences between actors are more obvious and immediate than similarities. (Compare for example, the Soviet Union with Lesotho or the United States with Tonga.) Even the formal condition of equality (all states are equally entitled to the rights of sovereignty) is really an expression of inequality in prac-tice, since the right to SELF-HELP that this implies will necessarily be dependent on the POWER that is at the disposal of those who wish to exercise it. RECOGNITION of a for-mal condition of equality has led inexora-bly to preserving what were regarded as natural and existing inequalities. Attempts have been made to rationalize the unequal endowments of the states, especially in LIB-ERAL theories of INTERNATIONAL RELA-TIONS, but with little practical effect on the process of DIPLOMACY. In fact, until com-paratively recently, inequality has been taken for granted in world politics not just as a reflection of how things actually are, but also as a valuable asset in a system which has no overall AUTHORITY to regu-late demands and resolve disputes. Because states are manifestly unequal, some inter-national disputes are that much easier to settle. In this sense the contribution of the great powers to the maintenance of INTER-NATIONAL ORDER can be seen as a direct function of inequality. If all states really were equal how could conflicts ever be settled?

The institutions of INTERNATIONAL SOCIETY, WAR, BALANCE OF POWER, inter-national law and diplomatic practice, while paying homage to the sovereign equality of states, nevertheless served to encourage and sustain the hierarchical order which allowed equality only between powers which were evenly matched. WAR, or capacity for waging it, was in this sense the great equalizer. The history of international relations has unfolded largely in these terms and whatever collective procedures for settling disputes existed, they did so because of inequality, not in spite of it. The VETO power given to permanent members of the SECURITY COUNCIL of the UN is an explicit recognition of this; and this has always been so. What the Athenians said to the MELIANS – that the powerful take what they can and the weak grant what they must – has thus been the starting point for some, and the stumbling block for others, in the quest for a satisfactory relationship between ORDER and JUSTICE in international relations. For THUCYDIDES this was an enduring (though not perhaps endearing) fact of international life: 'This is not a law we made ourselves, nor were we the first to act upon it when it was made. We found it already in existence, and we shall leave it to exist forever among those who come after us'.

The question of whether or not this basic condition of equality really is 'to exist forever' is precisely the issue that many people think bedevils statecraft in the last part of the twentieth century. The tension between the advanced industrialized states of the NORTH and the DEVELOPING states of the SOUTH, the demand for a redistribution of wealth, power and status within a NEW INTERNATIONAL ECONOMIC ORDER (NIEO) which goes far beyond the formal recognition of equality, coupled with the apparent decline in the utility of military power (especially in great and SMALL POWERS relations) has led to a re-evaluation of the traditional hierarchical structure of world politics. The expansion of the role of the GENERAL ASSEMBLY, in particular, has created a demand for a more egalitarian basis for international law and international politics. Though THIRD WORLD claims for

greater equality are unlikely to break the traditional mould of diplomatic practice some commentators have noticed a new political sensibility about the issue. The NON-ALIGNED movement and POLYCENTRISM are indications of this. However, it is difficult to escape the Orwellian conclusion that in world politics all states are equal but some are more equal than others.

## Espionage
*See*: INTELLIGENCE

## Ethnocentrism
This is the tendency to see one's own group, culture, NATION in positive terms and, conversely, other groups in negative terms. The term has sociological origins and, with some important exceptions such as Booth's work on strategy, ethnocentrism continues to be a socio–psychological concept which has important implications for international behaviour. The intensity of the attitudes that ethnocentrism gives rise to will vary between groups and over time. Similarly, the specific contents of the favourable/unfavourable IMAGE will also be time dependent. Ethnocentric attitudes may be passed down from generation to generation via the process of socialization. Much of this transmission will be informal but such biases can also infiltrate into the education system where both the formal and the 'hidden' curriculum can become transmission channels for these attitudes. In modern, large-scale complex societies, the mass media can reinforce and reflect ethnocentric views. Contact with out-groups and foreigners, far from 'broadening the mind', can confirm and strengthen these feelings.

Booth has suggested three applications of the term. First, as suggested already, the term is a shorthand means for reference to the near universal tendency of people to perceive others in relation to their own membership groups. Secondly, he suggests it can be used to refer to a faulty methodology. Booth has suggested, in a highly imaginative text, that STRATEGIC STUDIES may be criticized for evidence of ethnocentrism. In particular, the phenomenon of WORST-CASE ANALYSIS is at least partially explicable in these terms. Possibly the problem lies in the fact that strategic studies is a 'policy science' and its very proximity to DECISION-MAKERS leads to these biases. Thirdly, Booth suggests that the term is synonymous with being 'culture bound'. This is the condition where the individual or group becomes locked into its ethnocentrism so that it is unable to empathize with others and, therefore, is unable to see the world from their point of view.

Ethnocentrism is a consequence of the fact that politics is a group activity. Political socialization, which begins in the family, inevitably produces a discrete and distorted image of others. In the modern world ethnocentrism is closely related to NATIONALISM in both its statist and its ethnic forms. These attitudes can undoubtedly be manipulated by political leaders and ELITES for their own purposes. For this reason ethnocentrism, as a tendency, is often found to be contributing to tensions and hostilities that occur whenever groups conflict. Although better communication and closer contact will not of themselves reduce ethnocentrism, the reverse does appear to be the case, namely that communication failures and barriers do increase the scope for ethnocentrism to grow and flourish.

*See also*: DETERRENCE

## European Community (EC)

The central political organization which unites the executive bodies of the European Economic Community (EEC), the European Coal and Steel Community (ECSC) and the European Atomic Energy Community (EURATOM). The major institutions comprising it are the Council of Ministers, the Commission, the European Parliament and the COURT OF JUSTICE and taken together these represent the best example of INTEGRATION in contemporary WORLD POLITICS.

The process was a direct result of the devastation wrought by the Second World War and the realization that economic social and political recovery might best be achieved through closer union. The first major step in this direction was the creation of the ECSC in 1951 by the original six members: Belgium, France, West Germany, Holland, Italy and Luxembourg. The purpose was to coordinate coal and steel production under an independent SUPRA-NATIONAL authority which would be guided by collective interests rather than narrowly national ones. Plans for a European Defence Community came to nothing but the integrative process was strengthened by the establishment of the EEC and EURATOM which came into effect following the TREATY of Rome in January 1958. The rationale was to establish a coordinated economic policy and a CUSTOMS UNION. The United Kingdom applied for membership in 1961 and again in 1963 but was rejected mainly because of De Gaulle's suspicions of Britain's close relationship with the United States. The European Community as such was established formally in July 1967, bringing together these innovative institutions under the umbrella of a central organization. The United Kingdom eventually joined in 1973 along with Denmark and Ireland. Greece joined in 1981 and Spain and Portugal in 1986. The original six members had now grown to twelve, and it appears likely that Turkey will join in the near future.

Government of the EC consists of a complicated web of overlapping institutions. The main DECISION-MAKING body is the Council of Ministers which consists of representatives drawn from the governments of the separate member STATES. This is the political hub of the organization and as such is its least integrative component. The European Commission, which is chosen by the Council, is the secretariat of the EC and functions as the main supranational organ. Its main task is to initiate Community policy and to propose the annual budget. The European Parliament can dismiss the Commission and can reject the budget provided that a two-thirds majority is secured. Although in theory the Parliament is the legislative body of the EC, it is in fact its weakest institution, having no general powers to VETO laws drawn up by the Commission. Delegates to the Parliament have been directly elected since 1979 and are organized on a TRANSNATIONAL political party base rather than on strictly national lines. The Court of Justice functions as the final arbiter of community law and as such takes precedence over national laws.

Although the main thrust of EC policy has been internal, especially in the field of agriculture (the Common Agricultural Policy has by far the highest budget allocation), initiatives have also been developed in relation to external, non-Community affairs. The establishment of the European Political Cooperation process in 1970 was an important move in this direction. The first occasion in which the Political Cooperation machinery attempted to provide a fully coordinated FOREIGN POLICY perspective was at the conference on Security and Cooperation in Europe at HELSINKI in 1973. Since then common perspectives have emerged on many issues including East–West relations and the ARAB–ISRAELI CONFLICT. In 1975 the LOMÉ CONVENTION established special trading arrangements with forty-six developing states. However, the experience of Political Cooperation illustrates the difficulty of consensus politics even when there is broad agreement on general objectives. The lowest common denominator is often the furthest one can go and NATIONAL INTERESTS constantly intrude and frustrate efforts at presenting a genuinely united front. European foreign policy, as a consequence, tends to be reactive rather than innovative. The failure to agree on a comprehensive package of sanctions against South Africa clearly shows that Political Cooperation is not yet fully in place. Indeed, even taking into account substantial progress in the fields of economic integration and supranational organization, the EC is by no means a fully integrated, cohesive unit. The Single European Act which comes into force in 1992, and which seeks to provide the ground work for a greater measure of European unity, is regarded by many as a potentially crucial turning point in the integrative process, perhaps leading eventually to full political union.

### European Convention on Human Rights

Established since 1953 the Convention sought to create machinery for the protection of HUMAN RIGHTS among signatory STATES. To this end it is probably the most sophisticated MULTILATERAL TREATY so far in that it provides for a Commission which determines the admissibilty of petitions and a Court of Human Rights which sits at Strasbourg to provide rulings on the cases presented. Most observers agree, though, that the Convention and the institutions it established tend to favour 'the high contracting parties' (i.e. member states) rather than individuals. The decisions of the Court as to the violation of rights are binding but generally enforcement depends on voluntary compliance since few sanctions, short of outright expulsion from the COUNCIL OF EUROPE, are provided for. Apart from its intrinsic importance in the development of human rights legislation, the Convention is significant in that it can and does command wide media coverage and public interest, it does seek to provide outside protection for individuals against national governments and it could be seen as a role model for future world developments under the auspices of the UN.

### European Court of Justice (ECJ)

Probably the most integrative institution associated with the EUROPEAN COMMUNITY

(EC). It is the EC's only judicial tribunal and as such its task is to ensure that in the application and the interpretation of the Treaty of Rome, the law is observed and upheld. The members of the Court are chosen for six-year terms (renewable) by member governments and are usually people of high legal standing within the signatory STATES. The Court has a reputation for impartiality and INDEPENDENCE from political pressure and despite the fact that the ECJ's decisions are declaratory and not backed by sanctions, the degree of acceptance of its rulings is impressive. Indeed, only once has a state specifically refused to comply with a judgement: in 1979 when France rejected the ECJ's findings on their ban on lamb imports from the United Kingdom. The role of the ECJ is wide-ranging and involves, among other things, ruling on disputes between member states, between them and the Commission, between employees and the EC and on the validity of the EC legislation in relation to national courts. It is in relation to the latter that the ECJ has been innovative and some commentators allege that it has now created a 'new legal order' throughout the community, superimposed upon national law and superior to it. Its most important achievement is the development of the concept of direct enforcibility of EC law to such effect that a 'TRANSNATIONAL constitution' over and above national ones is now commonly regarded as well advanced. The issue of the precise relationship between national courts and the ECJ is unclear, but no one doubts that Community law under its direction has made significant inroads into traditional conceptions of SOVEREIGNTY.

## European Economic Community
*See*: EUROPEAN COMMUNITY

## Ex aequo et bono
A term in INTERNATIONAL LAW which allows decisions to be made on the grounds of fairness or equity rather than applying the rules of positive or customary international law. Article 38 (2) of the Statute of the INTERNATIONAL COURT OF JUSTICE (ICJ) indicates that the sources of law described in Article 38 (1) 'shall not prejudice the power of the Court to decide a case *ex aequo et bono*, if the parties agree thereto'. Although the ICJ has never decided a case *ex aequo et bono* arbitration tribunals have employed the concept, as they did in two Latin American BOUNDARY disputes in the 1930s (Guatemala–Honduras 1933 and Bolivia–Paraguay 1938).

## Exclusive Economic Zone (EEZ)
An important, and potentially explosive, development in MARITIME LAW which came to the fore at the UN Convention on the Law of the Sea in 1982. It involves claiming functional, though at present not territorial, SOVEREIGNTY over a 200-mile area adjacent to the coastal STATE. If universally adopted this would mean that 32 per cent of ocean space (28 million square miles) will be covered by some form of national administration (Booth, 1985). At present fifty-six states claim some form of exclusive rights in these zones, whereas others, including the United States, the Soviet Union and the United Kingdom who have rejected the EEZ concept, nevertheless claim 200-mile Exclusive Fisheries Zones. Technically, the 3-mile territorial jurisdiction limit still applies, but the widespread acceptance of EEZ throughout the 1970s portends some change in law. Also known as 'creeping jurisdiction' or 'territorialization' it represents a movement away from classical notions of *mare liberum* (open seas) towards *mare clausum* (closed seas). This closed sea principle and the doctrine of 'common heritage of mankind' which it embraces is not viewed as a welcome development by the older maritime powers and their belief in freedom of the seas and 'finder's keepers'. The conflict of interests is part of the NORTH–SOUTH debate although clearly it could find itself on the

agenda of SUPERPOWER relations if, for instance, the Soviet Union backed the claims of exclusive rights advanced by the emerging sea powers of the Southern Hemisphere. The 200-mile limit is an arbitrary one, having been arrived at initially by Chile, Ecuador and Peru in the Declaration of Santiago (1951). In this case, 200 miles happened to cover the productive fishing areas of their coastlines. The EEZ is an obstacle to the mobility of warships and aircraft overflights and is therefore viewed as a serious challenge to established naval 'blue water' strategies. This confrontation between the interests of the maritime powers in navigational freedom and the desire of coastal states to extend the range of their jurisdiction is likely to dominate future discussions on the law of the sea.

## Exile

The banishment of a person or group from one place to another. Exile may be self-imposed (e.g. ex-President Marcos of the Philippines, to Hawaii) or enforced (e.g. Napoleon to Elba and St Helena) but in either case it is usually viewed as a form of punishment. Originally used as such by the Greeks and Romans, it is now a common-place of WORLD POLITICS and is a special and dramatic variant of emigration. In cases where the LEGITIMACY of a REGIME is questioned, a government-in-exile may be formed and seek general RECOGNITION. Thus, the French government-in-exile was officially recognized by the United Kingdom from 1941–45 and was based in London. The nationalist government of Taiwan was officially recognized by the United States as the legitimate government-in-exile of China from 1949–79. The form of exile which involves loss of citizenship, whether voluntary or enforced, is known as 'expatriation'.

## Export

In the broadest terms an export is something which is transferred from one inter-national ACTOR to another, or from one actor to the global system. Thus it is possible to describe an intangible – such as NATIONALISM or socialism – being exported. Again it is possible to describe a tangible – such as manufactured goods – being exported.

The term is also used in a narrower, economically based sense. Here the reference is to the movement of goods and services between economic systems. It is important to note that with the growth of COMMON MARKETS and trading BLOCS the exporting actor need not be a STATE. Classical economic analysis, drawing upon the concept of comparative advantage, tends to the view that exporting goods and services is an efficient and, therefore, desirable activity. As a corollary, exporting encourages specialization and, left to itself, an international division of labour. Exporting states and trading blocs create wealth by this activity, which in turn provides for growth in incomes and possibly employment. The term *export led growth* has been a policy goal that many political elites have set for themselves and the systems they administer.

Recently, considerable attention has become concentrated upon the export of TECHNOLOGY – known as TECHNOLOGY TRANSFER. The argument has been advanced that the ability to export technology is not evenly spread throughout the INTERNATIONAL SYSTEM, but, rather, is largely located within the advanced industrial countries (AICs). These actors via agencies such as the multinational corporations (MNCs) have such an effective control over applied knowledge that they can often dictate the terms and conditions upon which the transfer takes place.

The example of technology transfer highlights another issue about exports and exporting. Success at this activity often provokes resentment and even fear among other actors. The bases for these sentiments are not entirely unfounded. Historically some of the most powerful and influential states in the system have been those which generated a considerable proportion of the GNP from exporting. Pre-eminent in this regard would be nineteenth century United Kingdom and twentieth century Japan. The two SUPERPOWERS, so-called, have relied less on exporting goods and services for their wealth creation, but, paradoxically, more upon exporting ideas – particularly political ideas – for their influence.


### Ex post ex ante
*See*: DETERRENCE


### Expropriation
Refers to the requisition of the property of ALIENS and the transfer of ownership to the STATE. A variety of NATIONALIZATION, although the latter can involve domestically owned property, whereas expropriation usually refers to foreign ownership only. Expropriation is a normal consequence of declaring a WAR. Under INTERNATIONAL LAW expropriation of alien property is legitimate provided certain conditions are met. It must be 'for reasons of public utility' and undertaken with due regard for the legal processes. In addition, 'prompt, adequate and effective compensation' must accompany the action. None of these conditions are precise and it is generally acknowledged that, as in so many other areas, international law is weak in this regard. Expropriation has been an important issue in twentieth century politics especially as a consequence of the decline of COLONIALISM and the development of COMMUNISM. The nineteenth century expansion of Western economies generated capital outflow and heavy investment in DEVELOPING areas, resulting in large segments of local economies coming under the ownership of foreign nationals. The success of the anti-colonial movement and the nationalization measures demanded by the communist IDEOLOGY (initially in the Soviet Union) led to conflict both over the right to

expropriate and to the amounts of compensation due. Retaliation by the aggrieved state can involve the entire range of diplomatic options – from protest to military sanctions and overt INTERVENTION in the internal affairs of the expropriating state (e.g. US reactions in relation to post-1959 Cuba, especially the BAY OF PIGS incident). Two considerations dominate international legal thinking on expropriation. First, capital-exporting states require some form of security before they are willing to invest. Secondly, the targets of such activity are entitled, according to rights associated with SOVEREIGNTY and INDEPENDENCE, to control their own economic destinies and under the doctrine of SELF-HELP are empowered to resist undue pressure. These conditions are not always reconcilable since many communist and THIRD WORLD states do not accept the provisos for compensation even though they may be embodied in TREATY form. The general weakness of international law in this regard was instanced in the Ugandan expropriation of Asian property in 1972.


### Extended deterrence
This is a special case of the general relationship known as DETERRENCE. In extended deterrence the Imposer is seeking to get a Target to abandon plans to attack or otherwise coerce a third party. Thus, analytically, extended deterrence is a triadic relationship between three ACTORS. It should be noted that the term 'active' deterrence is sometimes used in the literature to refer to this situation. It is a basic assumption in all extended deterrence situations that the problems of CREDIBILITY which exist in the two-person standard situation will be exacerbated in the triad. Conceptually three outcomes can arise in this context: deterrence will succeed and the third party will remain inviolate, deterrence will fail and the third party will suffer at the hands of the Target, deterrence will partially succeed but the Target's attentions will be

turned onto the Imposer which will be directly attacked itself. Historically problems of extended deterrence are not new but most observers are agreed that nuclear weapons have introduced new considerations into these calculations.

## Extradition

Legal term meaning the handing over of fugitives from one STATE to another. A criminal may take refuge in a state other than the one in which the offences occurred. The practice of extradition has evolved to deal with this. It involves a formal request from the injured state that the individual be extradited to be tried or punished for offences against its laws. In the absence of a specific TREATY there is no duty in INTERNATIONAL LAW to extradite. On the other hand states can, if they wish, extradite without a specific treaty obligation. Mutual interest and RECIPROCITY usually leads states to cooperate in these matters, but certain stringent provisions normally obtain. Thus, political, military and religious offences are usually exempt. The definition of 'political' of course varies and international affairs are replete with examples of controversy over the 'criminal/political' distinction. (UK requests to the United States for extradition of IRA members often fall into this category.) Most extradition treaties are BILATERAL and share certain provisions to safeguard individual rights. Among the most common are the following:

1. Double criminality principle, i.e. the crimes must be crimes under the laws of both states concerned.

2. Speciality principle, i.e. an extradited individual is not tried for a crime other than that for which he was extradited.

3. *Prima facie* evidence of guilt must be shown.

4. Requests are usually confined to 'serious' crimes (defined either in terms of length of punishment expected or in terms of type of offence).

5. The offence must have been committed on the territory of the requesting party.

6. It is not usual to be expected to extradite one's own nationals.

Extradition is a complex and delicate legal process impinging on the SOVEREIGNTY and INDEPENDENCE of states as well as on individual rights. The procedure is cumbersome and as such is in decline on a world-wide basis. However, DEPORTATION has proved to be a useful substitute.

## Extraterritoriality

A vital aspect of DIPLOMACY which refers to the exercise of legal jurisdiction by a 'sender' STATE within a 'received' state's territory. In modern usage it is bound up with diplomatic IMMUNITY. However, extraterritoriality has not always been mutual or reciprocal. During the period of European IMPERIALISM it was common practice for the imperial state to insist that its own expatriates be subject to their home-based legal system and not that of the locale in which they were placed. With the withering away of empires and colonies this unfair practice has all but disappeared. Apart from diplomats, it is common practice in ALLIANCE systems for the armed forces of one state which are present in the territory of another to enjoy the privileges of extraterritoriality. Agreements establishing this are referred to as 'status of forces' TREATIES (e.g. the NATO Status of Force Act 1951). Immunity from local prosecution can, of course, be waived by agreement.

# F

## Factor analysis

A means of analysing events in WORLD POL-ITICS mathematically by grouping them into clusters or bundles. Factor analysis is thus a statistical means of labelling events – a common enough procedure in all social explanation. The growth of INTERNATIONAL GOVERNMENT ORGANIZATIONS (IGOs) since 1945 has greatly increased the output and availability of moderately reliable statistical sources and this growth has undoubtedly increased the possible application of research methods such as factor analysis. An area of inquiry that has particularly interested scholars using this technique is the relationship between the occurrence of CONFLICT within states and conflict between states. Leading exponents of factor analysis have been Rudolph Rummel and Raymond Tanter.

## Fait accompli

A UNILATERAL act by one STATE, or group of states, that suddenly and dramatically changes the STATUS QUO. It usually carries the element of surprise and has the effect of breaking a diplomatic deadlock. In this sense, it can be regarded as an alternative to diplomatic NEGOTIATIONS. It is always a high-risk strategy since the onus is put on the other side to react or to acquiesce. Correct assessments of the likely responses of opponents are therefore crucial. Examples of notable successes are Hitler's remilitarization of the Rhineland (1935) and the Japanese occupation of Manchuria (1931). Failures include the placing of nuclear MISSILES on CUBA (1962) and the Argentinian occupation of the FALK-LANDS/MALVINAS (1982).

## The Falkland Islands (Malvinas)

A group of islands in the South Atlantic which are the subject of a long standing dispute between the United Kingdom and Argentina. Originally, possession was claimed by France, Spain and the United Kingdom, but by 1833 the United Kingdom had gained effective control. Argentina, by virtue of its proximity and also of its claim to be the natural successor to Spanish possessions, has consistently claimed SOVEREIGNTY over the islands since INDEPENDENCE in the 1820s. Talks about sovereignty have continued intermittently in the twentieth century, but were bedevilled by the islands' insistence on remaining under British protection. In April 1982 Argentina, without prior warning, occupied the Falklands and South Georgia, landing about 14,000 troops on the islands. The United Kingdom, after exploring a number of diplomatic initiatives including the UN, launched a counter-invasion. Argentine troops surrendered on 14 June. The affair, though fairly short in duration, was costly for both sides and Britain in particular faces a difficult task in maintaining its position as the sovereign POWER and providing permanent defence for the islands. Argentina has not dropped its claim to sovereignty and the dispute continues to disrupt normal diplomatic relations between the two states.

*See also*: DECOLONIZATION

## Fascism

Now used mainly as a multi-purpose term of abuse, but originally referred to political and ideological systems developed in Italy (1922) and Germany (1933). Historians disagree as to whether it is a nineteenth or twentieth century phenomenon, but agree that it is an IDEOLOGY of the extreme right which encompasses ideas about race, religion, economics, social welfare and LEADERSHIP which are directly and specifically opposed to COMMUNISM, socialism and LIBERALISM. It is not a coherent and self-contained political theory although its adherents regard Hitler's *Mein Kampf* as a fundamental text.

In INTERNATIONAL RELATIONS it is closely associated with IMPERIALISM, MILITARISM and NATIONALISM. The logic of belief in racial superiority leads to policies of conquest, domination and even elimination of lesser races. INTERNATIONAL LAW and MORALITY are subordinated to concepts of national necessity defined by the leadership and so 'might is right' and 'JUSTICE is on the side of the stronger' are central features of the approach. A semi-mystical belief in the destiny of the NATION is also a strong pointer, as is the involvement of the military in deciding national objectives. Political theorists most closely identified with the development of fascist ideas concerning international affairs are Gobineau, Sorel, Herder, Darwin, Nietzsche, Marinetti, Spengler and Chamberlain, although the ideas of more mainstream political philosophers such as MACHIAVELLI, Hobbes, Hegel and Trietschke are drawn upon and elaborated.

Although usually associated with prewar Italy and Germany, neo-fascist systems have appeared, among other places, in Spain, Portugal, Greece, Argentina, Brazil, Chile, Lebanon and South Africa, although the absence of a specific definition might render this judgement suspect.

## Federalism

This term is used in two contexts. First, to describe and explain how legitimate POWER is shared in constituent political units – the federation. Secondly, as an explanation and perhaps prescription of how INTEGRATION might be achieved between previously separate state ACTORS. Although explanation and prediction are linked, this LINKAGE is not a necessary one. Thus a federation of previously separate states might be achieved via FUNCTIONALISM as much as by federalism. However, both would recognize that the only viable and applicable working model for power-sharing in the newly integrated community was the federal one.

As a means of describing and explaining the division of legitimate POWER or AUTHORITY in federations, federalism postulates as an initial position a tension or conflict between centripetal and centrifugal forces. This conflict will be settled by the several parties signing a constitutional bargain which will stipulate where the jurisdictions of the centre and the periphery lie. Thus certain ISSUE AREAS will be reserved for the centre, others retained by the periphery. Normally DEFENCE, FOREIGN AFFAIRS and macroeconomic policy are handled exclusively at the centre. Conversely, the periphery will retain some revenue raising power, control over social and welfare services and some small discretion regrading penal codes and provisions. Federalism is a favoured system of government in large, culturally diverse states. Most of the largest states in the present system are federations.

Federalism as a balance between centripetal and centrifugal forces should be distinguished from decentralization or devolution in unitary systems. In federalism the centrifugal forces are already in place when the initial constitutional divisions of labour are effected. In decentralization the centrifugal forces come to the surface after the initial constitutional arrangement has been made. If these centrifugal tendencies become very strong and effective, decentralization can lead, by design or by accident, to federalism.

Federalism, as a theory of regional or even global integration, derives its inspiration from seeing the positive benefits of federalism as a system of state government. Its proponents argue that the inherent tension between centre and periphery and the 'unity through diversity' dialectic are appropriate working assumptions for inter-state unification efforts. Federalism, as a system of integration at these levels, has a good deal of ideological and prescriptive leaven therefore. In particular, in comparison with functionalist and neo-functionalist approaches, the federalists claim to be able to tackle the issue of legitimate power-sharing head on by proposing an empirically tested system for dealing with it.

In contemporary WORLD POLITICS the primary laboratory for testing federalism as a means towards integration has been Western Europe. After 1945 many individuals and groups among the ATTENTIVE PUBLICS in this region came to the view that the recent historical experience of the area demonstrated the need to set plans to move 'beyond the nation state' in the future. Specifically with the formation of the EUROPEAN COMMUNITY (EC) federalists have sought to broaden the basis of participation by a directly elected Parliament with real budgetary powers. Although federalists have had some limited success in this regard, their best endeavours have been frustrated by STATE-CENTRED organs of the Community, notably the Council of Ministers.

Federalism remains the only empirically tested theory of regional integration that combines unity with diversity. Implicitly it is also a theory of limited government. Whether it should proceed by the ELITIST or the populist modes is a point for debate within its adherents. By tackling the issues of HIGH POLITICS directly, the federalist approach to integration is the most ambitious and the most controversial. In particular it confronts the key issue areas of state SOVEREIGNTY and NATIONAL INTEREST by proposing a power sharing alternative which eventually becomes enshrined in a constitutional bargain.

## Feedback

A term originating in information theory. It refers to the inter-relationship between an organism and its environment, using these terms in the broadest sense. Thus through the mechanism of feedback an organism reacts to its environment and vice versa. Feedback allows the organism to increase its chances of goal attainment, and/or goal modification, by demonstrating that a particular behaviour pattern is likely, or unlikely, to lead to the desired goal. Feedback, accordingly, can either be positive or negative. The latter is particularly important if self-correction and adjustment of behaviour is to take place. According to information theory, therefore, negative feedback allows organisms to adjust to their environment and maintain stability through adaptation or HOMEOSTASIS. Homeostatic equilibrium is dependent upon negative feedback, therefore, if 'learning' is to be achieved. A seminal work that sought to apply these ideas to politics, and particularly POLICY-MAKING, was Karl Deutsch's *The Nerves of Government*. The influence and impact of these ideas can be judged from the extent to which the term feedback is used as a colloquialism.

## Fifth column

Term which originated during the Spanish Civil War (1936–9) meaning an organized and secret body working within enemy ranks which aims to subvert, sabotage and disrupt the WAR effort. Thus, during Franco's attack on Madrid he was said to have four columns of regular troops preparing for the frontal assault, while a fifth column of rebel sympathisers existed within the city ready to aid the cause. Fifth column activities are especially associated with ideological conflict and as such ought to be distinguished from practitioners of ESPIONAGE. A term closely associated with fifth column is QUISLING, which refers to a group of Nazi supporters who aided Germany's attack on Norway in 1941. This, though, carries pejorative overtones (i.e. traitor), whereas fifth columnists are often regarded as brave and honourable people. There is a sense in which both can be regarded as latter-day Trojan Horses.

## Final Act

An abbreviated reference to the document known as the Final Act of the Conference on Security and Cooperation in Europe signed in Helsinki, Finland on 1 August 1975. The document is also sometimes referred to as the HELSINKI ACCORDS. The document is not a TREATY and is, therefore, not binding on the signatories. It is, at best, a statement of good intentions and, as such has some persuasive significance.

The term is also used in connection with the Single European Act (1986) which seeks to widen the integrative process in relation to the EUROPEAN COMMUNITY (EC). As a diplomatic term, it was first used at the Congress of VIENNA in 1815.

## Finlandization

A GEOPOLITICAL term which refers to extending a STATE's influence through control of the domestic politics of the target country. It usually refers to aspects of Soviet FOREIGN POLICY and Finland is seen to be the model for this process. Whereas the US-inspired DOMINO THEORY places emphasis on direct military confrontation this notion asserts that take-overs can be achieved through other, more insidious means.

## First strike

The attempt to achieve strategic surprise by attacking an adversary first. First strike requires both CAPABILITY and intention. The former requires highly mobile forces with a high LETHALITY. The latter requires feasible and intelligible operational planning which will seek to rapidly disarm and therefore demoralise the adversary. It requires a DECISION-MAKING system that has a clear chain of command and decision-makers who are willing to run risks, able to tolerate considerable physical and psychological stress, and who regard defeating the adversary as the highest national goal.

The advent of NUCLEAR WEAPONS has increased both the attractions and the risks of a first strike strategy. The capability requirements for such a strategy, as outlined above, are now increasingly attainable. The advent of BALLISTIC MISSILE DEFENCES (BMDs) will further enhance the capability for a first strike. The major break on the growth of the TECHNOLOGY of first strike remains the decision systems. As long as leaders regard avoiding WAR, rather than winning it, as the highest national goal then the first strike option may be rejected. Paradoxically, it is possible to manipulate these factors through strategies such as BRINKMANSHIP to cause the adversary to make concessions, for instance during times of CRISES. There remains the possibility that a first strike may occur as a result of MISPERCEPTIONS and misunderstandings. It is a salutary reminder that no system is foolproof and that violence may occur by accident rather than design.

## First World

As the word 'First' implies, this categorization refers to those states that were, historically, in the vanguard of the MODERNIZATION process during the last two centuries. The United Kingdom was indubitably the first industrial state and its HEGEMONY led to a period of some stability in WORLD POLITICS at the time. This PAX BRITANNICA was effectively ended by the rise to prominence of the United States and the deleterious effects of the two World Wars. Hegemonial LEADERSHIP passed to the United States after 1945 and for a period of time, which is now almost certainly ended, that state was able to exert decisive influence over political, economic, strategic and cultural issue areas in the system. As a collective expression, the First World and the term advanced industrial countries (AIC) are coterminous.

The occurrence of the COLD WAR led to the term acquiring a more relativist connotation. It became usual when using the expression to explicitly contrast the 'First' and the 'Second' Worlds. In this usage the term was meant to refer to certain immutable values as well as a particular epoch in development. The rise of the THIRD WORLD in contradistinction to the First and Second has further exacerbated the sense in which these terms are now used in a relative rather than absolute context.

Economically the First World stands for capitalism and a belief in economic LIBER-ALISM. In the history of this development, change occurred as a result of internal processes rather than external pressure. Unlike the Second and the Third Worlds there was little deliberate planning involved in these changes. No central planning authority or international body set targets or goals for First World economic development. These shifts led to the growth of a bourgeoisie and for demands for political participation to be broadened to accommodate these new classes. In the United States this led to the movement for INDE-PENDENCE, while in Europe the progressive democratization of politics followed. Political structures in the First World are designed to provide for a system of participation that is at once broad based but minimal. Most individuals in these systems restrict their participation to voting in elections and in some instances, notably the United States, actual turnout is surprisingly low. In reality, the term 'democratic ELIT-ISM' is probably the closest approximation to an empirical stipulation of how these polities actually function.

Sociologically, levels of literacy are very high throughout the First World. Social mobility is also generally high, although many states in this category still show considerable evidence of class and status differences. Scientific innovation and technological change are important features of these societies and, again, they tend to be in the vanguard of most of these changes. The multinational corporation (MNC) is the unique non-governmental creation of the First World's value system and it has been the vehicle or transmission belt for distributing these values to the rest of the system. Life styles in the First World are urban-oriented but there is some evidence that this pattern is being reassessed as so-called 'quality of life' considerations are encouraging a new interest in ECOLOGY and environmental issues and the rise of GREEN POLITICS.

## Flag

An indication of affiliation or ownership, the flag typically symbolizes such relationships. Thus all STATES have their own flag as symbols of statehood. It will be carried by state airlines, warships and merchant ships as well as being prominently displayed on public buildings both within the home state and on embassies and missions abroad. The right to fly the flag of the state is embodied in INTERNATIONAL LAW and is known as *jus banderae*. In MARITIME LAW this refers to the norm that a ship's nationality is decided by the colours under which it sails and not by the nationality of the owner. Thus it is possible to grant the right to fly the flag of a state to non-nationals – 'flags of convenience'. This refers to a situation where a state will authorize vessels owned and operated by nationals from other states to fly their flags. The attraction of this practice is that it enables operators to enjoy regulations, and perhaps tax REGIMES, that are less onerous than those they would have to operate under in their own state, or else it is done for political/strategic reasons, as was the case in 1988 with the reflagging of Kuwaiti ships during the Gulf War. The system is not without its critics and in 1958 the Geneva Convention on the High Seas suggested that there should be a 'genuine link' between ship and state. However, the problem of identification persists and in 1982 the shipping committee of the United Nations Conference on Trade and Development (UNCTAD) produced these figures relating to registration: fifty-six countries representing 45 per cent of the world's deadweight tonnage had a significant degree of control and managerial involvement with vessels that flew their flag, five states (Liberia, Panama, Cyprus, Bermuda and Bahamas), representing 29 per cent of tonnage had open registration, while three states (the United Kingdom, Greece and Saudi Arabia) representing 18 per cent of the world's tonnage had a mixed system that lay somewhere between the open and closed varieties.

International ACTORS other than states may also have flags. Indeed, the most famous example is that of the INTERNATIONAL RED CROSS where the flag has become the title of the institution. In this instance the symbol is the reverse of the state flag of Switzerland.

Flags may also be used as signals rather than symbols, Before the growth of more advanced TECHNOLOGIES, flags were widely used by armed forces for signalling instructions or simply allegiance. Various colours indicate different signals, the 'white flag' being widely regarded as a signal of the willingness to SURRENDER or call a TRUCE in situations of armed combat.

## Flexible response

A term used in contemporary strategic analysis. It has two uses. First, at the strategic nuclear level, flexible response is a COUNTERFORCE doctrine which seeks to provide DECISION-MAKERS with a range of WAR fighting options, once the nuclear threshold is crossed. Secondly, flexible response is a NATO strategy which seeks to respond to AGGRESSION at an appropriate level and to escalate to a higher one if NATO forces are unable to hold the adversary at the initial level.

In its first use, flexible response (sometimes referred to as 'controlled response') grew from the increasing sense of dubiety about the CREDIBILITY of the doctrine of massive RETALIATION which was the basis of the United States' strategic policy during the first Eisenhower Administration. During Eisenhower's second term informed opinion began to favour a more selective DAMAGE LIMITATION use of American resources arguing that a counterforce approach would leave Soviet cities hostage to a second strike if hostilities continued beyond the initial phase. The newly elected Kennedy Administration in January 1961 was wholly persuaded by these ideas. One of the first acts of the new Administration was to revise the Single Integrated Operational Plan (SIOP) away from an all-out spasm attack on Soviet cities towards something more controlled and flexible. Notwithstanding McNamara's interest in ASSURED DESTRUCTION as a declaratory policy, flexible response ideas have remained the dominant influence upon US strategic thinking ever since.

In its second sense, flexible response is again associated with changes initiated under Kennedy. The new President had been persuaded that the policy of the Eisenhower Administration of cutting conventional CAPABILITIES, particularly the army, was a mistake. Encouraged by generals such as Maxwell Taylor, by the growing commitment to a COUNTER-INSURGENCY war in VIETNAM and by events such as the second BERLIN CRISIS, the Democrats began to expand America's conventional forces. At the same time the United States began to urge upon its NATO allies the view that substituting TACTICAL NUCLEAR WEAPONS for CONVENTIONAL forces, which had been a feature of NATO deployment policies in the 1950s, was a dangerous mistake. In May 1962 in a wide-ranging address to the NATO ministerial meeting in Athens, Robert McNamara made a forcible presentation of these arguments. The new emphasis upon conventional forces in NATO would give the ALLIANCE the ability to respond to a conventional initiative from the other side without having to initiate the early first use of nuclear weapons. NATO conventional forces were envisaged as being considerably more than simply a TRIP-WIRE in this view of McNamara's.

European reactions to these proposals were mixed but generally unenthusiastic. The most critical view in public was taken by the French Government, which argued that the logic of mutual nuclear DETERRENCE was forcing the United States to decouple itself from Europe. The French decision in March 1966 to withdraw from the joint military command structure of the alliance, but not to formally repudiate the North Atlantic Treaty was the logical corollary of these doubts and suspicions. With the French withdrawal, the most overt and coherent opposition to flexible response was removed. Changes of government in the United Kingdom in 1964 and in the Federal Republic of Germany in 1966 brought into office parties which were more sympathetic to the McNamara approach. In May 1967, five years after the original Athens speech, NATO adopted flexible response in directive MC14/3. In truth, the version of flexible response that was eventually to become NATO policy in 1967 was not the version proposed in 1962. Because the European members of the alliance were unwilling to commit the resources necessary to increase the conventional capability of NATO, the 1967 version of flexible response specifically directed NATO commanders to 'deliberate escalation' if they were faced with a WARSAW PACT attack which they could not hold. In effect, therefore, by writing the principle of escalation into the doctrine of flexible response the alliance was committing itself to the first use of NUCLEAR WEAPONS.

## Foco theory

A concept developed by the Cuban revolutionary leaders Castro and Guevara. The basis of the idea is that it is not necessary to wait until the objective conditions are right before commencing an INSURGENCY. Foco theory argues that a small group of armed insurgents can act as the focal point for discontents and thereby create manually the conditions for opposition. Guevara's subsequent campaigning in Bolivia failed to substantiate the theory and it remains, as of this writing, *sui generis* to the Cuban revolution.

## Foggy bottom

Irreverant American media term for the US Department of State which is said to be located in the foggiest quarter of Washington DC. Sometimes also used as an uncomplimentary synonym for American FOREIGN POLICY.

## Football war

Name given to the 5-day military conflict between El Salvador and Honduras which occurred in July 1969 and resulted in the deaths of over 3,000 people. Simmering hostility between the two states (mainly over BOUNDARY disputes) was ignited by the victory in June of that year of the Honduras national soccer team over that of El Salvador in the preliminary round of the World Cup. After OAS (Organization of American States) INTERVENTION a ceasefire was agreed and the El Salvador army withdrew from Honduras territory. The incident illustrates the thesis that the causes of WAR are many and wondrous.

## Force

Force is closely related to ideas about POWER and COERCION. It is usually connected in international affairs with the use of arms although this need not always be the case. In fact, it is a physical manifestation of how power relationships can spill over into a dimension of violence. Not all power relations involve the use of the threat of force so in this sense power is a much wider and more broadly based set of ideas. However, if power can be seen as covering a continuum of relationships, then force lies at one extreme, with perhaps IN-FLUENCE at the other.

As a member of the power family, force requires a CAPABILITY as a necessary condition. Normally this capability is expressed in terms of military resources. In INTERNA-TIONAL RELATIONS, as there is no monopoly of force held by a central agency, every ACTOR, in theory, can possess the means and capacity to use force should it so wish. Acquiring and maintaining such a capacity is expensive. Accordingly, those wishing to go down this path have to make conscious and continuous decisions about the allocation of often scarce resources. STATES, traditionally the actors most likely to seek to acquire such capabilities, have always distinguished themselves by how much of these resources they might be willing to allocate to maintain and increase their force capabilities. Indeed, an important variable in assessing position in the hierarchical structure of states (GREAT, MIDDLE or SMALL POWERS) is an estimation concerning the capacity and willingness to use force. One conditional variable in this process may be the state's ORIENTATION. Clearly a state that is ISOLATIONIST is less likely to feel threatened by others or feel the need to threaten others with the use of force. A second major constraint on the acquisition of force capability is likely to be the overall structure of the system. For example, the BALANCE OF POWER was, at its height, based on the assumption that the leading states in the system had the capability, individually or in coalition, to intervene forcefully if necessary to preserve the system and prevent its domination by one or a group of dissident states. These groupings were often referred to as STATUS QUO and REVISIONIST, as they were by E. H. Carr in *The Twenty Years Crisis, 1919–39*. Again, acquiring a force capability will require leaders within states to make choices as to the allocation of resources and, in particular, with the choice between force capabilities and other goals. The argument about 'guns versus butter' is clearly not confined to Stalinist Russia.

TECHNOLOGY has affected the role of force in a number of ways. First, the acquisition of a credible force capability is highly expensive. Modern weapons systems place a heavy burden on the economies of even the wealthiest states. Second, modern technology has increased the SCOPE and destructiveness of the violence available to the state that practices the use of force. The distinction between combatants and non-combatants is increasingly difficult to sustain and civilian deaths as a proportion of total WAR deaths have increased greatly. Since the gunpowder REVOLUTION the ultimate technological innovation to date has been the development of NUCLEAR WEAP-ONS. Indeed, the nuclear revolution in international affairs has caused further revisions to be made to our conception of the use of force. In particular, the distinction between force capability and force relationship is now sharper than ever. In nuclear weapons, states possess instruments of force which they would prefer not to use. As a result, DETERRENCE theorists have identified the problem of CREDIBILITY as being especially critical. Nuclear weapons have also blurred traditional distinctions between victors and vanquished. Consequently, the use of force, if it is to include nuclear weapons, is now beset by ambiguities and contradictions, the most blatant being the idea of its skilful non-use.

*International law and the use of force*
Restriction on the use of force has always been part of the rationale of INTER-NATIONAL LAW, and the twentieth century has seen the most concerted attempt yet to outlaw violence employed in the private interests of individual states. The LEAGUE OF NATIONS did not ban the use of force altogether but it did attempt to restrict it to tolerable levels and during the inter-war years there was a movement to achieve its

total prohibition which resulted in the General Treaty for the Renunciation of War (the KELLOGG–BRIAND pact) of 1928. However, even this was not a complete ban, as the right to SELF-DEFENCE and REPRISALS remained. WAR, of course, is not an exact synonym for force, and the CHARTER OF THE UN attempted to address the issue head on. Thus Article 2 (4) declared that 'All members shall refrain in their international relations from the threat or use of force against the territorial integrity or political independence of any state, or in any other manner inconsistent with the purpose of the United Nations.' The reference to 'force' rather than to 'war' was deliberate as it covers incidences where violence may be employed although perhaps falling short of a technical state of war. This is now part of customary international law, yet it is unclear whether the term includes not only armed force but other manifestations; for example economic force. This ambiguity was highlighted in 1973–4 with the use of the Arab oil weapon against states deemed friendly to Israel. It is not possible with any degree of certainty to establish whether economic or other forms of coercion are contrary to the Charter but expert opinion has it that international law is moving in the general direction of widening the definitional scope of the term.

Under the Charter the threat or use of force is illegal except in certain circumstances, and these are broadly the exercise of SELF-DEFENCE and the collective use of force by the organization itself. This doctrine of COLLECTIVE SECURITY led some to expect the UN to play a key role in the post-1945 system. In fact the intrusion of the COLD WAR into the working of the organization weakened the possibility and desirability of its providing a genuine international REGIME for the use of force. The KOREAN WAR (1950) is an exception to this but only because of the fortuitous absence of the Soviet Union from the SECURITY COUNCIL when the decision for collective coercive action was taken. Subsequently, the UN has developed a more modest PEACEKEEPING competence which seeks to avoid the active use of force and instead rely more on TRADITIONAL diplomatic techniques. The issue of TERRORISM has not so far produced a specific prohibitive TREATY mainly because of definitional problems associated with political preference. One man's 'terrorist' is another's 'freedom fighter' and so international law has not thus far been able to encompass the phenomenon.

The centrality of force in international relations has shown the inadequacy of international law, yet its use is hedged about with limitations. States possessing considerable military potential find its actual use more difficult to envisage and to enact. Force potential is not easily transferred into force relationships and when the transformation is made the resulting use of force is often self-defeating and costly. The attempt to establish international institutions which administer quasi-legal force has so far not been successful. As a result, although modern technology has placed enormous putative force into POLICY-MAKERS' hands, they have found its conversion into usable instruments highly contingent.

### Force de frappe

The French nuclear delivery system. The decision to develop an independent nuclear deterrent for France is normally associated with the Fifth Republic and, in particular, the Presidency of Charles de Gaulle. However, the original decision was made under the Fourth Republic. Unlike its UK neighbour, France has maintained a genuine independent force structure. France has land-based, sea-based and air launched delivery systems and has developed TACTICAL NUCLEAR WEAPONS as well. Closer nuclear collaboration with the United Kingdom has been actively discussed for a quarter of a century and might well become a viable policy option in the future. The term *force de dissuasion* is often used in preference, indicating more appropriately its deterrent intention.

*See also*: GAULLISM

## Force majeure

Diplomatic term referring to situations which arise out of unavoidable or unforeseen circumstances or else as a result of irresistible FORCE. Failure to comply with known INTERNATIONAL LAW, e.g. respecting territorial waters, may be excused on the grounds of *force majeure*. Used in this sense, it is the diplomatic equivalent of 'Act of God'. In another sense, it is frequently used to describe the application of superior or overwhelming force to settle a problem which hitherto had been a matter of consent, agreement or legal process. A group ruling through terror or repression alone could be described as ruling through *force majeure*.

## Foreign aid

A technique of ECONOMIC STATECRAFT where AID is used as an instrument of policy in order to achieve certain goals. Foreign aid implies a relationship between two ACTORS which may be stipulated on one hand as 'donor' and on the other as 'recipient', these words clearly implying that the relationship will be seen in positive terms by the participants. Although it will be argued here that aid relationships can become negative and coercive, the initial position will be that the sanctions involved are rewards rather than punishments. In summary, then, foreign aid may be seen as a form of POWER relationship. Accordingly, the donor must possess a CAPABILITY which can be converted into an aid relationship. For example, a STATE may possess large agricultural surpluses which it is willing to dispense to identified recipients. Similarly, the recipient must perceive that the goods and services offered will provide real additional resources. Both parties will look for tangible benefits from foreign aid relationships, therefore. In GAME THEORY terminology foreign aid expectations are positive sum.

States are not the only actors involved in foreign aid relationships, although they are the most important. International institutions such as the UN, through agencies such as the IBRD (WORLD BANK GROUP) and the IMF, also play an aid role. Moreover, it is certainly a mistake to see the activities of such bodies as being somehow 'non-political'. To the extent that such agencies get other recipient actors to do things that they would not otherwise do, then they may be said to be exercising political power relationships as donors over their identified recipients.

The precise political functions served by aid relationships are not always easy to uncover. The most overt political manifest function of aid will be evident from an examination of the conditions laid down by the donor. Indeed, such stipulations as laid down by agencies such as the IMF, for example, can specify the kinds of economic policies they expect the recipient to follow. IMF conditionality is rightly regarded as political, as well as economic, in its implications. This political connotation has led some commentators to criticize the Fund accordingly. Similarly, from the outset the MARSHALL PLAN had clear political implications. Important among these were: using US economic capability as a weapon in the COLD WAR, increasing cooperation among European states, assisting in the rehabilitation of Germany and boosting US exports in the post-war period.

Knorr (1975) has been responsible for directing the attention of analysts to the coercive function that foreign aid relationships can serve. The explanation for this is implicit in the initial characterization of foreign aid as a form of power relationship. A reward, once offered and accepted, can seem subsequently to be punitive if the donor threatens to withdraw or discontinue rewarding the recipient in the future. Because aid relationships exist over time, the opportunity for the donor to assume an intrusive and even coercive role *vis-à-vis* the recipient will increase. Furthermore, the donor may attempt to link in the aid relationship with other foreign policy ISSUE AREAS. Thus the United States used its Marshall aid link with the Netherlands to put pressure on the Dutch to come to terms with Indonesian nationalists in 1948–9.

A more general example of coercive LINKAGE is provided by the Hickenlooper Amendment of 1962, which is a blanket prohibition upon US aid to states that nationalize US assets without offering full and fair compensation. During the Nixon Presidency, when the United States was considering extending MOST FAVOURED NATION (MFN) status to the Soviet Union, the US Congress via the Jackson–Vanik Amendment sought to make this offer dependent upon recipient states allowing their nationals freedom of migration to other countries. (This stipulation was specifically aimed at Soviet citizens wishing to settle abroad, especially Israel.)

Whether conditions are stipulated, implied, altered or amended at some later date, the fact remains that donors will want to make some assessment of the aid relationship both with regard to their initial objectives and in order to assess the overall efficacy of the exercise. Judging how successful a particular instance has been in terms of NATIONAL INTERESTS is bound to be a subjective exercise. Thus the Marshall Plan was, at the time, regarded as a highly successful example of foreign aid working both in political and in economic terms. However, as Baldwin (1985) has recently pointed out, Marshall aid helped European recipients to do things that they probably would have done anyway and its influence declined towards the end of the programme. Additionally, it fostered the habits of European cooperation and, in the long term, created a powerful trading rival to the United States.

## Foreign Office

Originally a European innovation, it refers to an executive and administrative agency of STATE which is concerned with the formulation and conduct of FOREIGN POLICY. It goes by a variety of names including for-

eign ministry, ministry for external affairs, ministry of foreign affairs and state department, but the basic functions remain the same. These are: the gathering of INTELLIGENCE (usually through the diplomatic service), collating and evaluating information received, determining policy options available to government and communicating and explaining chosen policies to other governments and INTERNATIONAL ORGANIZATIONS. Since 'defence of the realm' is part of the rationale of politics, this agency is one of the most important in government. Most foreign offices are organized on geographical lines (an African desk, an Asian desk, etc.) and on functional lines (commercial, financial and administrative) and are coordinated by a Minister or Secretary who holds high rank and status in government and/or party.

## Foreign policy

The activity whereby STATE ACTORS act, react and interact. Foreign policy has been termed a BOUNDARY activity. The term 'boundary' implies that those making policy straddle two environments; an internal or domestic environment and an external or global environment. The POLICY-MAKERS and the policy system stand therefore at these junction points and seek to mediate between the various milieu.

The domestic environment forms the background context against which policy is made. Thus factors such as the resource base of the state, its position geographically in relation to others, the nature and level of development of its economy, its demographic structure, its IDEOLOGY and fundamental values will form the domestic or internal milieu. The international or external environment is where policy is actually implemented. Implementation of policy immediately involves other actors and their reactions will FEEDBACK into the policy-making system, thus forming part of the picture upon which future policy will be made. This attempt to create a reality upon which policy can be made is referred to as the DEFINITION OF THE SITUATION. It is a necessary prerequisite to understanding the environment and therefore to making policy decisions.

For most DECISION-MAKERS the international environment will be approached from a regional perspective. GEOPOLITICS sets the parameters for this REGIONALISM. States have to react to their neighbours in all aspects of policy and therefore this regional dimension will be crucially important. Even the most significant states in contemporary WORLD POLITICS, the superpowers, have regional interests, the United States in Latin America and the Soviet Union in Eastern Europe. COOPERATION and INTEGRATION often take place on a regional basis. Similarly many CONFLICT situations, including some of the most chronic and persistent, have their origins in regional rather than global politics. The ARAB–ISRAELI CONFLICT is a good example. The actual conduct of policy will be based within the institutional framework of the state. What are defined as vital matters of NATIONAL INTEREST will be handled by the head of government along with senior advisors. Such questions are normally referred to as HIGH POLITICS and would include matters of immediate PEACE and security as well as questions vital to the wealth and welfare of the state and its people. Conversely LOW POLITICS refers to matters of a routine and regular nature which, in point of fact, constitute the great bulk of normal and routine DIPLOMACY. An intermediate category, often called Sectoral Politics has been coined by some writers on foreign policy to cover those areas where particular interest groups perceived that they have vital interests at stake but where these cannot really be called 'national' without distortion. Clearly these categories are not hard and fast and a particular ISSUE AREA may change in its relative significance. For the United Kingdom this clearly happened in 1982 when the FALKLANDS issue moved rapidly from Low/Sectoral to High following the Argentinian initiative to occupy the islands UNILATERALLY.

Conventional wisdom might want to suppose that foreign policy is made on the basis of rational calculations of advantage and disadvantage with the policy makers acting as a unified system. There is good reason to doubt that this view is entirely valid. In recent years the bureaucratic politics approach has sought to emphasize that the organizations that make policy are not unified. Rather, key individuals tend to pursue their own version of the national interest often in conflict with others within the system. As a result the policy that emerges may represent a compromise between various points of view or the triumph of one organizational perspective over another. It is certainly plausible to see the ARMS RACE in terms of this view. If this is the case, then the ACTION–REACTION model suggested above needs to be modified to allow for the organizational context in which policy is made.

The implementation of policy decisions requires states to utilize instruments such as military and economic CAPABILITIES. The military instrument of policy has traditionally been seen as the most important where areas of High Policy are concerned. Recently, economic instruments have attracted increased attention. This is partly as a result of increases in INTERDEPENDENCE and partly because of some of the problems surrounding the use and the threat of the use of FORCE in contemporary politics. In the last analysis, however well endowed a state may be with the capacity to act to advance its interests, the skill and determination of its diplomats and the conduct of its DIPLOMACY may be crucial to the outcome. It is useful to distinguish diplomacy from foreign policy, since they are sometimes used synonymously in the more traditional texts. Whereas diplomacy refers to the manner of conducting one's relations, foreign policy refers to the matter. The latter remains the best term to use to encapsulate a state's relations with the outside world.

## Fourteen points

Speech by President Woodrow Wilson to Congress on 18 January 1918 which contained the ideological justification for the US WAR effort and which subsequently became the basis of the new INTERNATIONAL ORDER sought by IDEALISTS after the First World War. While undoubtedly representing the Wilsonian approach in INTERNATIONAL RELATIONS the speech owed its substance to a group of experts who had been assembled by Colonel E. M. House to draft proposals for the long-term settlement of international disputes. Among these was Walter Lippmann, who was subsequently regarded as one of the foremost American REALISTS. The speech contained a mixture of general and specific issues presented by the war and by the continued international ANARCHY. It called for new DIPLOMACY consisting of 'open covenants openly arrived at', freedom of the seas in PEACE and war, removal of TRADE barriers, reduction of armaments and impartial adjustment of colonial claims. No less than eight points applied the doctrine of SELF-DETERMINATION to political settlements in specific parts of Europe. The fourteenth point, which subsequently became the most influential, was the plea for the formation of a 'general association of nations' which would give 'mutual guarantees of political independence and territorial integrity to great and small states alike'. This LEAGUE OF NATIONS was the centrepiece of the whole programme, although it is ironic that the STATE that did so much to create it subsequently refused to join it.

The significance of the speech is that it contains, in a practical form, almost all the elements of a LIBERAL theory of international relations – MULTILATERAL diplomacy, the rule of law, the creation of INTERNATIONAL ORGANIZATIONS to mitigate ANARCHY, COLLECTIVE SECURITY, self-determination, FREE TRADE and DISARMAMENT. Despite the failure of the League of Nations, this programme has had a powerful influence on Western thinking about international affairs and elements of it form part of the general corpus of modern international law. In spirit, if not in substance, it still forms the essence of the liberal approach to WORLD POLITICS and represents the first specifically US contribution to the creation and maintenance of the international order.

## Forward defence

A form of extended DEFENCE where a STATE engages an enemy not on home territory but in some other (usually predetermined) location. It is still considered to be a variety of SELF-DEFENCE but is at one remove from the homeland, and as such is often regarded as less legitimate. It is often justified on the grounds of AID to an ally whose territory has been compromised or threatened. The United Kingdom's entry into both World Wars and the military basis on which they were prosecuted is a good example. Again, the TRUMAN DOCTRINE and CONTAINMENT are instances of the United States' use of this concept within the general framework of DETERRENCE. A feature of forward defence which is often overlooked (particularly by practitioners of it) is the resentment it can sometimes generate in the states upon whose territory the stand is to be made. Thus France, under General de Gaulle, was particularly anxious about this and other aspects of the US commitment to forward defence in Western Europe. The firmness of the commitment (would the United States regard an attack on Paris in the same light as an attack on Washington?) as well as the intrinsic asymmetry of the relationship (is France a mere dependency of the United States under this doctrine?) were issues that dominated French politics and strategic thinking during this period. Again, disquiet has been publicly expressed on a number of occasions throughout Europe that the adoption of forward defensive postures by both the United States and the Soviet Union means in effect that a TOTAL European WAR could be fought which had only limited impact on the territories of the major belligerents. For these reasons the adoption of such strategies needs to be accompanied by a measure of political and diplomatic sensitivity.

## Fourth World

A shorthand term for what the UN has called the LEAST DEVELOPED COUNTRIES. These STATES are distinguished by very low per capita Gross Domestic Products (GDPs), low levels of literacy and low levels of manufacturing development. Geographically, the Fourth World is confined to two continents: Africa and Asia. In Africa, the so-called 'famine belt' stretches across the middle of the continent from Mauritania to the Sudan, in this region the already vulnerable economies have recently been exacerbated by drought. In Asia the paradigm Fourth World state is Bangladesh where recent exacerbation has been caused by cyclone-provoked floods rather than drought. States can slip into this category as a result of man-made rather than natural conditions. AFGHANISTAN and Mozambique, states ravaged by revolutionary INSURGENCY and foreign INTERVENTION, can be cited here.

In terms of the global HIERARCHY of states, the Fourth World clearly refers to those ACTORS at the margin of the system. The UN and agencies such as UNCTAD, as well as influential bodies of private interests such as the BRANDT REPORTS Commission, have sought to draw the attention of ELITES and ATTENTIVE PUBLICS in the rest of the system to the plight of these states.

## *Francophonie*

A term used to describe common bonds among those STATES and communities that share the French language, culture and civilization. Originally a nineteenth century notion relating specifically to French North Africa it was revived by President Senghor of Senegal in 1960 and widely publicized in 1962 (the year of Algerian INDEPENDENCE) by a special issue of the journal *Esprit*. Its subsequent popularity in the French-speaking world led to the establishment of over two hundred private and public organizations, usually Paris-based, designed specifically to promote the idea of a shared identity and to maintain ties with the thirty-five states which accord some official status to the French language. Four main institutions or areas of activity sustain the idea of *francophonie*: the Agence de Cooperation Culturelle et Technique (ACCT, 1969), the annual Franco–African SUMMIT conferences, regular meetings of the Francophile States and the French Secretariat of State for Francophonie. The first occupant of this position, Madame Michaux-Chevy, defined it in this way: 'Francophonie is a fight . . . for a new international solidarity, for a new intricate and manifold cultural identity and for a common development.' Although its aspirations are somewhat vague, it does represent a coherent, if somewhat loose, movement in WORLD POLITICS and serves to demarcate and defend the French-speaking world from possible encroachments from the more dominant Anglo–Saxon civilization. In this sense it has often, albeit wrongly, been described as an agency of French FOREIGN POLICY or alternatively as an instrument of NEO-COLONIALISM.

## Free trade

A trading system between two or more ACTORS. The essence of free trade is that goods are imported without any restrictions, such as TARIFFS, being placed upon them. From an economic standpoint, free trade increases competition and efficiency. Producers have access to foreign markets, while consumers have access to IMPORTS. As a result of free trade greater specialization occurs in economic activity throughout the system. Individual members become less self-sufficient and more dependent upon others. As a result, free trade is often associated with the growth of INTERDEPENDENCE among actors. As a system of organizing economic relationships it may be directly contrasted with AUTARKY or self-sufficiency.

The advocacy of free trade is usually associated with economic LIBERALISM, at least in its classical phase. Many of these ideas were resuscitated after 1945 under the BRETTON WOODS system of international economic relations. Under the hegemonial influence of the United States, the major institutional framework for post-war relations was established. Similarly the later negotiations for an international trade REGIME, under the defunct International Trade Organization (ITO), and the substitute General Agreement on Tariffs and Trade (GATT) reflected the same liberal free trade philosophy. The same outlook influenced the MARSHALL PLAN and post-war tariff-cutting negotiations under GATT. The LIBERAL regime has not been able to resist the encroachments of NEO-MERCANTILISM of late, and increasingly GATT has had to combat the growth of non-tariff barriers to TRADE.

The philosophical assumptions behind free trade have been criticized by compensatory liberals and others. The rise of the THIRD WORLD has thrown these doubts into sharp relief because the alleged shortcomings are not simply a matter of intellectual fashion or preference. Writers such as Prebisch (1964) have argued that if the terms of TRADE penalize certain economies a system of free trade will leave some states permanently at a disadvantage. If those penalized are those that can least afford it, then free trade can exacerbate and widen inequalities within the system. Demands for a free trade regime that ignore such structural inequalities have been opposed by the Third World. The NEW INTERNATIONAL ECONOMIC ORDER (NIEO) and the United Nations Conference on Trade and Development (UNCTAD) have been used by this constituency to press for changes in the trade regime that will recognize and compensate for these difficulties.

## Free trade area

A form of economic union between STATES. In a FREE TRADE area the constituent members agree to abolish TARIFFS and other restrictions on stipulated goods between themselves. However, *vis-à-vis* the rest of the system they continue to maintain the structure of their existing tariffs. A free trade area is therefore a less integrated system than a CUSTOMS UNION because there is no common external tariff. Although a free trade area is less integrated it may prove to be just as complicated to implement because rules and procedures have to be agreed to prevent goods entering the area from outside via those member states with the lowest range of tariffs. Without clear rules about origin, the states with the lowest external tariffs will benefit most from a free trade area, because TRADE and production will be deflected in their favour. Logic would suggest that a free trade area works best where the members have a similar pattern of external tariffs, or where they agree to substantial HARMONIZATION of tariffs to reduce differentials. For this reason a free trade area is often seen as the preliminary stage in the formation of a full customs union.

During the 1950s considerable discussion took place among Western European state members of the Organization for European Economic Cooperation (OEEC) about the desirability of forming a free trade area. Agreement was not possible, however, and instead the membership became divided between those states wishing to proceed much further with INTEGRATION in order to form a customs union and the remainder, led by the United Kingdom, wanting to stay with the free trade area idea. The formation of the EUROPEAN COMMUNITY (EC) constituent institution, the European Economic Community under the Treaty of Rome in 1957, seemed to settle the issue. In retaliation the British formed the European Free Trade Association (EFTA) under the Stockholm Treaty in 1959. EFTA was a bargaining chip designed to force the EC to expand its membership and to lower the common external tariff. The EC refused to negotiate with EFTA *en bloc* and in 1961 the British defected to begin access negotiations with the Community.

Free trade areas, as forms of economic integration, are covered by General Agreement on Tariffs and Trade (GATT). Although it might seem that some aspects of the free trade area idea contradict the GATT principle of non-discrimination, exceptions were made in the Agreement for these types of groupings. Provided tariffs and other restrictions are eliminated on 'substantially all the trade between the constituent territories' the GATT stipulations are satisfied. Unfortunately the meaning of the phrase 'substantially all' has never been satisfactorily defined. In cases of conflict GATT has usually been unable to prevail.

## Free World

A term associated with the COLD WAR indicating those parts of the world not subject to COMMUNIST influence or domination. Sometimes used as a synonym for the West, although this is erroneous as it was clearly the intention of US POLICY-MAKERS to include non-Western and THIRD WORLD STATES under this rubric. The term is used rather loosely now but in the immediate post-war period the United States was the architect of a number of overlapping global ALLIANCES which John Foster Dulles referred to as the 'Free World Alliance'.
*See also*: CONTAINMENT; TRUMAN DOCTRINE

## Front

Generally used in a number of senses:

1. Referring to the scene of fighting, line of battle or the forward position of armed forces. A First World War variation on this was the notion of the 'home' front indicating that the WAR was TOTAL.

2. Organizations which come together with the specific aim of opposing or toppling a REGIME, e.g. the Patriotic Front (Zimbabwe) and the United Democratic Front (South Africa).

3. A group which is used, or deliberately set up, to feign allegiance to certain acceptable aims or institutions whereas in reality it is controlled by activists working for another cause. In this sense, 'front organizations' are generally associated with Soviet FOREIGN POLICY, more particularly with Leon Trotsky (1879–1940).

## Frontier

A zone of contact between two entities or social systems. It should be distinguished from BOUNDARY which implies more or less strict territorial limits. Frontier is a much vaguer concept and is projected outwards ('in front') rather than inwards ('within bounds'). A frontier zone therefore refers to an area of delineation between different DOMAINS. It is often used in a metaphorical sense ('the frontiers of knowledge') but in WORLD POLITICS is has tended to signify contact zones between one civilization or culture and another. Thus, the history of European IMPERIALISM is often presented as a record of pushing forward 'the frontiers of the known world'. Implicit in this notion was the implication that frontiers were not immediately or obviously subject to the post-WESTPHALIAN rules of international contact (NON-INTERVENTION, SOVEREIGNTY and RECOGNITION) that had been established by the boundary-conscious Europeans in their dealings with one another. This double standard has always been a feature of frontier politics especially as practised by, but not in relation to, the European STATE-SYSTEM.

The phrase 'frontier thesis' refers specifically to the work of American historian Frederick Jackson Turner who in 1893 argued that the closing of the American West as a frontier in the latter part of the nineteenth century would have important consequences for US politics, especially with regard to overseas expansion. Generally in world politics, frontier has been superseded by boundary, which with its connotations of cartographical territoriality, has brought into play the political and legal conventions associated with state SOVEREIGNTY. In GEOPOLITICS spatial frontiers have been converted into boundaries when two powers begin to approach each other's peripheral territory. This may lead to the creation of BUFFER STATES between the two competing systems as was the case, for example, with AFGHANISTAN which straddled the contact zone between Russia and British India. These regions, as the history of Afghanistan illustrates, are often extremely sensitive to sudden shifts in the overall configuration of world politics.

## Front-line states

Refers to those STATES that share a territorial border with the Republic of South Africa or are directly affected by its politics of DESTABILIZATION and which are committed to ending APARTHEID, securing majority rule and freeing themselves from DEPENDENCE. Originally the term referred only to Zambia, Botswana, Tanzania, Angola and Mozambique but after 1980 these five were joined by Malawi, Lesotho, Swaziland and the newly independent Zimbabwe. These nine states together established the Southern African Development Coordination Conference (SADCC) in order to resist South African attempts at creating a 'constellation' of moderate, non-Marxist states in Southern Africa. However, despite some initial successes, the Front-line states have found it extremely difficult to disengage from South Africa and so far, are noted more for their rhetoric than for any substantive achievement.

## Frustration

*See*: AGGRESSION

## Functionalism

Functionalism was originally conceived, as Claude suggests in his 1971 volume on International Organization, as an approach to PEACE. However, it has implications for INTEGRATION as well and these ideas have been taken up and developed of late – particularly by NEO-FUNCTIONALISM. Functionalism begins its analysis with the deceptively simple proposition that the provision of common needs can unite peoples across STATE boundaries. This has produced a concentration by functionalist writers on what has been called the wealth–welfare dimension in WORLD POLITICS and to the avoidance of HIGH POLITICS. The functionalist logic, that there are wide and significant areas for the provision of common services and for the meeting of common needs, served to inspire the UN to establish a host of Specialized Agencies – such as the WORLD HEALTH ORGANIZATION (WHO). By avoiding the most politically contentious issue areas and concentrating instead upon wealth–welfare provisions, functionalists tried to focus upon areas of unity rather than disunity between people and states. Functionalists assumed that a natural HARMONY OF INTERESTS existed in these matters.

David Mitrany's 1943 book is generally regarded as the first and most persuasive statement of twentieth century functionalist principles. Mitrany's intellectual milieu was Fabian, Social Democracy and his debt to this kind of thinking is clear, in particular in his belief that common needs should be met by public provisions of goods and services. Mitrany, in discussing functionalism, sought to draw explicit contrasts with FEDERALISM which he saw as being too locked into constitution building and considerations of POWER sharing rather than the provision of common needs. In this and in other ways Mitrany anticipated contemporary arguments in favour of transnationalism and INTERDEPENDENCE.

Functionalists believed that loyalties could be transferred away from the NATION STATE towards new functional organizations. This would occur because people would see that the provision of goods and services now depended upon transnational cooperation and, following a kind of utilitarian calculus, they would perceive that their best interests were now being served by the new arrangements. Among political ELITES also the experience of working in a cooperative framework with others would encourage mutual responsiveness in the future.

Secondly, functionalists saw 'enmeshment' or 'engrenage' occurring as states increased their cooperation to meet functional tasks. As states became more interdependent it would be increasingly difficult to pull out of these arrangements and increasingly costly to remain outside for any length of time. In this way the functionalists were anticipating the idea of SPILL-OVER which became a distinctive feature of the neo-functionalist literature in the 1950s and 1960s.

It should not be thought that functionalism, as originally conceived of by Mitrany, was a theory of regional integration. Indeed he was rather hostile towards such developments, believing that they would deflect peoples' attention away from the true goal of international integration. Moreover, Mitrany saw the possibility that regional FEDERATIONS might simply become super-

states or SUPERPOWERS. The old issues and the old problems of the NATION-STATE would simply be recast in new clothes. Instead, following the dictum that 'form follows function', the true functionalist should not arbitrarily foreclose on any possible arrangements for the future.

## Fungibility

A term used in the analysis of CAPABILITIES and POWER relationships. Literally a thing is held to be fungible if it is transferable or can be used in lieu of another. Thus the inability to achieve such conveyance is termed 'low fungibility'. Power theorists such as Baldwin (1979) have argued that capabilities or possessions suffer from low fungibility and that, as a result, considerable operational restraint will be experienced when ACTORS attempt to use these capabilities out of context. Baldwin has striven hard to establish the point that the attribute of 'powerful' should only be applied in a policy contingency framework.

## Futurology

*See*: ALTERNATIVE WORLD FUTURES

# G

## Game Theory

Game Theory is a formal, mathematical method of studying DECISION-MAKING in situations of CONFLICT. Being formal, it expresses its ideas in terms of how things *should* be, given certain assumptions. Notable among these are that those making decisions will act rationally. Being mathematical these ideas are expressed in quantitative, numerate form. Thus it is usually the case in this type of analysis for the decision problem to be represented in the form of a matrix with numerical values attached to the outcomes, as shown in Figure 1(a). Each player in the game has two choices, giving four possible outcomes. This binary choice situation is, clearly, a simplification of reality. It is a plausible simplification, however. It is possible to include more than two strategies in the

*(b) Prisoner's dilemma*

|  | +50 | +100 |
|---|---|---|
| +50 |  | −100 |
|  | −100 | −50 |
| +100 |  | −50 |

*(a)*

|  | −50 | +100 |
|---|---|---|
| +50 |  | −100 |
|  | −100 | +50 |
| +100 |  | −50 |

*(c) Chicken*

|  | +50 | +100 |
|---|---|---|
| +50 |  | −100 |
|  | −100 | −1000 |
| +100 |  | −1000 |

matrix and, obviously, to produce more than four outcomes. The numerical values attached to the outcomes are known as pay-offs and it is usual to read one player on the lower left (or south-western) row and the others on the top right (or north-eastern). It is important to note that each player must commit himself to a strategy without knowing what the other has done in advance.

Given these ground rules a number of consequences follow. Returning to the point about RATIONALITY made above, it can be seen that it is necessary to settle upon some agreed definition of what constitutes rationality, at least initially, if the analysis is to proceed. In game theory it is assumed that players will seek to maximize their gains or to minimize their losses. In other words, in this branch of social analysis rationality is defined in terms derived from microeconomics and with ideas about utility maximization and disutility minimization. In the language of game theory, this rule of rational behaviour is referred to as the MINIMAX principle.

Applying the minimax principle can be quite straightforward if the game situation is ZERO–SUM. The zero–sum situation can be identified when the pay-offs in the matrix added together equal zero, as shown in the first example. The zero–sum game is the game of pure CONFLICT, there is no co-operation on offer at all and the motives displayed are totally antagonistic. A gain by one party is seen as a loss by the opponent. In these circumstances minimax is a very useful rule guide to follow and a stable solution, or SADDLE POINT will be reached. This is stable because neither player can have any incentive to prefer another strategy.

A second class of games, known by a variety of terms, can be distinguished from the zero–sum game. Using mathematical criteria this second class can be termed non-zero–sum or variable sum games. Using psychological criteria they can be called mixed motive games. The essence of the difference is that the assumption of pure conflict is dropped from the game and the players face outcomes where they can both lose and both win, where coordination and cooperation emerge as alternatives to pure conflict. This switch has the merit, so its proponents allege, of being more isomorphic with reality. The switch has the shortcoming that the notion of minimax rationality can no longer be confidently applied to mixed motive games.

Furthermore, the situational characteristic that game moves are supposed to be made without prior knowledge of what the other side has done appears to be a real handicap when a more coordinated and cooperative strategy is sought. A classic mixed motive game known as the Prisoner's Dilemma (Figure 1(b)) raises these central issues in a direct way. Unlike the zero–sum game, this type provides no clear answer to the question, 'what is the rational strategy?'. As Rapoport (1974) has suggested, the Prisoner's Dilemma actually suggests two types of rationality, individual rationality and collective rationality. Moreover the Prisoner's Dilemma is interesting because it raises psychological issues about being both trusting and trustworthy.

Another variation within the mixed motive class of games is that known as 'Chicken'. Even the most cursory study of Figure 1(c), which is a matrix for this type of game, will show that outcome 2 : 11 is one which both players would want to avoid. Conversely outcome 1 : 1, implying some form of cooperation, appears attractive. However, the possibility exists in Chicken to exploit the common desire to avoid 2 : 11 to achieve 2 : 1 or 1 : 11. The pay-offs in the Chicken game therefore seem to imply that behaving in a deliberately risky, if not reckless, way can be rewarded if the other side gives ground thereby. The temptation to behave in this manner is built into the game situation. Just as the Prisoner's Dilemma has been held to raise parallels with ARMS CONTROL and DISARMAMENT negotiations, so Chicken is held to raise parallels with tactics that are sometimes used in CRISIS situations.

Game theory is not without its critics, as an examination of the works of Schelling (1960) and Rapoport (1964) show. By remaining a purely formal, quantitative set of percepts game theory retains its purity but in the process has little relevance as an IDEOLOGY or metaphor for certain real world situations. On the other hand, once the attempt is made to apply game theory to real-world situations its limitations are apparent. Rapoport has argued that in the field of mixed-motive games no unambiguous definition of rationality can be given and that, indeed, the playing out of the mixed motive game involves consideration of factors such as 'trust' which are not encountered in the zero–sum game. Its great value to social science must be as a heuristic device rather than a means of testing or VERIFICATION.

## GATT

The General Agreement on Tariffs and Trade (GATT) was signed by twenty-three states in October 1947. At the time it was envisaged that the treaty would become an integral part of the International Trade Organization but when the latter's charter was not ratified by the United States GATT became, by default, the only MULTILATERAL agreement covering international TRADE activities between states in the system. GATT represents, then, both a formal international convention and a DE FACTO international institution.

GATT was established to create and then maintain a FREE TRADE REGIME. This would be achieved by promoting the principle of TARIFF reductions through multilateral CONFERENCE DIPLOMACY, and by extending the ideas of the MOST FAVOURED NATION (MFN) and non-discrimination. Exceptions to these ground rules were permitted in the following circumstances: states with severe BALANCE OF PAYMENTS difficulties, CUSTOMS UNIONS and TRADE BLOCS and discrimination where it was intentionally adopted for security purposes, including COLLECTIVE SECURITY actions by the UN.

As a forum for trade negotiations, GATT has promoted what might be termed as 'tariff disarmament' at a number of bargaining rounds of which the most significant, to date, were the KENNEDY and TOKYO meetings in the 1960s and 1970s, respectively. The current Uruguay Round is planned to finish in 1990. Trade issues are no longer the exclusive concern of GATT. Since 1947 the creation of the Organization for Economic Cooperation and Development (OECD) and the United Nations Conference on Trade and Development (UNCTAD) has meant that a variety of bodies, representing differing interests, particularly those of the NORTH and the SOUTH, are now involved in this ISSUE AREA.

## Gaullism

A loosely structured set of approaches, aspirations and assertions associated with the political life and legacy of the French military and political leader, Charles de Gaulle (1890–1970). Gaullism is derived from three sources: de Gaulle's memoirs, his public utterances, speeches and press conferences and his policies, particularly in the period after he became the first President of the Fifth Republic in 1958.

In the language of contemporary analysis, Gaullism may be termed STATE-CENTRIC. It is thus a reassertion of the REALIST view that STATES are the primary ACTORS in WORLD POLITICS. In the context of the development of closer integrative ties within Western Europe after the formation of the European Coal and Steel Community (ECSC) and the EC, Gaullism sought to eschew supranationalism in favour of a more confederal arrangement based upon the state. This conceptualization became known as *Europe des patries*. The peremptory pursuit of these ideas led to considerable stresses and strains within the Community throughout the period of de Gaulle's presidency of France (1958–69).

De Gaulle sought to resist what he saw as the encroachments of the United States by creating Europe as a Third Force between the hegemonial aspirations of the two SUPERPOWERS. The United Kingdom was seen as part of this 'Anglo-Saxon' tradition and was ironically dubbed as the 'Trojan horse' for US INTERVENTION in the continent. As a result the UK application for membership of the Communities was VETOED by de Gaulle in 1963.

In the context of military security politics, Gaullism provided the rationale for the development of France as an independent nuclear power with the creation of the *FORCE DE FRAPPE*. Although the infrastructure for this development was created during the Fourth Republic, it is generally agreed that the elaboration of this into an independent arm was essentially gaullist. Similarly, the French decision to withdraw from the unified military command structure of NATO in 1966 was perfectly explicable in terms of gaullist precepts. Indeed the 1966 decision had been signalled a long time before.

Under de Gaulle, France developed a high profile as the leading European critic of US FOREIGN POLICY. This criticism extended across the whole range of ISSUE AREAS from the VIETNAM WAR to the role of the dollar in the international payments system, from US INTERVENTION in Central America to the role of multinational corporations (MNCs).

How far Gaullism endures beyond its founder is a moot point. It certainly constitutes, in its most enduring aspect, a fundamentally different approach to the question of European INTEGRATION than that represented by supranational enthusiasts and it may be noted somewhat paradoxically that since joining the EC in 1973 successive governments in the United Kingdom have been doggedly gaullist in their approach to these issues.

## General Assembly

One of the principal organs of the UN. As its main arena for general political debate, the Assembly is the nearest institution to a genuine world forum that exists in contemporary international affairs. Unlike the other organs (the SECURITY COUNCIL, the Economic and Social Council, the Trusteeship Council, the Secretariat and the INTERNATIONAL COURT OF JUSTICE (ICJ)) the General Assembly is the only one in which all member STATES are represented. Its main function is discussion and RECOMMENDATION. Article 10 of the CHARTER gives an extremely wide mandate in regard to the scope of its functions. It can cover 'any questions or any matters within the scope of the present Charter or relating to the powers and functions of any organs provided for in the present Charter.' Despite this seemingly generous remit, there are two important limitations. First, Article 12 confines the Assembly to discussion of, but not recommendation on, any dispute or situation which is simultaneously under consideration by the Security Council. Secondly, its authority is confined to recommendations that are not binding on individual member states. In addition to discussion and recommendation, the Assembly exercises a supervisory role in relation to all the activities of the UN, and acts as the central coordinating body for all the other organs and agencies. A third major function is financial. It has the AUTHORITY to consider and approve the overall budget and to make recommendations on the budgets of the SPECIALIZED AGENCIES. The Assembly also has sole power to elect the non-permanent members of the Security Council, the Economic and Social Council and the Trusteeship Council and jointly with the Security Council it selects judges for the ICJ. On the recommendation of the Security Council it also appoints the SECRETARY-GENERAL. Again, alongside the Security Council, the General Assembly has control over admission to membership of the UN. Finally, the Assembly has a role in the amendment and revision of the Charter, although this is subject to RATIFICATION by the permanent members of the Security Council.

The very broad range of powers and functions allocated, combined with the tendency to interpret them expansively, have led many observers to conclude that the Assembly is an inefficient and cumbersome body. Suggestions are frequently made on the need for streamlining or slimming down, but the primary rationale of being the only world forum where all members can be heard defeats all efforts at reform.

Despite its apparent impotence in the area of DECISION-MAKING, the Assembly has played a significant role in the maintenance of INTERNATIONAL ORDER, especially during periods of Security Council stalemate. The Charter provides for the calling of 'special sessions' and it is in this area that the Assembly has had most effect. In particular the Uniting for Peace Resolution of 1950, which enables the Assembly to initiate action if the Security Council is unwilling or unable to, has significantly upgraded its importance. There is no doubt that the Assembly has played a larger part in the process of peaceful settlement of disputes than a strict reading of the Charter would indicate. The Uniting for Peace Resolution has been the basis for calling a number of emergency special sessions dealing with CRISES in such divergent areas as the Middle East, South Africa, Eastern Europe, the Congo and AFGHANISTAN. It has been estimated that more than 22 per cent of all disputes submitted to the UN have been dealt with solely by the General Assembly, and another 75 per cent have been considered in conjunction with the Security Council. Clearly, while the Assembly is not the primary agency for the settlement of disputes, it has succeeded in interpreting its role in this regard in quite a different way to that envisaged in 1945.

## General theories

Theories of WORLD POLITICS which aim to provide all-embracing explanations of inter-state behaviour are sometimes called 'grand' theories. The search for overarching propositions which could explain, predict and evaluate the structures and processes of INTERNATIONAL POLITICS is a recurring one in the history of speculation about the subject. Yet despite a number of spirited attempts there is little in the literature, classical or modern, that even approaches a general theory. Indeed, many commentators question its very possibility in the social sciences where standards of verification and proof, objectivity and subjectivity and controlled experimentation are necessarily of a different order to those in the natural sciences. Indeed, such is the contemporary theoretical disarray within the field that there is no general consensus on either the subject of the inquiry or the proper method of speculating about it. The TRADITIONAL or 'classical' view that theories of world politics should revolve around the STATE and the structure and processes of the STATE-SYSTEM as they relate to WAR and PEACE, has been challenged, and to a large extent replaced, by increased awareness of the importance of TRANSNATIONAL processes, economic structures and non-state actors. Nevertheless, despite evidence of its increasing irrelevance, the classical approach (which reached its fullest expression within the school of political REALISM) is still, especially among practitioners, the most pervasive and popular of all the quests for a general explanatory theory of international politics. Concentration on the causes of war and the conditions of peace or security within a broad STATE-CENTRIC spectrum has by and large set the theoretical framework of the study, even among those who openly disavow its impressionistic and non-scientific base. The failure to provide a comprehensive, internally consistent and coherent conceptual base which is not overtly crude or simplistic has led to an incremental approach among most academic practitioners. The quest for totality of explanation has been replaced by partial theories which are grounded in inductive empirical research. BEHAVIOURALISTS, for example, believe that the acquisition of knowledge is cumulative and its collation will eventually reveal an inner structure or pattern which explains the mysteries of the entire universe. TRADITIONALISTS however, are sceptical of such grand syntheses and acknowledge that the contingent element in politics will always preclude sophisticated theoretical understanding.

## Geneva Conventions

*See*: CONVENTIONS ON THE RULES OF WARFARE

## Genocide Convention

The Convention was passed by the GENERAL ASSEMBLY of the UNITED NATIONS ORGANIZATION in December 1948 and came into force in January 1951. Genocide is defined in the Second Article as the act of destroying, in whole or in part, a national, ethnical, racial or religious group. Such acts are held to include: killing, seriously injuring or causing mental harm to members of such groups, inflicting upon such groups adverse living conditions so that the physical destruction of the group is threatened, deliberate attempts to prevent members of the group from having children, and forcibly transferring children from one group to another.

In addition to punishing genocide itself, conspiracy to commit genocide, incitement to commit genocide, attempts to commit genocide and complicity in genocide are punishable. Persons held to have committed any of these acts are liable under the convention, whether they are acting in an individual capacity, or as leaders, officials, or agents of governments.

In principle, therefore, the Convention appears to establish a broad based REGIME for outlawing genocide. It also represents a major extension of international criminal law into an area of WORLD POLITICS highlighted by the Nuremberg trials. It is one of the few instances where 'general principles of law recognized by civilized nations' (see

Article 38 of the Statute of the INTERNATIONAL COURT OF JUSTICE for details) can be said to have had a major impact on the law creating process.

In practice, as is the case so often in the most contentious areas of INTERNATIONAL LAW, enforcement or IMPLEMENTATION of the Convention is more contingent and qualified. In particular, where such acts are carried out as part of government policy, or where such acts have the tacit support of the government of the STATE concerned, it may be difficult to bring the criminals to account. Furthermore, the charge of complicity may be levelled against other members of the UN, who when confronted with such evidence fail to enforce the standards enshrined in the Convention.

## Geopolitics

A method of FOREIGN POLICY analysis which seeks to understand, explain and predict international political behaviour primarily in terms of geographical variables, such as location, size, climate, topography, demography, natural resources and technological development and potential. Political identity and action is thus seen to be (more or less) determined by geography.

According to Harold Sprout in a seminal article (1963) the word 'geopolitics' is a loose translation of the German word 'geopolitik' which meant the exploitation of knowledge to serve the purposes of a national REGIME. In other words, German geo-policy was an overt and subjective policy science designed to further the nationalistic interests of the STATE. In this way, it came to be associated with justifying the aggressive posture of the Third Reich. This identification has had an unfortunate effect on the study of geopolitics, particularly in the English-speaking world, where the concept of *LEBENSRAUM* came to be seen as having a malign and sinister effect on German policy. Many concluded that the study of geography in conjunction with politics meant an obsession with strategy, which in turn meant a predilection for WAR and conquest. The German study of geopolitics as a pseudo-science is associated with the work of R. J. Kjellen, Friedrich Ratzel and more especially with the founding in 1924 of the Institute of Geopolitics in Munich under Karl Haushofer. Haushofer had strong links with the Nazi party and after Hitler's rise to power in 1933, he became an influential academic policy advisor. Because Haushofer and the Munich Institute were regarded as exploiting geographical concepts for specific power-political purposes the whole enterprise was frowned upon in UK and US academic circles where the term 'political geography' was preferred to the more value-laden 'geopolitics'.

Nevertheless, a number of important hypotheses have been advanced concerning the geographical dimension of political relationships. These concern the global distribution of land and sea, climatic variations, the distribution of raw materials and the distribution of people and institutions. In relation to the spatial distribution of land and sea, two names in particular stand out, both of whom were writing at the turn of the twentieth century, Mahan (1890) and Mackinder (1919). The gist of Mahan's thesis, which had an important and acknowledged impact on the development of the US navy, was as follows: given that the sea and the great oceans are continuous and uninterrupted and given that sea transport was more efficient and cost effective than land transport, whoever controlled the sea would soon ascend to primacy in WORLD POLITICS. Ability to control the sea depended on possession of a powerful navy, strategically located overseas BASES, and an insular and defendable home base. Insular STATES with these properties (and he saw the United States as a 'continentally insular' state) would therefore play the major roles in establishing the future patterns of world politics. Mackinder, while agreeing with Mahan that the key to understanding world politics is the layout and configuration of land and sea, reached the opposite conclusion and saw control of the continental heartland as the vital objective if HEGEMONY was to be achieved.

Geopolitical hypotheses connecting climate (i.e. recurring patterns of weather) to political behaviour have a long history stretching back at least to the ancient Greeks. It is known, for example, that both Hippocrates (400 BC) and Aristotle (300 BC) made correlations between climate and human behaviour. It is a commonplace assumption (though no more than that) that the Mediterranean and milder North temperate climates are more conducive to the development of civilization and rapid technological growth than the more equatorial or Arctic conditions that prevail elsewhere. Therefore, cyclic fluctuations in climate are important (though not fully understood) variables in predicting political behaviour. This, of course, is why all states are concerned about the scientific possibility of effecting weather-controlling schemes; the geopolitical consequences are potentially enormous. Other hypotheses commonly advanced concern the distribution of natural resources and population distribution. Again neither are conclusive although it is assumed as a rule of thumb that state power is directly related to the ability to convert raw materials into military instruments of statecraft, and also that sheer manpower can be decisive ('God is on the side of the big battalions'). However, technological expertise and knowledge can and do whittle away at these premises.

The term geopolitics has now acquired some academic respectability although the subject is still not central to mainline INTERNATIONAL POLITICS courses. In the United States especially, it has had a number of outstanding practitioners, including H. & M. Sprout, J. Hertz and N. J. Spykman. It is still a somewhat neglected field but it has seen something of a revival in the area of military/defence analysis. One of the major pitfalls associated with the approach has been its avowedly determinist

character, although its more sophisticated adherents now stress that their hypotheses are 'possibilistic' rather than 'probablistic'.
*See also*: HEARTLAND THEORY

## GLCM

A Ground-Launched Cruise Missile. The platform for the CRUISE MISSILE in this mode would be a mobile transporter vehicle. The TECHNOLOGY of the GLCM is essentially the same as that for the air-launched cruise missile (ALCM) and sea-launched cruise missile (SLCM). Like these, the GLCM is in principle a dual-capable system, that is to say, it can carry either CONVENTIONAL or NUCLEAR warheads.

## Globalism

Globalism has two discrete and analytically separate meanings. First, it is used in the context of FOREIGN POLICY analysis to characterize an ORIENTATION taken by HEGEMONIAL STATES. Secondly, it is used in the context of WORLD POLITICS to identify a particular approach to issues perceived to be global.

In the first sense, therefore, globalism is the tendency to collapse the distinction between the NATIONAL INTEREST and ISSUE AREAS in the rest of the system. Accordingly, there is a high propensity for such 'globalist' states to evince interventionist tendencies when conducting their foreign policy. Globalism requires a significant CAPABILITY, particularly in the military and/or economic dimensions and the willingness to use such capability to secure perceived goals, often at considerable cost. Ideologically, globalism will be sustained and justified by reference to a world view which sees the global ACTOR as uniquely qualified to pursue interventionist behaviour. This perceptual sense has appropriately been termed 'nationalistic universalism'.

In the contemporary system, both the United States and the Soviet Union have shown, at times, globalist tendencies. Militarily, they are the most significant single state actors in the system. Economically, they offer competing 'models' for development, while ideologically, US exceptionalism and Soviet attachment to Leninist thinking about IMPERIALISM have encouraged the leaders in both states to follow interventionist policies, particularly in the THIRD WORLD.

Globalism in the second sense refers to the viewpoint which holds that such problems as POLLUTION, population or conservation can only be dealt with on a global scale. Moreover, this view sees the state-as-actor approach as being inadequate to the challenge these issues present. Non-state actors must be admitted into the policy process if the global challenge is to be met. This admission will take place at a number of stages. First, in the DEFINITION OF THE SITUATION non-state actors, including individuals, may be able to provide the expertise and the understanding to reach an adequate definition. Secondly, at the IMPLEMENTATION stage non-state actors, particularly INTERNATIONAL ORGANIZATIONS may be required to establish the ground rules and monitor the subsequent conduct of the participants.

While it does not necessarily lead to advocacy of WORLD GOVERNMENT, globalism does emphasize the extent to which cooperation must be conducted among a system of mixed actors. Accordingly it can be regarded as a form of PLURALISM. Many of the assumptions of globalism are derived from theories about collective goods. To the extent that it is optimistic or pessimistic in its prognosis, globalism is one of the chief constituents of FUTUROLOGY.

The presence of two globalist states in one system at the same time has led many observers to generalize these tendencies into a structural characteristic called bipolarity. The BIPOLAR system, particularly that variant termed 'tight' bipolarity, is both cause and effect of globalism. The latter gives a distinct bipolar effect to the system, while bipolarity causes the HEGEMONIAL states to engage in 'tit-for-tat' interventionism which typifies globalism. This circularity is quite usual in world politics and is termed a FEEDBACK loop.

Globalism is an extremely costly policy to implement, particularly for any length of time. Paradoxically the costs of globalism are greater in the military context if policies are seen to be failing, while in the economic context they are greater if policies are seen to be succeeding. The most traumatic example of the costs of globalism in the contemporary period must be that of US intervention in the VIETNAM WAR up to the final disengagement in 1973. The development and subsequent consolidation of policies based upon mutual nuclear DETERRENCE has caused further modification in the unmitigated pursuit of globalism. The existence of a significant, if somewhat heterogeneous, group of THIRD WORLD states has meant that at best globalism can be said to cause a 'loose' bipolar configuration.

## Gold exchange standard

A system of international payments where individual currencies are tied to a fixed exchange rate with a stipulated currency which is, itself, fully convertible into gold, also at a fixed rate. After 1945 under the BRETTON WOODS system, a gold exchange standard operated with the US dollar acting as a fully convertible store of value and means of exchange within the system. This system lasted for a quarter of a century and under its aegis international economic relations were rebuilt and rekindled. Impressive growth targets were achieved by individual STATES particularly amongst the ADVANCED INDUSTRIAL COUNTRIES (AICs) and overall world TRADE increased significantly as a result. The system collapsed in the 1970s when following the devaluation of the US dollar it became impossible to 'hold the line' on fixed parities and, instead currencies were allowed to fluctuate or 'float'.

With hindsight it can be seen that maintenance of the system was too contingent upon the strength of the dollar and the willingness of other international ACTORS to hold dollars and not to convert them into gold. France, in particular, was reluctant to cooperate in this fashion arguing that, in effect, other major trading states were being invited thereby to underwrite US FOREIGN POLICY. Economically, it could be argued that the system of fixed parities was too conservative and that it encouraged political and financial authorities to regard a particular rate as sacrosanct. Accordingly, when adjustments were made in rates the situational context would invariably be one of CRISIS.

Analytically, the post-war Gold Exchange Standard can appropriately be seen as correlated with US HEGEMONY in the system. This was clearly institutionalized in the IMF and given its first and perhaps clearest expression in the European Recovery Programme or MARSHALL PLAN of 1948–52. Similarly, the collapse of the system in the 1970s is also correlated with the relative decline in US ability to maintain the REGIME.

## Gold standard

A system of international payments where individual currencies are tied to a fixed exchange rate with gold. This pricing of individual currencies enables exchange rates between them to be calculated, pro rata, once their gold price is known. This rate, at which it is possible to exchange one currency for another, and/or for gold, is known as PARITY.

The international gold standard was an important mechanism for underwriting international TRADE and payments for almost two hundred years up to 1914. Indeed it reached its peak in the decades immediately before 1914, when the United Kingdom was the leading STATE in the international system under the HEGEMONIAL arrangement known as PAX BRITANNICA. The leading STATES in the system went off the standard during the First World War in order to finance the enormous expenditures caused therein.

An attempt was made after 1919 to return to the standard but the recession in economic activity known as the 'Great Depression' caused states to abandon the standard and to allow currencies to fluctuate or 'float'. Thus, the United Kingdom left the standard in 1931 and the United States in 1933. By accident rather than design, therefore, the system became in effect a GOLD EXCHANGE STANDARD during these rather uncertain years.

After 1945 a full-blown gold exchange standard was instituted under the BRETTON WOODS system. Reflecting the hegemonial position of the United States, the dollar became in effect 'as good as gold' as a store of value and means of exchange within the system. Like the old pre-1914 system parities were fixed against the dollar, while that currency had a fixed parity in terms of gold. This system itself collapsed in the early 1970s and, to date, no attempt has been made to reintroduce a system of international liquidity based upon gold. Apart from the economic drawbacks of such a move, politically, reinstituting gold would be resisted by all those who regard the Union of South Africa as an international pariah and would not want to see a windfall increase in that state's wealth effected so gratuitously.

## Good Neighbor

An attempt to reverse the traditional US policy of protectionism and INTERVENTION in Central and Latin America. Under the MONROE DOCTRINE (1823) and the Roosevelt Corollary (1904) the United States had sought unrivalled hemispheric superiority in the region to the extent that it reserved the right to intervene, by force of arms if necessary, in the internal affairs of sovereign STATES south of the Rio Grande. This policy, not unnaturally, attracted much criticism and resentment with the res-

ult that the United States in the twentieth century began to abandon direct methods of coercive control and moved towards a more subtle mechanism of dominance. (*See*: DOLLAR DIPLOMACY). In 1933 President Roosevelt inaugurated another more dramatic shift in American policy when he proclaimed the Good Neighbor doctrine. In his inaugural address he declared that he 'would dedicate this Nation to the policy of the good neighbor who resolutely respects himself and, because he does so, respects the rights of others'. No geographical region was mentioned, but it soon became clear that this policy initiative was directed at Latin America. Accordingly in 1933, at the seventh conference of the US states in Montevideo, the United States signed a NON-INTERVENTION treaty, in 1934 it abrogated the Platt Amendment which had placed restrictions on Cuban SOVEREIGNTY, in 1935 it withdrew troops from Haiti and in 1936 it signed a treaty with Panama terminating its right of military intervention outside the Canal zone. After the Second World War the Rio Treaty, the first general security pact created by the United States, was signed and this process culminated in the establishment of the Organization of American States (OAS) in 1948, which seeks to draw the states of the REGION closer together in social and economic matters and deals with security, principally the threat of the spread of COMMUNISM in the hemisphere.

Most analysts consider the Good Neighbor policy to be somewhat fraudulent. It replaced policies of overt military intervention and financial control with a more indirect form of US dominance, namely the enlisting of indigenous political, military and business ELITES to maintain US interests. The US Export–Import Bank has been used to lock the economic systems of the individual states firmly into the US economy, and the United States has trained and equipped local police and military forces with the specific purpose of suppressing national revolutionary movements which may threaten their dominance. US support for unpopular REGIMES coupled with instances of military intervention (Cuba 1961, Dominican Republic 1965, Grenada 1986, Panama 1989) have led many to question the CREDIBILITY of this policy. No one doubts though, that its purpose is to maintain US HEGEMONY.

## Good offices

A technique in INTERNATIONAL LAW relating to the involvement of a third party in the peaceful settlement of disputes. The procedure involves attempts by the third party to bring the opposing sides to NEGOTIATION. In theory it can be distinguished from 'mediation' which implies the active participation of the third party in the negotiation process itself, but in practice the two approaches often converge. Good offices is generally non-participatory and is limited to providing a channel of communication between the disputants, thus paving the way for direct BILATERAL DIPLOMACY. It differs from ADJUDICATION and ARBITRATION in that its object is to stimulate diplomatic dialogue between the contending parties and not to stipulate settlement provisions or to provide means for their implementation. The HAGUE CONVENTION of 1899 and 1907 tended to classify 'good offices' and 'mediation' together. Thus both 'are exclusively concerned with the giving of advice and are never of binding force'. In practice mediation tends to be more activist than good offices. All signatories to the Conventions were accorded rights to offer good offices or mediation in international disputes and the offer was not to be construed by the disputants as an unfriendly act. Examples of good offices would be Switzerland's role in formally ending hostilities between Japan and the United States in 1945, or the part played by France in initiating US–North Vietnamese negotiations in Paris in February 1970. An example of mediation would be the US role in the Middle East in 1973–4. In the latter case the third party played a much more

INTERVENTIONIST role than in either of the former cases.

It is useful to distinguish between 'good offices' and 'interest sections'. The latter usually refers to situations where diplomatic relations have been broken off and a third party embassy is entrusted with overseeing the interests of one side. Sometimes, a STATE may request that its own diplomats be allowed to operate from a third party embassy. This occurred during the FALKLANDS conflict when the United Kingdom established an interest section in the Swiss Embassy in Buenos Aires. Using the good offices of a neutral third state or establishing interest sections are common devices in a world characterized by extreme ideological hostility. Thus, Israel, Libya, Iran, South Africa, as well as the United States and the Soviet Union have all at some time found it convenient to establish direct contact with their opponents through friendly third-party intermediaries.

## Gorbachev doctrine

Western media term for new initiatives, particularly relating to SUPERPOWER cooperation in Soviet FOREIGN POLICY since 1985 under the tutelage of Mikhail Gorbachev. The reorientation of Soviet domestic society symbolized by the concepts of *glasnost* (openness) and *perestroika* (restructuring) were perceived to have important external consequences. In 1985–6 the Soviet DECISION-MAKING ELITE apparently concluded that superpower status and the ideological and political HEGEMONY that this implied carried a heavy economic cost with correspondingly little positive benefit. Despite the ostensible 'success' of the Brezhnev era which witnessed the US debacle in Vietnam, socialist REVOLUTIONS in Angola, Mozambique and Ethiopia as well as a heightening of revolutionary momentum in Latin America, the Soviet Union had made little tangible gains. In fact these initiatives proved burdensome. Angola and Mozambique quickly assumed debtor status, Ethiopia was ravaged by famine, and the 1979 invasion of AFGHANISTAN put increasing strains on the Soviet military and economic systems. An energy crisis in Eastern Europe in 1984–5 further exacerbated the problem, as did growing Soviet dependence on Western sources of high TECHNOLOGY and vital food commodities. In addition a renewal of the ARMS RACE with the United States and more especially disquiet at the proposed US Strategic Defense Initiative (SDI) and the economic costs that the installation of a reciprocal system would invoke, resulted in a fundamental reappraisal of the basic goals and direction of Russian foreign and defence policies. In particular, the Gorbachev doctrine has led to the Intermediate Range Nuclear Force (INF) TREATY signed in Washington in 1987, which is the most significant ARMS CONTROL measure since the beginning of the COLD WAR era in 1946. It has also led to direction-shifts in Soviet involvement in Afghanistan, Southern Africa, the Middle East and the Persian Gulf. In Afghanistan (the invasion of which Gorbachev declared to be 'a mistake') Soviet forces were withdrawn in 1989. In Southern Africa, it is widely believed that the removal of Cuban troops from Angola and its linkage with Namibian INDEPENDENCE from South Africa is a direct consequence of Gorbachev's 'new thinking' about the Soviet role in the REGION. In the Middle East it has led to new PEACE initiatives by the Soviet Foreign Minister Edvard Shevardnadze (a Gorbachev appointee) and the likelihood of a restoration of diplomatic relations with Israel. Similarly in the Persian Gulf region there have been attempts at a diplomatic RAPPROCHEMENT with Iran. All these directional changes have been perceived to be logical consequences of the 'revolution' in Soviet domestic, social and economic policies signalled by *glasnost* and *perestroika*. On the level of ecopolitics the relative openness of the Soviet authorities regarding the Chernobyl nuclear accident in 1986 is the most dramatic manifestation of the Gorbachev doctrine thus far. It is difficult

to assess the depth to which the doctrine has penetrated within Soviet DECISION-MAKING circles but most observers believe that a rationalization of the complex, compartmentalized and bureaucratic character of foreign policy formulation is now under way. Clearly, reconstruction and modernization of Soviet society has meant a large scale transfer of resources away from the military sector into the civil sector. This in turn has led to a new spirit of DETENTE in WORLD POLITICS. How long this lasts is a function of the success of *perestroika* and the political longevity of its principal architect.

Many analysts have argued that the liberalization of Eastern Europe which occurred dramatically in 1989 was a direct consequence of the Gorbachev doctrine, in particular its departure from the BREZHNEV penchant for active interference in the internal affairs of BLOC STATES. While this radical policy shift has been welcomed outside the Soviet Union the internal repercussions are a cause of great concern not merely over Gorbachev's own political future, but more seriously over the continued coherence of the Union itself and of the leading role of the COMMUNIST party within it. For over seventy years, the Communist party has been the unifying force which kept more than 100 different nationalities together within the largest country on earth, covering about one-sixth of the earth's surface, and with a total population of about 280 million. Growing nationalist unrest, ethnic rivalries and economic dissatisfaction – all of which have been exacerbated by *glasnost* and *perestroika* – have created secessionist movements in the rimland Republics which may well lead to the disintegration of the present structure of the Soviet empire. By the end of 1989 the Baltic Republics (Estonia, Latvia and Lithuania) had already signalled their interest to seek a new relationship with Moscow. The other 'autonomous' republics, Ukraine, Byelorussia, Moldavia, Armenia, Azerbaijan, Georgia and the Muslim republics of Kazakhstan, Kirgizia,

Tadzhikstan, Turkmenistan and Uzbekistan will undoubtedly follow suit. What form the new relationship between the periphery and the centre will take is not clear, but few doubt that the structure will be a much looser one involving varying degrees of limited SOVEREIGNTY. In the Muslim republics, which have a combined and rapidly growing population of nearly 50 million, which makes them the biggest underlying threat to the Slav identity of the Soviet Union, the problem is confounded by the rise of ISLAMIC fundamentalism and moves to open FRONTIERS with Iran and Turkey. Whether the Gorbachev doctrine can survive the possible dismemberment of the Soviet Union itself is a matter for debate.

## Great powers

Term associated with traditional, especially REALIST, analyses of INTERNATIONAL POLITICS. It refers to the ranking of STATES primarily in terms of their military and economic capabilities. Hence the hierarchical structure of WORLD POLITICS is often characterized as consisting of great powers (or today, SUPERPOWERS), MIDDLE POWERS, SMALL POWERS and MICRO-STATES. The term itself can be traced back to fifteenth century Italian politics but the first time it was formally adopted as an orthodox diplomatic concept was with the signing of the Treaty of Chaumont in 1817. As a result of the Congress of VIENNA (1815) five states, Austria, Britain, France, Prussia and Russia, had informally conferred on themselves great power status. The intention was that these states acting in concert would adopt a managerial role in relation to the maintenance of order in the European STATE-SYSTEM. The CONCERT SYSTEM with its emphasis on controlled MULTILATERAL management thus replaced the somewhat 'loose' BALANCE OF POWER system that had preceded the Napoleonic Wars. Throughout the nineteenth century there was a self-conscious effort by these states (they were

sometimes joined by Italy after 1860) to enforce, in their own interests, the 'PEACE and security' of Europe. The interests of lesser powers, for example Poland, were often sacrificed on the altar of great power unity. Outside Europe two other states came to be regarded as having great power status: the United States after its defeat of Spain in 1898 and Japan after victory over Russia in 1904–5. In the twentieth century the tendency to assign special status in diplomatic conferences continued and great power status was institutionalized in both the LEAGUE OF NATIONS and the UNITED NATIONS where five states (the United States, the United Kingdom, France, the Soviet Union and China) were given permanent membership of the SECURITY COUNCIL with the power of VETO. Since the Second World War the term 'great power' has given way to 'superpower' a word first coined by Fox (1944). The use of the latter term denotes the emergence of a new class of power which is clearly superior to the traditional European great powers. Today it is commonly recognized that the United States, the Soviet Union and perhaps China are superpowers, but although the nomenclature may have altered the managerial roles they seek to adopt remain in essence the same.

It is a matter of some dispute in the literature of world politics as to what constitutes great powerhood. In most discussions the military dimension is paramount: great powers (or superpowers) are generally those that can maintain their security independently and against all others. They are in the first rank of military prowess. This means, at the very least, a developed strategic nuclear CAPABILITY. It is sometimes alleged that economic strength alone can confer great power status. Thus, Japan is often spoken of in these terms. But although economic strength is a necessary condition, it is not generally regarded as a sufficient one.

In addition to military and economic strength, great powers normally have global if not universal interests and are usually characterized as possessing the political will to pursue them. The United States, for example, although long regarded by others as a great power, has not always displayed the political will to behave like one, especially during the period until 1917 and between 1921–41. It was only after the Second World War that the United States consistently and self-consciously adopted this posture. The United Kingdom and France, on the other hand, have frequently displayed the political will associated with great power status and also sometimes perceive themselves as having world-wide interests, but because they are not in the first rank in military and economic terms they are no longer considered to be members of the great power club. They are more properly regarded as MIDDLE or secondary powers even though they are still accorded the formal or institutional trappings of membership of this category in the UN.

## Green movement

Primarily a European phenomenon, at present there are Green parties in Austria, Belgium, the United Kingdom, Finland, France, Holland, Ireland, Luxembourg, Sweden, Switzerland and West Germany. They are political parties in the sense that they contest national and local elections but they also represent a TRANSNATIONAL movement which seeks to protect the environment and establish peaceful relations. According to the Greens environmental protection is not compatible with the modern industrial system either in its socialist or capitalist guise. Industrialization on a global basis will not only destroy the earth's ecological systems, but the intense resource-competition it generates will eventually lead to a build-up of political tensions to such a pitch that NUCLEAR WAR becomes a high probability. Linking ECOLOGY and PEACE in this way the aim of Green politics is nothing short of a transformation of INTERNATIONAL SOCIETY. The orthodox model of a multi-STATE-SYSTEM

characterized by economic competition and nuclear balance is rejected as indeed is the reformist view which seeks marginal systemic changes such as arms reduction and some wealth transfer from the NORTH to the SOUTH.

The Greens have been active for over a decade and although they have not achieved a significant measure of political support (apart, perhaps, from in West Germany) they have succeeded in highlighting a number of pressing environmental problems, especially the issue of air POLLUTION and acid rain. In this connection, in 1979, thirty-five STATES signed the Convention of Long-Range Transboundary Air Pollution and in 1980 Canada succeeded in getting the United States to monitor cross-border pollution drift. In 1983 West Germany began a ten-year plan to reduce acid rain emissions and also pressed for EC support. In 1984, the United States and the Soviet Union entered into talks about the acid rain problem and in 1985 the UN Economic Commission for Europe succeeded in establishing a PROTOCOL signed by nineteen European states (plus Canada) whereby they agreed to 30 per cent cuts in sulphur dioxide emission by 1993. The United Kingdom and the United States refused to join what became known as 'the 30 per cent Club'. In 1987 the leading industrial states signed the Montreal Protocol as a preliminary to controlling the emission of chlorofluorocarbons (CFCs) which have been identified as the major ozone-layer destroyers, and which are found in commonplace consumer items such as refrigerators, aerosol cans, air conditioners, foam furniture and packaging. A total ban on CFCs is envisaged by the year 2000. In 1989 a government-sponsored London conference on the problem was attended by representatives from 110 states and it soon became clear that this particular issue is confounded by the likelihood that developing states, including China, are now set to install hundreds of millions of refrigerators containing CFCs as part of their quest for MODERNIZATION. This conflict between ECOLOGY and development is a sensitive one but there are signs that in the developed world at least, the message of the green movement is set to penetrate even into the most conservative realms of political discourse. The assembling of a 'global repair kit' is now part of the survival agenda of WORLD POLITICS.

Thus, although the Greens initially appeared to lack mass popular support, in the strict electoral sense, the alternative strategies for survival they, among others, present may yet prove to be a significant shift away from conventional STATE-CENTRIC orientations. The Chernobyl disaster of 1986 demonstrated clearly that the global biosphere is indifferent to national BOUNDARIES, and that the sovereign state alone cannot, or will not, resolve migratory transnational problems of this kind.

## GRIT

Acronym for Graduated Reciprocation in Tension-Reduction, GRIT is intended as a series of policy moves made between adversaries that will lead to de-escalation and amelioration of the CONFLICT. It was first proposed in 1962 by the American psychologist Charles Osgood. Osgood argued that the measures envisioned by GRIT would be modest and limited but, by RECIPROCITY, would proceed on an incremental basis to cover more and more areas of the adversarial relationship. Osgood argued, rather neatly, for a reversal of the ARMS RACE dynamic. As tension–reduction actions are reciprocated then a downward spiral will produce a reduction in the perceived need for arms. GRIT was certainly not restricted to the ARMS RACE, however, and Osgood saw the possibilities for confidence-building actions across a whole range of economic, social, cultural, scientific and technical relationships. Although Osgood was specifically writing with the so-called COLD WAR in mind, the GRIT dynamic can, in principle, be applied to any chronic and persistent conflict situation.

Conceptually GRIT is a form of gradualism or INCREMENTALISM. That is to say POLICY-MAKERS should set themselves limited finite targets which can be achieved without significant redefinition of basic values and long term goals. The step-by-step approach, moreover, has the advantage, it is argued, of allowing policy-makers to avoid running too many or too great a series of risks when implementing the strategy.

## Grotian view of international society

Concept employed originally by Martin Wight and developed by Hedley Bull to describe a twentieth century view of INTERNATIONAL SOCIETY which appears to bear great resemblance to the classical presentations of Hugo Grotius (1583–1645) in *Mare Liberum* (1609) and *De Jure Belli ac Pacis, On the Law of War and Peace* (1625). Bull's view is that underlying much of the theory and practice of INTERNATIONAL RELATIONS since the First World War and enshrined in the Covenant of the LEAGUE OF NATIONS, the Paris Pact, the UN CHARTER and the charter of the International Military Tribunal at Nuremburg is a formula for orderly international conduct which is largely derived from the DOMESTIC ANALOGY as used by seventeenth century social contract theorists. The central Grotian assumption is that of the solidarity, or potential solidarity, of STATES with respect to the enforcement of INTERNATIONAL LAW. The doctrine seeks to establish WORLD ORDER by restricting the rights of states to go to WAR for political purposes and promote the idea that FORCE can only legitimately be used to further the purposes and goals of the international community as a whole. In other words, as in domestic society, the private use of violence is severely proscribed. The rules which Grotius devised were biased in favour of the 'just' party and therefore designed to support and encourage a solidarist conception of the international community.

The principle of collective security is the culmination of the neo-Grotian movement in twentieth century international thought, the idea being that, apart from SELF-DEFENCE, the legitimate use of FORCE is assigned to INTERNATIONAL SOCIETY itself and not its separate members. Of course, this formula depends for its success on the common RECOGNITION by states of a degree of communality, a willingness to forgo narrower conceptions of the NATIONAL INTEREST and a desire to promote the wider cause of international solidarity. None of these essential prerequisites operated during the inter-war years with the result that not only was the new Grotian world order not forthcoming but also that older devices for the maintenance of order (e.g. BALANCE OF POWER) were weakened to such an extent that they too failed to keep the PEACE. Bull's conclusion is that, although the attempt to apply the solidarist formula has failed in the twentieth century, this does not mean that conditions will never arise when it might succeed.

## Groupthink

Groupthink is the tendency, noted in some small group DECISION-MAKING situations, for individuals within a group to cease thinking for themselves and to merge their opinions with the prevailing group viewpoint. As a result, these individuals may fail to voice doubts and disagreements about decisions that are under consideration by the group. This tendency towards conformity and concurrence may so inhibit critical thinking that fundamental, and even fatal, errors will occur. In summary, then, groupthink is a theory of defective decision-making.

The US social psychologist, Irving Janis (1972), first used the idea. In his book, Janis compares and contrasts four FOREIGN POLICY 'fiascoes' with two successes – all the examples being taken from US FOREIGN POLICY in the twentieth century – and then draws certain inferences about groupthink

and how it might be avoided in the future. There is, for Janis, an inverse relationship between the groupthink syndrome and the effective performance of the group.

Janis argues that the primary causal condition for groupthink to occur is group cohesiveness. Loyalty to the group, and in particular loyalty to the leader, is likely to be important. Individuals may feel that taking an independent line will lead them into conflict with colleagues whose respect and friendship they value. This attitude will make the would-be deviant think hard before challenging the intellectual orthodoxy of the majority.

In the 1972 original, and in the 1982 revision, Irving Janis stipulates other antecedent conditions. The most significant of these are:

1. That the group is isolated from contradictory and critical opinions that would otherwise significantly criticize the policy.
2. That the LEADERSHIP within the group is 'directive', that is to say that the group has a strong committed leadership.
3. The existence of a high level of stress within the group caused by a PERCEPTION that the stakes at issue are high. In short, that the group faces a CRISIS.

These antecedent conditions are necessary, although not sufficient, conditions for the occurrence of groupthink. The principal defects caused by groupthink can be summarized as:

1. The group fails to survey a sufficient range of alternatives or objectives.
2. The group fails to examine the risks involved due to wishful thinking.
3. The group fails to re-examine courses of action that had been previously rejected.
4. The group fails to work out contingency plans.
5. The group shows poor information search and excessive bias in evaluating that information that is processed.

Janis's work on decision-making and the groupthink syndrome is certainly prescriptive. By contrasting 'fiascoes' and 'successes', by stipulating how groupthink might be avoided, Janis is clearly identified as an optimist who believes that errors can be avoided, or at least reduced in number and consequence, by more vigilant attention to process and procedure.

Other approaches to decision-making have avoided the dichotomy between 'good' and 'bad' that emerges from Janis's work. Thus at least one analyst has suggested that POLICY-MAKING consists, not of looking for the best solution, but rather for 'satisfactory' ones, following a procedure known as 'bounded rationality'. If one starts from the position that policy-making is the art of 'muddling through', then Janis's checklist of allegedly defective processes looks uneasily like the norm. Recent work on the bureaucratic structure in which policy is made has suggested that 'standard operating procedures' play an influential role in policy-making within the organizational milieu.

Irving Janis's groupthink ideas remain a provocative and perceptive view of how small groups of key decision-makers may reach decisions. Approaching the question from the very distinguished tradition of US 'group dynamics' ideas, he has pointed to the impact that close loyalties and affiliations can have upon all of us when placed in situations of great stress and strain.

## Guerrilla warfare

The word 'guerrilla' is derived from the Spanish and means literally a small WAR. Its original use refers to the involvement of Spanish irregular forces in the Peninsula War (1808–14) in support of Wellington. In this instance guerrilla war was adopted after the regular Spanish armies had been defeated by the French invaders. This early nineteenth century use of guerrilla warfare established many of the ground rules for this type of combat. First, the physical environment of the Iberian peninsula was sufficiently extensive and formidable to afford a suitable context for hit-and-run tactics.

Secondly, the local population were generally supportive of the guerrillas. This provided the Spanish with valuable INTELLIGENCE as well as material support. Thirdly, the Spanish enjoyed external support from Napoleon's opponents, in particular from Wellington's forces. These factors of isolation, support from the population and external assistance have remained important variables in successful guerrilla campaigns ever since.

Throughout the nineteenth century this type of irregular combat continued to be used as an adjunct to CONVENTIONAL warfare. A defeated ARMY might turn to guerrilla tactics to sustain some kind of opposition to the victors. The Second Boer War (1899–1902) was a precursor of things to come later in the twentieth century with regard to this kind of campaigning. It was truly an asymmetric CONFLICT in the sense used by writers on PROTRACTED WAR. Although not revolutionary in the sense that can be applied to PEOPLE'S WARS of later in the century, the Boers were strongly motivated by NATIONALISM and an opposition to British IMPERIALISM. Although they were ultimately defeated, the Boers demonstrated again the principles of mobility and a supportive population in the conduct of such campaigns. On the British side a strategy of isolating the guerrillas from the supportive population was tried and eventually found to be successful. At the same time the prosecution of the Boer War caused serious rifts and schisms within the British political system and between Britain and other states in Europe.

During the First World War, guerrilla warfare was used with some success by the Arab forces who rebelled against Turkish rule following certain British encouragement in 1915. The British promised Husain Ibn Ali, the Sherif of Mecca, RECOGNITION and support for moves towards Arab INDEPENDENCE in return for support for the British war against the Turks. The Arab Revolt that followed was chronicled by the enigmatic T. E. Lawrence in his *Seven*

*Pillars of Wisdom* (1926). Lawrence reiterated the by now standard operating procedures of the guerrilla exponent: mobility and a supportive population, the need for a protracted war and appropriate motivation.

Guerrilla warfare developed most of its technical characteristics between the Peninsula War and the Arab Revolt. Thereafter its character changed as it became the principal *modus operandi* for parties and factions seeking to effect REVOLUTIONARY changes in a STATE or a region. In particular, it was with Mao Tse-Tung and the ideas of People's War that the paradigm shift took place. Guerrilla warfare is now used by insurgents of all descriptions fighting protracted wars against incumbent systems. In the lexicon of protracted war, guerrilla methods occupy the second (of three) stages. The term is often used somewhat loosely when the user really intends to talk about INSURGENCY.

### Gunboat diplomacy

The phrase refers to the use of warships as an instrument of FOREIGN POLICY. It is particularly associated with British IMPERIAL policies in the nineteenth century. Britain's general naval strategy was to keep most of the fleet in home waters and occasionally despatch a squadron to a particular REGION so as to restore order, to enforce the payment of debts or engage in punitive INTERVENTION. The overall purpose was to initiate sudden, limited intervention to defuse a CRISIS and to discourage repetition of the alleged offence. In this way, gunboat DIPLOMACY is associated with active COERCION, albeit of a limited kind, rather than with a passive SHOW OF FORCE. The term is a species of 'naval diplomacy' though in contemporary strategic analysis, the latter normally refers to a 'signalling' role rather than one involving actual combat. Naval warships are used as highly visible symbols of POWER to reinforce policy directives or to deter possible obstacles to their success. Indeed, although the classical period of imperial gunboat diplomacy may be over, the use of warships as instruments of foreign policy short of all-out actual engagement is still considered important. Contemporary naval diplomacy involves a wide variety of tasks including the use of warships to signal intentions to an adversary, deploying them in order to negotiate from strength, or using them for display purposes ('showing the FLAG') to reinforce or create a more compliant or supportive mood. In this way, the high profile 'presence' of naval forces has become the rationale underlying their peacetime strategic utility.

# H

## Hague Peace conferences

These occurred in 1899 and 1907 and were self-conscious attempts by a major section of the international community (twenty-six STATES participated in the first conference, forty-four in the second) to clarify and codify rules relating to arms limitation and the occurrence of and conduct in WAR. They were significant in that they were a revival of the conference system that had monitored the 'PEACE of Europe' from 1815–54 (see CONCERT SYSTEM). But unlike the Concert system, they were not confined to the GREAT POWERS alone and their deliberations were much more specific and particular. They produced no substantive ARMS CONTROL measures (except for a rather vague resolution that all states should restrict their DEFENCE budgets for the 'welfare of mankind') but nevertheless are important as they represent the first general conference on DISARMAMENT and in this sense laid down the ground rules for subsequent initiatives on arms limitation. The most significant practical innovation produced at the Hague was the establishment of a PERMANENT COURT OF ARBITRATION, forerunner of the Permanent Court of International Justice and the INTERNATIONAL COURT OF JUSTICE. The conference also produced rules relating to conduct in war, treatment of PRISONERS OF WAR and the rights of neutrals, as well as codifying conventions relating to land and sea warfare. On a political level, the conferences were beset by great power rivalry, especially that between Germany and Britain, neither of whom were greatly interested in MULTILATERAL across-the-board reductions in FORCE levels. Despite this, and despite the fact that the Hague conferences failed to prevent the First World War or even to limit the excesses of the participants in it, they are an important development in INTERNATIONAL POLITICS and law as they prepared the ground for postwar attempts to regularize international behaviour. Participation was virtually universal; it was not confined to one class of state, and deliberations were conducted on the basis of sovereign equality. All these factors, plus the creation of a skeletal PEACEKEEPING body, constitute step-level functions in the development of INTERNATIONAL LAW and ORGANIZATION. The Hague conventions created the basis for the modern law of war in the sense that they codified existing state practice and customary international law. The norms and standards embodied therein are still binding as TREATY rules, except where later treaties (e.g. the GENEVA CONVENTION of 1949) have superseded them.

## Hallstein doctrine

Pronounced in 1955 by West German Minister Walter Hallstein, it declared that the Federal Republic of Germany would no longer maintain diplomatic relations with the states recognizing the German Democratic Republic (GDR). Its purpose was to isolate the GDR and to reinforce Chancellor Adenauer's insistence that the Federal Republic 'is the sole legitimate representative of the German people in international affairs'. Acceptance of the Adenauer position was part of the package of agreements reached by the Nine Power London Conference of 1954 which was ostensibly called to sort out the issue of German rearmament and membership of NATO.

The Hallstein doctrine worked as a deterrent for a number of years but it became increasingly difficult to reconcile with the Brandt policy of OSTPOLITIK. Establishing full diplomatic relations with other members of the WARSAW PACT, all of whom recognized the GDR, made the doctrine a dead letter. After the building of the Berlin Wall in 1961 following the second BERLIN CRISIS, it was increasingly implausible for the Federal Republic to claim to truly represent all Germans. In 1989 the massive exodus of East Germans into the Federal Republic coupled with the widespread demand for German unification has served to revive the central tenet of the Hallstein doctrine, albeit in a rather oblique and unexpected form; the idea of one Germany is now high on the agenda of European politics.

## Harmonization

A process whereby constituent ACTORS agree to coordinate their policies more closely than in the past. Typically STATES will be the actors involved in harmonization agreements and these arrangements will be formally stipulated in TREATY law. Harmonization involves an institutional infrastructure to superintend the arrangements which may take some time to effect. Normally, states agree to harmonization in specific ISSUE AREAS and these can be identified as ones showing a high degree of actual or potential INTERDEPENDENCE. Harmonization is sometimes thought of as a form of INTEGRATION. In particular the FUNCTIONALIST and the NEO-FUNCTIONALIST approaches to the subject of integration often take harmonization as a starting point. It is arguable whether the term integration is really appropriate, however, and it may be better to regard harmonization as close co-

ordination, as suggested above. For this reason harmonization processes are STATE-CENTRIC and where institutions are created to supervise harmonization the essence of the framework will be INTERNATIONAL rather than SUPRANATIONAL.

As with so many examples of coordination and integration in contemporary WORLD POLITICS, the best instances come from the post-war Western European context. In the field of HUMAN RIGHTS the EUROPEAN CONVENTION of 1950 is a good example of the consensual characteristics underlying harmonization. Similarly in the economic field the work of the OEEC sought to harmonize economic recovery on a regional basis, working in particular towards FREE TRADE among the members and convertibility of currencies. The subsequent EUROPEAN COMMUNITY has, of course, moved beyond harmonization towards integration and the merging of separate state-centred competences.

## Harmony of interests

*See*: LIBERALISM

## Haves and have-nots

Term coined by Cervantes in *Don Quixote* (1605–15): 'There are in the world two families only, the Haves and the Have-Nots.' Universally popularized in the twentieth century and used as a relative or comparative term whenever a commentator seeks to distinguish within a total population, two groups, classes, functions, peoples, STATES or coalitions of states. The classification clearly implies an unequal or hierarchical division as when it is used to indicate the great disparities of wealth between states, especially between those belonging to the rich industrialized NORTH and those belonging to the developing or underdeveloped SOUTH. The term also implies that due to the division, the system is likely to be unstable. Thus E. H. Carr, in

*The Twenty Years' Crisis*, discusses 'haves' and 'have-nots' in the context of peaceful change. Indeed, POWER theorists have often written in terms of STATUS QUO versus REVISIONIST, or 'satisfied' versus 'dissatisfied' ACTORS in order to highlight its unstable characteristics. The BRANDT REPORTS have a clear conception of where 'haves' and 'have-nots' can be currently located with regard to political economy. The relationship between VERTICAL and HORIZONTAL PROLIFERATION implies a similar dichotomy. The term clearly lacks precision, but it is nevertheless a convenient shorthand.

## Hawk

A hawk is a hard-liner. Like the term DOVE, this is a personality type which can be identified by reference to a number of typical components. The hawk is overly concerned with not appearing to be weak. The rationale for this view is provided by the hawk's PERCEPTION that what counts in INTERNATIONAL POLITICS and FOREIGN POLICY is POWER, and particularly the willingness to use it. According to the hawk, adversaries will only comply with one's wishes if they see firmness and resolution. In particular, the maxim that one should seek to 'negotiate from strength' is essentially hawkish. Hawks are more likely than doves to engage in WORST-CASE ANALYSIS and consequently to interpret ambiguous or unanticipated moves by the opponent as malevolent. Hawks are not afraid to look for 'showdowns' that is to say crisis situations that will be approached from a strategy of pure COERCION unless and until the adversary retreats to some more compliant position. The importance of correct handling of the showdown CRISIS is not simply intrinsic to the issues immediately at stake. Hawks see such as tests of resolve and reputation which, with success, will be enhanced for the next time. The hawk's dilemma is that, if he extends his self-IMAGE to the adversary, then the end result is violence and WAR. Two hawks, who are not bluffing, can only test each other's resolve by engaging in

the most reckless BRINKMANSHIP. The end result of hawkish behaviour can be the war that nobody wants but which nobody can back away from. The greatest danger with the hawkish mind set is that by being too provocative it produces the classic paradox – the SELF-FULFILLING PROPHECY.

## Health
*See*: WORLD HEALTH ORGANIZATION (WHO)

## Heartland theory

Probably the most well-known model associated with the GEOPOLITICS school illustrating the global relationship between land-based and sea-based POWER. It was first propounded by Sir Halford Mackinder in 1904 as 'The Geographical Pivot of History' and was subsequently refined in *Democratic Ideals and Reality* (1919) (where 'pivot area' became 'heartland') and added to again in 1943.

Mackinder's original model is drawn from a very wide and sweeping conception of world strategic history. The pivot area (or heartland) he identified as central Asia, from where horsemen dominated Asia and Europe. With the age of maritime discovery in the fifteenth century, however, the balance of forces shifted to the maritime powers, especially Britain. By the end of the nineteenth century this dominance of sea power was coming to an end and Mackinder predicted the reassertion of land-based power. Accordingly, he asserted that the STATE that could control the Eurasian landmass between Germany and central Siberia would be able to control the world. He expressed it in this way:

> Who rules East Europe commands the Heartland
> Who rules the Heartland commands the World Island
> Who rules the World Island commands the World.

In this representation central Asia is the 'heartland' and the 'world island' is Eurasia plus Africa – in all, over two thirds of the world's surface land area.

His theory was widely interpreted as a rationalization and justification for the traditional British policy of maintaining a European BALANCE OF POWER and of preventing heartland HEGEMONY by either Germany or Russia which would pose a direct threat to Britain's Empire. In this way the BUFFER STATES created by the Treaty of VERSAILLES (1919) were designed to drive a wedge between Germany and Russia and thus protect the strategic route to the Heartland. In 1919 his concern was to avoid German control of Russia. By 1943 the roles were reversed – Russian dominance now needed to be countered. Although the original work had stressed the strategic dominance of land power, Mackinder's final version in 1943 hinted at a revival of sea power. The US school of GEOPOLITICS, led by Nicholas Spykman, took this up and argued that the key area was the 'inner crescent', which was called the 'Rimland', control of which could NEUTRALIZE the power of the Heartland. US sea and AIR POWER therefore had a positive role to play in post-war WORLD POLITICS. The Heartland–Rimland thesis then became the conceptual basis for post-war US policy, CONTAINMENT being the effort to seal up the Rimland in order to hem in the Heartland (Soviet Union). The post-war ALLIANCES, NATO in Europe, CENTO in West Asia and SEATO in East Asia, were specific attempts to do this. Most of the post-war conflicts involving confrontation between the SUPERPOWERS developed in the Rimland – BERLIN, KOREA, the Middle East and VIETNAM being cited as the most dangerous. This thesis has obvious connections with the DOMINO THEORY whereby the 'fall' of one Rimland state will inevitably lead to the fall of adjacent countries until the 'World Island' itself becomes vulnerable.

That Mackinder's ideas persisted for so long in Western strategic thinking owes much to the fact that his simple spatial model provided a clear and coherent set of policy guidelines to the United States after 1945. The Heartland–Rimland thesis did indeed provide a global perspective to US strategic thought and dove-tailed neatly with their obsessive fear of COMMUNIST expansionism.

## Hegemonic stability theory

A theory developed within political economy by US academics in the 1970s and particularly associated with the writings of Kindleberger (1973, 1978), Krasner (1976, 1983), Keohane (1984) and Gilpin (1975). This scholarship has taken the concept of HEGEMONY as the independent variable and sought to correlate it with the idea of REGIME as the dependent variable. The hypothesis is that stable regimes, particularly in international economic relations, depend upon a hegemon establishing norms and rules and then superintending their functioning by enlightened use of its CAPABILITY to encourage other members to work the regime under its hegemonial power. Enlightened use of power requires the hegemon to use positive sanctions to create a structure of incentives for those further down the HIERARCHY to benefit and therefore stay in the system. This enlightened hegemony will eventually cause the downfall of the regime because REVISIONIST interests will challenge the position of the hegemon, either explicitly or implicitly, and destabilize the regime.

The two examples that, almost without exception, are invariably quoted by hegemonial stability theorists for the purposes of illustration and validation are nineteenth century Britain and post-1945 United States. In both cases the hegemonial control was short-lived. The UK impact upon the international TRADE SYSTEM lasted perhaps through the thirty-year period after the repeal of the Corn Laws in 1846, while US hegemony was seriously starting to wane in the early 1970s when the fixed GOLD/DOLLAR EXCHANGE rate system collapsed and OPEC successfully challenged the post-war international petroleum regime.

Hegemonial stability theory is firmly placed within the POWER tradition. Its leading exponents are clearly committed to the view that putative power or CAPABILITY is an important variable in both INTERNATIONAL POLITICS and WORLD POLITICS. While recognizing the low FUNGIBILITY of power as a resource, and therefore the highly contingent nature of power relationships, hegemonial stability theorists doggedly persist in their 'resource–power' perception notwithstanding the significant arguments posed by Baldwin (1979) and others against this somewhat static view.

Hegemonial stability theory is also exclusively concerned with relations within the ADVANCED INDUSTRIAL COUNTRIES (AICs) of the FIRST WORLD. No attempt is made to apply it to relations with the centrally planned economies, while in terms of the NORTH–SOUTH dichotomy the theoretical market place is already well stocked with economic LIBERALISM and DEPENDENCY theory. Finally hegemonial stability theory takes a rather truncated view of one of its central concepts – hegemony. The ideological implications of hegemony, a view stressed within the Marxist tradition, have been largely ignored by hegemonial stability theorists.

## Hegemony

A term which has been used in INTERNATIONAL POLITICS for some time, although rather intermittently. Its popularity has increased over the last two decades because it is now used by writers on political economy in connection with HEGEMONIAL STABILITY THEORY. Hegemony is a concept meaning primacy or LEADERSHIP. In an INTERNATIONAL SYSTEM this leadership would be exercised by a 'hegemon', a STATE possessing sufficient CAPABILITY to fulfil this role. Other states in the system would thereafter have to define their relationship with the hegemon. This they might do by acquiescing, by opposing or by remaining indifferent to its leadership. It is clear that sufficient numbers of states, out of the total system membership, must take the first option in order to establish hegemonial control. This acquiescence can be called 'hegemonic consent', therefore.

Since the role of hegemonial actor depends upon CAPABILITY, the concept of hegemony bears a strong family resemblance to the concept of POWER. It is important to remember that power has an ideational as well as a materialistic content. Capability analysis of hegemonial ACTORS needs to be constantly vigilant against crude REALISM which tends to operationalize the concept in strictly economic and military terms. Although these are important, it should be stressed that a hegemon's ability to lead is derived as much from what it stands for as from how it seeks to achieve its goals.

Writers are agreed that the United Kingdom in the nineteenth century and the United States in the twentieth constitute examples of hegemons. UK hegemony began after the repeal of the Corn Laws and continued for thirty years until it started to wane in the 1880s, when the United States and Germany challenged its industrial supremacy. US hegemony began in 1945 and ended in the post-VIETNAM syndrome, with Japan and the EUROPEAN COMMUNITY emerging as TRIPOLAR rivals, at least in terms of political economy.

Ideationally, both STATES represent similar world views. They can appropriately be seen as standard bearers for what has come to be called the FIRST WORLD and for the values of economic LIBERALISM. Currently some writers on the subject see possibilities for a reassertion of hegemony taking place via TRILATERALISM. Ideationally there is no particular problem here, because the United States, Japan and the EUROPEAN COMMUNITY all subscribe to the same ideas about the nature of economic and political systems. The main departure from the past would be that the assumption that a hegemon was a single state actor would have to be dropped.

## Helsinki Accord

To some commentators the diplomatic agreement signed in Helsinki in 1975 at the conclusion of the Conference of Security and Cooperation in Europe (CSCE) represented, at the time, the highest achievement of DETENTE in East–West relations. The conference, which lasted from 1972–5, was proposed by the Soviet Union and was attended by representatives of thirty-three European states (the only exception being Albania), as well as the United States and Canada. The Accord, also known as the Helsinki Final Act, was divided into four areas or 'baskets' of common concern; Basket I covered questions of security in Europe and the Mediterranean, Basket II dealt with cooperation in the fields of economics, science, TECHNOLOGY and the environment, Basket III was concerned with humanitarian matters, HUMAN RIGHTS, culture, education and the free flow of people's ideas and information throughout Europe, and Basket IV provided for the holding of review conferences to oversee progress in these areas and to continue MULTILATERAL cooperation. Subsequent meetings have taken place in Belgrade (1977), Madrid (1980–3) and Ottawa (1985), which was specially convened to review progress on HUMAN RIGHTS. The Accord was not a TREATY as such, but was an agreement which all parties undertook to implement. International agreements which are not law are known as 'Non-binding International Agreements – the Helsinki Accord was clearly of this genre, since officially it was a political statement of intent rather than a legally binding document. Nevertheless, 1 August 1975 must be regarded as a historic date if only because the agreement signed represented the formal end of the Second World War, in the sense that the political and territorial FRONTIERS of Europe (including the border separating the two Germanies) were formally recognized by all parties. In return for RECOGNITION of Soviet domination of Eastern Europe, the West succeeded in putting human rights (Basket III) firmly on the agendas of East–West relations alongside the traditional concerns of TRADE and security, something which Moscow has since had cause to regret. Other matters covered by the Accord included an increase in economic, technical and cultural relations between the two BLOCS, a specification of prior notification of and the exchange of observers at large scale military operations by both sides, provisions relating to environmental protection and the establishment of monitoring groups to oversee performance in all sections of the Final Act.

The overall configuration of the agreement was characterized by the anxiety of the Soviet Union to legitimize its HEGEMONY in Eastern Europe and the determination of the West to exact a price for this. Thus, while the Soviet Union stressed the principle of NON-INTERVENTION (Principle VI) as being the crux of the agreement, the West has continually focused on human rights (Principle VII) as the heart of the matter. The post-Helsinki debates have been conducted largely in terms of these to issues: the Soviet Union insisting that no foreign government or group or individuals had a right to interfere in areas of its own SOVEREIGN jurisdiction and the West insisting that the non-intervention principle was not an obstacle to monitoring respect for human rights within the Soviet domain.

Developments in the Soviet Union and throughout Eastern Europe in the second half of 1989, in particular the spectacular demise of COMMUNISM, the opening of the Berlin Wall, the re-emergence of the issue of German unification and the impending fragmentation of the WARSAW PACT, have made it likely that a new, thirty-five NATION summit will be called to decide the future political shape of Europe. If this is the case, then in all probability it would be called under the auspices of the Conference of Security and Cooperation in Europe

(CSCE). High on the agenda of such a conference would be the whole question of the political ORIENTATION of a united Germany coupled with a redefinition of the relationship between NATO and the remnants of the Warsaw Pact. 'Alternative' security arrangements – involving multistructured political ACCOMMODATION and tolerances rather than BIPOLAR nuclear confrontation and suspicion – may well emerge to form the basis of PEACE and stability in Europe in the 1990s. The Helsinki framework, which broke new ground in SUPERPOWER relations in 1975, could yet become the instrument that finally signals the end of bipolarity in Europe and its replacement by a multipolar, pluralist structure where traditional military/security issues take second place to political, economic, social and humanitarian issues.

## Hierarchy

A hierarchy is a system of stratification. The basis of this stratification will differ between social systems. In the INTERNATIONAL SYSTEM, stratification is based upon POWER and INFLUENCE. Taking these two dimensions as independent variables, it is possible to stipulate hierarchies based upon models which take power and influence to be possessions which are distributed unevenly between member STATES and, secondly, it is possible to stipulate hierarchies based upon models which take power and influence as relationships which produce unequal outcomes between member STATES in the system.

Viewed as possessions, power and influence produce differential distributions of CAPABILITIES between states in the system. This can be shown for purposes of illustration by taking a number of indices currently available to compare and contrast state ACTORS in the contemporary international system. Thus, taking the variable of population, China, India, the Soviet Union and the United States account for nearly half the world's population. Conversely al-

most one-quarter of the present UN membership are, in demographic terms at least, micro-states with populations of less than one million people. Taking the dimension of GNP, almost two-thirds of the world's is generated by the ADVANCED INDUSTRIAL COUNTRIES (AICs) while, per capita, the GNP of this group of states is more than ten times higher than the African average. The United States and the Soviet Union account for approximately one-half of all the military expenditure in the international system and, together with France, the United Kingdom, Italy and West Germany, these six states are responsible for more than 90 per cent of the ARMS TRADE. Again the ISSUE AREA of TECHNOLOGY TRANSFER demonstrates how much scientific and technical knowledge is generated within the AICs.

Such illustrations as those offered above show that, from the point of view of power and influence as possessions, the international system is hierarchical, a small number of state actors having a disproportionately large amount. When the state actor perspective is modified and evidence from the world system is included then the most striking non-state actor in terms of these kinds of 'profiles' is the MNC. Ranking states according to GNP and MNCs according to Gross Annual Sales, the finding shows that the MNC possesses more putative economic power than many states. The conclusion from empirical studies of the MNC would seem to suggest that, outside its own corporate system, the MNC wields influence rather than power. In pure power terms the state is still able to provide countervailing power *vis-à-vis* the MNC.

Once hierarchy is approached from relationships rather than possessions, a number of categories emerge. There is first the relationship within the AICs. In this group the post-war hierarchy has been established under the hegemonial leadership of the United States. HEGEMONIC STABILITY THEORY sees benefits in this kind of hierarchy. As the relative power position of the United States has shifted, notably in the field of political economy, the hierarchy has become more broadly based. TRIPOLAR tendencies and TRILATERALISM are contemporary configurations. These relationships are predominantly characterized by INTERDEPENDENCE, both in the military–security policy area and in the wealth–welfare area. Since INTERDEPENDENCE is closely related to ideas about POWER and influence, and since it has already been argued that these are critical dimensions in international and global hierarchies, then it is quite consistent with all that has been adduced so far to see this as a key characteristic in the relationships within the AIC/FIRST WORLD group of states.

Relationships between the group of states discussed above and the centrally planned economies (ceps) grouped in COMECON and the WARSAW PACT are non-hierarchical. In the military–security field PARITY and equality are characteristics. In the wealth–welfare field potentialities for hierarchy are evident, but to date are not exploited. Within the ceps themselves the hierarchy established by the Soviet Union in the military–security and the IDEOLOGY fields shows signs of erosion. POLYCENTRISM and PLURALISM are producing a more diffused system.

Within the THIRD WORLD hierarchical tendencies are strong. Both the OPEC cartel and newly industrialized countries (NICs) show this in the field of political economy. These groups can possibly play a substitute role within the Third World structure by replacing the historical hierarchy of DEPENDENCY upon the First World. In the military–security field, NON-ALIGNMENT is an attempt to escape from hierarchy by avoiding coalitions that would be dominated by hierarchical actors from AICs or ceps. The evidence of hierarchies within the Third World just alluded to, shows the continued utility of the hierarchical idea and the extent to which structural inequalities continue to be a feature of WORLD POLITICS.

## High Commissioner
Term used specifically by COMMON-WEALTH states to refer to AMBASSADORS or heads of mission sent by one member country to another. The use of this term instead of 'ambassador' indicates the SPECIAL RELATIONSHIP that is thought to exist between members of this international sub-community.

## High frontier
A US DEFENCE policy interest group and political lobby. The name comes from General Graham (1982). The FRONTIER referred to is space and the work is an extended argument for BALLISTIC MISSILE DEFENCE. Graham envisages a multiple defence CAPABILITY using space-based systems and ground-based interceptors. In particular, this strategy envisages intercepting Soviet missiles during the boost phase using space-based systems. There is no doubt that Graham's energetic lobbying for ballistic missile defence (BMD) and the speech of President Reagan on 23 March 1983 announcing a long-term research and development plan to remove the ballistic missile threat – the so-called 'Star Wars' speech – were not coincidental.
*See also*: SDI

## High Politics
This term is used in two contexts. First, in FOREIGN POLICY analysis, where it is used as a collective expression for certain issue areas of crucial importance. Secondly, high politics is used in the study of INTEGRATION where, borrowing from the first usage, theorists again identify certain issue areas which are highly resistant to integration processes. Both meanings imply a horizontal division and an explicit contrast with LOW POLITICS. The idea that foreign policy is structured in terms of hierarchies in this way is also evident in the analysis of elites. Here, of course, the hierarchy is about 'who makes foreign policy?' rather than about issue areas.

In its first usage, high politics implies that in cases of a CONFLICT foreign policy issues take precedence over domestic. The idea of the primacy of foreign policy is certainly a tradition within many states. In representative systems this primacy leads to injunctions that 'party politics should stop at the water's edge' and competing political parties are often encouraged to seek out areas of BIPARTISANSHIP, certainly in the high politics areas. At a minimum, high politics involves the maintenance of core values – including national self-preservation – and the long-term objectives of the STATE. Clearly these are not transient or temporary concerns and indeed in many systems they will show remarkable continuity over time. CRISES situations are, by definition, issues of high politics, because one of the situational characteristics of the crisis is that important values will be threatened. Similarly, significant changes in the ORIENTATION of the state – for example the UK decision to apply for membership of the EUROPEAN COMMUNITIES, or the INDEPENDENCE issue of a THIRD WORLD state – will involve high politics.

In terms of elite structures, high political questions will be dealt with by the formal office holders. In some states, notably the USA, formal pronouncements by the national leadership on matters of high policy are often referred to as 'doctrines'. Once a decision has been made in principle and the IMPLEMENTATION stage has been reached, high political issues will be increasingly handled within the bureaucratic and organizational context. Thus the UK decision to apply for membership of the EUROPEAN COMMUNITIES, although taken after soundings at the highest levels, was quickly 'bureaucratized' once the decision had to be implemented and access negotiations began.

High politics in the second sense has been used as an implied critique of both FUNCTIONALIST and NEO-FUNCTIONALIST theories of integration. The argument here is that by ignoring the distinctive character of high politics, certain integration theories are overly optimistic about their chances of success. Integration theorists have been too willing to assume that economic motives for change would dominate political motives for the STATUS QUO. In particular via the idea of SPILLOVER, it was thought that a kind of automatic and irresistible momentum would be created. Such high political principles as state SOVEREIGNTY have proved much more tenacious than was sometimes thought. To their credit the federalists have been instinctively ready to tackle these high policy issues directly and have not assumed that the functionalist/neo-functionalist disregard for high politics was justified or wise.

## Hijack

The theft or temporary capture of means of transport, usually aircraft, by terrorist groups in order to further their aims. Aircraft are the preferred targets for this type of activity and the term 'skyjacking' is sometimes used to distinguish this behaviour from hijacking in general. Hijacking requires total secrecy up to the moment of commitment, careful planning, good INTELLIGENCE and great determination. Hijacking is a small group activity usually committed for political rather than criminal motives. Once the hijack is under way the perpetrators become highly visible and sacrifice their secrecy and anonymity. This makes hijacking a rather special form of TERRORISM because usually the terrorist will attempt to retain the element of secrecy throughout the operation. Hijackers may use their captives and captured property as 'bargaining chips' to secure some concession from the STATE whose assets they have seized and/or from the state(s) whose nationals they hold.

States will attempt to combat hijacking by increasing security at airports, seaports and other embarkation points by coordinating their policies and sharing information and, in some cases, by publicly committing themselves to a HAWKISH position on the issue of NEGOTIATING with terrorists. As transportation methods proliferate, particularly in the THIRD WORLD, the opportunity for hijacking increases. Hijacking does not take place in a political vacuum, nevertheless, and the most spectacular instances in contemporary WORLD POLITICS have been associated with radical nationalist/ethnic movements such as those inspired by the ARAB–ISRAELI CONFLICT.

## Hiroshima

The first ATOM BOMB was dropped on the Japanese city of Hiroshima at 8.15 a.m. local time on 6 August 1945. The device was a URANIUM-based bomb, in the KILOTON range. The bomb was dropped from a single, modified B29 aircraft from a height in excess of 30,000 feet. The weapon airburst above the city at slightly under 2,000 feet. The death and destruction wrought by the immediate explosion was extensive. Due to the scale of the disruption caused to rescue services, many of the most severely wounded died subsequently. In February 1946 Supreme Allied Headquarters indicated that its estimate of the casualties were: dead 78,150; still missing 13,983; seriously wounded 9,428; slightly wounded 27,997. These figures may well err on the side of caution.

The bomb was not tested before it was used, so Hiroshima could be regarded as reality testing. Most commentators are agreed that, like most difficult decisions, a complex of factors was involved. The United States was certainly anxious to avoid an opposed invasion of the main Japanese islands and to end the WAR, if possible, before the Soviet Union carried through its pledge to declare war on Japan. The bomb's use was a demonstration of the awesome potential of NUCLEAR WEAPONS, although at that time the US stockpile was too small to amount to more than a putative CAPABILITY. It should also be remembered that the United States had total air superiority *vis-à-vis* Japan. The implication

that the United States could destroy large urban targets at will was reinforced at Hiroshima.

Since 1945 Hiroshima has come to symbolize the dawn of the nuclear age. Proponents of NUCLEAR WEAPONS regard it as a salutary reminder of the potential POWER which concentrates the minds of would-be transgressors upon the DETERRENT threat. Opponents of such weapons see in Hiroshima the need to escape from a system of relations based upon threats and REPRISALS which are too costly to carry out.

## Hobbesian

Along with MACHIAVELLIAN this is probably the most well known and well worn categorization of the REALIST approach to WORLD POLITICS. It is not difficult to see why. Thomas Hobbes's (1588–1679) account of relations between STATES is drawn largely from his identification of this with the condition of man in the 'state of nature' before the establishment of civil society (*Leviathan*, ch. xiii). Hobbes's state of nature is anarchic and warlike where the life of man is 'solitary, poore, nasty, brutish and short'. Using this DOMESTIC ANALOGY he suggests that states, like individuals, are in a state of nature, which is a state of WAR:

> But though there had never been any time wherein particular men were in a condition of warre one against another; yet in all times Kings, and Persons of soveraigne authority, because of their Independency, are in continual jealousies, and in the state and posture of Gladiators; having their weapons pointing, and their eyes fixed on one another; that is their Forts, Garrisons and Guns, upon the Frontiers of their Kingdoms; and continual Spyes upon their neighbours; which is a posture of war (p. 65).

This account of ANARCHY and the SECURITY DILEMMA each individual (and therefore each state) faces is the conceptual basis of what might be termed the 'pure' realist school. It appears to contain all its essential elements. Man is aggressive and egotistical, the state seeks only its own ends, interest is defined in terms of POWER, conflict is natural and the social environment is anarchic/chaotic. There is no law or morality to speak of and actions are limited, if at all, by prudence, which in any case is little more than enlightened self-interest.

Following the domestic analogy, the logical way out of this condition is the creation of a 'Leviathan amongst Leviathans', but Hobbes resisted this step towards world empire or WORLD GOVERNMENT and most adherents to this view argue that survival ultimately rests on a form of BALANCE OF POWER. Hobbes himself was not concerned with inter-state relations; his observations about them are an off-shoot, a subordinate part, of his explanation of domestic politics and his justification for government. It is somewhat surprising therefore that his few and brief references to world politics have been so influential. This is partly due to the vivid and forceful style of presentation, partly because it appears in outline to fit the simple realist model, and partly because of the general paucity of philosophical speculation about INTERNATIONAL RELATIONS.

However, not a little controversy surrounds this orthodox interpretation of the Hobbesian view. It is possible to argue that Hobbes himself was not a 'Hobbesian' in the traditional sense. Hobbes describes the state of nature where men live without a common power 'to keep them all in awe', as a war of all against all, and then like Locke after him, forestalling the argument that such a condition never existed, he points to the relations between states as exemplifying it. But he adds this sentence, which makes all the difference to his view of international relations. He says of the state of war between states . . . 'But because they uphold thereby the industry of their subjects; there does not follow from it that misery which accompanies the liberty of particular men.' Therefore, although he clearly defines the state of nature with relations between states, the external conditions of states are not the same as those of individual men (i.e. they are less miserable). INTERNATIONAL POLITICS is in a state of nature because there is no government, but this ANARCHY, this absence of government, does not lead to chaos as it clearly does for individuals. Anarchy in its international context is therefore not as intolerable as in its domestic context. It may in fact be compatible with the idea of an INTERNATIONAL SOCIETY of states (the 'anarchical society'). In addition, Hobbes specifically identified the laws of nature – which dictate that PEACE should be sought wherever possible – with the laws of nations. This suggests that far from being a bleak, unrelenting battle for daily survival, inter-state relations are capable of sustaining communal, cooperative endeavours based on reason and mutual respect for law (see: Hedley Bull (1966)).

## Holy Alliance

A vague and somewhat mystical mutual AID and assistance agreement signed in 1815 between the monarchs of Russia, Austria and Prussia, subsequently joined by all other European rulers except the Pope, the Sultan and the British Monarch. The Alliance was significant in that it represented a reactionary and supposedly Christian, anti-liberal movement in WORLD POLITICS and was designed as a MULTILATERAL instrument of INTERVENTION in the affairs of newly independent STATES. Fears of Holy Alliance interference to restore imperial rule in Latin America was a contributory factor in the promulgation of the MONROE DOCTRINE. The Alliance was all but destroyed by internal dissention over the Greek war of INDEPENDENCE (1821–29). Attempts were made, especially by Metternich (who represented Austria, the most cosmopolitan and vulnerable empire), to turn the Alliance into a collective international police force under the aegis of the CONCERT SYSTEM, but this came to nothing. Differences over the SCOPE of GREAT POWER collaboration, over the merits of collective intervention, and over ideological orientation meant that the Alliance was never as cohesive as its originators had intended.

## Homeostasis

A term used in CYBERNETICS. Homeostasis is to cybernetics what equilibrium is to mechanics; that is to say, it conceptualizes how an organism maintains an even state with its environment. In cybernetics this is achieved by processing information about the environment in relation to the goals being pursued by the organism and adapting behaviour patterns accordingly. Since the flow of information into the system is continuous – this is one of the basic principles of cybernetics – homeostasis is an ongoing process itself. Unlike the term FEEDBACK – itself also taken from cybernetics – homeostasis has not passed into the currency of standard political analysis. The major reference work on these ideas remains that of Professor Karl Deutsch (1966).

## Horizontal proliferation

NUCLEAR PROLIFERATION proceeds along two axes: the horizontal and the vertical. VERTICAL PROLIFERATION is the deliberate increase and refinement of existing nuclear CAPABILITIES by STATES already 'in the club'. Horizontal proliferation is the term used to identify the spread of NUCLEAR WEAPONS from existing states to new states. The issue of horizontal proliferation used to be referred to as the 'Nth country problem' because it was assumed at the time that this phrase was in fashion (the early 1960s) that, given the putative POWER, states would more or less automatically and instinctively decide to develop nuclear weapons. Some of the WORST-CASE scenarios of that period have not occurred. Instead the growth has been slow, if steady. Moreover

in July 1968 the NON-PROLIFERATION TREATY (NPT) was opened for signature and for the first time a concerted effort was made to establish a REGIME which would tackle both horizontal and vertical types.

Between 1945 and 1964 horizontal proliferation proceeded steadily taking in the United States, the Soviet Union, the United Kingdom, France and China. In each case the decision to 'go nuclear' was based upon a complex of factors both internal to the states concerned and external to their political and strategic situation. Moreover, in some cases there seems to have been a discernible ACTION–REACTION dynamic in these decisions, the French decision being influenced by the UK, the Soviet by the US and the Chinese by both the US and the Soviet. In all instances important bureaucratic and vested interests, including the military and scientific communities, were behind the DECISION-MAKING. In the United Kingdom the political decision to make a fission bomb was taken by the Labour Government in 1947. This decision was itself one of a sequence going back to 1941 when the Maud Committee Report was accepted by the coalition government. Maud had argued that 'no nation would care to risk being caught without a weapon of such decisive possibilities'.

Both the UK and French decisions were, additionally, prompted by self-perceptions of their status in the post-war system and the need to confirm or maintain this via membership of the nuclear club. Both were concerned about US commitments under NATO and in keeping with EXTENDED DETERRENCE thinking, the French, in particular, arguing that once the US homeland became vulnerable, their guarantee was no longer credible. Strategic questions also influenced the Chinese decision. They had already experienced the coercive potential of nuclear weapons during the latter stages of the KOREAN WAR. The growing difference with the Soviet Union from the late 1950s onwards merely confirmed their perception that for strategic reasons the Chinese leadership needed access to its own nuclear weapons system. In this way horizontal proliferation is causally related to the SECURITY DILEMMA.

Since Chinese accession and the Treaty on the Non-Proliferation of Nuclear Weapons (NPT), horizontal proliferation has occurred in areas outside the COLD WAR confrontation zones and for reasons which have more to do with regional conflicts than global conflicts. The paradigm here is the Indo–Pakistan situation. India did not sign the NPT and instead, under the so-called Sarabhai Profile, conducted a peaceful nuclear explosion (pne) in the Rajasthan desert at Pokhran in 1974. Pakistan has been associated with the 'Islamic bomb' conception and it is certain that a Pakistan pne would be regarded as highly provocative in India. Since an Islamic bomb would also have implications in the Middle East the possibility of the action–reaction dynamic surfacing again is apparent. Clandestine nuclear weapons projects were under way in Israel at the same time as the NPT was under consideration, and it seems clear that both Israel and the other clandestine power, South Africa, see their weapons programme again in terms of regional CONFLICT situations. Nuclear weapons in the hands of Israeli or South African leaders might be seen as 'last resort' systems if their security problems became very acute in the future.

Horizontal proliferation raises the issues behind DETERRENCE both as a theory and a policy. All those states which have joined the nuclear 'club' since 1945 have seen their possession of these weapons as necessary for them to pose contingent threats *vis-à-vis* a perceived adversary. Moreover, apart from the two SUPERPOWERS these systems have been seen as punishment rather than denial deterrents. As has already been mentioned, the French and the UK saw problems inherent in extended deterrence ideas being solved by their national systems. Indeed, there would seem to be a positive correlation between independent nuclear systems and NON-ALIGNMENT. There is certainly an inverse relationship between these weapons and ALLIANCES. Waltz (1981) has argued that the steady spread of nuclear weapons may replicate the kind of stability that many identify as a key characteristic that nuclear weapons possession has given to the existing club members. This unusual conclusion would certainly remove many of the worst fears of the Nth country scenarios of the 1960s.

## Hot-line agreement

Difficulties involving communications during the CUBAN MISSILE CRISIS of 1962, which had brought the United States and the Soviet Union to the brink of NUCLEAR WAR, led both sides to reconsider the question of direct communication links between Washington and Moscow. Proposals in the 1950s to establish mutual land observation posts and aerial surveillance of each side's military facilities had generally floundered in the stormy seas of COLD WAR suspicion and hostility, but the events of the missile crisis convinced the United States and the Soviet Union that improved direct communication networks were a vital feature of modern CRISIS MANAGEMENT and avoidance of NUCLEAR WAR by accident, miscalculation or misunderstanding. Accordingly, at Geneva on 10 June 1963, a Memorandum of Understanding was signed under which an official teletype communications link was established between the two capital cities permitting direct and immediate contact between heads of government during a CRISIS. In 1971 this agreement was modified to take into account the new means of communication by satellite. Similar communication links were established between Moscow and Paris in 1966, and Moscow and London in 1967. The advantages of the hot-line are that during the most crucial phases of international crisis, DECISION-MAKERS can bypass the slower and more formal diplomatic channels and communicate their intentions and policies directly to the other side, thus reducing possibilities of misunderstanding or garbled third-party messages. There is evidence that the hot-line has played a significant role in recent East–West relations, particularly in regional conflicts where either side may be anxious to reassure the other as to the extent of its involvement. The ARAB–ISRAELI war of 1967, for example, was one such occasion when the hot-line was used to good effect.

## Hot pursuit

A legal doctrine usually associated with MARITIME LAW but now used more widely to cover activities on land, air and sea. It refers to the right to pursue an offender outside the territorial limits of one's own national JURISDICTION. The adjective indicates that the exercise of this right is a limited one in circumstance, time and place. Thus, the action must begin within the jurisdiction of the violated party, is undertaken only by its authorized agents, is engaged in until the offender is arrested and is broken off when the offender reaches its own territorial area or that of a third STATE. It is justified as an enabling device for the reasonable exercise of territorial jurisdiction.

## Human rights

The notion that human beings have rights because they are human beings and not because they are citizens of STATE X or state Y is, in terms of the practice of WORLD POLITICS, a relatively new one. Traditional thinking has it that INTERNATIONAL LAW is concerned primarily with states rights – in particular rights associated with post-WESTPHALIAN ideas about SOVEREIGNTY and its corollary, NONINTERVENTION. Human rights, in so far as they were acknowledged, were subsumed under states rights, conventional wisdom being that international law was law between states whereas municipal law was law between individuals. Although the distinction has never been quite as clear as this – the rights of ALIENS and foreign nationals

have long been a matter for concern, for example – orthodox accounts of INTERNATIONAL POLITICS and law have always been more or less STATE-CENTRIC in this way. However, the distinction between the two has become increasingly blurred and contemporary world politics has witnessed a dramatic upsurge in the question of human rights and their place in the STATE-SYSTEM. It may be said that whereas the innovation of seventeenth century world politics was the creation of the society of states, the REVOLUTION of the twentieth century is the creation of a prototype WORLD SOCIETY in which individuals have equal standing with states and where states themselves acknowledge that issues connected with the fundamental rights of human beings are as legitimate a part of FOREIGN POLICY concerns as the more traditional preoccupations with PEACE, security and economic well-being. This process was formally heralded by the establishment in 1946 of the United Nations Commission on Human Rights, and on 10 December 1948 (which was designated Human Rights Day) the GENERAL ASSEMBLY passed the Universal Declaration of Human Rights. This was unopposed, although South Africa, Saudi Arabia and the Soviet BLOC abstained. The commission worked on two covenants designed to give substance to the general declaration: the first was on economic, social and cultural rights and the second on civil and political rights. The first was passed by the General Assembly in 1966 (although it did not become operative until ten years later) but the second covenant has had a much more difficult ride and the investigatory Committee established has constantly run up against recalcitrant governments insisting on the overriding principle of states rights (Israel, for example, refused to cooperate with its investigations into possible violations in occupied territories after the Six-Day War). Thus, the INTERNATIONAL SYSTEM has clearly laid down a code of established human rights and attempted to create judicial machinery which can investigate infringements but the problem of enforcement remains a thorny one. States can, and do, ignore them. Yet as a statement of principle, and perhaps of positive world morality, these proposals clearly have an effect on WORLD PUBLIC OPINION and the standard they set is used as a yardstick to measure, and also to beat, states which consistently fail to comply. Rhodesia and South Africa have borne this brunt most often in recent times.

On a REGIONAL level, as distinct from the international, provision for human rights implementation has been more successful. The EUROPEAN CONVENTION ON HUMAN RIGHTS (1953) sought not only to delineate these rights but also to enforce them. A commission and a court of human rights has been established to which individuals can bring action against their own governments. In the American continents there are similar developments. The American Convention on Human Rights (1978) created a commission and a court which again contained provision for individuals to present grievances. In Africa the Banjul Charter on Human and People's Rights (1981) is somewhat weaker than its European and American counterparts, mainly perhaps due to the different African conceptions of human rights – a conception which stresses the rights of collectivities and groupings ('peoples') rather than individual rights as such. In all these incidences, whether provision for enforcement is present or not the power of PUBLIC OPINION is an important sanction in the conflict between individuals and the sometimes overbearing POWER of the state. Other regional innovations have not been as successful as those in Europe or the United States. The 1975 HELSINKI ACCORD, which included provision for human rights, has not so far made much headway in the Soviet bloc partly because Helsinki is not legally binding on its signatories. The Arab Commission on Human Rights (1969), too, has made little progress mainly because in ISLAM the rights of the community come before the rights of the individual; for Muslims duty to God, from whom all human rights emanate, is

logically prior to obligations to individuals.

Of the non-governmental institutions concerned with this issue Amnesty International (founded in Britain in 1961) stands out. This group actively specializes in seeking to obtain freedom for prisoners of conscience and has been instrumental in campaigning for the rights of thousands of unfortunates on a world-wide basis. Other specialist organizations in this field are the Minority Rights Group, the Anti-Slavery Society and the INTERNATIONAL COMMITTEE OF THE RED CROSS – all of which are concerned with specific aspects of individual rights.

Clearly, although the twentieth century has seen a greater movement towards acceptance of human rights as an integral part of world politics than at any other time, there is a great deal of debate as to where the emphasis should be placed. In the West the rights of individuals to be free from the interference of others is paramount, whereas in the East economic and social rights take precedence over civil and political rights. Liberty in socialist states is expressed primarily in social and economic terms: in liberal states it is largely a civil and political affair. Therein perhaps lies an important dimension of the tension between the two systems, and because of its emphasis on economic development rather than the legal protection of civil liberties the THIRD WORLD tends to prefer the socialist view. After all, subsistence and basic needs are often a more immediate and pressing concern than constitutional niceties and protective legal procedures (*see*: R. J. Vincent, 1986). Whatever ideological differences can be delineated, though, no one doubts that the human rights issue has altered, probably for ever, the classical conception of INTERNATIONAL RELATIONS.

**Humanitarian assistance**
Traditionally associated with acts of assistance undertaken by STATES in response to natural disasters of a temporary kind: that

163

is earthquakes, floods, fires, famines and so on. In classical international legal theory it is associated with the idea of *offices d'humanité* developed in particular by Vattell. It is not regarded as a duty under INTERNATIONAL LAW, rather is it rendered as a matter of 'grace or bounty'. Some modern theorists have argued that the concept should be extended to cover not just natural and temporary disasters, but also social and endemic disasters. In addition, the rendering of humanitarian assistance should be regarded as a positive duty and consequently could be demanded by sufferers as a right derived not only from the doctrine of 'shared humanity', but also as a logical consequence of membership of the international community of states. Thus the provision of, for example, minimum subsistence to all should be viewed not as a voluntary act of charity, but as a legal requirement under the doctrine of distributive JUSTICE.

*See also*: HUMAN RIGHTS

## Hydrogen bomb

The hydrogen bomb is the most powerful weapon invented by man – to date. Its energy is generated by the fusion of hydrogen isotopes. Hence it is sometimes referred to as the 'fusion' bomb, although the weapon as developed actually combines fission and fusion processes. A small ATOM BOMB is exploded to act as a trigger for the fusion of the hydrogen. This two-stage process has led some to refer to 'thermonuclear' weapon instead of hydrogen weapon. The size of the hydrogen weapon is limitless – at least in theory – and larger yielding weapons are measured in the MEGATON range. This exponential increase in destructiveness has led some to argue that the real REVOLUTION is thermonuclear rather than nuclear. The difference between fusion weapons and fission weapons is greater than the difference between fission and CONVENTIONAL weapons.

Although scientific interest in the fusion process dates from 1942, the political impetus to development came from the ARMS RACE. In particular, the Soviet testing of an atomic weapon in 1949 provoked the United States Administration into serious consideration of the research and development implications of thermonuclear weapons. The Soviet atomic test, achieved several years in advance of their anticipated CAPABILITY, had so alarmed the United States that they felt unable to stand aside from the possible development of fusion weapons themselves.

Policy discussion over the so-called 'super' took place within the Truman Administration between three agencies: the Defense Department, the State Department and the Atomic Energy Commission. Unanimity between the three over the development of the 'super' was far from complete. Indeed there were powerful voices inside the Administration and outside in the scientific community arguing against development of hydrogen weapons. In particular it was felt by many that if the United States went ahead with development and production of these weapons any remaining chances for an international control REGIME, such as that proposed under the BARUCH PLAN would be lost. Additionally many critics of the hydrogen bomb argued that such a destructive weapon used against civilian targets would be quite indiscriminate in its effects. In a remarkably prescient anticipation of the debates over mutual assured destruction (MAD) these early fears warned against the development of such a COUNTERCITY CAPABILITY by the United States.

The decision to go ahead with the development of fusion weapons led to the first test in 1951, further testing in 1952 and the Bikini test of March 1954 which confirmed the power of the weapon. By the time of the Bikini test, the Soviet Union had already commenced their programme. In retrospect the decisions over the 'super' in the early 1950s look tantalizingly like a window of opportunity situation.

# I

**IBRD**

*See*: WORLD BANK GROUP

**ICBM**

An intercontinental BALLISTIC MISSILE. The SALT process stipulated that the range of a MISSILE should be not less than 5,500 km, approximately 3,000 miles. ICBMs are exclusively land-based systems. Their basing mode would normally be a hardened silo, although in the past the early developments of ICBM systems were stationed above the ground. In the jargon a silo is regarded as a 'hard target', which means that it is invulnerable to all but the most accurate, and therefore direct, of hits. Recently the SUPER-POWERS have developed mobile basing modes for their ICBMs and this has enhanced their survivability further. Of the two STATES, the Soviet Union has a larger proportion of its offensive weapons in the ICBM category. The United States has preferred a TRIAD of force structures with a mix of 'air-breathing' and sea-launched systems. These two states are in a class of their own as regards the ICBM launcher. The continued refinement and improvement of these weapons and their warheads has been an important and unfortunate destabilizing factor in the ARMS RACE and has done much to contribute to the problems of VERTICAL PROLIFERATION in recent decades.

**IDA**

*See*: WORLD BANK GROUP

**Idealism**

Sometimes called 'utopianism', and with less accuracy, 'rationalism' or 'LIBERAL-ISM', it refers to an approach to INTER-NATIONAL RELATIONS that stresses the importance of moral values, legal norms, INTERNATIONALISM and harmony of interests as guides to FOREIGN POLICY-making rather than considerations of NATIONAL INTEREST, POWER and independent STATE survival within a multi-state decentralized system. According to E. H. Carr (1946), its foremost critic, the central fallacy of idealism was its tendency to indulge in wishful thinking at the expense of rigorous empirical analysis, to the extent that it was characterized by 'the inclination to ignore what was and what is in contemplation of what should be' (p. 11). Thus, excessive emphasis on abstract principles rather than factual realities led, according to Carr, to an inability especially in the Anglo–American world both to comprehend and to control international events during the inter-war period. Theorists such as Arnold Toynbee, Norman Angell and Alfred ZIMMERN, as well as practitioners such as Woodrow Wilson, consistently failed to grasp that the mainsprings of state action and behaviour revolved around considerations of power and national interest rather than ethics and universalism. Policies based on such fallacies (e.g. general DISARMA-MENT, international cooperation and INTERNATIONALISM were bound to fail because 'these supposedly absolute and universal principles were not principles at all but the unconscious reflections of national policy based on a particular interpretation of national interest at a particular time'. In fact, although Carr was among the first to identify 'idealism' as a particular school or approach which dominated thinking in the period following the First World War (and which, in effect, created INTERNATIONAL RELATIONS as a separate academic discipline) the tradition was well established in the history of international thought long before the twentieth century. Thus Locke, Bentham, Rousseau, Kant and J. S. Mill were all regarded as 'idealists' of one sort or another since all of them, albeit on various levels and with varying degrees of conviction, expressed faith in 'reason' and 'conscience' as harbingers of perpetual PEACE and universal harmony. The doctrine of the DOMESTIC ANALOGY, whereby conditions which created order within the state could be reproduced on the international plane, was a central assumption of the approach and this led directly to the advocacy of COLLECTIVE SECURITY and the creation of a LEAGUE OF NATIONS which would forever resolve the SECURITY DILEMMA associated with an unstructured and untutored international ANARCHY. For the idealists, therefore, peace was both indivisible and achievable.

The 'realist–idealist debate' which dominated the discipline (especially in the United States) in the late 1940s and early 1950s has largely been superseded in academic commentaries, but is now regarded as a suitable (if somewhat naive and dated) general introduction to the outer parameters of the subject.

## Ideology

An ideology is a set of assumptions and ideas about social behaviour and social systems. Its application to political studies has been far-reaching, particularly since the French Revolution. In politics these assumptions and ideas are often referred to as doctrines. Thus a political ideology can be defined as a set of doctrinal assumptions and ideas about the past present and future states of affairs in political systems, including the INTERNATIONAL SYSTEM and the world system. Political ideologies are usually thought of as being very explicit philosophical systems such as MARXISM/LENINISM. This is almost certainly too narrow a view. NATIONALISM is quite clearly an ideology in the terms used above, yet it is often much less explicit than Marxism/Leninism and it is certainly more specific and relative to a particular political culture. All political ideologies will contain components which seek to describe and explain how a particular state of affairs came into being; sometimes in addition a political ideology will seek to stipulate what FOREIGN POLICY analysts would call long-term goals for the future. In this sense political ideologies are also predictive and prescriptive.

Ideologies fulfil a number of functions:

1. Ideologies are a source of CONFLICT in INTERNATIONAL POLITICS. Rosecrance (1963), in his study of nine European systems from 1740, found that four, including the two most recent, showed elements of ideological conflict. Ideological conflicts show great intensity between the parties, unwillingness to compromise and marked tendency to become total. According to Kaplan (1957) system structure tends towards a tight BIPOLARITY. Ideological conflict in the contemporary system, often referred to as the COLD WAR, has diminished in intensity over the period. The refusal of large numbers of new states to commit themselves to one side or the other, preferring policies of NON-ALIGNMENT and positive NEUTRALITY, has been an important contributory factor. Many of the postwar regional conflicts have had ideological dimensions, usually nationalism. The ARAB–ISRAELI CONFLICT is a good example.

2. Ideologies as a source of CAPABILITY in INTERNATIONAL POLITICS. The REALIST tradition of separating POWER and ideology has tended to obscure the possibility that ideology may be a source of putative power. Ideology contributes towards what Spiegel calls motivational power. Although neither a necessary nor sufficient condition

for an active foreign policy, a high level of ideological self-righteousness will be conducive to active INTERVENTIONIST foreign policies. Of the two SUPERPOWERS the United States perhaps shows this tendency more than the Soviet Union.

Ideology is also a source of capability within the STATE and this internal dimension can 'spill over' into the external environment. States come to represent a particular ideology within the international system as a reflection of their internal beliefs and values. Charismatic LEADERSHIP relies upon an ideological base. This type of leader derives considerable power and influence from the success with which he or she appears to encapsulate in their personality the aspirations of particular classes or peoples. Classic twentieth century examples would be Lenin, Mao, Ghandi and Mandela. The routinization of charisma occurs when the principles and practices of the leader outlast the life of the individual and become part of an ideological tradition.

3. Ideologies as an influence upon policy-making. In this use of ideology, the concept becomes much more subjective. Ideology becomes a kind of lens through which policy makers perceive their various environments and react accordingly. The process of reaching a DEFINITION OF THE SITUATION will bring ideological influences to bear upon the policy process. These ideological influences will be generalized rather than specific but in the process of specifying their relevance to a particular ISSUE AREA differences may arise between individuals and groups. Explanations of US foreign policy have often been sought in terms of the ideologies of ISOLATIONISM and INTERVENTIONISM/INTERNATIONALISM. In terms of the current discussion these would become the 'lenses' through which policy goals, particularly in the long term, would be defined. The decision after 1919 to reject Wilsonian IDEALISM is sometimes presented as a reversion to politics of self-interest. The ideological approach instead would see it in terms of isolationism suggesting

one course and interventionism/internationalism another.

These ideological influences are a product of socialization influences as much as intellectual fashion. Socialization, both in childhood and adult life, is important in two ways. Manifest socialization, including indoctrination, occurs in all social systems and begins in the family. Latent socialization, by placing individuals in a particular milieu, occurs throughout life. Political sociology has tended to concentrate upon totalitarian societies when examining the role of socialization in the creation and maintenance of ideological factors. Totalitarian systems are, however, only the most overt and extreme instances of what is a general tendency.

4. Ideologies as ways of looking at the subject. In this aspect intellectual preferences come to the fore. Little and McKinlay (1986) approach ideology in this way. They identify three ideal types: liberalism, socialism and realism. Gilpin (1975), in writing about political economy, has identified the same three although his terminology is different and his exemplification is somewhat narrower. Writers in an earlier period have spoken of realism and idealism/utopianism. Recently a WORLD SOCIETY perspective has become fashionable.

In this usage ideology is perhaps interchangeable with 'perspective' or 'intellectual tradition'. It is a way of looking at politics both domestically and externally. Indeed, in the World Society perspective it is a way of collapsing that distinction. It is more concerned with the subject as studied on the campus rather than the subject as conducted by the FOREIGN OFFICE, but the two activities are interdependent.

## IFC
*See*: WORLD BANK GROUP

## IGO
Intergovernmental Organizations. Some-

times rendered as International Governmental Organizations. To all intents and purposes, the meaning is the same. IGOs are founded by governments representing STATES. These organizations are established to engage in problem-solving in the interests of, and possibly on behalf of, their member states. The specificity of the problem(s) to be solved will have a bearing upon the SCOPE and DOMAIN of the organization. The broader the range of problems, the more multi-purpose the organization must be. Thus, the best known contemporary IGO is the UNITED NATIONS (UN) established by a multilateral TREATY known as the CHARTER. The UN aspires to universal membership and in this regard has been far more successful than its predecessor, the LEAGUE OF NATIONS. It is made up of a number of organs plus the SPECIALIZED AGENCIES, Commissions Funds and Programmes. It has attempted problem-solving in all the major ISSUE AREAS in contemporary INTERNATIONAL RELATIONS.

The greatest proliferation of IGOs since the inception of the UN in 1945 has been at the regional level. Regional cooperation and regional INTEGRATION have produced a host of IGOs in all the major identifiable regions of the world. Unlike the UN, most of these organizations are single purpose. They may operate in the area of military security, economic integration and cooperation, cultural exchanges, HUMAN RIGHTS questions and so on. The possibility of 'regional arrangements' of this kind was anticipated in the UN Charter, although the scale of the proliferation almost certainly was not.

Finally in this categorization, there are those IGOs which seek to articulate and aggregate the interests of a particular class of states within the total STATE SYSTEM, but which cut across regional demarcation lines, e.g. the Organization of Petroleum Exporting Countries (OPEC) and the COMMONWEALTH. Both of these IGOs draw members from a number of regions, yet neither can claim to be universal with-

in its class – there are oil exporting states outside OPEC and there are former British colonies outside the Commonwealth. Both are fairly 'loose' ASSOCIATIONS by comparison with the types mentioned above but both have been sufficiently successful to encourage emulators, rivals and opponents.

IGOs of all types are important channels of communication between representatives of their member states and governments. Particular importance is attached to the potentialities and possibilities for informal face-to-face contact. The cloakroom conference and the cocktail bar bargain are valuable activities which often go unreported by journalists and unrecorded by historians, but which enable DIPLOMATS to talk about talks and exchange information with others. More publicly IGOs can sometimes attempt to mediate in conflicts that occur between their members.

Thus NATO has attempted to ameliorate differences between Greece and Turkey, while the Organization of African Unity (OAU) has sought to mediate in a number of African conflicts including the protracted CIVIL WAR in Nigeria. This kind of internal conflict may, hypothetically, occur in any IGO. In the special case of the UN, because it is near universal all CONFLICT between member states can be seen as internal. In another sense, though, if the UN is viewed as an autonomous ACTOR conflict between the UN and a state or group of states can occur. Some of the most controversial moments in the UN PEACEKEEPING record have left the IGO as one of the parties to the conflict with member states in opposition to the Organization.

The above discussion raises the most fundamental question about IGOs. To what extent can they be regarded as autonomous actors in INTERNATIONAL POLITICS? REALISTS are inclined to deny the IGO any AUTONOMY. For them, the organization is little more than the sum of its constituent parts and is particularly susceptible to domination by the most powerful and influential state members. The IGO thus becomes an expression of and an extension of the FOR-EIGN POLICY of the dominant state or coalition. This rather limited view of IGOs is questioned by those who argue that the very existence of these organizations can affect, mould and even modify the policies of state members. Moreover the fact that states are concurrently members of a plurality of IGOs may mean that a cumulative impact will be generated over time which, effectively, sets limits upon what a state can or cannot do, or even say, on an ISSUE AREA. In this respect IGOs become what Pentland (1973) has called 'systemic modifiers' of state behaviour. To what extent are they autonomous actors?

There are two ways of looking at the autonomy question; one is institutional, the other issue-orientated. Institutionally, if an IGO develops a secretariat which can act independently of governments then this can lead to greater autonomy. This happened briefly to the UN under Hammarskjold but it was controversial and produced a reaction from, among others, the Soviet Union, which proposed to replace him with a troika system of international civil servants. This autonomy is more prevalent in economic IGOs such as the IMF and the United Nations Conference on Trade and Development (UNCTAD), a reflection of the greater amount of INTERDEPENDENCE in economic relations. Genuine INDEPEN-DENCE in the secretariat, as opposed to the quasi-independence above, is evident in regionally based IGOs such as the EUROPEAN COMMUNITY (EC). Since the EC has SUPRA-NATIONAL implications, the role of the secretariat is bound to be more significant in this case.

IGOs may gain autonomy because there are issue areas in WORLD POLITICS which can only be dealt with on a MULTILATERAL basis. These issue areas tend to be Prisoner's Dilemma situations where there are strong collective motives for cooperation, POLLU-TION, proliferation of NUCLEAR WEAPONS and access to the world's oceans being examples. If states are to act collectively in these areas with any likelihood of success

then they must establish a system of rule-governed relations, including a system of sanctions, that can be implemented by IGOs. By definition this will involve allowing the organizations a degree of autonomy.

## Image

An image is a subjective assessment made by an individual or a group of its physical and social milieu. An image is a psychological construct that is an amalgam of cognitive and affective processes. For this reason, there will always be a sense in which the image can be distinguished from 'reality'. This discrepancy may be trivial or it may be critical to any subsequent behaviour patterns. An image, moreover, contains elements of past, present and future.

The most basic image identifiable in WORLD POLITICS is the image that a people have of themselves expressed through their concept of nationality and the ideas of NATIONALISM. Thus the first tangible images that most people have are of their own national or ethnic reference group. As with so many political attitudes, these self-images will be the result of upbringing and socialization. In most NATION-STATES these images are reinforced by the mass media and sometimes manipulated for PRO-PAGANDA purposes. As suggested above, images are affective as well as cognitive; they can therefore arouse feelings of amity or enmity. Hostile and/or friendly images of other national and ethnic groups are an important factor in the impact they can have upon world politics. Indeed, a number of studies have shown the tendency for images to be reciprocated: hostility begets hostility, friendliness begets friendliness. This tendency is referred to as the MIRROR IMAGE.

The study of national images has been wholly advanced within the SOCIAL SCIENCE APPROACH. K. E. Boulding's 1956 work is widely regarded as the first, and now seminal, contribution to the literature. Subsequently, images have been particularly studied by those favouring a psychologically orientated approach to the subject and by students of PUBLIC OPINION.


## IMF

The International Monetary Fund (IMF) was established as part of the BRETTON WOODS system in 1944. Subsequently it became part of the UN structure. In conjunction with the WORLD BANK, the IMF was regarded as one of the central institutions for the management of post-war economic relations.

The IMF, as the name implies, was intended to supply international liquidity to member STATES finding themselves in BALANCE OF PAYMENTS difficulties. In addition the Fund was to manage a system of stable (rather than fixed) exchange rates. A particular currency would have a 'par value' which was expressed in terms of dollars. Alteration of that rate would be effected, with the approval of the Fund, if the STATE's external payments balance was held to be in 'fundamental disequilibrium'. As already stated, in addition to its supervision of the exchange rate REGIME, the Fund lends money to member states in balance of payments difficulties. It is always assumed that the monetary authorities of the recipient state would take appropriate measures to correct such imbalances and indeed it has become a feature of IMF lending that so-called 'conditionality' stipulations would be part of the 'rescue package'. Recognition of the right to lay down such conditions is indicated by the recipient government issuing a 'letter of intent' to the IMF. This whole procedure – of laying down conditions which are then accepted in the letter – is clearly a significant erosion of state SOVEREIGNTY. Although an accepted and expected feature of the IMF's conduct it is not without controversy. The IMF has a tradition of requiring states in receipt of its loans to make internal adjustments to rectify the disequilibrium. Thus raising taxes and interest rates and cutting public expenditure, including subsidies, are typical IMF-preferred policies.

The linchpin of the original Bretton Woods arrangement was the US dollar. The gold/dollar exchange rate had been fixed at 35 dollars per ounce in 1934 and it was assumed that this exchange rate was, to all intents and purposes, fixed and immutable. During the early post-war period of reconstruction the principal concern about the dollar was its shortage. Although the US balance of payments began to move into deficit during the 1950s it was not regarded as serious. As long as the dollar shortage remained other states in the system were willing to see the United States running deficits which were financed by the export of dollars. The IMF system was, in fact, a GOLD EXCHANGE STANDARD with the dollar regarded as being 'as good as gold' for these purposes. The IMF system of stable exchange rates established as a fundamental principle of the system after 1944 began to be seriously questioned towards the end of the 1960s. By 1961 the great emerging problem was the US deficit. By running a deficit the United States was funding the system but was equally running the risk that, if confidence collapsed, then a forced devaluation of the dollar would be necessary.

When the collapse of confidence in the dollar eventually came in 1971 it was both spectacular and momentous. Speculative attacks upon the dollar were encouraged by a series of poor TRADE figures which seemed to suggest that the link between gold and the dollar might have to be suspended or ended altogether. In August 1971 the US President announced that the convertibility of the dollar into gold was temporarily suspended. At the end of the year a joint meeting of the Group of Ten (G10) and the Executive Directors of the Fund agreed to devalue the dollar 10 per cent against the other currencies in the Group. These decisions effectively brought down the Bretton Woods system of stable exchange rates. Following a second dollar devaluation in February 1973 the system was abandoned and the new era of 'floating' rates replaced it.

Cautious and considered deliberations of these changes were reduced by the first OIL SHOCK in 1973–4. Suddenly states were moving massively into credit or debit on their balance of payments. Any chance of structured reform was abandoned and floating continued into the future. The Jamaica Agreement of January 1976 amended the Articles of Agreement of the Fund to legitimize floating. In reality there has been a good deal of 'management' of the float by the central banking authorities of the principal G10 states since. The Jamaica Agreement also confirmed that for the future the SPECIAL DRAWING RIGHTS (SDR) would be the principal reserve asset of the Fund.

At the time of writing the major ISSUE AREAS facing the Fund are THIRD WORLD DEBT and the new OSTPOLITIK in Eastern Europe. Because the international economic system is so bifurcated between the NORTH and the SOUTH the IMF has tended to reflect that structural division. Membership of the Fund now exceeds 150 states but, unlike the political organs of the UN system, the IMF DECISION-MAKING structure operates upon a system of weighted voting. Voting power depends upon the amount of quotas the state has with the Fund. IMF quotas are credits rather than money but, in addition to determining voting power, they also determine the amount of foreign exchange a state can draw from the Fund. Thus the most economically significant states contribute the greatest quotas, but get the most from the system. The Group of Five states within the Fund membership are in effect at the top of the HIERARCHY. In effect the United States, the EUROPEAN COMMUNITY and Japan can, through their voting power (which only reflects their economic significance) effectively influence the working of the Fund. THIRD WORLD states represented by the Group of 24 cannot match this putative power.

## Immigration

Refers to the movement of people from their home STATE to another state, usually to seek employment, to improve wages, to join family members or to escape from adverse living conditions. The immigrant is distinct from the REFUGEE in that the move is voluntary rather then forced. The issue of international migration impinges directly on central concepts such as SOVEREIGNTY, NATIONALITY and HUMAN RIGHTS and as such has important implications for INTERNATIONAL RELATIONS. For example, migrants may be a source of conflict between sending and receiving countries (as is the case between AFGHANISTAN and Pakistan). Immigration may also pose security problems in the receiving state, especially where cultural and IDEOLOGICAL differences between host and sender are great. In addition, movement across INTERNATIONAL boundaries can have unsettling economic and financial consequences arising from the international flow of capital, savings and investments. Most discussions of immigration centre on economic conditions as the main initiator of population movement but political factors are also crucial. Population movement is often impelled or encouraged by governments (e.g. Kenyan Asians after independence, or bourgeois Cubans after Castro's REVOLUTION); it is often prevented by governments (e.g. Jews in the Soviet Union) and of course, it is governments who decide whether immigrants should be allowed to enter the state of their choice. Political determinants are therefore crucial. Forced emigration has often been used as a means of achieving cultural homogeneity or ethnic dominance and can be linked with the rise of NATIONALISM in Europe and the rise of post-colonial new states in Africa and Asia. Remittance from migrant workers is often of great importance for the economies of many THIRD WORLD and developing states. Zimbabwe, Botswana, Lesotho and Mozambique are, in varying degrees, dependent on such sources of returning income. The host state (in this case South

Africa) is never reluctant to use this economic weapon to gain leverage over the sending states.

INTERNATIONAL LAW relating to human migration has tended to defer to the good will of sovereign states or else is bound up with specific TREATY commitments. Generally, states have no legal duty to admit all immigrants, and most impose selective restrictions on entry, most of which relate, at least ostensibly, to possible threats to the public safety, security, welfare or institutions of the recipient state. Often these restrictions serve to mask racial or geographical discrimination. However, there is a growing body of opinion that the moral duty of states to admit immigrants under certain conditions is incontestable. Greater concern for human rights may lead to more open boundaries but as yet, each state jealously guards its sovereign right to adjudicate such issues.

*See also*: ORBITER

## Imperialism

Derived from the Latin word 'imperium' it refers to the relationship of a hegemonic STATE to subordinate states, NATIONS or peoples under its control. An imperial policy therefore usually means a deliberate projection of a state's POWER beyond the area of its original jurisdiction with the object of forming one coherent political and administrative unit under the control of the HEGEMON. This assertion of dominance is associated with, but can be distinguished from, COLONIALISM. An empire can result in full economic and political integration of its subjects in the form of a SUPRANATIONAL entity whereas colonies are exploitive by definition. In practice though, the two concepts often overlap.

Territorial expansion is an age-old phenomenon but in the modern world it is usual to identify two distinct phases: (a) mercantilist or dynastic imperialism which dates roughly from 1492–1763 and which saw the Western hemisphere and much of

Asia come under European control and (b) 'new' imperialism, 1870–1914, which witnessed the subjugation by Europe of most of Africa and parts of the Far East. The period between is dormant in the sense that domestic issues such as BALANCE OF POWER, FREE TRADE, NATIONALISM and the industrial revolution were the major preoccupations of the European states. In the development of theories of imperialism it is the second phase that has attracted most attention. The first major effort in this direction was J. A. Hobson's *Imperialism* (1902), which linked the phenomenon with the demands of maturing capitalism for markets, investment opportunities, raw materials and cheap labour. Hobson's thesis was revived by Lenin in *Imperialism: The Highest Stage of Capitalism* (1917), which subsequently formed the basis of the COMMUNIST view of INTERNATIONAL RELATIONS and of the causes of WAR. The competitive urge generated by monopoly capitalism would inevitably result in generalized imperialist world wars which in turn would destroy capitalism itself, thus preparing the way for the establishment of socialism. The equation capitalism = imperialism = WAR has had enormous influence in the twentieth century world, although its explanatory power is rather limited. Many analysts have disputed the necessary connection between capitalism and imperialism and point to the frequency of imperial conquest and war long before the development of modern capitalism (see Schumpeter (1919)). Furthermore, it is as difficult to subsume the expansionist record of the Soviet Union under this formula as it is the apparent lack of imperial drives in advanced capitalist societies such as Switzerland or Sweden.

Alternative explanations, casting doubt on the MARXIST/LENINIST insistence on the link between economics and politics, abound in the literature on the subject. Thus, the demands of POWER-POLITICS, strategic imperatives, diplomatic manoeuvrings, the search for honour and prestige, the rise of assertive NATIONALISM, changes in military TECHNOLOGY, the shift in sea-power from sail to steam, developments in communications, the growth in the power of the media, the extension of the railway system, the invention of the telegraph – all these have been identified as factors in the rise of modern imperialism, as indeed have humanitarian or missionary impulses and racial IDEOLOGIES (a phrase which neatly couples the two is 'white man's burden'). Clearly, the phenomenon is not susceptible to a mono-causal or deterministic explanation; it is more likely to result from a combination of a number of often disparate elements which existed in some imperialisms, but not in others. Besides the Marxist/Leninist view, another which emphasizes the determinist nature of imperialism is the REALIST school where imperialism is regarded as a natural, and if not curbed, inevitable consequence of the anarchic, multi-state INTERNATIONAL SYSTEM (see H. J. Morgenthau, 1948).

In contemporary usage the word has become politicized and now denotes *any* form of sustained dominance by one group over another. 'Cultural' or 'economic' imperialisms are phrases frequently used to describe more subtle forms of relationship that do not involve overt political control. Notions of neo-imperialism, neo-colonialism and DEPENDENCE have accelerated the process of moving the term away from its traditional meaning, to such an extent that to many the term is now a political slogan so vague and wide-ranging that it is devoid of any practical or theoretical utility in the study of international affairs.

## Implementation

Implementation is a facet of DECISION-MAKING. While not every decision requires implementation – for instance, a decision to do nothing – every implementation act presupposes a previous decision. Thus when the United States decided in October 1962 to institute a QUARANTINE during the CUBAN MISSILE CRISIS, this decision required implementation by their military forces. Implementation may be seen as a set of discrete acts or as a process. Either way, it involves the agents of a particular ACTOR in carrying out certain behaviour repertoires at the instigation of the DECISION-MAKERS themselves. Of course, in the limiting case the decision-makers may implement their own decisions. This is more likely to occur in cases of HIGH POLITICS where core values and long-run goals are at stake in a particular policy outcome. Again in the example of the Cuban missiles, the US and Soviet leaders communicated directly with each other in order to manage the CRISIS successfully.

Analytically, then, implementation is that stage of a policy decision that comes after formulation. Additionally, the results of the implementation process will constitute FEEDBACK into the decision system. Policy makers should be enabled to decide thereby whether their policy is likely to achieve the goals they set when the initial formulation took place. For the decision system to work in this way it is necessary for what Halperin (1974) calls 'faithful implementation' to take place. Only very rarely is implementation a 'one-shot' affair. Usually it requires coordination between a number of departments of the government and cooperation between a number of governments, and non-state actors, if it is to stand any chance of working as intended.

The UK Government's decision to enter into negotiations to join the EC in 1961 was a highly complex decision to implement, because it involved the negotiating team in coordinating several different departmental interests within the government and several different external interests – including the COMMONWEALTH – at the same time. The French VETO cut short an implementation process that was proving extremely difficult to effect as the policy-makers had intended.

In large organizations – such as those involved in implementation of FOREIGN POLICY decisions – the process is treated as a standard operating procedure (sop). Sops may be highly resistant to change because

173

they represent the routines of the organization. They can also lead to a certain rigidity with the result that policy formulation may not be perfectly transferred into policy implementation as desired by the decision-makers. Halperin comments that this flexibility means that large organizations find it difficult to develop new plans quickly or to implement plans developed in a different context.

The possibility that faithful implementation may not occur because officials are unwilling to implement in the manner requested must be faced. In those political systems where the leadership is subjected to regular and routine electoral scrutiny the tendency is very apparent for senior bureaucrats to regard themselves as permanent fixtures and their political masters as transient and temporary occupants. In this way a bureaucracy can create its own ethos, rules of the game, procedures and so on. These will effectively reduce and constrain the initiatives available to decision-makers freely to implement their own policy decisions.

## Import

In the broadest terms an import is something which is introduced into an international ACTOR from the external environment. Thus it is possible to describe an intangible – such as democracy, NATIONALISM, feminism – being imported into a STATE, or a REGION from outside. It is equally possible to describe a tangible – manufactured goods – being imported.

The term is generally used in a narrower, economically based sense. Here the reference is to the movement of goods and services for which there is an identifiable demand into a specified economic system. Again with the growth of COMMON MARKETS and trading BLOCS the importing actor need not be a state.

Common sense indicates that one actor's imports are another's EXPORTS and, consequently, the level of imports into any system has to be monitored by policy makers

and their advisors. At any one time there will always be some actor in the system seeking to alter the balance between its imports and its exports. This disequilibrium may be short-term and temporary or long-term and structural. POLICY-MAKERS may seek to remedy this by discouraging imports and/or encouraging exports. The former policy is known as 'import substitution'.

Import substitution has a number of political advantages. If the market within the system is actually or potentially very large then import substitution will increase the self-sufficiency of the system *vis-à-vis* the external environment. For example, the establishment of CUSTOMS UNIONS such as the EUROPEAN COMMUNITY has led to extensive import substitution in the agricultural sector of the economy. In this example import substitution has led to over-production and to such measures as DUMPING of surpluses in other markets. Import substitution also affects positively the terms of TRADE between the actor and the environment.

Import substitution has the important additional advantage of reducing the actor's DEPENDENCE upon the external environment. Because it can lead to great uncertainties and vulnerabilities, dependency is often held to be an undesirable state of affairs. It can certainly place an actor that is so dependent in a situation where leverage, pressure and even coercion can be exerted by those providing goods and services. Thus, although import substitution is sometimes inefficient and is contrary to FREE TRADE ideas, it does have considerable political advantages and attractions.

## Incrementalism

A theory of DECISION-MAKING first developed by David Braybrooke and Charles E. Lindblom (1963). This was then incorporated into later works by Lindblom in 1965 and 1977. In the original discussion by the two authors the theory – called therein a 'strategy' – was termed 'disjointed incrementalism' but the shortened version is widely used. The essential arguments for incrementalism are outlined in the fourth chapter of the joint work. The authors, using the idea of a continuum, suggest that decision-making can be analysed using two variables: the degree of information that is available at the time of decision and the degree of change that is effected by the decision. Combining the two variables four typologies emerge: decisions effecting large change where the available information is good, decisions effecting small change where the available information is good, decisions involving small change where the available information is poor and decisions involving large change where the available information is poor. What is termed 'incremental politics' is identified as type three above: decisions effecting small change made with a low level of information.

It is suggested that incrementalism is typical or 'normal' decision-making. POLICY-MAKING is seen as solving problems, issues are approached on a step by step basis, the evaluation of alternatives is restricted and the goals sought after are short-term rather than long-term.

Incrementalism has been well described as like moving away from outcomes that are undesired, rather than towards outcomes that are desired. Policy-making, according to the incremental model, proceeds through a series of approximations which is why it is characterized as 'problem solving'. Where long-term change is effected it comes about through sequential rather than sudden movement.

Although the above-mentioned texts were not written specifically with FOREIGN POLICY-making in mind, the theory of incrementalism has recognizable features with this context. In general terms it has served to direct attention away from what have been called rational ACTOR models of policy-making towards viewing the organizational and bureaucratic contexts as important to the policy process. Graham T. Allison (1971) pays due respect to the innovations of the earlier books.

## Independence

This term has normally been used in two senses in the analysis of INTERNATIONAL POLITICS and FOREIGN POLICY. First, it is used in a quasi-legal sense to indicate that a STATE exercises exclusive authority over a tract of territory and that, moreover, this exercise of authority is recognized by other ACTORS in the system. In this first sense, independence is a corollary of SOVEREIGNTY. Secondly, the word is used to describe a POLICY GOAL pursued by individuals, interests and factions which seek independence or SELF-DETERMINATION for an identifiable group which will often comprise a NATION or a putative nation.

The two usages become fused when a state is declared independent. This has been a common occurrence in twentieth century international politics, particularly as former COLONIAL powers have relinquished control over peoples and territories that were previously part of their imperial systems. This process is known as DECOLONIZATION. Thus the term independence marks a historical turning point in the political history of the majority of state members of the contemporary system. In most cases this transition was marked symbolically to demonstrate the transfer of AUTHORITY. In THIRD WORLD states the history of the period is often referred to as the 'struggle' – as in the idea of the struggle for independence – while the mobilization of people in support of these goals produces the 'movement' – as in the idea of the independence movement. Some analysts have pointed to the dangers of being too easily seduced by these symbols and have argued that in many important respects – particularly economic – DEPENDENCE not independence was the reality. This idea that colonial control continues in other forms is known as NEO-COLONIALISM.

The quasi-legal use of the term independence is exclusively reserved for state actors. It is therefore part of that approach to the subject known as STATE-CENTRISM. Discerning analysts of this approach accepted that political independence had to be safeguarded in a system that was SUB-SYSTEM dominant. Traditionally this was achieved by BALANCE OF POWER DIPLOMACY which was dedicated to the preservation of the political independence of, at least, the dominant actors in the system. Complete political independence was probably only available to those states committed to ISOLATIONISM. Even then it was difficult to sustain in all ISSUE AREAS of policy, particularly in the field of international economic relations where the benefits of INTERDEPENDENCE were demonstrated by the classical economic LIBERALS of the nineteenth century. As the system has become more of a mixed actor structure, the applicability of the term independence – in the first sense outlined above – has been reduced. The term AUTONOMY is certainly more appropriate for the non-state actors.

## Influence

A term which has strong connotations with POWER, influence is used in two senses. First, it is used as a non-coercive form of power. Like power is can be analysed both as a CAPABILITY and as a relationship. Influence relationships, moreover, are similar to power relationships in the sense that they seek to 'cause' someone to do something that he/she would not otherwise do. In the case of influence relationships, however, sanctions are not overtly employed. The target is persuaded to change its mind instead of being coerced into doing so. Influence relationships, in this non-coercive sense, are likely to be particularly prevalent among ACTORS that are accustomed to expecting and receiving a high level of responsiveness in their relationships. ALLIES rather than adversaries, coalition partners rather than CONFLICT parties, actors with 'special relationships'; it is in these situations that influence rather than power will be the preferred way of securing agreement. What has been called sensitivity INTERDEPENDENCE is often thought of in terms of

responsiveness within an existing relationship and the two concepts – influence and interdependence – may be linked in this way. Alternatively influence relationships may be identified in a HIERARCHY, provided that the actors further down the 'pecking order' accept the leadership of the 'top dog'; then the latter will be able to exercise influence over the rest, but conversely will be susceptible to influence in return. Again the responsiveness will be present but the relationship will be closer to what has been called 'vulnerability interdependence'. In a hierarchical system influence will be prone to shade off into power when and if actors seek to manipulate perceived vulnerabilities in a coercive manner.

Secondly, influence may be identified within the power relationship itself, rather than as an alternative to it. The term can thus be used to describe power relationships which fail to produce compliance, but do produce some reaction from the target to the imposer's attempts. Because influence is seen as a kind of power failure, in this second usage the two concepts are much less distinct. 'He failed to get the target to do what he (imposer) wanted, but he still caused the target to change its behaviour' would be an example of influence in this way. In this second context the CAPABILITIES for influence and the capabilities for power are identical. 'He thought he had power but he only had influence', could plausibly be said of someone in this second sense. Thus any ACTOR that is unable to overcome resistance and to secure its goals is merely 'influential', but not 'powerful', the distinction between this use of 'influence' and the use discussed earlier being in the role played by sanctions. In one use of the term influence sanctions play no role whatsoever, in the other they are present in the relationship but fail to secure compliance.

*Influence without power* and *influence within power* are difficult ideas to operationalize and to observe empirically. Many distinguished authorities have not even tried. Dahl (1984), one of the foremost writers on power within political science itself, lumps 'power' 'authority' 'control' all together as 'influence terms'. In this way influence truly becomes the paradigm 'portmanteau' term. This approach has been avoided here by defining influence in two ways which are admittedly close to power but which can, at least analytically, be distinguished from it.

## INF treaty

This convention, signed on 8 December 1987 between the United States and Soviet Union, eliminates a class of missiles variously described as Intermediate Range Nuclear Forces (INF) or Long-Range Theatre NUCLEAR WEAPONS (LRTNW). The essence of the TREATY is the agreement to remove all ground-launch BALLISTIC MISSILES and CRUISE MISSILES from Europe. The systems stipulated cover ranges of between 500 and 5,000 km. Thus, at the lower end of the range the agreement strays beyond the limits of what is normally regarded as a LRTNW. In detail the systems covered are: on the American side Pershing II and Pershing IA ballistic missiles and GLCM. On the Soviet side: SS-4, SS-5, SS-20, SS-12, SS-23 and SSC-X-4. In purely quantitative terms these reductions heavily favour the US position. Additionally the treaty involves the contracting parties in a highly incursive system of INSPECTION.

The 1987 Treaty was the culmination of some six years of ARMS CONTROL negotiations instigated by the United States with a set of proposals known as the 'zero option'. For a long time it looked as if the zero option proposal was hopelessly optimistic and even cynical in its declaratory stance. However, the dogged persistence of the Reagan Administration to negotiate from strength combined with the leadership changes in the Soviet Union culminated in agreement.

The momentum generated by these events could well spill over into an agreement to reduce tactical or battlefield

nuclear weapons. Certainly it is going to make it very difficult for those wishing to 'modernize' these systems to realize this goal in the future. As such the piecemeal denuclearization of NATO would become a distinct possibility. It would also throw into sharp relief the commitment by NATO to the FIRST USE of nuclear weapons.

## Innocent passage

The right of foreign sea-going vessels to traverse the territorial waters of another STATE without interference provided 'it is not prejudicial to the peace, good order or security of the coastal state' (Article 19 of the 1982 UN Convention On the LAW OF THE SEA). This includes the right to stop and anchor but only in accordance with the ordinary navigational requirements or if occasioned by FORCE MAJEURE or distress. The 1982 Convention initiated a twelve-mile innocent passage REGIME for all vessels, although some states (e.g. the Soviet Union) require prior authorization for passage of warships. In INTERNATIONAL LAW, vessels in innocent passage are subject to the laws of the coastal state and the usual rules relating to transportation and navigation. Submarines must normally travel on the surface and show the FLAG. However, the Convention was somewhat ambiguous in the provision for underwater vehicles since the problem of inspection and detection is difficult even for the most technologically advanced coastal states. Sweden and Norway, for example, are known to be particularly concerned about the difficulties of tracking the illegal submerged passage of Soviet submarines in Scandinavian waters.

The exact meaning of 'innocent passage' has never been clear but the Convention did attempt to clarify it and provide specific criteria for assessment. Thus, the character of the mission must be understood (is it threatening or dangerous or contrary to international law?). Secondly, the activities of the vessels during passage must conform to certain standards (are they engaged in weapons practice or information gathering?). Thirdly, the passage must comply with environmental, fishing and research requirements (are they engaged in wilful POLLUTION or illegal sea-bed exploitation?). All these criteria were intended to strengthen the hand of the coastal state and to ensure that only activities which had a direct bearing on passage were permitted. Critics have argued that the concept is a vague and ambiguous one and that it seriously impedes global naval mobility. In particular, the territorialist trend towards greater coastal jurisdiction of adjacent waters caused some concern to the larger naval powers. Nevertheless, most commentators agree that in relation to innocent passage, the Convention achieved a fine balance between traditional naval interests and coastal states' aspirations towards greater control of the sea.

*See also*: LAW OF THE SEA

## Inspection

Inspection is a form of VERIFICATION. It is that form of verification that takes place on-site. Inspection thus differs from surveillance. Surveillance is also a form of verification but it involves observing rather than inspecting. In an efficient verification system, inspection would properly follow surveillance. The latter would suggest that something was wrong, inspection would either confirm or deny this assumption. Inspection is thus a means of providing information and INTELLIGENCE. It helps to establish that an ACTOR is doing something, or refraining from doing something. Inspection may be carried out by the parties to a relationship or by a third party – such as the UNITED NATIONS – brought into the relationship because of its perceived NEUTRALITY and impartiality. In a relationship of total co-operation and trust, inspection would not be regarded as either appropriate or necessary. In a relationship of pure CONFLICT and total hostility, inspection would not be possible. Inspection functions essentially along a continuum between these two polar positions.

Inspection is important to most ARMS CONTROL and DISARMAMENT agreements. In addition to providing the information and intelligence function referred to above, inspection helps to deter evasion of arms control and disarmament agreements. If it is impossible for parties to agree to a system of inspection then they may find it impossible to agree to arms control and disarmament *per se*. Alternatively, and in the absence of agreement about inspection, the parties will have to rely upon other means of verification, such as the so-called national technical means. For example, when it proved impossible to get agreement on the number of on-site inspections that would be permissible, the United Kingdom, the United States and the Soviet Union agreed to a PARTIAL TEST BAN TREATY in 1963. The only kinds of NUCLEAR WEAPONS tests needing inspection were those conducted underground (to avoid confusion with earthquakes) and this class of testing was left out of the final agreement. Inspection systems are normally institutionalized in the terms of the agreement between the contracting parties. For example, under the NON-PROLIFERATION TREATY which came into force in 1970, the International Atomic Energy Agency (IAEA) is empowered to make periodic and *ad hoc* inspections of national facilities in order to maintain the safeguards regime. If a full-blown agreement to initiate general and complete DISARMAMENT became possible, it would require an international inspectorate, among other things, to ensure that agreements were being kept. Inspection is part of the family of international institutional repertoires that includes fact-finding, observation and supervision duties. All of these quasi-diplomatic functions require some measure of support and cooperation from the parties being inspected or supervised if they are actually to be efficacious.

## Insurgency

Insurgency is an armed unsurrection or rebellion against an established system of government in a STATE. If the violent challenge by the insurgents is forcefully resisted by the incumbents, and it normally is, a CIVIL or internal WAR situation will result. Such outcomes lead to PROTRACTED violence between the parties. Insurgencies are normally aimed at one of two goals. Centripetal insurgencies seek to replace the incumbent REGIME with a system of government more conducive to the interests and inclinations of the insurgents. Typical within this category are movements for the INDEPENDENCE of colonial peoples and territories which seek via the insurgency to end formal colonial control. Because colonial systems relied upon coercion rather than consent as their principal means of social control, even a fairly low level of insurgent violence will be perceived by the authorities as a threat which has to be resisted. Centripetal insurgency is also a typical form of violent opposition to authoritarian REGIMES within states that are formally independent. In this sense the term is isomorphic with the idea of REVOLUTION – although not all revolutions take the form of insurgencies, of course. Centrifugal insurgencies, on the other hand, are aimed at secession from the incumbent state and the formation of a new entity. In the present system centrifugal insurgencies are likely to be associated with the expression of ethnic NATIONALISM. Although less common historically than centripetal insurgencies, contemporary instances such as Eritrea and the Southern Sudan show the salience of this category.

Individuals and groups are recruited into insurgency movements by two principal appeals: (a) to their sense of ethnic identity and (b) to their political allegiance. These two appeals may fuse, as they did in the case of the Malay Communist Party after 1948, if affective and cognitive attitudes come together. Social groups that are recruited into insurgency movements include the intelligentsia and the rural peasantry.

This fusion was explicitly recognized in the idea of PEOPLE'S WAR and the Chinese and VIETNAMESE revolutions which exemplified this model.

Insurgencies proceed by using the strategy of unconventional warfare, including GUERRILLA WAR, particularly in their earlier stages. Centripetal insurgencies normally move beyond this guerrilla mode in their later stages when it becomes necessary physically to 'liberate' areas of the disputed territory from the control of the incumbents. Eventually the violence may become essentially CONVENTIONAL if there is no short cut available to removing the last vestiges of the STATUS QUO. Anti-colonial insurgencies usually succeeded well before this point of finality was reached. In all cases insurgency situations are paradigm instances of the CLAUSEWITZIAN tradition of viewing the military instrument as the means of achieving political goals.

Since insurgencies are protracted conflicts, external or third party INTERVENTION is the norm rather than the exception, certainly in the macropolitical system post-1945. Third party intervention tends towards one of three typologies. First, a third party may attempt to mediate between the insurgents and the incumbents. Diplomatically such intervention requires giving at least DE FACTO RECOGNITION to the insurgent movement. Secondly, intervention may occur because the external actor has been drawn into the violence as an ally or protector of one of the parties. If this intervention is made on the side of the insurgents then they will look to the ally to provide them with a sanctuary or BASE area, safe and secure, from which operations against the STATUS QUO REGIME can be conducted. For the latter, on the other hand, the most important role an ally can play is diplomatic support and economic AID to assist in prosecuting their campaign against the insurgents. During the 1960s this prosecution came to be called COUNTER-INSURGENCY. Thirdly, an outside party can use an insurgency to penetrate the state concerned militarily and/or economically for its own interests. This can occur as a SPILL-OVER from alliance links or it may be quite independent of the parties. As a result the target state becomes in effect a client or satellite, whatever the outcome of the civil war.

## Integration

Integration is both a process and an end state. The aim of the end state sought when actors integrate is a political community. The process or processes include the means or instruments whereby that political community is achieved. There is an important proviso which must be entered immediately. The process of integration should be voluntary and consensual. Integration which proceeds by FORCE and COERCION is IMPERIALISM. Although historically empire-building has some of the characteristics currently attributed to integration, modern scholarship has been insistent that the process of integration should be regarded as non-coercive. Taking a historical perspective, the most significant attempts at building political communities in the past have been directed towards the creation of NATION-STATES. Nationalist sentiments have often preferred to describe this as unification rather than integration, moreover. Current scholarship, with its emphasis upon integration between STATE actors, can present a truncated view of the process if due regard is not paid to the nation-building purposes of earlier eras.

An integrated political community must possess certain structural characteristics. Thus typically among STATES integration will produce a collective configuration of DECISION-MAKING that will be closer to the SUPRANATIONAL ideal type rather than the INTERNATIONAL. For instance, collective decisions might be taken by a majority of the membership and the strict UNANIMITY principle would be abandoned. The need for policy integration will be particularly important if the nascent community is responsible for the allocation of goods and services between the constituent units. This will certainly be the case in those instances where political community building is predicated upon economic integration via CUSTOMS UNIONS and COMMON MARKETS. This aspect of community building has particularly exercised the interest and attention of students of integration in the post-1945 period.

At a minimum, integration presupposes the existence of a SECURITY COMMUNITY, that is to say a system of relationships which has renounced force and coercion as means of settling differences. Beyond this requirement, economic INTERDEPENDENCE will encourage the putative participants to engage in the kinds of collective action referred to above in order to promote mutual interests. REGIONALISM – expressed both in terms of similarity and proximity – will further enhance these tendencies. As integration proceeds new tasks, responsibilities and mandates will be taken on by the central institutions. This 'organizational task expansion', as it has been called, will be positively correlated with the integration process.

In an integrated community, political processes will take on characteristics often associated with intrastate, rather than interstate, politics. For instance, political parties and interest groups will start to press demands and articulate interests at the centre as well as at the periphery. Indeed, eventually they will prefer to concentrate upon the former locus of POWER. Groups representing economic, social, environmental and religious interests will develop in addition to more traditional party arrangements. If economic integration has been a key preliminary to political community building then these groups may well be associated with wealth–welfare issues. The 'rules of the game' for these groups will broadly include a willingness to work within the system in order to achieve their goals and specifically a commitment to PLURALISM as a political style. This pluralist characteristic of the political processes will give rise to TRANSNATIONAL politics as an increasingly significant section of the population within the member states perceive that more and more of their expectations and aspirations are being met within the integrated structure.

A political community must command the loyalties and affections of the majority of the population of its constituent units. Historically in the formation of nation-states, NATIONALISM provided the IDE-OLOGICAL and attitudinal infrastructure for this loyalty transfer. Contemporary efforts at building communities 'beyond the nation state' have the double task of providing a new focus while combating the centrifugal impulses of nationalism. FUNCTIONALISM and NEO-FUNCTIONALISM have paid particular attention to this aspect of integration; the functionalist's logic tries to suggest that there will be a progressive transfer of loyalty away from the constituent states towards the new community on the basis of a utilitarian calculation of where the wealth–welfare policy issues are really being handled.

Integration is a highly persuasive process in the contemporary MACROPOLITICAL system. Its development since 1945 has been largely on a regional basis with the greatest advances being made within Western Europe. The development there of a security community following the Second World War was an important prerequisite. Externally the active encouragement of the United States from the MARSHALL PLAN onwards was an important contributory factor in the emergence of new entities in the continent. As the number of actors involved in the European experiment has increased some observers have seen the dynamic being diluted. On the other hand the SCOPE of integration – as measured by the number of sectors/issues involved in the integration process – has increased.

## Intelligence

Since knowledge is POWER, the gathering of information about another's CAPABILITIES and intentions is a vital aspect of STATE behaviour, both internally and externally. It can be open or covert, strategic or non-strategic. In all cases, its purpose is to acquire, analyse and appreciate data in order to facilitate POLICY-MAKING. While the acquisition of confidential information is the prime function of the intelligence community, other roles associated with it are counter-intelligence (to prevent others acquiring information), deception (the spread of disinformation) and covert action (political warfare or subversion). Intelligence is gathered in two ways, technical and human. Technical intelligence is referred to as *sigint* (signals intelligence) and *elint* (electronic intelligence); human intelligence is called *humint* and refers primarily to espionage. It is a mistake to assume that technical intelligence (through the use of spy satellites, sensitive listening devices, early warning aircraft and spy ships) has rendered human intelligence obsolete. There are some kinds of information (classified documents or likely intentions of DECISION-MAKERS) that are not externally detectable, however sophisticated the TECHNOLOGY involved. An 'agent in place' or a highly trained individual on the spot who is able to eavesdrop, purloin or otherwise glean sensitive information, is still an essential instrument of intelligence services. In any case, since the problem of avoiding strategic or political surprise lies more in analysis than in gathering information, human intelligence will always be paramount. Faulty analysis of relevant information has resulted in some spectacular and well known political and strategic disasters. Among them are the following: The German attack on the Soviet Union in 1941 (Operation Barbarossa). PEARL HARBOR 1941, the North Korean–Chinese offensive 1950, the BAY OF PIGS 1961, the Tet Offensive 1968, the Yom Kippur War 1973 and the FALKLANDS/MALVINAS War of 1982. Intelligence failures of this kind are often followed by political upheaval and measures of organizational reform, but given the complexity and volume of data available, as well as the constraints of time, it is doubtful that they can be eliminated altogether. Scholarly analysis of these events suggests that the problem usually lies with the consumer of intelligence rather than with the producer. Bureaucratic inertia, complacency, internal rivalry and above all, a fixed image of an adversary's likely behaviour, are the most common faults.

Intelligence is often referred to as the 'missing dimension' of diplomatic history and INTERNATIONAL RELATIONS. Apart from the very nature of the enterprise, one of the reasons for this is that intelligence successes are rarely made known outside the professional circles involved in them, and then only when the outcome cannot be affected. One of the outstanding successes of modern intelligence was undoubtedly the deciphering of German wartime codes (the Enigma machine). This, it was subsequently claimed, considerably shortened the Second World War. However, we have no means to substantiate this: in matters of intelligence failure is easier to gauge than success.

## Interdependence

Interdependence in WORLD POLITICS implies that ACTORS are interrelated or connected such that something that happens to at least one actor, on at least one occasion, in at least one place, will affect all the actors. Thus in any given system of relations the more actors, the more places and the more occasions, the greater the interdependence. As Keohane and Nye (1977) point out, interdependence always implies sensitivity, in the short term at least. The above definition is also congruent with this idea of sensitivity. Whether all actors in a system are affected equally will define whether the interdependence is symmetrical or not. Symmetry is usually seen as a benchmark against which actual instances may be judged. In reality it is not likely to be perfect. Conversely if one actor in a system is relatively indifferent about some

change in relationships while another is crucially affected by it, then the interdependence is asymmetric. This can lead to a highly manipulative set of relations with one actor or group being totally dependent upon some other actor or group. This highly vulnerable position is again recognized by Keohane and Nye as a longer-term and structurally determined effect of interdependence. It also bears a strong family resemblance to POWER analysis.

Although ideas about interdependence became very fashionable during the 1970s, more discerning writers recognized that interdependence, as a characteristic of relationships, could be identified with one of the most persistent features of the STATE SYSTEM – the ALLIANCE. It is quite clear that the activities of ally seeking and alliance construction presage interdependence. In the alliance situation the degree of interdependence will depend upon how much the allies need each other and how dependent they are upon each other's CAPABILITY to meet the external threat. In the twentieth century recognition of the importance of interdependence in military–security ISSUE AREAS was taken a stage further with the idea of COLLECTIVE SECURITY. In terms of the concept of interdependence, collective security took the motivation that produces ally seeking a stage further and sought to establish a security REGIME which would be more organized than the traditional alliance. At the same time both institutional responses recognized the significance of interdependence.

As the Keohane and Nye book (1977) shows, more recent scholarship on the idea of interdependence has tended to focus primarily upon wealth–welfare economic issue areas rather than those referred to above. The explanation for this is not hard to find. As a general rule interdependence increases directly as industrialization and MODERNIZATION take place. Moreover, if and when these processes commence, regular and routine access to markets will be required to achieve and sustain economic growth. Interdependence increases further and a complex FEEDBACK loop is set up between certain economic goals and the consequences of interdependence. The TRADE SYSTEM is usually taken as the paradigm example of this process of economic interdependence. The larger the ration of trade to GDP the more dependent the state is upon the international trading system.

Recent scholarly interest in interdependence is a reflection of this economic fact of life rather than the military–security issue area mentioned earlier. Indeed, a whole perspective or paradigm on MACRO-POLITICS – the PLURALIST – has been built upon recognition of this as a persistent and pervasive process in the system. Ideas about REGIMES and empirical analysis of regime construction have, again, been primarily influenced by this sector of macropolitical activity.

*See also*: COMPLEX INTERDEPENDENCE

### International

The word was coined by Jeremy Bentham and first appeared in *An Introduction to the Principles of Morals and Legislation* (1780). He invented the word to give a more accurate rendering of the Latin phrase *ius gentium* or 'law of nations':

> The word 'international', it must be acknowledged, is a new one; though, it is hoped, sufficiently analogous and intelligible. It is calculated to express, in a more significant way, the branch of law which goes under the name of the law of nations; an appellation so uncharacteristic that, were it not for the force of custom, it would seem rather to refer to internal jurisprudence.

There has been some scholarly dispute as to whether Bentham was actually translating the Latin term, but what is beyond dispute is that he believed that a new adjective was needed to describe the system of law between SOVEREIGN STATES – 'international' LAW thus contrasts and ought not to be confused with, 'internal' law.

### International Court of Justice (ICJ)

This was established by the UN as its 'principal judicial organ' and as such is the most far-reaching attempt yet to apply the rule of law to international disputes. Its Statute, which is annexed to the Charter, is similar to its predecessor the PCIJ and all members of the UN are automatically members of it. The Court consists of fifteen judges who are elected by the GENERAL ASSEMBLY and the SECURITY COUNCIL voting separately. The elections are staggered to ensure continuity, and judges are elected for a period of nine years. Permanent members of the Security Council always have a sitting judge, but if a STATE appearing before the Court does not have a judge of its own NATIONALITY on the Court, it may appoint an *ad hoc* judge. The Court elects a president and vice-president for a three-year term, and it sits in the Hague.

The jurisdiction of the ICJ is twofold: settling international disputes and giving Advisory Opinions. Only states may be party to cases before the Court but non-state ACTORS, such as private individuals or international organizations, may be able to obtain advisory opinions. States which are not members of the UN, for example Switzerland, may under certain conditions acede to the Statute. The so-called Optional Clause (Article 36) was designed to strengthen the Court's competence and required that all signatory parties recognize the compulsory nature of the Court's jurisdiction. This has not proved very successful. It had been estimated that up to the 1980s less than half the members of the UN accepted this 'compulsory' jurisdiction.

Article 38 of the Statute of the Court stipulates that the law to be applied should be: international conventions (i.e. TREATIES), international custom and 'general principles of law recognized by civilized nations'. In practice, the Court has been extremely cautious about applying this last source of law to disputes that have been referred to it. In mitigation it has to be recognized that as the membership of the UN has more than trebled since the inception of the Court, the chance of any positive consensus emerging about these general principals has receded. Because the Court has cautiously based its judgements on convention and custom, the Court's main impact upon litigation has been to clarify existing law-creating processes rather than to boldly push for juridical innovation. The rather different situation on Advisory Opinions is referred to below.

A number of contentious cases have been heard and ruled upon by the ICJ but its decision has not always been complied with. For example, in the dispute between the UK and Albania over damage to ships and loss of life in the Corfu channel (1946), the Court awarded nearly a million pounds damages to the UK against Albania. Albania, though, has consistently refused to accept this judgement and pay the damages awarded against her. Although doubts abound as to the value of raising major international disputes before the ICJ (partly because of the difficulty of enforcing decisions), the Court has had many successes in laying down principles by which disputes may be judged. Notable in this context are the principles for drawing base lines concerning territorial waters, fishing rights and the method of calculating the continental shelf beneath the sea. Generally, though, the record of the Court is a mixed one in contentious cases.

Besides these, the Court has given a number of important Advisory Opinions which have helped set the tone of post-war international affairs. The most important of these was that concerning South West Africa/Namibia. In 1970 the Court, revising an earlier decision, gave an opinion to the effect that South Africa's presence in Namibia was illegal and that other states were under an obligation to take no action which recognized South Africa's legal authority there. South Africa continued to dispute this view, arguing that the UN did not succeed to the League's power of supervision over the mandate which was given to South Africa. In 1989, however, South Africa finally agreed to accept UN Resolution 435 which called for Namibian INDEPENDENCE. In this instance extraneous political factors, such as the GORBACHEV DOCTRINE and the US policy of CONSTRUCTIVE ENGAGEMENT, rather than pressure from the ICJ, produced the policy change.

The GENERAL ASSEMBLY OF THE UN is charged with the responsibility for 'developing' INTERNATIONAL LAW (Article 13) and there can be little doubt that the ICJ is a crucial component in this process. However, a number of important criticisms and constraining factors have mitigated against its development. Only a limited category of cases are brought to the Court – in general, those that do not affect fundamental interests. On issues that are likely to give rise to international conflict – issues connected with the COLD WAR, for example – the Court has not been brought into play. The lack of enforcement power is clearly a basic handicap and although under Article 94 the Security Council has power to give effect to the Court's judgements, it has never done so. In the work and even in the composition of the ICJ the 'political' and the 'legal' elements often appear to be at odds. In this connection, developing states in particular have been critical of the Court, seeing it as an instrument to further the interests of FIRST WORLD or Western or European states. Notwithstanding these criticisms, few would doubt that the ICJ is one of the most important attempts in international history to establish the rule of law in the settlement of international disputes.

### Internationalism

Refers to a wide variety of doctrines and IDEOLOGIES which aim to transcend STATE-CENTRED politics and focus instead on universal, or at least, transnational interests. It is usually associated with IDEALISM or utopianism in international thought and as such is presented as a rational and moral alternative to the narrow conception of NATIONALISM alleged to pervade REALIST thinking. However, the NATIONAL INTER-EST and the international interest are not always presented as alternatives. Under the liberal HARMONY OF INTERESTS doctrine the two are coterminous. American LIBERALISM, for example, has often asserted that 'what's good for America is good for the world'. This somewhat spurious identification of individual interests with those of the wider community is not confined to the United States. Most STATES, whatever their professed ideology, have at one time or another asserted if not believed similar sophistries. Indeed, a major theme of E. H. Carr's seminal text, *The Twenty Years Crisis* (1946), was the exposure of the use of the concept of internationalism to justify the ascendancy of the GREAT POWERS in the nineteenth and twentieth centuries.

Besides liberalism, other important examples of internationalist doctrines are MARXISM/LENINISM and PACIFISM. For the Marxist, the end product is 'the withering away of the state', for the pacifist it is the abolition of CONFLICT and warfare, but both are premised on the obstructiveness and volatility of state-centred political behaviour. In this sense, internationalism could be seen as a REVOLUTIONARY creed, not just in terms of ultimate goals but also in terms of the strategies envisaged to achieve them. Whereas state-centred theories could be said to be horizontal (i.e. state-to-state relations), internationalism is primarily vertical, appealing as it does to a universalist conception of the human condition. In the study of international affairs, its most recent manifestation is in the WORLD SOCIETY and WORLD LAW approaches where concepts of a common humanity and universal HUMAN RIGHTS replace more traditional perspectives. Internationalism is by no means a recent phenomenon in WORLD POLITICS and the history of international thought is replete with examples, mostly drawn for the NAT-URAL LAW tradition, of universalism or cosmopolitanism. Erasmus (1466–1536) is perhaps the most well known example, but

Kant (1724–1804), too, is central to this tradition.

Another, narrower conception of the term is when it is used as the antithesis of ISOLATIONISM. Thus, it is often alleged that during the nineteenth century, US foreign policy moved 'from isolationism to internationalism'. In this sense the term refers to American entry into full political and diplomatic participation in world affairs (e.g. it was not until 1863 that the United States attended and participated in an international conference). Internationalism here refers merely to greater cooperation and involvement with the international community. It does not necessarily carry universalist aspirations, though in the US case, the two did ride in harness.

## International law

The term was coined by Jeremy Bentham in 1780 and refers to the system of rules that are regarded as binding on STATES and other agents in their mutual relations.

It is usual to distinguish between two branches, 'public' and 'private'. Private international law, which is sometimes called 'conflict of laws', has to do with the rights and duties of individuals as they are affected by overlapping jurisdictions so is an adjunct of law within states rather than between them. Public international law on the other hand sees states themselves as legal entities and consists of the sum total of the rules, principles, customs and agreements that these entities accept as having the force of law in their relations. It is public international law that is dealt with here.

There is a great deal of confusion and often dismay concerning international law since the tendency to compare it with municipal law is often irresistible. International law has not been able to solve the problems of CONFLICT, AGGRESSION and WAR despite the hopes of idealists of the 'peace-through-law' approach who believe that law and institutions could form the basis and inspiration for a COMMON-

WEALTH of states. It is clear that international law differs in many respects from other types of law, so much so that some allege that it is not 'law properly so-called', but is at most 'positive morality' (Austin, 1832). Since the international system is characterized by an absence of a legislature, judiciary and executive, it is argued that there cannot therefore be a legal order. There is, of course, the GENERAL ASSEMBLY of the UNITED NATIONS (UN) comprising delegates from all member states, but their resolutions are not legally binding except on certain UN agencies. There is no system of courts and although the INTERNATIONAL COURT OF JUSTICE exists it can only decide cases where both sides agree and it has no enforcement powers. There is no governing body in INTERNATIONAL RELATIONS since the SECURITY COUNCIL – which is the nearest institutional equivalent – is handicapped by the VETO possessed by five states (the United States, the Soviet Union, China, France and the United Kingdom).

Notwithstanding these ultra-realist objections international law does exist even if it has limited applicability in the high profile areas of controlling aggression, conflict and war. It has over the centuries played a vital part in shaping the character of INTERNATIONAL SOCIETY, having developed an elaborate system of rules and procedures covering the land, the sea, the air, outer space, DIPLOMACY, NEUTRALITY, warfare, HUMAN RIGHTS and so on – almost every aspect upon which one state's existence impinges upon another.

## Sources

As may be expected given the absence of a written constitution and an international legislative body, the sources of international law are varied. They can be divided into four categories in order of importance: (a) agreements or TREATIES; (b) custom; (c) reason; (d) authority. With regard to (a) treaty law is founded on the principle of *PACTA SUNT SERVANDA* which means that treaties which are in force should be observed. There is a rider to this, *REBUS SIC STANTIBUS*, which does allow a party to nullify a commitment if there have been significant changes in the conditions existing at the time the agreement was originally entered into. Under international law a treaty normally prevails over a national law which may conflict with it. Regarding (b) an important part of contemporary law arises from the customary practice of states over many centuries. This may or may not be translated into MULTILATERAL treaties or codes of conduct. Categories (c) and (d) above are invoked when appeals to agreement and customary practice both fail to indicate the rights and obligations of states. In this case recourse is made to logical deductions from established principles or opinions of legal authorities and jurists. Underlying all this and giving force and credibility to international law is the principle of RECIPROCITY – the notion that it is in the mutual interest of all states to follow the established conventions.

## History and development

It is something of an exaggeration to say that Hugo Grotius (1583–1645) is the father of international law as paternity suits can be served at least as far back as the Romans, but it is generally acknowledged that, as with so many concepts in international relations, it was seventeenth century Europe that cradled, nourished and developed modern international law. Grotius certainly played a vital part in this process as it was his *De Jure Belli ac Pacis* (1625) that put international law on a secular basis and made the somewhat daring assertion that law between states was based not on theology but on reason. The emergence in Europe of INDEPENDENT and powerful NATION-STATES with incessant local rivalries and insatiable appetites for territorial expansion increased the need for legal demarcation of rights and duties and an important area of law which was refined during this period was that relating to the occurrence of, and conduct in, warfare. Theories of the JUST WAR abounded and although this has now disappeared from modern treaties on international law it still underlies approaches to aggression and SELF-DEFENCE.

Two predominant schools of thought evolved concerning the foundations of law: the 'naturalist' school, which identified international law with the law of nature based on reason, and the 'positivist' school, which held that law is man-made and therefore the consent of states is its sole basis. Positivist theories dominated the nineteenth century, the idea being that international law depended upon the will of the sovereign states and its purpose was to establish order and stability in an anarchical society rather than to promote values such as JUSTICE or fair play. In the twentieth century, especially as a result of experiencing two world wars, these assumptions began to be questioned and the NATURAL LAW tradition made something of a come-back. THE LEAGUE OF NATIONS was created in 1920 and although it was a lamentable failure in the prevention of continuing international conflict, it did help to break the untrammelled authority claimed by the sovereign states and prepared the way for the establishment of the UNITED NATIONS (UN) in 1946. The PERMANENT COURT OF INTERNATIONAL JUSTICE was set up in 1921 (succeeded by the International Court of Justice in 1946), the International Labour Organization was also established at this time and many other inter- or supra-national bodies were created which in theory at least were designed to water down the purer notions of SOVEREIGNTY which had hitherto dominated the field.

International law is now in a state of flux. It appears to be moving away from being premised on a system of sovereign states towards the development of a common law for a world community of individuals. In the past states were the sole legal persons; in the twentieth century this hard shell has been breached and international law now concerns itself not just with states but also with individuals. This development was substantiated by the Allied Tribunals of 1946 which found enemy per-sonnel responsible for 'crimes against humanity'. The process has continued to this day, most notably with recent multilateral declarations and conventions on HUMAN RIGHTS.

However, although international law appears to be moving in the general direction of WORLD LAW it is important to remember that the absence of a supranational enforcement agency, coupled with the continued insistence on state sovereignty and states rights, means that a radical revision of the basis of international law is unlikely in the near future.

*Communist views*
The emergence of the Soviet Union in 1917 wedded to MARXIST/LENINIST notions of the relationship between law and politics, has surprisingly had little effect on the orthodox system of international law described above. Since classical international law was founded on 'the state', this revolutionary IDEOLOGY appeared to demand that it, too, should 'wither away'. However, Soviet attitudes to international law have amounted to a modification rather than a denial of traditional practice. Soviet realism under Stalin suggested that the international legal order could not be changed overnight, however desirable that goal might be. Therefore, as a temporary expedient, the Soviet Union would recognize the validity of the system yet reserve the right to view it as a strategy of capitalist exploitation. In the Khrushchev era this 'transitional stage' was replaced by the international law of PEACEFUL COEXISTENCE, which was based on five principles: renunciation of war, NON-INTERVENTION, respect for territorial integrity and sovereignty, development of economic and cultural cooperation and recognition of the principle of EQUALITY. This package is not so far removed from Western notions and it indicates that the Soviet Union has abandoned the notion that 'capitalist' and 'socialist' international law are radically different from one another. Yet since these declarations were accompanied by a firm

commitment to the continuance of the international class-struggle and the willingness to use violence to this end ('wars of liberation'), the idea of peaceful coexistence has met with a high degree of scepticism in the West.

## The THIRD WORLD

Given the IMPERIAL and COLONIAL background, which incidentally was legitimized by the prevailing international legal system, it is hardly surprising that the principles and practices associated with international law would be challenged. The Christian and Eurocentric nature of this legal order would not, at first sight, appear to suit the needs of these newly independent states. However, traditional international law has proved to be remarkably resilient and pliable, and in recent years the new states have embraced the concepts of sovereignty, territorial integrity, non-interference, non-aggression and equality with all the fervour of the original participants at WESTPHALIA in 1648. The interests of the new states are often in direct conflict with the older members of the international community but so far they have been anxious to work within the existing framework rather than create a new one. The quest for a NEW INTERNATIONAL ECONOMIC ORDER (NIEO) has not so far been accompanied by a formal quest for a New International Legal Order, although some inroads have been made on past practice, especially in the direction of ideas associated with collectivism and 'common heritage'. These notions are at the forefront of the Third World approach and are a frontal assault on the more individualist and libertarian foundations of the old order.

*See also*: LAW OF THE SEA

## International Law Commission

A subsidiary organ of the UNITED NATIONS. The Commission was established in 1947 with fifteen members elected by the GENERAL ASSEMBLY. Since then the membership has been steadily expanded to reflect the growth in STATES in the Organization in general. Thus in 1956 the Commission was increased to twenty-one members, in 1961 to twenty-five and in 1981 to thirty-four. These members are distinguished legal authorities who sit in a personal capacity, not as representatives of governments.

The Commission is intended to implement Article 13 of the CHARTER which speaks of 'the progressive development of international law and its codification'. Codification refers to the process whereby existing conventions and customs may be stipulated in a more systematic form. Progressive development implies the extension of the international legal REGIME to areas where the law is nascent. It could be argued that it has been in the area of codification that the Commission has been most successful. For example, the Vienna Convention on Diplomatic Relations (1961) had its origins in the work of the Commission, as did the various conventions on the LAW OF THE SEA. In respect of the codification process, the Commission may be seen as working in the same tradition as the Committee of Experts for the Progressive Codification of International Law established by the LEAGUE OF NATIONS in 1930.

The existence and activity of the International Law Commission raises fundamental questions about the law-creating processes in the INTERNATIONAL SYSTEM. Perhaps an appropriately cautious view would be to say that, in comparison with the judgements of the INTERNATIONAL COURT OF JUSTICE, the reports of the Commission are of secondary importance as evidential value. As these proposals have the status of recommendations, it is unlikely that any radical reform of INTERNATIONAL LAW will arise *directly* from the work of the Commission. Rather, it is a more plausible conclusion to see this body working indirectly to change the parameters within which international law and its development is assessed.

## International morality

A traditional term, closely related to the notions of INTERNATIONAL ORDER and INTERNATIONAL SOCIETY, which implies that INTERNATIONAL RELATIONS are, or should be, conducted on the basis of certain shared ethical values, assumptions or norms which are not necessarily embodied in INTERNATIONAL LAW. The issue has been a contentious one throughout the history of international thought; indeed, the question of whether or not there are ethical limits to political action is central to the TRADITIONAL or classical approach to WORLD POLITICS. At one extreme, political REALISM, taking its cue from the MACHIAVELLIAN or HOBBESIAN models, argues that INTERNATIONAL POLITICS is essentially amoral; that notions such as JUSTICE or EQUALITY or freedom can only have proper application within the STATE. The INTERNATIONAL ANARCHY dictates that SELF-HELP and self-interest are key values in DECISION-MAKING. To think otherwise would not just be unwise or foolish, but irrational. In this view states create their own morality and the highest morality of all is the NATIONAL INTEREST and *RAISON D'ÉTAT*. A watered-down version of this extreme sceptical view is the relativist argument that moral obligations do impinge on world politics, but that the context within which it takes place renders it imperfect. The stress here is on the issue of national survival and on the instrumental value of order; in matters of policy formulation the outcome of order is more important than the principle of justice. Pursuit of BALANCE OF POWER therefore takes priority over the pursuit of justice, equality, HUMAN RIGHTS or freedom. This is the view adopted by most modern realists, including E. H. Carr, H. J. Morgenthau, R. W. Tucker and Henry Kissinger; order is a necessary precondition of justice and since the unrestrained pursuit of the latter could well lead to disorder and chaos, prudence rather than moral principle should guide state policy. Sometimes known as the 'morality of the lesser evil' this position rests on the belief that the moral requirements or

states, existing as they do with no common political superior, are of a different and perhaps lesser order than those of individuals within an orderly civil society. This is not to say that they do not exist or are not important; it is just that other more pressing values and considerations, usually revolving around security issues, are always likely to intrude.

In contrast, THE IDEALISTS or universalists hold that if human beings have moral obligations to one another, then so too must states, which after all are social collectivities. The idea of context is irrelevant; right conduct is universal and therefore what is considered good or evil in one context is, *ipso facto*, good or evil in another. This view identifies 'absolute' values such as the promotion of universal justice, human rights or SELF-DETERMINATION which override parochial concerns with interest or self-advantage. The society of states is in reality a society of people; BOUNDARIES exist but this does not diminish or alter the moral position. Rights of subsistence, for example, are universal, therefore traditional STATE-CENTRIC doctrines evolving around SOVEREIGNTY and NON-INTERVENTION are barriers to progress which must in the end be breached. Adherents to this approach, or variants of it, can be found in a tradition which includes Kant, Woodrow Wilson and some of the more modern WORLD SOCIETY theorists. Underlying it is a belief in the idea of a common humanity which brings with it a common set of rights, duties and obligations. Accompanying this there is a corresponding belief that the present social and political institutions that characterize the INTERNATIONAL SYSTEM are seriously defective: global unity and planning are therefore essential if the moral issues of peace, security, harmony and environmental well being are to be resolved.

Between the two basic realist/idealist positions there are innumerable variations and mutations on the meaning and significance of international morality, and most contemporary commentators take their stand on a compromise or synthesis between the two extremes. That is, that TRANSNATIONAL obligations and rights are important and certain obligations of common humanity undoubtedly exist, but their realization is circumscribed by the character of the international political system. An international community of sorts exists, but it is not cohesive enough to generate operational definitions of rights and obligations. Poverty, hunger, starvation and natural catastrophes elicit genuine international concern and action, but this is never undertaken at the expense of serious deprivation in the home base. Altruism is not entirely absent from world politics, but the political significance of state boundaries inevitably takes precedent over universal moral claims.

## International Non-Governmental Organization (INGO)

INGOs are TRANSNATIONAL, non-profit-making organizations. Thus the multinational corporations (MNCs) are specifically excluded at the outset, since they are profit making, and merit special attention on their own. INGOs are particularly prolific in the following issue areas: economic and commercial relations, arts and leisure, medicine, science TECHNOLOGY and education, youth and women's organizations and humanitarian relief work. Although INGOs' constituent members are states, the state representatives are non-governmental. Although some government representation may be allowed within the definition, the majority of the members should not be agents for any governmental interest. The separation from the STATE-CENTRED perspective is further enhanced by the fact that INGOs will necessarily have their own secretariat which will be internationally recruited – but from outside governmental structures.

Some relative assessment of the size and significance of INGOs can be obtained by applying the criteria of DOMAIN and SCOPE.

Domain will give an indication of the membership size. Scope will give an indication of the issue areas covered by these organizations, and therefore of the functions which they perform. Over the post-1945 period the domain of INGOs has increased by an average of 5 per cent per annum. The increase in the state membership of the system over the same period is, undoubtedly, an important contributory factor. However, increases in the scope of INGOs over the same period have also had a FEEDBACK effect upon domain. The most significant increases during this period have been in the economic and commercial sectors and in humanitarian relief, youth and women's movements. The distribution of INGOs within the regions of the world is highly uneven. Thus the advanced industrial countries (AICs) are heavily represented. Among THIRD WORLD states, Latin America is the most prolific participant. Conversely the lowest levels of participation come from the formerly centrally planned economies of Eastern Europe and from Asia. The majority of the headquarters offices of INGOs are located in the AICs. The conclusion would appear to be that a high level of political and economic development is a necessary condition for effective participation in INGOs. Political development leads to PLURALISM and the growth of interest groups within societies. These groups may then seek to establish links across state boundaries, thereby creating the basic prerequisites for INGO development. At the same time economic development creates the conditions wherein this development can take place. In summary, then, political development provides the ideological nexus, while economic development provides the infrastructure.

The growth of INGOs since 1945 has forced analysts to re-examine the extent to which the state can still be considered the dominant actor in WORLD POLITICS. If the system is indeed a MIXED ACTOR MODEL then INGOs share the stage with states, MNCs and intergovernmental organizations (IGOs). Detailed analysis of the political role of the INGO probably requires a case study, policy contingent type of approach. The majority of INGOs are not political ACTORS *per se* but rather functionally specific groups which may 'cross over' into politics when the opportunity or the need arises. Thus the World Council of Churches has taken a very public position on APARTHEID, while the INTERNATIONAL RED CROSS has abandoned its traditional NEUTRALITY on the ARAB–ISRAELI CONFLICT and HUMAN RIGHTS issues in the occupied territories on the Gaza and the West Bank. INGOs can collaborate with governments in order to improve or discourage relations between states that are in conflict. Sino–American relations were improved in the early 1970s by the development of sporting contacts, including table tennis. Conversely pressure has been exerted via the UK COMMONWEALTH and the UN to discourage sporting links with South Africa.

In theory the growth of INGOs is limitless. There are not the territorial restraints evident with the growth of NATION-STATES. If present trends continue, there will be close to 10,000 INGOs in the world system by the twenty-first century. Such impressive growth will inevitably have implications for the future.

## International order

Sometimes used as a synonym for INTERNATIONAL SYSTEM it usually refers to the pattern of activities or the set of arrangements that characterizes the mutual behaviour of STATES. In this sense it has a number of formal attributes – political, diplomatic, legal, economic, military – which provide method and regularity to WORLD POLITICS. The contemporary international order is based on the European STATE-SYSTEM established at WESTPHALIA in 1648: a multiplicity of sovereign states coexisting in a condition of ANARCHY which nevertheless recognize common standards of behaviour and interaction. There have been other international orders, such as empires, suzerainties and tribute systems with different components and attributes, but the contemporary order, which is now global, is premised on a rejection of WORLD GOVERNMENT and a presumption in favour of state SOVEREIGNTY. It is said to display 'order' in the sense that it recognizes regulating elements (e.g. BALANCES OF POWER, DIPLOMACY, LAW) which provide a framework within which interaction takes place. The periodic resort to armed CONFLICT is not incompatible with this order since violence itself is circumscribed by known rules. However, in any type of international order stability is a key value. This does not necessarily mean that the order is static. Change and development (for example the emergence of new states) can and do occur, but these are generally accommodated by the process of adaption or adjustment. Some commentators argue that the rationale of order is security; that the purpose of the regulating arrangements is to provide protection for the states themselves and for the system of which they are a part. This REALIST or conservative view favours the STATUS QUO and is generally averse to claims that order is or ought to be synonymous with JUSTICE. Others again argue that no international system can be legitimate without the just ordering of affairs. Thus, pressures for a NEW INTERNATIONAL ECONOMIC ORDER stem from a belief that the contemporary arrangements are inequitable and should be changed. In the present order, this demand stems principally from THIRD WORLD or developing states. The argument for justice as the central value is often accompanied by the idea that the international order (order between states) should give way to a world order (order between individuals or non-state groupings of people). In this way, emphasis on diplomatic–strategic issues are viewed as inseparable from global social, cultural economic and TECHNOLOGICAL issues. Instead of relating primarily to matters of national and international security, order is organically bound up with the issues of human suffering, poverty, hunger, social justice and ecological balance. The conditions for PEACE rest on the fulfilment of basic human needs and in relation to this the present arrangement of POWER and AUTHORITY in world politics is hopelessly inadequate. Yet another use of the term concentrates on the establishment of INTERNATIONAL ORGANIZATIONS and central institutions as being characteristic features of order. Order cannot properly exist between states until central authoritative institutions commanding the loyalty of all have been created. However, as some commentators have pointed out, the use of the term 'international order' in this context is inappropriate since with the establishment of WORLD GOVERNMENT, the bases for order would be internal not international.

## International organizations

Formal institutional structures transcending national BOUNDARIES which are created by MULTILATERAL agreement among NATION-STATES. Their purpose is to foster international cooperation in areas such as security, law, economic and social matters and DIPLOMACY. They are a relatively recent phenomena although many commentators, from the Ancient Greeks onwards, have advocated their creation in one guise or another. In fact they began to emerge in the context of the nineteenth century European STATE-SYSTEM where there were specific and self-conscious attempts to facilitate international intercourse and to provide a functional enabling procedure for common international endeavours. The first of these was the Central Commission for the Navigation of the Rhine in 1815 and the most well known was the International Telegraph Union of 1865 which was the precursor of the modern International Telecommunications Union (ITO). In the twentieth century these organizations have proliferated to such an extent that on almost every issue, over and above the traditional state-to-state diplomatic network, there exists a more or less permanent framework of institutions through which collective measures can be realized.

Modern international organizations are of two basic types, the 'public' variety known as intergovernmental organizations (IGOs) and the 'private' variety, the international non-governmental organizations (INGOs). Foremost examples of the former would be the LEAGUE OF NATIONS and the UNITED NATIONS and of the latter, the INTERNATIONAL RED CROSS and Amnesty International. Common characteristics of both types are voluntary membership, permanent organization, a constitutional structure, a permanent secretariat and a consultative conference. In addition, IGOs are established by TREATY and in deference to state SOVEREIGNTY, normally limit their competence to recommendation rather than compulsion. In this way, although states retain ultimate AUTHORITY, international organizations not only provide a means for cooperative action but also multiple channels of communication which on varying levels overlie traditional diplomatic structures. For example, it has been estimated that at present over 380 public and about 4,700 private international organizations are operative on a day-to-day basis in WORLD POLITICS.

The theory of international organization has evolved from developments in such areas as INTERNATIONALISM, transnationalism, COMPLEX INTERDEPENDENCE, the study of REGIMES, FUNCTIONALISM, FEDERALISM and INTEGRATION. The central focus of all these concerns is an attempt to get beyond the political, social and economic fragmentation which has traditionally characterized the more parochial and individualistic views of classic REALISM. While it is not easy to assess the extent to which international organizations have contributed to the growth of internationalism, two basic views can be identified. On one hand, they are seen as early prototypes for an emerging WORLD GOVERNMENT, and on the other they are regarded as ineffectual and largely symbolic subterfuges for UNILATERALISM, which is the 'real' or 'proper' source of international behaviour. Neither extreme adequately captures the role of international organizations in contemporary world politics. Although doubts persist as to whether they are autonomous international ACTORS with a defined legal personality, few deny that they have made an enormous contribution to the management of INTERNATIONAL RELATIONS. The underlying governing structure of world politics may not have been seriously impaired, but its behavioural process has clearly undergone a radical transformation.

### International politics

This term is used to identify those interactions between STATE ACTORS across state BOUNDARIES that have a specific political content and character. These interactions will be handled by governments directly or by their accredited and accepted representatives. The term 'international' rather than 'interstate' is used because the latter has confusing connotations with FEDERALISM and federations. The term may immediately be compared with INTERNATIONAL RELATIONS. It is generally accepted usage to regard international politics as a class or category of international relations. The relationship between international politics and FOREIGN POLICY is also close. If the former is concerned with interactions, the latter is concerned with actions and reactions. From the FOREIGN POLICY perspective, international political relationships are created by states engaging in the activity of making policy.

International politics implies that states are the dominant actors in the field. If other actors are identified then their ability to 'act' autonomously must be seriously questioned. The moment the assumption about state primacy ceases to be possible, then the term 'international' begins to look seriously deficient and some other designator – such as 'world' or 'global' – has to be used in conjunction with politics in its stead. Con-

siderable confusion has been caused over recent decades because this terminological requirement has not been observed and authors have persisted in using 'international politics' when they mean WORLD POLITICS.

Discussions on international politics are also made more difficult because there is no agreed definition of what the word 'politics' means. Indeed, some writers have wanted to define politics very narrowly in terms of the 'polity'. Without the polity one cannot have politics. Since there is no international polity, there is no international politics. This, albeit briefly, is the nub of the argument. Other definitions of politics, which stress the centrality of POWER considerations, are much more compatible with international politics. They are also intuitively acceptable to the extent that they confirm the importance of the power variable in international politics and foreign policy. Some definitions of politics favour a more DECISION-MAKING approach. Thus, in one famous aphorism, politics has been defined as 'who gets what when why and how?' In terms of state behaviour this definition certainly re-establishes the links between foreign policy and international politics. However, it is necessary in this instance to insist on the STATE-CENTRED character, otherwise an INTERNATIONAL ORGANIZATION deciding to lend money to a state becomes an international political actor.

As Young (1968) has noted, there are significant discontinuities in international politics once empirical analysis starts to be made. State interactions are in most instances heavily biased towards particular REGIONS. This obvious empirical finding assumes greater significance once attempts are made to identify or superimpose structural characteristics upon the field. The idea of structure is examined in the context of the INTERNATIONAL SYSTEM but it will suffice to note that the regional level of activity is, for most states, the one where most foreign policy ISSUE AREAS are related to.

The study of international politics has been and remains at present highly eclectic.

What is often called 'grand theory', that is to say attempts at all-embracing explanations of the field, have usually relied on the concept of POWER as their chief building block. Morgenthau was arguably the most famous of this genre. The development of SOCIAL SCIENTIFIC APPROACHES has produced a different kind of grand theory – SYSTEMS ANALYSIS. However, since the early efforts by Kaplan and others, systems analysts have not been particularly interested in international politics, preferring to see MACROPOLITICS in world or global political terms.

The central issue which this scholarship has raised has been the applicability and desirability of basing analysis upon the state-centred tradition. If the system has moved towards a MIXED ACTOR MODEL then the grand theorist will have to shift his gaze away from state towards these other actors in order to obtain a valid picture. As a result concepts such as SOVEREIGNTY become less central and AUTONOMY more significant. Foreign policy analysis remains fairly viable because the researcher can broaden his field to include non-state actors without abandoning his foothold in the foreign policy tradition. The same is not the case with analysis of international politics and its utility for descriptive, explanatory and even predictive purposes is being steadily eroded.

**International Red Cross**

Initially known as the International Committee for Aid to Wounded Soldiers, it was founded in 1863 by a group of Swiss citizens who were influenced by Henry Dunant (*see* H. Dunant, 1947). Formed a year before the first GENEVA CONVENTION its role has been to work for the application of the principles of humanitarian conduct agreed at the various international conventions on the rules of warfare. It began with the care of the sick and wounded on the battlefield, extended its operations to PRISONERS OF WAR (1929) and twenty years later achieved a major breakthrough in international cooperation when the Red Cross Convention, designed to protect civilians in occupied territories, was adopted (1949). In 1977 its scope was again widened to include humanitarian protection and assistance to victims of interstate or internal conflicts and other disasters.

The movement consists of three sections – the International Committee of the Red Cross (ICRC) which is its official title, the Red Cross or Red Crescent societies (139 in all) and the League of Red Cross and Red Crescent Societies formed in 1919. These three meet once every four years as The International Conference of the Red Cross. The ICRC is a neutral and independent institution (membership being confined to Swiss citizens) and performs an intermediary role in situations of armed CONFLICT. For example, it was in place during the most dangerous phase of the conflict between Federal Nigeria and BIAFRA (1967–70) when it lost fourteen delegates in the fighting. Suggestions were made that the ICRC should supervise the withdrawal of Soviet missiles from Cuba in 1962 under the auspices of the UNITED NATIONS but this was defeated by the refusal of Cuba to allow ICRC inspection of its ports. The main task of the ICRC, besides being an impartial intermediary, is in providing medical supplies and personnel during wartime and in attempting to protect civilians and noncombatants. To this end it seeks to establish 'hospital' or 'neutral' zones in battlefield areas. It also provides assistance to PRISONERS OF WAR and attempts to oversee treatment of political detainees. Given the ubiquity of armed conflict in twentieth century WORLD POLITICS, the humanitarian role of the ICRC cannot be underestimated and virtually all states recognize its value (*see*: D. P. Forsythe, 1977).

**International relations**

This term is used to identify all interactions between state-based ACTORS across STATE

BOUNDARIES. The term can immediately be compared with, though is broader than, INTERNATIONAL POLITICS. Indeed, the latter is subsumed as one, and certainly one of the most important, sub-fields of international relations. Thus INTERNATIONAL LAW is part of international relations but not international politics. Law is, after all, certainly in its customary form, created by interactions between state-based actors. Similarly international economic relations are part of international relations but not international politics. This is not to say that political calculations will not intrude into these areas, but only that they can be separated for purposes of analysis.

International relations is thus an interdisciplinary and heterogeneous area of study. It has no unifying methodology because, taken with three examples mentioned above, international economics is an empirical social science, international law is far more normative than most social sciences while international politics is eclectic, borrowing from a number of traditions and divided in many minds into a rather unruly flock of activities. It should also be noted that the above listing is illustrative rather than exhaustive, diplomatic history, which again has its own methodology, being an obvious omission.

International relations, as a term of discourse, is much less used today than it was in the immediate years after the Second World War. At that time the STATE-CENTRIC tradition was still holding the stage and researchers and teachers regarded the state as the key to much analysis. As the SOCIAL SCIENTIFIC APPROACH gained ground new insights and new evidence were being introduced from subject areas that were not traditionally thought of as international relations subjects. GAME THEORY and SYSTEMS ANALYSIS, to name but two of these approaches, were not part of this tradition. Systems analysis was particularly disturbing to these more traditional ways because it suggested that via the concept of system it was possible to link together subject areas that had previously been thought of as separate.

Coincidentally with these changes in methodology the principal area and object of study – the state – was undergoing changes which seemed to question the old verities. The idea that the state was a clearly defined, hard-shelled unit of analysis – sometimes referred to as 'the billiard ball model' – was being questioned. Increasing evidence that the INTERNATIONAL SYSTEM was a MIXED ACTOR MODEL in important respects and that TRANSNATIONAL relations were an area of growing importance encouraged moves away from the older orthodoxies. Finally, some of the constituent subject areas of international relations became subjects for critical scrutiny. International law has an alleged 'eurocentric' bias, international economics should not avoid the issues raised by international political economy while international politics itself has had to share the stage with WORLD POLITICS and other more heterodox approaches such as the WORLD SOCIETY perspective.

### International society

Ever since GROTIUS posited his concept of a 'great society of states' as the bedrock upon which INTERNATIONAL LAW, ORDER and cooperation would be built, scholars have debated the very existence of a genuine 'society' or 'community' beyond the NATION-STATE. There is no hard empirical evidence that the practice of international relations has generated a society or community in the usual senses of the words at all, and most scholars cautiously preferred to speak of an INTERNATIONAL SYSTEM of STATES which, although displaying a regularized pattern of interaction within a specified environment, did not attain the degree of integration necessary to warrant the appellation 'society'. However, to theorists in the classical tradition, the notion of an international society which forms the basis for INTERNATIONAL ORDER is fundamental. The misnamed ENGLISH SCHOOL OF INTERNATIONAL RELATIONS is predicated upon it:

its principal members, Charles Manning, Martin Wight, F. S. Northridge, Hedley Bull and Alan James are all alleged to belong self-consciously to the 'international society' or 'international community' approach. That is, they all assert that the proper object of study is the conditions of social order present and possible within the prevailing international ANARCHY. As such, the approach is regarded as a variant of the REALIST school which focuses on the 'state-as-actor' axiom within a broad framework of institutionalized 'unity-in-diversity', i.e. the anarchical society. Thus Hedley Bull (1977), its most prominent advocate, asserts that 'a society of states (or international society) exists when a group of states, conscious of certain common interests and common values, form a society in the sense that they conceive themselves to be bound by a common set of rules in their relations with one another and share in the working of common institutions' (p. 13). The institutions which are said to create or foster this order are international law, DIPLOMACY, INTERNATIONAL ORGANIZATION, and BALANCE OF POWER. In this way the autonomy of international relations as a separate field of forces is alleged to be established as is the distinction between this and a 'system' which merely involves contact and interaction without the concomitant communal values, mutuality or RECIPROCITY involved in the society approach. The theories advanced are primarily normative although great pains are taken to establish their empirical relevance. Further, and in contrast with the systems approach, it is not SUB-SYSTEM dominant; that is, in many important respects the international society itself conditions the behaviour of the actors within it.

Whether or not international society is fictional or exists only in the mind, few would doubt that its image has underpinned mainstream classical international theory since at least the Second World War. The behavioural/systems movement, which for a short period dominated US approaches, is now beginning to acknowledge the vitality and persistence of the older traditions of analytical philosophy, jurisprudence and diplomatic history which first identified and elaborated the societal perspective. The US concept of 'international REGIMES' could therefore be seen as an implicit acknowledgement of this, since 'regime' in this context is a specific attempt to identify the intervening and perhaps autonomous institutional structures which sometimes have decisive effects on national strategies and perspectives.

## International system

The concept of an international system is derived from SYSTEMS ANALYSIS. The system is made up of interacting units which, in this case, are STATES. Thus the term STATE-SYSTEM is interchangeable with the term 'international system' used here. At the level of the international system, the state is a SUB-SYSTEM. At the level of the state, groups and interests within the state may be regarded as sub-systems. This constant movement upwards from sub-systems to systems, or downwards from systems to sub-systems, is one of the essential characteristics of systems analysis. In the particular case of the international system, following Kaplan we may note that the system is sub-system dominant. FOREIGN POLICY, which is the activity whereby states act and react to each other, is made against an external environment which is the international system. Because the international system is sub-system dominant, the activity of making and implementing foreign policy will have a significant effect upon the system, particularly in the case of those major state ACTORS in the system traditionally referred to as GREAT POWERS.

Discussion of the concept of the 'great power' raises directly the issue of the structure of the international system. Because the system is sub-system dominant, its structure or configuration will crucially depend upon the nature of the 'pecking order'. Thus an international system with only two great powers and a large number of non-aligned, neutral and isolated states will be quite different structurally from a system of four or five competing great powers each with their own ALLIANCES and BLOCS. Some writers on the international system have argued that it is upon the number of great powers and upon the nature of their relationship that the system structure depended. The two most popular structural types have been the BIPOLAR and the MULTI-POLAR systems, the classical BALANCE OF POWER being a paradigm example of the multipolar system. In this way it is possible to come to a better definition of the idea of the great power, at least in relation to system structure. The great power is the state actor of such significance that its removal from the system would change the structure of the system.

If system structure was dependent upon the sub-system domination of the state, so too was system process. Two fundamental and, in some senses, antithetical processes can be distinguished in the international system. These processes are CONFLICT and cooperation, discord and collaboration. These may be seen as being ranged along a continuum marked at one extreme by ZERO SUM relations of pure conflict and at the other by positive sum relations of close coordination, harmonization and even IN-TEGRATION. Given these macropolitical processes, states in their foreign POLICY-MAKING need to address these issues through their ORIENTATIONS. In this way certain broad policy orientations can be seen as responses to the systemic processes, ally seeking on the one hand and NEUTRAL-ISM AND NON-ALIGNMENT on the other being examples. With regard to the point made earlier about system structure, where a state finds itself structurally may deter-mine its response to the systematic pro-cesses of conflict and cooperation.

The international or state system de-veloped in Europe from the sixteenth cen-tury onwards. As basic state structures became established, people's loyalties and allegiances to these new actors developed through NATIONALISM. Thus the European state system spawned the concept of the NATION-STATE. This fused together the political–sociological concept of the nation and the political–legal concept of the state. The idea was exported thereafter, with im-portant changes, from Europe to the rest of the world. In the twentieth century the growth of state members of the system has been impressive, at least superficially, if quantitative factors are the main criteria. Paradoxically, as the membership of the system has increased, the very basis of the system has been questioned.

In particular, the territorial basis of the state has been eroded and even removed altogether. Military TECHNOLOGY and eco-nomic INTERDEPENDENCE have been par-ticularly erosive. States are increasingly vulnerable to these systemic changes while at the same time they have set for them-selves new goals and targets – particularly in the wealth–welfare ISSUE AREAS – which can only be met with outside assistance and cooperation.

In an effort to come to grips with the perennial systemic processes of conflict and cooperation states have engaged in institu-tion building. This has developed furthest in the wealth–welfare fields, but even in re-lation to military–security questions global organizations such as the UNITED NATIONS and regional organizations such as the ARAB LEAGUE have developed repertoires. The extent to which these intergovernmen-tal organizations (IGOs) can be regarded as actors is hotly debated. However, it is diffi-cult to escape the conclusion that they do act to modify and alter the system and, by so doing, to affect the environment within which the states operate. If, as seems prob-able, the system is no longer simply the sum of all state interactions then it may be inap-propriate to regard it as an international or state system totally. A plausible com-promise is to retain the term 'international system' for use as originally conceived and to recognize the need to analytically distinguish a world system to cover this new MIXED ACTOR situation. Following the precepts of systems analysis, the international system becomes a sub-system within the world system.

## Internment

Properly, the forced detention of ALIENS and PRISONERS OF WAR during wartime, but the term has also been used to describe the enforced resettlement, encampment or imprisonment of dissident nationals in peacetime. The HAGUE CONVENTION of 1907 obliged neutrals to intern alien troops, vessels and military aircraft. Specific conditions governing the treatment of internees were outlined in the Geneva Conference on Prisoners of War and the Protection of Civilians in August 1949 and were subsequently developed by the INTERNATIONAL RED CROSS Conference at New Delhi in 1968. Cases of internment which fall outside the scope of the Hague and GENEVA CONVENTIONS are now regarded primarily as HUMAN RIGHTS issues.

## Intervention

A portmanteau term which covers a wide variety of situations where one ACTOR intervenes in the affairs of another. The relationship has been the source of much scholarly interest. Lawyers, basing their arguments on the starting point that there is an international norm of NON-INTERVENTION, have sought to establish ground rules which allow intervention to take place legally. Strategists have sought to establish operation rules which allow intervention to be successful. Diplomatic historians have sought to understand why particular interventions, usually of a controversial and possibly of an influential nature, took place, while political scientists have sought to identify and stipulate the characteristics that link these discrete events into that class of conduct we call intervention.

Under the classical sovereign STATE-SYSTEM, established after WESTPHALIA, interventionism as a behaviour pattern had to

be restricted and hedged about with legal and diplomatic restraint. If STATES and statesmen intervened willy-nilly in each other's affairs then the very idea of sovereign EQUALITY and territoriality would be undermined. Accordingly the BILLIARD-BALL MODEL of the state actor developed to enshrine and enhance the idea that what lawyers called DOMESTIC JURISDICTION would prevail. This meant that certain matters and concerns were 'off limits' to the society of states. Key areas where this prohibition was held to apply were referred to by terms such as 'territorial integrity' and 'political independence'. In essence these ideas attempted to safeguard the territorial and governmental STATUS QUO in the sovereign state. Territory and governmental structure were both intrinsically and symbolically important to states and statesmen. Thus intervention in these matters was supposedly prohibited by the sovereignty principle.

How far behaviour had to go to constitute 'intervention' is a moot point. Certainly under the classical system, military FORCE was the most widely available instrument for this purpose. It can be used to gain admittance to both the territory and the political structure of a target state. Its impact in this respect is often dramatic and sometimes decisive. Once the force option has been taken, it becomes difficult to retreat from it. INFLUENCE, having been established by force, is subsequently maintained by force. Because force was such a threat to the exclusivity of state sovereignty an antidote had to be found. Conceptually, as we have seen, this was the doctrine of non-intervention. Diplomatically, if this proved to be inadequate, then recourse was taken to the BALANCE OF POWER. Although the balance of power sometimes involved interventionist tactics, it also served to inhibit and restrain intervention, or was supposed to. This preventive function was achieved through the mechanism of DETERRENCE. States in the system could act to prevent others from intervening in their affairs, as well as those of third parties, by threatening some credible sanction. Such sanctions were, again, usually manifested in military terms. The balance system is often held to have reached its fullest expression during nineteenth century European DIPLOMACY, in particular in the period after the defeat of France in 1815 and before the First World War. During this same time frame other developments were taking place in INTERNATIONAL POLITICS which were to significantly increase the potentialities and possibilities for states to intervene in matters essentially within the parameters of domestic jurisdiction.

First, the rise of the liberal–democratic state in western Europe and North America created a type of political system which was much more open to intervention. Ideas about FREE TRADE implied the free movement of goods and services across states. Ideas about political freedom and representative democracy implied the free movement of ideas. The availability of more rapid and effective means of communication and transportation assisted these developments. Writers on INTERNATIONAL POLITICS characterize these systemic changes as INTERDEPENDENCE.

Secondly, the growth in the number of actors in the INTERNATIONAL SYSTEM has created an environment where intervention might flourish. It should not be thought that these actors are exclusively states, either. The development of intergovernmental organizations (IGOs), particularly in the twentieth century, means that these actors can adopt interventionist policies and attempt implementation thereafter, the persistent intention of the majority membership of the UNITED NATIONS to discuss APARTHEID, notwithstanding the invocation of DOMESTIC JURISDICTION defences by the state government, being a case in point.

The growth in actors also presents an increase in the number of targets for intervention. Many of the newer THIRD WORLD states are polyethnic arrangements often with a fragile and corrupt governmental structure. These fragmented states are, clearly, more susceptible to intervention. It is often not difficult to find an interest group or faction within the ruling ELITE willing to collaborate with the outside party and, in this way, access to the policy centre is achieved. The paradigm example is the civil strife situation where authority is actively and openly contested and where ally seeking activity with external parties is endemic. The intervener's objectives will thus be predetermined by the factions themselves while the instruments of intervention will run the gamut from diplomatic support to economic assistance to military operations. US involvement in VIETNAM is a good example of this process.

Thus, starting off from an initial position in favour of non-intervention, the ground has shifted to the present position where intervention is endemic among international actors. Clearly, instruments of intervention cover a continuum from the use of force at one extreme to the most conventional forms of DIPLOMACY at the other, but how confidently can we stipulate the objectives of intervention? At the outset the intervener believes he can materially alter the situation to his advantage or prevent the situation from becoming more disadvantageous by his actions. However, it is important to remember that intervention is rarely a one-shot operation and that having embarked upon interventionist policy a threshold is crossed and the tendency is to continue with more of the same rather than to be constantly reassessing the rectitude of the original decision. Moreover, the reaction of the Target can affect the perception of objectives. Original objectives may be altered, entirely new ones may be undertaken as a result of the dynamic between an intervention intitiative and a Target response. Again, the point about the time frame within which intervention is to be implemented appears to be crucial to understanding objectives.

Reference was made at the outset to scholarly conceptions of intervention. One of the most ambitious attempts to provide a synoptic view was that made by political scientist, J. N. Rosenau. In a series of influential papers written twenty years ago, Rosenau (1968, 1969a) stipulated that intervention had two characteristics: it appeared as a break from conventional or normal behaviour and it was intentionally directed at the structure of political AUTHORITY.

Viewing intervention as a sharp break from previous behaviour has much to commend it. It reflects the legal tradition, already referred to, which tended to take non-intervention as the norm. Seen from this perspective intervention is a break.

Unfortunately, contemporary behaviour by international actors appears almost to argue the opposite. Intervention is now the norm, not vice versa. Moreover it has been argued that the instruments are much more refined and sophisticated than in the past. This makes intervention more pervasive and insidious. Emphasizing intervention as a break diverts attention from the point of view which stresses gradualism and INCREMENTALISM as characteristics of interventionary behaviour. It would avoid the rather contentious, not to say dubious, argument advanced by Rosenau that US intervention in VIETNAM began with the bombing campaign of February 1965.

Stipulation that the target for intervention should be the *structure* of government looks more promising. A plausible starting point might be to say that intervention occurs when the authoritative allocation of values within an actor's internal environment is made by, or made with the assistance and approval of, persons and parties representing other international actors. This definition covers such activities as the IMF team arriving in the state capital and insisting upon a more balanced budget before they open a credit line. It covers the activities of the PLO in Beirut as well as the substantial American funding of the French counter-insurgency war in Indo–China fifteen years before the commencement of overt US bombing.

## IRBM

An abbreviation of Intermediate Range Ballistic Missile. Usually thought of as covering the range 2,500–5,500 km. These types of systems, and the shorter range medium range ballistic missiles (MRBMs), would now be referred to as Long Range Theatre Nuclear Forces, at least within NATO. The placement of these types of weapons in Cuba in 1962 was held to have contributed to the subsequent October CRISIS between the United States and the Soviet Union.

## Iron curtain

A phrase usually associated with Winston Churchill but actually first used by Nazi PROPAGANDA minister Joseph Goebbels, to describe the deliberate isolation of Eastern Europe from the West by the Soviet Union. It was popularized by Winston Churchill in his famous Fulton, Missouri speech of March 1946 where he said: 'From Stettin in the Baltic to Trieste in the Adriatic, an iron curtain has descended across the Continent'. The speech, and the implications of Soviet expansionism it appeared to contain, made a powerful impression particularly in the United States and many commentators allege that the image it projected underpinned Truman's policy of CONTAINMENT and that it provided justification for HAWKISH Western policies during the COLD WAR. In fact the speech was less pugnacious than popularly believed and Churchill went on to say '. . . I do not believe that Soviet Russia desires war. What they desire is the fruits of war and the infinite expansion of their power and doctrines'. This observation clearly echoed the thoughts of the more LIBERAL US supporters of containment who argued that the Soviet Union should be opposed by diplomatic, ideological and political means rather than straightforward military confrontation (*see*: X). This speech served to increase Soviet fears of ENCIRCLEMENT and effectively ended any hope of a revival into the post-war period of East–West cooperation.

## Irredentism

The term originates from nineteenth century Italian politics and specifically from a political movement called the Irredentists. The movement sought to advance certain GEOPOLITICAL claims to territories outside the Italian STATE structure. The basis of these claims could loosely be called NATIONALISTIC, although in some instances, for example Corsica, a separate ethnic identity could be distinguished in the territory itself which might have found Italian irredentism uncongenial.

The term has passed into general political and diplomatic discourse in the twentieth century, It is used, sometimes pejoratively, to characterize policies which seek to alter the STATUS QUO in a particular territory on the basis of nationalistic or ethnic criteria. Irredentism is particularly likely to occur where legal, state-based FRONTIERS straddle and divide an ethnic group. The 'irredenta' then becomes that territory 'lost' to the ethnic group as a result. Irredentism can, therefore, become a source of potential or actual CONFLICT between international actors. An apposite recent example has been the claims made by Somalia to incorporate Somali peoples in Ethiopia and Kenya into a single ethnic state. Other examples in contemporary politics of irredentism are the claims for *enosis* or union with Greece by some Greek Cypriots and the claims for a united Ireland.

## Islam

Islam is one of the three great monotheistic RELIGIONS of the world. Founded in the seventh century AD it is also the most recent and, some would say, the most vital. It rapidly expanded from Mecca and Medina in the Arabian Peninsula throughout the Middle East, North Africa, Central Asia and Southern Europe in the century that followed the death of Mohammed, the Prophet. Uniquely among the three religions, Judaism, Christianity and Islam, its founder showed great political skill as well as great spiritual commitment. This fusion of political, legal and spiritual into one complex system is the singular achievement of the Islamic tradition. The Christian dichotomy of sacred/secular, Church/State, rendering to Caesar and rendering to God, is not really recognized as such within Islam. Certainly in its classical period Islam was a total expression of allegiance to a way of life that impinged upon all aspects of society.

Islam is sectarian, the main division being between Sunni – orthodox – and Shia – heterodox. These divisions date from the fourth Caliphate and are as much political as spiritual in origin. The breakdown of Islamic unity thereafter allowed the Ottoman Turks to succeed to the Caliphate and for STATE-CENTRIC tendencies to manifest themselves. When Shiism became the official religion of Persia (Iran) in the sixteenth century this established a trend which has continued as the STATE SYSTEM developed from its European nexus to cover the world. In the contemporary system it is thus possible to identify Islamic populations within particular STATES as being either predominantly Sunni or Shia and also to define followers of Islam within a particular state in relation to other religious groups. In the modern LEBANON indeed a whole political system was devised which recognized this confessionalism and sought to reflect it in a 'spoils system'.

In terms of WORLD POLITICS, therefore, Islam can be identified as operating at two levels. First, there are a group of states which by tradition and affiliation can be termed as 'Islamic' whether their internal arrangements are sacred or secular. Currently these states can be identified by their membership of the Islamic Conference Organization, which numbers forty-six states, including AFGHANISTAN whose membership was suspended in 1980 following the INTERVENTION of the Soviet Union. These states seek to coordinate and harmonize their policies on ISSUE AREAS such as the ARAB–ISRAELI CONFLICT where a joint Islamic position might be expected.

Secondly, there are states wherein followers of Islam are a distinct, visible and significant minority. The two key examples in this category are the Soviet Union and India. The latter has the larger Muslim population – almost 76 million as opposed to 55 million in the Soviet Union – but the proportion of Muslims to the total population is much larger in the Soviet Union. Moreover, the differential birth rate between Muslim and non-Muslim in the Soviet Union favours the former so that this proportion is likely to increase further in the future. Both states have histories of communal tension between Muslim and non-Muslim ethnic groups. In the case of India this centres on the disputed territory of Kashmir, in the Soviet Union on the southern republics.

## Isolationism

Term particularly associated with the FOREIGN POLICY of the United States, but also used to describe phases of UK foreign policy. It refers to the deliberate avoidance of political, diplomatic or military commitments to other STATES. In the case of the United Kingdom it was a strategy associated with diplomatic mobility and flexibility following the dictum of 'no permanent friends, no permanent enemies, only permanent interests'. In the United States, however, after the Washington administrations (1789–97) it was raised to the level of a political dogma rather than a set of practical policy guidelines to suit a particular set of circumstances. Isolationism in the United States, almost from the start, was bound up with its geographical insulation from the main centres of political activity, with its uniqueness as a LIBERAL state and with its belief in the moral superiority of the US way of life. In this way it was directed at Europe rather than the Western Hemisphere, the Pacific or the Far East. However, even in relation to Europe it did not imply commercial, cultural or intellec-

tual separation as it clearly did in the case of nineteenth century China and Japan.

The use of the term has aroused much debate among US diplomatic historians, some of whom have argued that because of the absence of economic isolationism the whole notion is mythical. Mainline historians, on the other hand, argue that US foreign policy from 1783 onwards can best be understood in terms of a more or less permanent tension between the forces of 'isolationism' and the forces of 'interventionism' both of which spring from shared assumptions about the exceptionalism of the US political experience. The high-water mark of US isolationism was the Senate's rejection of the Treaty of VERSAILLES as well as membership of the LEAGUE OF NATIONS and the subsequent public endorsement of this policy in the elections of 1920. The inter-war years (1919–41) which witnessed a succession of NEUTRALITY acts in 1935, 1936 and 1937 was evidence of the general consensus in the United States that isolationism was its natural and orthodox position in WORLD POLITICS. As a result of World War Two, especially with the rise of the Soviet Union as a global POWER, isolationism was replaced by CONTAINMENT and INTERVENTIONISM. The rhetoric associated with the earlier policy still exists as when domestic opponents of active US involvement in WORLD POLITICS are frequently referred to as 'neo-isolationists'.

## Issue area

Sometimes rendered issue-area, this classificatory term was first introduced into empirical political science by Robert Dahl (1961a). In what was fundamentally a piece of political sociology, Dahl sought to show how the composition of key local ELITE groups was crucially dependent upon the issue area chosen. Dahl identified the three key issue areas in New Haven as: public education, urban redevelopment and party nominations for local elective offices.

Dahl used his research to argue for a PLURAL-IST conception of ELITE structures but later in the decade the concept of issue area was taken up by writers on FOREIGN POLICY analysis.

James Rosenau is generally agreed to have broken new ground in applying these ideas. In his chapter in R. Barry Farrell's 1966 volume and then in his own 1967 edition on domestic sources of foreign policy Rosenau sees the concept of issue area as a vertical BOUNDARY in politics. The stipulation of an issue area thus enables the researcher to link discrete ACTORS, processes and outcomes into one functionally significant whole. In the Farrell volume Rosenau suggested four issue areas in his 'pre-theory': territorial, status, human resources and non-human resources. In the 1967 work he attempted to reach an assessment of the validity of distinguishing domestic policy issues from foreign policy issues.

The term issue area has now passed firmly into the lexicon of policy analysis. It is, for instance, difficult to envisage any study of UN voting patterns proceeding very far without a primary designation of key issue areas in the organization. Again, approaching the ARAB–ISRAELI situation as an issue area immediately sensitizes the researcher to the need to establish an early identification of who the parties are in that particularly complex situation.

# J

## J-curve

Term employed by J. C. Davies (1969) of the University of Oregon to indicate graphically the de Toqueville notion that REVOLUTIONS are more likely to take place when a period of prolonged rising expectations is followed by a period of sharp reversal. The frustration which is generated by the gap between expectations and gratificatons is, at its most intolerable point, likely to result in violent REGIME change. As a broad generalization it has proved useful in analysis of revolutionary situations, but the problem of uniqueness and its general inability to distinguish between 'revolution' and 'rebellion' (which does not necessarily involve change of regime) has severely curtailed its predictive capabilities. In addition, it is primarily a psychological explanation and as such does not address itself directly to the political, social and economic milieu within which change takes place.

The term is also used in economic analyses to indicate certain consequences of devaluation on the BALANCE OF PAYMENTS issue.

## Jingoism

A general term indicating HAWKISH or bellicose policies in dealing with other STATES. It has been suggested that the term is of Basque origin ('Jainko' is the name of the supreme god of the Basques) and was first used by mercenary Basque soldiers in the employ of Edward I in his thirteenth-century Welsh campaigns. It was popularized in an English music hall song by G. W. Hunt in 1878: 'We don't want to fight, yet by Jingo! if we do / We've got the ships, we've got the men, and got the money too.' In this instance, it became a rallying cry for those who supported armed British resistance and the use of GUNBOAT DIPLOMACY against the Russian advance into Turkey in that year. Now generally used as a synonym for chauvinism or extreme and pugnacious patriotism. It is sometimes associated with a variety of ISOLATIONISM as when J. F. Kennedy spoke of 'belligerent jingoism and narrow isolationism' as characterizing a periodic and unhealthy trait in US FOREIGN POLICY.

## Johnson doctrine

Sometimes known as the Johnson–Mann doctrine, this was formulated in 1965 by President Johnson and his under-secretary of state for Latin American affairs, T. C. Mann. It stated that the KENNEDY DOCTRINE of giving support only to those STATES in Latin America with representative governments (i.e. those formed through general elections) would cease and would be replaced by a pledge that the United States would henceforth support any Latin American government whose interests were deemed compatible with those of Washington. It was composed in the wake of US military INTERVENTION in the Dominican republic and in this sense was a revival of the Dulles–Eisenhower policy preferences in relation to Latin America. Its general purpose was to reassert US willingness to combat the 'clear and present danger of the forcible seizure of power by the Communists'.

## Junta

Originally a Spanish term referring to a ruling committee or administrative council such as those established in Spain in 1808 during the Peninsula War in opposition to Napoleonic rule. Now more generally used to refer to military government (*junta militar*) especially, though not exclusively, in the Hispano–American world. In Latin America during the period of liberation from Spanish and Portuguese IMPERIAL rule, representative governments were frequently established by military conspiracies. Usually the junta consisted of several officers drawn from all the services and was in effect a joint ruling cabal, but in the twentieth century the term is most often used in relation to the dictatorial rule of a single dominant military commander, as it did in relation to the administration of General Pinochet in Chile after September 1973.

## *jus ad bellum/jus in bello*

These mean literally 'justice in going to WAR' and 'justice in the conduct of war'. This distinction between the ends for which war is fought and the means by which it is conducted is an essential part of the JUST WAR doctrine. *Jus ad bellum* was of more concern to the ancient and medieval worlds, whereas in modern times *jus in bello* receives more emphasis, perhaps because of the greater acceptance of the ACT OF WAR as a necessary consequence of the establishment of secular SOVEREIGN STATES. The GENEVA and HAGUE CONVENTIONS, for example, were concerned with identifying precise conditions of *jus in bello* rather than with occasions on which *jus ad bellum* operated. The recent ISLAMIC revival of the Jihad, or Holy War, is in this sense a return to pre-modernist conceptions of *jus ad bellum*.

## *jus cogens*

Refers to a body of principles or norms in INTERNATIONAL LAW which override or supersede others and 'which cannot be set aside by treaty or acquiescence but only by the formation of a subsequent norm of contrary effect' (I. Brownlie, 1973a). According to this, which has its origins in the writings of GROTIUS, a TREATY or commitment would be void if it was contrary to certain basic principles of international law. The technical name given to these (unspecified) principles is 'peremptory norms of general international law' and it is enshrined in Article 53 of the VIENNA Convention on the Law of Treaties, 1969. Examples of such overriding rules would normally include the outlawing of GENOCIDE, the principles of SELF-DETERMINATION and the banning of piracy. Recently, radical international lawyers have argued that *jus cogens* applies in relation to the Republic of South Africa. They argue that, notwithstanding laws relating to the rights of NEUTRALITY or non-interference in internal affairs, APARTHEID is such an affront to the public interest of the world community that all STATES have a positive and active duty to oppose it. The precise applications of *jus cogens* is not universally agreed upon, but its revival in international law is an indication of its evolution from the notion of law based on the consent of STATES, to a WORLD LAW established on certain fundamental principles which are considered binding and not discretionary.

## Justice

As with other subjective terms, there is no widespread agreement either on the meaning of justice in the international context or even on its general applicability to WORLD POLITICS. For the HOBBESIAN, the recognition of a decentralized international STATE-SYSTEM characterized by an absence of a single legitimate AUTHORITY inevitably means that justice takes a back seat to considerations of ORDER. Indeed, its very existence on this view is structurally dependent on the prior realization of orderly relations. For IDEALISTS, on the other hand, not only can justice be defined but it is also a prerequisite of a stable and lasting order. The question of order versus justice therefore is a central and often divisive issue in traditional international theory. On one hand, REALISTS argue that the issue is secondary and derivative while on the other, non-realists argue that it is primary and constitutive.

The term 'international justice' usually refers to moral standards over and above those prescribed by law which confer rights and duties on ACTORS irrespective of size or importance. They may be embodied in INTERNATIONAL LAW (e.g. the rule of NON-INTERVENTION or sovereign equality) but this is not necessarily the case. Demands for justice, for example, can refer to the redistribution of the world's resources based on criteria which are not yet embedded in contemporary international law (e.g. the notion of the 'common heritage of mankind' and its implications for ownership or possession of resources which are not covered by established rules of territorial jurisdiction). Sometimes the terms 'international justice' and 'inter-state justice' are used synonymously, though clearly the latter is more specific and may even exclude from its purview considerations of fair play to non-state ACTORS.

The right of SELF-DETERMINATION, for example, can and does frequently clash with the rights associated with SOVEREIGNTY. Indeed, a major feature of the development of the international legal REGIME is the present tension between STATE-CENTRED considerations of justice derived from customary or positive law and individual or human justice derived from the NATURAL LAW tradition. It is often asserted that the natural law tradition, in so far as it challenges the positivist conception, is potentially subversive in the sense that it is designed to erode the principle of sovereignty upon which international order ultimately rests.

In contemporary INTERNATIONAL RELATIONS, dissatisfaction with the traditional state-centred views (which reach their extreme manifestation in phrases such as 'justice is on the side of the stronger' or 'might is right') has led to a growing body of opinion that justice must be cosmopolitan and universal. Supporters of ecopolitics, for example, argue that since TECHNOLOGY has outgrown the limits of state boundaries and since INTERDEPENDENCE is now a fact and not an ideal, considerations of justice should be tied to concepts of a common humanity and should entail at least minimum standards of welfare and environmental concern. 'World' justice on this view must take precedent over the inter-state or individual varieties. However, there is as yet no evidence of substantial inroads into the traditional view expressed most forcibly in, for example, the MELIAN DIALOGUE in THUCYDIDES' fifth-century BC account of the Peloponnesian Wars. The persistence and intrusion of questions of POWER and order into considerations of justice appears to be endemic and will remain so for as long as states are the main ACTORS in WORLD POLITICS.

## Justiciable/non-justiciable disputes

Terms used in INTERNATIONAL LAW to distinguish between those disputes that are capable of legal resolution through, for example, ADJUDICATION or ARBITRATION and those which are resistant to it. The distinction reflects the lack of autonomy of international law and the existence of two basic categories of international disputes, the legal and the political. Political disputes sometimes involve matters of HIGH POLITICS and NATIONAL INTERESTS which, although often capable of settlement, are not usually thought of as susceptible to legal resolution. International law may be applicable to such disputes, but the party or parties involved may not wish to be bound by such decisions. In such cases, where a settlement is sought the means employed are generally non- or quasi-legal, e.g. BILATERAL or MULTILATERAL DIPLOMACY, mediation, GOOD OFFICES or in the last resort, WAR. The distinction between the two categories rests ultimately on the importance STATES attach to the issues involved. Generally, the more important the issue the less likely its justiciability.

## Just War

The attempt to justify WAR in one set of circumstances and not in another has its origins in Christian ethics, in particular in the fourth century AD which witnessed a transition from PACIFISM to beliefs in the right or duty to fight for a just cause. The early Christians did not bear arms but by the time the Roman Emperor (Theodosius 1, in 38 AD) declared that Catholic Christianity was the state RELIGION of the empire, canon law began to move in the direction of a just war doctrine. St Augustine (AD 354–430) is commonly held to be the first major propagandist for these ideas, which in essence have remained a part of western civilization ever since. Definitions of the Just War have periodically altered but the general purpose remains the same: that is, to give some wars legal and moral justification, to condemn those that do not comply with the requisite specifications and also to impose restrictions on the actual conduct of war.

The formal terms given to this enterprise are JUS AD BELLUM and JUS IN BELLO. Emphasis on the latter, referring to right conduct in warfare, indicates that an important aspect of the Just War doctrine is that just wars must not be pursued by unjust means, e.g. the indiscriminate slaughter of non-combatants. The medieval view of the Just War is best represented by St Thomas Aquinas (1225–74), who wrote that war may be justified if three conditions are satisfied: (a) it must be waged by a proper sovereign AUTHORITY; (b) there must be a just cause and (c) the intentions must be pure, so that they intend to promote good and not pri-

vate aggrandisement. Further conditions which were generally agreed upon later were that in wars which were not fought strictly in SELF-DEFENCE there must be a reasonable prospect of victory and that every effort must have been made, prior to the use of FORCE, to resolve the issue by peaceful means. In relation to conduct in war, the innocent (i.e. the non-combatants) should be immune from direct attack and the amount of FORCE used should not be excessive. The legal dimension of this doctrine owes more to GROTIUS than to any other single theorist. His *De jure belli ac pacis* (1625) is still regarded as a classic statement on the just war and the means of waging it. Against the backdrop of NATURAL LAW and the customary law of nations, Grotius delineated four causes which make a war just: (a) self-defence; (b) to enforce rights, (c) to seek REPARATIONS for injury; and (d) to punish a wrongdoer. Grotius held that a war cannot be just on both sides and also warned that even a just war can become unjust if intentions are wrong and if unjust acts are committed. Grotius' main contribution to the development of this theory was to put on a secular, pragmatic basis what had previously been considered to be a matter of theology or ethics. He accepted that a multi-state INTERNATIONAL SYSTEM would inevitably mean the occurrence of wars. His purpose was to limit their incidence and to limit the damage or harm that was bound to occur. These twin purposes have subsequently been the rationale for the various international conventions on the rules of warfare in the nineteenth and twentieth centuries as well as INTERNATIONAL ORGANIZATIONS such as the LEAGUE OF NATIONS and the UN. In modern times a number of problems have arisen in relation to the doctrine. In particular, the following ought to be considered: the PREVENTIVE WAR or the pre-emptive strike, can this be justified on a principle of extended self-defence? (Israel, for example, justified its actions in June 1967 on these grounds); counter-INTERVENTION, is it permissible to intervene against the prior intervention of other STATES? (the United States sometimes used this pretext in relation to VIETNAM); humanitarian intervention, is it justifiable to intervene against acts that are morally reprehensible (for example against APARTHEID in South Africa)? These and other issues such as GUERRILLA WARFARE and TERRORISM raise doubts about the continued validity of rules and principles drawn up in more civilized periods of international history. Indeed, it might be claimed that the decline of the Just War doctrine in the twentieth century, especially in the nuclear age where the concept of DETERRENCE rests on the threat of deliberate mass slaughter of the innocent, is related to technical developments in warfare which at least blur and at most obliterate traditional distinctions between combatants and non-combatants. One area where the doctrine, or an extreme bastardization of it, has been revived is in the notion of the Holy War. This is a war which, because it is commanded by God or his earthly representatives is, without question, just. ISLAMIC fundamentalists, especially under the leadership of the Ayatollah Khomeini, are at present involved in a Jihad on behalf of Allah. President Reagan too, when he railed against the evil empire of COMMUNISM, especially in Central America, seemed to be reviving the spirit of the early Christian crusades and their sacred duty to uphold the spirit of righteousness. Indeed, political REALISTS have long been critical of the dangers involved in the application of varieties of the just war doctrine in WORLD POLITICS. A. J. P. Taylor (1979) summed it up well: 'Bismark fought "necessary wars", and killed thousands; the idealists of the twentieth century fight "just" wars and kill millions'. Apart from these extreme manifestations, in the twentieth century the doctrine of the Just War, for reasons given above, has tended to be rather muted and confined to Christian (usually Catholic) theology, although the VIETNAM war and the uncertain basis on which the United States was involved did generate some soul-searching on the issue (*see*: Walzer, 1977, 1978).

# K

## KAL 007

Korean Air Lines flight KE007 (popularly referred to as KAL 007) was shot down over the Soviet Union on 1 September 1983. At the time of its interception by the Soviet forces, the plane was more than 300 miles off course. All the passengers and crew were lost.

The shooting down of KAL 007 raises two issues immediately, First, the question of the plane's position at the time of the interception, and secondly the reaction of the Soviet authorities. The most plausible explanation for the first question would seem to be pilot error. Most air accidents are caused by MISPERCEPTION and there is no reason to suppose that this case is the exception. Various 'conspiracy theories' have been elaborated to try to explain why the plane was so far off course. These range from the HIJACK theory to the ESPIONAGE one, but all are highly speculative.

The second issue raised by the KAL 007 incident concerns the Soviet reaction. Again, the most plausible explanation appears to be that the Soviet authorities were applying standard operating procedures. All intrusions into Soviet air space were unacceptable and the fact that this intrusion was by a civilian air liner was a coincidence. Additionally, applying a kind of 'reverse conspiracy theory', the Soviets might have assumed that the flight was an INTELLIGENCE-gathering mission or might have confused it with an intelligence-gathering mission in an area – Sakhalin Island near Hokkaido – which is sensitive. The actual decision to engage the aircraft appears to have been taken at the Far Eastern command headquarters after contact with the national command centre. There is no reason to suppose that this decision was not made on strictly military criteria, having regard to procedures and rules of engagement.

## Kellogg–Briand pact

Also known as the General Treaty for the Renunciation of War or the Pact of Paris. It was a MULTILATERAL TREATY signed in 1928 initially by fifteen signatories which later rose to sixty-eight. It began life as an attempt by French Foreign Minister Briand and US Secretary of State Kellogg to bring the United States, which had refused to join the LEAGUE OF NATIONS, back into the INTERNATIONALIST quest for world PEACE. It contained two main proposals. First, that all signatories renounce WAR as an instrument of national policy and secondly that all disputes should be settled by peaceful means. However, a number of STATES. including the United Kingdom, insisted on reservations regarding the right to take military action in cases of SELF-DEFENCE. For the United Kingdom this right extended to protection of the British Empire. The United States, for their part, did not envisage the enforcement of the MONROE DOCTRINE to fall within the terms of the treaty. Although the pact was an attempt to strengthen the League's position on the issue of COLLECTIVE SECURITY, its articles were far too general and hedged about with too many reservations for it to have any significant impact on developments in

WORLD POLITICS, either between the signatory states themselves or between them and non-signatories. The failure to distinguish operationally between wars of AGGRESSION and wars of SELF-DEFENCE allowed the pact to be interpreted permissively. As one contemporary observer put it, 'to a much greater degree than is true of most treaties, it is a scrap of paper binding no one to anything' (Schuman, 1933). Nevertheless, violations of the Pact of Paris were integral to the prosecution cases at the WAR CRIMES TRIALS in Nuremburg and Tokyo after the Second World War.

## Kennan plan

A short-lived and highly controversial proposal by American diplomat George Kennan (*see*: x) concerning the reunification of Germany. The proposal was spelt out in the BBC's prestigious Reith lectures of 1957 and was broadcast world-wide. Kennan's plan involved a general TREATY specifying the withdrawal of all armed forces from western and eastern Europe, a severe armament limitation on the new united Germany and its prohibition from participation in any existing or future military BLOC. It was opposed by all interested states, in particular by the United States (Dean Acheson called it 'mystical' and 'quite fantastic') and West Germany where it was regarded as 'scurrilous'. REALISTS saw it as disruptive of the BALANCE OF POWER and regarded the NEUTRALIZATION and DEMILITARIZATION of Germany as idealistic, artificial, and inherently dangerous. They argued that a neutral and disarmed Germany would lead to its FINLANDIZATION, a process by which it would inevitably fall into the orbit of Soviet military and political INFLUENCE. However, the impending collapse of COMMUNISM in East Germany in late 1989 has led to renewed and strident calls for German unification. Should this happen, it is very likely that the Kennan plan, or something similar to it, will form the framework of the new German state's relationship with the rest of Europe and the SUPERPOWERS.

## Kennedy doctrine

A short-lived LIBERAL proviso to conservative US interpretations of their role in Latin America under the MONROE DOCTRINE and specifically an attempt to encourage continental economic development coupled with democratic IDEALISM in the hemisphere. It was enunciated on 5 July 1961 by President Kennedy in a speech to the Conference of the Alliance for Progress in Punta del Este and consisted of a pledge that the United States would give economic and military assistance only to those STATES with representative governments established through general elections and the democratic process. It was regarded as an advance especially by HUMAN RIGHTS campaigners who were concerned about US AID to regimes in Latin America with dubious records both in relation to individual rights and to the democratic ideal. The general purpose was to align the United States with reformist movements in the hemisphere and to stave off COMMUNIST-inspired social REVOLUTION. It was superceded by the JOHNSON DOCTRINE in 1965.

## Kennedy round

The Kennedy Round is the name given to the sixth session of multilateral TARIFF negotiations held since 1947 under the aegis of GATT. The negotiations lasted from May 1964 to June 1967. Fifty-four STATES participated in these negotiations including the EUROPEAN ECONOMIC COMMUNITY, which negotiated as a single ACTOR. Although the US President who gave his name to these deliberations was dead before they even started, conventional usage has retained this reference. In addition, the original Trade Expansion Act, which gave the US negotiators their mandate, was presented to Congress in 1962 during the Kennedy Presidency.

The Kennedy Round negotiations were significant in terms of TARIFF-cutting DIPLOMACY because for the first time it was proposed that tariffs should be reduced on what was known as the 'linear' method as opposed to the previous practice of negotiating item by item. The linear method would envisage cutting tariffs on certain items by, for example, 20 per cent across the board. If it works properly, the linear method can be much more expeditious than the item by item approach. It is also more difficult for vested interests to oppose linear tariff negotiations because particular items have to be 'opted out' or made out to be exceptions to the general rule. The linear, across-the-board method had been successfully implemented by the EEC in their CUSTOMS UNION negotiations after 1958. As a general rule, the linear approach is favoured by those seeking to liberalize TRADE by the most efficacious method.

At the opening session of the Kennedy Round in 1964 it was proposed that a 50 per cent cut in industrial tariffs would be a good round figure to aim for during the subsequent negotiations. Unfortunately what looked like an intelligible and LIBERAL benchmark for the subsequent negotiations was steadily whittled away via the tactic of exceptions. It was always agreed that parties to the negotiations would want to enter certain exceptions to the linear cuts. The most usual reason for claiming exceptions was that 'significant tariff disparities' existed between the parties claiming exception and the rest. An example will illustrate the point. State A with a tariff of 10 per cent and State B with a tariff of 25 per cent would, applying a linear principle of 50 per cent reductions end up with 5 per cent and 12.5 per cent, respectively. Their relative positions are exactly the same after the linear cuts as before. Very often, therefore, objections to linear tariff cuts come from low tariff systems wishing to reduce the relative tariffs between themselves and the high tariff systems. During the early stages of the Kennedy Round the EEC made over 1,000 claims for exception to the linear principle against the United States.

The average cuts in industrial tariffs eventually negotiated as a result of the Kennedy Round were closer to 35 per cent than the original 50 per cent proposed in the 1962 Act. In fact this average of 35 per cent conceals the fact that on some items reductions in excess of 50 per cent were achieved, while on others no appreciable movement was possible at all. In particular above average cuts (i.e. more than 35 per cent) were achieved on the following: chemicals, machinery, transport equipment, precision instruments and non-ferrous base metals. The cuts were to be effected between 1968–72 with the United States lowering its tariff one-fifth in five reductions starting on 1 January 1968. A slightly different timetable was worked out for the European Community states and the United Kingdom (which was not at the time of the Round a member of the EEC).

The Kennedy Round negotiations were initiated in order to address a particular set of problems arising from the formation of the western European CUSTOMS UNION and the putative membership of that grouping by the United Kingdom. In this light it is perhaps unfair to criticize the Kennedy negotiations for not paying sufficient attention to the problems of the LEAST DEVELOPED COUNTRIES (LDCS). In any case by the time the Kennedy cuts were agreed the United Nations Conference on Trade and Development (UNCTAD) had been formed and was quickly taking shape as a sounding board for THIRD WORLD concerns. In particular the demands for what were to become known as the Generalised System of Preferences – in effect non-reciprocal tariff cuts in favour of the LDCs – were first being voiced during the period of time covered by the Kennedy Round.

More telling, perhaps, are the criticisms that Kennedy did nothing to tackle the growing problem of non-tariff barriers (NTBS) to trade and the issue of temperate agriculture. The issue of the NTB was postponed to the TOKYO ROUND while the temperate food question exacerbated differences between the EC and the United States over the Common Agricultural Policy and the consequential over-production of food. Temperate food production has powerful lobby groups behind it on both sides of the Atlantic and it proved possible to negotiate agreements in this ISSUE AREA only with respect to cereals.

## Kiloton

A measure of the destructive power of NUCLEAR WEAPONS. The kiloton, or KT, is held to be the equivalent of 1,000 tons of TNT. Both of the weapons used against Japan in 1945 were in this category, although by today's standards their kilotonnage would be of the TACTICAL rather than the STRATEGIC category. As missiles have become increasingly accurate, warhead size had decreased so that most intercontinental ballistic missiles (ICBMS), certainly on the Western side, would carry kiloton rather than MEGATON sized weapons.

## Korean war

The Korean War began in June 1950 and ended in July 1953. It originated as a CIVIL WAR and thereafter expanded to draw in the UNITED NATIONS (UN) and the People's Republic of China (PRC). Hostilities commenced in the final week of June 1950 when a substantial incursion of North Korean forces across the 38th parallel occurred. Korea had been divided since 1945 following the defeat of the Japanese forces in Asia (the Japanese had annexed the territory in 1910). The somewhat arbitrary line of the 38th parallel thus divided what were a single people with a strong sense of territorial identity. It is certain that in 1945, given a free choice, the majority of the Korean people would have chosen national INDEPENDENCE and UNIFICATION. Like Germany, Korea became divided as a result of being occupied by the SUPERPOWERS

after 1945. As a result their division became caught up in the COLD WAR rivalry between the two sides. They could regard themselves as less than fortunate in this respect.

Before the civil war broke out an attempt had been made under the aegis of the UN to achieve the reunification of Korea. A temporary commission was appointed by the GENERAL ASSEMBLY in November 1947 and the following year elections were held – but only in the South. Political power in the North had been effectively exercised since 1946 by a COMMUNIST regime under the leadership of Kim Il-Sung, while in South Syngman Rhee, a veteran NATIONALIST, assumed power after the 1948 elections. The Soviet Union thereafter withdrew their forces from the North and the United States did likewise in the South. Given the intense Cold War rivalry of the time, the chances of an agreed process for Korean unification seemed remote.

After the withdrawal of US forces in June 1949 the United States continued to support the REGIME in the South with substantial amounts of AID. However, doubts about how far the Truman Administration would go in support of the Koreans emerged in January 1950 when Secretary of State Acheson appeared to exclude both Korea and Formosa (Taiwan) from the defence perimeter that the United States was seeking to establish in Asia under the policy of CONTAINMENT. The US Congress attitude to the Korean commitment was shown to be equally ambiguous and ambivalent during the spring of 1950, the House first rejecting and then accepting the Korean aid bill. Overall the impression coming from the US policy ELITE was that Korea was not vital to US interests. As Paige (1968, p 76) puts it in his standard work on US policy at the time: 'It (Korea) was tucked down somewhere below the surface of crucial attention.'

The sequence of events which began on 25 June 1950 may be said to constitute a surprise attack within the meaning of that term, at least as far as US perceptions were concerned. Three factors seem to have contributed to this MISPERCEPTION. First, the United States was working on the assumption that Korea was one of a number of flashpoints and that it was not the most likely. Secondly, that an attack in the other direction, i.e. from the South against the North, was equally feasible since the Rhee regime was not that stable and was itself committed to reunification. Thirdly, skirmishes and border incursions had been a persistent feature of relations between the two halves of Korea for eighteen months prior to the invasion and that, in communications terms, there was considerable 'noise' in the system which might diffuse the ability of POLICY-MAKERS to draw the correct inferences. As a result, strategic surprise was almost perfect and nearly decisive. The Southern forces were driven into a small pocket around Pusan and it was fully three months before the UN forces, as they had become in the interim, were able to break out and to successfully counter-attack.

If the US Government was surprised by the events of the last week of June 1950 in the Korean peninsula, then the Soviet Union was equally surprised by the US response. As Paige shows in his study, the United States responded to what was a classic CRISIS situation with a sequence of rapid decisions in the days that followed. By the end of the month the Administration was committed to the reintroduction of ground forces back into Korea and the UN was committed to significant enforcement measures under Chapter 7 of the Charter. The Truman Administration never perceived the Korean War as purely or essentially a civil war. Rather, the United States became convinced that the Soviet Union was behind the North Korean moves and that the United States was being 'tested' to assess its CREDIBILITY to resist perceived AGGRESSION. Parallels with the 1930s and the 'lessons' of the APPEASEMENT period were frequently drawn by US leadership who would have been particularly influenced by that inter-war decade. Given that the United States was being 'tested' therefore the appropriate response was resistance. The only question remaining was whether this should be BILATERAL or MULTILATERAL. As Paige demonstrates, the decision to take the Korean crisis to the UN was made very early in the first week.

The involvement of the UN in the Korean War was controversial. Meeting in emergency sessions on 25 and 27 June, the SECURITY COUNCIL passed a series of resolutions fixing the blame for the commencement of hostilities on the North Koreans, called for a cease-fire and the withdrawal of forces to their original positions and, when compliance was not forthcoming, recommended enforcement action under Chapter 7 of the CHARTER. It is now generally accepted that the Korean vote was *sui generis*. The Soviet Union was absent from the Council throughout these proceedings (it was protesting at the refusal of the organization to accept the credentials of the PRC). The Soviet absence undoubtedly enabled the Council to take a number of decisions, at the height of the crisis, which served to legitimize what was, in truth, a US-inspired response to the Korean War. The Council did, however, side-step the legality of its DECISION-MAKING by making recommendations to the membership. At the time of the Korean situation the United States and its allies commanded considerable voting support in the UN. It should be remembered that the bulk of the THIRD WORLD STATES had still to join the Organization and many states in the Organization were at that stage in post-war politics still oriented towards the West. The fact that both Cuba and China voted in support of the US-sponsored resolutions on Korea in the June crisis is instructive of how far the institution was dominated by these interests.

The UN decision to extend the war into North Korea in the autumn of 1950 provoked the second major crisis of the war. If the original involvement of the UN was controversial because the Organization was seen to be taking sides in a Cold War confrontation, the extension of the fighting across the 38th parallel clearly exceeded the spirit if not the letter of the first Security Council resolution '. . . to repel the armed attack and to restore international peace and security in the area'. Moreover, in implementing that decision the UN provoked Chinese INTERVENTION in support of the North Koreans. As a result there was a significant escalation of the war. Far from achieving the unification of Korea by this adventure, the UN forces were repulsed from the North with significant losses and the North Koreans and the Chinese 'volunteers' drove the UN forces back to the original 38th parallel dividing line. Initially, it seemed as if they were going to repeat the stunning gains of June. The intervention of the Chinese locked the conflict into a STALEMATE situation until a permanent cease-fire was agreed in 1953.

The Korean War has provided valuable case study material for research in a number of areas. Obviously, its relevance to the crisis literature is apparent. Students of FOREIGN POLICY analysis and of STRATEGIC STUDIES have used Korea to examine certain ideas. In the policy analysis field particular interest has been shown in the decision to escalate the war in the autumn of 1950 when the UN forces crossed the 38th parallel into North Korea. Janis (1972), writing in the context of GROUP-THINK ideas, has called this decision Truman's BAY OF PIGS. DETERRENCE theorists have also looked at these events in the light of the seeming failure of the PRC to deter the UN from this step. The Chinese Communists issued repeated warnings that if the 38th parallel was crossed they would assist the North Koreans. In summary, studies of this period in the Korean conflict, aimed particularly at the US decision system, seem to suggest the following

conclusions: (a) the Truman Administration took excessive risks in their escalation decision; (b) they seemed to hold stereotypes of the Chinese LEADERSHIP which seemed to suggest that the latter's capacity for independent judgment was limited and, following on from this, that the Soviet Union, the PRC and the North Koreans could be regarded in effect as a single ACTOR where decisions on the war were concerned; (c) the escalation decisions were bitterly opposed within the Administration by some of the most senior and respected foreign policy-making staff, including George Kennan (see: X).

Halperin (1963) has suggested that Korea was a paradigm of LIMITED WAR in the postwar system. This conclusion is rather contingent upon where the analyst stands. From the perception of the United States, the Soviet Union and the PRC, perhaps Korea was a limited war fought for limited ends. From the perspective of the Koreans, however, the war was comprehensive in its impact and significant in its implications. This is because the war was a civil conflict and these situations are by nature total.

The limits on the use of NUCLEAR WEAPONS are perhaps fairly meaningless. The US stocks of these weapons were low until the latter stages of the war and as ATOMIC weapons became more available during the Eisenhower Administration the United States became more willing to contemplate their use. The US view that the three COMMUNIST states were acting as one is now widely regarded with great scepticism. The Chinese were not involved in the war until the escalation decision of the autumn of 1950, while the Soviet absence from the Security Council for the crucial votes in June 1950 hardly confirms the theory that the attack was a Communist 'conspiracy'.

# L

## Landlocked states

Those STATES that do not possess a coastline. These are: AFGHANISTAN, Andorra, Austria, Bhutan, Bolivia, Botswana, Burkina Faso, Burundi, Central African Republic, Chad, Czechoslovakia, Hungary, Laos, Lesotho, Liechtenstein, Luxembourg, Malawi, Mali, Mongolia, Nepal, Niger, Paraguay, Rwanda, San Marino, Swaziland, Switzerland, Uganda, Vatican City, Zambia and Zimbabwe. Most of these states have felt disadvantaged by the traditional LAWS OF THE SEA which for obvious reasons favour those states with coastlines. The revision of the law of the sea in 1982, UNCLOS III, attempted to give even landlocked states some maritime rights, especially concerning the resources of the seabed, under the 'common heritage of mankind' doctrine. However, UNCLOS III has not been universally ratified.

Landlocked states are susceptible to economic warfare techniques as a result of their geographical position. Thus the entrepôt position of the state controlling access to the sea can be used to apply pressure to the landlocked state by withholding or reducing the availability of goods and services. Zambia and Zimbabwe are, at the time of writing, certainly aware of this type of economic leverage, while Lesotho is double landlocked, in so far as it is totally surrounded by the Republic of South Africa, in addition to its geographical position as a landlocked state.

## Land reform

A policy whereby the ownership and use of land is changed. The changes associated with land reform involve the redistribution of land held in large estates – *latifundia* – to small farmers and tenants and/or to landless farm workers. A variation of land reform, particularly favoured in centrally planned economies, is to redistribute land to cooperatives and collectives rather than to individual farmers. Politically, land reform is seen by its proponents as weakening or even destroying the POWER base of the traditional landed oligarchy or *rentier* class. As a policy therefore land reform is particularly associated with radical and reformist ideas. Alternatively it may be seen as a means whereby a traditional system can avoid violent upheaval by instituting change in order to mitigate the worst excesses of the system. Such a judgement might appropriately be made of the attempts at land reform in Russia before 1917.

In contemporary WORLD POLITICS land reform is certainly seen in reformist if not REVOLUTIONARY terms. There are many examples from the THIRD WORLD of land reform programmes being initiated by LESS DEVELOPED COUNTRIES (LDCs) since 1945. Ideologically, these measures are usually seen in these STATES as representing the desire to place land ownership in the hands of those who actually work the land. Widespread support for these changes has come from organizations such as the UNITED NATIONS, particularly in those organs of the UN where THIRD WORLD concerns are well represented.

Economically, land reform can make a great deal of sense. It leads to a redistribution of income in favour of groups who might reasonably be expected to spend their money at home rather than abroad. It can lead to a redirection of land use in favour of producing cash crops for domestic urban markets rather than internationally marketed commodities, which is a feature of the *latifundia* system.


## Launch-on-warning

A term used in strategic analysis for a FIRST STRIKE. As the term implies, in this conception the initial strike is triggered by a DIPLOMATIC or INTELLIGENCE warning that indicates that one is about to be attacked. Such a warning should be unambiguous, its source should be reliable and it should be susceptible to checking and VERIFICATION. In the real world this may seem like a counsel of perfection. In any case, all these variables may be of little avail if the mind-set of the key DECISION-MAKERS is unable to accept the implications of the evidence. A famous example of repeated warnings failing to provoke an appropriate response is the Barbarossa (1941) case study, as Whaley (1973) shows.

The advent of NUCLEAR WEAPONS has greatly increased the stakes implicit in the launch-on-warning situation. TECHNOLOGY may assist in this regard by making missiles more accurate and by providing the intelligence systems with more sophisticated means of monitoring other ACTORS. Conversely it was argued in the late 1950s that SECOND-STRIKE invulnerability of delivery systems reduced the incentives to launch-on-warning. Additional measures of CRISIS MANAGEMENT such as the HOTLINE should give key decision-makers more 'thinking time' before they make irrevocable commitments.
*See also*: PRE-EMPTION


## Law of the sea (Maritime law)

The attempt to apply general rules to cover over two-thirds of the earth's surface has always been fraught with difficulty, no less so in the twentieth century than in the seventeenth when this issue was first systematically tackled by jurists. From the outset the matter of control and jurisdiction of the seas was a power-political affair. Throughout this period the major maritime NATIONS have oscillated between attempting to claim huge tracts of the high seas as part of their proper territorial domain and devising a principle of 'open seas' which would preclude appropriation and give free access to all. The latter view (freedom of the seas) eventually prevailed mainly because of the interests of the European maritime states in exploration and commercial exploitation of the Orient and elsewhere. The Dutch scholar Hugo Grotius, in his *Mare Liberum* (1618), is generally credited with elaborating the first systematic doctrine of 'the freedom of the seas'. Grotius' brief was to sustain the right of Dutch navigation and commerce in the East Indies against Portuguese claims to monopoly. From the outset the Grotian doctrine was regarded as a permissive one by the major states who saw themselves as having virtual *carte blanche* over the great oceans. On the other hand, it was regarded as an oppressive and pernicious doctrine by the smaller, weaker STATES who were concerned with the expansion of their territorial rights rather than with free passage. This division between the interests of the more powerful and less powerful states has remained a fundamental one in Maritime law to this day.

Once enunciated, freedom of the high seas rapidly became one of the basic principles of INTERNATIONAL LAW. This freedom was not unlimited, however, for it was regarded as permissible for a coastal state to claim a maritime belt around it shores ('territorial waters') which was treated as an integral part of its territorial jurisdiction. The subsequent history of the law of the sea from the seventeenth century onwards has largely to do with finding precise demarcation lines to establish these limits of control. Originally limits were based on the 'cannon-shot rule' which meant in effect that the dividing line between the high seas and territorial waters was the extent to which the coastal state could exert military domination. Modern practice favours a 12-mile territorial sea, although this is not universally the case, as some states claim 3, 4, 6, 15, 20, 30, 35, 50, 70 and even 200 nautical mile limits defining their territory. Given this, it is hardly surprising that many commentators refer to the chronic untidiness of the law of the sea. In addition to 'territorial waters', other aspects which compromise the basic principle of freedom are 'belligerents' rights' and the right of HOT PURSUIT, both of which purport to give states temporary privileges in certain defined circumstances, though this is often a matter of dispute as it is sometimes claimed that the 'right of INNOCENT PASSAGE' takes precedence.

The trend in maritime law has been in the direction of extending JURISDICTION over portions of the high seas and this has resulted in the elaboration of special claims to 'Contiguous Zones', 'Economic Exclusion Zones', 'Maritime Exclusion Zones' and even 'POLLUTION Zones'. This shift in emphasis is clearly a reflection of the increased awareness of the economic and ECOLOGICAL potential of the sea and the anxiety of some states and some MULTI-NATIONAL COMPANIES (MNCs) to exploit this to the full.

However, alongside this tendency towards ANNEXATION of the sea a counter-movement has developed, particularly among THIRD WORLD states, which proclaims the seas and the riches therein to be part of 'the common heritage of mankind' and therefore beyond the range of the individualistic aspirations of the more acquisitive states. This phrase and the sentiments it expresses was popularized in 1967 by Ambassador Arvid Pardo of Malta and was quickly endorsed by the GENERAL ASSEMBLY OF THE UN. The fear was that with the discovery of raw materials in the sea-bed and with the rapid growth in TECHNOLOGICAL capability that renders these materials extractable, the poorer, less de-veloped states, not to mention the LANDLOCKED STATES, would once more lose out if there was a general free-for-all of the kind implied in the original doctrine of freedom of the sea. Combined with increasing concern about the depletion of the world's resources this has led to a demand for a fresh look at the underlying philosophy of the law of the sea.

The result is that at present two competing ideologies – freedom of the sea versus common heritage – vie for general approval by the international community. A number of recent conferences on the law of the sea, UNCLOS I (1958), UNCLOS II (1960) and UNCLOS III (1974–82), have attempted to resolve the differences between the two positions. Indeed, UNCLOS III has come so close to revising the traditional approach that it is regarded by some observers as being the first significant step in the direction of a NEW INTERNATIONAL ECONOMIC ORDER. So far, over 120 states have appended their signatures to the new maritime REGIME. But the old divisions remain and major maritime users, such as the United States, the United Kingdom, Japan, West Germany and Italy, among others, have so far rejected the proposals. It remains to be seen whether this minority of traditionalists eventually accede to the collectivist view or whether they will continue to cling to the libertarian and permissive principles of the Grotian tradition.

## Leadership

Considerations of leadership occur in two contexts in WORLD POLITICS. At the level of MACROPOLITICS, certain ACTORS seem to enjoy DE FACTO positions of leadership. In this usage, the term is coterminous with HEGEMONY. In the second sense, leadership is used in FOREIGN POLICY analysis to direct attention towards the personalities holding leadership roles at the head of organizations. The remaining discussion will concentrate upon this latter usage.

Studying the influence of personality

raises methodological issues. Historians are inclined towards a contextual analysis of particular individuals and time periods, while psychologists prefer to stipulate personality types in general before looking at individual cases. The two approaches become synthesized in the so-called 'psychobiography' which attempts to correlate an individual case study with more general ideas about the relationship between personality, upbringing, self-perception, etc., and the individual. The George's 1964 study is a good example of this approach.

Personality types have been more overtly synthesized with policy preference in Eysenck's (1954) two-dimensional, tough-minded versus tender-minded and conservative versus radical treatment. Barber (1985), likewise, used the two-dimensional idea in his discussion of US Presidential personality. Looking more explicitly at foreign policy outcomes, Stoessinger (1985) identified two types of policy maker: the crusader and the pragmatist, while Paige (1977), taking the variable of change, argued that this produces three attitude types: conservative, reformist and revolutionary.

An overly psychological orientation to the issue of individual leadership is probably inevitable. Certainly, as the above citations show, it is a popular approach. It is well to remember that leadership is exercised within an organizational context. In many political systems, moreover, leadership roles and positions are competitively sought after. Thus for every group of POWER holders there may be an identifiable group of power seekers as well. This competitive environment will affect the leaders' perceptions of issues and how they handle them, particularly if the leadership is likely to face electoral judgement upon their DECISION-MAKING in the future.

Leadership also implies 'followership'. The consequential question, 'what causes followers to respond positively rather than negatively to a leadership?' can appropriately be raised. Here Weber's (1947) seminal trichotomy of charismatic, traditional and rational–legal ideal types may point towards an answer. Charismatic leadership is derived from the kind of individual, personality characteristics discussed already. The charismatic leader is the revolutionary, the warrior, the prophet, the demagogue, the national hero, etc. Such leadership styles surface during times of great social change to confirm or challenge the STATUS QUO and to provide an inspiring vision of the future. This ability to mobilize the followers is clearly an important facet of leadership and, in the case of the charismatic type, it seems to inhere in the individual. On the other hand, Weber's other two types depend upon the social and legal nexus for their leadership capabilities. Recent studies of THIRD WORLD polities has done much to increase interest in the traditional or patrimonial leadership types.

## League of Nations

Probably the most significant innovation of twentieth century INTERNATIONAL RELATIONS, the League was created in 1920 with the specific object of establishing procedures for peaceful resolution of international disputes and conflicts. The immediate catalyst for its formation was the First World War and the TREATY OF VERSAILLES which followed it but its origins go back to IDEALIST and LIBERAL dissatisfaction with the international ANARCHY, BALANCE OF POWER and the concept of SELF-HELP which had hitherto characterized the STATE-SYSTEM. It was intended to be a global organization though it was handicapped from the outset by political and IDEOLOGICAL realities. The United States refused to join, the Soviet Union was ostracized by the others, France and the United Kingdom gave only lukewarm support and Germany, Italy and Japan operated outside the principles established in the Covenant. Nevertheless, its brief history (1920–46) is testimony to the break-up of the old system and the almost universal desire in the twentieth century to establish international institutions which would go some way towards establishing a legal REGIME for the orderly conduct of international affairs. The UNITED NATIONS is its successor and between them these organizations have added a new dimension to WORLD POLITICS.

The League consisted of three main organs: the Council (fifteen members, including France, the United Kingdom and the Soviet Union as permanent members) which met three times a year, the Assembly (all members) which met annually, and a Secretariat which functioned as an international civil service. All decisions had to be by unanimous vote. The underlying philosophy of the League was the principle of COLLECTIVE SECURITY which meant that the international community had a duty to INTERVENE in international CONFLICTS: it also meant that parties to a dispute should submit their grievances to the League or the ARBITRATORS. If the League or the arbitrators failed to reach a unanimous decision within six months the disputants could, after a further delay of three months, go to WAR. The PERMANENT COURT OF INTERNATIONAL JUSTICE, although separate from the League, acted in concert with it. The centre-piece of the Covenant was Article 16, which empowered the League to institute ECONOMIC or military SANCTIONS against a recalcitrant STATE. In essence, though, it was left to each member to decide whether or not a breach of the Covenant had occurred and so whether or not to apply sanctions. This is regarded by commentators as a major weakness, yet although the League failed in respect of German, Italian and Japanese AGGRESSION in the 1930s, it did succeed in resolving some disputes in more minor cases (notably in the Balkans and South America). The settlement of international conflict was its rationale but the League also concerned itself with other matters and subsidiary bodies were set up dealing in areas such as MANDATES, DISARMAMENT and economic and social cooperation.

History might have dealt harshly with the League's overall record of achievement but none can doubt that its very existence was a major and radical step in the development of modern international relations. The argument that it failed in its purpose has to be balanced against the notion that it was never really tried. The member STATES, particularly the more powerful European ones, were locked into traditional concepts of SOVEREIGNTY and DIPLOMACY and in matters of HIGH POLICY bypassed the League system altogether. However flexible the provisions of the Covenant might have been, unless it received the full cooperation of the major powers in implementing decisions it was bound to be something of a non-starter in the matter of resolving international conflict.

## Least developed countries (LDCs)

This term has been used for some two decades within the UNITED NATIONS to describe those STATES at the bottom of the HIERARCHY, at least in terms of economic criteria. The UN defines these states as those having the lowest per capita GDP, the lowest levels of literacy and the smallest share of secondary or manufacturing industries input into GDP. The colloquial term FOURTH WORLD is sometimes used to refer to these states. Bangladesh, with something like one-quarter of the total population of the LDCs, is a paradigm of this class of states. In many instances they show negative growth rates of per capita income annually and they run the real risk of 'dropping out' of the system altogether if their prospects cannot be improved.

## Lebanon

A Middle Eastern state which has experienced COMMUNAL CONFLICT and violence of increasing intensity since 1975. The Lebanon does not fit into the classical European conception of the NATION STATE because there is very little isomorphism evident between the political–legal concept of the STATE and the political–behavioural concept of the NATION. The Lebanon is thus a multi-ethnic arrangement.

The territorial basis of the modern Lebanon was the product of European INTERVENTION. During the First World War, Britain and France each decided to establish a SPHERE OF INFLUENCE in the area. After the war the area known as Syria was the object of two MANDATES granted under the League of NATIONS. In the south the British were given Palestine, while in the north, the French retained the term 'Syria' for the rest. In the summer of 1920 the French created a separate ENCLAVE – the Lebanon – from Syria. From its inception the Lebanon represented a balance of forces between Christian and Muslim elements.

This balance was enshrined in the so-called National Pact of 1943. In that year, France somewhat reluctantly agreed to Lebanese INDEPENDENCE. The resulting political arrangement could be described as a power-sharing framework. It was hoped that all ethnic groups would feel sufficiently committed to the system to make it work within the rules of the game. Specifically, it was agreed that offices should be distributed according to ethnicity. For example, the President of the republic was to be a Maronite Christian, the Prime Minister a Sunni Muslim, the speaker of the Parliament a Shiite, and so on. The term most often used to describe this arrangement is 'confessionalism'. In addition to the divisions at the centre, each confessional group had, or sought to establish, geopolitical POWER bases within the territory of the state. Thus particular parts of the country are identified as being the fiefdoms of particular ethnic groupings. This had undoubtedly led to the 'cantonization' of the Lebanon with the implicit threat that these centrifugal forces might eventually cause the break-up of the state completely. The political system inherent in the National Pact and the concepts of power sharing broke down briefly in 1958, and totally after 1975. Internally, the most decisive factor that eroded this arrangement was

demography. Stated simply, the birth rate among Muslims was higher than among Christians, thus eventually the latter would become a minority while the former would come to expect more of the benefits of majority status to accrue to them. Furthermore, the prosperity of the 1950s and the 1960s – which was based mainly upon service industries – was not distributed evenly. In particular a growing Shiite sense of relative disadvantage was producing schisms within the Muslim community and the growth of radical politics among the underprivileged. Because of the divisions within the majority Muslim population it has proved impossible for any one group to provide a centripetal counter-weight to the centrifugal forces of sectarianism. The consensus that created the National Pact has gone and Lebanese politics has moved into a more ideologically structured framework. Politics in the Lebanon has also become more violent. All the major sects have their own MILITIAS; these have been used to enforce a kind of DE FACTO sectarian SOVEREIGNTY and to enhance cantonization. In addition, all the sects have sought AID and assistance from outside parties. INTERVENTION from outside parties has been a feature of Lebanese politics. Three are particularly crucial and merit attention: the Syrians, the Israelis and the Palestinians. Historically, Syria has had a deep and enduring INFLUENCE in the Lebanon. Geographically, it represents the Lebanese hinterland, the two economies are INTERDEPENDENT and the revival of service industries in the Lebanon would be greatly helped by an open and peaceful border with Syria. Politically Syria can play a number of roles in the Lebanon: honest broker, peacemaker, defender of minority rights, mediator, IRREDENTIST. As with any FOREIGN POLICY ISSUE AREA, the outcome will be a complex of factors over which no party has total control.

The Israelis have been drawn into the Lebanon ostensibly in pursuit of the Palestinians. They have also sought allies within the Lebanese sectarian system. Finally, they have been drawn into the Lebanon to play a military role – both overt and covert. There is little doubt that Israeli intervention has increased the polarization among the sects in the Lebanon. The use of FORCE by Israel has been costly and controversial.

The Palestinians have lived in the Lebanon since the inception of the state of Israel in 1948. In 1969 the Lebanese government signed an accord with the PLO which recognized the right of the latter to use the territory of the Lebanon as a BASE for political and paramilitary operations. The Israelis indicated that the Cairo Accord effectively nullified the cease-fire agreement of 1949 between themselves and the Lebanon. A solution to the Palestine question would remove a major irritant from the Lebanon. The Palestinian presence in the state has drawn the attention of the Israelis to the Lebanon and moreover has significantly alienated the Christian and Shia sects. The Palestinians have sometimes operated as a 'state within a state' and this has weakened the AUTHORITY and prestige of the central government in Beirut. The complexities of Lebanese politics are exacerbated by the Palestinian factor.

The Lebanon remains a complex and intractable issue. It is typical of a whole class of contemporary conflicts in that its origins lie within one particular territorial state. Through ally seeking and external intervention outside parties have been drawn into this vortex. Like the ARAB–ISRAELI CONFLICT, it has drawn in the SUPERPOWERS and the UN. At the time of writing a stable self-sustaining resolution of this conflict still seems some way off.

## Lebensraum

German GEOPOLITICAL term meaning 'living space'. The term can be credited to General Karl Haushofer (1869–1946) and his team at the Institute of Geopolitics in Munich, but was popularized by Adolf Hitler in *Mein Kampf*. Originally, it was an adjunct of the HEARTLAND theory and referred to control of central and eastern Europe. Hitler used it as part of his thesis that it was Germany's destiny to control the East and therefore other STATES must accede to her request for *lebensraum*. Territorial expansion was deemed necessary because of Germany's overpopulation and need for foodstuffs; therefore, the Ukraine, for example, was seen as a German 'granary'. *Lebensraum* also has overtones of racial superiority, the Aryan master race having a mystical right to dominate those around it.

## Legalistic–Moralistic

Term that gained wide currency as a description of American FOREIGN POLICY after publication of George Kennan's *American Diplomacy, 1900–1950* (1957) where he stated that this approach 'runs like a red skein through our policy over the past fifty years'. Kennan argued that in the twentieth century, unlike the nineteenth, American POLICY-MAKERS tended to lose sight of POWER considerations and a limited conception of the NATIONAL INTEREST and substitute instead a belief in legal and moral contractual engagements as the solution to WORLD ORDER problems. The DOMESTIC ANALOGY (arguments drawn from the internal American experience) plus a feeling of moral righteousness, encouraged a serious misunderstanding of the realities of WORLD POLITICS. Woodrow Wilson's policies and speeches are said to be the best illustration of this approach.

## Legation

Originally an ecclesiastical term denoting someone deputed to represent the Pope but now more commonly used to indicate a DIPLOMATIC mission of the second order where the head of mission does not hold the titular rank of AMBASSADOR. Thus, while it is usual to style an ambassador as 'Ambassador Extraordinary and Plenipotentiary', the head of a legation is likely to be called 'Envoy Extraordinary and Minister Plenipotentiary'. The term is also used to refer to the building in which the minister resides and the area immediately surrounding it. In this sense, the legation is usually immune from the JURISDICTION of the host STATE and subject only to the laws of the sending state. It can, and frequently does, therefore serve as a place of refuge. For example, black political activists in South Africa have used the UK and West German legations as places of sanctuary.

*See also*: DIPLOMATIC IMMUNITIES AND PRIVILEGES

## Legitimacy

In international affairs this is bound up with notions of RECOGNITION and as such is more often a political matter rather than a strictly legal one. The doctrine of legitimacy is sometimes called the 'Tobar doctrine' which takes its name from the Foreign Minister of Ecuador who elaborated the idea in 1907. The suggestion was that governments which came to POWER by means other than those laid down in the constitution should not be recognized by the international community. Thus a COUP D'ÉTAT or a REVOLUTION would render a STATE illegitimate and therefore beyond the range and scope of INTERNATIONAL LAW and the conventions of DIPLOMACY. The concept is especially associated with American FOREIGN POLICY in relation to Latin America which, in accordance with the MONROE DOCTRINE, it regards as a special area of interest and concern. Under President Woodrow Wilson this was given added precision through the policy of 'democratic legitimacy'. This was a refinement of the Tobar method in that it invoked the idea of popular support: if the new REGIME was popular, it would be granted legitimate status; if it was not, it would not. Although this principle and the IDEOLOGY associated with it is still a feature of American foreign policy (most notably in the case of non-recognition of the People's Republic of China) it is generally regarded as an unsatisfactory and unrealistic way of determining full membership of the international community.

The term is also used in a more general sense referring to the framework of the INTERNATIONAL SYSTEM. Thus Henry Kissinger (1964), for example, writes of a 'legitimate international order' implying that all the major powers have accepted established conventions of dealing with one another and agree on the parameters of foreign policy aims and methods. A legitimate order is stable, as contrasted with a revolutionary system, where a major power or powers is dissatisfied and seeks to rearrange the STATUS QUO. The period from 1789–1815 was a revolutionary one, whereas the system that was established between 1815–1914 was legitimate.

## Lend-lease

The Lend-Lease Act was inaugurated in March 1941 and was designed to render assistance to the Allied powers fighting the Second World War through a system of deferred payment for goods. This programme, inspired by F. D. Roosevelt, effectively ended the NEUTRALITY of the United States even though it was nine months before the United States actually entered the WAR. Roosevelt felt that the United States should become 'the great arsenal of democracy' and to this end proposed that it should 'lease, lend or otherwise dispose of' arms and supplies to the amount of seven billion dollars to states whose DEFENCE was regarded as vital to America's interests. From 1941 to 1945 it has been estimated that the United States provided more than fifty billion dollars' worth of weapons, raw materials, food, machine tools and other strategic supplies to aid the hard-pressed Allies in Europe – the bulk going to the United Kingdom and the Soviet Union. In the post-war period repayment of Lend-Lease became a contentious issue particularly between the United

States and the Soviet Union and contributed to the climate that produced the COLD WAR.

## Less developed countries (LDC)

A term of relative economic development which is normally used with reference to the THIRD WORLD of Africa, Asia and Latin America. In this context it has become widely accepted by analysts and commentators. It would be possible to identify an LDC using such economic indicators as gross domestic product (GDP), *per capita* GDP, *per capita* growth and so on. LDCs tend to be recipients of AID rather than donors. They tend to play a disproportionately small role in world TRADE. In short they tend to be dependent upon advanced industrial countries (AICs). Identification of this grouping has led to the characterization of economic relations as being divided on a NORTH–SOUTH axis with the LDCs corresponding to the South.

It should be acknowledged that the term is a blanket one and covers a large number of states with a fair degree of imprecision. Thus some writers have attempted to characterize the very poorest as the FOURTH WORLD while others have identified a small group of rapidly growing economies, in Asia, as Newly Industrialized Countries (NICs). These subdivisions are tacit recognition of the imprecision referred to above.

## Lethality

A composite measure used in order to compare nuclear forces. The term has been particularly applied to the nuclear relationship of mutual DETERRENCE between the United States and the Soviet Union. Lethality is a function of the ACCURACY of a missile and its yield. Of the two factors mentioned above, it is generally agreed that accuracy is the more significant. Lethality is held to be particularly important when considering a COUNTERFORCE strategy. In addition to its implications for targeting, lethality is also used whenever attempts are made to compare the missile capabilities of the two states, for example, for the purposes of ARMS CONTROL.

## Level of analysis

A methodological term. Its implication is that in studying WORLD POLITICS, INTERNATIONAL POLITICS and FOREIGN POLICY awareness should be shown towards the units which are being studied. In traditional analysis these units were taken to be: the individual, the STATE and the system. One of the first, and seminal, outlines of this division was made by Singer in 1961. Waltz (1959) in his study of WAR applied this triad. Over the years since, particularly with the growth of social science approaches, the value of early and explicit recognition of the operational level of analysis has been generally recognized by scholars. It would be difficult to conceive of anyone writing in the fields of, for instance, CONFLICT or INTEGRATION who did not use these units to sort and arrange ideas at various stages in the research. It is testimony to their efficacy that they have become good habits rather than self-conscious decisions. To avoid excessive parochialism, it is well to remember that other social sciences, in particular economics and sociology, similarly recognize the requirement to operate at various levels in pursuit of their studies.

## Liberalism

The liberal tradition in international affairs can be traced back at least as far as John Locke (1632–1704) but it is in the nineteenth and twentieth centuries that liberalism has had its most enduring impact. Indeed, the development of modern WORLD POLITICS would be incomprehensible without an appreciation of the part played by the liberal approach. For example, the role of INTERNATIONAL ORGANIZATIONS such as the LEAGUE OF NATIONS and the UNITED NATIONS can be directly attributed to the liberal quest for the elimination of the international ANARCHY and the inauguration of the rule of law. It could be argued that the success of liberalism in the twentieth century is due to the influence in world politics of its most powerful proponent, the United States, but this would be to deny one of the basic tenets of its belief system – the idea that progress is inevitable and that the TRADITIONAL REALIST responses to the question of WORLD ORDER are atavistic and inherently dangerous.

The liberal theory of INTERNATIONAL RELATIONS contains a number of propositions, most of which derive from the DOMESTIC ANALOGY concerning the relationship between individuals within the state. Among the most important are the following:

1. PEACE can best be secured through the spread of democratic institutions on a world-wide basis. Governments, not people, cause WARS. Democracy is the highest expression of the will of the people, therefore democracies are inherently more pacific than other political systems. An INTERNATIONAL SYSTEM composed of democratic STATES would, in consequence, lead to a condition of perpetual peace, where CONFLICT and WAR would disappear. This is self-evident and based on reason. Best known proponents of this view are Kant and Woodrow Wilson, both of whom believed that the solution to the problems of world order and security lay in the spread of the democratic ideal. In this connection 'consent' is the only legitimate grounds for government, therefore IMPERIALISM is immoral. SELF-DETERMINATION is a condition of democracy, just as the final bar at the court of world judgement is PUBLIC OPINION which in the last resort is the safeguard of peace.

2. Bound up with this, and underpinning it, is a belief in the 'natural HARMONY OF INTERESTS'. If people and states make rational calculations of their interests and act upon them, something akin to Adam Smith's 'invisible hand' would ensure that the NATIONAL INTEREST and the INTERNATIONAL interest would be one and the same. The free market and the perfectibility of human nature would encourage INTERDEPENDENCE and demonstrate conclusively that 'war does not pay' (Angell, 1910).

3. If disputes continue to occur, these would be settled by established judicial procedures, since the rule of law is just as applicable to states as it is to individuals. An international legal REGIME based on common voluntary membership of international organizations would begin to fulfil the functions of a legislature, executive and judiciary, while still preserving the freedom and INDEPENDENCE of the states.

4. COLLECTIVE SECURITY would replace notions of SELF-HELP. The assumption here is that just as it must always be possible to identify an AGGRESSOR so also must it be possible to organize a preponderant collective coalition of law-abiding states to oppose it. The League of Nations and the United Nations were founded on this premise; security being conceived of as a collective, communal responsibility rather than an individual one.

These are core beliefs of liberalism but liberals themselves often disagree as to the advisability of particular courses of action. In this context, it is instructive to distinguish between INTERVENTIONIST and NON-INTERVENTIONIST liberals. The former, among whom Woodrow Wilson figures prominently, believe that although 'progress' is historically inevitable, it is sometimes necessary to help it along. Thus, war on behalf of the liberal ideal may occasionally be required to rid the world of illiberal and persistent opponents. The JUST WAR or the crusade are perfectly permissible policies provided the object is to further the cause of democratic liberalism. This attitude to war was put most succinctly by R. H. Tawney: 'either war is a crusade, or it is a crime. There is no half-way house.' The non-interventionists, on the other hand, believe that a liberal WORLD ORDER is implicit in history and that the virtues of liberalism itself would spread without any active prodding by its adherents. Nineteenth century American traditions of ISOLATIONISM were often expressed in these terms; the new politics of the New World would, by dint of its own obvious superiority, sweep all before it. However, the emergence in the twentieth century of two powerful anti-liberal ideologies, FASCISM and COMMUNISM have rendered the NON-INTERVENTIONIST stance somewhat anachronistic. Since the Second World War and the defeat of fascism, the liberal stand has been taken on the ground of CONTAINMENT which argues that the future of liberal democracy rests on its ability first, to stop the spread of communism and second, to eliminate it altogether. Containment, which is still the official orthodoxy of US FOREIGN POLICY, can thus be seen as a compromise between INTERVENTIONISM and non-interventionism, but it is as well to stress that liberalism, whether active or passive, on the battlefield or in the market place, envisages the eventual defeat of the forces of illiberalism in whatever garb it decks itself. It is this self-righteousness and spirit of moral omnipotence that is one of the weaknesses of contemporary liberalism, as it all too easily leads to policies of sustaining the STATUS QUO almost at any cost. US foreign policy, in particular, has come under repeated criticism for supporting regimes with appalling records on HUMAN RIGHTS on the sole grounds that these regimes are anti-communist. The VIETNAM WAR may yet prove to be something of a watershed in the history of liberalism, particularly of the interventionist variety.

The dark side of liberalism is its chronic inability to come to terms with the use of FORCE for particular and specific ends. REALISTS have never been slow to point this out. The brighter side is that it honestly and self-consciously intends to work for a brave new world where human rights and the well being of individuals are given a higher priority than state's rights and the narrower conceptions of NATIONAL INTEREST which characterize the more traditional approaches. Whether this is regarded as unduly idealistic or utopian depends upon one's general political orientation.

*See also*: ECONOMIC LIBERALISM

## Liberation theology

A branch of Christian theology which emphasizes the important role that the Church can play in the achievement of social justice and ameliorating the conditions of the poor and oppressed. Employing a MARXIST or socialist view of social, economic and political conditions, it calls for activist INTERVENTION on the part of the clergy in the struggle against exploitation both from internal and external sources. It has had a profound impact on THIRD WORLD politics generally, but it is in Latin America that it has achieved its greatest political impact. At a conference of Roman Catholic bishops of Latin America at Medellin in Colombia in 1968 there was near-unanimous support for the aims of the movement despite opposition from the VATICAN, which considered it to be a dangerous intrusion into politics and perhaps an unwitting instrument of communist PROPAGANDA. Outside Latin America, it has had an important effect on the developments in southern Africa and the World Council of Churches has on a number of occasions publicly endorsed its general aims. In South Africa in particular, Archbishop Desmond Tutu (Nobel Peace Laureate in 1984), and Dr Allan Boesak (president of the World Alliance of Reformed Churches) have given liberation theology a high international profile in the general opposition to APARTHEID. Liberation theology is also sometimes known as 'revolutionary theology' although most of its adherents have tended to shy away from this appellation due to its connotations of condoning violent change.

## Limited nuclear war

This term is used in two contexts. First, that NUCLEAR WEAPONS could be used in a limited WAR situation such as KOREA. Secondly, that if mutual nuclear DETERRENCE fails it would be possible and preferable to attempt to 'limit' the subsequent nuclear exchange between the United States and the Soviet Union. The two uses are linked because they both involve crossing the nuclear threshold. They raise the central question about all LIMITED WAR situations: how can one reach tacit understandings about 'limits' that are stable?

The advent of nuclear weapons after 1945 obviously provides the background to this question. The development of very powerful fusion or HYDROGEN weapons and conversely the development of low-yield tactical weapons in the 1950s increased political, strategic and scientific interest in exploring the potentialities of these refinements. Additionally, US membership of NATO after 1949 and the crucial question of the role of nuclear weapons within the ALLIANCE added a political immediacy to these speculations, particularly after 1954 when NATO became committed to the battlefield use of nuclear weapons.

Using nuclear weapons in a limited war situation will always have attractions for STATES that perceive themselves facing an adversary that can overwhelm them conventionally. It is after all a particular instance of the general proposition about substituting TECHNOLOGY for manpower. In order to reduce collateral or accidental damage the weapons should be of a low yield – at the lower end of the KILOTON range. Additionally, such use makes more sense if the adversary does not possess such weapons and, moreover, does not have access to other states which might make them available. The use of nuclear weapons against the Japanese at HIROSHIMA and NAGASAKI is a rough analogy to this situation.

Provided always that the appropriate weapons are available and that targets can be identified, using nuclear weapons in a limited war context against a non-nuclear state might be considered plausible. The problem, at least from the perspective of limited war, is that using such CAPABILITIES demolishes a clear and unambiguous limit without replacing it with another of equal clarity. Notwithstanding the Japanese example, such uses are largely uncharted waters. Such moves are clearly escalatory and possibly highly provocative.

Limited nuclear war between nuclear armed adversaries is a more recent development. It is causally related to the situation of perceived PARITY between the SUPERPOWERS and to doctrines of deterrence and the belief that if deterrence looks like breaking down the outcome could be controlled within 'limits'. Clearly, if a nuclear exchange is to be controlled, the parties themselves must demonstrate self-control or restraint. This is the working definition of limited war. Thus, such views as these are part of the limited war tradition, although they have been adapted to the special circumstances of mutual deterrence. Limited nuclear war, or limited nuclear options, have attracted increasing interest among US strategists since the Nixon Administration and the pronouncements of Defense Secretary Schlesinger. They reflect growing rejection of mutual assured destruction (MAD) as a declaratory policy, as well as a policy outcome, and the belief that the *EX POST EX ANTE* problem requires implementable options.

## Limited war

A term used in strategic analysis. Limited WAR is the deliberate exercise of restraint by parties engaged in military operations. As Brodie (1965) has emphasized, the qualification of intentionality is crucial. If a party lacks the CAPABILITY to fight a TOTAL WAR then this is not an example of limited war within the definition. Empirically establishing that restraint is deliberate is not easy. One method might be the case study approach used by Paige (1968) in the

KOREAN WAR decision. Clearly evidence that DECISION-MAKERS eschewed certain options in order to observe limits would constitute a reliable test. Colloquially, limited war is akin to someone fighting with one hand tied behind their back – they have a capability which remains potential rather than actual.

Restraint leading to deliberate war limitation may be observed in a number of dimensions. First, restraint may operate with regard to means. Certain weapons available to a party are not used or are used in moderation. Schelling (1960), probably the foremost contemporary thinker on limited war, has argued that 'break points' or 'fire breaks' should be qualitatively distinct and salient. Thus 'no nuclear weapons' or 'no gas' are objectively distinct. Limits within classes are less easy to operate than limits between classes. This is particularly important if such limits are to be reached by tacit understanding rather than explicit convention. Over time, Schelling argues, it should be possible to establish such limits or 'thresholds'. In bargaining terms, deliberate war limitation is a way of signalling or communicating with the adversary. Schelling can also be credited with establishing the idea that many forms of conflict behaviour are instances of bargaining. Establishing limits of war limitation is an example of this genre.

Bargaining in a limited war does not stop at the establishment of initial limits because, by raising or lowering the limits, the parties are attempting to communicate with each other. In the WORST-CASE situation, if a party perceives that the war is going badly it will want to review the limits and revise them upwards. The United States' conspicuous failure to realize any of its policy goals in VIETNAM after 1961 led to the steady revision of limits, specifically by instituting an AIR WAR and then by introducing ground forces.

If means are one type of limit, DOMAIN and SCOPE are others. By domain here is meant limitations on the number of parties, limits on the commitment of parties and limits on the geographical area of operations. By scope is meant limits on the issues at stake and ultimately limits on the objectives being pursued by the parties in fighting the war in the first place. Schelling argues that UNCONDITIONAL SURRENDER is a limit, 'unconditional annihilation' is not. If this is not trailing the coat, it is certainly stretching what most would intuitively regard as the boundary between limited/unlimited. Schelling is surely right to argue, however, that tacit limits are often more viable than explicit agreements.

Establishing limits to war by tacit bargaining depends in the final analysis upon the PERCEPTION of the parties. If there is sufficient overlap then collaboration and even coordination is possible. If perceptions do not overlap then tacit bargaining may fail to establish the parameters for limitation. In the Vietnam War the limiting process failed to work. This experience is a salutary reminder that much of the highly speculative and imaginative writing about limited war depends upon certain fundamental assumptions about the DEFINITION OF THE SITUATION between the parties.

## Linkage

The term appears in two senses, first in analysis and secondly in DIPLOMACY. Analytically linkage, or linkage theory, argues that hard and fast boundaries cannot be drawn between, for instance, domestic policy and FOREIGN POLICY, between what happens at the national level and what happens at the global level. It has already been noted that foreign policy is a 'boundary' problem and international theory suggests that one reason for this state of affairs is that there is a lack of clarity about where the boundary should be. Through a system that communications theorists would recognize as a FEEDBACK loop, events internally influence events externally and vice versa.

Linkage ideas have influenced that group of writers currently arguing for a WORLD

SOCIETY perspective. They see the idea of the STATE as a clearly defined unit being redundant as a result of, among other things, the erosion of the concept of external SOVEREIGNTY because of the linkage between national systems and other ACTORS. State actors are seen as being 'penetrated' to such an extent that they often cease to be effectively operating units. Linkage ideas were first advanced in a significant way in the 1960s by James Rosenau (1969b). They form part of the milieu of PLURALISM which has increasingly questioned the validity of traditional models of state-biased politics.

Linkage may also be used in the diplomatic sense where as a negotiating tactic one side may seek to 'link' concessions in one field to those in another. For example since the HELSINKI Final Act politicians in some states in the WESTERN ALLIANCE have particularly tried to link ARMS CONTROL and HUMAN RIGHTS in negotiations with the Soviet Union.

### Local war

A geopolitical term for a class of violent CONFLICT that is either internal WAR or regional conflict with very limited participation. Empirically it would be difficult to envisage a local war involving more than three states as parties. Beyond this demarcation the violence would become regional as well as local. This 'regionalization' or 'internationalization' of local war situations occurs via INTERVENTION.

The concept of local war is a classificatory idea. Accordingly, a wide variety of conflict types can be grouped under this heading. Typical examples of local wars would be:

1. Border wars: disputes about BOUND-ARIES and FRONTIERS are likely to arise between states in systems where significant change has occurred or is occurring – such as DECOLONIZATION. The Indo–China border war of 1962 is an example of this type of local violence.

2. Anti-colonial wars: while the process of decolonization was generally achieved within a low theshold of violence, this was not always the case and often violence escalated significantly. This usually occurred in colonial situations where communities were polarized, either between ethnic groups (as in Cyprus 1952–60) or where white settler communities complicated the picture (as in Algeria after 1954). Where polarization continues into the INDEPEN-DENCE period the local conflict becomes an example of type 3.

3. Communal conflicts and civil wars: polarized communities may spill over into violence and civil strife. If third parties are drawn into the violence it may be difficult to prevent the conflict becoming 'regionalized'. Cyprus after 1960 and Palestine after 1947 are examples. The latter became 'regionalized' in the way suggested in 1948 when the ARAB LEAGUE states intervened.

4. Proxy wars: these are local wars initiated by manipulation of one or both of the parties by outside interests. This category is marginal to the local war idea because the outside parties are typically thought of as SUPERPOWERS or significant regional actors. The BAY OF PIGS 1961 is a good example.

### Lomé conventions

The agreements whereby the EUROPEAN COMMUNITY has sought to identify and assist a group of LESS DEVELOPED COUNTRIES (LDCs) known collectively as the ACP (African, Caribbean and Pacific) states. Lomé is the capital of Togo in West Africa, a former French colony. At the time of writing Lomé 3 is terminating. The Lomé conventions are a combined TRADE and AID system which grew out of the earlier YAOUNDÉ CONVENTION.

The Lomé conventions are part of what is called the NORTH–SOUTH system. There is little doubt that the ACP states need Lomé (or something like it) more than the Europeans. The latter do more trade with THIRD WORLD states outside the Lomé conventions than in. Defenders of Lomé would argue that the Europeans have tried from the outset to accommodate the concerns of the ACPs with systems such as stabex which explicitly recognizes that Third World producers have little control over their EXPORT prices unless they can establish OPEC-type cartels. As the ACP group grows bigger they will find it harder to coordinate their own bargaining position so that they can present a united front to the Europeans throughout the detailed negotiating period, which is likely to be 18 to 24 months on past evidence. In any case it must be appreciated that the Europeans have more bargaining leverage, because they have greater economic POWER potential, than the ACP states. The latter contain some of the poorest states in the system.

## Loose bipolarity

A variation of the BIPOLARITY model of WORLD POLITICS. This derivation is generally associated with the writings of Morton Kaplan (1957). Kaplan sought to make this model, like the BALANCE OF POWER, isomorphic with a particular historical example. In the case of loose bipolarity this isomorphism was with the post-1945 system of hierarchical BLOCS, NON-ALIGNED states and intergovernmental organizations (IGOs) such as the UN. Kaplan elaborated a set of rules for the system to follow and compared and contrasted it with both the balance of power and the 'tight' bipolar system. Some years later, Kaplan sought further refinement with the idea of a 'very loose' system (Rosenau, 1969).

In both the original 1957 presentation and in the subsequent modification Kaplan was anxious to make this particular instance of SYSTEMS ANALYSIS relevant to a particular historical epoch. Although this increases the immediacy of the analysis it probably weakens its long-term theoretical viability. Other writers favouring the bipolar approach such as Waltz (1964) have probably achieved more influence with their model building by avoiding this tinkering. Critics have highlighted the inherent problems associated with the idea of 'loose' as a term in systems analysis. Beyond a certain point a system becomes so loose that it takes on the characteristics found in a MULTIPOLAR system.

## Low politics

A term used in the analysis of FOREIGN POLICY. Issues are held to be low politics if they are not seen as involving fundamental or key questions relating to a state's NATIONAL INTERESTS, or those of important and significant groups within the STATE. Low politics issues tend to be dealt with by the bureaucracy employing standard operating procedures. In the last analysis, whether an issue is perceived as low politics depends upon the DEFINITION OF THE SITUATION and how other key ACTORS similarly 'define their situations'. The FALKLANDS prior to 1982 and post-1982 is a good example, from the UK context, of how an issue traditionally defined as 'low' can suddenly escalate to take in the most fundamental values of HIGH POLITICS.

## LRTNW

Long-range theatre NUCLEAR WEAPONS, sometimes rendered as 'forces' instead of 'weapons'. Also often colloquially referred to as 'Euromissiles' because of the history of their deployment. These are weapons systems of between 1,000 and 5,500 km range. The term thus covers what were previously called intermediate range and medium range BALLISTIC MISSILES. LRTNW occupy an indeterminate grey area between the purely strategic and the purely tactical systems. They can be used to strike at an opponent's infrastructure and his economic and social systems or they can be used in support of CONVENTIONAL WARFARE in a tactical mode.

## LRTNW

The concept of the LRTNW developed from the forward-based systems that the United States reintroduced into Europe in 1949. Until the B52 intercontinental bomber became available, the United States required basing facilities in Europe and Asia to threaten the Soviet Union. In December 1957 NATO decided to deploy the first generation of LRTNW missiles in Europe with the Thor and Jupiter systems.

The original Soviet response to these developments was to produce and deploy two systems in the late 1950s and early 1960s, namely the SS-4 and SS-5 missiles. The Soviet decision to modernize their LRTNW by introducing the SS-20 into service caused NATO to respond with the 1979 decision to station ground-launched cruise missiles (GLCMs) and Pershing II ballistic missiles in Western Europe. These deployments led to the INF TREATY following a difficult period in East–West relations which was consequent upon the original deployments.

# M

**Machiavellism**

Term which symbolizes the ruthless pursuit of objectives regardless of conventional moral values. Niccolo Machiavelli (1469–1527), in his best known works *The Prince*, the *Discourses* and the *Art of War*, outlines a theory of RAISON D'ÉTAT whereby the use of any technique is permissible so long as it achieves the desired end. Associated with a cynical, pessimistic view of politics and INTERNATIONAL RELATIONS, it is often and incorrectly identified with the realist view with which it shares family resemblances. The essence of Machiavellism is that every other value is subordinate to the survival of the state:

> Where the very safety of the fatherland is at stake, there should be no question of reflecting whether a thing is just or unjust, humane or cruel, praiseworthy or shameful. Setting aside every other consideration, one must take only that course of action which will secure the country's life and liberty.

The absence of a moral dimension is linked to the concept of 'necessity': the state is necessary, POWER is necessary to its survival, and in order to secure power it may be necessary to act immorally. 'A prince must also learn how not to be good; this is the demand of necessity which rules the whole of human life' (*see*: F. Meinecke, 1957, p. 49).

**Macropolitics**

A term used to identify a LEVEL OF ANALYSIS. The prefix 'macro' connotes the 'whole' and is often used in contradistinction with the prefix 'micro' connoting individual or several parts. This distinction is widely used in the social sciences and is particularly favoured by economists where the macro/micro dichotomy is well known. Given a particular field of study, macroanalysis therefore begins with the field *per se* and works inwards thereafter to examine individual case studies. Macroanalysis has been particularly favoured by SYSTEMS THEORISTS as part of the SOCIAL SCIENTIFIC approach to the field. Morton Kaplan (1957) was one of the first scholars within this burgeoning tradition to apply macroanalysis, while the distinguished political geographers Harold and Margaret Sprout (1971) must be credited with much of the earliest, ground-breaking work on the relationship between man and his milieu.

Macropolitics is, then, that study of politics which centres upon the milieu or the environment rather than the individual ACTOR. As such it is coterminous with WORLD POLITICS. Unlike terms such as world or INTERNATIONAL POLITICS, macropolitics is uncommitted on the central issue of whether the STATE is any longer the most significant actor in the system. Used in this way macropolitics may be taken to be as 'value free' as any expression can be in the analysis of social systems.

**MAD**

An acronym for Mutual Assured Destruction. The term is used in strategic analysis with particular reference to US policies of nuclear DETERRENCE. The term is derived from ASSURED DESTRUCTION, the additional factor being the mutual or RECIPROCAL nature of the threats and outcomes implied. Thus MAD implies a situation of PARITY where both the SUPERPOWERS possess invulnerable SECOND STRIKE delivery systems which enable them credibly to threaten each other with a level of devastation that is rationally assumed to be unacceptable.

MAD is the outcome of the period in the 1960s when assured destruction became feasible. In the case of the United States, which to a considerable extent was the trendsetter in these developments, the era is particularly associated with period of office of US Secretary of Defense Robert McNamara. At this time the developments of intercontinental ballistic missiles (ICBMs) like the Minuteman and submarine-launched ballistic missiles (SLBMs) such as Polaris led firstly to assured destruction and then, as the Soviet Union was encouraged to follow suit, to MAD as declaratory policies. The logic of MAD dictated that both sides should avoid taking active or passive defensive measures that would reduce the other's chances of wreaking offensive havoc upon their respective civilian populations. In the jargon of the strategists, MAD presupposes the 'hostage cities' situation. Each side, knowing that it can destroy the other's major population centres, is thus deterred from crossing the nuclear threshold. Thus the term 'mutual VULNERABILITY' may be regarded as a more accurate, if less dramatic, alternative rendition of MAD.

MAD enshrined the basic assumptions of that version of deterrence theory which holds that by threatening near certain and totally unacceptable costs an adversary will be deterred – deterrence by punishment, as it is called. Moreover, in the absence of any effective defensive capabilities, MAD was achievable with finite forces and within acceptable budgets. Once the parties had achieved MAD, stability in the ARMS RACE was possible if not certain. By accepting what might be called the 'cult of the offensive' MAD seemed to exemplify many of the implications of the advent of NUCLEAR WEAPONS, in particular that the balance between offence and defence predominantly favoured the former.

It is important to understand that MAD was a declaratory policy, not an action policy. It is clear from the documentary evidence now available that the United States never intended to implement MAD as part of its WAR planning if the nuclear threshold was ever crossed. Analysis of the single integrated operational plan (SIOP), first promulgated in the United States in 1960 and revised at regular intervals ever since, shows that US war plans were to attack nuclear and CONVENTIONAL military targets in the first instance. If this is the case then MAD may legitimately describe a state of affairs which could arise after a nuclear exchange. The hostage cities outcome would be reached, not by implementation of MAD, but by controlled COUNTERFORCE strikes which would, perforce, exclude cities. MAD was thus a doctrinal inclination, or a state of affairs, rather than an action programme.

As a doctrine MAD is essentially BIPOLAR in its logic. Unfortunately the real world situation facing US POLICY-MAKERS is more complicated. In particular, because the United States has important ALLIANCE commitments, issues of EXTENDED DETERRENCE are raised which MAD is ill-equipped to tackle. Mutual VULNERABILITY, which is built into MAD, implies that the United States can never convincingly threaten to sacrifice its own cities to save those of its allies – particularly in Western Europe – and thus MAD is not enough. Of course doctrines of FLEXIBLE RESPONSE and LIMITED NUCLEAR WAR have been promulgated in order to meet this deficiency.

MAD may look tenable as a doctrinal inclination but should deterrence ever fail, or appear to be failing, MAD raises acute problems regarding its implications. This is known in deterrence theory as the EX POST EX ANTE problem. Since MAD offers the alternative of national suicide to that of national SURRENDER, its logic breaks down when it is most needed – at the point of war. Again the tendency in the United

States has been to look for more 'implementable options' and this has moved mainstream US strategic thinking away from MAD towards more limited and contingent threat systems since the 1960s. These moves have been enhanced by the knowledge that MAD was never accepted by the Soviet Union as a plausible or appropriate doctrine. The Soviet tradition, being much more self-regarding, instinctively reacted against the mutual hostage relationship assumed in MAD.

## Maginot Line

The Maginot Line was a system of FRONTIER fortifications built by France after 1929 to defend their borders with Germany. The principal fortifications covered the area from Luxembourg to the Vosges. South of the Vosges, secondary fortifications stretched down the Rhine valley towards the Swiss frontier. Although the Line bears the name of the French Minister of War at the time, the idea of fortfications along the north-eastern borders had been favourably discussed for some years previously. The Line was completed in 1934. In construction it represented an elaborate system of gun emplacements, underground bunkers, storage and living facilities and transportation networks.

The strategic thinking behind the Maginot Line was derived from the French experiences during the First World War. It was argued that heavy and concentrated fire power plus determined resistance would always check and then defeat an enemy offensive. In DETERRENCE terms, the Maginot Line, and indeed the Maginot mentality, was a nearly pure example of deterrence by denial. By making an enemy attack too expensive to contemplate in terms of manpower and material losses, the enemy would be deterred from launching it in the first place.

In the event, the Line proved to be an expensive irrelevance in 1940. Using BLITZKRIEG tactics, and fighting a WAR of great movement and bold offensive, the German invading armies swung north of the line through Belgium. The Line remains testimony to the fallacy of refighting the last war and ignoring strategic and TECHNOLOGICAL changes in the interim. The term 'Maginot Line mentality' is sometimes used – usually in a pejorative way – to describe over-reliance upon defensive techniques and approaches.

## Mandate system

*See*: ADMINISTERED TERRITORY AND TRUSTEESHIP

## Manhattan project

The code name adopted after August 1942 for the project to build an ATOM BOMB. Scientific research thereafter came under the aegis of the political and military control of the US Government. The normal rules of academic research were abandoned and the strictest secrecy prevailed. The fact that the team was headed by a professional soldier, General Leslie Richard Groves, is indicative of the primacy of military/security issues over the usual canons of scientific scholarship.

Notwithstanding the reference to New York in the code name, research on the bomb project was conducted at three centres: Oak Ridge, Hanford and Los Alamos. Oak Ridge was an enrichment plant, Hanford a PLUTONIUM reactor and Los Alamos in New Mexico was chosen by Groves and Robert Oppenheimer as the location for the testing and production of the actual bomb. This test took place in July 1945 at Alamogordo, New Mexico.

## Maoism

A system of ideas and assumptions about politics, economics and society in general associated with the life and thought of the Chinese NATIONALIST and COMMUNIST leader Mao Tse-tung (1893–1976). Mao was the popular, indeed charismatic, leader of the Chinese REVOLUTION which eventually overthrew the Kuomintang in 1949, thereby establishing the People's Republic of China. It should be understood at the outset that Maoism is not specifically a corpus of ideas about INTERNATIONAL and/or WORLD POLITICS; rather like MARXISM/ LENINISM, it is a system of ideas which has implications for the field.

Maoism has made two distinct contributions to world politics. First, in the period up to 1949 Mao developed and applied a theory of revolution which emphasized the fusion of GUERRILLA WARFARE as an instrument with the mobilization of the peasants as the mainspring of the revolutionary movement. It was this fusion which was unique about Maoism. Previously guerrilla warfare had not been specifically seen as the means whereby an INSURGENCY could overcome an incumbent REGIME, nor had the rural peoples been seen as the appropriate basis of support for such changes. It was Mao's genius that made the connection. Mao's theories of guerrilla warfare are often referred to as PEOPLE'S WAR and the distinctive historical experience of the Chinese under his leadership led to the belief in the positive benefits, as well as the dire necessities, of a PROTRACTED WAR.

The second contribution of Maoism was to develop a world view and FOREIGN POLICY ORIENTATION that was distinctly different but which still had roots in the Chinese tradition. These ideas were developed in the period of power after 1949 when the People's Republic of China (PRC) had to respond to the putative LEADERSHIP of the Soviet Union and the considerable hostility and suspicion of the United States. At the same time the process of DECOLONIZATION in Asia presented the new Chinese leadership with the opportunity to implement theories about the 'intermediate zones' and the 'three worlds' in the decade of the 1950s. Maoism, among other factors, was instrumental in creating a new self-consciousness among THIRD WORLD ELITES while at the same time establishing a

definite role for the PRC within the Third World movement.

Maoism also developed a TRIPOLAR configuration between the PRC, the Soviet Union and the United States after 1949. Indeed, Chinese orientations towards these two SUPERPOWERS underwent a full 180-degree about-turn between the establishment of the PRC and the death of Mao in 1976. An initial period of amity with the Soviet Union, when Mao himself personally negotiated the Sino–Soviet Treaty of 1950, and hostility towards the United States, when China intervened in the KOREAN WAR in the same year, had by 1976 changed into hostility towards the former ally and DETENTE with the former enemy. The split with the Soviet Union under Mao and the RAPPROCHEMENT with the United States during the Nixon presidency were significant aspects of this orientation towards a more TRIPOLAR relationship.

## Maritime Law
*See*: LAW OF THE SEA

## Marshall Plan
The Marshall Plan, or European Recovery Programme, takes its popular name from the US Secretary of State, George C. Marshall, whose address at Harvard in June 1947 contained the original idea. Marshall proposed that the United States establish a programme of economic assistance to help European governments and peoples rebuild their economies that had been shattered as a result of the Second World War. By the summer of 1947 it was clear that the early, post-war optimism about European recovery was not justified. BILATERAL US AID to states such as the United Kingdom had been rapidly dissipated and existing international institutions, such as the International Bank for Reconstruction and Development (IBRD) were not appropriate for the task. Marshall specifically proposed a MULTILATERAL regional

initiative rather than a variation of the previous BILATERAL programmes. To this end the US Government stipulated that the European states should immediately consult together to assess their needs and provide the donor American government with specific statistically based requests.

The consultation that took place among European states during the summer of 1947 was important for two outcomes. Economically, it provided an early example of cooperation in an ISSUE AREA which was to become increasingly important to Europeans, particularly in the West, in the decades ahead. The Organization for European Economic Cooperation (OEEC) was formed for this purpose in 1948. Politically, it showed that there was a clear division of opinion between the free market approach led by the United Kingdom and France and the centrally planned approach led by the Soviet Union. As a result effective Soviet consultation and cooperation in these matters ceased after July 1947.

The Soviet perception of the Plan was that it constituted an infringement upon their economic SOVEREIGNTY. There is no doubt that the Marshall scheme would have meant that outside parties would have been able to pass an opinion on the Soviet economy and on the manner in which it was run. A tradition had been established under Stalin of planning for self-sufficiency, with a particular emphasis upon manufacturing industry and a managed market. The whole tradition established under US HEGEMONY was the very antithesis of this. Whatever the intentions of its framer, the Plan undoubtedly became caught up in the COLD WAR. By the time that the Plan had been approved by Congress in the spring of 1948 attitudes had hardened on both sides and the programme had become politicized into part of the repertoire of instruments available to the United States and its friends. By exerting counter-pressure upon Eastern European states to reject the Plan, the Soviet Union confirmed its own hegemonial intentions in the East and helped to confirm the division of Europe and the consequent demolition of European INTERDEPENDENCE which had been a feature of the region before 1938. The Soviet Union responded to the specific challenge of the Marshall Plan by the Molotov Plan which led to the formation of COMECON in January 1949. The formation of these rival economic institutions, outside the competence of the UN Economic Commission for Europe – which was the only pan-European institution – signifies the importance that the COLD WAR was to have in the politics of international economic relations after 1945.

It is beyond dispute that Marshall assistance was directed towards a very real and pressing economic need. The Second World War had turned Europe from a creditor into a debtor within ten years. WAR damage was considerable and the transition from a war economy to a peace economy was daunting in its implications. Additionally, Germany, the engine room of the European economy before 1938, was divided and if the Soviet Union had its way would be subjected to an onerous REPARATIONS programme. At the same time Europe had been the continent which had pioneered economic development in the previous centuries and thus the infrastructure for recovery was present. Although generous, nearly three-quarters of all Marshall aid was spent on purchasing goods from the United States, so that the US economy was indirectly subsidized as a result. The long-term recovery of the economies of western Europe were such that with the formation of the EC, the region became a serious trade rival and competitor to the United States. Notwithstanding these somewhat mixed results for US interests, the Plan must be regarded as one of the major successs of post-war economic assistance policies.

## MARV

An acronym for the Manoeuvring Re-entry Vehicle, the latest refinement upon the multiple independently targeted re-entry vehicle (MIRV). In the MARVd system the warheads can actually adjust their trajectories because they carry their own guidance systems and propulsion means. Improvements in missile ACCURACY through 'mirving' and now 'marving' enhance the CAPABILITY of the side possessing such refinements to contemplate COUNTERFORCE, damage limiting options. While technically impressive, such advances may add little to overall stability and, if the case of the MIRV is any indication, they can exacerbate VERTICAL PROLIFERATION and the ARMS RACE.

## Marxism/Leninism

A number of commentators have remarked on the difficulty of establishing a Marxist/Leninist theory of INTERNATIONAL RELATIONS. Martin Wight (1966), for example, asserted that 'neither Marx, Lenin nor Stalin made any systematic contribution to international theory; Lenin's *Imperialism* comes nearest to such a thing, and this has little to say about international politics.' While this may be so, it is possible to provide an outline of the main thrust of the COMMUNIST approach, especially in relation to IMPERIALISM, WAR, social conflict and REVOLUTION. The essential elements of Marxism are as follows:

1. All history is the history of class struggle between a ruling group and an opposing group.
2. Capitalism gives rise to antagonistic classes, the bourgeoisie and proletariat, with the bourgeoisie in control.
3. Capitalism uses war to further its own ends.
4. Socialism, which destroys classes, must also destroy war.
5. Once the STATE has withered away, so too must international relations.

On this view all political phenomena are projections of underlying economic forces. So whereas LIBERAL and REALIST theories are *horizontal* (relations between states) the Marxist/Leninist view is *vertical* (relations between classes). In this sense, many argue that Marxism/Leninism is a theory of domestic politics rather than INTERNATIONAL POLITICS. Certainly, the approach denies the separateness of international relations and views it as an extended manifestation of the quest for economic gain or advantage. Given that 'capitalism' and 'the state' are both seen as the villains of international affairs, it is not clear from the Marxian analysis if one or both must be abolished to bring about permanent peace. K. N. Waltz (1959) points to this as a major ambiguity and argues that socialist theory in the twentieth century has had to adapt or revise the original all-encompassing propositions. Lenin (1870–1924) is a major figure in this process, so much so that the official orthodoxy is now termed Marxism/Leninism rather than simply Marxism.

Lenin's *Imperialism: the Highest Stage of Capitalism* (1917) owes much to the pioneering work of J. A. Hobson in 1902. For Lenin, imperialism is an inevitable consequence of capitalism. It is 'decaying' capitalism where competition has been replaced by monopolies, and at this stage states come to live more and more on capital exports; because of lack of opportunity within the capitalist countries themselves, the export of capital to achieve a high rate of investment return is essential. The drive towards political or military control of markets and sources of raw materials results in a general capitalist scramble for colonies. This has the added bonus of providing cheap sources of labour and a guaranteed market for surplus goods. The general result is that advanced capitalist states are driven through imperial policies into CONFLICT with one another over possession of underdeveloped areas. Because markets and sources of raw materials are not unlimited, international conflict between capitalist states is endemic and although there may be temporary agreement between these exploiting states as to the ownership of territories or SPHERES OF INFLUENCE, in the end these states are bound to clash. The First World War is seen as proof of this thesis. The solution to the problems of continuing international conflict and the establishment of PEACE is the elimination, through revolution, of capitalist states themselves. A peaceful WORLD ORDER can only be achieved through attacking the domestic economic systems of states. 'World proletarian revolution' is thus the means to effect this change.

Capitalist states will not 'wither away' overnight, so socialist states are established in the interim, and the conviction is that an international socialist system of states would be free of conflict since socialists agree on basic questions of resource allocation and are not tainted by the MILITARISM which characterized the old order. (Many critics however, have pointed out that this does not seem to have occurred in quite the way the theory suggests, as the Sino–Soviet CONFLICT of the 1950s and 1960s was just as bitter as any between capitalist states.) An associated idea is the notion of capitalist ENCIRCLEMENT which Stalin in particular saw as a likely strategy of the capitalist world, and indeed this took on a new significance with the adoption of policies of CONTAINMENT by the United States in the post-1945 era. Eventually, though, according to Khrushchev, this would give way to socialist encirclement as the forces of capitalism weakened. Another important revision of Marx's original thesis is the idea of PEACEFUL COEXISTENCE which was first used by Lenin and Trotsky in relation to the Treaty of Brest–Litovsk (1917) and which came to signify ACCOMMODATION with capitalist states, but did not altogether abandon the commitment to undermine them through WARS OF NATIONAL LIBERATION.

Lenin's analysis of imperialism is the backbone of the communist theory of international relations, and although modifications have been made in the face of the changing pattern of WORLD POLITICS in the twentieth century it is likely to remain as the theoretical prism through which socialist states view the outside world. Critics of the equation Capitalism = Imperialism = War are legion and most point out that

Lenin built a universal system out of a limited set of historical experiences. While the theory throws light on the period between 1870 and 1914, it lacks explanatory power both before this time and after it. Very little attention is given to the causes of international conflict other than the economic one (e.g. political, psychological, cultural, ideological, religious or personal causes). The assertion that a world of socialist states would be non-imperial and peaceful has been questioned. The element of the 'inevitability of war' with the capitalist world remains but the increasing importance of DETENTE and ARMS CONTROL agreements between the two camps has the effect of watering even this bastion down.

However, while many criticisms may be made of the internal coherence of the arguments and of their external application no one can doubt that Marxism/Leninism has had an enormous influence on the twentieth century world, not least among THIRD WORLD states. The charge that Western capitalism and imperialism deliberately suppressed the economic development of the underdeveloped world is often irresistible as is the model of 'socialist revolution' and the idea that full development can only occur after the introduction of central planning, MODERNIZATION and the politicization of the masses. In addition, in the wider area of the subject matter of international relations itself, there is a sense in which Lichtheim's (1971) observation that 'to some extent we are all Marxists now' is true since the tendency of Marxism/Leninism to shift attention away from the sovereign state towards an emphasis on non-state ACTORS (particularly of the economic variety) is now firmly embedded in the discipline. Marxism/Leninism may not amount to a theory of international relations, but its observations on world politics have succeeded in restructuring the focus of the discipline to the extent that for some scholars historial materialism is now one of its central paradigms. Without doubt the sociological and behavioural aspects of the subject as well as concepts of

INTERDEPENDENCE have a direct debt to pay to this movement. Although economic determinism may offer only a partial explanation of international behaviour, the movement towards a structural/functional analysis and away from the entrenched STATE-CENTRIC position would not have been possible without the groundwork laid by adherents of this view. For a thorough recent analysis *see*: V. Kubakalova and A. Cruickshank (1980).

## Massive retaliation

Part of the 'New Look' DEFENCE policy of the first term of the Eisenhower Presidency (1953–7), Massive Retaliation was the first serious attempt to elaborate a strategic doctrine for the nuclear age. The most famous enunciation of Massive Retaliation was contained in John Foster Dulles's remarks to the Council on Foreign Relations in January 1954 (Bobbitt *et al.*, 1989). The Secretary of State announced that henceforth the United States would rely upon the 'great capacity to retaliate, instantly by means and at places of our choosing . . .'. A few months later Dulles toned down the rhetoric in an article which appeared in the journal *Foreign Affairs*. In a text that was largely drafted by the State Department's Policy Planning Staff, Dulles warned against the PERCEPTION of Massive Retaliation as a policy for all seasons. By the time the Foreign Affairs article appeared the damage caused by the earlier speech had been done. The IMAGE that Dulles had conjured in the January address of the United States 'unleashing' its Strategic Air Command (SAC) against the Soviet Union or China was now indelibly imprinted in the minds of informed PUBLIC OPINION in the United States and its allies.

Massive retaliation was designed to meet the needs for a DETERRENT posture that would capitalize upon the technical advantages the United States then possessed over the Soviet Union, in particular in its offensive bomber capabilities. At the same time it was intended that the policy would oper-ate within budgetary constraints which would allow the United States to put most of its strategic eggs in the basket of SAC while running down expenditure on the army and the navy as a corollary.

Massive Retaliation was part of an 'all-purpose' nuclear strategy adopted by the United States during the 1950s. Rapid technical progress had been made in the development of smaller 'tactical' or 'theatre' atomic weapons as well as the massively destructive HYDROGEN BOMB. Eisenhower was personally willing to regard this developing arsenal as available for use in time of WAR as well as available for deterrence in times of PEACE. The idea that NUCLEAR WEAPONS were somehow qualitatively different from CONVENTIONAL and that, accordingly, a significant 'firebreak' could be identified at this junction was not at this time a particularly influential point of view. Deliberate moves to raise this threshold were made in the 1960s when the Democrats were returned to office at the end of Eisenhower's second term.

In the event the Republican Administration failed to live up to the more dire predictions of nuclear BRINKMANSHIP that the earliest statements on Massive Retaliation might have suggested. In a particularly pithy critique of the doctrine, Kaufmann (1989) argued that 'the minimum requirements of credibility have not been fulfilled . . .'. The studied ambiguity of the intention to choose one's places to retaliate was turned against the doctrine by its critics. Moreover, by implying that the Soviet Union and/or China were behind every perceived challenge to the interests of the United States, the commitment was made to a rather naïve BIPOLARITY which saw 'COMMUNIST conspiracies' in every violent CONFLICT situation. It was this kind of perception which produced the DOMINO THEORY in the context of VIETNAM during the same period.

Although the administration never formally renounced the doctrine, by the second term it had become more symbol than substance. In any event the new TECHNOLOGIES of BALLISTIC MISSILES, dramatically demonstrated by the launching of the Soviet 'Sputnik' satellite, suggested that the future lay with these systems rather than the manned bombers which had been the backbone of the US delivery system when Massive Retaliation was first announced. Additionally such expert reports as those published by the Killian and Gaither committees seemed to suggest that VULNERABILITY was to become a benchmark for the future assessment of delivery systems and in this context again the manned systems of the United States did not show up too well. Also, after 1956 US INTELLIGENCE information on the CAPABILITIES actually possessed by the Soviet Union – as opposed to those claimed – showed that while the Soviet Union was not following the United States down the path of building a large offensive air force, their air defences – both active and passive – were considerably enhanced during the period. This again increased US concerns about the reliability of their SAC forces. Indeed as the decade closed the terms 'graduated' or 'measured' rather than 'massive' might be better prefixes for the nature of US retaliatory capabilities and intentions.

## MBFR

An acronym for Mutual and Balanced Force Reductions. These conventional ARMS CONTROL negotiations were formally opened in October 1973 following exploratory and preparatory talks which began in January of that year. They were terminated, without reaching the formality of a TREATY, in February 1989. Many of the issues under discussion during the MBFR years have now been subsumed under the Conventional Armed Forces in Europe (CFE) negotiations which, at the time of writing, are still continuing.

MBFR negotiations were inspired by a NATO invitation to the WARSAW PACT to discuss CONVENTIONAL reductions made in the summer of 1968. MBFR bears a strong family resemblance to the various proposals for DISENGAGEMENT in Central Europe, associated with such ideas as the RAPACKI PLAN. Following upon the NATO commitment to FLEXIBLE RESPONSE the previous year, the idea of reducing conventional forces to an approximate PARITY made good sense for NATO strategists. Without such moves to reduce the Warsaw Pact's superiority in conventional manpower and equipment, the NATO commitment to flexibility and its implied freedom to escalate meant that rather than risk losing a conventional WAR, NATO would initiate the first use of nuclear weapons. Obtaining Warsaw Pact agreement to conventional reductions was thus an indirect route towards reducing the risks of NUCLEAR WAR in Europe. Additionally, conventional force reductions would be welcomed *per se* for the direct and opportunity cost savings they would achieve. At the time of their inception the MBFR negotiations meshed in with the developing DÉTENTE process between the United States and the Soviet Union and the West German intitiative towards OSTPOLITIK.

The full title given to the MBFR talks was the 'Negotiations on the Mutual Reduction of Forces and Armaments and Associated Measures in Central Europe'. The so-called 'reduction zone' was stipulated as embracing the territory of the two Germanies, Benelux, Czechoslovakia and Poland. The STATES actually deploying forces within this geographical demarcation were the 'direct' participants. Other NATO and Warsaw Pact states were to be 'special' participants. Spain, at that time not in NATO, and France, in the ALLIANCE but not participating in its joint command structures, were the only current members of NATO not participating either in the January preliminaries or the full autumn 1973 discussions on MBFR.

From the outset the talks were plagued with two difficulties. First, there were considerable differences, statistically, between the figures for ground and air forces personnel being used by NATO and the figures being used by the Warsaw Pact. Not surprisingly, the Western PERCEPTION was of lower NATO numbers and higher Warsaw Pact numbers, while the Eastern view was a MIRROR-IMAGE of the West. Secondly, equally serious differences existed between the two sides over the issue of INSPECTION. While accepting that national means would have to be supplemented by on-site inspection, agreement could not be reached on the number of inspections accorded under the draft treaty on each side.

Because the MBFR process never produced a TREATY for RATIFICATION it is often dismissed as a squandered opportunity. This is perhaps too harsh. A number of 'side-benefits' were unquestionably obtained. For instance, the Nixon Administration was able to use the MBFR process to hold at bay Congressional pressures for UNILATERAL US troop reductions in Europe. The Soviet Union's acceptance of the principle that national technical means were insufficient bases for an inspection REGIME was an important concession. Above all the MBFR process kept the idea of disengagement alive and provided important experimental data on how this goal might be achieved. The target of 700,000 personnel available for 'active duty' discussed under the MBFR process may look conservative and cautious in the future if the best intentions of the CFE negotiators are realized. Indeed, the startling events of late 1989, the demise of COMMUNISM in Eastern Europe, the revival of the idea of German unification as well as the visible weakening of the Warsaw Pact, appear to have created new opportunities for substantial and truly radical FORCE cuts on both sides. Clearly, this issue is now high on the agenda of East–West relations and it is likely that target figures for troop emplacements on both sides will be substantially lower than those indicated above.

### Megaton

A measure of the destructive power of NUCLEAR WEAPONS. The megaton, or MT, is held to equal one million tons of TNT. This measure is usually applied to fusion weapons. As a general tendency the Soviet Union has tended to produce more missiles capable of carrying heavier warheads than the United States.

### Melian dialogue

A much quoted section of THUCYDIDES' *Peloponnesian War* (Book V, Ch. 7) which is used by many commentators to illustrate the indifference of POWER POLITICS to moral argument. Ignoring a desperate plea from the Melians that they wished to remain NEUTRAL in the conflict with Sparta (431–404 BC), the Athenian envoys asserted that 'the standard of justice depends on the equality of power to compel and that in fact the strong do what they have the power to do and the weak accept what they have to accept.' The Athenians then besieged Melos and eventually executed all the men of military age and sold the women and children for slaves. In a chilling rider to the idea that JUSTICE is on the side of the stronger the Athenian diplomat added: 'This is not a law that we made ourselves, nor were we the first to act upon it when it was made. We found it already in existence, and we shall leave it to exist forever among those who come after us.' The idea that the powerful take what they want and the weak grant what they must has been a pervasive one in INTERNATIONAL POLITICS and has constantly intruded into discussions on the EQUALITY of STATES in the INTERNATIONAL SYSTEM.

### Mercantilism

A school of thought connected with political economy. Mercantilism flourished in Western Europe in the centuries between the Renaissance and the Industrial Revolution. Its impact upon the developing system of INTERNATIONAL POLITICS was considerable because its basic contention that foreign economic policy should reflect STATE interests was compatible with the trend towards STATE-CENTRED thinking evident at the time. Mercantilism may be contrasted with ECONOMIC LIBERALISM which, as originally articulated by Adam Smith, was a frontal assault upon the assumptions and implications of the mercantilists. Whereas the liberals emphasized policies and philosophies that favoured cooperation, the mercantilists were wholly self-centred and self-regarding in their approach. In particular mercantilists argued that state policy should seek to increase EXPORTS and decrease IMPORTS relative to a given level of economic activity. Since one state's exports are another state's imports, this doctrine of seeking selfish advantage has come to be called 'beggar-my-neighbour' policy.

Mercantilism is also associated sometimes in the popular mind with so-called 'bullionist' theories. This line of reasoning argued that great significance was attached to the accretion of precious metals as a source of wealth and a store of value. Accordingly the self-centred pursuit of a favourable TRADE balance was important because it enabled the payments balance thereby generated to be converted into bullion. Again the economic drawbacks of frankly hoarding precious metals and not recycling them through the system was easily demonstrated by the subsequent liberal critique.

It should not be thought that mercantilism is completely archaic because of the above remarks. PROTECTIONISM and NEO-MERCANTILISM as practices and policies show that this is not the case. Moreover, the mercantilists' fundamental ideological commitment to the view that foreign economic policy is about the accretion of wealth, CAPABILITY and putative POWER is still valid today. Their belief that economic capabilities provided the 'war potential' for the state was widely accepted within the STRATEGIC STUDIES tradition as a fundamental tenet. Their contention that international economic relations were, at bottom, inseparable from political considerations continues to receive much endorsement today.

## Micro-state

Micro-states, according to UN and COMMONWEALTH definitions, are those STATES with under one million inhabitants. Of the Commonwealth's forty-nine members twenty-seven have been officially identified as micro-states. These are as follows: *Europe*, Cyprus and Malta; *Caribbean*, Guyana, Barbados, Bahamas, Belize, Antigua-Barbuda, St Lucia, Grenada, St Vincent, Dominica, St Kitts-Nevis; *Africa*, Mauritius, Botswana, Gambia, Swaziland, Seychelles; *Asia*, Brunei, Maldives; *Pacific*, Fiji (present status uncertain), Solomon Islands, Western Samoa, Vanatu, Tongo, Kiribat, Tuvalu and Nauru. In all, there are over forty of these very small states dotted around the globe sometimes occupying strategically important locations. The problems of DEFENCE and avoiding outside INTERVENTION are acute, particularly so for island micro-states in the Caribbean, Indian and Pacific oceans. The recent (1983) US invasion of Grenada has spawned great interest and concern that these micro-states are not economically viable and are potential trouble-spots in WORLD POLITICS. What is 'viable' is often a reflection of one's own prejudices but certainly the possession of full voting rights in the UN and its agencies by these states is something that the international community as a whole will soon have to monitor. The United States, in particular, is beginning to question the wisdom of granting equal rights to all states regardless of size or development.

## Middle powers

Middle powers are those STATES which are generally regarded as secondary only to GREAT POWERS. Martin Wight (1978) defines them in this way:

241

. . . a power with such military strength, resources and strategic positions that in peacetime the great powers bid for its support, and in wartime, while it has no hopes of winning a war against a great power, it can hope to inflict costs on a great power out of proportion to what the great Power can hope to gain by attacking it.

France, with its FORCE DE FRAPPE, clearly belongs in this category, as perhaps does the United Kingdom. But because of Wight's emphasis on military CAPABILITY this definition appears to rule out other states, such as Japan and West Germany whose military capability may be limited but whose economic strength, in particular, is vast. The problem of definition is a complex one and C. Holbraad (1984), looking mainly at GNP, population and armed force levels for 1975, lists eighteen states as belonging broadly in this category: France, the United Kingdom, China, Japan, West Germany, Canada, Italy, Brazil, Spain, Poland, India, Australia, Mexico, Iran, Argentina, South Africa, Indonesia and Nigeria. The list is a controversial one and reasons for inclusion or exclusion might not always be clear but these states and perhaps others, such as Israel, Syria, Pakistan, East Germany and South Korea, may be regarded as sharing some minimal common characteristics. They usually have large populations, they are relatively DEVELOPED, they possess credible armed forces and are reasonably wealthy. They are also REGIONAL powers of some stature. Yet any characterization that groups Spain alongside West Germany, or Poland alongside Canada, or Mexico alongside the United Kingdom is imprecise. In recognition of this middle powers are sometimes subdivided into 'upper middle powers' (the first five in Holbraad's list) and 'lower middle powers'. Other commentators prefer a separate categorization for those in the upper bracket and use the terms 'secondary powers' or 'regional great powers' to distinguish them from middle powers. In this way S. Spiegel (1972), identifies secondary powers as 'those states which are able to challenge the

superpowers in particular areas of activity'. Middle powers are then 'those states whose level of power permits them to play only decidedly limited and selected rôles in states and regions other than their own'. The fact that, for example, the United Kingdom could reasonably be slotted into both these categorizations indicates the difficulty of the enterprise. In most assessments of position in the international HIERARCHY five elements of CAPABILITY are usually considered: material or economic power, military power, motivational power, achievement and potential. Since some, if not all, of these indices involve subjective evaluations, agreement on particular classification will always be contentious.

## Militarism

Militarism is the subordination of civil society to military values and the subordination of civilian control of the military for military control of the civilian. Typically the two processes may occur together whenever the military institutions take over the political system. A necessary condition for the emergence of militarism is the establishment of armed forces – particularly ARMIES – of sufficient size and complexity to play a significant and lasting role in the political system. One reason in the past for resisting large permanent military establishments has been the awareness that this can lead to militarism. In what might be called the Anglo–American tradition, political leaders and commentators sought to eschew large armies, in particular, to avoid this kind of occurrence. In other traditions – notably European socialism – the MILITIA was seen as an acceptable alternative to the standing army, which was perceived as reactionary and STATUS QUO orientated.

The growth of STATES and INTERNATIONAL SYSTEMS combined with the TECHNOLOGICAL changes associated with the Industrial Revolution has increased the scope for militarism. States usually establish and maintain standing armies and the military is the one sector in society which, perforce, will be technologically orientated. Additionally, the MODERNIZATION process has further enhanced the relative importance of the military in society. Obsolescence of ideas, equipment and training is the Achilles heel of the armed forces. In all states the military, as an interest group, will fight its corner, campaigning for more equipment, better pay and an expanded complement. In some instances this activity may lead to the growth of a MILITARY–INDUSTRIAL COMPLEX (MIC). In unstable political systems it may lead to the growth of militarism. In short, militarism thrives on political instability. INTERVENTION by the military will often be justified, to both domestic and international audiences, on the grounds that it will promote stability in a system that would otherwise decay.

Militarism in contemporary INTERNATIONAL/WORLD POLITICS is particularly associated with the THIRD WORLD. Within that very broad classificatory grouping, the Latin American region is probably the paradigm example of the phenomenon. Militarism has been virtually endemic in much of Latin America since the Wars of Independence at the start of the nineteenth century. Where military leaders have taken power over the last two centuries it has usually been with the assistance of or in ALLIANCE with the more conservative social forces in the REGION. Alternatively the military has remained more in the background, exercising VETO POWER in the system by the constant threat of intervention.

External developments have also influenced Latin American militarism. In the 1920s and 1930s FASCISM in Italy and Spain provided contagious role models. After 1947 the COLD WAR was a new justification for intervention – to prevent or check the spread of COMMUNISM, a move which, additionally, re-established the militarists alliance with the conservatives. On many occasions – for instance recently in Argentina and Chile – the military have

seemed to regard themselves as above the law, or at least outside it, in their suppression of opposition and infringement of HUMAN RIGHTS. The military may be indicted on the grounds of widespread corruption and excessive personal enrichment, even populist regimes like Perón's (1945–55) in Argentina, were susceptible to this failing.

## Military–industrial complex (MIC)

A term given wide currency by US President Dwight Eisenhower when he issued a warning about the 'unwarranted influence' of the military–industrial complex in his farewell address in 1961. Intellectually the idea can be seen as having two derivations: political sociology and political economy. Political sociology provides the idea of ELITE and in particular C. Wright Mills's (1956) characterization of political economic and military circles in the United States forming 'overlapping cliques'. Mills saw the COLD WAR having an important causal connection with the POWER elite and in this respect he shares with the political economists the view that the 'permanent war economy' established in the United States after 1945 created the infrastructure for the MIC.

The leading figure in the political economy tradition is undoubtedly Melman (1985). He argues that between 1941 and 1945 what he calls an 'ideological consensus' emerged in the United States about the relationship between military expenditure and economic activity. In brief this consensus holds that military expenditure generates employment and prosperity, boosts the economy and reduces unemployment. This creates a permissive climate among the mass public for maintaining high levels of DEFENCE expenditure during peacetime. As a result the 'overlapping cliques' about whom Mills wrote in the *Power Elite* are able to manipulate and dominate the system.

The idea of the MIC firmly locates the

explanation for ARMS RACES within the domestic structure of the states concerned. In this respect it is a distinct break with those ACTION–REACTION theories that have rested upon external, state-to-state behaviour patterns. A particular difficulty with the MIC is deciding whether it is *sui generis* to the United States or whether it can be applied to other social systems. Not surprisingly, attempts have been made to apply it to the Soviet Union and South Africa, although few have been satisfactory. Scholars have also recently analysed Israel in terms of these ideas.

Critiques of the US version of the MIC have come from two directions. First, political sociologists writing within the PLURALIST tradition have suggested that the power structure is not as monolithic as the elitists suggest and that considerable competition for power and INFLUENCE goes on at the top. Political economists, meanwhile, have attacked the permanent WAR economy on the grounds that it is inefficient. There are considerable direct and opportunity costs for society in supporting the MIC. Evidence is adduced from the recent experience of states such as Japan which would appear to show that fast economic growth is not correlated positively with high, but rather with low, levels of defence expenditure. Indeed, according to this view there is very little statistical evidence to substantiate a positive link between growth, employment, inflation or favourable external payments accounts and high levels of military expenditure.

## Militia

Locally raised, part-time forces used to supplement or to replace the regular ARMY in an emergency situation. This might be an external threat to the STATE, such as that posed by an invasion. Alternatively civil strife and even CIVIL WAR can pose an internal threat of such magnitude as to require the INTERVENTION of the militia. Allowing the local population to bear arms in this way requires a considerable act of confidence by any political LEADERSHIP since an armed population may defy the civil authorities rather than support them. At the same time the principle of the nation-in-arms has attracted considerable support and carried considerable appeal over the centuries from NATIONALISTS and COMMUNISTS alike. For some advocates of the militia, the right to bear arms is regarded as almost 'inalienable'.

Strategists have been interested in the role of the militia since MACHIAVELLI and debate has continually raged about the relative merits of professional armies versus locally raised forces. The development of MARXISM/LENINISM added a further IDEOLOGICAL dimension to the issue. Many communists, following the lead provided by Engels, have argued that the militia is the best type of military organization for this type of political system. With the establishment of the Soviet Union the debate had an empirical point of focus. In this case the issue was decided in favour of the regular army and the term 'militia', although still used in the Soviet Union, now refers colloquially to sections of the civilian police forces.

Among other European states, a similar kind of debate took place in the years between 1919 and 1939. Again the principle of the 'nation-in-arms' was central to French thinking. Additionally it was felt that the militia was essentially a defensive system and that, in conjunction with the MAGINOT LINE, its existence would send appropriate signals to the Germans about French intentions. Other European states with a tradition of relying upon militias include Switzerland and Finland, both states with a neutralist ORIENTATION in their FOREIGN POLICY.

## Minimax

A term derived from GAME THEORY. The term is sometimes written as *maximin*. Either rendition means the same. It refers to the assumption that, in the game, the players will seek to maximize their gains or to minimize their losses.

Minimax assumptions are necessary, in this type of analysis, to deal with the issue of what constitutes RATIONALITY. Without making these assumptions it is impossible to stipulate how a player might act in the abstract. Minimax assumptions have been particularly helpful in dealing with ZERO SUM gaming situations. In these the structure of the game allows fairly confident assumptions to be made about rationality.

## Minimum deterrent

A term used in strategic analysis to characterize a NUCLEAR WEAPONS CAPABILITY that could be used in a SECOND STRIKE mode against an adversary that was perceived to be both threatening and superior to oneself. Just how 'minimum' such a DETERRENT has to be to retain CREDIBILITY is thus a moot point. It depends almost totally upon the relativities of the relationship between the two STATES. Moreover, like all relationships it is prone to change over time. In this way the deterrence impact of such a capability is dynamic and may have to be altered to account for changing circumstances.

It is generally agreed that the United Kingdom's nuclear weapons are held to constitute a minimum deterrent *vis-à-vis* the superior capability of the Soviet Union. For a quarter of a century this was achieved through the Polaris A-3 system obtained from the United States. While insufficient to achieve assured destruction levels, it was assumed that this force could actually reach the Soviet homeland in a situation of dire national emergency. The element of uncertainty about how much damage could actually be caused by this small force was held by its proponents to be part of the deterrent effect. In the case of the United Kingdom, minimum deterrence was forced upon the state given the financial constraints against which nuclear policy was made.

The example of France shows that a MIDDLE POWER need not perforce adopt this posture. The *FORCE DE FRAPPE* is much more like a scaled-down version of the US TRIAD. There is some evidence that as a result France is closer to perceiving its capability in a COUNTERFORCE war-fighting mode than the United Kingdom. These asymmetries between the two European nuclear states would have to be resolved if nuclear cooperation between them was to be significantly increased in the future.

## Mirror image

Sometimes rendered as 'mirror percept'. The term is clearly derived from the psychological idea of IMAGE and PERCEPTION as important dynamic qualities affecting the way individuals and groups 'see' their world, particularly their social world. The necessary conditions for the mirror image effect are: first, a situation of social CONFLICT within or between groups and, second, a situation of POLARIZATION about the cause and conduct of the conflict. Given these antecedent conditions, mirror-imaging occurs when antagonistic groups attribute exactly the same 'diabolical' characteristics to their opponents. Thus the two groups may come to the independent judgement that the other is attempting to 'surround' or 'encircle' them. They may be equally convinced that the other is 'cheating' or 'dissembling'. During NEGOTIATIONS they may present data which appear to suggest that while they are negotiating in good faith the adversary is not. In short, mirror-imaging is a form of perceptual distortion or MISPERCEPTION.

The American psychologist Bronfenbrenner (1961) is generally credited with some of the earliest social scientific work on mirror image effects. His publications in the early 1960s seemed to substantiate the phenomena in Soviet–American relations both among mass and informed publics. More recently J. W. Burton's interest in the possibility of 'controlling communication' between adversaries via third party activities has resuscitated the mirror image effect. In the context of CONFLICT RESOLUTION, of course, mirror images stand in the way of self-sustained solutions. Unless and until they can at least be substantially modified, if not totally altered, these perceptions will exacerbate hostilities and antagonisms between parties in conflict.

The development of MIRVs has undoubtedly fuelled the ARMS RACE. It has made the IMPLEMENTATION of effective ARMS CONTROL measures more difficult, not least because it has complicated the VERIFICATION processes. Counting warheads – which is what MIRV technology implies – is intrinsically more difficult than counting missile silos.

## MIRV

Multiple independently targeted re-entry vehicle. As the name implies, the MIRV is a development of the multiple re-entry vehicle (MRV). The main qualitative difference is that MIRVs can be aimed at different targets. MIRVs are carried on a post-boost vehicle or 'bus'. The bus separates from the final rocket stage and proceeds to eject warheads at selected targets. Having completed the mission, the bus burns up as it re-enters the earth's atmosphere. MIRV TECHNOLOGY was evolved as a consequence of the need to launch multiple earth satellites for the space programmes of both the SUPERPOWERS.

The United States began to introduce MIRVs into its intercontinental ballistic missile (ICBM) force in 1970 with Minuteman III. This was followed by the Poseidon submarine-launched ballistic missile (SLBM) the following year. The Soviet Union tested a MIRV in August 1973. The SALT I agreement was concluded at this time without specific RECOGNITION being given to this new TECHNOLOGY, an omission which, it is generally agreed, seriously damaged the efficacy of the TREATY.

The dynamic relationship between technology, strategy and ultimate political goals is well illustrated by the MIRV case. Because MIRVs enable more targets to be covered, this increased the viability of a COUNTERFORCE rather than COUNTERVALUE targeting mode.

MIRVs also increase the viability of a FIRST STRIKE, and can be seen as more effective means of penetrating ABM defences.

## Misperception

A misperception is a misinterpretation or misunderstanding. Its usage assumes that there is a 'correct' or 'more accurate' PERCEPTION from which a deviation has occurred. Since both terms – 'perception' and 'misperception' – are subjectively defined concepts, it may be quite difficult to establish what is 'accurate' or 'correct' in these matters. On many occasions such a conclusion can only be reached after the event when, with hindsight, it can be said that certain ACTORS 'misperceived' the situation. Like the term perception, misperception directs the analyst to individual and small group levels of ANALYSIS. It probably makes little sense to speak of a NATION misperceiving a situation and it certainly makes no sense to speak of a STATE doing so, since the latter would be an unwarranted reification.

There are a number of causal factors which can be identified as increasing the probability that an actor will misperceive the aims and intentions of others when conducting FOREIGN POLICY. Situationally, information that reaches DECISION-MAKERS is often ambiguous and susceptible to a number of interpretations. In extreme circumstances other actors may deliberately seek to enhance this ambiguity and uncertainty by deliberate deception. Secondly, political leaders are often under time pressure to make up their minds and given this pressure, and the inherent ambiguity already referred to, POLICY-MAKERS may 'rush to judgement'. This can lead the policy-makers to foreclose prematurely on fresh information, particularly if it appears to be contradictory, and to make decisions without sufficient reference to it. A potentially unsatisfactory occurrence will then be made worse as psychological defence mechanisms come into play and fresh information is distorted to fit into the existing picture. If this becomes the 'official view' it may be hard for diplomats and advisers to break through an increasingly inappropriate DEFINITION OF THE SITUATION with dissonant arguments and ideas. A spiral of misperception is then built into the decision-making process. Sometimes it is only possible to break out of this situation by some traumatic event, such as a change of LEADERSHIP. In retrospect it becomes clear that serious misperception has occurred and this becomes part of the 'why?' factor in subsequent explanations.

Misperception is also causally related to IMAGES. Actors' images, both of themselves and of others, will enhance the chances of misperceptions affecting policy-making. In particular, images may encourage actors towards certain tendencies which produce misperceptions. Actors sometimes overestimate their own ability to influence outcomes and they wrongly attribute a change of policy by another actor to their own efforts. Actors sometimes show a tendency to see discrete happenings as part of an overall plan, to apply a crude 'conspiracy theory' where none may be justified. In strategic relations there is the tendency to assume another actor's intention upon the basis of his capabilities – known as WORST CASE ANALYSIS.

Misperception, like perception, is affected by emotional factors as well as cognitive factors. Stress and strain may build up within a decision-making group, particularly in a CRISIS situation, and this can increase the extent to which decisions are made in an atmosphere that is emotionally charged. In particular the tendency towards 'wishful thinking' has been noted by a number of psychologists as being positively related to an increase in affective as opposed to cognitive factors.

Recent research by historians and social scientists has sought to direct attention towards the relationship between misperception and the occurrence of WAR. Taking the distinction between capability and intention as central to the analysis, researchers have examined how misperception of capabilities and/or misperception of intentions are causally related to the decision by actors to go to war. In many of these studies the issue of where misperception begins and perception ends is, unfortunately, not always clarified. This problem was identified at the outset of the discussion and it remains the case that such distinctions can often only be established *ex post*.

## Missile

A rocket or projectile with its own propulsion and guidance systems. Its payload would normally be a warhead but unarmed missiles could be used for reconnaissance purposes. Modern missile TECHNOLOGY was first developed during the Second World War when Germany produced the so-called V1 and V2 weapons. The V1, or 'flying bomb', was a small pilotless aircraft. It would now be called an 'air-breathing' system and was a precursor of the CRUISE MISSILE. The V2 was a BALLISTIC MISSILE with a range slightly in excess of 200 miles, which would make it a short-range system by contemporary standards.

Since 1945 advances in missiles have been made with regard to propulsion systems, guidance mechanisms and warheads. When combined with ATOMIC and HYDROGEN BOMBS, the offensive missile is a potent system indeed. Defensive technologies have not, generally speaking, kept pace with offensive systems since 1945. Thus the advent of modern missiles has had the tendency to tip the balance in favour of the putative attacker.

## Missile Gap, The

The Missile Gap – written in capitals with

the definite article – refers to a particular period of time in the nuclear ARMS RACE. In August of 1957 the Soviet Union announced that it had successfully tested an intercontinental ballistic missile (ICBM) and two months later the Soviets launched the first earth satellite SPUTNIK. These events are generally agreed to have been the immediate causes for the growing US perception that it faced an adverse 'missile gap' *vis-à-vis* the Soviet Union. This pessimism was given semi-official credence when in the same month as Sputnik, the Gaither Committee presented a secret report to President Eisenhower which emphasized the growing PERCEPTION that the United States' means of delivery, in particular its Strategic Air Command (SAC) forces, were becoming increasingly vulnerable to a surprise attack. The Gaither Committee Report – its main arguments were widely 'leaked' to the media during the winter of 1957–8 – undoubtedly gave the go-ahead to those in the United States wishing to engage in WORST-CASE ANALYSIS. During the summer of 1958 some wildly inaccurate figures were published in the US press suggesting that by 1960 the Soviet Union would be substantially ahead of the United States in this CAPABILITY.

The issue of The Missile Gap became a party political one in the months and years that followed and it reached its most strident tones during the Presidential election campaign of 1960. A number of leading Democratic party contenders seized upon the issue to berate the Republican party and its candidate for the Presidency, Richard Nixon. His period in office as Eisenhower's Vice President made him quite susceptible to the general criticism of Republican neglect of US DEFENCES.

The accession of John Kennedy to the White House in January 1961 led to the rapid demise of the worst fears of the United States about their relative capability. It was made quite clear to the new Administration by the INTELLIGENCE community that the United States enjoyed a favourable gap rather than faced an adverse one. Moreover it was clear that the second generation of MISSILES – solid fuel systems such as Polaris and Minuteman – would be available in the US arsenal well ahead of their perceived adversary. It was to be this new, less vulnerable, capability which was to serve the United States so well in the 1962 CUBAN MISSILE CRISIS. What one commentator called the 'Alice-in-Wonderland' belief in an adverse Missile Gap was officially recognized among the ELITE in the autumn of 1961.

The period from the autumn of 1957 to the autumn of 1961 may appropriately be taken as the start and finish points for The Missile Gap. There can be little doubt that President Eisenhower had been provided with information from the Central Intelligence Agency, following the commencement of U-2 spy flights in 1956, that would have confirmed that the Soviet Union was not ahead. What could not have been predicted at the time was the significant lead the United States would subsequently establish. At the same time it should be appreciated that other agencies in the US government had a vested interest in inflating their own intelligence figures and that opposition politicians found that the whole argument provided an irresistible opportunity to attack their opponents in the White House.

## Mixed actor model

A term used by Oran Young (1972) in a seminal contribution to a book of essays appropriately dedicated to Harold and Margaret Sprout. Young's argument was that is was no longer possible or desirable to base the analysis of MACROPOLITICS upon a single ACTOR model – such as the STATE-CENTRIC idea of INTERNATIONAL POLITICS – and accordingly that heterogeneity was the order of the day. In this way Young also challenged the idea that the concept of HIER-ARCHY could usefully be applied to the field of macroanalysis. Again, no doubt in part under the influence of the Sprouts,

Young suggested that questions of domination and submission should be settled on a policy-contingency, ISSUE AREA basis rather than by deductively stipulating that certain actors were intrinsically dominant. Young's mixed actor perspective also enables a basic distinction to be made analytically between relations containing actors of the same type and relations between different types of actors – for instance between states and intergovernmental organizations (IGOs) or between IGOs and INTERNATIONAL NON-GOVERNMENTAL ORGANIZATIONS (INGOs). However, unless these mixed relationships are demonstrably growing in importance much of the force of Young's argument is weakened.

In some respects the mixed actor idea leaves something to be desired. In particular it leaves open the question of how a relative comparison is to be made of different actors if an idea of their ranking or 'weighting' is to be achieved. What Young achieved was to point scholars towards an increasingly significant perspective – usually referred to as PLURALISM – which appeared to influence macropolitical thinking in the 1970s.

## MNC

An abbreviation of Multinational Corporations. The term TRANSNATIONAL Corporations is sometimes used. It is interchangeable with Multinational, although the latter is more popular. The abbreviation 'Multinational' is sometimes used, in singular or plural forms. Finally the MNC sometimes appears as 'Multinational Enterprise'.

Although they are in one sense INTERNATIONAL NON-GOVERNMENTAL ORGANIZATIONS (INGOs) MNCs are usually excluded from the category of INGOs, because they are profit-making. Their growth and contemporary significance in WORLD POLITICS also merits special and separate treatment from the INGO. The SCOPE and DOMAIN of their operations have led some commentators to welcome their activities, while others have warned against their self-regarding pursuit of corporate INFLUENCE. The UN and some of its SPECIALIZED AGENCIES, the governments of STATES, interest groups such as trade unions have all conducted analyses and investigations into MNCs in general or into specific cases. These inquiries are a measure of the seriousness with which informed opinion in world politics takes the Multinationals. A recent collection of academic essays on them was subtitled 'the new sovereigns' (Said and Simmons, 1975). Others have seen the MNC as one of the main corrosive agents attacking the STATE-CENTRED view of the system. The arrival of the MNC on the stage of world politics has clearly provoked much activity.

MNC may be defined as a profit-making organization which controls assets in at least two states. These may be identified as the home state (the state where the company is incorporated) and the host state (the state where the company has branches or affiliates). The activity of establishing or taking over branches/affiliates is referred to as *direct foreign investment* and is a further characteristic of the MNC. This kind of investment pattern may be contrasted with portfolio investment, which was a feature of the nineteenth century investment pattern under British HEGEMONIAL influence.

Gilpin (1975), among hegemonic stability theorists, has sought to establish a link between the hegemonial position of the United States after 1945 and the rapid growth of the MNC thereafter. In the decades immediately after 1945 the link between US domination of the system of political economy and the burgeoning of MNCs was close. This domination has now declined, but MNCs are still predominantly incorporated in one of the states in the advanced industrial countries (AIC) region. This domination is now TRILATERAL, with the EC and Japan emerging as important home bases for their own respective MNCs. Indeed, if the AICs can be regarded as an economic system, then a considerable amount of inward investment is evident within it. Paradoxically, at present the United States is almost as important as a host state for other's investment as it previously was a home state from which others could invest.

MNCs can be identified operating in primary, secondary and tertiary sectors of economic activity. The classic primary sector MNC is the OIL COMPANY. MNCs have also been important in extractive industries, notably in bauxite/aluminium production. Historically, the primary sector was the first to develop to prominence, the impulse to develop on a transnational basis being largely dictated by geography, the natural location of the raw materials determining the move abroad. Extractive industries have often been seen by critics of the MNC as the most exploitative. Their impact upon the local economy of the host state may be minimal and their managerial structure may tend to be ETHNOCENTRIC. MNCs operating in primary sectors of economic activity tend to invest in THIRD WORLD hosts rather than AICs. The history of OPEC shows that these host states need not be passive recipients of this kind of investment system. Provided that the market conditions are favourable, host states can do much to combat the worst excesses of the MNC by requiring more local participation in production, by acquiring a greater share in profits generated from local activity, by negotiating an agreed and guaranteed price for the products and even by nationalizing some or all of the locally based activities of the MNC. (Clearly they can do little about the MNCs activities outside their FRONTIERS.)

Manufacturing, or secondary economic activity, is without question now the most important area of MNC activity. The growth of manufacturing has increased the relative importance of the AICs or the NORTH as recipients for corporate investment. In the Third World this kind of manufacturing investment is very selective indeed in its location, with the newly indus-

trialized countries (NICs) predominating. In many areas of manufacturing investment TECHNOLOGY TRANSFER is a key subsidiary factor in the MNCs operations. The first BRANDT REPORT highlighted the extent to which, via control of patents, the MNCs exercise control over technology.

The location of manufacturing activity is not controlled and constrained in the same way as extractive industries are by geography. In deciding where to locate a foreign subsidiary, an MNC can 'shop around' to some extent. Moreover, if there are strong vested interests in the putative host state that would welcome this investment, the MNC may be offered positive inducements by the national government to come into the state. This naturally increases the bargaining power of the MNC and may mean that 'side benefits' – such as a favourable arrangement with the labour unions – can be obtained as part of the final agreement. In general terms, manufacturing activity tends to be more integrated into the economic and social life of the host state. It should not be thought from the above discussion that the MNCs experience a complete free choice situation. In the case of an integrated market like the EC, for instance, MNCs from Japan and North America may be very anxious themselves to establish subsidiaries in such a buoyant REGION.

With regard to their activities in the Third World, concern has been expressed that the technology exported with manufacturing investment may not be the most suitable. Systems of production that encourage high productivity of labour may be less appropriate for an economic system where there is no shortage of labour and where wage rates are, comparatively, low in any case. The recent attempts by the UN and its agencies to establish a code of conduct for MNCs has been particularly concerned with this 'appropriate technology' dimension.

MNCs are increasingly important in the tertiary or service industry sector, banking, insurance and other financial services being one growth point, leisure and tourism being another. Service industry expansion overseas tends to follow manufacturing as would be natural with a 'service' sector. Investment is concentrated in the AICs and selected Third World states.

The impact of the growth and development of the MNC upon world politics in the most recent decades has been considerable. Opinion is divided about the advantages and disadvantages of this state of affairs. Economic liberals tend to welcome the MNC, as Gilpin argued, as 'partners in development'. DEPENDENCY theorists, with their gaze more firmly set on the Third World and on the extractive sector, see the MNC as part of a HIERARCHY of exploitation. Others are more sanguine seeing nationalization as the ultimate weapon which, if the circumstances are propitious, the state can use to 'fight back' against the more intrusive and self-regarding activities of the MNC. In this way nationalization is less an expression of a commitment to collectivism and more an expression of a commitment to NATIONALISM and the perceived need for greater participation in the economic life of the nation.

## Mobility

A term used in military strategy. Mobile forces are regarded as important for both DEFENCE and offence. Defensively, MOBILITY makes it harder for an adversary to seek out a defender's forces in order to destroy and defeat them. Ships at sea rather than in harbour, aircraft on patrol rather than on the ground, ARMIES on the move rather than encamped are all more elusive. If an ACTOR fears a surprise attack then mobility will reduce the damage that can be caused even if warning time is very short.

Distinction may be made between CONVENTIONAL force mobility and nuclear force mobility. In conventional modes, mobility is partly a function of the kinds of weapons possessed. This in turn depends

upon procurement decisions taken years in advance of the actual contingency. Thus acquiring AIRLIFT mobility means, in the first instance, having sufficient transport aircraft and helicopters ready and available to lift men and materials into or away from a particular area. Even something as elementary as maintaining equipment at a high state of readiness can enhance mobility. In general terms a good defensive strategy should combine fixed and mobile CAPABILITIES. Mobile forces can plug gaps and breakdowns that can occur in fixed positions and prevent the total collapse of the defence that can happen if a fixed position is breached or circumvented. The experience of France and the MAGINOT LINE in 1940 is surely instructive here.

Nuclear mobility is inversely related to VULNERABILITY. That is to say the more mobile the nuclear forces, the less vulnerable they are. The submarine-launched ballistic missile (SLBM) Polaris system was the first delivery system to be specifically recommended and required in order to enhance mobility. Recent US interest in the Midgetman small intercontinental ballistic missile (ICBM) is prompted by its enhanced mobility over the Minuteman and MX systems. The difficulties encountered by the United States in deciding upon a 'basing mode' for the MX have also been partly a function of the perceived need for mobility.

Issues of mobility play an entirely different role in GUERRILLA WARFARE. One of the defining characteristics of this type of combat is the need for the guerrilla forces to practice mobility in order to trade space for time. Guerrilla war, at least in its more prevalent 'countryside' version, seeks by employing a strategy of PROTRACTED WAR to harrass and wear down the adversary. Once guerrilla war ceases to employ mobility it ceases to be guerrilla war and moves instead into the more conventional idiom already discussed. Classical guerrilla war literature accepted that, if the method was to be used to achieve political change, then such a transition to the conventional mode was inevitable.

## Modernization

This term is used in two contexts. First, modernization is used to identify certain processes of social change that historically first occurred in Western Europe and which now appear to be a near universal phenomenon in the WORLD SYSTEM. Second, modernization is used in STRATEGIC STUDIES to identify changes and developments in the procurement of weapons systems. Often these changes have important effects upon ARMS RACES and ARMS CONTROL agreements.

Modernization as a type of social change is not specifically political in its character. Rather the argument is that as societies become more modern these antecedent conditions will produce changes in the structure and function of their polities. In particular modernization will produce demands for increases in political participation which will be met by changes in the character and availability of political institutions. Modernization is indeed a multi-faceted process involving, in addition to politics, changes in economic, cultural, technical, psychological and intellectual aspects of human relations. Examples of such changes often cited include: the weakening of the extended family in favour of the nuclear, increased importance of money as a means of making payments and settling debts (as opposed to payments in kind) an increase in secular as opposed to sacred values, the replacement of cottage industries with large scale mass production, the spread of literacy and the growth of urbanization.

These changes are certainly not uniform, nor are they inevitable. Moreover, the somewhat simplistic view that they represent 'progress' has certainly been rejected by most discerning observers. What does, however, seem to be the case is that, as trends over the last two centuries, these modernizing characteristics appear to be highly significant and near universal. Since modernization is a global process which all social systems experience to some extent it has tended to increase levels of INTERDEPENDENCE and even INTEGRATION across STATE FRONTIERS and between different peoples. Among individuals and groups these changes appear to have the most impact upon ELITES and LEADERSHIP groups. These sections of society seem to embrace a more cosmopolitan attitude towards modernization tendencies and, as a result, their POWER and status is often enhanced because they seem to be in the vanguard of these changes. The more far-sighted of these modernizing elites see modernization as supplementing rather than supplanting traditional society and there is considerable evidence, particularly from the THIRD WORLD, of modernity and tradition coexisting in the same social system. The growth of GREEN POLITICS in some of the advanced industrial countries (AICs) of late shows that modernization is not perceived by all as an irreversible process. In its most strident manifestations, green politics appears to represent a rejection of the view that modernization trends cannot be reversed.

Modernization in the sense used by strategists is much narrower than the usage discussed above. Here the term refers to qualitative improvements in weapons systems or in classes of weapons. Because such changes can have destabilizing effects upon state relations – for instance by provoking or exacerbating an ARMS RACE – attempts have been made to control their impact. Indeed, in the SALT II TREATY specific provision was made for the contracting parties – the United States and the Soviet Union – to modernize their weapon systems provided that this modernization was controlled and that it did not lead to certain quantitative limits being infringed. Currently NATO is much exercised by proposals before the members to modernize certain short-range THEATRE NUCLEAR WEAPONS.

## Monroe doctrine

Originally intended as a warning to European STATES not to intervene in the New World, it has become the conceptual basis of US policy in Central and Latin America.

In 1823 and for a considerable period afterwards it was little more than wishful thinking, as the United States did not possess either the naval POWER or the diplomatic status to enforce what Bismark came to call 'this extraordinary piece of insolence'. Throughout the nineteenth century it was the convergence of US and UK interests in the REGION and, in particular, UK sea power in the Atlantic and Caribbean that permitted a 'free' Latin America and prevented a resurgence of political and military INTERVENTION from the European imperial powers. In fact the early violations of this NON-INTERVENTION doctrine were by the United Kingdom, as when UK troops occupied the FALKLANDS/MALVINAS islands in 1833, despite protests from the Rio de la Plata (Argentina). It was not until the end of the century that the United States acquired the military, diplomatic and economic power to act as the self-appointed guardian of the southern half of its hemisphere. In 1904 the Roosevelt corollary took the doctrine an imperial step further and declared that misgovernment (or 'chronic wrongdoing') within the Latin American republics themselves would invite active armed US intervention. Henceforth, the United States took upon itself the roles of both moral tutor and policeman in the area south of the Rio Grande (see: WILSON DOCTRINE).

Outside the United States, the doctrine has not been a popular one and they have been anxious to disguise its rather obvious HEGEMONIC character (see: DOLLAR DIPLOMACY; GOOD NEIGHBOR). However, within the United States the Monroe doctrine has been revered as an article of faith akin to the notion of 'manifest destiny'. In fact, the two beliefs are coupled in the national psychology; just as the United States was destined for continental westward expansion, so too did it seem predestined to dominate the entire hemisphere. The UNILATERAL projection of US power into Latin America has legal as well as moral overtones. For example, it was used to justify the BLOCKADE of Cuba in 1962 to force the withdrawal of Soviet missiles and although Khrushchev dismissed its validity most Americans continue to believe that it is now part of the general corpus of INTERNATIONAL LAW relating to the region. After the Second World War it became MULTILATERAL in character with the formation of the Organization of American States (OAS) and the Rio Treaty. The reference in the UN CHARTER to 'regional arrangements' being kept apart from UN jurisdiction appears to reinforce the idea that outside intervention in hemispheric matters is not permissible.

When President Monroe first proclaimed it, the doctrine was ISOLATIONIST in character and appeared to offer a *quid pro quo*; that the Europeans keep out of Latin America and the United States for their part would not interfere in Europe. Since the formation of NATO the United States have been actively involved in Europe, therefore many believe that, apart from US power, there is no legal or moral justification for continued outside exclusion. Because of these changes Dexter Perkins (1955), echoing Bismark, urged that the doctrine should be discarded as its words 'convey a definite impression of hegemony, of supercilious arrogance, of interference'. It is extremely unlikely that this will happen as the United States continues to demonstrate that the Western Hemisphere is firmly within its own SPHERE OF INFLUENCE. The Soviet Union has largely accepted this as part of a tacit trade-off for a free hand in Eastern Europe. Whether Latin Americans themselves will continue to accept the strictures of the 'Collossus of the North' is another matter and it may well be that in the long term the Monroe doctrine becomes the United States' Achilles heel.

## Mood theory

A term used in PUBLIC OPINION analysis. It refers to what has been called 'the mass public' and seeks to establish links between attitudes and inclinations among this group and the DECISION-MAKERS. The term was originally discussed in Almond's (1966) standard work on the subject. The word 'mood' clearly implies a generalized and somewhat imprecise set of predispositions. Clarification is possible through such techniques as opinion polling, of course. Care must be taken not to build too many hopes upon public opinion polling. It might tell us what the prevailing mood is on a particular issue. It cannot explain how those opinions came to be held, nor can it describe what relationship there might be, if any at all, between opinion and policy.

Writers on the subject of public opinion, particularly within the SOCIAL SCIENTIFIC APPROACH, have been considerably exercised by the fact that the majority of the adult population, even in democratic systems, do not appear to hold consistent, coherent or informed opinions about FOREIGN POLICY, INTERNATIONAL or WORLD POLITICS. On particular issues the precise percentage will clearly vary, but Holsti (1983) talks of '70 per cent or more'. Rosenau (1961a) speaks of estimates varying from 75 to 90 per cent. In purely quantitative terms, then, it seems that the mood theory applies to a very sizeable majority of the population.

Examples of public 'moods' on issue areas most often cited include: the apparent 'WAR-weariness' of many people in the United Kingdom after the First World War, the so-called 'MAGINOT mentality' in France during the inter-war period, the 'ISOLATIONIST impulse' in the United States after Woodrow Wilson, the alleged 'Kith and Kin' sympathies with Rhodesian Whites after the Unilateral Declaration of Independence (UDI) in 1965 shown by UK citizens, the 'FALKLANDS Factor' in 1982 and so on. In these examples public mood seems to be a distillation of recent historical experiences, particularly those of perceived national triumph or tragedy, plus a somewhat impressionistic concept of the fundamental ORIENTATIONS and long-range goals of the STATE. The mood sets permissive limits beyond which decision-makers may be reluctant to go, at least in the short term.

Mood theory clearly implies that membership of the mass public does not mean that people are totally passive *vis-à-vis* POLICY-MAKING processes. Mood theory also leads to the tentative rejection of the view, favoured by many IDEALISTS, that mass public opinion on these issues is inherently pacific. Although most of the examples quoted above might seem to suggest a non-belligerent mass public – apart from the Falklands case – this conclusion should not be drawn. Mood theory implies that innovative thinking about foreign policy and the external environment will not come from the mass public. In a sense this is tautological because it is built into the idea of the 'mass' as opposed to the ATTENTIVE PUBLICS. Nonetheless, it is worth reiterating that mood theory is reactive rather than innovative. It seems valid to conclude that the mass public will tend to favour the STATUS QUO and, in consequence, be one step behind the policy-makers when it comes to agreeing changes in a state's policy goals and ORIENTATIONS.

## Moratorium

A temporary suspension of relationships or activities by ACTORS in order to give one or more parties a respite or 'grace period' in which to effect changes. The moratorium may be legally binding or *ad hoc* and persuasive. The device is particularly used in political economy where creditors give debtors more time to repay debts by declaring a moratorium. It is hoped thereby that during the moratorium measures will be taken to reschedule the payments or take other steps to alleviate the debtor's circumstances.

Moratoria may, in principle, be declared in any relationship. Thus STATES NEGOTIATING ARMS CONTROL agreements may stipulate a moratorium on some activity which they consequently hope to include in a more permanent agreement. The PARTIAL TEST BAN TREATY was preceded by a moratorium on testing in 1958. Although the moratorium was subsequently broken, it did demonstrate that the three states concerned – the United States, the Soviet Union and the United Kingdom – were potentially amenable to such an agreement. After a further round of testing, the Treaty was eventually signed.

### Most favoured nation (mfn)

This fundamental principle of international TRADE seeks to establish and advance the principle of EQUALITY of treatment and non-discrimination among trading STATES. The principle may be illustrated by taking a BILATERAL situation thus: under mfn principles the parties will extend to each other the same advantages that they have extended to other third parties in the past, or are extending to others concurrently, or intend to extend in the future. Most favoured nation principles are typically applied to TARIFFS and if these principles are applied consistently, they should lead to mutual and balanced tariff reductions.

It is generally agreed that the mfn principle began to be applied to international trade in the eighteenth century, reaching its peak in the last decades of the nineteenth. The First World War and the events thereafter led to the weakening of its application but with the formation of the General Agreement on Tariffs and Trade (GATT) in 1947 a concerted attempt was made to resuscitate these ideas by writing them into the first article of GATT. At the same time GATT allows important exceptions to the mfn principle. Crucially TRADE BLOCS, FREE TRADE areas and COMMON MARKETS are all exempt. The emergence of the United Nations Conference on Trade and Development (UNCTAD) in the 1960s further weakened the mfn principle because the THIRD WORLD called for a system of positive discrimination in their favour to replace it. This call has been recognized with the establishment of a generalized system of preferences between advanced industrial countries (AICs) and the Third World.

The mfn principle remains a testament to those who believed in a liberal, equal, non-discriminatory international trading system (it is usually rendered mfn, not m.f.n.).

### MRBM

An acronym for medium range ballistic missile. Normally thought of as covering a range from 1,000–2,500 km. This term has been replaced by the more comprehensive Long Range Theatre Nuclear Weapon (LRTNW). The placement of MRBMs in Cuba by the Soviet Union in the autumn of 1962 was held to be part of the proximate causes of the CUBAN MISSILE CRISIS of that year.

### MRV

An acronym for multiple re-entry vehicle. The MRV was the precursor to the multiple independently targeted re-entry vehicle (MIRV). Like the latter, it is a multiple-warhead missile, but unlike it the MIRV is directed at a single target area. The MRV is thus one unit carrying a cluster of warheads (and decoys) which are released at the same time, rather like the pellets from a shotgun. The analogy with some of the more spectacular of firework rockets, which burst open into clusters, is not inappropriate to give an idea of the MRV's function.

The most appropriate example of a MRVd system still in operation is the Polaris A3 missiles of the UK Royal Navy which carry the Chevaline MRVd warhead. The US Navy has long since abandoned this warhead system for the MIRVd Poseidon and Trident missiles. MRVs are believed to have a limited CAPABILITY to penetrate ballistic missile defences (BMDs). Their relative inaccuracy makes them well suited to a SECOND STRIKE COUNTER-CITY or counter-value method of targeting. MRV TECHNOLOGY is more than a quarter of a century old and the persistent VERTICAL PROLIFERATION by the SUPERPOWERS now makes it look rather dated.

## Multilateralism

A policy of acting in concert with others to achieve objectives particularly with regard to DIPLOMACY, DEFENCE and DISARMA-MENT. Since the expansion of the INTER-NATIONAL SYSTEM from twelve sovereign STATES in 1648 to over one hundred and sixty today, multilateralism has replaced UNILATERALISM and BILATERALISM as the dominant pattern of activity in most ISSUE AREAS. The increased INTERDEPENDENCE of states in economic, political and military matters coupled with rapid industrial, scientific and TECHNOLOGICAL developments in the twentieth century has led directly to the growth of permanent multilateral diplomatic institutions such as the LEAGUE OF NATIONS and the UNITED NATIONS. In the area of defence the concept of COLLECTIVE SECURITY in its various guises is an aspect of multilateralism which has replaced the notion of SELF-HELP implicit in the unilateralist approach. With regard to disarmament the multilateralists argue that progress is most likely if arms reduction is undertaken by all states simultaneously and in concert rather than through the one-sided initiatives preferred by unilateralists.

## Multipolarity

A type of system structure with at least three 'poles' or ACTORS being identified as predominant. Since the TRIPOLAR system is a recognized variation of multipolarity the following discussion will concentrate upon those structures with four or more 'poles'. The actors that dominate a multipolar system need not be STATES: BLOCS or coalitions may qualify. The classic historical example of a multipolar system is the BALANCE OF POWER. Here the polar actors were individual states engaging in ally seeking in order to maintain the DETER-RENT balance. If this ally seeking proved to be successful the system could tip into something more akin to a BIPOLAR configuration. This will potentially occur in a multipolar arrangement if a violent CON-FLICT leads to POLARIZATION around one key ISSUE AREA.

Academic opinion is somewhat divided about whether the contemporary system is multipolar and, if it is, whether that is to be welcomed or not. The issues for and against are well represented in James Rose-nau's (1969) collection of readings. Here, David Singer and Karl Deutsch argue persuasively that stability is the crucial variable in assessing such systems and on that count multipolarity comes out ahead of its main BIPOLAR rival as a preferred arrangement.

# N

## Nagasaki

Three days after HIROSHIMA, a second atomic weapon was used against the Japanese industrial city of Nagasaki. Unlike the first device, the fissile material in the Nagasaki bomb was PLUTONIUM. A similar device had already been tested at Alamogordo, New Mexico in July 1945. The Nagasaki bomb could not be justified on 'testing' grounds in quite the same way as Hiroshima, therefore; like the first weapon, the Nagasaki bomb was in the KILOTON range and was air-burst over the target. The United States had originally intended to use the second bomb on Kokura but poor visibility over the area caused them to bomb Nagasaki instead.

The decision to use the second bomb on Japan so soon after the first indicates that having made the decision in principle to begin atomic bombardment of Japan, the United States intended to continue with that policy as long as bombs were available and until Japan surrendered. How far the use of the ATOM BOMB against Japan actually caused its surrender has remained to be debated. Controversy has continued ever since over these two incidents and their implications.

## Nation

Although probably the most pervasive concept of the contemporary world, this is a vague notion which refers to a social collectivity, the members of which share some or all of the following: a sense of common identity, a history, a language, ethnic or racial origins, religion, a common economic life, a geographical location and a political base. However, these criteria and characteristics are often present in different degrees and combinations. None is either necessary or sufficient for definition. Nations can exist without a distinct political identity (e.g. the Welsh nation), they can exist without a defined territorial base (e.g. the Jewish nation during the Diaspora) and they can exist without common linguistic, cultural, religious or ethnic components (e.g. the Indian nation). Usually, though, there is a strong sense of common identity and unity. Yet even this apparently most basic requirement may be lacking (hence the emphasis on 'nation-building' which is widely regarded as a vital ingredient in the MODERNIZATION process and developmental politics relating, in particular, to post-COLONIAL Africa). The difficulty of definition is compounded by common political usage which tends to blur the distinction between the social and legal aspects of the term. Thus, membership of the UNITED NATIONS refers specifically to political entities defined by spatial territorial BOUNDARIES. Those peoples or groupings who fall outside this rubric (e.g. the Kurds) appear therefore not to possess the relevant criteria. In this connection the term NATION-STATE may be more precise though even here some states (e.g. the United Kingdom) may comprise several nations. In the modern world everyone 'belongs' to a particular nation (the word itself derives from the Latin verb *nasci* – to be born), and so ubiquitous is the concept that it is even employed to convey ideas which to some extent run counter to its general meaning (e.g. INTERNATIONAL, SUPRANATIONAL, 'multinational'.

## Nation-state

The nation-state is the dominant political entity of the modern world and as such can be considered to be the primary unit of IN-TERNATIONAL RELATIONS. However, it is a comparatively recent phenomenon. It developed in Europe between the sixteenth and nineteenth centuries after the collapse of the Holy Roman Empire and the emergence of the centralized STATE claiming exclusive and monopolistic AUTHORITY within a defined territorial area. Absolute political power within the community and INDEPENDENCE outside it are characteristic features. With the emergence of a number of such political formations the modern framework of international relations began to take shape, that is, separate political units interacting within a context where no final arbiter or authority is recognized or indeed present. Historically, the fusion of 'nation' and 'state' post-dated the process of political centralization and it was the nineteenth century that witnessed the dovetailing of political organizations with a particular social grouping which constituted the 'nation'. The people comprising the nation became the ultimate source of the state's LEGITIMACY and the national idea itself became the natural repository of, and focus for, political loyalty. Thus, it was during this period that the coincidence of the boundaries of state JURISDICTION and the characteristic elements that made up 'nationhood' took place. In the twentieth century this process became a universal one, though it should be noted that nations can exist without states and that states are not always composed of ethnically homogeneous social, cultural or linguistic groups. The nation-state, which is commonly regarded as the 'ideal' or 'normal' political unit, is in fact a particular form of territorial state – others are CITY-STATES

and empires – and many commentators regard it as a disruptive force in the modern world. In particular, its obsessive emphasis on NATIONALISM, on SOVEREIGNTY and on RAISON D'ÉTAT has tended to mitigate against the development of a cohesive and pacific international community. The twentieth century has witnessed what appears to be a growing trend towards SUPRANATIONAL forms of political organization, especially on a regional basis, yet the nation-state is still a potent force in WORLD POLITICS. However, its detractors have argued that although it may have been the most effective political formation in terms of providing economic well being, physical security and national identity, there is no guarantee that this will continue. After all, the nation-state is an artificial, not a natural, construct and it may well be that despite its near-universality, it may already be something of an anachronism.

*See also*: NATION; NATIONALISM.

## National interest

Used generally in two senses in WORLD POL-ITICS: as an analytical tool identifying the goals or objectives of FOREIGN POLICY and as an all-embracing concept of political discourse used specifically to justify particular policy preferences. In both senses it refers to the basic determinants that guide STATE policy in relation to the external environment. It applies only to sovereign states and relates specifically to foreign policy: the internal variety usually being characterized as 'the public interest'. According to Charles Beard (1934), the first scholar to produce a sustained analysis, the term entered the political lexicon in sixteenth century Europe and began to replace the older notion of RAISON D'ÉTAT in harness with the development of the NATION-STATE and NATIONALISM. It expressed no particular dynastic or state-familial interests but the interests of the society as a whole and as such was linked with the idea of popular SOVEREIGNTY and the LEGITIMACY of the state. Thereafter it came to represent the entire rationale for the exercize of state power in INTERNATIONAL POLITICS.

As an instrument of political analysis it is particularly associated with the school of political REALISM and its most influential advocate was Hans Morgenthau (1951), for whom the concept was of central importance in understanding the process of international politics. Morgenthau's thesis that the acquisition and use of POWER is the primary national interest of a state had a profound effect on a generation of scholars in the 1950s and 1960s and consequently on the development of the discipline as a whole. For Morgenthau, the idea of national interest defined in terms of power as the central motif of state behaviour had an objective and therefore discoverable reality. However, his emphasis on military and economic dimensions to the virtual exclusion of other factors (especially the notion that principles or moral values could play a dominant part in formulating policy) led to a reappraisal of the concept and a rejection of the presumption that it was synonymous with the pursuit of power. Since then the idea of the national interest as the key to foreign policy analysis has largely been superseded; DECISION-MAKING theorists in particular argued that far from having objective reality the interests that guide foreign policy are more likely to be a diverse, PLURALISTIC set of subjective preferences that change periodically both in response to the domestic political process itself and in response to shifts in the international environment. The national interest therefore is more likely to be what the policy-makers say it is at any particular time. Its value in ANALYSIS has been further eroded by the move away from STATE-CENTRISM and the strategic–diplomatic milieu and the emergence of models of COMPLEX INTERDEPENDENCE and WORLD SOCIETY. The term has consequently been largely ignored in recent literature on INTERNATIONAL RELATIONS.

In essence, at the root of the idea of the national interest is the principle of national security and survival. The defence of the homeland and the preservation of territorial integrity is basic to it. It is presumed that all other policy preferences are subordinate to this one. The term 'vital interest' is often used in this connection, the implication being that the issue at stake is so fundamental to the well being of the state that it cannot be compromised and so may result in the use of military force to sustain it. However, vital interests may not relate solely to questions of national survival. The VIETNAM WAR, for example, was regarded, at least by some administrations, as involving a vital interest of the United States yet at no time was the territorial homeland threatened. Other considerations involved in the concept which are equally if not more value-laden are the ideas associated with economic well-being, the promotion of ideological principles and the establishment of a favourable WORLD ORDER or BALANCE. All these, either singly or in combination, could be regarded as vital depending (among other things) on the dominant perceptions of the decision-makers at the time. Attempts have been made to develop models or matrices of the varying levels of intensity an interest may be expected to generate (e.g. is it a 'survival' issue, a 'vital' issue, a 'major' issue or a 'peripheral' issue?) but these have floundered on the bedrock of subjectivism. One ACTOR'S peripheral interest may well be a matter of survival to another. In sum, the concept does highlight important factors in foreign policy analysis and continues to be used in political discourse, but its value as a research tool is extremely limited.

## Nationalism

This term is used in two related senses, first, to identify an IDEOLOGY and secondly, to describe a sentiment. In the first usage, nationalism seeks to identify a behavioural entity – the 'nation' – and thereafter to pursue certain political and cultural goals on behalf of it. Pre-eminent among these will be national SELF-DETERMINATION. This may be empirically defined in a number of ways. IRREDENTISM, INDEPENDENCE, secession, are all goals that may be sought under its rubric. In its second usage, nationalism is a sentiment of loyalty towards the NATION which is shared by people. Elements of cohesion are provided by such factors as language, religion, shared historical experience, physical contiguity and so on. In the last resort such bonds must be integrated into a perceptual framework which subjectively defines a group of people as different from their neighbours and similar to each other. Empirical instances continually show that it is perfectly possible to create such a sense of national identity in the absence of some of the above factors. In short, it is difficult to stipulate convincingly that there is any cohesive factor that is necessary or sufficient for the creation of such sentiments.

The ideological origins of nationalism are to be found in the political history of Western Europe after the collapse of feudalism. It reached its clearest statement of intent during the French REVOLUTION and thereafter the nineteenth century saw it reach its zenith in Europe. The Italian Risorgimento was perhaps the precursor of the twentieth century phenomenon of nationalism as a resistance movement against foreign domination. In general, intellectual opinion in the nineteenth century was inclined towards the view that the nation represented a 'natural' bond amongst humans and that, accordingly, nations should form the basis for STATES. This fusion of the nation and the state into the NATION-STATE idea became such an influential factor that it gave rise to a whole category of relations – INTERNATIONAL POLITICS – and a complete perspective on activities – that of STATE-CENTRISM.

Nationalism as an ideology was exported during the nineteenth and twentieth centuries from Europe to the rest of the world. The fact that European IMPERIALISM hypocritically failed to extend to others what it was willing to claim for itself – the right of national self-determination – meant that the nationalist ideology was turned against European control and used as a weapon of national liberation. In addition to turning against the foreigner, nationalists turned against their own parents and made the issue one between generations as well as between rulers and ruled. This sense of grievance created by Europeans among their subject peoples at the discrepancy between theory and practice produced what historically came to be called the nationalist movement. As a form of protest anti-COLONIAL nationalism began as an ELITE expression of dissatisfaction and spread downwards thereafter to the masses. The immediate demand in all instances was for independence and the turning over of control of the territory to the indigenous elite. In the process of using nationalism to wrest authority away from external control a subtle change in the relationship between the idea of 'nation' and the idea of 'state' occurred. The THIRD WORLD states that were turned over to their own fates with the ending of formal colonial control were not homogeneous nations at all. Most contained at least two ethnic groups – for example the tribal system in Africa – and many contained three or more. As a result the fusion of the nation with the state was not carried over into the non-European context. So prevalent is this characteristic in Third World nationalism that most writers on the subject make a clear distinction between state nationalism and ethnic nationalism. The classic European assumption that nations must have states and that, if possible, states must have one homogeneous nation, has been completely abandoned in the process of diffusing the nationalist ideology from Europe to the rest of the world. This distinction is often referred to in the literature as the difference between nation-states and state-nations.

Nationalism in the second sense – as an attitude or sentiment – varies between individuals and groups within the extant or putative nation. Elites – intellectuals, political leaders and the military especially – are likely to show clear evidence of nationalist attitudes. Among the rest of the population nationalism will vary along a number of dimensions. Recent research by SOCIAL SCIENTISTS into extreme forms of nationalism such as FASCISM seems to show that there is often a positive correlation between certain personality types and extreme nationalist sentiments. Nationalism, like other political ideas, is diffused and spread among a population via the mechanism of socialization. The growth of mass education and the mass media in the twentieth century has created important transmission belts for this process but socialization processes start in the family and it is reasonable to assume that in many instances nationalistic attitudes are transmitted in this primary group setting.

Nationalism is often encouraged and enhanced by contact with foreigners. This contact may take place at the personal level or it may be mediated via the media and other channels. It is clearly possible to manipulate these sentiments to create a climate of PUBLIC OPINION favourable to a political leadership, faction or party. Once mobilized these attitudes are often difficult to control and a particular leader or LEADERSHIP may become permanently invested with a kind of aura as a result. The term 'charismatic' is often used to identify this fusion of a peoples aspirations in one individual. Although over-used it can be applied to a number of twentieth century figures.

Many political analysts see nationalism as a divisive force in WORLD POLITICS. Indeed, IDEALISTS of many sorts have argued that nationalism was a temporary phenomenon and with the imperative of economic INTERDEPENDENCE would be replaced by INTERNATIONALISM and cosmopolitanism. In particular, the Marxists argued that nationalism was primarily a bourgeois IDEOLOGY and that the rise of the nation-state was inseparable from the requirements of early capitalism. As capitalism developed and became more international, nationalism would be replaced by the 'class struggle' which would in turn break down national boundaries. These assumptions were not borne out by political developments and the First World War, in particular, destroyed the idea of class solidarity against the nationalist principle. Thereafter, Marxian analysis of nationalism has associated it with anticolonialism and the struggle against imperial or foreign domination and exploitation. As such the first major revolution that combined nationalism with revolutionary socialism was the Mexican revolution (1910–17) which subsequently was regarded as the model for the anti-colonial movement.

Liberal analysts have warned of the inherent dangers of unrestrained nationalism. Whereas in the first half of the nineteenth century it was associated with democracy and LIBERALISM it later took on an aggressive, militaristic form and came to be identified with imperialism, fascism and totalitarianism. This form of 'integrative nationalism' according to liberal thought is a distortion. There is no necessary connection between nationalism, CONFLICT and WAR. In fact nationalism, properly understood and fostered, is a positive development in world politics leading to the liberation of colonial peoples and subject national minorities.

Although there is no general theory, there is a broad consensus that nationalism both as a form of consciousness and as a political ideology has been the single most important factor shaping the structure and the process of the modern world. The ideas of the nation-state and self-determination, from which it is inseparable, have formed the recognized foundation for the practice of international relations and although there are movements towards supranational forms of cooperation and political organization, few doubt that its effects have yet to be fully worked out.

The process of nation-building and emancipation from the old dynastic, multinational and imperial states has redrawn the world political map, first in Europe and the Americas between 1815 and 1920 and then in Asia and Africa after the Second World War, so that now, with the exception of Antarctica, all the earth's land surface is divided into nation states. Up to 1914 the international system consisted of about fifty sovereign states in all. By the end of the war ten new states emerged. When it was founded in 1920 the LEAGUE OF NATIONS had forty-two members. The UNITED NATIONS in 1945 had fifty-one but membership rose to 135 in 1973 and to 159 in 1988. Estimates vary, but such is the continued force of the ideas of nationalism and national self-determination that by the end of this century it is likely that the international system will comprise some 200 sovereign states. Since there are no optimum requirements concerning size or population (most of the new states will in fact be 'micro-states') it is impossible to assess what the ultimate number of independent political units will be. Clearly, nationalism is not only the most potent force in world politics, it is also, judging by mere numbers, the most successful.

## Nationality

Often described as the connecting link between the individual and INTERNATIONAL LAW, nationality indicates the status of belonging to a particular STATE. By virtue of this, an individual may be entitled to certain benefits and obligations under municipal and international law. There is no universally accepted definition of nationality, and as a general rule each state is free to define who its nationals are, though this discretion can be circumscribed by specific treaties (e.g. TREATIES concerning the elimination of STATELESSNESS). Thus, Article 1 of the 1930 Hague Convention on the Conflict of Nationality Laws stated that:

> it is for each state to determine under its own law who are its nationals. This law shall be recognized by other states in so far as it is consistent with international

conventions, international custom and the principles of law generally recognized with regard to nationality.

The most important of these principles concerning the acquisition of nationality are first, descent from parents who are nationals (*JUS SANGUINIS*) and secondly, the territorial location of birth (*JUS SOLI*). Nationality may also be acquired by marriage, adoption, legitimization, naturalization or as a result of transfer of territory from one state to another. It should be noted that since international law recognizes the primacy of the state in this regard, the practice of acquiring nationality varies considerably. As well as being acquired, nationality can also be lost or denied. Thus denial of nationality to blacks in South Africa can be seen either as deprivation on racial grounds by Pretoria or as the result of the transfer of territory (i.e. as a consequence of the creation of the 'homelands'). As with most concepts in international law, the political element is the dominant one, and the condition of statelessness is not uncommon. Conversely, and by the same token, DUAL or multiple NATIONALITY, usually arising from overlapping applications of the *jus sanguinis* and *jus soli* rules, has long been accepted practice. In addition to individuals, companies, ships and aircraft are regarded as having nationality, usually relating to the state in which they are registered. The practice of flags of convenience has grown to exploit the lack of uniformity in this regard.

## Nationalization

An act of economic policy by a STATE ACTOR whereby foreign owned economic assets are expropriated by the authorities of the state concerned. Nationalization has always been recognized under INTERNATIONAL LAW as an appropriate and proper exercise of SOVEREIGNTY provided always that fair and prompt compensation is offered. Failure to make such restitution makes the act of nationalization tantamount to confiscation.

It should not be thought that governments necessarily resort to nationalization as a result of any commitment to collectivism or socialism. Although this may on occasions be a factor in such policies, it is more often the case that such measures are an expression of NATIONALISM and spring from a desire to curb and control the activities of foreign interests and to seek preferment for one's own nationals. Expropriation, or at least the threat of it, is seen as an effective way of controlling the activities of multinational companies (MNCs), moreover.

*See also*: OIL COMPANIES

## NATO

An acronym for the North Atlantic Treaty Organization. The North Atlantic Treaty was signed in Washington DC in April 1949. The original parties were: Belgium, Canada, Denmark, France, Iceland, Italy, Luxembourg, Netherlands, Norway, Portugal, the United Kingdom, and the United States. Greece and Turkey joined in 1952, the Federal Republic of Germany in 1955 and Spain in 1982. In 1966 the French Government informed the Organization that it was withdrawing its forces from assignment to the Organization and as a corollary requested that all units, BASES and headquarters not controlled by the French be removed from its territory. France has not, of course, repudiated the TREATY.

NATO is sometimes identified as a COLLECTIVE SECURITY organization, although this is a misuse of the original idea behind the concept. It is more accurate to regard NATO as a military ALLIANCE and as such it is typical of an important class of INTERNATIONAL ORGANIZATIONS that have been a characteristic of the STATE SYSTEM. In keeping with the stipulations of the UN CHARTER, NATO is a defensive arrangement and, like the WARSAW PACT of 1955, it is an ideological alliance. That is to say it represents a grouping of like-minded states with similar political and economic systems. Given this ideological connotation, it can be seen that the COLD WAR and the policy of CONTAINMENT of Soviet POWER and INFLUENCE in Europe was, and remains, the essential rationale for the formation of NATO. The proximate cause for NATO was the BERLIN CRISIS of 1948–9 and the PERCEPTION among UK and French leaders in particular that some antidote to the conventional military capability of the Soviet Union was needed if Western Europe was to avoid Soviet coercion or worse in the deteriorating relations after 1945.

Like most alliances, NATO is based upon the idea of DETERRENCE. Article Five of the North Atlantic Treaty states that: 'The parties agree that an armed attack against one or more of them in Europe or North America shall be considered an attack against them all'.

Since an attack upon North America was not considered a significant possibility in 1949, it is clear that the framers of the Treaty intended that the main deterrent effect of their convention would be a US pledge to defend rather than liberate Western Europe in the event of war. The United States assumed that Europeans would be willing to engage in a good deal of SELF-HELP as well but the onus to provide the deterrent capability lay across the Atlantic in 1949.

As a result of this arrangement NATO took on two characteristics which have remained permanent features: first, the most powerful and influential member of the Alliance is not a European state and secondly, that the Alliance would perforce be strong in those military CAPABILITIES in which the United States was strong: AIR POWER and NUCLEAR WEAPONS, which left NATO with a strategy which was based upon nuclear deterrence of conventional attack from the outset. This lack of symmetry was recognized very early in the Alliance's history and strenuous efforts were made, notably by setting CONVENTIONAL force levels at Lisbon in 1952 far in excess of existing

CAPABILITIES, to persuade NATO members to redress the balance within the Alliance between nuclear and conventional in favour of the latter.

It has to be said that, apart from a brief period after the second Berlin crisis, NATO has never looked like matching Warsaw Pact conventional numbers. Indeed, among the European states there was a marked reluctance to do so. NATO military commanders were forced by the circumstances to devise strategies that would allow for this gap between available conventional forces and desirable conventional forces. This was achieved, often very successfully, in two ways: by relying upon the first use of nuclear weapons and by substituting TECHNOLOGY – particularly air power – for ground forces. GEOPOLITICALLY, if WAR was to occur between NATO and the Warsaw Pact, Germany would be the first and most important area of land operations. Having regard to German interests, therefore, NATO became committed to the 'forward defence' principle in order to prevent, if at all possible, the devastation of German territory by a conventional campaign. The twelve German divisions which it was planned to add to NATO's conventional capability following German membership were envisaged as part of the conventional 'shield' for the nuclear 'sword' but not as the means to fight a purely conventional war.

NATO's nuclear addiction, as it has been called, remains the defining characteristic of the alliance. The development of so-called independent nuclear forces by, first, the United Kingdom and then France (two of the most important European members of NATO) only served to enhance this trend towards nuclearization. Under Robert McNamara the United States tried to wean NATO away from this addiction with ideas about FLEXIBLE RESPONSE only to find these notions being reinterpreted to suit nuclearization in 1967. The North Atlantic Council's decision in 1979 to introduce new long range theatre nuclear weapons (LRTNW) into Europe raised the issue of nuclear weapons anew. The response of a number of European publics was critical and the deployment of these theatre weapons was the subject of successful, if protracted, ARMS CONTROL negotiations which produced the INF TREATY. At the time of writing it is difficult to envisage NATO members being willing to agree to any further modernization of its nuclear arsenal. The initiative is currently very much with the arms controllers and to this end NATO may assume a more diplomatic role in future negotiations with the Warsaw Pact.

Institutionally, NATO is a complex of civil and military organizations. The highest political AUTHORITY in the Alliance is the North Atlantic Council. The Council provides a means whereby fundamental issues concerning the Organization can be discussed. All member states are represented on the Council by their ambassadors and, in this way, the Council can remain in virtually permanent session. Meetings of the Council are chaired by the SECRETARY-GENERAL who is, like the UN counterpart, an international civil servant. Although formal voting in the Council is not used, in reality a DE FACTO UNANIMITY principle operates through the need to reach a consensus. The Defence Planning Committee, despite its name, is more than simply a committee of the Council. It would be better to describe it as a collateral committee. The Nuclear Defence Affairs Committee and the Nuclear Planning Group, established in December 1966 under the aegis of the Defence Planning Committee, reflect the nuclearization of the alliance and the need to establish some consultative machinery whereby all the members can have an input into nuclear DECISION-MAKING even though they do not possess nuclear weapons themselves.

The military organization of the Alliance is headed by the Military Committee. The command structure is tripartite: European, Atlantic and Channel. Allied Command Europe is located in Belgium, Allied Command Atlantic at Norfolk, Virginia and Allied Command Channel at North-wood, United Kingdom. France and Iceland are not fully represented on the Military Committee. France has a kind of observer status following it's withdrawal, while Iceland, having no military forces, is represented by a civilian observer.

## Natural law

Refers to the idea of a natural system of law existing independently of customary or positive law. Thus human beings, and by extension states, are subject to a universal set of rules which are derived from nature (or God) and which are discernible through reason. The natural law tradition underlies the formative period of INTERNATIONAL LAW and although its antecedents can be traced to Roman and Greek thought (especially in the idea of *jus gentium*) it is during the period from the fifteenth to the seventeenth century that it exerted most influence. International legal theorists associated with this school are Vitoria (1480–1546), Suarez (1548–1617), Gentili (1552–1608), Grotius (1583–1645), Zouche (1590–1660) and Pufendorf (1632–94). All these writers agreed that the essence of INTERNATIONAL SOCIETY was a respect for mutual social rights and duties which were not man-made but were implicit in the natural order of things. However, despite its apparent universalism, the natural law tradition and the values associated with it were basically Christian (although Grotius, arguing that natural law was the main source of the law of nations, conceded that this law would remain valid even if God did not exist). In this way, differentiations were made between Christians who shared a common conception of the divine origins of law and those such as the Ottomans who did not. The essence of the doctrine was that law was derived from universal principles of JUSTICE and therefore natural law was accorded primacy over conventional or positive law. In the eighteenth and nineteenth centuries the positivist conception that law was man-made and that as a result law and justice were the same thing became the accepted orthodoxy and the natural law school faded away except in the Roman Catholic Church, where it is still held to be the official philosophy of law. In the twentieth century there have been a number of secular attempts to revive it as the basis for international law (*see* especially J. L. Brierly, 1958, and H. Lauterpacht, 1950). The fact that this doctrine does not distinguish between states and individuals and is consequently ambiguous on the question of membership of the international society has made it especially attractive to HUMAN RIGHTS theorists and those who regard the doctrine of SOVEREIGNTY as an obstacle to the achievement of social justice in WORLD POLITICS.

## Natural resources

These are normally thought of as the physical assets of the planet which can be divided into land-based and sea-based categories. The most basic of the former is the land itself. Sea-based assets may be divided between those pertaining to the ocean – such as fish stocks – and those pertaining to the sea-bed. Natural resources are territorially divided between states and are legally owned as public or private goods. The major exception to this state of affairs is the oceans. Under the traditional principle of the freedom of the seas and under the contemporary idea of the common heritage of mankind the seas were made exceptions to this STATE-CENTRISM. Whereas the principle of the freedom of the seas was exclusive, that is to say, that beyond the territorial waters nobody had control, the principle of the common heritage is inclusive; that is to say, beyond the JURISDICTION of the coastal states the natural resources of the oceans belong to all.

On land there is no equivalent to the common heritage principle, although significant moves are currently being made to provide a more global perspective on such issues as the tropical rain forests. De-forestation of the land is a serious problem in much of the THIRD WORLD. It is becoming increasingly clear that a purely self-centred NATIONAL INTEREST approach to these problems is no longer appropriate and that solutions must be sought that reflect legitimate global as well as state-centred concerns.

Natural resources are allocated in an asymmetric way between STATES in the system. In the past, and indeed at the present, this produced and still produces disparities rather than equalities. Theorists interested in such concepts as CAPABILITY and POWER tend to try to build these disparities into their analyses. In this way resource allocation becomes part of the explanation for what many see to be a situation of HIERARCHY and stratification. This tendency is especially marked when more traditional analyses based upon INTERNATIONAL POLITICS are involved.

The endemic disparities in resources between states has often been held to be a precipitant cause of CONFLICT in international politics. Quarrels between actors over land are among the most fundamental and prevalent. These disputes do not only or always involve natural resources. Indeed, land can have an important symbolic significance quite separate from its inherent resources. However, where quarrels over land are pursued for largely economic reasons it is plausible to assume that the parties are disputing access to and control over natural resources.


## Negotiation

Negotiation is the process whereby macro-political actors interact in order to effect a number of goals that can only, or most effectively, be realized by joint agreement. If an actor has the CAPABILITY and the willingness to effect an outcome independently then no negotiation is required. To this extent entering into the negotiating process is a tacit recognition by the parties that their interests are complementary.

Fred Charles Iklé (1964), in his standard work on the subject, suggests that it is possible to establish five analytical categories when looking for reasons why actors negotiate to effect outcomes. First, in order to extend an agreement that is already in force between them where the original understanding had a time limit. In this way the SALT II agreement was an extension of SALT I. Secondly, to normalize relationships as when two ACTORS re-establish diplomatic relations. Thirdly, a redistribution agreement involves situations where parties agree to change a particular STATUS QUO. Redistribution agreements are common after the ending of a WAR situation. The parties to the CONFLICT may make such arrangements. Fourthly, innovation agreements may be reached to establish new actors. The San Francisco Conference approved the establishment of the UN. The Balfour Declaration viewed with favour the establishment of a home for the Jews in PALESTINE in 1917. Finally, negotiations may be entered into for what Iklé calls 'side-benefits'. Parties may negotiate simply in order to establish a clearer PERCEPTION of each other's goals, and to make PROPAGANDA for themselves and their position.

These categories are made for purposes of analysis and empirically they may be combined. Thus a cease-fire agreement can be said to normalize a situation. However, to the extent that during such ARMISTICE negotiations the acceptance of a cease-fire line involves a change of territory, then redistribution has taken place. Equally it is possible for parties renewing an agreement to introduce new clauses thus innovating. It is also possible to redistribute values when renegotiating agreements. This is particularly likely when actors are involved in TARIFF bargaining, the essence being to renew an agreed tariff position but to redistribute at the same time. The process of negotiating for side benefits may be implicit in any of the other four processes.

Formal negotiating begins with the statement of positions by the parties.

Sometimes these formalities are preceded by negotiations about who are to be included as parties and even about the physical arrangements for the meetings. Once all sides are in possession of the other's demands then three basic choices are available: to accept agreement on the available terms, that is to say upon the terms other parties put forward; to attempt to improve the available terms by bargaining; to break off negotiations because neither of the previous choices are acceptable.

The essential tactic in negotiation is for a party to convince all others that its current offer is the best available and that there is no point in bargaining around the terms in order to improve them. The actual behaviour whereby terms are modified and outcomes evolved is the essence of the bargaining process. There are a variety of stratagems that parties can use to reach the bargain. It may be possible to reach agreement by setting a deadline or dateline for the terms offered or by giving the impression that these terms may harden if agreement is not reached.

An essential variable in the process of negotiation will be the way the issues are defined by the parties. This perception of the issues can determine the likelihood of negotiations ever taking place, let alone whether they succeed or not. As a general rule the smaller the issue difference the greater the chance of negotiations succeeding. Conversely, the more issues are seen as fundamental matters of principle, the harder compromise becomes. Sometimes parties deliberately manipulate the issues to make agreement easier or harder, the deliberate widening of issues into matters of principle being the most obvious. If all parties can agree in principle at the outset, that impediment is removed and details can be filled in during the bargaining. Sometimes parties will couple issues together. This may be done in order to be constructive, for example by offering to reciprocate concessions, or it might be destructive, widening

the agenda of discussion in order to exert pressure.

The way in which issues are perceived by the parties is likely then to have an important bearing upon the outcome of the negotiations. The broader the structure of the ISSUE AREA the smaller the chances of success but the greater the pay-offs if the negotiations do succeed. Conversely reducing the issue area increases the chances of success but reduces the significance of what is agreed. If the negotiations fail in the latter case, the chances of reviving the negotiations at some later date is almost certain to be greater. This kind of INCREMENTALISM stands frequent repetition.

The whole question of the relationship between CAPABILITY and negotiation is a complex one. It is sometimes simplified into the aphorism that parties should seek to 'negotiate from strength'. This view has much superficial validity, and appears to be intuitively sound. Upon closer examination, however, the injunction looks flawed. Kenneth Boulding (1962) has observed that parties 'dictate' rather than negotiate from positions of strength. A position of PARITY is more likely to be conducive to success in negotiations than great diversity in strength.

It is often necessary to differentiate between amity and enmity as background conditions in negotiations. It seems intuitively valid to suggest that between friends the parties are likely to be more accommodating than between foes. Whereas ACCOMMODATION between friends is likely to be the outcome, at least in part, of positive values between the parties, accommodation between foes is more likely to be dictated by expediency. In particular, negotiations between friends are more likely to evince the attitude of 'negotiating in good faith'. In essence this carry-over from an international legal concept means to negotiate with a real desire to reach agreement rather than to negotiate for 'side benefits'. More specifically, 'negotiating in good faith' involves not maintaining a dogmatic position that precludes agreement and accepting the principal rule of accommodation, which is the willingness to make concessions in order to secure agreement.

Agreements are most usually reached through compromise if negotiations are not to break down. In order to compromise parties agree to a partial withdrawal from their initial positions. This withdrawal need not be symmetrical and it is not infrequent that one side will appear to submit to demands made of it without seeking an adequate *quid pro quo*. The essential point about compromise, as Kenneth Boulding has pointed out, is that all parties must appreciate that the price of continued CONFLICT is higher than the costs of reducing demands. Compromise is, in fact, a two-step process, the first being that all sides withdraw some of their demands in preference for a continuation of the STATUS QUO and, having made this move, the bargaining for the actual terms of the compromise can take place. These two stages can be termed 'the commitment to compromise' and the 'compromise bargain', respectively.

The physical environment against which negotiations take place can be significant. Under this rubric such factors as the venue, the number of parties and the degree of secrecy or openness can be significant. The choice of venue will often be dominated by considerations of NEUTRALITY. Other considerations may be good access to communications and the nature of the issues to be negotiated. BILATERAL negotiations are, for obvious reasons, more manageable but run the risk that by excluding third parties, important interests will not be consulted and will therefore not feel constrained to support any agreement. Conversely MULTILATERAL negotiations are more unwieldy but have the advantage of allowing all parties to be represented. The debate between open and secret negotiations is an old problem about which strong views were held by both IDEALISTS and REALISTS. The dichotomy is empirically overdone. No contemporary negotiation is completely open or secret. In this respect the open/secret categories mark the ends of a continuum between which actual negotiations can be ranged. Factors that are likely to affect the movement towards one end or the other will include: the level of amity/enmity between the parties, the reasons for the negotiations and the perceived need for public support during the process itself.

## Neo-colonialism
*See*: COLONIALISM

## Neo-functionalism
An academic theory of INTEGRATION originally suggested by Haas (1958) as a result of his work on the European Coal and Steel Community. As the term implies, neo-functionalism is a modern variant of FUNCTIONALISM. Both theories are based upon the view that integration proceeds best by working from areas of mutual and overlapping interest in a piecemeal fashion. This is often referred to in the literature as the 'sector approach'. Both theories assume that these sectors will in all probability be located in the ISSUE AREA of political economy. Both theories assume that people's loyalties to their existing NATION-STATES will be steadily eroded as they see that integration has many positive benefits and that these can best be obtained, and sustained, by the new nexus.

Neo-functionalism differs from functionalism in a number of important respects. First, it is a theory of regional rather than global integration, and specifically a theory of how this process has been achieved in Western Europe since 1945. By concentrating upon a region in this way the neo-functionalists have been able to achieve great parsimony of concepts and theories. The main weakness inherent in the regional concentration is that a certain breadth of vision is thereby lost. Secondly, neo-functionalists have been much more concerned with institution building than were the original functionalists. With this in mind, Mitrany (1975) dubbed them 'federal–functionalists'. Notwithstanding, neo-functionalism is distinctly oriented towards the political aspects and implications of integration. Central to this view is that once commenced, sector integration will lead to a SPILLOVER effect into other cognate areas of activity. In particular, in those issue areas where high levels of INTERDEPENDENCE actually or potentially exist, spillover integration will be difficult to resist. Moreover, as interest groups within the member states begin to see the positive benefits of the process, they will actually initiate moves for further integration. Spillover, therefore, may be semi-automatic or manually operated.

The events in western Europe in the 1950s seemed to confirm the explanatory significance of neo-functionalism. The formation of the European Coal and Steel Community (ECSC) was followed by further attempts at the sector method of integration. Although the European Defence Community failed to secure the RATIFICATION of all its putative members, the formation of the EUROPEAN ECONOMIC COMMUNITY and of Euratom in January 1958 seemed to confirm the logic of neo-functionalist thinking. Within the institutional structure of the Community, neo-functionalists place their greatest confidence in the Commission. Although nominated by the member states, the Commissioners represent the SUPRANATIONAL rather than the STATE-CENTRIC tendencies in the arrangement. Fresh initiatives for integration and recognition of spillover tendencies are likely to come from the Commission. The initiation of a directly elected European Parliament after June 1979 further strengthened the neo-functionalist institutions within the Community.

Neo-functionalism comes from the same intellectual stable as the US school of political sociology known as PLURALISM. Like the pluralists, they assume that politics is a group activity and that in advanced industrial societies POWER and INFLUENCE will be diffused among a number of competing groups. Because competition rather than CONFLICT is the norm, the nature of the political activity will be circumscribed by a basic underlying consensus. Differences of degree rather than differences of kind will identify these groups and politics will be a bargaining process often identified as INCREMENTALISM. These pluralist assumptions fit well together with the point mentioned above, that neo-functionalism tends to concentrate upon the issue area of political economy as particularly susceptible to integration. Since advanced industrial societies tend to be preoccupied with wealth/welfare questions, the whole set of assumptions are self-reinforcing. It is not surprising to find that the neo-functionalists expect politics at the supranational level to be similar to politics at the national level. Both are dependent upon the same pluralist conceptions.

In the 1960s Western European neo-functionalism encountered GAULLISM. As a result the assumptions, particularly about the dynamic tendencies of spillover, were called into question. It became clear that the ideas derived from pluralism, referred to above, were in themselves dependent variables and that political ELITES with fundamentally different perceptions would not be able to work the same system in the same way. Moreover to the extent that these elites exercised constitutional authority within their own states, they were able and willing to exercise VETO POWER over groups such as the Commission. It is now accepted by neo-functionalists that the Council of Ministers and the European Council represent this veto power and that, with the accession of the United Kingdom after 1973, a further enhancement of Gaullist tendencies took place.

## Neo-mercantilism

Neo-mercantilism or new mercantilism is,

as the term implies, the resurgence of MER-CANTILISM. Historically, two examples of this regeneration are usually cited. First, the period between 1919–39 and, within that time frame, the period after the Great Depression of 1929–33. Second, the period since 1970 when the BRETTON WOODS system of TRADE and payments began to break up as the US HEGEMONY looked more questionable. The link between these two periods is that in both instances states used PROTECTIONISM in various forms as an economic instrument to insulate themselves from external events and circumstances, the aim, as ever, being to produce a surplus on the current account trading position by exporting more than is imported at a given level of economic activity.

Since the idea of mercantilism was first promulgated and a link was thereby established between foreign economic policy and overall goals and ORIENTATION, important changes have taken place in the conventional expectations that individuals and groups have about the proper role of the STATE, both internally and externally. In particular, the growth of ideas about the welfare state, and the growing acceptance that wealth/welfare issue areas are central tasks for governments to tackle and central aspirations for peoples to have, caused a quantum shift in the SCOPE and DOMAIN of governmental activity. Whereas in the sixteenth century protectionism was seen as a means of increasing STATE power, it is now often seen as a means of protecting the standard of living, the employment prospects and the growth targets of states. Mercantilism, or the new mercantilism, serves more masters than it did and, therefore, is seen as more benign that it once was.

The first twentieth century neo-mercantilism experiment ended with the Second World War and the emergence of the United States as the HEGEMONIAL actor immediately afterwards. The consensus at the time of the Bretton Woods negotiations was that ECONOMIC LIBERALISM was positive and that any deviation from that norm – such as might be implied by a move to-wards protectionism/neo-mercantilism – should be resisted. In general terms the General Agreement on Tariffs and Trade (GATT) system ought to encourage these liberal tendencies but by allowing states to form CUSTOMS UNIONS and COMMON MARKETS under the same REGIME, GATT was strengthening the protectionist tendencies within the system.

The GATT dispensation weakened LIBERALISM and encouraged neo-mercantilism in two respects: First, it promoted the formation of BLOCS of states based upon regional affinities and secondly, within the bloc structure, it allowed the participating states to discriminate against those outside the TRADE BLOC/common market. This discrimination reached its height in the Common Agricultural Policy (CAP) of the EUROPEAN COMMUNITY. CAP is a paradigm example of neo-mercantilism on a number of counts: it seeks to protect domestic interests and lobby groups from external competition, it artificially raises prices within the market *vis-à-vis* world prices, it leads to overproduction by marginal/uneconomic units, and it encourages DUMPING which further distorts the world market. In terms of what might be called 'classical' mercantilism, CAP encourages people to think in terms of security of supply rather than economy of production and efficiency of price. At the same time it provides stocks of surplus food which can be distributed in the form of economic AID for political purposes.

It should not be thought that the European Community is the only standard-bearer of neo-mercantilism in the present system. One of the characteristics of this type of political economy is that it provokes retaliation, tit-for-tat measures and even trade wars. From the perspective of the economic liberal, neo-mercantilism becomes a bad habit which others quickly learn to emulate.

## Neutralism
Increasingly replaced in the vocabulary of

WORLD POLITICS by the term NON-ALIGNMENT, neutralism refers to a declaration of non-participation in specific conflicts and of treating all parties impartially. Such a policy need not necessarily apply to all international conflicts since neutrals can belong to regional alliances; it is therefore possible to be neutral *vis-à-vis* a particular conflict and an active participant in another one. India, for example, declared itself neutral in the COLD WAR yet maintained strong regional commitments. Neutralism is often regarded as a useful posture to serve the security interests of new and relatively weak STATES in the INTERNATIONAL SYSTEM. Not taking sides may maximize the possibilities of genuine INDEPENDENCE in a BIPOLAR world. It may also serve an important domestic function in that DECISION-MAKING ELITES can avoid the charge that they are tools of one international faction or another and of course it also has the advantage of giving freedom of action and flexibility to the practising state. Indeed, one of the benefits of noncommitment during the Cold War was that it helped to undermine rigid bipolarity and force the SUPERPOWERS to widen the SCOPE of their policies. In particular, economic, social and developmental issues have been highlighted at the expense of narrower confrontational policies. This has been especially evident in the GENERAL ASSEMBLY of the UNITED NATIONS ORGANIZATION.

Neutralism should not be confused with NEUTRALITY which has a specific legal connotation nor should it be confused with ISOLATIONISM which usually involves complete separation from and perhaps indifference to, international affairs.

## Neutrality

Unlike NEUTRALISM with which it is often confused, neutrality is a legal concept which involves established rights and duties, both for the STATE which refrains from taking part in a WAR and for the belligerents themselves. Like other international legal concepts, the laws of neutrality were formed mainly by TREATIES in the seventeenth and eighteenth centuries, subsequently entered customary law and were then codified by judicial rulings and international conventions in the nineteenth and twentieth centuries. Under the UN CHARTER, although neutrality is recognized no member can assume the posture of a neutral if the SECURITY COUNCIL has sanctioned a proposed action against an aggressor. In this sense, it can conflict with notions of the JUST WAR. Generally, a state is presumed neutral if by word or deed it has not declared support for one or other of the belligerents. In that case certain specific rights and duties are delineated. For example, belligerents must not violate the territorial integrity of neutrals. Their commercial activities on land, sea and in the air are to be respected so long as they are sanctioned by INTERNATIONAL LAW. In return, neutrals are to remain impartial, they are not to aid any of the belligerents directly or indirectly and they are expected not to allow their citizens to do so. In particular, they should not permit neutral territory to be used for war purposes. Clearly these rights are always enjoyed precariously and neutrality must not be confused with DEMILITARIZATION. In fact, because of the conditions imposed by international law, neutrality involves the ability to defend one's territorial integrity.

Neutrality can be proclaimed in unilateral declarations, as the United States did in 1793, but also in multilateral treaties. In 1815, for example, The Perpetual Neutrality of Switzerland was guaranteed by the Congress of VIENNA; this was later reaffirmed by the VERSAILLES TREATY in 1919, and by the LEAGUE OF NATIONS in 1933. In 1830 the London conference proclaimed the neutrality of Belgium (it was in violation of this that the United Kingdom formally entered the First World War). In 1907 the Second International Hague Peace Conference reaffirmed the territorial inviolability of neutrals and codified their rights and obligations at sea. Difficult areas in this respect involve the laws of BLOCKADE, the definition of contraband and the whole process of neutral shipping plying between ports of the belligerents. The issues of trade and commerce are notoriously thorny and the general rule of thumb is encapsulated in the phrase 'free ships give freedom to goods'. In other words, the nationality of a ship determines the status of its cargo. Enemy goods on a neutral ship, if they do not fall into the category of contraband, are thus not subject to seizure. However, as with so many things 'contraband' often lies in the eye of the beholder, and belligerents have rarely hesitated to intervene if there is any possibility at all of neutral activity giving aid and succour to the enemy. The rights of neutrality have been largely ignored in both World Wars and few states – with the continuing exceptions of Switzerland and Sweden – saw neutrality as a viable policy for maintaining INDEPENDENCE. In TOTAL or NUCLEAR WAR conditions, neutrality appears a very quaint proposition. However, in 1955 the Austrian Peace Treaty provided for the perpetual NEUTRALIZATION of Austria. Although technically this was self-neutralization, it was directly promoted by the Soviet Union and agreed to by the United States, the United Kingdom and France. The extent of Austrian AUTONOMY rather than mere acquiescence in this regard is difficult to assess.

Other concepts associated with neutrality are 'neutral territories' and 'neutral zones'. The former usually refers to uninhabited territories that divide two states and which are under joint supervision, for example, the desert territory on the borders of Iraq and Saudi Arabia or that between Saudi Arabia and Kuwait (which was in fact divided in 1965 after the discovery of oil pools). 'Neutral zones' refer to sanitary or security zones formed during a war, to protect civilian populations under the supervision of the INTERNATIONAL RED CROSS. These were first established at Madrid during the Spanish Civil War of 1936 and have since become common practice especially in CONFLICTS in the Middle East. Article 14 of the Geneva Convention of 1949 provided for the establishment and recognition of sanitary and security zones which were specifically designated for the wounded and the sick (whether they were combatants or non-combatants) and for the protection of civilian populations.

## Neutralization

Neutralization is permanent NEUTRALITY. It is a status concept and is usually applied to STATE ACTORS, although in principle any territory can be neutralized. Since the requirement of neutrality is permanent in this instance, the diplomatic ground rules extend into PEACE as well as WAR. Thus a status of neutralization may, in exceptional circumstances, be regarded as totally incompatible with membership of some intergovernmental organizations (IGOs) even though they are not ALLIANCES. The paradigm example of this limiting case of neutralization is Switzerland. In addition to eschewing alliances, that state has also regarded full membership of the UNITED NATIONS as incompatible with its neutral status.

Neutralization is usually implemented by an agreement between a number of interested state actors – often referred to as guarantors – and the state that is to be the subject of the neutralization understanding. Occasionally neutralization can be self-imposed – as in the case of Austria after 1955 – but again the tacit support of outside parties is still required. As such neutralization may be regarded as the assumption of reciprocal rights and duties. The particular state actor declares itself neutral and in return the outside parties agree to respect this situation. It can be seen that from the perspective of extraneous interests, neutralization can be an effective method of insulating disputed territory and deterring outside INTERVENTION. It may appropriately be regarded as a system of CONFLICT MANAGEMENT as a result. It should not be confused with

DEMILITARIZATION and in fact neutralized states have rarely been demilitarized.

Demilitarization involves deprivation of organized military force; it does not necessarily involve external guarantees about independence or territorial integrity. NEUTRALISM, too, is a different phenomenon although it does share family resemblances. Unlike neutralization, a posture of neutralism can involve external military, diplomatic and political commitments.

Neutralization was a popular method of conflict management under the BALANCE OF POWER system. In particular, during the nineteenth century a number of agreed initiatives were taken to establish states as permanent neutrals. Switzerland was the first but the example of Belgium is possibly better if a specific instance of balance of power consequences is sought. Belgian neutrality and independence was established in the 1830s. This status was seen, particularly by the United Kingdom, as constituting a BUFFER STATE, first to French and then to German interests in the region. Indeed it was the violation of Belgian neutrality in 1914 that lead to the British intervention in the continental violence of that summer.

Neutralization has continued to have its proponents in the contemporary system and the example of Austria demonstrates how this technique can be applicable in a BIPOLAR rather than in a balance of power system. Probably the most significant drawback with this status is that it imposes severe restraints upon the FOREIGN POLICY makers in the neutralized state. As the case of Switzerland indicates it can inhibit full participation in IGOs and more generally it requires a good deal of consensual agreement among the foreign policy ELITE about the fundamental orientations of the state. With the exception of Laos, it has not been popular in the THIRD WORLD where the more dynamic orientation of NON-ALIGNMENT is preferred. At the time of writing increasing interest is being shown in neutralization as a possible future status for a united Germany.

## New International Economic Order (NIEO)

The NIEO is a THIRD WORLD manifesto for revision of the global system of economic relations. It was first mooted by the leaders of the NON-ALIGNED Movement at their Algiers summit in the autumn of 1973. Subsequently the issue was taken up by a Special Session of the GENERAL ASSEMBLY of the UNITED NATIONS in May 1974. The Assembly adopted a Programme of Action for the establishment of a NIEO. At the autumn meeting of the regular Assembly Resolution 3281 on the Economic Rights and Duties of States was passed by 120 votes to six (the opposition including the United Kingdom and the United States) with ten abstentions. Both the Action Programme and the Charter on Economic Rights reiterated ideas about revision and restructuring which had been under discussion in the United Nations Conference on Trade and Development (UNCTAD) since its inception in 1964. The whole package produced by the CONFERENCE DIPLOMACY of the period 1973–4 might appropriately be regarded as a series of basic negotiating demands or bids from which more detailed and specific agreements could follow.

The tabling of the demands for a NIEO concurrently with the first OIL SHOCK and the emergence of OPEC was no coincidence. The possibility that the oil weapon presaged a more fundamental shift in bargaining power away from the NORTH towards the South could not be ignored. The emergence of clear divisions within the Northern states – particularly between the United States and France – in 1975 seemed to confirm this.

The reforms demanded under the aegis of the NIEO can be grouped into the following classes: (a) reforms in the terms of TRADE and in access to the markets of the advanced industrial countries (AICs); (b) reforms in the major global economic institutions, particularly the IMF; (c) recognition of the burgeoning problem of Third World DEBT; (d) demands for greater economic assistance and recognition of the issue areas of TECHNOLOGY TRANSFER; and (e) recognition of the rights pertaining to economic SOVEREIGNTY of states particularly with regard to NATIONALIZATION and the control of the activities of multinational companies (MNCS).

International TRADE reform has been called the priority item on the NIEO agenda. Specifically, two demands have been made, first, for a system of pricing for primary products or commodities which would, at a minimum, even out adverse fluctuations so that the export earnings of less developed countries (LDCs) are not damaged by adverse movements. A Common Fund agreement was eventually worked out under the auspices of UNCTAD in June 1980 which seeks to stabilize commodity prices on stipulated items. Secondly, deliberate and intentional preferences should be granted in favour of the LDCs to secure their access to the market economies of the AICs for their manufacture. Since this runs counter to the whole principle of the General Agreement on Tariffs and Trade (GATT), and particularly the MOST FAVOURED NATION (MFN) idea, its implementation into a generalized system of preferences represents a major departure from the strategy of trade liberalization.

Judgement on the NIEO should not entirely rest with its implementation. Like any manifesto this is certainly one criteria for evaluation; however, it is also profitable to assess the documents in terms of the ideas lying behind them. As Cox (1979) argued in his review article in *International Organization*, while the NIEO is at one level a set of negotiation demands – or a manifesto – at another it is about the fundamental structure of the global system of economic relations ('global' rather than 'international' because non-state actors are involved). At a third level it is about the kinds of analytical frameworks that should be used to address these issues. Frameworks such as ECONOMIC LIBERALISM, MERCANTILISM, NEO-MERCANTILISM, REALISM and MARXISM. In this sense the NIEO is about IDEOLOGY and POWER.

## NIC

An acronym for Newly Industrialized/ Industrializing Country (both tenses are found in the literature). There is some debate and discrepancy about membership of this grouping but four unequivocal NICs can be identified in the REGION of East Asia: South Korea, Taiwan, Hong Kong and Singapore. Other putative NICs in other regions of the system are referred to below. In passing it should also be noted that of the above four, Hong Kong is *sui generis*. Its status is that of a DEPENDENT TERRITORY, not a STATE: it is scheduled for repatriation to China in 1997. Nor does its undoubted economic prosperity make it typical of the NICs. Unlike the other three, Hong Kong has developed as a key financial and business centre, playing an entrepôt role *vis-à-vis* China and East Asia in general.

Notwithstanding the Hong Kong case, the NICs have been able to expand their manufacturing sectors because they have enjoyed advantageous comparative costs *vis-à-vis* the market leaders, the advanced industrial countries (AICs). They have a high level of entrepreneurial skill among their populations, an open economy regarding foreign investment and stable, if undemocratic, political regimes. The emergence of the NICs exemplifies a real shift in productive resources from the NORTH to selected sites in the South. Typical examples of manufacturing growth can be cited in such fields as: cars and trucks, consumer electrical goods, shipbuilding, steel and textiles. Among THIRD WORLD states the NICs stand out for their achievement of self-sustained, export-led economic growth. They have, moreover, avoided the kinds of debt problems associated with the recent economic performance of the putative NICs of Latin America.

The evident success of these NICs has had two effects upon relations in the field of political economy. First, their success has weakened the concept of Third World solidarity. Ideologically the NICs have achieved their impressive economic performance by applying the principles of

ECONOMIC liberalism and by following the example of Japan. They have been willing to see multinational company (MNC) investment in their economies and have often facilitated such capital flows by offering a permissive taxation REGIME to the corporations. Their political systems, if stable, have poor HUMAN RIGHTS records and limited and restricted opportunities for participation.

The second consequence of NIC success has been that it has provoked a backlash among the AICs. One form this has taken has been for increases in PROTECTIONISM on the grounds that 'cheap' imports are flooding into home markets from these areas. A second response, particularly favoured in the United States, is to argue that the NICs have 'graduated' into the first division and that henceforth they should cease to regard themselves, or be regarded by others, as THIRD WORLD states requiring special consideration. Institutionally their appropriate destination would seem to be the ORGANIZATION FOR ECONOMIC COOPERATION AND DEVELOPMENT (OECD) according to this perception.

Four unequivocal NICs were identified earlier. Putative members for the next decade might include Brazil, Malaysia, Mexico and Thailand. Observers also await the possible sighting of the first African NIC. Such lists are, of course, speculative. As examples of FUTUROLOGY they depend upon the confidence with which certain trends, presently cited, can be extended into the future.

## Nixon doctrine

Originally known as the Guam doctrine since in outline it was first articulated in a number of informal statements at Guam in the Philippines in July 1969. Although rather vague and ambiguous, these briefings about the future US global role received world-wide media coverage and subsequently the Nixon administration elevated these policy guidelines into a full-blown presidential doctrine. According to Henry Kissinger (1979) the President's VIETNAM address of 3 November 1969 deliberately re-echoed these themes in order to ensure that the doctrine was named for the President rather than for the location in which it had first been expressed. In essence the doctrine contained three major policy themes:

1. It pledged that the United States would maintain all existing TREATY commitments.
2. It promised to 'provide a shield' should a nuclear power threaten an ally or any other state whose survival was deemed important to US interests.
3. In cases involving other non-nuclear types of AGGRESSION, the United States promised to provide military and economic assistance with the important proviso that 'we shall look to the nation directly threatened to assume the primary responsibility of providing the manpower for its defense.'

The doctrine should be viewed in the context of the desire for DISENGAGEMENT from Vietnam and its central purpose was to reaffirm the primacy of US global commitments while simultaneously avoiding further activist participation in future land wars in THIRD WORLD regions. The immediate antecedent of the doctrine was Nixon's article (1967) entitled 'Asia after Vietnam' where the two major policy initiatives of the new administration were clearly foreshadowed: the emphasis on the development of indigenous regional security systems and the RAPPROCHEMENT with China. However, from a larger philosophical and intellectual perspective few doubt that the main architect of the new policy perspective was Dr Henry Kissinger. His central ideas were formed from his studies of nineteenth century European DIPLOMACY and as such were anchored in the notions of BALANCE OF POWER, MULTIPOLARITY, PLURALISM, STATUS QUO, orderly change and resisting REVOLUTION (*see* especially *A World Restored*, 1964). In particular, his conception of a 'legitimate order' and a 'stable structure of peace' involved a radical reappraisal of the traditional BIPOLAR and very muscular US conceptions of the modalities of CONTAINMENT as expressed in the TRUMAN DOCTRINE. Thus, in the new doctrine, although the overall objectives of containing the main adversaries and promoting US interests on a global scale remained intact, the means–ends formula was altered. Containment was to be sought through MULTIPOLAR NEGOTIATION rather than through direct bipolar confrontation. Clearly the rationale of the Nixon doctrine was to restore operational flexibility to US FOREIGN POLICY after the disastrous adventure in Vietnam, while at the same time redistribute the burdens of the global security commitments that the nation had to support.

## No-first-use

This proposal is usually taken to refer to the issue of NUCLEAR WEAPONS. It states that an ACTOR possessing such CAPABILITY will renounce the option to be the first to cross the nuclear threshold. It is thus both a declaration of principle and a statement of doctrine. The no-first-use issue, or debate, has been held to be particularly relevant to Europe where on the NATO side the strategy of FLEXIBLE RESPONSE commits that alliance to be the first to use such weapons in certain circumstances. In theory a first use/no-first-use dichotomy could arise with any weapons system of a controversial nature.

Early proposals for no-first-use of nuclear weapons were made by the Soviet Union in 1955 and the Soviet Union continued to support such ideas diplomatically whenever they were raised in such forums as the GENERAL ASSEMBLY of the UNITED NATIONS. In 1982 the Soviet Union unilaterally renounced the first use of them in Europe. At the same time public discussion of the idea in the West was promoted by the publication in the journal *Foreign Affairs* of an article by four American diplomats: McGeorge Bundy, George F.

Kennan, Robert McNamara and Gerard Smith (1984). The authors suggested that even the limited use of nuclear weapons in Europe could not be controlled and that the nuclear threshold must be preserved as the firebreak. Accordingly, the four recommended a declaratory and action policy of no-first-use. The corollary to this suggestion was that CONVENTIONAL forces, particularly on the central front, would need to be strengthened to compensate.

The Foreign Affairs article by Bundy *et al.* is really the EX POST EX ANTE problem in a different guise. In effect the authors argue that what looks plausible before the event looks implausible afterwards. Not surprisingly, these ideas were subjected to a good deal of critical and sceptical scrutiny by European policy ELITES. The proposal for an increase in conventional forces, somewhat *sotto voce* in the original article, was poorly received. Fundamentally, European opposition to the no-first-use idea centres upon the issue of war prevention *per se* – rather than NUCLEAR WAR prevention – and insists that precluding the former must continue to rest with nuclear weapons in a punishment mode of DETERRENCE. Such European criticisms of the no-first-use position of the United States is founded upon what Buzan (1987) has called the 'easy' school of deterrence. In the circumstances of 1982, European opinion argued that a doctrine of no-first-use was a tacit signal to the Soviet Union that the alliance would rather fight and lose a CONVENTIONAL war than risk a nuclear conflagration.

In analytical terms the no-first-use debate is about the key question, which may be posed rhetorically: 'What are nuclear weapons supposed to deter?' If the answer, and the only answer, is a nuclear attack, then a no-first-use policy becomes a special case of SECOND STRIKE. It may thus pose no special problems. However, if nuclear weapons are supposed to deter conventional attack – which has always been the NATO position – then a no-first-use policy is less credible because it can make conventional war more likely. In such circumstances a viable no-first-use policy depends upon the side adopting it being willing to increase its conventional forces, or the side against whom it is directed being willing to adopt conventional DISARMAMENT.

## Non-aggression pact

As the name implies, an agreement between two or more STATES not to engage in hostilities, usually for a specified period. The ACTORS involved normally share a border or are in dispute over issues which could involve the use of armed force in their resolution. The issues of contention are not resolved by the agreement. The Nazi–Soviet pact of 1939 is a good example. This was specified to last for ten years (in fact it lasted less than two years) and contained a secret PROTOCOL which divided Eastern Europe into Russian and German SPHERES OF INFLUENCE. For both sides the pact represented a convenient breathing space. For Germany it offered security on the Eastern front. For the Soviet Union it bought valuable, albeit temporary, time for rearmament and strengthening its Western defences. Non-aggression pacts are often regarded as a useful means of reducing international tension while not deviating from basic positions. They have also been used as a means of inducing small or weak states to comply with the wishes of a regional HEGEMON. Thus in 1970 South Africa, seeking to combat a perceived regional COMMUNIST threat offered non-aggression pacts to its black neighbours. In return for an assurance of non-interference from Pretoria, South Africa expected its neighbours to deny insurgent facilities for operations against it. At the time there were no takers, but in the early 1980s P. W. Botha revived the offer as part of his efforts to create a 'constellation of states' around South Africa. In 1984 the Nkomati accord was signed between South Africa and Mozambique. The essence of this was that while South Africa committed itself to end support for RENAMO, Mozambique agreed to end the ANC military presence in its territory. This accord, and a similar accord signed with Swaziland in 1982, was regarded by Pretoria as a blueprint for a series of regional non-aggression pacts with surrounding black states, which as well as creating a 'Pax Pretoriana' would considerably ease the internal security problems of the South African government.

It should be noted that non-aggression pacts do not commit signatories to the active defence of the other party. The only commitment is to forego the military option as a means of resolving a dispute. They are not 'treaties of friendship' though given time and mutual compliance, they could conceivably develop into them. However, as in all treaties, the principle of REBUS SIC STANTIBUS is deemed to apply as it clearly did in the German case and may well yet do in the South African example.

## Non-alignment

A FOREIGN POLICY ORIENTATION that has been widely adopted within the current INTERNATIONAL SYSTEM by STATES of the THIRD WORLD. Non-alignment, as the term implies, seeks to avoid BLOCS, coalitions and ALLIANCES. Specifically it is a rejection of the system of competitive groupings established around the COLD WAR confrontation zones in the post-1945 system. In particular non-alignment was a resistance movement against attempts by the United States and its allies to produce carbon copies of NATO in the THIRD WORLD after 1949. More generally, non-alignment is an assertion of the INDEPENDENCE of the state and its immediate attraction to those new members of the system produced by the DECOLONIZATION process should be apparent. Having recently thrown off the COLONIAL yoke, the newly independent were concerned to maintain a respectable distance from alliances dominated by the FIRST WORLD. At the height of the Cold

War some in the West saw this orientation as equivocal and even immoral. More relaxed attitudes now prevail and non-alignment has come to be accepted as the standard operating PERCEPTION of their external environment by the overwhelming majority of Afro–Asian ELITES. Latin American commitment is less evident or total.

Non-alignment differs from traditional policies of NEUTRALIZATION by being an orientation that is assumed or taken up by the parties themselves, rather than being guaranteed and assured by outside interests. Moreover, non-alignment is not essentially a form of CONFLICT MANAGEMENT like neutralization. By insulating themselves from SUPERPOWER conflicts the non-aligned seek to be part of the solution rather than part of the problem. Non-alignment neither requests nor requires outside guarantees beyond the accepted commitment towards PEACEFUL COEXISTENCE, a principle established at the BANDUNG CONFERENCE.

During the 1950s the term positive NEUTRALISM was sometimes used as an alternative for non-alignment. The prefix 'positive' is instructive here. Far from opting out of the system – like a traditional neutral state – the non-aligned enthusiastically exercised their SOVEREIGNTY, immediately asserting a more independent role diplomatically in events such as the KOREAN situation and enhancing their influence in intergovernmental organizations (IGOs) such as the UN. The early ascendancy of Asian leaders was reflected at the Bandung meeting but thereafter African and Middle Eastern elites became more involved. Following the BELGRADE meeting in 1961, the Non-Aligned Movement was established and agreement was reached on triennial meetings. CONFERENCE DIPLOMACY, indeed, has been a specific characteristic of non-alignment. By combining their voting power into BLOCS such states can command effective working majorities in organizations such as the UN.

By definition the non-aligned position is inappropriate in the context of wealth–welfare, NORTH–SOUTH issues since the non-aligned are one of the poles in the BI-POLAR structure. As a result non-alignment as an orientation is only relevant to military security questions and, even within that category, to threats posed externally from outside the state by the activities of the superpowers and their allies. Accordingly the value of the term 'non-alignment' as an explanatory device is reduced and it reverts to being a taxonomy or label for a large, but divisive, group of states.

## Non-intervention

A pivotal notion in the WESTPHALIAN STATE-SYSTEM where rights associated with INDEPENDENCE and SOVEREIGNTY logically implied corresponding duties of non-intervention. Thus, the claim to exclusive DOMESTIC JURISDICTION represented by the principle of *cuius regio eius religio* extended to its corollary – freedom from external interference. Primarily an eighteenth century European idea, the rule of non-intervention in INTERNATIONAL LAW and public diplomatic practice is especially associated with the writings of Wolff (1749) and Vattel (1758). Most early writers on the subject tended to regard it in absolute terms, seeing it as an indispensable prop to STATE sovereignty and therefore an argument for liberty against earlier HEGEMONIC and IMPERIAL claims. However, just as the rights of sovereignty are not absolute, so the duty of non-intervention is circumscribed by reservations and qualifications (even Wolff, for example, claimed that it could be compromised by collective action – the *civitas maxima*).

While non-intervention is now widely regarded as a rule which states ought to adhere to, it is often thought to be more honoured in the breach than in the observance. Indeed, many scholars have noted that in the post-1945 period INTERVENTION appears not only to be endemic in INTERNATIONAL POLITICS (to the extent that it can be regarded as 'structural' in character), but may even be coterminous with it. That is, if all states complied all the time with the requirements of non-intervention, INTERNATIONAL POLITICS as we know it would disappear. In this way, modern debates centre not around the existence of the rule, but rather the nature and SCOPE of exceptions.

The legitimacy of intervention in the internal affairs of another state clearly depends on a number of factors including purpose or cause, means employed and the authority under which intervention takes place. Generally, unilateral intervention is regarded as suspect although intervention by invitation (e.g. the Soviet intervention in AFGHANISTAN in 1979), or counter-interventions (e.g. Cuban assistance to Angola up to 1989 to counter South African aid to UNITA forces), or even pre-emptive intervention on the grounds of SELF-DEFENCE (e.g. the Israeli bombing of a nuclear installation in Baghdad in 1981) – are all regarded as more or less justifiable exceptions to the rule. Again, interventions in support of SELF-DETERMINATION or WARS OF NATIONAL LIBERATION are often advanced as legitimate exceptions, especially from the THIRD WORLD perspective. In addition, 'humanitarian' intervention, either unilaterally or collectively, is a right that is frequently invoked especially by supporters of the emerging law of HUMAN RIGHTS. To many the doctrine of non-intervention, representing as it does the ultimate expression of states' rights, is not just inimical to the development of INTERNATIONAL ORGANIZATIONS but also to the general acceptance of human rights as an integral feature of international relations. The rigidity of the doctrine, at least in its original form, allows 'pariah' or 'rogue' states like South Africa to survive behind quasi-legal technicalities associated with the more exclusive versions of sovereignty and domestic jurisdiction.

Clearly, non-intervention is bound up with the idea of a decentralized STATE-SYSTEM composed of sovereign, independent units who are nominally equal. The survival of the rule is therefore linked to the survival of this particular form of WORLD ORDER. The concentration or centralization of POWER and AUTHORITY in one source, or else in a number of regional centres, would severely limit its scope and effectiveness. For the present, despite a number of corrosive forces eating away at its edges, non-intervention is still acknowledged to be a bulwark against unwarranted outside interference. As such, it seeks to define the FRONTIER between internal and external affairs and to express, however hazily, the proper and permissible limits of contact between one state and another.

*See also*: CALVO DOCTRINE; INTERVENTION

## Non-tariff barriers (NTBs)

Non-tariff barriers to trade fall into two categories. First, there are QUOTAS, quantitative restrictions deliberately designed to protect domestic interests. These are a clear breach of the principles behind the General Agreement on Tariffs and Trade (GATT), although there are certain exceptions to this prohibition. The secondary category of NTBs is not always or intentionally a form of TRADE restriction. The impact of these upon trade will often be latent rather than manifest so their separation from quotas can be justified. The discussion of NTBs that follows will concentrate exclusively upon this second category.

Under this rubric, NTBs are of four broad types: internal taxes, administrative barriers, health and sanitary regulations and government procurement policies. An internal tax can be used to discriminate against IMPORTS if a deliberate differential is exercised between domestic and imported products which, to all intents and purposes, are the same. Routine and regular administration of importing, as an activity, can become discriminatory if importers appear to be required to submit to excessive and time-consuming paperwork, delay due to documentation problems, etc.

Health and sanitary regulations which are perfectly legitimate in themselves can be used to discriminate against imports. Government procurement policies, by deliberately encouraging individuals and institutions to, e.g., 'buy British' or 'buy American' not to 'export jobs', can have a discriminatory effect.

This rather heterogeneous category of activities is subsumed under the idea of NTBs which have a latent rather than manifest impact upon trade. In many instances – such as government procurement policies – the original articles of GATT were virtually silent in identifying and prohibiting the discriminatory impact of these activities. It has only been since the KENNEDY ROUND of GATT negotiations that increasing attention and concern has been directed at the NTBs. It is reasonable to assume that this ISSUE AREA will continue to exercise GATT negotiators.

## North

The term 'North' is a loose, portmanteau concept used the advanced industrial countries (AICS). It is particularly popular in political economy and, in terms of developmental models, it may be regarded as being synonymous with the growth of the FIRST WORLD. SYSTEMS ANALYSIS tends to juxtapose it with the equally amorphous concept of the SOUTH. Indeed, the popular title of the first BRANDT REPORT was NORTH–SOUTH.

## North–South

A dichotomous term used in MACROPOLITICS to identify one of the most pervasive BIPOLAR divisions in the current global system. Relationships between the NORTH and the South have grown in significance since the collapse of COLONIALISM and the emergence of the THIRD WORLD in the 1950s. The visceral commitment of these new states to FOREIGN POLICY ORIENTATIONS

variously described as positive NEUTRALISM or NON-ALIGNMENT meant that in the ISSUE AREA of security politics – often thought of as HIGH POLITICS – the South would rigorously oppose attempts by the North to secure their adhesion to Northern dominated COLD WAR coalitions.

The South's attempt to throw a cordon sanitaire around the Cold War was not totally successful. The United States, in particular, has sought on occasions through policies of INTERVENTION to carry these issues into the Third World. Justification was found, for example, in the bipolar PERCEPTION of the DOMINO THEORY. On other occasions it must be conceded that factions and tendencies within the South sought and encouraged Northern intervention in violent CONFLICT situations. The Soviet BLOC – not usually thought of as part of the North – has also played the interventionist card and during the 1970s in particular it was clear that the DÉTENTE relationship between the United States and the Soviet Union was not inhibiting the latter from pursuing such strategies.

Many commentators argue that, notwithstanding the above analysis, the true ISSUE AREA for the North–South dichotomy is to be found in wealth/welfare, political economy. Certainly in this context a very different picture emerges from that already discussed. The dependence of the South upon the North for AID and TRADE in order to generate income to meet developmental goals has meant that in this context the term 'North–South' refers to the BILATERAL and MULTILATERAL relationships that are entailed. It should not be thought, moreover, that these relations are exclusively STATE-CENTRED. The multinational companies (MNCs) based in the North and involved in primary or secondary industrial production in the South are an equally valid picture of North–South interactions. These relationships have been variously analysed using different models and the DEPENDENCY or dependencia perspective is one of the most compelling.

From the early 1960s onwards the Southern states began to use their burgeoning majority in the UNITED NATIONS to press for greater attention to be paid to their aspirations and concerns. It was pressure from the South that largely created the United Nations Conference on Trade and Development (UNCTAD) in 1964 and it was Southern economists such as Prebisch that provided the intellectual framework for the series of demands for a new deal on world trade that accompanied the UNCTAD process. Until the success of OPEC in the early 1970s, the terms upon which North–South economic relations were conducted were very unequal. The OPEC cartel seemed to point to new possibilities for strengthening the bargaining position of the South and a comprehensive checklist of demands was presented under the rubric of the NEW INTERNATIONAL ECONOMIC ORDER (NIEO).

Retrospectively, OPEC and the first OIL SHOCK would seem to have been a window of opportunity which was not entered. Conservative forces within OPEC collaborated with the Northern financial system to recycle petrodollars and oil-importing advanced industrial countries (AICS) were able in the short term to finance their debits accordingly. Other commodity cartels were not established and indeed, by accident, the OPEC action hit Southern oil importers harder than their Northern counterparts. The petrodollar recycling exercise, moreover, was a precipitant cause of the subsequent DEBT CRISIS in Latin America.

The unintended consequence of OPEC and the first oil shock was to drive a line between oil producers in the South and the rest. The growth of the newly industrialized countries (NICS) and the putative NICs constitutes another break in Southern solidarity. Antithetically, the realization that a FOURTH WORLD of extreme poverty and deprivation existed in an identifiable 'famine belt' removed a further prop from the homogeneity of the South. The OPEC exercise of commodity cartel POWER remains the best instance, to date, of the South being able to back their demands for

change with something more substantial than a rectitude based upon perceptions of equity. Realism would suggest that unless and until the South can produce more bargaining chips of the OPEC genre they will have a difficult time wringing agreement from the North on structural change.

Within the North the main systemic changes are associated with the loss of US hegemonial CAPABILITIES to determine systemic outcomes. The United States now shares predominance with the EUROPEAN COMMUNITY and Japan. This has meant that on certain key occasions the North has spoken with a number of voices *vis-à-vis* the South. This was notable in the aftermath of the first oil shock, when the United States wanted to pursue a more confrontational policy than either the Europeans or the Japanese. With regard to the continuing area of trade reform, the North has shown a clear preference for the GATT system rather then UNCTAD.

It should be noted that the North–South dichotomy is only one of a number of relationships that can be identified between these two 'poles'. North–North relations and indeed South–South relations are both evident. It is certainly possible to discern structures and processes in MACROPOLITICS which might encourage both the analyst and the POLICY-MAKER to think in terms of these alternatives in the future.

## NPT

An acronym for the Treaty on the Non-Proliferation of Nuclear Weapons. This multilateral ARMS CONTROL agreement was opened for signature in July 1968 and came into force in March 1970. The NPT seeks to achieve three principal goals. First, to stop the HORIZONTAL PROLIFERATION of NUCLEAR WEAPONS from states possessing them to states that do not have this CAPABILITY. The first and second Articles of the NPT cover this contingency. Secondly, to allow for the continuation of TECHNOLOGY TRANSFER regarding civilian NUCLEAR

POWER facilities. The signatories established a safeguards system allowing the proliferation of peaceful nuclear TECHNOLOGY under the aegis of the International Atomic Energy Agency (IAEA). Included in the NPT safeguards system is the notion that the Agency will have full and open access to the civilian nuclear programmes of all non-nuclear states, including the right to conduct periodic INSPECTIONS of all their plants and facilities. Thirdly, the NPT sought to control the trend towards further VERTICAL PROLIFERATION by enjoining the signatories to 'pursue negotiations in good faith on effective measures relating to cessation of the nuclear arms race at an early date and to nuclear disarmament'. Article Seven of the Treaty encouraged the establishment of NUCLEAR FREE ZONES. Article Eight committed the contracting parties to meet at five-yearly intervals to review progress made in establishing and extending the REGIME. At the time of writing, three review conferences have been held. The TREATY itself will be reviewed in 1995 and the proliferation regime may, or may not, continue on a multilateral legal basis thereafter.

Critics of the NPT point to the fact that it discriminates between two classes of states, those that had tested and deployed nuclear weapons before the treaty was concluded – the United States, the Soviet Union, the United Kingdom, France and China – and the non-nuclear rest who are expected to confirm this status by signing away the option of 'going nuclear'. It is the case that the NPT contains an escape clause stipulating that a signatory can repudiate the convention after three months but, since that applies to nuclear states as well as non-nuclear, its insertion is not specifically made in the interests of the latter. Not surprisingly the inventory of non-signatories of the convention – referred to as the 'hold-out' states – is a roll-call of those who dissent from this state of affairs for ideological and/or for NATIONAL INTEREST motives: Argentina, Brazil, China, India, Israel, Pakistan and South Africa.

Since the Treaty was signed horizontal proliferation has slowed down but not stopped. India has conducted its peaceful nuclear test. Pakistan, or interest groups within that state, seek to develop the so-called 'Islamic bomb'. Israel has a small clandestine stockpile and South Africa is believed to have conducted a test explosion in 1979. Not everyone, of course, thinks that 'more would be worse'. Professor Waltz (1981) has been a notable heretic on these matters, However, arguments that horizontal proliferation increases stability are anathema to supporters of the NPT. They argue that nuclear weapons in the 'wrong hands' (a term which is often defined in highly subjective terms) could quickly destabilize the regime established under the Treaty.

The idea that a sharp dividing line can be drawn between nuclear weapons and nuclear power – which is clearly central to the NPT – flies in the face of historical evidence. All the existing nuclear states have deliberately and unashamedly used PLUTONIUM produced in their civilian power programmes for military purposes. Indeed, the United Kingdom has exported the material to the United States. Moreover, the new generation of fast breeder reactors can reprocess plutonium up to weapons grade, while laser TECHNOLOGIES can enrich URANIUM for the same purposes. In the light of past experience, therefore, the idea that nuclear power advances will not leak into nuclear weapons production seems overly optimistic. More plausible is the hope that nuclear power will itself become less attractive for both economic and environmental reasons and that these trends will help to foreclose the proliferation of peaceful nuclear energy as well as the strategic.

Since its inception in 1970 the NPT has functioned to make it politically awkward and technically difficult for 'near-nuclear' states to make the decision to develop nuclear weapons. The NPT has increased the confidence that nuclear weapons states can have, that cooperation with non-nuclear states to establish and advance their nuclear power programmes need not lead to 'leakage' of technology into military activities. In this respect the working of the various supplier's groups can reassure nuclear states that competition to win markets for nuclear power exports will not lead to infringements of the NPT safeguards.

It should be recognized that the presence of the 'holdout' states precludes the NPT regime from achieving universality. In 1995 the parties will have to make irrevocable decisions about the continuation, or otherwise, of the convention.

## Nuclear accidents

Nuclear accidents fall into two categories: first, civilian accidents, which invariably mean accidents in nuclear reactors; and second, military accidents, which involve malfunction and breakdown of nuclear devises, including nuclear powered systems, during peacetime conditions. Excluded from this discussion are those 'accidents' (such as the accidental launch of a missile) that might lead to WAR or ACCIDENTAL WAR.

The main risks with both civilian and peacetime military accidents is that innocent third parties will be affected by environmental POLLUTION and degradation. The increasing use of NUCLEAR POWER to generate energy for industrial and domestic purposes has meant that such facilities have proliferated. As a result serious breakdowns often cannot be controlled or restricted to an area within the confines of the power plant. Worse still, they cannot be confined within the territorial borders of the STATE wherein the plant is situated. Thus the Chernobyl accident of April 1986 was not confined to the Soviet Union and pollution and contamination spread outside its borders. The first inclination that something significant had occurred came when Swedish and Finnish monitors reported high levels of radioactivity two days after the explosion. Truly, the Chernobyl impact has been to confirm the extent to which INTERDEPENDENCE is a key characteristic of contemporary MACROPOLITICS.

Accidents in nuclear reactors have been depressingly regular occurrences since 1952, when the first reactor accident occurred at Chalk River, Ottawa, Canada. Significant contamination of the environment occurred in 1957 at Windscale in the United Kingdom, while a catastrophic local incident took place in the Kasli/Kyshtym area of Chelyabinsk region of the Soviet Union in the same year as Windscale. The Three Mile Island incident at Harrisburg, Pennsylvania in March 1979 was the most serious, to date, in the United States and, in company with Chernobyl, it showed the importance of human error as a factor in explaining such malfunctions.

Attempts are currently being made by the nuclear power industry to improve global safety standards following Chernobyl. An intergovernmental organization (IGO), the World Association of Nuclear Operators, was formed in the spring of 1989. Military installations are specifically excluded from the remit of this new body. Four early warning centres will be established in the United States, the Soviet Union, France and Japan. Information, expertise and, in the worst case, remedial advice will be shared on a TRANSNATIONAL basis by this IGO.

Incidents of a military kind are much more difficult to uncover and therefore assess. All the NUCLEAR WEAPON states tend to be very reluctant to admit to such incidents occurring or to ask for international assistance thereafter. Particularly drastic are naval accidents. Controlling pollution may be difficult if not impossible if a vessel sinks to the sea-bed. Collisions at sea between ships carrying nuclear weapons and/or powered by nuclear reactors are hazardous. To date, the most serious of such incidents involved the US Navy. In 1975 the USS Belknap and the USS John F. Kennedy collided in the Mediterranean off the Italian coast. The subsequent fire on board the Belknap came within 40 feet of missile magazines.

## Nuclear decapitation

An unanticipated, and therefore surprise, attack upon the command, communications and control structure of a STATE. The attack would be made with NUCLEAR WEAPONS and this factor, plus the surprise element, could make the initiative decisive. The purpose of such a move would be to eliminate the ability of the political and military command centres in the target to coordinate an effective response. Decapitation might be so effective as to preclude any retaliation. More plausibly, however, such decapitation would degrade and confuse the retaliatory CAPABILITIES of the target; coordination and direction of the residual forces would be made more difficult as a result. Retaliation by the target would tend to take place on an individual *ad hoc* basis with forces acting independently of central control.

Concern about the ability of the major COLD WAR adversaries to engage in nuclear decapitation has grown of late. It is part of the increased emphasis upon Command, Control, Communications and Intelligence ($C^3I$). Most informed opinion tends towards a set of pessimistic conclusions on the issue of the survivability of national command centres in the event of a major nuclear exchange.

## Nuclear-Free Zones (NFZ)

A NFZ is a REGION of the world where the states in the area and/or extra-regional states with territorial interests in the area agree not to test, manufacture or stockpile NUCLEAR WEAPONS. The term 'nuclear-free' is something of a misnomer, therefore, and it is more accurate to call these agreements Nuclear-Weapon-Free Zones. Indeed intergovernmental organizations (IGOs) such as the UNITED NATIONS have specified that peaceful nuclear developments should be allowed to take place under the rubric of the NFZ/NWFZ idea. It is also generally accepted that such zonal arrangements will require at least the tacit cooperation of all five of the existing nuclear weapon states:

the United States, the Soviet Union, China, France and the United Kingdom.

Three specified zonal agreements have, to date, been reached and these are all currently operating in their respective parts of the globe. Historically, the first such zonal agreement was the ANTARCTICA TREATY of 1959. In some ways the most far reaching and comprehensive of the three extant treaties, the Antarctic Treaty demilitarizes as well as denuclearizes the continent. This was followed in 1967 by the Treaty of Tlatelolco which seeks to prohibit the introduction of nuclear weapons into Latin America. Tlatelolco was the first NFZ/NWFZ convention to cover inhabited areas of the globe. Following the UN principles, as well as the inclinations of the parties, no attempt was made to extend the provisions to cover peaceful nuclear development. Indeed the official name of the treaty was changed from 'Treaty for the Denuclearization of Latin America' to 'Treaty for the Prohibition of Nuclear Weapons in Latin America' in order to allow for such peaceful nuclear developments.

All the states in the region, save Cuba, have adhered to Tlatelolco. The strength of the commitment of Argentina, Brazil and Chile is in some doubt since none of these states have signed the TREATY on the Non-Proliferation of Nuclear Weapons (NPT). Moreover, since the contracting parties can repudiate the treaty after only 3 months' notice, the possibility of a 'break-out' of the Tlatelolco system by one of these 'threshold' states is always possible. Two PROTOCOLS to the treaty enabled states with international responsibilities for territories within the region: the United Kingdom, France, the United States and the Netherlands, and the five nuclear weapon states – referred to above – to adhere to either or both Protocol I and Protocol II. There is some evidence to suggest that during the subsequent FALKLANDS crisis of 1982 the United Kingdom infringed both the spirit and the letter of the Tlatelolco system by introducing naval forces into the region carrying nuclear weapons.

The third NFZ/NWFZ agreement currently in operation is the Treaty of Rarotonga which established a South Pacific Nuclear-Free Zone in August 1985. Membership of the South Pacific Forum is a necessary condition for signing the Treaty of Rarotonga. In some respects Rarotonga seeks to improve upon Tlatelolco. It is unequivocal in banning 'peaceful nuclear explosions' (which Tlatelolco is not) and it prohibits the dumping of nuclear wastes. Conversely the Latin American treaty is GEOPOLITICALLY more feasible because it covers large areas of land which are, in principle, susceptible to the control of the contracting parties. Rarotonga covers vast stretches of ocean and high seas which the contracting parties are unable physically or legally to control. Moreover, the attachment of the most powerful state in the South Pacific, Australia, to the ANZUS agreement with the United States has meant that such existing security arrangements must necessarily weaken the commitment of any Australian government to a radical interpretation of Rarotonga. Thus the contracting parties must have been unable to take a united position on the issue of visits to home ports by ships believed to be carrying nuclear weapons.

The most contentious aspect of Rarotonga has been and remains the continued use by France of its territories in the area for nuclear testing. France has tested both in the atmosphere and underground since 1966. These tests have mainly been conducted at Mururoa Atoll and there is no sign that the conclusion of the Rarotonga Treaty will produce a change of direction of this issue from France. Failure to persuade France to abandon testing within the area covered by the treaty must be regarded as the major failure of Rarotonga.

From the systemic perspective, proposals for NFZ/NWFZ can be seen as assisting the moves to check HORIZONTAL PROLIFERATION. This linkage was formally acknowledged in the NPT. Article Seven of that Treaty specifically encouraged the establishment of such zones. It is surely no accident of DIPLOMACY that all the working examples of such zoning have been confined almost completely to the southern hemisphere. The major challenge facing supporters of such zonal agreements must be to extend the process into the North in the decades ahead.

## Nuclear power

A term used for the generation of electricity by a nuclear power plant or station. It was recognized very early in the nuclear age that the heat produced in a nuclear reactor could be converted into steam to run turbines. The world's first nuclear power station was established at Calder Hall, United Kingdom in 1956. At the time great optimism was evident about the future possibilities for nuclear power, particularly among ATTENTIVE PUBLICS in the advanced industrial countries (AICs). It was seen as preferable to coal on the grounds of cost and preferable to oil on the grounds of political economy. The 1956 Suez CRISIS had shown how easy it was to interrupt oil supplies following a crisis in the REGION.

Since the 1950s nuclear power has become an important energy source for some STATES but overall the early optimism has not been justified. Approximately 15 per cent of the world's electricity is now generated in this way. Three-quarters of this capacity is situated in the OECD states. In the THIRD WORLD, the Asian newly industrialized countries (NICs) have major power programmes, as does India. For the rest of the THIRD WORLD nuclear power has proved to be too expensive an option to contemplate. The cost-saving expectations of the earlier period are now seen to be too sanguine. Within the OECD group, France stands out as the state most dependent upon nuclear power for its energy requirements. More than two-thirds of French electricity is generated by nuclear power plants.

# NUCLEAR PROLIFERATION

The developments in nuclear power referred to above have raised two ISSUE AREAS within MACROPOLITICS: first, that of NUCLEAR PROLIFERATION; and secondly, that of NUCLEAR ACCIDENTS. Of the two issue areas, the proliferation question shows considerable commitment to norm-acceptance and institution-building. As such it is valid to regard the nuclear proliferation concern as a REGIME – in particular with the International Atomic Energy Agency (IAEA) and the Treaty on the Non-Proliferation of Nuclear Weapons (NPT) in mind. On the other hand, no similar stipulation could be made about NUCLEAR ACCIDENTS. Accordingly it seems reasonable to assume that INTERNATIONAL and TRANSNATIONAL cooperation on this aspect of nuclear power must soon be faced.

## Nuclear proliferation

One of the most significant and controversial processes of twentieth century MACROPOLITICS, nuclear proliferation is a portmanteau term which covers two interrelated developments: HORIZONTAL PROLIFERATION, or the spread of NUCLEAR WEAPONS, and VERTICAL PROLIFERATION, deliberate increases in the stockpile of weapons and/or their diffusion into regions and areas that had previously been NUCLEAR-FREE ZONES (NFZs). Buzan (1987) regards nuclear proliferation as one of the main concepts of STRATEGIC STUDIES, thereby placing it in the front rank of mainspring influences upon the subject matter of this field of study. It is also generally regarded as a mixed blessing and many would share the value judgement that the world was a safer place before the nuclear genie escaped the vessel.

Efforts to control the process date from the early post-1945 attempts to internationalize nuclear weapons through proposals such as the BARUCH PLAN. As the first nuclear state, the United States did much to encourage and continue this inter-national institutional approach through the establishment of the International Atomic Energy Agency (IAEA) in the 1950s. However, at the same time the Republican Administration was encouraging horizontal proliferation by its active collaboration with the United Kingdom under the broad aegis of the SPECIAL RELATIONSHIP. Vertical proliferation also began in earnest in the 1950s with the development of the HYDROGEN BOMB, tactical nuclear weapons and continued refinement via testing in the atmosphere.

Once the United States found that it had to live in adversarial partnership with the Soviet Union as well as ALLIANCE partnership with the United Kingdom, serious efforts were made by the three states in the 1960s to establish a REGIME that would at least control horizontal proliferation. Once it was clear that the Treaty on the Non-Proliferation of Nuclear Weapons (NPT) had failed to stop the spread to THIRD WORLD STATES – highlighted by the Indian peaceful nuclear explosion of 1974 – the chief exporting states formed the Nuclear Suppliers Group or London Group to tighten up the leakage on TECHNOLOGY from civilian to military programmes. This attempt to impose oligopoly rules on the regime so infuriated the 'holdout' states, led by India, that the 1980 NPT Review Conference, held in the aftermath of the London Group guidelines and the passing by the US Congress of the 1977 Nuclear Non-Proliferation Act, was an acrimonious affair. Specifically the issue of vertical proliferation was raised directly and the argument was put that the existing nuclear weapons states were not taking their commitments under Article Six sufficiently seriously.

Nuclear proliferation must be judged an irreversible process. Probably the single most constructive step that could be taken to halt further vertical proliferation would be a COMPREHENSIVE TEST BAN, while horizontal proliferation control must continue under the NPT regime or its replacement after 1995.

## Nuclear umbrella

A form of EXTENDED DETERRENCE. In this instance a STATE possessing a NUCLEAR WEAPONS CAPABILITY pledges to extend to another state or group of states the protection perceived to be afforded by these weapons. Empirically the NATO and WARSAW PACT ALLIANCES are examples of the umbrella idea. The United States pledged to Western Europe and the Soviet Union to the Peoples Democracies – making a MIRROR IMAGE. Historically the United States pledge was the earlier and, arguably, throughout the post-1949 period was the more significant.

Under certain conditions – usually referred to in the literature as 'punishment deterrence' – a nuclear umbrella system cannot provide DEFENCE at all and the state(s) covered under its protection cannot expect that their territories will be defended. A system of nuclear umbrella based upon mutual assured destruction (MAD) would be of this genre. As such a nuclear umbrella is no substitute for CONVENTIONAL capabilities if a defence as well as deterrent function is required.

The NUCLEAR WINTER thesis suggests that if the nuclear threshold is crossed the results may be equally damaging for friend and foe alike and the activation of the threat behind the umbrella may be largely indiscriminate. Moreover, if nuclear deterrence is based upon the punishment variation referred to above, the umbrella states may have to make the difficult choice between suicide, if war starts, or SURRENDER if the guarantees are not honoured.

It should be noted that in NATO parlance the term 'coupling' is sometimes used to refer to the nuclear umbrella idea. In this idiom, the United States is 'coupled' with Western Europe under the umbrella.

## Nuclear war

Notwithstanding the use of NUCLEAR WEAPONS against Japan in 1945, war between STATES possessing nuclear weapons has never occurred. Of course, the whole basis of nuclear DETERRENCE thinking is to argue that the threat of nuclear WAR can be manipulated to secure the prevention of war. Since 1945 nuclear weapons have proliferated and spread from the original US monopoly position to the current situation where states outside the original COLD WAR confrontation zones – such as Israel – have developed a nuclear weapon CAPABILITY. As a result nuclear war may occur not solely from the BIPOLAR relationship between the SUPERPOWERS but as a result of violence in the THIRD WORLD spilling over into the nuclear mode.

Conceptually nuclear war might occur in two ways. First, a CONVENTIONAL conflict might become 'nuclearized', as one side initiated the use of these weapons – as happened in 1945. Deterrence theory would imply that this is more likely to occur if the side utilizing these weapons has a monopoly. However, if deterrence breaks down or seems to be breaking down – then the use of nuclear weapons between states might occur as a policy of strategic surprise or first strike. Again in theory a first strike might take place without the accompanying conventional exchange referred to above.

Because of the very great destructive potential of nuclear weapons, a full-scale nuclear war would be difficult to control. Even before the promulgation of the NUCLEAR WINTER thesis it was widely accepted that civilian casualties would be of pestilential proportions. The wholesale breakdown of social control and the need for draconian executive authority in the post-attack situation are probable consequences. Because a full-scale nuclear war would be so unlimited and indiscriminate, some commentators have argued that its legal status is dubious. The twentieth century has seen unparalleled attempts to codify the laws of war. In general terms these developments have attempted to set restrictions upon the use of certain types of weapons, such as poison gas and to set restrictions upon certain types of targets, such as churches and hospitals, as well as neutral states and their nationals. It is difficult to see how nuclear war could ever be sufficiently discriminatory to meet these requirements. It should of course be noted that declaratory statements about INTERNATIONAL LAW may be one thing and enforcement and implementation of these principles quite another. This is a general deficiency probably inherent in the subject of international principles and their effectiveness. It must be admitted that there are other instances in the twentieth century of states not observing the letter or the spirit of the humanitarian principles of the laws of war. Furthermore, as the recent history of the Middle East shows, it is not only the most powerful states in the system which ignore and infringe these principles.

Some writers have attempted to distinguish between the use of nuclear weapons – nuclear warfare – which is probably illegal and their possession which might not be. It has been noted elsewhere in this volume that the nuclear age is evidently paradoxical. Here may be another one. To possess nuclear weapons may not be illegal, whereas to use them probably is. Moreover their deployment is a grey area between possession and use. Again, deployments such as mutual assured destruction (MAD) would seem to be illegal because they are, by definition, indiscriminate. In other respects, MAD, since it is a retaliatory rather than first strike strategy, is probably legal. It can be justified as a REPRISAL. Deterrence theorists will argue that as long as the threat system works the potential illegality of nuclear war can continue to be debated. If it fails, the few who survive may have more pressing concerns than the legal status of the disaster that has befallen the planet.

### Nuclear weapons
Weapons that employ the fission and/or the fusion principles to destroy their targets.

The only two nuclear weapons that have actually been used in WAR are the two ATOMIC BOMBS dropped on Japan in 1945. The development of the fusion or HYDROGEN BOMB has added a whole new dimension to these types of weapons. In theory the destructive power of the fusion weapon is limitless, although in practice, the production and installation of very large weapons may be of dubious value. Nuclear weapons are now designed for all contexts from the battlefield to the intercontinental. Thus a broad, if somewhat arbitrary distinction is often made between STRATEGIC and TACTICAL WEAPONS, while recently, with the European context in mind, politicians and strategists have spoken of an INTERMEDIATE range. All these distinctions tend to be justified upon two criteria: technical and functional. Thus technically, tactical weapons would be thought of as single-shot systems, of very limited range, with a small warhead. Functionally such weapons, as their name implies, would be used on or close to the battlefield in support of more CONVENTIONAL types of forces. Tactical weapons are highly mobile and thus very easy to conceal. At the other extreme strategic weapons are now usually thought of as multiple warhead, long-range systems which operate at intercontinental distances. Functionally, there is considerable dispute about whether these strategic systems have any effective or plausible end other than to be used to threaten an adversary.

This last point is held by some commentators to be one of the most significant points of departure in thinking about strategic nuclear weapons. As Professor Glenn Snyder (1961) argued in his seminal work, nuclear weapons have led to a new emphasis upon DETERRENCE at the expense of DEFENCE. Thus nuclear weapons, particularly of the strategic genre, can inflict great punishment upon an adversary but, unlike more traditional types of weapon systems, they cannot deny a potential enemy from inflicting great costs in retaliation. They have great offensive potential but little defensive potential, at least, so it has seemed until recently. The so-called Strategic Defense Initiative (SDI) may properly be seen as an attempt to redress this imbalance between offence and defence.

This paradox has been termed the 'nuclear revolution', the term being intended to convey the very radical way in which nuclear weapons have changed the system of relations, at least between those possessing them. In the language of GAME THEORY nuclear weapons have greatly increased the incentives to cooperate – to avoid a totally destructive war – but, at the same time, have increased the incentives to manipulate this threat to force the adversary to be the one to make the necessary concession. This threat manipulation is elegantly analysed in such classic games as Chicken and the Prisoner's Dilemma.

The implications of the nuclear revolution have thus had profound effects upon conventional wisdom on the military instrument of FOREIGN POLICY. It has created a new interest in theories about LIMITED WAR. It has, as already noted, created a new interest in the possibilities of new defensive TECHNOLOGIES and systems. It has created a new interest and concern in the potentialities of surprise attack or FIRST STRIKE. Finally, it has created a new concern and impetus towards ARMS CONTROL and DISARMAMENT.

In terms of the long history of INTERNATIONAL POLITICS, therefore, nuclear weapons have profoundly altered the costs and benefits which, rationally considered, states could expect to gain or sustain from the use of FORCE. Moreover, in the language of POWER analysis they appear not to be very fungible. That is to say, states possessing them seem to have difficulty in making their nuclear CAPABILITIES freely available to support and sustain foreign policies in areas other than those most obviously governed by nuclear DIPLOMACY. It would appear to be the ultimate paradox of nuclear weapons that they confer great potential or putative power but little effective or usable power beyond the deterrent relationship already identified. Attempts to realize the potential of nuclear weapons are often referred to as 'conventionalization', that is, the attempt to think of these weapons in terms of familiar traditional canons of strategy that would have been used prior to HIROSHIMA. In short, to deny or overcome what was earlier called the nuclear revolution. This tendency has been evident at various stages in the COLD WAR from both the SUPERPOWERS. For instance, in the United States much thought has gone into devising options for the use of nuclear weapons that might seem to avoid the 'suicide or surrender' alternatives. This strategy is often referred to as COUNTERVAILING.

## Nuclear winter

As the term implies, the nuclear winter thesis postulates that a significant and potentially catastrophic change in the climate of the earth would follow upon a large scale nuclear exchange, particularly if that exchange was in a countervalue rather than COUNTERFORCE target mode. The argument runs that the smoke and dust raised into the atmosphere by a series of nuclear explosions would obliterate the sun's rays and cause a lowering of the surface temperature of the Earth. This additional climatological factor would compound the effects of NUCLEAR WAR that are already known and accepted. If the thesis is at all tenable – and there is clearly no acceptable way of reality testing it – then a nuclear war would be an even greater disaster for the planet than had previously been supposed. The thesis depends upon a simultaneous, rather than sequential, triggering of the major arsenals of the nuclear STATES. The thesis also rests upon a 'threshold' concept – above the threshold serious climatic consequences occur; below the threshold they do not. This threshold idea is one of the more controversial aspects of the thesis, not least because the threshold is an imprecise and variable concept. Notwithstanding this imprecision, the threshold ideas suggest the conclusion that pre-emptive FIRST STRIKE upon an adversary's forces that crosses the threshold would have the paradoxical effect that, via the nuclear winter, the attacker would suffer along with the victim; in short that the effects of nuclear war are indivisible.

It should be understood that the theory of the nuclear winter is not an established and tested scientific fact but rather a series of hypotheses which have been derived from research on such things as volcanic activity and the effects of large-scale conventional bombing on cities. The likelihood of the nuclear winter outcome depends upon such variables as the types of targets, yield of the weapons, number of weapons used simultaneously, and even the time of the year when the attack occurs. Thus a no-cities targeting strategy that uses accurate, low-yield weapons might be more benign. Similarly, heavy rainfall might reduce the dust and smoke in the atmosphere, even if it can do little to 'cleanse' in other ways.

It is clear that the theory of the nuclear winter is not without controversy. As with so many ideas, proponents of particular positions tend to take what they want from the structure of the arguments and leave the rest. Thus the theory can be used to argue against DETERRENCE, in respect of NUCLEAR WEAPONS. It can be used to argue for significant arms reductions and a policy of minimum deterrence; that deterrence using nuclear threats is enhanced; that strategies involving nuclear BRINKMANSHIP and risk manipulation are still feasible.

# O

## OAPEC

*See*: OPEC

## OAS

The Organization of American States was formed in April 1948 when twenty-one founding states established the Organization by signing its Charter at a conference in Bogota. The founding members were: Argentina, Bolivia, Brazil, Chile, Colombia, Costa Rica, Cuba, the Dominican Republic, Ecuador, El Salvador, Guatemala, Haiti, Honduras, Mexico, Nicaragua, Panama, Paraguay, Peru, the United States, Uruguay and Venezuela. Following the REVOLUTION, Cuban membership was suspended. The OAS is a typical intergovernmental organization (IGO) with a small permanent Secretariat and a SECRETARY-GENERAL elected by the General Assembly for a five-year term.

The Bogota Pact attempted to stipulate some ground rules for the future conduct of inter-American relations, most notably in its 15th and 16th Articles which explicitly prohibit external intervention in the affairs of member states as well as the use of economic and political COERCION. These constraints were specifically aimed at the United States which had developed INTERVENTIONIST inclinations – particularly in Central America – since 1898. The idea that the Americas were an area of special interest and attention for the United States went back to the MONROE DOCTRINE and the somewhat vague REGIONALISM known as Pan-Americanism. There is no doubt that under the surface of inter-American unity a significant bifurcation exists between the United States and the other state members of the Organization. The United States has tended to see the OAS as a means for collectively legitimizing US policy in the region, while the Latin states have seen it as a means of restricting and restraining US interventionist tendencies by obtaining their adherence to the code of conduct in the Charter.

The advent of the COLD WAR after 1945 and the clear emergence of the United States as the one unequivocal SUPERPOWER in the system were important situational factors which inhibited rather than enhanced the chances of the OAS working as its Charter intended. US interventionism could now be justified in terms of the global IDEOLOGICAL struggle with international COMMUNISM and the emergence of a revolutionary REGIME in Cuba after 1959 simply confirmed this PERCEPTION. The United States has saved its most contentious interventions for Central America: notably the CIA-inspired toppling of Arbenz in 1954 and the Dominican Republic operation of 1965.

In retrospect Dominica proved to be a watershed as far as the OAS was concerned. Diplomatically the United States now finds itself in a minority or in isolation on key issue areas involving the letter and spirit of Articles 15 and 16. Thus during the FALKLANDS/Malvinas crisis of 1982, the majority of OAS members supported the Argentinian position. The following year, the Organization refused to support the Grenada operation launched by the Reagan

291

administration. Increasingly in recent years the Organization has turned to FUNC- TIONALISM and to encouraging regional co- operation between member states.

## OEEC

The Organization for European Economic Cooperation (1948–61). This regional in- ternational institution was established on 16 April 1948 when the Convention for European Economic Cooperation was signed by the foreign ministers of sixteen states. The original members were: Austria, Belgium, Denmark, France, Greece, Ice- land, Ireland, Italy, Luxembourg, the Netherlands, Norway, Portugal, Sweden, Switzerland, Turkey and the United King- dom. West Germany and Spain acceded to the Convention in 1949 and 1959, respec- tively. The United States and Canada be- came associate members in 1950.

The OEEC was the institutional expres- sion of the MARSHALL PLAN or European Recovery Programme. The Truman Ad- ministration had stipulated that US aid un- der this scheme would be conditional upon suitable multilateral coordination being evinced by European STATES and peoples. The existing United Nations Economic Commission for Europe was ignored in the process. The US LEADERSHIP had also ex- pressed the hope that the Plan would act as a catalyst for closer European cooperation and even INTEGRATION. In summary, there- fore, the OEEC may be said to have had two broad functions: the implementation of the ERP through the years 1948–52 and the IMPLEMENTATION of agreed schemes for freeing European TRADE and establish- ing closer coordination, leading to actual integration.

The principle DECISION-MAKING organ within the OEEC was the Council on which all member states had equal representation and equal voting rights. All obligatory deci- sions required UNANIMITY. Under the broad aegis of the Council there was a series of Committees, headed by the Execu-

tive Committee. The organization was staffed by an internationally recruited sec- retariat, headed by a SECRETARY-GENERAL.

Given its area of discretion, the OEEC was more successful in implementing the task of superintending the ERP than in furthering integration. A major ideological division became evident from the earliest days of the OEEC between the UK position on integration and that of France. The British decision to remain outside the Euro- pean Coal and Steel Community (ECSC) and to absent itself from the discussions on the formation of an EEC was substantive evidence of this division. Indeed the forma- tion of the EEC in January 1958 drew the OEEC into a series of abortive discussions in the so-called 'Maudling Committee'. These meetings, at the behest of the United Kingdom, explored the possibility of a FREE TRADE AREA in industrial goods.

The division within the OEEC member- ship between the six states in the EEC and the eleven outside meant that the Organiza- tion had contradicted its basic rationale. In January 1960 it was agreed that the origi- nal Convention had to be revised and after a period of consultation a new Convention was agreed at the end of 1960 establishing the ORGANIZATION FOR ECONOMIC CO- OPERATION AND DEVELOPMENT (OECD) which came into being on 30 September 1961.

## Oil companies

The paradigm example of a primary in- dustry multinational corporation (MNC) for many members of both informed and mass publics is the TRANSNATIONAL oil com- pany. The mid-twentieth century corporate structure of the oil company was first de- veloped in the United States in the last two decades of the nineteenth century and the first decade of the twentieth. Oil companies are vertically integrated economic ACTORS specifically and essentially involved in three activities: exploration for and production of crude oil, transportation and refining of the same and, finally, marketing of finished oil products. In the past this has resulted in great structural power accruing to the companies and enhancement of this position was possible by individual companies co-operating to maintain their market position. Consequently, free market principles have never really applied in this industry and instead oligopoly has been the typical and accepted structure.

Oil companies are divided into three groups: majors, independents and nationals. The majors are, as the term suggests, the biggest. Seven corporations are always included in this category: Standard Oil of New Jersey, Standard Oil California, Texaco, Gulf, Mobil, Royal Dutch/Shell and British Petroleum. The French CFP (*Compagnie Française des Petroles*) is also sometimes included in this grouping. The independents are the late entrants, smaller, privately owned companies such as Amoco or Occidental without the same extensive vertical integration outlined above.

The ability and willingness of these independents to employ 'spoiling' tactics by offering host states more favourable terms than the majors was to prove a crucial variable in breaking the POWER of the latter to control the market after 1970. As a result when the OPEC challenge was made to wrest control from the majors the presence of the independents assisted OPEC and weakened the 'seven sisters'.

The final group of companies, the nationals, are as the term suggests those state-owned enterprises established by NATIONALIZATION and EXPROPRIATION. Examples here would be Kuwait Petroleum Company, Petrobras of Brazil or Petroleos de Venezuela. Nationalization of foreign-owned oil assets was first attempted in Mexico before the Second World War. The most celebrated pre-OPEC instance after 1945 was the Iranian nationalization of UK assets in 1951. Expropriation is now accepted as an effective and legitimate method for increasing local and national participation while reducing or at least curbing the

putative power of the majors and independents.

The structure of power in the oil industry is now TRIPOLAR. The majors are no longer able to set production and pricing targets as in the past. The independents are increasingly important, particularly in so-called 'downstream' operations. The nationals represent a resurgence of STATE-CENTRED attitudes and a desire to counterbalance the archetypical MNC represented by the 'sisters'.

## Oil shocks

A convenient shorthand term for a number of significant changes in the supply, and therefore the price, of oil. The first shock occurred in 1973/4 when, as a result of OPEC/OAPEC action, price increases and supply interruptions were coordinated. The second shock emanated from the Iranian revolution of 1979. OPEC was able to seize this opportunity to substantially raise prices over the period 1979–81. The third shock followed the abandonment by Saudi Arabia of its role of 'swing producer' within the cartel in 1985. The OPEC gains of 1979–81 were expunged and for a brief period the price plunged to 1974 levels (which in real terms meant that it fell even lower). Some modest price restoration since the third shock is latterly apparent.

In all instances adaptive behaviour by other members of the oil REGIME followed in the wake of each shock. The two price rises have encouraged exploration and development of non-OPEC reserves and the search for alternative energy sources. The events of the first shock also produced significant institution building, notably among the advanced industrial countries (AICs) through the formation of the OECD-sponsored International Energy Agency (IEA). The price fall after 1985 confirmed the trend away from OPEC manipulation towards a more MIXED ACTOR situation. These reductions were welcomed for their deflationary effects among consumers, while the producers hardest hit were those with large and growing populations. Their per capita incomes were reduced accordingly.

It would be unwise to be too sanguine about the future. Further shocks – whether deliberately manipulated or accidental – cannot be ruled out. Oil will continue to play an important role in the global political economy for the future. The reserve position still favours OPEC. The world's major reserves are situated in the Middle East which continues to evince political instability. At the same time these reserves are not situated close to the main areas of economic activity. Transportation of oil will also continue to be a major potential political and ecological hazard. The experience of the three extant shocks is a reminder of how relative political outcomes can be – one person's shock is another's opportunity.

## OPEC

An acronym for the Organization of Petroleum Exporting Countries. OPEC was established in 1960 by five STATES: Iran, Iraq, Kuwait, Saudi Arabia and Venezuela. It is an intergovernmental organization (IGO) with a small headquarters staff in Vienna headed by a SECRETARY-GENERAL. In economic terms its intention was to establish a cartel arrangement between the commodity producers in the oil industry to maintain a price structure that would reflect the perceived interests of its member states, rather than the OIL COMPANIES which had set prices and production levels hitherto.

OPEC was established at a time when the BALANCE OF POWER within the oil industry preponderantly favoured the consumers. The unilateral initiative by the Iranians to nationalize UK oil interests in 1951 had failed. During the Suez crisis of 1956–7 an attempt at concerted action to use the 'oil weapon' against the West had been foiled by the oil companies and their home governments. Rationing oil and bringing supplies in from the Americas had diffused the situation. In real terms, oil prices were declining throughout the 1950s. Economic recovery, rapidly under way in Western Europe and Japan, was considerably assisted by this cheap, non-renewable energy source.

In 1968 the OPEC issued their 'Declaratory Statement on Petroleum Policy' which identified two ISSUE AREAS between themselves and the oil companies. First, OPEC wanted more control over pricing policy. The membership rejected the role of price-taker in favour of that of price-maker. Secondly, OPEC rejected the existing participation agreements. The traditional role of the host states, as tax collectors in respect of their oil concessions with the companies, no longer sufficed. In the same year that OPEC issued their declaration of intent. three conservative Arab states: Kuwait, Libya (prior to the revolution) and Saudi Arabia formed the Organization of Arab Petroleum Exporting Countries (OAPEC) to shadow the multi-ethnic OPEC.

Within five years from the OPEC statement and the formation of OAPEC a series of actually discrete but potentially interrelated events occurred which served to redress the bargaining power of the oil producers and the companies in favour of the states and against the majors. In chronological order rather than order of significance, these events were as follows.

1. The revolution of September 1969 in Libya which replaced the conservative monarchy with a Revolutionary Command Council.

2. The radicalization of OAPEC following the Libyan changes and the admissions of Algeria and Iraq.

3. The increasing dependence of the advanced industrial countries (AICS) as a whole and crucially the United States within that group, upon Middle Eastern oil. This meant that any significant interruption in supply and/or significant rise in prices would have a most damaging multiplier

impact upon the economies, and the polities, of these DEVELOPED STATES.

4. The increasing instability of the dollar as a reserve currency and a store of value. Oil prices are quoted in dollars and any weakening or devaluation of the dollar had an adverse effect upon the dollar export earnings of the OPEC states. The dollar devaluations of 1971 and 1973 meant that the oil producers had to raise prices simply to prevent a deterioration in their earnings.

5. A further round of international violence in the unremitting ARAB–ISRAELI CONFLICT signified another attempt by the Arab states through OAPEC to use the oil weapon against those among the AICs perceived to be sympathetic towards the Israeli position. This led to an EMBARGO being instituted against the West which had some effect in producing a more sympathetic attitude towards the Arab position in general and the Palestinian position in particular. It is important to remember that, although the embargo occurred at the same time as the OPEC initiative on prices (which is discussed below), from a causal perspective the two events can and should be kept separate.

OPEC's move into the centre ground as the price-maker for crude oil came in two stages. Following a successful Libyan initiative in the autumn of 1970, OPEC as a group negotiated increases with the companies at Teheran during the early months of 1971. Further increases, necessitated by the falling value of the dollar, were negotiated at Geneva a year later. Agreement was reached later that year on the question of participation which had not been covered in the talks at Tripoli, Teheran and Geneva. It was anticipated that majority participation by the host states would be achieved by 1982. Although it was not clear at the time, this agreement was the end of the first stage of OPEC's assumption of the price-maker's role. Thereafter price increases would be imposed *unilaterally* by the OPEC membership rather than bilaterally via negotiations.

Approaching the watershed events of 1973–4, OPEC had increased its membership from the founding five to include Abu Dhabi, Algeria, Dubai, Ecuador, Gabon, Indonesia, Libya, Nigeria, Qatar and Sharjah. (Abu Dhabi, Dubai and Sharjah later became the United Arab Emirates (UAE)). Within the OPEC membership two state oil-producer profiles may be discerned. First, there are those states with large oil reserves and small populations who can afford to adjust their production downwards if required without experiencing significant and unpleasant domestic consequences. Typical of this category are Saudi Arabia – often referred to as the 'swing producer' – Kuwait and the UAE. Secondly, there are those states such as Algeria, Iran, Iraq and Nigeria with high populations, smaller reserves per capita, and a vested interest in maximizing their production.

In October 1973 OPEC acted for the first time to raise oil prices unilaterally. A second rise was announced in December to take effect from January 1974. The domination of the Western-based oil companies and the era of cheap non-renewable energy based upon this industry was ended in less than twelve weeks. Equally rapid and sweeping changes were effected on the issue of participation. Nationalization and EXPROPRIATION measures have been used, not in pursuit of some collectivist commitment to socialism but rather as an expression of NATIONALISM. National-owned oil companies now play an important role in the industry as a result.

The four-fold increase in oil prices to more than eleven dollars per barrel as of January 1974 is often referred to as the first OIL SHOCK experienced by the world system during the 1970s. Reactions to these events were vigorous. The NORTH–SOUTH dichotomy can conveniently be used to identify these repercussions.

Among the Northern states, the United States took the initiative in re-tabling a proposal that those states in the OECD should act in concert to confront the producers' cartel with a countervailing consumers group. These ideas were subsequently to culminate in the establishment of the International Energy Agency (IEA). Although this IGO is not exclusively concerned with petroleum, this is indubitably its original rationale and main function. Indeed, other energy sources are seen as means for reducing dependency upon oil and oil products. Japan and the leading Western European AICs (except France) subsequently succeeded in modifying the confrontational IMAGE of the IEA and directing it towards a more cooperative PERCEPTION of its relations with OPEC.

The greatest economic damage from the OPEC initiative on prices was felt by the oil-importing Third World. These states did not have the CAPABILITY to cushion the fall-out or make adjustments in the way of the AICs. These were long-term effects, however, and immediately OPEC seemed to the rest of the Third World like nemesis. Other commodity producers were encouraged to look towards the OPEC experience and form their own producer cartels. To date none have achieved the successes enjoyed by OPEC in the 1970s.

OPEC also encouraged the Third World to go onto the offensive in the UNITED NATIONS by presenting a whole raft of proposals and initiatives under the rubric of the NEW INTERNATIONAL ECONOMIC ORDER (NIEO). The 1970s was officially stipulated the Second UN Development Decade and many of the ideas presented under the NIEO were familiar from the first decade and the early debates within the United Nations Conference of Trade and Development (UNCTAD) in the 1960s. It would be a mistake to attribute too much weight causally to OPEC in these matters. The demand for fundamental restructuring of the world political economy had a much longer and more diverse pedigree. What OPEC did give the Third World's leaders was a new sense of confidence in themselves and the rectitude of many of their arguments. It should be noted also that some of the leading members of the Third World movement – such as Algeria – were also influential in OPEC.

Oil prices continued to rise throughout the 1970s and then after the second oil shock they peaked during the winter of 1980–1 at three times their January 1974 level. Subsequently the price has fallen steadily towards the marker put down by OPEC after their second unilateral move. Statistically the period 1970–90 looks like a classic cyclical pattern. The rising price throughout the first part of the cycle encouraged the exploration and development of marginal oil producing areas – such as the North Sea – and the content of non-OPEC oil now traded by the industry has increased accordingly. Collateral effects have been to increase interest in energy saving and alternatives to oil as an energy source. As a result OPEC's share in the industry has been almost halved since 1973–4.

The world's oil industry is entering the last decade of the century evincing many characteristics of a MIXED ACTOR MODEL. There are a number of key ACTORS but none can individually restore stability. Cooperation depends essentially upon an agreement about ground rules and if parties are pursuing mutually exclusive goals this may be impossible. OPEC's relative importance has slipped from what now looks like the peak of the mid-1970s, yet no other group exists to replace it. On the company structure, nationals now account for three-quarters of all production, replacing the pre-OPEC domination of the majors. Centrifugal tendencies would seem to be ascendent at least for the present.

## Open door

Used in a general sense it refers to policies that favour the encouragement of FREE TRADE. More specifically, the Open Door doctrine refers to a series of notes issued by US Secretary of State John Hay in 1899 and 1900 which invited various governments to adhere to the principle of equal economic opportunity in China. The notes stated that while the United States recognized the existence of SPHERES OF INFLUENCE in China, it did not accept that this should lead to a discrimination against US interests in respect of railway tariffs, harbour dues and other commercial matters. This policy was supported by the Committee on American Interests in China, an influential lobby of business interests which was based on the claim that the United States was disadvantaged in Chinese markets by the spheres of influence system.

This policy, while overtly anti-imperialist and pro FREE TRADE, actually signalled a new US intention to play a positive role in mainland Asia. The acquisition of the Philippines following the United States' victory over Spain in 1898 was a watershed in this process. The Open Door principle thus provided the rationale for US interests in the area and indicated a new role for rapidly developing US naval power. US military participation in the international expedition that retook Peking from Chinese revolutionary and anti-foreign forces – known as 'Boxers' – in 1900 confirmed that US interests would be advanced or protected by the use of FORCE if necessary.

The United States' emergence as an ACTOR in Asian affairs dates from this period. Theodore Roosevelt's reference to the REGION as 'America's Achilles heel' is indicative of the changing ideological framework which influenced the Open Door DIPLOMACY. The strategic and economic lure of China remained an important element in this PERCEPTION throughout the century and helps to explain the perceived 'loss' of China after 1949.

## Operational environment

A term used in FOREIGN POLICY analysis. 'Milieu' is sometimes substituted for 'environment' in this usage. The essence of the concept is that a distinction can be made between the perceptual world of the DECISION-MAKER and the unperceived context within which these essentially psychological processes take place. This latter contextual factor is what is meant by the term operational environment/milieu. The term psychological environment is reserved for the former and the symmetry is thus complete.

The idea of the operational environment was introduced into the literature by the US political geographers Harold and Margaret Sprout. In their 1956 essay, and later in their 1965 book, the idea formed part of an extended discussion of environmental factors in both geography and WORLD POLITICS. The UK academic Frankel (1963) incorporated it into his analytical text, while Brecher (1972) used the distinction in his 1970s study of foreign POLICY-MAKING in Israel.

The operational environment can best be seen as a constraint or limitation upon what the policy-makers can or cannot achieve. Although it is not perceived as relevant at the time of decision, at the implementation stage its impact will be felt. If the operational environment then begins to spill into the psychological via the process of FEEDBACK, adaptive behaviour by the DECISION-MAKING system should be possible. Adjustment and correction can be made and a closer correlation between the two milieu should be achieved. Conversely continued lack of congruence between the two environments leads to MISPERCEPTION.

## Orbiters

HUMAN RIGHTS jargon for REFUGEES unable to find a STATE willing to accept them. The United Nations High Commission for Refugees (UNHCR) reported an upsurge of refugees seeking POLITICAL ASYLUM in the late 1980s, particularly among Eritreans, Somalis, Sri Lankans, Kurds, Iraqis and Iranians. Many are held by local immigration authorities and subsequently sent back to their last place of call or put on onward flights to other destinations. Under the terms of its remit UNHCR can award 'mandated' status to such refugees and assume responsibility for resettlement, but in practice this has proved difficult to enforce.

Efforts to nominate Austria (because of its traditional hospitality and geographical location) as a central pooling point for orbiting refugees has so far failed since UNHCR cannot obtain the necessary international guarantees that the Austrian government demands. The term was first used in connection with the expulsion of 50,000 Ugandan Asians in 1972, but in that case the United Kingdom was ultimately responsible for resettlement. The problem became acute when immigration quotas and movement restrictions began to tighten up on a world-wide basis.

### Organization for Economic Cooperation and Development (OECD)

The OECD grew out of the OEEC. Both the membership and the tasks of the new body were expanded in the process. The OECD includes three significant economic ACTORS excluded from the OEEC: the United States, Japan and Canada. The functions covered by the intergovernmental organization (IGO) were similarly expanded. Development was stipulated at the outset as a central concern of the new organization. Since its inception in 1961 further task expansion into more specific issue areas such as multinational companies (MNCS), TECHNOLOGY TRANSFER and relations with groups such as OPEC have been taken on.

The OECD was established by a convention signed by twenty states in Paris on 14 December 1960. The original signatories were: Austria, Belgium, Canada, Denmark, France, Germany (Federal Republic), Greece, Iceland, Ireland, Italy, Luxembourg, the Netherlands, Norway, Portugal, Spain, Sweden, Switzerland, Turkey, the United Kingdom and the United States. Japan joined the organization in 1964. Currently the membership includes, in addition to the above, Australia, Finland and New Zealand.

Unlike the EUROPEAN COMMUNITY, the OECD was intended to be and remains an INTERNATIONAL rather than SUPRANATIONAL organization. Provision for binding DECISION-MAKING is extremely hedged about and in reality OECD makes recommendations to its members. Article 6 of the Convention of voting can only be interpreted as a restatement of the UNANIMITY principle, albeit *sotto voce*. The Organization has a small permanent secretariat headed by a SECRETARY-GENERAL whose powers are stipulated under Articles 10 and 11.

In terms of its economic principles, the OECD may be said to broadly reflect the ideas associated with the term ECONOMIC LIBERALISM of the compensatory, reform or Keynesian kind. Its clear commitment in the Paris convention to such goals as economic growth, trade liberalization and development show this. As such it stands in opposition to NEO-MERCANTILISM and PROTECTIONISM. Its expansion to include Japan in 1964 meant that all the most significant advanced industrial countries (AICS) were among its members. The admission of Australia and New Zealand has neatly rounded this off.

Internally the OECD works to assist its member states to coordinate their policies to achieve the goals set out above. It is an invaluable source of economic and statistical information for its members and ATTENTIVE PUBLICS. It works efficiently at the TRANSGOVERNMENTAL level where high officials seek HARMONIZATION of policy. All this presupposes a commonality of interest, of course, but it was suggested above that such a broad ideological consensus could be discerned within the Organization.

The formal equality of its members is somewhat contradicted by the existence of the so-called Group of Seven (or G7) states. These are: Canada, the United States, the United Kingdom, France, Germany, Italy and Japan. The political ELITES of these STATES meet periodically under the auspices of the OECD in what are popularly referred to as 'economic summits'. Although substantive issues of political economy are covered at these meetings, topics such as TERRORISM have also concerned the leaders.

Externally, the OECD states represent a powerful interest group in global bargaining. It was felt quite appropriate, therefore, that when the perceived OPEC challenge was made the OECD members should co-ordinate their energy policies through the International Energy Agency (IEA). In MACROPOLITICAL terms this might be seen as an attempt at the restoration of HEGEMONY. Certainly with the NORTH–SOUTH dichotomy in mind, the strategy was consistent with the need to confront Southern solidarity with an equally united front. Currently the Organization is showing great interest in the newly industrialized countries (NICS) and other middle income economies (referred to within the Organization as 'Major Developing Economies'). Again the ideological link with economic liberalism is apparent. These states represent the anticipated embourgeoisement of the THIRD WORLD. Membership of the OECD for selected major developing economies (MDEs) in the future cannot be ruled out.

## Orientation

Part of the vocabulary of FOREIGN POLICY analysis, orientation is used in INTERNATIONAL POLITICS to describe and explain in the broadest terms how and why POLICY-MAKERS approach issues in the external environment. An orientation may be viewed as a frame of reference or paradigm which exerts a broad directional influence upon policy. This INFLUENCE is generalized rather than specific and, accordingly, it may be difficult to extrapolate a STATE's orientation from a specific policy decision. Occasions will arise when an issue is seen as a watershed, of course, and in these circumstances policy will be made with clear implications for the orientation. Thus the United Kingdom's decision to seek full membership of the EUROPEAN COMMUNITY, first announced in the summer of 1961, implied a change in orientation away from the relationship with the United States and with

the COMMONWEALTH towards its neighbours in Europe. Similarly, US membership of NATO after 1949 represented an orientation towards membership of an extra-hemispheric ALLIANCE which remained a US commitment for decades afterwards.

K. J. Holsti (1983) uses the idea of orientation as an explanatory variable in his standard text. He suggests that there are 'at least' three orientations: ISOLATIONISM, NON-ALIGNMENT, coalition making and alliance construction. Holsti's triad is extremely broad and the categories are not mutually exclusive. However, his subsequent discussion tends to substantiate the idea suggested above that orientation may be seen as a portmanteau, frame of reference term.

Orientations are important for DIPLOMATS and statesmen as well as for scholars. Practitioners tend to use them to establish a tradition with the past, or as a point of reference for the future. A particular political LEADERSHIP can be expected to imbibe these ideas as part of the socialization process and they may be invoked at times of perceived CRISIS when a state's fundamental goals and prevailing orientations will be challenged or confirmed.

## Ostpolitik

This term refers to the series of policy initiatives taken by the Federal Republic of Germany (FRG) in the late 1960s and early 1970s to achieve greater normalization in its relations with the Soviet Union, Poland and Czechoslovakia and the German Democratic Republic (GDR). The policy is particularly associated with the name of Willy Brandt who, first as Foreign Secretary under Chancellor Kiesinger, and later as Chancellor himself, took this policy through to fruition in a series of BILATERAL agreements between 1970 and 1973. Ostpolitik replaced the HALLSTEIN DOCTRINE developed under Chancellor Konrad Adenauer. It accepted the implications of the post-war distribution of POWER in Europe, including the existence of two German states. It took the issue of the reunification of the two Germanies off the immediate political agenda and it accepted the post-war frontiers with Poland and Czechoslovakia. Ostpolitik represented a significant shift in the ORIENTATION of the FRG towards Eastern Europe. It was also important in making a contribution towards the DETENTE policy between the US-led Western BLOC and the Soviet-led Eastern bloc. In particular, the CONFERENCE ON SECURITY AND CO-OPERATION IN EUROPE (CSCE) – and the mutual force reduction talks – MBFR – are important dimensions of European detente. Agreement on the status of BERLIN was a substantial achievement of the period that witnessed the Ostpolitik. The upheavals of 1989 in East Germany, especially the dramatic opening of the Berlin Wall on 9 November has led to a reawakening of the debate on the status of the two Germanies and consequently of Berlin. The call for the unification of Germany, possibly to its 1937 territorial boundaries, is now firmly at the top of the new European agenda. If this comes about Ostpolitik will take on an entirely new meaning.

*See also*: YALTA

## Outer Space Treaty

Signed in 1967. Its full title is the Treaty on Principles Governing the Activities of States in the Exploration and Use of Outer Space, including the Moon and Other Celestial Bodies. The main provisions of the Treaty are that the contracting STATES agree not to place weapons of mass destruction, such as NUCLEAR WEAPONS, in space or on celestial bodies. It also envisages that the exploration and utilization of this environment should be for peaceful purposes. Some ninety states have signed the TREATY since it was opened for signature on 27 January, 1967. There are no provisions in the Treaty

for institutional VERIFICATION that the provisions are being respected, nor is there any machinery for the ADJUDICATION of disputes between the parties. The latter can repudiate the Treaty after twelve months' notice.

Since the inception of the Outer Space Treaty, the environment of space has become increasingly important for security purposes. The use of earth satellites for INTELLIGENCE gathering and the development of anti-satellites or anti-satellite (ASAT) weapons as a counter-measure is one indication. Another is the renewed interest in BALLISTIC MISSILE DEFENCE (BMD). With regard to this innovation, it is clear that at some stage in the testing and installation of a BMD, the spirit, if not the letter, of the Outer Space Treaty would be broken.

## Overkill

A term used with reference to the destructive capacity of NUCLEAR WEAPONS. Specifically, it refers to the ability to destroy one's opponent more than once. The term is imprecise and often used in a polemical sense to suggest that a halt to the manufacture and installation of weapons is long overdue. Such a position implies acceptance of the strategy of minimum DETERRENCE espoused by the French and UK delivery systems, unless the advocate rejects nuclear deterrence totally as an instrument of policy.

Overkill is imprecise because it fails to take account of targeting and operational planning requirements. It also ignores the relatives in the nuclear relationship. With the latter in mind 'mutual overkill' might be a better expression to use. Recently a new dimension has been added to overkill-type arguments against nuclear weapons with the NUCLEAR WINTER idea. Both terms imply that there is a threshold beyond which the stockpiling and projected use of nuclear weapons give diminishing returns.

# P

## Pacifism

This refers to the bundle or mosaic of attitudes, ideas and opinions concerning the indictment of WAR and the use of violence or physical FORCE on human beings. It is not a coherent political IDEOLOGY or doctrine. Rather, two distinct but related meanings can be identified: (a) the 'absolutist' notion which rejects war and the use of physical violence under all circumstances as a means of settling conflicts; (b) the 'relativist' notion which is more discriminating and specific in its rejection of violence. It was, for example, in the second sense that International Socialists rejected the First World War but participated in the Second. Pacifism, in both its uses, is associated with non-violent resistance as a means of implementing its aims. However, in the absolutist use non-violence is a matter of principle in all circumstances. In the relativist use it is not regarded as immutable. Again the absolutist will regard the opponent with respect, good will and even love; the relativist, on the other hand, may be indifferent or even hostile. We may note that pacifism, in both senses, has been embedded in international thought since earliest times.

In ancient China the writings of Lao-Tzu and Confucius are said to belong to this tradition and in the western world, Judaism and Christianity, on some interpretations, question the validity of the need for violence and warfare. The Christian pacifist tradition is somewhat controversial and most commentators agree that by the fourth century the early absolutist strain of pacifism which forbade Christians joining the Roman Army began to die out. In the Middle Ages, the doctrine of the JUST WAR, while retaining some pacifist elements, saw the religious or spiritual aspect move from the personal to the public domain.

In the modern world, from the seventeenth century onwards, it became particularly associated with the Society of Friends or QUAKERS which established, in line with these ideas, a disarmed colony in Pennsylvania. However, it was in the nineteenth and twentieth centuries that pacifist ideas began to spread widely, partly because of the new practice of conscription into national ARMIES. During the period when STATES employed small professional military forces it was relatively easy for pacifists to avoid compromising their beliefs, but with the development of mass armies from the Napoleonic Wars onwards, pacifism and conscientious objection became a persistent response to conscription and an important feature of contemporary political discourse. Most pacifists since have shown a willingness to cooperate with the authorities to the extent of fulfilling non-combatant duties within the armed services, or taking positions in civilian life vacated by conscripts.

The impact of the twentieth century on pacifism has been profound. As noted earlier, the First World War was attacked by many International Socialists using MARXIST/LENINIST ideas about the connection between capitalism and war. Their refusal to participate in it marks their protest as being within the pacifist tradition, although in other respects this group was, and still is, highly selective in its approach to non-violence.

In the aftermath of the First World War, the development of INTERNATIONAL INSTITUTIONS dedicated to the search for non-violent solutions to conflict and the encouragement given to moves towards DISARMAMENT have a family resemblance to pacifism. This period saw pacifism at its height. For example, the so-called 'Oxford Oath' when thousands pledged never to fight for King and Country was its greatest public success. One of the criticisms of the pacifist movement made later by writers in the REALIST tradition was that by promulgating these ideas, especially in the United Kingdom and the United States, conditions of military and psychological unpreparedness were developed which served to encourage Germany, Italy and Japan to pursue policies of aggrandizement and conquest. The movement was attacked on the grounds that, as it was blind to the ubiquity of evil and POWER POLITICS, it served to foster illiberalism and tyranny (*see:* Reinhold Niebuhr, 1940).

Perhaps the most eminent twentieth century pacifist was Mohandas K. Ghandi (1869–1948). Although Ghandi supported the United Kingdom in the First World War on the grounds that this might accelerate Indian independence, failure to achieve this led him to organize the Satyagraha (truth-force) campaigns of non-violent resistance to continued UK rule. Between 1919 and 1947 under Ghandi's leadership the Satyagraha captured the world's imagination and demonstrated that pacifist ideas were not confined to matters of individual conscience but could be successfully organized at the level of group relations. Under Ghandi, non-violent resistance and mass civil disobedience became powerful tools for the conventionally powerless in their quest to change the prevailing order. His success in gaining Indian independence in 1947 led to a re-appraisal of the techniques of non-violence and a stress on planning, organization and discipline, all of which Ghandi possessed to a high degree. It was Ghandi, more than anyone, who demonstrated how civil disobedience could be utilized by the dispossessed and disaffected as an effective sanction. In so doing it became an instrument of mass political protest and direct action.

The heirs to this tradition can be identified in mass political and social protest movements in both the West and the East. Thus the American civil rights movement under Martin Luther King and the African National Congress (ANC) movement in South Africa in the 1950s owned a direct and acknowledged debt to Ghandi. The Solidarity movement in contemporary Poland shows that even in non-democratic states, the techniques of civil disobedience and non-violent direct action can have significant results.

The advent of NUCLEAR WEAPONS in 1945 and the new era of potential NUCLEAR WAR has not surprisingly evoked a strong response. Pacifists of both the absolutist and the relativist varieties have united to oppose these developments and to propose alternatives to the nuclear STATUS QUO. As a result they have become part of the peace movement, that loose confederation of interests which seeks radical change in INTERNATIONAL POLITICS. The first concern of these 'nuclear pacifists' has been to halt the ARMS RACE.

Some have suggested that this can be assisted by states acting in a unilateral way – for example by UNILATERAL DISARMAMENT – others have stressed BILATERAL and MULTILATERAL measures. Many see the first as a step towards the second, in any event. Secondly, pacifists have sought to reduce international tensions and to encourage structures and processes that would improve international cooperation. Thirdly, they have been prominent in the encouragement of more academically orientated studies of how to encourage strategies for PEACE rather than war. The growth of peace studies and PEACE RESEARCH have resulted from this new emphasis. It should, of course, be understood that pacifists are not alone in championing some or all of the above trends.

It is clear that pacifism is not a uniform,

coherent or formal doctrine. Its origins as well as its manifestations are diverse. It has spiritual, theological, humanitarian and utilitarian aspects. In addition, it encompasses refusal to countenance all forms of violence, civil disobedience, peace movements, nuclear disarmament, strikes, BOYCOTTS and a wide variety of alternative schemes for replacing FORCE as an arbitrator of INTERNATIONAL RELATIONS. Despite this eclecticism, pacifism is a vital feature of contemporary WORLD POLITICS and is likely to continue to be relevant in the future.

## Pacta sunt servanda

Probably the oldest principle in international law this asserts that TREATIES are binding on the parties to them and must be executed in good faith. This proposition is often regarded as the basic and validating norm of the international legal REGIME and it is not difficult to see why. Without a minimal belief that agreements will be carried out the very existence of communal law is placed in doubt. The principle asserts that a STATE cannot release itself from treaty obligations at will: if this was so the already fragile structure of INTERNATIONAL LAW would all but disintegrate. Provision is made for the termination of treaties but this itself is rule-bound. The Vienna Convention on the Law of Treaties 1969, which is the most ambitious attempt yet to codify customary treaty law, reaffirmed both the importance of the rule of *pacta sunt servanda* and the need to clarify provisions for termination. Thus Article 26 asserts: 'Every treaty in force is binding upon the parties to it and must be performed by them in good faith'. Article 42(2) of the Convention contains the proviso that: 'The termination of a treaty, its denunciation or the withdrawal of a party, may take place only as a result of the application of the provisions of the treaty or of the present Convention.' In fact, most treaties contain provisions for termination or withdrawal either by the inclusion of a time factor or else through extenuating circumstances (REBUS SIC STANTIBUS).

## Pan-nationalism

A type of NATIONALISM which is TRANS-NATIONAL in its implications. This apparent paradox arises because in pan-nationalism the idea of the 'nation' as a defined group is larger than the existing political units. In other words pan-nationalism seeks to unite a number of supposedly separate units into a greater whole. Like other varieties of nationalism, pan-nationalism uses certain cohesive factors to establish this unity. Elements such as language, religion, shared historical experience and physical contiguity, familial ties to nationalists in general, are used by pan-nationalists in the same way. For example, in the case of pan-Arabism, language binds whereas religion divides. Thus a Christian Arab can aspire to the ideal by speaking Arabic as the first language and living in the Arab lands.

Because pan-nationalism cuts across NATION-STATE boundaries it should be considered closer to ethnic nationalism. Both these types erode the STATE-CENTRICITY of the nation-state matrix. Politically pan-nationalism produces ORIENTATIONS and goal-seeking behaviour which seeks to unite disparate territories into larger communities. Sometimes pan-nationalism leads to IRREDENTISM but this is not its most usual format. It is more likely that pan-nationalism will be conducive to REGIONALISM, regional cooperation and even INTEGRATION. It can also be used as a FOREIGN POLICY instrument by individual political ELITES for expansionist or HEGEMONIAL ends. Imperial Russia was often thought of as using pan-Slavism in the nineteenth century in order to advance Russian claims to protect the Slav-speaking peoples under the aegis of the Ottomans. Finally, pan-nationalism has been linked to DECOLONIZATION in both the Arab and the African instances. Pan-Arabism and Pan-Africanism were part of the resistance movement against foreign rule which culminated in the ending of formal COLONIAL control in the twentieth century.

## Para bellum

This refers to the age-old idea that 'if you want PEACE, prepare for WAR'. The doctrine assumes that military preparedness is a prerequisite of security and stability in a hostile environment. Notwithstanding its dubious validity in the history of INTERNATIONAL POLITICS, *para bellum* has undergone a revival in strategic theory, especially in DETERRENCE and WORST-CASE scenarios. It is usually associated with REALISM, its most extreme variation being 'the best form of defence is attack'. Beloved of militarists and HAWKS throughout time.

## Paradigms

*See:* SOCIAL SCIENCE APPROACH

## Parity

Parity is equality or essential equivalence. It has two uses in WORLD POLITICS. In the context of international monetary relations it refers to the rate at which it is possible to convert a currency into gold or into a national currency, such as the dollar. Under the GOLD STANDARD parities were fixed against gold and therefore exchange rates could be calculated between national currencies, *pro rata*. Under the BRETTON WOODS system, instituted after the Second World War, parities were again fixed. This time, since the system was not a pure gold standard, they were usually quoted in dollars. The dollar parity was, of course, still quoted in gold. In effect the dollar was 'as good as gold' until the system collapsed in the 1970s.

Under the current system of floating exchange rates, parities may now be quoted in any fully convertible currency, or against a collection or 'basket' of currencies. Within important economic blocs like the EUROPEAN COMMUNITY a system of fixed parities may operate. Normally in these regional arrangements a dominant currency will be the benchmark for the rest. Fixed parity regimes are usually associated with periods of relative political and economic certainty, as, for example, under a hegemonial ACTOR system.

Parity is used in a second sense in world politics in STRATEGIC STUDIES in particular in the acquisition and control of arms. Discussions of the idea in this context lack the quantitative foundations that they have in international economics. The attempt under the SALT processes to compare dissimilar weapons systems under the aegis of 'parity' are a case in point. Allegations that such conventions were 'fatally flawed' were made as a result.

Strategic parity also depends upon a system that is BIPOLAR. Of course this bipolarity can obtain between two alliances just as well as it can between two states. Parity, however, cannot tolerate third or fourth parties of equivalent CAPABILITY acting as independent units because *ad hoc* coalition formation will demolish parity very quickly. Indeed in tripolar or multipolar worlds seeking and maintaining parity is a recipe for great instability.

The advent and spread of NUCLEAR WEAPONS would appear to have created special problems for the application of ideas about parity. The concept is wholly dependent upon relativities. Nuclear weapons, and indeed nuclear DETERRENCE, are in some respects absolutes. Their possession by states such as France does not depend upon ideas of parity for its rationale. Indeed these conceptions of minimum deterrence recognize and accept the asymmetry with more powerful nuclear states and look instead to nuclear weapons as a means of overcoming their lack of parity.

**Partial test-ban treaty**

This convention, properly known as the Treaty Banning Nuclear Weapon Tests in the Atmosphere, in Outer Space and Under Water, entered into force on 10 October 1963. Its prohibitions are clear from the full title of the agreement. It contained no provision for periodic review, unlike the Treaty on the Non-Proliferation of Nuclear Weapons (NPT). It contained no provision for INSPECTION and for this reason underground nuclear tests were specfically excluded. The TREATY contains an escape clause, moreover. After three months' due notice has been given, parties can unilaterally repudiate the convention if they feel that vital national interests are at stake.

Since the Treaty came into operation the three NUCLEAR WEAPON states that signed it, the United Kingdom, the United States and the Soviet Union, have continued to observe its prescriptions. France and China, which were not signatories, continued testing in the atmosphere. France subsequently suspended atmospheric testing in 1975, having by that time conducted over forty tests. Of the rest, over 100 non-nuclear states have signed the Treaty since it was opened for signature on 5 August 1963.

The issue of nuclear testing in the atmosphere was first raised by the Japanese Government following the US HYDROGEN BOMB test at Bikini atoll in 1954. Subsequently the question was taken up at the BANDUNG CONFERENCE of 1955 and by the UN GENERAL ASSEMBLY in its tenth session (1955–6). By 1958 the three nuclear states that were eventually to sign the Treaty had indicated their willingness to begin negotiations and, to this end, a MORATORIUM on testing was observed. This moratorium was broken by the first French test in February 1960. By the autumn of 1961 the moratorium had, in effect, broken down with the Soviet resumption of atmospheric testing. The United States resumed underground testing at the same time and then atmospheric testing in April 1962. After

one more round of testing the three states worked out an agreement in the Soviet Union in July 1962.

The Partial Test Ban Treaty significantly failed to stop VERTICAL PROLIFERATION of nuclear weapons. Indeed, by implicitly sanctioning the testing of nuclear weapons underground it encouraged the process. The main impact of the 1963 Treaty was to reduce the environmental damage caused by the debris from such testing. Additionally, it can be counted as one of the successes of the post-CUBAN MISSILE CRISIS DETENTE between the United States and the Soviet Union. The gap on the issue of inspection between the two SUPERPOWERS was never closed in 1962, although it is not accurate to suggest that the Soviet Union was opposd *per se* to inspection. A comprehensive test ban with only three inspections – which was as far as the Soviets were prepared to go – would probably not have passed the US Senate.

*See also:* COMPREHENSIVE   TEST-BAN TREATY (CTB)


**Partisan**

A partisan is an irregular soldier conducting GUERRILLA WARFARE on behalf of a REVOLUTIONARY, MARXIST/LENINIST cause. The first instance of partisan warfare occurred during the Civil War in the Soviet Union that followed the Bolshevik Revolution of 1917. Following the invasion of the Soviet Union by Germany in 1941, the call went out for the resuscitation of partisan warfare in the lands being occupied by the Wehrmacht or being threatened with invasion. In fact partisan warfare had been largely neglected since the Revolution and these operations took some time to achieve any scope or significance. As the tide of battle turned slowly in favour of the Soviets, the partisans were able to come into their own and by 1943 they were certainly holding down substantial numbers of German troops. In the final offensive against Germany on that FRONT such operations became more peripheral again.

Politically a more influential instance of partisan warfare is the Yugoslav resistance to the AXIS invasion of their territory during the same time period. Under the LEADERSHIP of Tito, the Yugoslav partisans fought off both the invading Axis and their own royalist opponents. No other STATE-based COMMUNIST party succeeded in gaining and holding power in the manner of the Yugoslav partisans. In this one instance INTERVENTION by the Soviet Union, and in particular the Red Army, was not required to achieve the revolution. The infusion of NATIONALISM with revolutionary Communism, which was a feature of the Yugoslav partisan movement, produced one of the first instances of the war of national liberation. The subsequent break with Stalin after 1948 and Yugoslavia's successful resistance to Soviet ECONOMIC SANCTIONS served to strengthen this sense of uniqueness.

Partisan tactics are generally similar to the basic principles of guerrilla warfare: avoid pitched battles, trade space for time and attack the enemy where he is weakest – for instance, his lines of supply. The existence of partisan forces in an area will deter the local population from collaborating with the enemy and, if partisans can win over the 'hearts and minds', the local population can provide additional INTELLIGENCE about enemy dispositions as well as material support for the partisans. As the case of Yugoslavia shows, the partisan forces may go even further in 'liberated' territories, actually setting up the infrastructure of political control. As the example of the Soviet Union shows, partisans can be used more simply as auxiliaries on the fringes of the regular forces. Such tactics are very much within the guerrilla warfare tradition.

**Pax Britannica**
Literally means PEACE imposed by British

dominance. Used correctly therefore it can only refer to that period in the recent past when Britain was the dominant STATE in the STATE SYSTEM. Most scholars are agreed that this domination began in the wake of the defeat of France in 1815, was at its peak in the middle decades of the nineteenth century and declined thereafter. The decline was disguised for the reason that no other state immediately emerged to replace Britain as the dominant ACTOR. Eventually, the United States did, but this occurred in the 1940s after a long period when the system lacked a dominant state.

The bases of Pax Britannica were military, economic, diplomatic and intellectual. Militarily, Britain was a naval power. The possession of huge naval forces and the concomitant insistence upon the 'two-power standard' – whereby the British navy was able to cope with the combined strength of the next two ranking powers – were the outcome. As a result of this POWER base, Britain established a vast global network of naval bases. Particularly important, in addition to the home bases, were those in the Mediterranean, in South Africa and in Singapore. Possession of such a powerful CAPABILITY was an important DETERRENT to other European powers to move into areas of perceived British interest. For example, there is no doubt that, without the British navy, the MONROE DOCTRINE would have been merely a declaratory statement of future intentions.

Economically, Pax Britannica was possible because Britain was the first STATE to adopt modern techniques of industrial production. The wealth created by this revolution enabled Britain to establish a commercial system of banking and foreign portfolio investment based upon the capital, London. A system of international TRADE and payments was thereby created in the nineteenth century, a system based upon INTERDEPENDENCE in economic relations. Intellectually this was justified by a belief in FREE TRADE and by the advocacy of

LIBERAL ideas about individualism and free enterprise. Diplomatically, the Pax Britannica was dependent upon the European BALANCE OF POWER working to prevent the rise of hegemonial challenges from the continent. To assist this Britain sought to act as the balancer in this system. Outside the European context, Britain sought to advance and protect its interests either by seeking direct control over territories or through a SPHERES OF INFLUENCE policy. Paradoxically, the European states that sought to challenge this system, France and Russia, became in time Britain's chief allies in European politics. Intellectually this system was an affront to the liberal/individualistic and democratic/nationalistic tendencies in British political life in the nineteenth century.

Like any system based upon a single dominant actor, the Pax Britannica was dependent upon Britain maintaining that position. By the end of the nineteenth century Britain's economic domination had been lost, for good, to the United States and Germany. The great financial strains placed upon the British economy by the First World War further exacerbated this decline. Britain's decline as a naval power was formally recognized by the Washington Naval Treaty of 1921. Britain's imperial system was challenged by the Boers and the Irish. Finally, the intellectual ideas of individualism and liberalism were contested by collectivist thinking, which in some manifestations manipulated or rejected parliamentary democracy altogether.

*See also:* HEGEMONIAL STABILITY THEORY; SPHERES OF INFLUENCE

## Peace

Absence of WAR. Broadly, three conditions of international affairs can be identified: war, non-war and peace. The first indicates a condition of actual hostilities whereas the third signifies either their cessation or absence. In this sense the word carries a negative connotation although popular usage, as well as INTERNATIONAL LAW, assume it to be a positive value and indeed regard it as the prevailing or orthodox expression of inter-state relations. Accordingly, peace is simultaneously the fundamental assumption upon which international law is based as well as being both the subject and object of the institutions associated with it. The second condition, non-war (which is sometimes rendered as 'the condition of neither war nor peace'), is by no means a new one in WORLD POLITICS, although it gained considerable impetus as a result of post-war SUPERPOWER postures. Thus, the COLD WAR and the development of ideas associated with PEACEFUL COEXISTENCE reflected a belief that while the advent of NUCLEAR WEAPONS had rendered war irrational as an instrument of policy, CONFLICT and competition between the major ACTORS would continue to form the framework of relations. The fact that a condition of actual BELLIGERENCY did not exist did not mean that, by default, peace could be said to be established. The idea of non-war is an implicit recognition that an absence of organized armed conflict is a necessary, but by no means sufficient, part of the definition of peace. In classical international theory this is often expressed in HOBBESIAN terms: 'So the nature of War, consisteth not in actuall fighting, but in the known disposition thereto, during all the time there is no assurance to the contrary. All other time is Peace.' (*Leviathan*, Ch. 13).

When accompanied by the definite article the word 'peace' is often used as a synonym for TREATY. For example, the treaties of Munster and Osnabruck in 1648, which are widely regarded as marking the beginnings of the modern international STATES-SYSTEM, are more commonly referred to as the Peace of WESTPHALIA. It is not unusual, either, to speak of 'peace treaties', indicating the RATIFICATION of a treaty ending a particular war and distinguishing this type of international agreement from others. Associated with this kind of usage is the Latin word *pax*. This normally denotes an *imposed* settlement (usually by means of conquest or the exertion of superior POWER) as it did, albeit in different ways, in the following: Pax Romana (2 BC), Pax Ecclesiastica (AD 12), Pax Britannica (nineteenth century) and Pax Americana (post-Second World War). In these instances, the idea of 'pacification' by a hegemonic power is central to its meaning.

Notwithstanding the difficulty of a positive definition in world politics, the quest for peace has dominated international thought, if not practice, since earliest times. According to F.H. Hinsley (1963) (whose *Power and the Pursuit of Peace* is a seminal study of the search for conditions of peace in the modern state-system), although 'the aim cannot be much less old than the practice of war', it was in the late nineteenth century that for the first time, peace proposals began to proliferate as a consequence of the fear of the destructive power of war rather than simply the result of its outbreak. This tendency has continued into the twentieth century when the avoidance of war and the maintenance of peace became a first-order problem of political thought rather than, as hitherto, being relegated to its outer edges. An important exception to this is Kant's *Perpetual Peace* (1795) which is widely regarded as the most coherent statement of the LIBERAL or INTERNATIONALIST approach to the problem of causes of war and the mechanics of the maintenance of peace. The Kantian emphasis on republicanism, constitutionalism, law, civil liberties and judicial methods of settling disputes has been described as representing, par excellence, the bourgeois or Western view of the establishment of peace and as such is wholly consistent with the continuation of capitalism and its social, economic and governmental manifestations. Indeed, Kant's idea of 'a federalism of free states' as well as his commitment to universal HUMAN RIGHTS could conceivably be regarded as an early prototype of the CHARTER of the UNITED NATIONS for which 24 October, the day it was founded in 1945, is now officially deisgnated as Peace Day. The MARXIST/LENINIST notion of peaceful coexistence should not be seen as an endorsement of the Kantian view, since although it rules out violent conflict between the major STATES, it envisages the continuation of violent conflict between classes as well as legitimizing the propagation of WARS OF NATIONAL LIBERATION and REVOLUTION. In this way, its focus is on 'relative' or 'comparative' peace rather than on the somewhat idealistic 'absolute' variety sought by the Kantians.

*See also:* PACIFISM; PEACEKEEPING; PEACE MOVEMENTS; PEACE RESEARCH

### Peaceful coexistence

Peaceful coexistence is a FOREIGN POLICY doctrine which attempts to reconcile ideological divisions with the practical political needs. As a form of pragmatism, peaceful coexistence was developed by Soviet and Chinese DIPLOMACY following the emergence of a BIPOLAR INTERNATIONAL SYSTEM after 1945. Although the Soviet version of peaceful coexistence can be traced to the founders of the 1917 REVOLUTION, its elaboration into a distinctive WORLD VIEW was the work of Stalin's immediate successors: Malenkov and Khrushchev. Before the period 1952–4 peaceful coexistence was simply tactical RECOGNITION that war, although inevitable, was not imminent. After Malenkov and Khrushchev peaceful coexistence was seen far more as an immutable fact of life. In essence what Stalin's heirs argued was that the advent of NUCLEAR WEAPONS made WAR unthinkable as a rational instrument of policy and that, as a result, the revolutionary spread of MARXISM/LENINISM could not be predicated upon that fact. Different economic and social systems – particularly the COMMUNIST and capitalist – would have to coexist in a situation of non-war, therefore. Although violent CONFLICT between states such as the Soviet Union and the United States was ruled out, violent conflict between classes was not. Contradictions within societies would continue and WARS OF NATIONAL

LIBERATION would arise through inevitable historical processes which the Soviet Union should support. Peaceful coexistence should, thus, not be confused with DETENTE. It was a doctrine that fully expected CONFLICT and competition to continue – particularly in the THIRD WORLD. In this way the attempt at what US diplomacy called 'LINKAGE' in the 1970s was quite alien to the conceptualization of peaceful coexistence in the 1950s by the two Soviet leaders.

The Chinese view of peaceful coexistence was first enumerated in the Sino–Indian agreement of 1954 which identified five principles of peaceful coexistence. These were:

1. Mutual respect for each other's territorial integrity and SOVEREIGNTY.
2. Non-aggression.
3. Non-interference in each other's internal affairs.
4. Equality and mutual benefits.
5. Peaceful coexistence.

These ideas were later to be incorporated into the BANDUNG CONFERENCE of Non-Aligned states.

An attempt was made, particularly by Soviet international lawyers, to incorporate peaceful coexistence into ideas about INTERNATIONAL LAW in the 1960s. The argument was adduced that legal relations between the Soviet Union and the West should be governed by the principles of peaceful coexistence and that, to this extent, the idea should be regarded as an international legal concept.

Peaceful coexistence remains an important example of the need that ideologues find to reconcile their concepts with empirical reality. As a historical fact peaceful coexistence doctrine was an early attempt to reconcile Marxist/Leninist unity with an increasingly complex and centrifugal international system. It fell victim to the Sino-Soviet dispute of the late 1950s onwards and became associated in a perjorative way with REVISIONISM.

## Peacekeeping

As a general expression peacekeeping is a third party role played by an ACTOR in a violent CONFLICT situation. Having identified the parties and the issues, the putative peacekeeper attempts, by using a repertoire of behaviour, to stabilize the conflict situation at least to the extent of eliminating the overt violence from the relationship. Thus typically a peacekeeper will assist in the establishment and supervision of a cease-fire or TRUCE. In effecting this outcome the peacekeeper may find itself expediting the withdrawal of forces, the repatriation of prisoners and the interposition of its own contingents into a *cordon sanitaire*. In this way peacekeeping can be viewed as a function of DIPLOMACY and indeed when the UN began to develop a significant repertoire of peacekeeping devices during the 1950s the then SECRETARY-GENERAL coined the phrase 'preventive diplomacy' to characterize this approach to CONFLICT MANAGEMENT.

Everyday usage of the term 'peacekeeping' however implies another type of response which might be termed instead 'keeping the PEACE'. In this latter usage a more active role is envisaged for the peacekeeper. Here the third party may attempt to suppress or deter parties to violence from continuing with their behaviour. In this more activist usage peacekeeping is perhaps more akin to law enforcement and less to DIPLOMACY. The size, composition and mandate for a peacekeeper of this latter type will be much larger than the type discussed above. Forces may be equipped to engage in fighting, the mandate may sanction the use of FORCE to effect certain outcomes and so on. As is so often the case these two 'ideal types' – one diplomatic, the other more a compellent or deterrent – merge into one as a situation develops. Part of the undoubted controversy surrounding the UN operation in the Congo (Zaïre) after 1960 was that model one peacekeeping shaded off into model two when the operation was faced with the secession of the province of Katanga.

Optimistically viewed, peacekeeping

should lead to peacemaking but such hopes are frequently not realized. Peacekeeping techniques, particularly cease-fires, interposition and NEUTRALIZATION, have the tendency of 'freezing' situations. Empirically it is the case that peacekeeping simply does not lead to peacemaking in each and every instance, as even the most cursory examination of the ARAB–ISRAELI CONFLICT shows. Hypothetically the field is wide open for any actor in WORLD POLITICS to assume a peacekeeping role provided that actor has the confidence of the parties. The best example available up to the present is that of the UN which, as already stated, developed such a role during the 1950s under the incumbency of Dag Hammarskjold as its second SECRETARY-GENERAL.

A good point of departure in examining the role of the UN in peacekeeping operations is indeed to identify the 'Hammarskjold approach' at the outset. This was based upon the following assumptions: (a) that violent conflicts outside the COLD WAR confrontation zones were amenable to UN peacekeeping; (b) that, in contrast to Chapter 7 of the Charter, this approach was not coercive and certainly did not look towards the COLLECTIVE SECURITY model at all. Consent of the host government was important and CRISIS MANAGEMENT rather than military enforcement was emphasized; (c) this approach relegated the VETO powers in the SECURITY COUNCIL to a more passive role as far as the operations themselves were concerned. However, it was recognized that the active help of the VETO states was necessary both constitutionally and financially in these operations; finally (d) this approach expanded the executive and administrative role of the Secretary-General and his office.

Under the leadership of Hammarskjold and with the backing of the new NON-ALIGNED members of the Organization, the UN played a crisis management role in Suez (1956), the LEBANON (1958) and the Congo (1960). Partly because of the complex and chaotic internal political situation in the Congo and partly because the

precedents of Suez and the Lebanon proved inadequate, Hammarskjold's consensus of support began to collapse and he was subjected to much criticism from the veto powers, in particular the Soviet Union which proposed replacing him with a *troika* arrangement of three Secretary-Generals.

It would appear from the three early examples cited above that the minimal requirements for the operation of any consensus on peacekeeping should include support from the following parties: (a) the host state to the UN operation; (b) the parties to the dispute if they were not covered in (a); (c) the veto powers in the Security Council; and (d) the parties supplying forces to the operation. Furthermore, that this consensus should provide (i) a workable set of directives to the Secretary-General; (ii) regular and reliable financial support; and (iii) reasonable latitude to the Secretary-General to play an executive and administrative role on a day to day and week to week basis. When this consensual framework collapsed in the Congo it had a disabling effect on the whole operation.

The Organization emerged from the Congo experience more cautious about the future of peacekeeping. When a UN force was sent to Cyprus in 1964 the costs of the operation were met by voluntary contributions and the mandate had a time limit (which was renewed). Again for the first time troops from one of the permanent members of the Security Council were used (British) contrary to the earlier ground rules. The enlargement of the size of the Security Council to fifteen states made it more representative and it seemed to make good organizational, as well as constitutional, sense to retain the primary initiative for sanctioning peacekeeping with the Council.

The UN continued to be involved in peacekeeping operations in the 1970s and the 1980s but throughout the modified version of the original ground rules continued to obtain. GEOPOLITICALLY the THIRD WORLD has been the area of concentration and, with the possible exception of the Congo, the character of UN peacekeeping has been the preventive diplomacy model discussed earlier. Great stress has to be laid upon the consensual nature of all these operations. Over time a consensus can change or evaporate altogether and in these circumstances sustaining an operation can be difficult. This tendency is likely to be exacerbated because peacekeeping tends to freeze situations. The relationship between peacekeeping and peacemaking can indeed be tenuous.

## Peace movements
*See:* PACIFISM

## Peace research
Peace research is that branch of human inquiry which seeks to improve the prospects – in the present and in the future – for the establishment of PEACE. Peace research is thus not a value-free branch of inquiry; indeed, values intrude into peace research in two distinct ways. First, those engaged in the activity ('peace researchers') are philosophically committed, a priori, to the view that peace is both attainable and desirable. Secondly, the peace researcher eschews strict empiricism in favour of social engineering. Thus by simply conducting peace research the goal of peace may be moved closer to realization. In this way peace research can be seen as an applied study rather than the pursuit of knowledge for its own sake.

Intellectually there are two broad approaches to the subject matter of violent CONFLICT and its eradication within the peace research tradition. First, there are those who concentrate upon the psychological environment and take an essentially subjectivist view of the subject matter. This is the 'war begins in the minds of men' tradition. Emphasis is placed upon PERCEPTION and MISPERCEPTION and the rela-

tionship of these psychological processes to the tensions that cause violence. It is often assumed that if parties to a conflict can be made to review their DEFINITION OF THE SITUATION non-violent resolution is attainable. This approach tends to concentrate upon ELITES and informed publics as the crucial target populations wherein redefinitions must be effected. Sometimes, peace researchers argue, this is only possible by changing a whole LEADERSHIP structure.

The second approach concentrates upon structures at the outset rather than as a consequence. This view may be said to look towards the OPERATIONAL ENVIRONMENT, therefore, as the main locus of inquiry. Structures within state actors and within the INTERNATIONAL SYSTEM are emphasized in the belief that it is the objective conditions within systems of interaction that produce violent conflict behaviour.

Both approaches are agreed, however, that violence is only the most extreme manifestation of conflict and that a valid self-sustaining condition of peace must begin by an understanding of conflict *per se*. In this respect, at least, peace research and CONFLICT RESEARCH are interested in the same basic processes. The modern peace research tradition has been dependent upon the insights of the social scientific conflict researcher for its own resuscitation.
*See also:* STRATEGIC STUDIES

## Pearl Harbor
The Japanese attack on the US naval base at Pearl Harbor, Hawaii, on 7 December 1941 ensured that the United States entered the Second World War on the Allied side. The term has come to symbolize, at least in Western eyes, both the inherently treacherous nature of WORLD POLITICS and the constant need to guard against surprise attack. The slogan 'no more Pearl Harbors' for the post-war US DEFENCE establishment was as least as effective in increasing global

US military expenditure and commitments as the cry 'no more Vietnams' in the 1970s was in curtailing them. In the two-hour raid the Japanese sunk seven battleships, killed 2,403 citizens, wounded another 1,178 and destroyed or put out of commission most of the US air-strike force parked on the runways of the island of Oahu. As a consequence of what Roosevelt called this 'dastardly' attack which would live on in history as 'a day of infamy', the United States declared WAR on Japan. Three days later Hitler honoured his pledge under the Tripartite Pact (signed by Germany, Italy and Japan on 27 September 1937) and joined the fray against the United States. This gave the Roosevelt administration justification for converting an informal ALLIANCE with the United Kingdom into a formal one, and led indirectly to his 'Europe first' policy – that the European war would take precedence over the war in the Pacific.

Since 1941 historians and DECISION-MAKING analysts have disagreed both concerning the reasons for the high-risk Japanese attack and concerning possible US presidential complicity in it. Regarding Japanese motivation, most concede that domestic factors, especially the rising influence of MILITARISM within Japanese society in the 1930s, had a decisive effect on the growing militancy of Japanese FOREIGN POLICY. However, it has been suggested that regardless of domestic factors, developments in the international economic and strategic order meant that Japan as a late industrializer had to accelerate the process of acquiring cheap sources of raw materials and guaranteed markets in a REGION already crowded with established imperial actors. Thus, Japanese fears of an 'ABCD' (American, British, Chinese and Dutch) ENCIRCLEMENT led directly to Pearl Harbor. With regard to possible US high-level complicity, revisionist historians argue that since the Japanese codes had been deciphered long before the event, the US government in effect encouraged the Japanese to attack in the interests of manoeuvering the United States into the European war. A variant of this is that it was the United Kingdom which had prior knowledge of the attack and that UK decision-makers had deliberately not informed Washington of it in the sure hope that, as a consequence, the United States would be forced to join them in their battle for survival against Hitler's Germany. Other analysts, especially Roosevelt's biographers, have tended to deny these charges and allege that the attack contained all the elements of 'surprise'. In an innovative and influential study, Wohlstetter (1962) clears Roosevelt of complicity but argues that the US decision-makers, inundated with a wealth of information from decoded Japanese messages, failed to identify the 'signals' (the worthwhile information) from the general 'noise' (the mass of conflicting reports) and were therefore caught cold.

## Penetrated state

Term associated particularly with James N. Rosenau (1969b) and is a corrective to the traditional concepts of the 'territoriality' and 'impermeability' of the SOVEREIGN STATE. The separation of domestic and FOREIGN POLITICS of a state, for so long a cardinal feature of the classical approach to INTERNATIONAL RELATIONS, is now regarded as naïve and myopic since few, if any, states are completely shut off either from the outside world or from domestic consequences of their own foreign relations. All states are to some extent 'penetrated' by actors from the outside. This may range from overt military support for a particular REGIME (e.g. the United States and the Philippines) or it may refer simply to the activities of foreign lobbyists on behalf of governments or multinational firms. In either case, the virginal purity of the traditional 'hard-shelled' state has been compromised.

## People's War

A term used in the analysis of REVOLUTION

which is specifically derived from the experience in China under the LEADERSHIP of Mao Tse-tung. It would be hard to dispute the contention that the defeat of the Japanese invaders and the overthrown of the Kuomintang by the Chinese COMMUNISTS ranks as one of the paradigm examples of revolutionary change. The very essence of this significance stems from the appreciation that the Chinese actually *changed* the paradigm in effecting their revolution. The Chinese revolution has often been referred to as the 'countryside' version, in contradistinction with the Soviet example. This is because, in the former case, the peasants were actively mobilized in support of the Communist leadership and the programme of economic and social change. This was both possible and desirable because the instrument of change was the campaign of GUERRILLA WARFARE conducted by Mao and his followers against the incumbent REGIME and the Japanese invaders. The successful conduct of this campaign required a supportive population, hence the emphasis upon the need to mobilize the countryside. Traditional Marxist/Leninist dogma had been based on the assumption that it would be among the urban proletariat that the main engine of change would come. The Chinese revolution appeared to suggest that an alternative paradigm was viable.

The Chinese Communists were able to broaden the nature of their appeal after the Japanese invasion and claim to represent the only effective vehicle for the expulsion of the interventionist forces and the achievement of national liberation. This represented the fusion of the class struggle with the national struggle. With the increasingly open identification of the United States with the Kuomintang position, the Communists were able to claim that their struggle was against the resurgence of IMPE-RIALISM and COLONIALISM from the West as well as from fellow Asians.

People's War is thus a sort of ideological shorthand for this historical experience. In addition it came to be regarded as a model for others to follow, or at least to refer to in their own revolutionary endeavours. For scholars of international and comparative politics it became a set of analytical benchmarks which could be used to compare and contrast. For the forces of the STA-TUS QUO, People's War became a phenomenon to be resisted and, if possible, defeated. In order to achieve this goal understanding it was the first prerequisite.

The decade of the 1960s became the decade of People's War because of two factors: the VIETNAM WAR, or the second Indo–China War, and the Cultural Revolution in China. The latter led to the vigorous assertion by, in particular Mao and Lin Piao, that the concept was universally valid where all subject peoples, particularly in the THIRD WORLD, were attempting revolutionary changes against incumbent regimes supported by the West. The former, the Vietnam War, is widely regarded as a test case of People's War. In retrospect, most analysts are agreed that it diverges from the Chinese model in a number of important respects. Vietnam was a much more 'internationalized' conflict than the Chinese revolution. In particular through the phenomenon of INTERVENTION outside parties were drawn in to give AID and assistance, and even to act as allies. Secondly, more attention was perhaps paid by the Vietnamese to the potentialities for psychological warfare and the need to erode the adversaries' will to fight. In particular, a distinctive feature of the Vietnamese version of People's War was the high profile initiative which would publicize the conflict and, perhaps by achieving strategic surprise, prove to be militarily damaging or even decisive. Such an initiative was the Tet Offensive of 1968. The Vietnam War was not a vindication for guerrilla warfare seen as a means of overthrowing an incumbent regime. After Tet, the fighting became increasingly conducted between CONVENTIONAL units. Rather, Vietnam appears as a vindication of the theory of PROTRACTED WAR which is often seen by strategists as having a family resemblance to guerrilla war.

Like so much of the language of political

discourse, People's War begs the important question: to whom does the term 'People' apply? Politicians, for their own purposes, might wish to claim that almost any insurgency that appeared to have a popular basis was, therefore, a 'people's' conflict. An historically circumscribed alternative has been offered here. People's War – in capitals – is another way of talking about the Chinese Revolution and certain stipulated successors and emulators.

## Perception

Perception is a basic psychological process whereby individuals relate to their environment. A distinction is usually made in psychology between the perception of things and the perception of people, the latter process being referred to as 'social perception'. It is a fundamental characteristic of the act of perceiving that selection is involved. Certain stimuli are noted and others ignored. A variety of factors will affect this discrimination including the individual's past experiences, his current physical and psychological state and the frequency and familiarity with which cognate experiences have occurred. How people perceive each other clearly has a considerable bearing upon how their behaviour towards each other is determined.

Taking account of perceptions in WORLD POLITICS involves the study of behaviour at the individual LEVEL OF ANALYSIS. In particular, the investigation of DECISION-MAKING and how key 'players' perceive their situation will form a large part of the analysis. As such, perception is the basic psychic process that leads to the DEFINITION OF THE SITUATION. All perceptions in decision-making are conditional assumptions or inferences about another person or persons. These inferences will seek to attribute certain intentions to the other and, upon that basis, certain responses will be made. Perception of another's intentions is a difficult procedure because these are states of mind which can only be inferred by indirect evidence.

Psychologists argue that individuals seek to maintain cognitive consistency or balance and that, accordingly, person perception tends to assimilate new information into existing IMAGES. Jervis (1976), in his work on the subject of perception and MISPERCEPTION, argues that this tendency to seek consistency in perceiving is inevitable: 'intelligent decision-making in any sphere is impossible unless significant amounts of information are assimilated to pre-existing beliefs' (p. 145). The policy maker in world politics faces potential inundation by the complexities of the environments in which policy is made if this kind of perceptual screening is not effected. These pre-existing beliefs will be both immediate, contingent concerns ('evoked sets') as well as more deeply held attitudes and images.

The study of perceptions in world politics has been wholly advanced under the SOCIAL SCIENCE APPROACH in the post-1945 period. As Jervis points out in the opening chapter of his book such approaches depend upon recognition of the decision-making level of analysis as relevant. A complete picture of why particular decisions were taken requires scholarly reconstruction which will necessarily have to take account of how those authoritatively placed to take decisions 'saw' the situation. At the same time a total commitment to subjective phenomenalism should be avoided. As the distinction between the psychological and operational environments suggests, there is a world beyond the perceptual horizon.

## Permanent Court of Arbitration

This was set up by the Hague Convention for the Pacific Settlement of International Disputes in 1899 and revised in 1907. The name is misleading since it is not really a permanent or fixed court. It is rather a panel of jurists who are ready to act as arbitrators in particular cases referred to them. Each STATE party to the convention nominates four persons to serve and each party to a dispute selects two of these, only one of whom may be a national. The four arbitrators chosen then select one more from the panel to act as an umpire. The Permanent Court of Arbitration, because it is not a standing court and because its composition varies from case to case, has been criticized since for these reasons it cannot develop a coherent body of case-law. However its value, like most international institutions, lies in its very existence; its provision of a machinery to settle disputes should the parties desire. Its most active period was between 1900 and 1932 when twenty cases were decided, but since then its use has been limited and it has been largely superseded by the PERMANENT COURT OF INTERNATIONAL JUSTICE (1921) and its successor the INTERNATIONAL COURT OF JUSTICE (1946).

## Permanent Court of International Justice (PCIJ)

This was formed under the auspices of the LEAGUE OF NATIONS in 1921. It was the first systematic attempt to create a world court to provide judicial settlement of international disputes, and unlike the PERMANENT COURT OF ARBITRATION its judges were chosen not by the parties of the dispute but were elected by the League. The PCIJ was superseded in 1946 by the INTERNATIONAL COURT OF JUSTICE which has virtually the same statute and jurisdiction.

## *Persona non grata*

Term normally associated with DIPLOMACY whereby a receiving STATE declares that it is unwilling to accept or receive a diplomatic representative of another state. This may occur at the initial stage of appointment (*agréation*) or more usually it may occur some time after the granting of *persona grata* (acceptability) when the diplomat concerned has violated the rules of normal diplomatic behaviour. The declaration of

*persona non grata* represents a serious diplomatic initiative since it involves expulsion or at least a request that the diplomat be recalled to his country of origin. Tit-for-tat expulsions are not an uncommon feature of contemporary WORLD POLITICS.

## PLO

An abbreviation of the Palestine Liberation Organization. The PLO was formed in 1964 following an agreement in principle the previous year at an Arab League Summit. The Charter of the Organization adopted at the time envisaged that the liberation of Palestine from Israeli occupation would be achieved in conjunction with the Arab states of the Middle East and North Africa rather than by independent action. This strategy, which might appropriately be called 'Pan-Arabism', was later to be challenged and rejected following the comprehensive defeat of a number of Arab FRONT LINE STATES following the June 1967 WAR with Israel. The original leadership of the PLO under Ahmed Shukairy was removed in 1967 and a more radical and independent (independent of the Arab states) group of leaders emerged thereafter to take control of the Organization. As a result the PLO underwent a fundamental change of ORIENTATION.

The PLO became in the late 1960s what it remains to date – an umbrella organization for a variety of resistance movements to the STATUS QUO in the Middle East. Indeed some of the more radical elements in the PLO, such as George Habash's Popular Front for the Liberation of Palestine (PFLP) wanted to see radical changes in some of the Arab states – notably Jordan – as well as in the territory known diplomatically as Palestine since 1917. The principal resistance movement in the PLO is El Fatah (the Palestine National Liberation Movement). El Fatah was formed under the leadership of Yasser Arafat to pursue a policy of 'liberation' via Palestinian SELF-HELP rather than by relying upon Pan-Arabism to achieve Palestinian demands in its 'coat-tails.' In 1965 Fatah established a military wing – Asifah – and began *fedayeen* (commando) operations against Israel. At the fifth session of the Palestine National Council (PNC) at Cairo in February 1969 Fatah gained majority control of the PLO and Arafat became Chairman of the Executive Committee.

Since the eclipse of the old guard and the take-over of the Organization by the *fedayeen* groups the PLO has enjoyed mixed fortunes. As a GUERRILLA WARFARE operation the Organization has never had more than a nuisance value. High profile HIJACK operations, armed incursions into Israel proper and/or the occupied territories on the West Bank and the Gaza Strip, and out-and-out TERRORISM have been the typical methods of operation. The PLO faces a powerful adversary in Israel; the occupants of the West Bank have not been able to provide the supportive infrastructure for guerrilla operations while the Arab states have not always proved reliable, the crushing of the PLO in Jordan in September 1970 and the CAMP DAVID negotiations between Egypt and Israel being instances where NATIONAL INTEREST was put before support for the PLO. Militarily the Organization's greatest defeat came after the 1982 Israeli incursion into the Lebanon, which was intended to remove PLO bases from Lebanese territorty and the Organization's influence upon Lebanese politics.

Diplomatically the PLO under Arafat's LEADERSHIP has done much to compensate for its military track record. The Chairman has shown great resilience, a deft touch, a willingness to 'trim' to prevailing winds and a flair for publicity. RECOGNITION of the PLO as a legitimate party to any settlement/resolution of the ARAB–ISRAELI CONFLICT has been steadily achieved since 1969. The Rabat Summit of Arab states of October 1974 recognized the Organization as the sole legitimate representative of the Palestinian people, ending effectively any Jordanian hopes in that direction. During the autumn of 1974 the UN GENERAL AS-SEMBLY accepted the right of Palestinian SELF-DETERMINATION and national INDE-PENDENCE (Resolution 3236) and admitted the Organization to the UN on observer status (Resolution 3237). In 1980 at the Venice meeting of EUROPEAN COMMUNITY leaders the Palestinians were recognized as parties. In the closing weeks of the Reagan Presidency the United States moved towards a dialogue with the Organization on an official basis following Arafat's declaration that the PLO accepted the right of Israel to exist within secure borders.

These achievements have been realized at some cost diplomatically. In effect the officially recognized representatives of the Palestinian diaspora now accept the partition of mandate Palestine between themselves and the Israelis, a solution proposed in 1947 by the UN and rejected by the Arab side. Moreover, any Palestinian state that is established will be considerably smaller than that envisaged in 1947. Any solution still requires the Israelis to recognize the PLO as legitimate parties to the negotiations. An 'internal' settlement attempt by Israel would certainly be condemned by the Organization and would probably not be self-sustaining given the current level of civil strife in the occupied territories evidenced by the two-year-old *intifada* (uprising).

## Pluralism

This term is used in two senses in WORLD POLITICS. First, as a perspective on the structure of the system. Here pluralism may be taken as a portmanteau term covering all those who reject the assumptions of STATE-CENTRISM in preference for some kind of MIXED ACTOR MODEL. Secondly, pluralism is derived from political sociology where it is used to identify political systems where power is shared amongst a plurality of competing parties and interest groups. Pluralism is thus a theory both of inter-state and intra-state politics.

Pluralism in the first sense argues that the

assumptions of the traditional state-centred view of world politics were derived from a period when the level of interconnectedness between states was significantly lower than at present. Pluralists argue that there has been a massive erosion in the impermeability of the STATE during the twentieth century in a number of directions. This erosion is explained in the pluralist literature by reference to the idea of INTERDEPENDENCE, particularly in the issue area of economic relations. Pluralists indeed believe that certain economic goals – often bundled together as 'wealth/welfare issues' – can only be realized by states becoming more collaborative with other state and non-state ACTORS. Thus the state is seen as more integrated into the global system by pluralists than by REALISTS. Because the system is one of mixed actors, the defining characteristic of the actor becomes AUTONOMY rather than SOVEREIGNTY. The pluralists argue that actors such as the IMF or the PLO can be said to enjoy a measure of autonomy and should therefore be included in any model of world politics. For pluralism the concept of actor is relative: it cannot be fixed by some legal principle such as sovereignty; rather, it depends upon the context of the ISSUE AREA. Pluralists also hold that the billiard ball metaphor gives a distorted picture of intrastate politics. Blackboxing or reifying the state misrepresents the domestic political process. Because pluralism is also a theory of how domestic politics works – at least in those systems which are pluralist – then holding to this perspective produces a rather different picture of POLICY-MAKING as well as MACROPOLITICS. In particular, pluralists are far more willing to build the bureaucratic and organizational context of the policy system into their modelling and, conversely, to abandon or modify ideas about RATIONALITY.

The growth and development of ethnic self-consciousness and the emergence of subnational and TRANSNATIONAL interests associated with the same have, according to the pluralists, had important implications for the idea of the NATION-STATE as the typical actor in macropolitics. Any idea that there is a neat and tidy fit between the state and the nation must be revised in the light of widespread evidence of ethnic nationalism as a centrifugal force working in many states against state-centred NATIONALISM. Some conception of the ethnic diversity of many states can be demonstrated by an examination of language as a variable. On this criteria only a small minority of states are ethnically homogeneous. If loyalty to and identity with the state, through the instrument of nationalism, is not guaranteed in the present system then, at a minimum, the billiard ball model needs revision, if not abandonment.

Pluralists argue that many problems in macropolitics, such as combating POLLUTION or PROLIFERATION, cannot be resolved by states taking a narrow, self-centred view. If these problem-solving tasks are so approached the result will be self-defeating. Instead states must recognize a common interest and engage in cooperation, HARMONIZATION and even sectoral INTEGRATION in order to produce positive-sum solutions. States may engage in institution-building which will further erode their autonomy.

## Plutonium

An artificially created fissile material. Plutonium was discovered in 1941 when it was produced by bombarding URANIUM 238 with neutrons. Plutonium 239, as it is known, is a fissile material like uranium 235, but unlike the latter its production is easier and cheaper. This facility has undoutedly contributed to the PROLIFERATION of NUCLEAR WEAPONS since 1945.

## Polarity

A concept used in SYSTEMS ANALYSIS, polarity implies that within a definable system certain ACTORS are so important that they constitute 'poles' against which other actors have to respond (by joining coalitions or remaining non-aligned). Thus a polar actor is one which is so significant that its removal would alter the contours of the system. Conversely a new polar actor would be one which, by entering the system, also altered the contours. In the past entry and exit from polar positions has usually been effected as a result of WAR. Polarity is a relatively new term in the analysis of WORLD POLITICS and is often used in conjunction with the term POWER. Thus a BIPOLAR system would consist of two powers, a TRIPOLAR of three, and so on.

Use of the concept of polarity can only proceed with confidence if the term is explicated further to uncover the preconditions that appear necessary and/or sufficient. Traditionally, military power was regarded as a necessary precondition for stipulation as a 'pole'. Although military potential is not easily or cheaply converted into effective instruments of INFLUENCE, its possession does give the actor considerable negative or VETO power. For this reason, no satisfactory discussion of the bases of polarity can avoid taking into account the military factor.

Economic potential as a determinant is important, both for its own sake and as a contributory factor in the 'war potential' of actors. Economic power is more malleable than military since it can be used for both positive and negative sanctions. INTERDEPENDENCE, although identifiable in the military–security ISSUE AREA, is far more prevalent and pervasive in economic relations.

The determinants of polarity should include an ideational factor. Such factors may be explicit statements akin to IDEOLOGIES, or they may be implicit and imprecise 'ground rules'. Indeed, the two are different facets of the same thing. Thus in the contemporary system, the THIRD WORLD states have sought to change the ground rules of the international political economy through such demands as those contained in the call for a NEW INTERNATIONAL ECONOMIC ORDER (NIEO). At the same time, there is a more structured set of ideas about the nature of economic power, institutions and relationships behind these demands.

In discussions on polarity in the literature the issue of stability is often raised in order to facilitate comparison between different configurations. Some writers have seen bipolarity as more stable, others argue for MULTIPOLARITY. In these discussions stability is often defined by the limiting condition of an absence of war between the polar actors. In any event, given that in all systems change is endemic, stability is at best a relative not absolute term.

## Polarization

A process that occurs during CONFLICT situations, particularly if the conflict is violent, or threatens to become so. Polarization leads to vertical divisions being established within a system of relations so that parties to the conflict tend to coalesce together to form coalitions. The most usual form of polarization is the straight bifurcation of a system into two competing groups. In WORLD POLITICS this is what is meant by BIPOLARITY and is also the limiting case of polarization. Once a system has become polarized in this way contact within the 'poles' increases while contact between the 'poles' decreases; thus polarization can lead to the exacerbation of conflict over time. Polarization is particularly likely if the conflict is perceived to be about fundamentally different IDEOLOGIES or value systems. In such circumstances the parties conflict over what the other 'stands for' rather than what the other wants out of the dispute. ACCOMMODATION and COMPROMISE become increasingly difficult as a result.

It should not be thought that polarization always or of necessity produces an approximate equality between the 'poles'. Thus in the bipolar case one side may be clearly superior to the other in size and significance. Ideologically one may be defending the STATUS QUO, the other seeking to change it. Polarization may lead to greater stability or it may be unstable. In world politics academic opinon has been firmly divided between the proponents of bipolarity on one hand and MULTIPOLARITY on the other. One of the key variables in this dispute has been the relative stability of the systems under review.

*See also:* POLARITY

## Policy-making

An actor that is a collectivity makes policy. Thus the UN, through organs such as the SECURITY COUNCIL or the GENERAL ASSEMBLY, makes policy. The PLO makes policy. State ACTORS, most obviously, make policy. The IMF makes policy. Policy-making is, in short, the decision to embark upon certain programmes of action (or inaction) in order to achieve desired goals. Policy-making is the activity of individuals and groups holding role positions within organizations. Because of this behavioural connotation with policy-making, the activity is crucially dependent upon a DEFINITION OF THE SITUATION. Since the policy maker's environment is itself a complex of other actors, potentially also making policy, FEEDBACK processes are crucial and must be ongoing if the policy process is to have a point of reference with this environment. The actual process of carrying out policy decisions is referred to as IMPLEMENTATION.

It can be said that policy-making is one of the basic processes of WORLD POLITICS. Methodologically students of the subject have sometimes wanted to regard it as a 'policy science', accordingly. This move has been resisted by scholars wishing to maintain a discrete distance between the campus and the cabinet room. In short, the policy science approach, although valuable, is not to everybody's taste or inclination. One of the best working examples of the 'policy science' approach is STRATEGIC STUDIES. Its

students have never been shy of a close relationship with the chancellery.

## Political asylum

This refers to the granting of a place of refuge. It is a contentious issue in INTERNATIONAL LAW since it is generally thought that the rights of asylum referred to the rights of STATES to grant, rather than the rights of individuals to demand it. However, Article 14 of the Universal Declaration of HUMAN RIGHTS appears to give individuals the right of political asylum as a general principle of international law. To strengthen this approach, a declaration on the Right of Asylum was prepared by the UN Human Rights Commission in 1960 which asserted that it was a duty of states to accept people demanding asylum except for 'overriding reasons of national security or safeguarding population'. However, this has not been formally adopted by the GENERAL ASSEMBLY. There are special and legally complex problems associated with asylum in embassies and warships (*see*: D. P. O'Connell 1970, pp. 808–15) and international law has not, as yet, evolved a universally agreed norm.

## Pollution

Pollution is the contamination, degradation and eventual destruction of vital parts of the environment of the planet. In all instances this polluting process is caused by the activities of man, predominantly in the economic sphere. Because pollution makes such activities more costly, it makes them less sustainable. Pollution in this way can be said to have a negative FEEDBACK effect upon its originators. Unfortunately pollution also frequently affects third parties. The territoriality of the STATE is irrelevant to the pollution process. It is customary to divide pollution into air, land and water or atmospheric, terrestrial and aquatic. In fact the three evironments are linked and the separation below is used purely to assist exposition.

Atmospheric pollution has increased substantially over the last one hundred years and more gradually over the last three hundred. Atmospheric pollution occurs as a result of the discharge of gases into the environment. Thus historically two of the oldest pollutants have been methane and carbon dioxide. Such gases are produced by both primary and secondary production. In particular, the mining and burning of fossile fuels, rice cultivation and animal breeding (both sources of methane) and deforestation. The familiar picture of such atmospheric pollutants is the so-called 'smoke-stack' industrialization process associated with the industrial revolution that began in Britain.

Atmospheric pollution currently is creating three issue areas: global warming, acid rain and ozone depletion. Scientists have identified a range of pollutant gases – known as 'greenhouse gases' – which are responsible for these temperature changes. It is likely that global warming – which is already under way – will produce significant changes in natural vegetation patterns and sea levels by the next century unless significant steps are taken to slow it down. Stopping it altogether is now impossible.

Acid rain is an example of how the atmospheric and aquatic environments interact. Oxides of sulphur and nitrogen combine with moisture in the atmosphere to fall as sulphuric and nitric acids. Acid rain is also an instance of how third parties can be affected by pollution. Prevailing winds carry the pollution across state frontiers with regularity. This problem is particularly severe in parts of Europe and Eastern Canada; in these instances the major pollutors – the United Kingdom and the United States – are not the major recipients of the pollution.

Recent studies have shown that the emission of chlorofluorocarbons (CFCs) into the atmosphere is resulting in the depletion of the earth's ozone layer. CFCs are used as refrigerants, aerosols, solvents and foams.

Their damaging impact was first noted over the Antarctic and the term 'ozone hole' has been used to model this depletion. Ozone is the atmospheric gas that prevents solar radiation in the ultraviolet band from reaching the earth's surface. The effect of increased ultraviolet radiation resulting from this depletion would be to increase skin cancers and depress the human immune system. The effects would be undiscriminating and global.

The major form of land pollution is desertification. In 1984 the United Nations Environment Programme survey suggested that some 35 per cent of the land surface of the planet is threatened with desertification. The following are the main causes of this process: overgrazing and over-cultivation, salinization of irrigated lands and deforestation. Underlying these causal factors is a more fundamental CONFLICT, between population and available land. It may be that the 'carrying capacity' of the land is insufficient for the population density, or it may be that LAND REFORM is needed to establish greater equity. Finding a solution is not easy. Removing land that is marginal from cultivation is only really an option for advanced industrial countries (AICS). In the THIRD WORLD this option is not really available. Population pressure must be eased in the long term but measures can be taken to check the process of desertification and to restore the land to better conditions.

The quality of water is degraded in two ways: by organic and by industrial waste. Historically organic waste – human and animal excreta and agricultural fibre – have been discharged into rivers, lakes and seas for centuries. In theory organic waste can be broken down by microbes and potentially organic waste is a problem of quantity rather than quality. Above certain levels the receiving environments cannot biodegrade organic waste without causing excessive oxygen depletion. This can then have a damaging effect upon fish stocks and even the human food chain.

Industrial pollution of lakes, rivers and seas is potentially more damaging. Heavy metals and pesticides are not easily degraded. Instead they persist and accumulate in the global water cycle. Pollutants enter this cycle in one of three ways: by deliberate discharge, by leaching through the soil into the water table and via the atmosphere.

Pollution issues can only be appropriately addressed by states defining their interests in ways which make cooperation, HARMONIZATION and even INTEGRATION possible behavioural responses. This in turn will lead to norm creation and institution building. Thus in September 1987 twenty-four states signed the Montreal Protocol on Substances that Deplete the Ozone Layer. The PROTOCOL provides for staged reductions in CFC production to reach 50 per cent of 1986 levels by 1988. Unfortunately, it seems likely that unless controls are made more stringent, the protocol will be a classic instance of 'too little too late'. It is clear that only by virtually eliminating CFC production will remedial action be sufficient to prevent further depletion of the ozone layer.

Pollution issues have been widely taken up within the AICs where GREEN POLITICS has become a major ISSUE AREA. In this way pollution problem-solving can be seen to bridge the divide between domestic politics and FOREIGN POLICY. As already noted the territoriality of the state is irrelevant to both causes and effects of pollution and as such this issue area seems closer to that approach to WORLD POLITICS termed PLURAL-ISM rather than the STATE-CENTRIC paradigm.

## Polyarchic

Literally 'government by the many'. The term is usually employed as a description of STATES which are not 'centrist' (one-party authoritarian states) or 'personalist' (personal dictatorships). Thus, western democracies would be regarded as polyarchic states. These terms are often used in discussions of the relationship, if any, between type of REGIME and external behaviour. In this way it is often argued that polyarchic states are more pacific than centrist or personalist states, since domestic opinion will exercise a restraining influence on adventurous POLICY-MAKERS. Contemporary research, while emphasizing that that type of regime does appear to affect FOREIGN POLICY actions, in no way affirms the absolute validity of such generalizations.

## Polycentrism

A structural expression used in connection with the INTERNATIONAL POLITICS of the BLOC of states under the HEGEMONY of the Soviet Union after 1945. Polycentrism literally means that a plurality of autonomous DECISION-MAKING centres has emerged within the Soviet BLOC and that assumptions about bloc unity – the idea in some Western minds of a COMMUNIST 'monolith' – needs to be questioned. Polycentrism is also an ongoing process and a number of suggestions will be adduced below to account for its development.

The term itself is generally credited to the Italian Communist leader Togliatti who first used it publicly in 1956. If this is the case then the developments which produced the terminology began almost a decade earlier. The year 1948, and the break in relations between the Soviets and the Yugolsavs, is the point at which most observers retrospectively date polycentrism. The Yugoslavs subsequently and successfully resisted Soviet pressure, including diplomatic and ECONOMIC SANCTIONS, to get them to change direction. During the following decade other so-called 'peoples' democracies' in Eastern Europe attempted in a more or less ad hoc way to establish what the parameters were for permitted deviation from bloc policy. Poland was able to make internal changes within the ruling ELITE in 1956 but the Hungarian attempt to leave the WARSAW PACT for an ORIENTATION closer to NEUTRALISM was resisted by Soviet military INTERVENTION. In the

1960s the Rumanian leadership succeeded in establishing a more independent FOREIGN POLICY position on a number of key ISSUE AREAS including the Middle East and COMECON planning. However, no other Eastern European state could emulate the success of the Yugoslavs who remained outside all these institutional groupings throughout the period. Indeed, under Tito's leadership Yugoslavia went further than any other European state – East or West – in establishing a clear and genuine non-aligned orientation.

The event of greatest significance in confirming polycentrism as a major factor in communist international politics was the Sino–Soviet split. Unlike other examples referred to above, the schism between the two most powerful and influential communist STATES in the system had a qualitatively different impact from anything that had gone before. The Chinese provided a completely different point of reference and intellectual tradition – exemplified by MAOISM – from the Soviet Union and the other Eastern European states. Indeed the schism between the two states became so wide, public and hostile that by the end of the 1960s a genuine TRIPOLAR system between the People's Republic of China (PRC), the United States and the Soviet Union was evident. Notwithstanding the 'fraternal invasion' of Czechoslovakia in 1968 by Warsaw Pact forces and the promulgation of what Western observers called the BREZHNEV DOCTRINE in the same year, polycentrism continued to be a valid way of identifying important structural characteristcs within the international politics of communist states thereafter.

As a process, polycentrism seems to be dependent upon the emergence of independent national communist parties free from overt ties with Moscow. In this respect it demonstrates again the importance of domestic factors in affecting foreign policy outcomes. The Yugoslav and Chinese examples both point to this conclusion. In both these instances national ELITES came to occupy positions of political power without the intervention of the Soviet Union. In the case of the Chinese, Stalin was extremely equivocal about supporting the Communists at all before 1949. In the rest of Eastern Europe, Rumania stood out for pursuing an independent foreign policy within the institutional structures established and directed by Moscow. Domestically great changes are, at the time of writing, under way in the whole of the bloc, with Hungary and Poland leading developments towards PLURALISM. Events throughout Eastern Europe in late 1989 have raised the issue of the very survival of the communist parties themselves, and not just their relations with Moscow. Among Western European parties, polycentrism has been defined as taking a line that is ideologically and diplomatically independent of Moscow. The Italian Communists have probably gone furthest in this regard and the term 'Eurocommunism' began to be used increasingly in the 1970s to refer to such developments within the communist parties of the EUROPEAN COMMUNITY states.

## Power

Power is one of the essentially contested concepts in the study of FOREIGN POLICY, INTERNATIONAL and WORLD POLITICS. Unfortunately its usage in the past and at the present often betrays an ambivalence and confusion. As a term it has affinities with coercion, INFLUENCE and so on. It has been described by one author as a portmanteau concept and accordingly it is difficult, if not impossible to define with any precision. Rather it is seen as something covering a range of eventualities from the FORCE/coercion mode to the influence/AUTHORITY mode. Baldwin (1979) has argued that greater clarity and precision had been achieved in recent years by regarding power as a causal concept. McClelland (1966) saw fresh hope in the possibility of borrowing from the community power literature. Unfortunately, political sociologists are not in any more agreement among themselves than any other discipline about power, as Waste (1986) has shown.

The power tradition in international politics, at least, is now indelibly associated with the REALIST tradition and the writings of Morgenthau (1948). REALISM is covered elsewhere but two points should be noted in passing. First, Morgenthau defines power in the broadest possible terms. This catch-all approach is definitely *de rigueur* today. Second, Morgenthau was not without his critics within the realist tradition and that, accordingly, his qualification to be their spokesperson should not go unchallenged. Much of the realist discussion of power has consisted of a debate between Morgenthau and his critics.

Most post-realist discussions of power now begin by making a basic distinction between power meaning a CAPABILITY or possession and POWER meaning a relationship. Thus Knorr (1973) speaks of putative and actualized power. Some writers have suggested indeed that confusion might be reduced if the term CAPABILITY was used in the first sense above and that 'power' be reserved for the relational usage.

Capability analysis has a long and distinguished tradition informed in particular by political geography and political economy. Factors such as GNP and GNP per capita, population size and land area, level of literacy and size of armed forces, skill and morale of the LEADERSHIP and the diplomatic service come to mind whenever people engage in capability analysis. The idea of HIERARCHY depends upon a differential spread of capabilities. The Sprouts (1971) sought to emphasize that capability analysis should always take place within 'some framework of policies and/or operational contingencies actual or postulated' (p. 176). Dahl (1984), with his stress on DOMAIN and SCOPE, adds the reminder that power relations operate over someone (domain) with regard to a particular ISSUE AREA (scope). Baldwin has argued in the above-cited article that this approach to the capability/power idea is based upon recognition that capabilities have, generally, low FUNGIBILITY and that it is for this reason that attention needs to be paid to domain and scope.

Capability is a necessary condition for the power relationship. Without such possessions it is impossible for an ACTOR to obtain compliant behaviour and the aim of the power relationship is to seek and secure compliance. Compliant behaviour may consist of doing something different or it may consist of continuing with a behaviour pattern that an actor really wishes to drop. Moreover, in power relations the expectation is always made that compliance will have to overcome resistance from the target. In summary then, power relations involve one actor or group of actors in overcoming the resistance of another actor, or group, and securing compliance thereby. Power relationships are confined to situations of social opposition. Their distinguishing characteristic is that sanctions will be used to secure compliance. A sanction can be either positive or negative, that is to say, it may offer rewards or it may threaten punishments. To make either, or both, these contingencies available the actor(s) must possess the capability, which is why it was stated earlier that putative power is a necessary condition for actualized power.

Because power relationships involve the use of sanctions to overcome resistance they can properly be seen as coercive. In this way it is possible, at least analytically, to distingush, for instance, the power relationship from the influence relationship. Influence is then, in one sense, a non-coercive form of power. Because power relationships involve coercion they can have unpredictable results on the actor(s) being coerced. Rather than securing compliance, sanctions can stiffen resistance and make a target actor determined to 'tough it out' in the face of threats and/or bribes. Moreover, threats cost more if they fail while rewards cost more if they succeed. A threat that fails to produce compliance has to be carried out in order to maintain CREDIBILITY. A reward that succeeds has to be carried through for the same reason. It can be seen, then, that positive and negative sanctions do not work in the same way or within the same psychological framework. On this latter point perceptions play an important role in determining how a target actor will respond. Rewards can be seen as punitive in certain circumstances. A state which has been receiving foreign AID can see a sudden suspension or reduction in its aid quota as a punishment if the cessation is linked to demands for compliant behaviour.

Power relations exist over time and perceptions of the past can influence reactions in the present or anticipation for the future. Moreover this mixing of past, present and future will be multidimensional. Actors will generalize about experiences with each other and with third parties in a form of 'learning theory'. The UK reaction to proposed ECONOMIC SANCTIONS against APARTHEID is not solely a desire to protect vested interests. Following their perceived and controversial failure over Rhodesian UDI, sanctions are seen by some received opinion as being slow working and misdirected. US anguish during the VIETNAM INTERVENTION was in part explicable in terms of their failure to be seen to be securing any of their objectives but also in terms of their perception that failure would adversely affect their 'standing' as a loyal and trustworthy ally. In both these examples it would seem that generalizations about power in one relationship can, as it were, 'cross over' into other relationships.

## Power politics
*See:* REALISM

## Pre-emption
Pre-emption occurs when an ACTOR commits itself to a course of action that is crucially influenced by anticipation of what another actor intends to do. It has been widely applied to the area of STRATEGIC STUDIES where it is envisaged that an actor might pre-empt an attack upon itself by striking a putative adversary first. In effect, therefore, pre-emption is a special case of FIRST STRIKE or surprise attack. Writers like Richard Betts (1982, 1987) have argued that US policy-makers and defence planners were attracted to the logic of this strategy during the period of greatest COLD WAR tension and that in certain CRISIS situations – notably over Cuba – it would have been initiated. Betts argues that pre-emptive attack is easier to justify politically than PREVENTIVE WAR but that the latter may be more viable militarily.

Like all decision-making situations, pre-emption relies upon good intelligence about an enemy's capabilities and a shrewd assessment of its intentions. Conversely MISPERCEPTION of either or both can be damaging. Stalin's desire not to provoke a pre-emptive strike from Germany in 1941 led the Soviet Union into a level of military unpreparedness which was most detrimental when the German preventive strike actually came.

Recent discussions of how STATE actors should react to TERRORISM have included suggestions that pre-emption must be available to the target states as part of their repertoire. It may be concluded that pre-emption is akin to the old sporting adage that you should 'get your retaliation in first'.

## Preventive war
Preventive WAR is the deliberate decision to initiate military violence because the initiator perceives that he has a preponderance of CAPABILITY in his favour. Furthermore, the initiator believes that this favourable imbalance is purely transient and that, if he delays, his putative adversary may catch up and even overtake him in the future. In effect, then, initiating preventive war is a deliberate, premeditated action based upon

a perception of temporary advantage. In general terms preventive warfare involves the use of an ACTOR's military capability in an offensive rather than defensive mode.

Two points may be noted about this definition. First, preventive warfare is one of that class of actions – MASSIVE RETALIATION being another – which depends upon what might be called the 'cult of the offensive'. Second, preventive warfare is in broad terms illegal under the CHARTER OF THE UNITED NATIONS and is out of line with the general twentieth century trend to sanction the use of FORCE only for individual and collective SELF-DEFENCE purposes.

Preventive war is based upon two assumptions about relationships and circumstances. The first is that war is in some senses inevitable. The second is that striking first will be decisive. The inevitability of war may be described as a particularly pessimistic DEFINITION OF THE SITUATION which politicians, DIPLOMATS, strategists and military leaders sometimes hold about the future. Such pessimism is deeply entrenched in thinking about INTERNATIONAL POLITICS and, until the advent of NUCLEAR WEAPONS and DETERRENCE in the nuclear age, adherents to REALISM as a paradigm were inclined in general towards such views.

The concept of FIRST STRIKE is dealt with elsewhere. Suffice it to add here that preventive war will be plausible in those circumstances where putative adversaries have a significant first strike capability yet lack an active and/or passive DEFENCE against each other. Feasibility is enhanced by possessing good INTELLIGENCE about the disposition of the opposing forces and by achieving surprise.

The constraints upon preventive war are formidable. As defined above, it is certainly illegal under present concepts of INTERNATIONAL LAW. It places key DECISION-MAKERS in the unenviable position of having to strike first, which is morally and psychologically difficult to justify, and it requires political leaders to make a considerable act

of faith in their intelligence communities and their military establishments.
*See also:* PRE-EMPTION

## Prisoners of war

Throughout the history of warfare the issue of the appropriate treatment of those taken captive as a result of the hostilities has been a thorny one. The most fundamental problem arises because the captives are under the effective POWER of a hostile ACTOR. The captor may thus dispose of them at the most convenient moment and by the most convenient process. In this way death or slavery were frequent fates suffered by captives. Wealth and/or status could sometimes buy a ransom, of course. In the last analysis the main traditional restraint upon gratuitous bestiality was RECIPROCITY. Captors would be constrained by the probability that the enemy would wreak retribution upon their own people if and when they fell into his hands.

Through the process of reciprocity, therefore, the issue of a code of conduct was developed on an *ad hoc*, local and specific basis; that is to say that agreements were undertaken by specific BELLIGERENTS in particular WARS as to the treatment of captives. In 1758 the French lawyer Vattel suggested a minimum standard of treatment when he proposed that '. . . as soon as your enemy has laid down his arms and surrendered his body you no longer have any right over his life'. The next two centuries have witnessed attempts to establish a more humanitarian REGIME for the treatment of prisoners of war. An attempt which finds its parallel in other aspects of the laws of war.

The treatment of prisoners of war was considered at the Brussels Conference of 1874 and at the HAGUE PEACE CONFERENCES of 1899 and 1907. The Hague meetings were important for establishing the principle that prisoners of war are the responsibility of the hostile government which therefore becomes responsible, in law, for their subsequent treatment. It also established a series of recognized rules for the appropriate treatment of prisoners during hostilities and for their speedy REPATRIATION afterwards. These provisions were supplemented in 1929 by the Geneva Convention on the Treatment of Prisoners of War.

The events of the Second World War, especially but not exclusively in relation to prisoners held by Japan, showed that the regime required further elaboration. The result was the 1949 Geneva Convention on the Treatment of Prisoners of War. Running to 143 Articles it represented the most detailed attempt to stipulate a code of conduct for those authorities detaining captives. It remains, at the time of writing, the major contemporary statement of INTERNATIONAL LAW on this question.

Two areas of recent controversy should be noted in conclusion. First, the question of repatriation. Events in Korea in the 1950s, in VIETNAM in the 1960s and 1970s and in the FALKLANDS in 1982 have raised certain questions about repatriation. Principally these concern a possible clash of interests between a STATE wanting its prisoners to be repatriated and the captives not wanting to return. The Falklands raised issues of third parties wanting prisoners to be detained as law-breakers where repatriation to their home state might allow them to escape justice. In brief, speedy repatriation of able-bodied prisoners might not be quite as unambiguous as the 1949 Geneva Convention suggests.

The second area of controversy relates to the increasing use of GUERILLA WARFARE, INSURGENCY and PARTISAN operations either in support of CONVENTIONAL methods or in their stead. These operations are, by definition, irregular and unorthodox. As such they raise the question of what should be the appropriate treatment for members of such forces captured during hostilities. The tendency since the advent of guerrilla warfare as a recognized mode has been not to extend to captured persons the protection of the prisoner of war regime. The re-turn to less civilized methods in respect of this category can be justified on a number of grounds. First, the guerrilla often uses deception and concealment; in short, he does not carry weapons openly. Secondly, the guerrilla does not, himself, observe the rules on the humanitarian treatment of captives. Thirdly, the guerrilla does not wear a recognized uniform. Because the irregular insurgent is usually the standard bearer of a revolutionary IDEOLOGY it is unlikely that state actors and their authorities will ever be able to incorporate this kind of warfare under the aegis of the 'civilizing' tendencies referred to earlier. As such its import is that a significant type of interstate and intrastate violence will not be so rule-governed as regards the treatment of captives.

## Propaganda

Propaganda is an instrument of policy. It is potentially available to any actor having the means to promote and disseminate it. Propaganda is the deliberate attempt at persuading people, either as individuals or in groups, to accept a particular DEFINITION OF THE SITUATION by manipulating selected non-rational factors in their personality or in their social evironment, the consequent effect of this attempt being to change and mould their behaviour into a certain desired direction.

TECHNOLOGY has been of great assistance to the propagandist. The development of printing, which allowed the propagandist to use newspapers, leaflets, pamphlets and books, was the first. The twentieth century development of wireless telegraphy enabled propagandists to broadcast actual sounds, including the spoken word, across state frontiers and to 'target' whole populations. The Nazi REGIME that came to power in Germany in 1932 was one of the first twentieth century leaderships to appreciate the importance of having radio receivers widely available to target a particular population. Picture transmission via television has been a further development in telegraphy since 1945. Film propaganda, intrinsically important in urban societies, has also been further enhanced by television.

There are a number of techniques and factors inherent in the propagandist's methodology. First, propaganda simplifies issues. This is partly to make things more intelligible but in the process of simplification censorship and distortion can be effected. Secondly, propagandists will appear to exercise a 'cultural proximity' judgement. Propaganda will concentrate upon issues in the external environment where people have some identification; geographic, cultural or political. Thirdly, the propagandist will sensationalize. Sensationalism is literally appealing to the senses. Propaganda is thus emotionally arousing or disturbing. This involves presenting issues which are personalized, dramatized, nationalistic and often immoderate. This sensationalism is particularly prevalent during CONFLICT situations where tensions are heightened in any event. The propagandist will be greatly assisted by being able to manipulate stereotypes that a target audience holds of other groups, societies and nations. Stereotypes of out-groups are widespread within social systems. They tend to be over-simplified in content and not amenable to change in response to changes in the OPERATIONAL ENVIRONMENT. These stereotypes, which are present in all social groupings, are therefore amenable to the influence of propaganda.

The classic instance of the kind of sensationalism referred to above is the *atrocity story*. The essence of this event, or series of events, is to manipulate the target audience into the PERCEPTION that the instigators of the atrocity are inhuman. This will be easier if there is already a high level of tension and hostility between the groups – such as would be expected during a WAR. An atrocity can be defined as a behaviour sequence which so violates the norms as to shock and arouse a sense of horror among those witnessing or hearing the incident. For the propagandist the first requirement is to convince the audience that the atrocity was actually committed. This can be facilitated greatly if independent witnesses are available to corroborate. Thereafter the propagandist must present the atrocity in such a way as to arouse the active concern and implied condemnation of the target audience. Normally the more the victims appear to have been defenceless and without military or political significance, the easier is the propagandist's job. If an atrocity appears to be racially motivated or if a whole group of people appear to have been indiscriminate victims – all the inhabitants of a village, for example – the atrocity will look worse. If the victims suffered other indignities before death – such as rape – the sense of outrage may be greater.

Propaganda is more likely to prove effective if the propagandist is the sole or major source of information for the particular target audience. Propaganda is more effective when directed at a population which shares, at least in part, the attitudes of the propagandist. It is easier to confirm existing attitudes, to strengthen prevalent beliefs than to effect radical change. Propaganda is more effective if it can be directed through other agencies of socialization, such as the family or the education system. These agencies can reinforce the message and provide a socio-cultural matrix which supports the propagandist. There is considerable evidence to suggest that people are more susceptible when in crowds, political rallies, etc. The manipulation of the non-rational side of the personality, which is the essence of the propaganda influence attempt, appears to be assisted in these circumstances.

## Protectionism

The use of TARIFFS and NON-TARIFF BARRIERS (NTBS), such as QUOTAS, to 'protect' a market that might otherwise be vulnerable to IMPORTS. Traditionally tariffs had been the most widely used instruments for protectionism, but latterly NTBS have been increasingly preferred particularly since the establishment of the General Agreement on Tariffs and Trade (GATT). Protectionist measures may be taken by STATES acting individually, or in concert, as in a TRADE BLOC or COMMON MARKET system. Accordingly, political economists have tended to see states, and their leaders, faced with a choice between FREE TRADE or protectionism. Classical ECONOMIC LIBERALISM came down firmly in favour of the former. Complete FREE TRADE has in point of fact always been an 'ideal type' to which the actual policies of states more or less approximated at particular times. Hegemonic stability theorists have recently pointed to a positive correlation between free, or freer, trade and the presence of a hegemonial ACTOR in the system willing and able to support the establishment of ground rules leading to this state of affairs. By implication, therefore, the absence of such an actor leads to the growth of protectionist sentiments and policies.

Protectionism is advocated by those thinkers favouring NEO-MERCANTILIST approaches to political economy. This tradition, like the MERCANTILIST approach beforehand, endorsed a STATE-CENTRED approach to such ISSUE AREAS as trade and payments. Accordingly it is quite appropriate for the leaders of states to think and act in these self-regarding terms. Liberals argue that if all actors in the system behave in this 'beggar my neighbour' manner then all will lose out since protectionist measures in one state will be cancelled out by reciprocal measures in another.

In contemporary WORLD POLITICS protectionism is a favoured policy among THIRD WORLD leaders. These states, their leaders argue, face a trading system that favours the established advanced industrial countries (AICs). Without countervailing measures they will find it difficult to redress the balance of disadvantage. Operation of such schemes as the generalized system of preferences amounts to explicitly recogizing this structural disadvantage and shows a willingness to modify the liberal ortho-

doxy towards what is variously called 'compensatory' or 'Keynesian' liberalism.

Protectionist pressure is also likely to be strong in those states where important and influential interest groups can successfully lobby for their particular needs to be met by a policy of protectionism. The Common Agricultural Policy (CAP) of the EUROPEAN COMMUNITY illustrates how a small but well organized group can lobby in defence of its perceived interests.

## Protocol

A term associated with DIPLOMACY which carries a number of meanings. It can refer to the original draft of a DIPLOMATIC document or TREATY or it can refer to a record of agreement between STATES which is less formal than a treaty or convention. Thus the agreement signed in 1920 at Geneva to establish the PERMANENT COURT OF INTERNATIONAL JUSTICE was described as a 'protocol'. In modern usage the word is universally employed as a generic term for diplomatic etiquette and rules of procedure. (Although the eminent diplomatist Harold Nicolson (1950) argues that the proper term in this second sense is 'protocole' meaning 'correct form of procedure' or 'ceremonial'.) An important ingredient of protocol is rank or precedence since matters of prestige and honour have always been central to diplomatic communications. At the Congress of VIENNA in 1815 four diplomatic ranks were established and subsequently formally adopted by the European diplomatic system. The hierarchy of rankings was, and is, as follows: (a) ambassadors and papal nuncios; (b) envoys extraordinary and ministers plenipotentiary; (c) ministers resident; (d) CHARGÉS D'AFFAIRES. At the Congress of Aix-la-Chapelle in 1818 it was further established that among diplomats of the same rank precedence was to be established on the basis of length of service in a posting rather than on the POWER or importance of the government the diplomat represented. The 'doyen' or dean of the diplomatic corps, regardless of state affiliation, thus heads ceremonial processions. Protocol in this wider sense embraces procedural matters, diplomatic language and formal aspects of the negotiating process and although modern developments in diplomacy have tended to bypass traditional courtesies it still has an important part to play in the business of communication between states.

## Protracted war

This term has two distinct meanings. Almost any WAR can become protracted if a STALEMATE occurs between the parties. In this sense it is the antithesis of BLITZKRIEG. However, the term can also be used in a second sense to refer to a deliberate strategy. In this usage the protraction is caused not by stalemate arising from symmetry of forces but stalemate arising from an inferiority of forces. It is thus closely related to the GUERRILLA WAR situation. Indeed, the deliberate extension of the violence by the inferior guerrilla or insurgent forces is a standard response. The inferiority of the insurgents forces them to opt for the indirect approach; trading space for time, harassing the incumbent's forces and denying them the chance of a decisive engagement, eroding their morale, physically exhausting them and so on. The essence of protracted war is encapsulated in the familiar dictum that the guerrilla wins if he does not lose: the conventional force loses if it does not win.

The most influential articulation of the importance of protraction in the guerrilla war is that of Mao Tse-tung in his writings on the Chinese experience of PEOPLE'S WAR. He argued that in their struggle against their opponents the Chinese Communists made a virtue of necessity by organizing resistance in the most remote rural areas, avoiding potentially decisive engagements, 'liberating' areas from their opponents' control and gradually encircling the urban areas from the countryside; all this in the expectation that, faced with a long campaign, contradictions and fissures would appear in the ranks of opposition. There is no doubt that by employing these methods with skill and determination, a force of insurgents can tie down a conventional force, many times its own size, for an indeterminate period of time. Mao himself saw the balance of forces between incumbents and insurgents gradually changing over time until the latter were in the position of taking the offensive, across the board, against the incumbent forces. It is important to a full understanding of protracted war, therefore, to appreciate that it is a dynamic and malleable instrument which, if effective, will eventually lead to the defeat of the incumbent forces and the downfall of their REGIME. It is part of the means for implementing revolutionary change.

Protracted War thus arises from a situation that has been defined as 'asymmetric conflict' (see: Mack, 1975). It has been widely employed by statesmen and strategists since the Chinese REVOLUTION and an examination of its several applications – both successful and unsuccessful – would have to cover the cases of VIETNAM after 1959, Malaya, Algeria, Cuba and a number of instances in Africa, South of the Sahara.

## Public opinion

Public opinion is a key variable in the domestic or internal environment of STATE ACTORS, particularly those which have some core value commitment to pluralist DEMOCRACY. Notwithstanding these democratic norms, there is considerable empirical evidence available to confirm the view that even in such participatory systems the mass of the population, in whose name policy is made, are not actively involved in the process in any regular and routine way. In the area of foreign POLICY-MAKING the vast majority of the population are probably ruled out from exercising any effective or significant influence. This is primarily because they simply do not know enough about what is going on, when it is going on, to have any influence.

There are a number of situational reasons for this lack of information and therefore lack of INFLUENCE. First, in all political systems FOREIGN POLICY is widely perceived as an area of executive predominance. Foreign policy or statecraft was traditionally regarded as the prerogative of rulers from the inception of the STATE-SYSTEM. Notwithstanding the attempts of twentieth century IDEALISTS to democratize the process, this influence of tradition is still significant in the contemporary system. In some states indeed this executive bias is strengthened by the amount of secrecy and confidentiality which surrounds policy-making. Secondly, it must be recognized that, particularly in the field of LOW POLITICS, many foreign policy decisions are made on the basis of rather specialist knowledge which is not available to the general public and which would probably not interest them if it was available. Thirdly, some foreign policy decisions are essentially reactive in character. Time may very well be at a premium and decisions may need to be made quickly with the minimum of consultation. Fourthly, the tendency in many democracies for foreign policy issues to be approached from a bi-partisan perspective means that the customary DEFINITION OF THE SITUATION provided by party politics is not available. In all systems the mass of the electorate do not have access to sufficient information to develop and then maintain sophisticated attitudes about foreign policy issues. The mass media often contribute to this relative ignorance by reducing their coverage of foreign affairs, or by presenting issues in a highly simplified form.

It can be concluded, therefore, that public opinion tends to be structured in a hierarchical fashion with an ATTENTIVE PUBLIC mediating between the mass public and the policy-making ELITE. Two communication patterns therefore become evident in public opinion terms. First, there is horizontal communication within the elite and between the elite and the informed public. Second, there is vertical communication between the LEADERSHIP and the mass of the population. Thus bureaucrats in the elite and interest or lobby groups in the informed public will probably have regular and routine channels of communication. Provided that there are no significant divisions within the elite this consensual communication pattern can be maintained. If, on the other hand, significant cleavages emerge within this structure the mass public may be mobilized in support of one or more factions and parties within the elite.

The foregoing discussion shows that the mass public need not remain passive on foreign policy questions. The mass of the population are likely to become mobilized when a split occurs within the policy-making elite. Secondly, the idea of unrelieved passivity is contradicted by the MOOD THEORY. This argues that the mass public can exert a negative and constraining influence by their prevailing mood, setting limits beyond which the leadership cannot easily go.

# Q

**Quadruple Alliance**
*See:* HOLY ALLIANCE


**Quaker**
*See:* PACIFISM


**Quarantine**
Term referring to the compulsory separation or isolation of people, animals, plants or merchandise arriving from abroad at sea or airports, usually for a specified period, its general purpose being to guard against the spread of contagious disease. Until the First World War, customary INTERNATIONAL LAW decreed that the period of quarantine should be forty days on board a ship anchored away from other ships in port. In 1926 and 1933, partly due to the relatively new practice of air travel, new regulations were introduced by the Sanitary Convention; these were amended by the PROTOCOL of 1946 and by the Convention of the Co-operation in Quarantine and Protection of Plants of 1959. These in effect diversified the practice to include long-stay isolation hospitals and temporary observation centres.

The term has also been used in a metaphorical sense as in Roosevelt's Quarantine Doctrine of 1937, where he declared that the WAR-like FASCIST STATES of Europe and imperialist Japan should be quarantined by the international community since 'war is a contagion, whether it be declared or undeclared'. The effects of the imposition of total mandatory ECONOMIC SANCTIONS on a state is often described in these terms: that the outside world should impose total isolation on an offending state until such time as the 'contagion' (usually APARTHEID) is cleared. In this sense the term is used to signify punishment rather than precaution, and is therefore less accurate than BOYCOTT or enforced isolation. The term took on a novel meaning in 1962 when the US government, under J. F. Kennedy, instituted a naval quarantine around the island of Cuba as a deliberately coercive move in the course of the CUBAN MISSILE CRISIS of October. One of Kennedy's biographers (Schlesinger, 1967) says of the decision: 'Since a blockade was technically an act of war, it was thought better to refer to it as a quarantine' (p. 624). This American finesse of the distinction is now the most commonly cited example of the use of the quarantine instrument.


**Quisling**
Synonym for collaboration with an occuping POWER, taken from the name of the Norwegian Prime Minister, Vidkun Quisling (1887–1945), as a result of his active acquiescence and cooperation with Nazi Germany. The word quickly passed into the vocabulary of WORLD POLITICS. In 1946, for example, a UN GENERAL ASSEMBLY Resolution recognized 'the necessity of clearly distinguishing between genuine refugees and displaced persons on the one hand, and the war criminals, quislings and traitors on the other'. The term Vichy is also sometimes used in this connection,

being derived from a French resort which from 1940 to 1944 was the seat of Marshall Petain's collaborationist government.

## Quota

A NON-TARIFF BARRIER (NTB), the quota is a quantitative restriction upon TRADE. It works by setting a physical limit beyond which IMPORTS cannot go and it is implemented by the central authorities of the ACTOR concerned – which may be a STATE, CUSTOMS UNION, COMMON MARKET and so on. Quotas are highly protectionist because, unlike tariffs, they work to completely remove goods from markets and leave the ground free for the preferred products – if any are available. In extremis they can be used as one of the weapons of economic control in a so-called 'siege economy'. That is to say, in an economic system that is run on highly autarchic, self-defensive lines. Siege economies are sometimes forced upon states during WAR conditions, but in addition they may be deliberately chosen goals by states following an ORIENTATION of ISOLATIONISM. A situation of internal war or REVOLUTION may, perforce, produce a siege economy.

As Baldwin (1985) notes quotas are accepted instruments of economic statecraft to be used, for instance, as part of a package of ECONOMIC SANCTIONS. Support for such coercive measures may additionally come from vested economic interests within the actor that willy-nilly benefits from such impositions. Quotas have been particularly favoured as policy instruments by agricultural interests and can be used to combat perceived policies of DUMPING by other actors. Quotas are widely used to control BALANCE OF PAYMENTS deficits. Unfortunately they can provoke retaliation and simply store up demand for goods and services which spills out once they are removed.

The General Agreement on Tariffs and Trade (GATT), while containing a general prohibition upon quota restrictions, made an exception in the case of signatory states with balance of payments difficulties. Quotas are restrictions upon FREE TRADE and therefore the GATT position on this issue is fully congruent with its ECONOMIC LIBERAL assumptions. GATT is not the only intergovernmental organizations (IGO) to face the issue of quotas in the post-1945 system. Both the OEEC and the EUROPEAN COMMUNITY worked to liberalize trade between member states. On the other hand the growth of such trade BLOCS and common markets has lead to the use of quotas against third parties outside the arrangement. The issue of quotas, as well as other NTBS, continues to exercise GATT negotiations at the time of writing.

# R

## Radar

A detection system which works by transmitting and receiving very short wave radio signals. Radar is actually an acronym for Radio Detection and Ranging. The ability of radar to collect information as well as to transmit it means that, in communication terms, it is a FEEDBACK system. This complexity means that radar can be used for 'position-fixing' and, as a result, it has great significance for military operations. It is also used in civilian transportation systems as a navigational device.

Early work on radar began in the 1930s in Western Europe and the United States. The advent of the Second World War provided fresh impetus for its development. Radar played a key role, for example, in the 1940 AIR WAR between the United Kingdom and Germany known as the 'Battle of Britain'. UK ground-based radars were able to provide early warning of incoming German air formations for the RAF interceptor squadrons. Radar was primarily used for defensive operations until the later stages of the WAR when both the US and the UK bomber forces used it for directional purposes in raids over Europe.

The advent of the COLD WAR rivalry between the SUPERPOWERS and the ensuing ARMS RACE after 1945 led to new developments in radar techniques. Very large ground-based radars were developed on both sides to furnish early warning of hostile movements by the adversary. The advent of missile TECHNOLOGY provided a further impetus for the evolution of radar.

Warning time of an impending FIRST STRIKE can be so brief that accurate and early detection of incoming missiles is a prerequisite.

## Radiation

The most common form of radiation is electromagnetic: infra-red, ultra violet and cosmic radiation being examples. Recent theories of physics, in particular quantum theory, have suggested that radiation should be conceived of as involving the emission of particles as discrete units rather than in continuous waves, as thought previously. Radiation occurs naturally on earth and in outer space but it is radiation that is deliberately produced by the activities of man that creates the most damaging effects. The twentieth century revolution in nuclear physics has greatly enhanced these CAPABILITIES. Irradiation caused by NUCLEAR POWER accidents and/or the deliberate use of NUCLEAR WEAPONS threatens POLLUTION of the planet on a scale some find unacceptable. In the case of nuclear power, of course, the irradiation is unintentional, usually the result of some human error compounding a technical malfunction.

The use of nuclear weapons is deliberate. Here the irradiation is much more severe and in extreme cases, such as the NUCLEAR WINTER, beyond man's capability to control. The actual explosion of an ATOM or HYDROGEN BOMB produces immediate radiation of heat, gamma rays and so on. The longer term irradiation, or fallout, can result in the release of isotopes which can continue to irradiate for centuries or even millennia. This irradiation time scale is known as the 'half-life' of the isotope and is a measure of the time it takes the substances to irradiate half its energy. Some of the isotopes produced by a nuclear explosion such as PLUTONIUM, have very long half-lives.

## Raison d'état

Reason of state. This doctrine is intimately bound up with political REALISM, POWER politics and REALPOLITIK and is concerned with the primacy or centrality of the STATE. It asserts that the question of necessity overrides ordinary considerations of morality; that where the well-being of the state is deemed to be at stake all other considerations are subordinate to its interests. As such, it is organically related to the concept of the NATIONAL INTEREST and its natural tendency is towards a utilitarian calculation of advantage for the state. According to Friedrich Meinecke's (1957) classic study of the idea the phrase was first used in the works of Archbishop Giovanni della Casa in 1547 where it was rendered as *ragion di stato*, but it was MACHIAVELLI who developed the first modern exposition of the idea in *The Prince* and *Discourses*. Machiavelli's central proposition was that every other value is subordinate to the survival of the state. In *Discourses* 111, 41, for example, he captures its essence in this way:

> Where the very safety of the fatherland is at stake, there should be no question of reflecting whether a thing is just or unjust, humane or cruel, praiseworthy or shameful. Setting aside every other consideration, one must take only that course of action which will secure the country's life and liberty.

In the world of practical politics, as distinct from political philosophy (assuming such a distinction can exist in this case where 'practice' clearly created 'theory'), it is particularly associated with the policies of Cardinal Richelieu in seventeenth century France. Domestically it justified the assertion of central AUTHORITY over powerful local interests and in FOREIGN POLICY it allowed France to form ALLIANCES against, rather than with, the Habsburgs with whom they shared a general religious-cum-ideological affinity. In its utilitarian guise, it reached its fullest expression in the expansionist policies of Bismark (though here the distinction between *raison d'état* and REALPOLITIK is somewhat blurred).

Apart from rational calculation of interests in the service of the state, the idea can be seen to have an ethical dimension, given a particular view of the means–ends formula. If the end to which policies are directed (e.g. the survival of the homeland) is itself deemed to be a moral one, then the tensions between public and private morality which have so damned the doctrine in the eyes of modern LIBERALISM disappear: reason of state is then simultaneously reason of God or of the moral ideal. However, as a number of commentators have pointed out, although on occasion 'doing what is right' and 'doing what is in your own interests' might happily coincide, there is no certainty that this will be so, nor is there a built-in guard against its unscrupulous employment. For these reasons, coupled with the fact that in the first half of the twentieth century it tended to speak with a pronounced German accent, the doctrine has been generally discredited, at least in public. However, in so far as the state is still central (though by no means unique) in WORLD POLITICS, the idea of *raison d'etat* can never be totally discounted.

## RAND Corporation

The RAND Corporation, Santa Monica, California is the archetype of the US policy-orientated research institute – the so-called 'think tank'. An acronym for Research and

Development, RAND began life as 'Project RAND' during the winter of 1945–6. The project was officially initated by US Army Air Force contract MX-791 on 1 March 1946. At that time sponsorship was shared between the USAAF and the Douglas Aircraft Corporation. Project RAND extended into the post-1945 world the close collaboration between the military and the scientific community that had been a feature of the period from 1941–5. Specifically Project RAND was to continue the 'scientific study and research on the broad subject of air warfare . . .' that had been so successfully initiated during the earlier period.

The connections with Douglas were severed in 1948 and in May of that year the RAND Corporation came into existence. Funded now by the Ford Foundation, RAND was to be an independent, non-profit making organization still working on Air Force contracts. In the autumn of 1947 the Social Science and Economics divisions of RAND were established. With this task expansion the RAND became in effect a STRATEGIC STUDIES rather than operational research institute. Thereafter RAND's influence in this key policy area grew into one of great significance. Some of the foremost minds in strategy were enrolled into RAND and some highly innovative studies were produced in the years that followed. Names such as Brodie, Kaufmann and Wohlstetter may be cited to substantiate the point (Bobbitt, 1989). Many of these scholars were subsequently recruited into a closer relationship with the POLICY-MAKING centre under the incumbency of Robert McNamara, the Secretary of Defense for much of the 1960s. Probably the greatest testament to the influence of RAND among strategists of the nuclear era is the attempt to 'conventionalize' nuclear weapons via such doctrines as COUNTERFORCE. The tradition of 'thinking about the unthinkable' was established early in RAND's existence and the ideas and assumptions associated with this approach to nuclear strategy had become conventional wisdom by 1980.

There is no doubt that in the strict academic sense RAND is not independent. Its close symbiotic relationship with the US military and the need to observe strict cannons of confidentiality – in order to have access to classified information – means that, in many respects, RAND represents a 'cross-over' from pure academic research to policy-orientated inquiry. This is a fairly familiar problem with STRATEGIC STUDIES in general and the history of institutions such as RAND demonstrate the premiums and the pitfalls of a close relationship with the policy centre.

## Rapacki plan

A Polish proposal for a NUCLEAR FREE ZONE in Central Europe which was first made public in the UNITED NATIONS GENERAL ASSEMBLY in the autumn of 1957 by the Polish Foreign Minister, Adam Rapacki. The basis of the Plan was the elimination of all NUCLEAR WEAPONS and their support facilities from the two German STATES, Poland and Czechoslovakia. The plan required that states within the zone should refrain from any policies which might lead to their production of NUCLEAR WEAPONS, while states outside the zone should refrain from introducing nuclear weapons of their own into it. In later versions of the plan, phased reductions in CONVENTIONAL forces were also included. The plan envisaged establishing a control authority to monitor the implementation of the agreement and the establishment of an INSPECTION regime to implement it.

The Rapacki plan was greated with a good deal of scepticism and some outright hostility in the West. By 1957 the states in NATO had become committed to the early and first use of nuclear weapons, at least of a TACTICAL dimension, in any future WAR in Europe. The failure of the Alliance membership to implement seriously any of the agreed policies for increases in conventional forces had perforce compelled

NATO to adopt this strategy. The TRIP-WIRE concept of CONVENTIONAL forces simply reinforced NATO's nuclear dependence. As such Rapacki looked like an attempt to undermine the one credible CAPABILITY that NATO could set against its perceived inferiority *vis-à-vis* the WARSAW PACT.

### Rapid deployment force (rdf)

A product of strategic thinking in the 1970s when many observers were writing of a 'new' COLD WAR, a rapid deployment force (rdf) was conceived as an instrument of Western INTERVENTION in THIRD WORLD violent conflicts. As the term implies, the thinking behind the rdf was that in certain circumstances speed would be of the essence if perceived interests were to be defended. The intervention of the Soviet Union in AFGHANISTAN was the catalyst, but in general terms the conception of the rdf is typical of that type of thinking which sees political problems in terms of military solutions.

Implementing the idea has proved to be more difficult than conceiving it. France has a small, ELITE force – the *force d'intervention* – which has been used to support French interests in Africa and the Pacific. The United States' much larger rdf – properly called the Rapid Deployment Joint Task Force – was set up in 1980. Unlike the French force, the US rdf draws existing forces from all of the services – including the Marine Corps – and has a generalized mandate to respond to any non-NATO contingency. These 'out of area operations' cover a very broad spectrum. A total available force in excess of 100,000 may be more than enough for intervening in an army mutiny in some Pacific island, but be totally inadequate for a major regional crisis in the Middle East that appears to threaten oil supplies. The difficulty is the conversion of available CAPABILITY into effective instruments of POWER. Until an appropriate DEFINITION OF THE SITUATION is reached it is impossible to match CAP-ABILITIES to requirements and even then the assessment may be negative.

Notwithstanding these caveats the following strategies for the US type of rdf can be envisaged:

1. An rdf could act as a TRIP-WIRE force. In this role it would symbolize the intention of the United States in particular, and the West in general, to escalate up the ladder once the 'trip' had been set off.
2. An rdf could be used in an internal WAR situation to support an incumbent regime – this is one role where ex-COLONIAL states such as the United Kingdom and France have used their forces in the past. The 'learning experience' of the VIETNAM WAR is instructive here, however.
3. An rdf force could be used in a specific case of economic crisis where threats to vital economic interests are perceived to be at stake. This role has been described as 'asset-seizing', although others might see it as 'asset-stripping'. The usual scenario here is a seizure by the rdf of Middle Eastern oil fields.
4. An rdf could be used as a proxy PEACE-KEEPING force. Here the intention would be NEUTRALIZATION and insulation of a violent conflict and the rdf would play the role of a 'law and order' force. The political question of whose law and order was to be enforced and for how long would still need to be settled.

How far a Western orientated and supplied rdf could operate in a Third World environment characterized by an ORIENTATION towards NEUTRALISM and NON-ALIGNMENT remains a moot point. However, the minimum ground rules for such a capability to operate at all should include: (a) having sufficient contingents available and trained for such operations; (b) having the support of states in the 'target area' so that, for instance, basing facilities would be available; (c) having a clear and unambiguous chain of command to the political DECISION-MAKING centre; and (d) a political centre with a clear idea of its goals and a mandate for achieving them.

## Rapprochement

Diplomatic term of French origin meaning the renewal of normal relations after a period of disharmony or CONFLICT. Thus, US–Chinese relations after 1979 could be described as 'rapprochement'.

*See also:* DETENTE

## Ratification

Usually refers to the treaty-making process. A TREATY is not confirmed or valid until the procedure for ratification is complete. This process can vary according to the constitutional requirements of the signatory states. In the United Kingdom ratification is by the Crown, in the United States the President negotiates treaties but under the provisions of the 'separation-of-powers' doctrine they cannot be ratified without the approval of a two-thirds voting majority in Senate. Most treaties are duly endorsed but an important example of non-ratification was the Senate's failure to approve the LEAGUE OF NATIONS Covenant in 1919, thus preventing US participation in the organzation. Since treaty-making is vital to the development of INTERNATIONAL LAW and is regarded as one of the great achievements of DIPLOMACY instruments of ratfication are regarded as crucial. A treaty is not in force until such instruments have been exchanged or deposited in a specific location. The twentieth century has seen an enormous increase in bilateral and multilateral treaties (the United Kingdom and the United States are parties to over 10,000 each) and the treaties registered with the UN extend to over one thousand volumes (*see:* Adam Watson, 1982). Ratification therefore has the effect of creating a new body of rules for those involved, and is part of the general dynamic of INTERNATIONAL SOCIETY.

## Rationality

Considerations of rationality frequently arise in the context of the study of WORLD POLITICS, particularly when the DECISION-MAKING LEVEL OF ANALYSIS is influencing description and explanation. The question 'are decision-makers rational?' is really fundamental to this approach. Indeed, many would argue that this question is one of *the* fundamental challenges facing any study of human behaviour, whatever approach is being used.

Discussions of rationality now usually take as their starting point the view, derived from economics, that rationality can be defined as utility maximization. This is sometimes presented as the way in which 'efficient' decisions should be made. Such stipulations are clearly prescriptive and still leave open the empirical question of whether in actual cases efficient choices are made. GAME THEORY in particular has sought to build upon a series of generalizations based upon this utility maximization approach. Here 'being rational' means following the MINIMAX precept: one maximizes gains or minimizes losses. To do anything else would be irrational. When game theoretical approaches are broadened to include mixed-motive games the problem of stipulating rationality becomes more complex. In particular the classic Prisoner's Dilemma game actually involves two concepts of rationality. Individual rationality prescribes to each player the course of action most advantageous to him under the circumstances, while collective rationality prescribes a course of action to both players simultaneously. The 'dilemma' intrinsic in the game is that if both act on the basis of collective rationality, then each is better off than the individual would be if acting on the basis of individual rationality. One of the key variables in resolving the dilemma in this game is the extent to which each player can 'trust' the other, but clearly considerations of trusting and being trustworthy take the analysis beyond the concept of rationality. If efficiency of choice as a criteria for evaluating rationality leads to paradoxes such as the Prisoner's Dilemma then this approach to the question of what constitutes rationality may be a mixed blessing.

An alternative view is taken by those who look at the way decision-makers reach estimations about the choices they have to make. If these individuals and groups can make an optimum estimation of the outcomes of all available courses of action then they can be said to be acting rationally. This idea of optimum estimation has been attacked by organization theorists such as Herbert Simon (1965). Simon developed the idea of 'bounded rationality' as an alternative to optimum rationality in these situations. He argued that decision-making problems are so complex that only a limited number of aspects of each problem can be attended to at any one time. Indeed, psychologically decision-makers identify and formulate problems within a particular framework so that the perceived solution, if there is one, is built into the framework.

Additionally, Simon argued that decision-makers rarely seek optimum solutions. They do not consider all the alternatives and pick the best one; rather, they find a course of action that is good enough for present purposes that satisfies. Simon called this 'satisficing' and said that this is more plausible than the idea of maximization. Simon's thinking about rationality implies that terms like 'finding the best possible policy' have little operational meaning because the search for alternatives is always limited and finite. It is impossible to consider all alternatives so POLICY-MAKERS tend to consider the most obvious, most attainable, most reasonable, etc. Of course, as the actual decision process proceeds other alternatives may occur or originally conceived alternatives may disappear.

It would appear that confident stipulations about rationality in the field of study are set about with qualifications. Deductive approaches such as maximizing subjective utilities are flawed by inductive, empirical studies which often show that in the particular event these requirements were not followed. The Prisoner's Dilemma shows that such deductive approaches may not produce stable solutions. Any discussion of rationality has to take account of the factor of subject PERCEPTION if it is to be empirically relevant and Simon's studies have shown how much this perspective can lead to modifications.

### Reagan doctrine

Term used to describe the FOREIGN POLICY of President Reagan from 1980 to 1988. This 'doctrine' was never officially promulgated as a series of coherent policy initiatives in the sense that the NIXON and TRUMAN DOCTRINES were. To a large degree it was a matter of style and IMAGE rather than policy or substance. The term itself was popularized in 1985 by Karl Krauthhammer of *Time* magazine and its central propositions involved overcoming 'the VIETNAM syndrome', restoring the nation's pride and self-confidence, and re-armament to the point that the United States could achieve a comfortable margin of security over its main adversaries. From the outset President Reagan was determined to halt the expansion of Soviet power that had occurred in the 1970s and to reaffirm both the utility and the legitimacy of the use of US power in pursuit of national objectives.

His overall goal was to break out of the straitjacket of mutual DETERRENCE in order to give the United States greater freedom of action in responding to global developments. Thus, although the doctrine itself appeared to be focused on proclaiming the rights of INTERVENTION against illegitimate (especially Marxist/Leninist) governments, it is inseparable from the larger issue of the strategic balance between East and West. Three broad policy objectives can be identified:

1. The creation of a new INTERNATIONAL ORDER where the LEGITIMACY of governments is linked to conformity to the democratic process. This meant that the United

States had a 'moral responsibility' to support anti-COMMUNIST insurgencies wherever they appeared, either through direct military intervention as in Grenada in 1983, or by supplying economic or military aid as in Pakistan, AFGHANISTAN, Angola, and most notoriously, in Nicaragua. The punitive air strike against Libya in 1986 was also part of this process of legitimization. By 1986 it has been estimated that the United States spent over one billion dollars in military AID and over four billion dollars in economic aid for the specific purpose of checking, and if possible reversing, the growth of Soviet and communist influence in the THIRD WORLD.

2. To restore a favourable military and strategic balance so that 'no enemy will dare threaten the United States'. The centrepiece of this process of rearmament was the Strategic Defense Initiative (SDI) but it also involved expanding the MX missile programme, Trident submarines and the Rapid Deployment Force (RDF), all of which originated during President Carter's ill-fated administration. In addition, the expansion of US CONVENTIONAL forces to enhance US regional intervention CAPABILITIES was undertaken. To improve communication and command systems, CENTCOM, a new central command structure, was established in 1983 with the specific task of overseeing and coordinating US deployments in the Middle East and Asia. Naval forces were also expanded and during the Reagan administration the combat fleet increased from 485 ships to 600. In all, by 1987 defence expenditure rose by 45 per cent.

3. The Soviet Union was to be denied access to advanced Western TECHNOLOGY. Reagan sought to exert pressure on the Soviet economy by exploiting its dependence on Western imports. To this end, the United States' European allies were encouraged (not always with success) to withdraw from existing commitments and abolish the favourable credit arrangements previously undertaken with the Soviet Union.

As the doctrine relied on a constant evocation of the Soviet threat ('the evil empire') it lost much of its force and thrust after 1985 when the 'new thinking' implicit in the GORBACHEV DOCTRINE began to take effect. Indeed, Presdent Reagan himself began to modify his COLD WAR stance and in the words of George Schultz, his Secretary of State, the doctrine had now evolved into 'constructive confrontation' where NEGOTIATION with the Soviet Union on ARMS CONTROL was linked to progress in HUMAN RIGHTS and regional issues. The culmination of this RAPPROCHEMENT was the INF TREATY signed in Washington in December 1987.

## Realism

Sometimes called the 'power-politics' school of thought, political realism in one form or another has dominated both academic considerations of WORLD POLITICS and the thinking of foreign POLICY-MAKERS themselves.

The ideas associated with it can be traced to the ancient Greeks, and THUCYDIDES' *History of the Peloponnesian War* is widely regarded as the first sustained attempt to explain the origins of international conflict in terms of the dynamics of power-politics. MACHIAVELLI in *The Prince* (1513) and HOBBES in *Leviathan* (1651) also provided crucial components of this tradition, especially in their conceptions of interest, prudence, and expediency as prime motivators in the essentially anarchic arena of world politics. As a theory, or a set of propositions about the individual, the STATE and the STATE-SYSTEM it reached the height of its appeal, especially in the Anglo-American world, in the years between the 1940s and the 1960s. Thereafter it was challenged by the BEHAVIOURAL or SOCIAL SCIENCE approaches, but reappeared in the 1980s in the guise of neo- or structural realism. Among its most prominent early adherents were E. H. Carr, R. Niebuhr, H. J. Morgenthau, G. Schwartzenberger, M.

Wight, N. Spykman and G. F. Kennan, all of whom continue to exercise an influence on the development of the field despite the basic weakness of the concepts and the methodology that they employed. This group spawned a generation of distinguished scholars who continued to approach world politics from a power-political framework. Among these are R. Aron, R. Rosecrance, A. Wolfers, K. W. Thompson, K. N. Waltz, H. Kissinger, H. Bull, R. E. Osgood and R. W. Tucker. The recent re-emergence of its central concepts (*see:* Keohane, 1986) testifies to its enduring appeal both on the campus and in the chancery. Without doubt, political realism is the most successful and perhaps the most compelling of the classical paradigms that shaped the development of the discipline.

The tradition focuses on the NATION-STATE as the principal ACTOR in world politics and its central proposition is that since the purpose of statecraft is national survival in a hostile environment the acquisition of POWER is the proper, rational and inevitable goal of FOREIGN POLICY. INTERNATIONAL POLITICS, indeed all politics, is thus defined as 'a struggle for POWER'. 'Power' in this sense is conceptualized as both a means and an end in itself, and although definitions are notoriously loose and slippery its general meaning is the ability to influence or change the behaviour of others in a desired direction, or alternatively the ability to resist such influences on one's own behaviour, so what a state can do in world politics is a function of the power it possesses. The idea of SELF-HELP is central as is the notion of SOVEREIGNTY which emphasizes the distinction between the domestic and the external realms. The addition of an 's' to the word 'state' creates not just a plural, but involves crossing a conceptual boundary. States answer to no higher authority and so must look to themselves to protect their interests and to ensure survival. The NATIONAL INTEREST therefore is defined in terms of power, to the virtual exclusion of other factors such as the promotion of ideological values or of moral principles. The nature of the anarchic state-system necessitates the acquisition of military CAPABILITIES sufficient at least to deter attack, and the best means of self-preservation is a constant awareness and reiteration of the worst-case scenario. Since all states seek to maximize power, the favoured technique for its management is BALANCE OF POWER. Stability and order are the result of skilful manipulations of flexible ALLIANCE systems: they do not stem from the authoritative force of INTERNATIONAL LAW or ORGANIZATION, which in any case is minimal. The approach is system-dominant in the sense that state behaviour is seen as a derivative of ANARCHY, but some adherents also claim that since the quest for power and self-interest is inherent in human nature, the states-system is a logical consequence as well as a reflection of it. The realists emphasize the persistence of CONFLICT and competition in WORLD POLITICS; cooperation is possible but only when it serves the national interest. The structure of the international system gravitates towards a HIERARCHY based on power capabilities and the notion of EQUALITY is at a discount except in the formal sense that all states are equally states.

Criticisms of the realist paradigm have been legion. It has been attacked for lack of methodological consistency, imprecision in the definition of key terms and for its ethical implications and overall policy costs. Its obsession with HIGH POLITICS and its presumption about the impermeability and centrality of the state have led to alternative approaches where non-strategic diplomatic issues and non-state actors are highlighted. Critics have also pointed out that political realism did not accurately describe, let alone explain, some of the major developments in the post-Second World War period, in particular the cooperative and integrative movements in Western Europe and elsewhere, as well as the apparent disutility of military force in increasingly larger ISSUE AREAS of INTERNATIONAL POLITICS. However, it remains an important WORLD VIEW and one which for generations of scholars and practitioners, best captures the essence of the international political system. The states-system is still anarchic, states are still the central actors and the GREAT POWERS are still the most dominant. Recognition of this as well as a keen appreciation of the methodological shortfalls of traditional realism led some scholars to re-examine the role of power in the system, in particular its role in achieving cooperation under conditions of anarchy. K. N. Waltz's (1979) influential *Theory of International Politics* is the most far reaching theoretical attempt so far to re-establish, albeit in a more rigorous form, the central tenets of realism. For Waltz the central feature of a theory of international politics is the distribution of power. It is the structural constraints of the global system itself which to a large extent explain state behaviour and dictate outcomes. This 'structural realism' argues that changes in actor behaviour are explained in terms of the system itself rather than in terms of a variation in attributes that actors may display. This concentration on the level of the international political system rather than on its component units has become part of the current 'neo-' or 'structural' realist revival. While concentration on TRANS-NATIONAL relations and COMPLEX INTER-DEPENDENCE challenges key assumptions of political realism (especially that nation-states are the only important actors) the ideas associated with power and its distribution are still central to any sophisticated understanding of world politics. The nature of power may have changed, but not the uses to which it has traditionally been put.

## Realpolitik

A nineteenth century German term referring to the adoption of policies of limited objectives which had a reasonable chance of success. It gained popularity as a result of the disillusionment felt in some quarters with the lack of REALISM in policies pursued by liberals during the 1848–9 REVOLUTION. It has been most often used to describe Bismark's policies and indicates a shrewd attention to detail, an inclination to moderation and a willingness to use FORCE if necessary. It is often used wrongly as a synonym for POWER POLITICS and in twentieth century literature it carries negative connotations because of its association with the non-negotiable demands of the Third Reich.

## *Rebus sic stantibus*

Refers to a fundamental change of circumstance, normally used in relation to TREATY law. If such a change is deemed to have occurred then a party to an agreement may withdraw from or terminate it; if circumstances remain the same (*rebus sic stantibus*) then the treaty is binding (*pacta sunt servanda*). This doctrine has been subject to much criticism by international lawyers since it can operate as an escape clause and may be used to evade all sorts of treaty obligations. Modern practice is to severely limit its scope. The notion of 'fundamental change' is a slippery one and Article 62 of the Vienna Convention has confined it to changes 'not forseen by the parties' and changes which 'radically transform the extent of obligations'. Thus, for example, the election of a COMMUNIST government in Britain might be regarded as 'a fundamental change of circumstance' in relation to membership of NATO, whereas the election of a Labour government would not, since the Labour Party was in office when the treaty was signed.

## Reciprocity

The principle of give-and-take or *quid pro quo* (something for something) used mainly in two senses in INTERNATIONAL RELATIONS: (a) as a fundamental premise of INTERNATIONAL LAW. The logic of reciprocity is regarded as essential to the development of international law since it tends to inhibit unreasonable unilateral claims as these can set precedents for others. 'What's sauce for the goose is sauce for the gander', as Canada showed when it used the US Pacific nuclear tests in the 1950s to justify claims to jurisdiction in the Arctic seas. Canada asserted that if it was permissible to claim exclusive use of the high seas to test weapons, then it too could claim exclusive use of the Arctic seas for POLLUTION control. Reciprocity is an important factor in the observance of international law since self-advantage is never confined to one state. In the long term it is mutual, as the benefits obtained from DIPLOMATIC IMMUNITY have shown. (b) As an important practice in international TRADE and commerce. Reciprocity is regarded as the basis for negotiating mutual trade concessions, especially in relation to TARIFFS. Dissatisfaction in 1987 with Japanese trade practices hinges on its apparent refusal to enter into the spirit of reciprocity. This may result in a trade WAR between the West and Japan. The Reciprocal Trade Agreements Act of 1934 in the United States was an attempt to break world-wide economic NATIONALISM and put tariffs on an even keel. The General Agreement on Tariffs and Trade (GATT) negotations between 1947 and 1979 resulted in the removal of most tariffs between the major trading partners. However, LESS DEVELOPED COUNTRIES often seek the removal of reciprocity as a means of encouraging their own economic growth as part of the quest for a NEW INTERNATIONAL ECONOMIC ORDER (NIEO).

## Recognition

One of the most difficult and complex issues in INTERNATIONAL LAW. It is at once a legal and a political condition. The act of recognition or non-recognition of a STATE or government is clearly a political matter (e.g. for ideological reasons the United States refused to recognize the People's Republic of China, 1949–79), but it also has legal consequences (in this case Taiwan legally became China). Deciding whether to recognize a new state or government involves a pledge to deal with the new entity as a full member of the international diplomatic community and in this sense can mean conferring LEGITIMACY. It does not, though, necessarily convey approval. Thus, Britain recognized the People's Republic of China on the principle that the COMMUNIST government had effective control over the territory and fulfilled the factual requirements of being a state and a government (the so-called Lauterpacht doctrine), yet this did not mean that Britain approved of the 1949 revolution. Britain has generally been realistic in its approach to the question, whereas the United States has tended to be idealistic; one basing its judgement on an assessment of factual situations, the other on moral or IDEOLOGICAL grounds.

There are two broad doctrines relating to this issue: the 'constitutive' theory and the 'declaratory' theory. The former maintains that the international community endows a state with legal personality, thus conferring recognition, while the latter believes that it is the factual situation of the existence of the state itself that matters. These two views correspond closely to IDEALIST theories of INTERNATIONAL RELATIONS (which ascribes particular functions to INTERNATIONAL SOCIETY as a whole) and REALIST theories (which concentrate on states and assign a minimal role to the wider community). Modern practice involves an admixture of the two approaches: international law tends to view community acquiescence and empirical reality as proper guidelines for conferring recognition. But it must be emphasized that the whole process is highly political and therefore contingent. Most commentators now regard the 'declaratory' approach as the better since non-recognition for ideological or constitutive reasons could logically infer that the non-recognized state has no obligations at all under international law. For example, the refusal of the Arab world to recognize Israel could entail Israel not being bound by international rules covering, say, AG-GRESSION or the laws of warfare. This has not in fact happened so that even those states which adopt the constitutive view have recognized its limitations.

Recognition is bound up with DE FACTO and DE JURE interpretations. The issue is also an important consideration in relation to territorial claims and recognition of BEL-LIGERENTS in a CIVIL WAR. In these matters, political considerations intrude to such an extent that international law itself can offer no hard and fast rule of procedure (*see:* M. Akehurst 1984).

## Recommendation

A non-binding decision. The hallmark of DECISION-MAKING within the intergovern-mental organization (IGO) is that such out-comes have the status of recommendations and that, accordingly, member states need not feel bound by them. Thus the statute of the COUNCIL OF EUROPE is replete with refer-ences to the making of recommendations by the principal organs of that institution. The UNITED NATIONS CHARTER clearly stipulates that the GENERAL ASSEMBLY is a body which will essentially recommend and deliberate rather than make binding decisions. Further-more, under Article 18 of the Charter, re-commendations of the Assembly on important issues have to be approved by a two-thirds majority. Like any decision-making competence, recommendations may be made by simple majority or by some sys-tem of weighted voting.

## Re-entry Vehicle (RV)

That part of a BALLISTIC MISSILE which re-enters the earth's atmosphere at the terminal stage of the flight. The re-entry vehicle will carry the payload, which will consist of a warhead, decoy, etc. Most bal-listic missiles now carry multiple RVs on a bus or post-boost vehicle.

*See also:* MRV; MIRV; MARV

## Refugee

Someone who is forced to move from his or her country of origin or of residence. Re-fugees are an anomaly in STATE-CENTRED INTERNATIONAL LAW since they are tech-nically 'stateless' until ASYLUM is granted. Although not a twentieth century phenom-enon, the refugee problem has multiplied alongside the increase in ideological war-fare and TERRORISM. The LEAGUE OF NATIONS created a High Commissioner for Refugees in 1921 to help displaced persons, mainly those who had fled from the Soviet Union after 1917. The Nansen passport was introduced during the League period to enable refugees to cross national bound-aries. Since the Second World War, the UN has taken over responsibility for the wel-fare of refugees and a UN High Commis-sioner for Refugees (UNHCR) was estab-lished in 1951. UNHCR can only afford temporary protection and the office is mainly concerned with liaising with mem-ber states to find more permanent solu-tions. In addition, a UN Relief and Works Agency (UNRWA) is dealing with the mas-sive task of providing respite and relief for over a million Arab refugees in the Middle East who have been displaced as a result of the ARAB–ISRAELI CONFLICT.

Many commentators argue that the 1951 UN definition of refugee is too restrictive. This confines the condition to those fleeing their home states for reasons of persecution (or a reasonable fear of it) because of their 'race, religion, nationality, membership of a particular social group or political opinion' (Brownlie, 1981, p. 51). In addition, the cri-teria apply only to individuals, not to groups, and exclude economic migrants and the victims of armed combat. Increasingly the distinction between enforced and volun-tary movement is difficut to sustain. In the case of the VIETNAMESE boat-people, for ex-ample, it is extremely difficult to distinguish between fugitives from political despotism rather than economic hardship since the quest for a better life often involves the im-plicit belief that political freedom and pros-perity are bound up together. The 1951 definition is the only one to have gained widespread international acceptance but recent transformations in WORLD POLITICS, especially the demise of COMMUNISM, have led to greater emphasis on the economic and humanitarian categories. Thus, West Germany recognizes the migration rights of East Germans and the Organization of African Unity has specifically recognized the humanitarian category of refugee (i.e. victims of wars, famines, communal violence and other social or ecological upheavals). Rigid adherence to the 'pure' refugee criteria of 1951 may make the screening process easier for reluctant governments, but this serves to conceal a problem which actually and potentially is vast in WORLD POLITICS. For example, it has been estimated by the US Committee for refugees that at present the world contains over 15 million people who could conceivably be labelled refugees, though only a very small proportion of these conform to the original definition. In 1951 the refugee problem (mainly the result of the Second World War) seemed containable, especially as most non-European and non-communist fugitives were not a matter of great concern to the West. Since then however the explosion of migrancy on a worldwide basis has created a problem which the international community is at present woefully ill-equipped to deal with. *See also:* IMMIGRATION; ORBITERS

## Regime

This term, derived from INTERNATIONAL LAW, has increasingly been applied to the study of MACROPOLITICS of late. Keohane and Nye (1977) linked the concept of INTERDEPENDENCE to the idea of regime and sought to examine regime change in stipulated ISSUE AREAS. Krasner's (1983) work, a substantial reprint from the journal *International Organization*, developed these ideas in a broad-based, multi-faceted treatment.

A regime is a framework of rules, expectations and prescriptions between ACTORS in WORLD POLITICS. This framework is based upon recognition of a common perceived need to establish cooperative relations based upon the principle of RECIPROCITY. A regime operates within a clearly defined issue area and behaviour patterns will be regulated through common membership of special purpose organizations. This membership will potentially be open to all relevant actors – whether they are STATE actors or not. In point of fact most of the empirical examples of regime discussed in the literature are based wholly or predominantly upon state actor membership. Decisions upon appropriate membership will depend upon the policy contingency framework and cannot be identified a priori and in advance.

Regime analysis is currently in vogue, particularly among US scholars. It is analytically dependent upon the concept of interdependence because interdependent units require cooperation and coordination of policies to produce a positive sum outcome. Conversely, once a regime has been established, a complex FEEDBACK loop is created and maintenance of the regime may require further policy decisions which have the effect – even unintended – of increasing levels of interdependence. As a result, regime creation can lead to instances of functional INTEGRATION between actors. The greater the SCOPE of the regime, the more likely is this outcome to occur.

Regime analysts have been concerned to explore three facets of the subject: how regimes are created, what institutional actors can do to maintain the regime and how, in the long run, regimes are transformed or abandoned. Because regime analysis assumes that cooperation and coordination of policies is feasible, it has been argued that identifying regimes shows that macropolitics is not an ANARCHY. The working assumption that the creation and maintenance of regimes necessitates behaviour patterns that are norm-governed is incompatible with dogmatic realist assumptions about anarchy. It should be noted that some scholars have seen an explanatory link between the three facets outlined above and HEGEMONIC STABILITY THEORY. In this version, the HEGEMON is seen to play a crucial role in the creation and maintenance of regimes. Collapse or removal of the hegemon, conversely, is a necessary condition for regime transformation or redundancy.


## Region

This term is used in a number of contexts with a number of meanings in WORLD POLITICS. Sometimes these meanings overlap: sometimes they contradict one another. The primary, common sense usage connotes physical contiguity. Indeed proximity seems to be a necessary, although not sufficient, condition for confident stipulation of a region. Within state actors physical contiguity or proximity seems to be an important prerequisite for creating and maintaining a sense of unity. The example of the failure of the two halves of Pakistan to maintain a united STATE when separated by the territory of the state of India and its dismemberment into Pakistan and Bangladesh in 1971 is surely instructive here. What is called elsewhere centrifugal INSURGENCY is clearly assisted by geographical isolation and remoteness.

Between state actors, contiguity as a variable in delineating regions produces mixed results. For example, there is a core area contained within the concept of 'Western Europe' which incudes the founding six of the EUROPEAN COMMUNITY. At the periphery things become more confused. Iceland and Ireland presumably mark the western fringes but where is the eastern fringe? Similarly, with the region of the 'Middle East'. A core area can be identified but is Libya part of it, or of North Africa? Is Turkey part of Europe or part of the Middle East? Michael Edwards (1962) opens his work on Asia with a chapter on the theme 'Asia: Does It Exist?' Clearly, more is needed than proximity to confidently stipulate the meaning of region.

Between state actors, indeed, it is possible to arrive at groupings based upon homogeneity. Social homogeneity may be defined as involving socio-cultural factors such as race, religion, language and history. Factors which, within the state, can contribute to a sense of NATIONALISM, between states can contribute to a sense of REGIONALISM. Economic homogeneity may be defined as involving factors such as level of economic development, evidence of trade blocs and COMMON MARKETS and possibilities of economic INTEGRATION. Political homogeneity relies upon one predominant variable: type of political system and its degree of stability. External homogeneity may be defined as the extent to which states in their foreign POLICY-MAKING seek to cooperate, coordinate and harmonize their goals and the degree to which this leads to institution building, BLOC politics and the formation of regional organizations. In this respect homogeneity or similarity, as defined above, may reinforce or revise ideas about region based upon proximity.

The variable of social homogeneity is very evident in the Middle Eastern region where ISLAM and Arabic are powerful factors in the regionalism. At the same time this criterion perforce excludes Israel and makes Turkey and Iran peripheral actors. Latin America is closer than Europe to the Middle East on these dimensions. In Western Europe on the other hand these cultural factors are divisive, particularly on language and RELIGION, and Western Europe scores very high on economic homogeneity. Indeed it would be valid to say that this region is the paradigm example of economic homogeneity throughout the global system. Conversely, this same economic factor which is so unifying in Western Europe pulls Japan out of its geographical context. Through the OECD and the IMF Japan is economically part of the West.

Political homogeneity is also high in Western Europe. Taking a historical perspective this is not surprising: the strong centralizing tendencies that produced the

STATE and the STATE-SYSTEM first occurred in that region. Later, following the French and US revolutions, the expansion of political participation followed the MODERNIZATION of political structures on both sides of the Atlantic. Thus it is possible to identify a Western European/North Atlantic region of political homogeneity. No other region matches this one on the criteria of politics. In the past Latin America has evinced a strong tendency towards MILITARISM as a distinctive regional characteristic but this is now weakening. Eastern Europe which was for four decades a distinctive political region is, as of this writing, highly diffused and unstable. The possibility exists that it may move closer to the Western European/US type in the future.

Studies of voting behaviour in the GENERAL ASSEMBLY of the UN show the extent to which external homogeneity is reflected in the phenomena of the voting bloc. Further evidence for the growth of this variable throughout the global system is produced by the increase in regional organizations since 1945. This growth can be correlated with the idea of REGIONALISM. Western Europe would seem to head the field although in the ISSUE AREA of military–security policies the region is linked via NATO with the United States. Proposals for a European Defence Community failed to gain sufficient support when moved in the 1950s and the Western European Union has only very limited military sigificance without NATO.

On the basis of the criteria of proximity and homogeneity discussed here it seems to be valid to conclude that some regions are more 'regional' than others. In all instances, though, it also seems valid to distinguish what have been called 'core areas' within the region from peripheral areas. It should be noted that the idea of periphery is not wholly or essentially geographic. Thus the United Kingdom's peripheral role *vis-à-vis* Western European regionalism was more the result of a lack of external homogeneity than anything else. This attitude persisted in the United Kingdom throughout the 1950s and only changed slowly and somewhat hesitantly thereafter. *See also:* SUB-SYSTEM

## Regionalism

Regionalism is to REGION what NATIONALISM is to NATION. A complex of attitudes, loyalties and ideas which concentrates the individual and collective minds of people(s) upon what they perceive as 'their' region. Regionalism exists both within states and between states. Within states it can be one manifestation of ethnic nationalism and the political goal of separatism and INDEPENDENCE. On the other hand, regionalism may simply reflect an organizational desire to increase efficiencies and make administration more accountable to the population. Regionalism within STATES is thus a very broad-based set of ideas and aspirations which may see much or little conflict between the concept of region and the concept of centre.

Between states regionalism is positively correlated with the idea of REGION. It has to be said that, in the conduct of their FOREIGN POLICY, leaders of states frequently approach their external environment wearing 'regional' lenses. This DEFINITION OF THE SITUATION is widely reflected among mass publics as well; the mass media will reinforce this tendency in reporting and covering foreign news. On the issue areas of military–security policies and wealth/welfare policies, problem solving is often perceived in terms of regional solutions. Thus regional arrangements such as ALLIANCES, ENTENTES, COMMON MARKETS, and FREE TRADE AREAS are typical institutional responses.

The attempt in the twentieth century to establish global international institutions such as the LEAGUE OF NATIONS and the UNITED NATIONS was seen, by some, to be a task that was inhibited by regionalism. This came to a head when the framers of the UN CHARTER found that the primacy of the SECURITY COUNCIL in matters involving

PEACE and security might be challenged by regional pacts and arrangements. Chapter VIII of the Charter entitled 'Regional Arrangements' represents a compromise formula between universalism and regionalism. In retrospect this *modus vivendi* was almost certainly prudent. The UN has failed to substantiate the COLLECTIVE SECURITY provisions of the Charter and the post-1945 system saw a renewal of regionalism.

The same tendency has been apparent in global economic relations. Regional cooperation and INTEGRATION via the wealth/welfare dimension has been one of the most distinctive features of MACROPOLITICS, and the UN system has been permissive. The General Agreement on Tariffs and Trade (GATT) has made specific provisions for these trading arrangements to be effected. Western Europe has, at the time of writing, gone as far as any region in building economic regionalism into a complex of institutions. The EUROPEAN COMMUNITY is now a powerful economic ACTOR in its own right and it has certainly functioned as a systemic modifier accordingly. It seems plausible to suppose that these trends will continue into the immediate future and that other actors will seek to improve the prospects for regionalism.

## Religion

Despite its neglect by contemporary scholars religion has had, and continues to have, an enormous effect on WORLD POLITICS both in the structural sense and as part of its process. The neglect has not been total; there have been a number of studies of the influence of belief systems and IDEOLOGIES, for example, but the apparent secularization of twentieth century politics has tended to marginalize its overall significance. Where it has been considered in, for example, explanations of the Iranian REVOLUTION of 1979 and its subsequent FOREIGN POLICY, it has usually been seen as an atavistic aberration which has temporarily distorted more orthodox explanations of state behaviour. REALISTS in particular have tended to subsume religion under the all-embracing concept of ideology which in any case only conceals the true nature of foreign policy (i.e. Morgenthau's (1948) 'interest defined in terms of power'). Where it has been given serious consideration, usually by sociologists, it has been defined largely in terms of its social functions as a set of ideas or beliefs which bind people into distinct social groups and in this way has been extended to include ideas such as NATIONALISM and COMMUNISM.

In fact, religion and the notions of law and JUSTICE it generated had a significant influence on the development of the classical STATE-SYSTEMS of Europe, Islam, India and China. The idea of *RES PUBLICA CHRISTIANA*, to take one example, underpinned the WESTPHALIAN codification of an association of states. Christianity became the dominant religion in Roman Europe in the fourth century. Subsequently, with the disappearance of the empire, the single most important binding force (the word religion comes from Latin *religare* – to bind) was Christianity. Although in the later conflicts between Church and State the temporal power was almost universally successful, the ideas that had been generated, especially concerning SOVEREIGNTY, law and MORALITY persisted. The state was the victor, but the state itself was premised on religious ideas. Despite the distinction drawn in the New Testament between God's domain and Caesar's, religion provided the justification for claims to state SOVEREIGNTY, whether this was divine rights for kings, or later for peoples. Apart from its role in state-building and system building it also had an incalculable effect on the development of modern INTERNATIONAL LAW. From the Romans onwards, Christian teachings and precepts were used to codify rules for mutual relationships and dealings. The GROTIAN conception of INTERNATIONAL SOCIETY is in essence a Christian one. The ideas of religious INTERNATIONALISM, which is the tendency to organize a multinational society around identical legal and moral principles, is integral to the development of modern INTERNATIONAL ORGANIZATIONS. In sum, the structural effects of religion on world politics is by no means marginal.

On a more empirical level, its effect on the process of world politics is no less important. At the beginning of the 1980s, according to UN data, the world contained more than one thousand million Christians, around six hundred million Moslems, four hundred and fifty million Hindus, two hundred and fifty million Buddhists, one hundred and seventy million Confucians, and nearly seventeen million Jews. The notion of religious freedom was recognized internationally for the first time in the Oliva Peace Treaty of 1660, and was subsequently endorsed in Roosevelt's Four Freedoms in 1941 and by the UN Commission on the Rights of Man (1955–60). Despite this, the sheer weight of numbers and the diversity of beliefs is bound to affect the stability of the contemporary INTERNATIONAL ORDER. No theory of state behaviour can afford to ignore it, or to relegate it to the outer edges of the discipline. *See also:* ISLAM LIBERATION THEOLOGY

### Renversments des alliances

Diplomatic term meaning 'reversal of alliances'. It refers to the practice of abandoning an ally and entering a new ALLIANCE with a recent enemy. The Nazi–Soviet pact of 1939 is sometimes regarded, not altogether correctly, as *renversments des alliances*. The practice was much more common in the non-ideological or classical period of BALANCE OF POWER in the eighteenth and nineteenth centuries. Indeed, in the REALIST view of INTERNATIONAL POLITICS, flexibility of alignments is a fundamaental requirement of successful power management. This practice was specifically endorsed in the Washington Doctrine of Unstable Alliances promulgated by President Jefferson in his inaugural speech to Congress on 7 January 1801. Following George Washington's strictures against entangling alliances, Jefferson argued that the United States should regard their WAR alliances as temporary and change or reverse them as soon as interest dictated. Sometimes, of course, *renversments* can occur not as a result of the general configuration of power and interest, but as a consequence of a REVOLUTION or a change of REGIME. In these cases, *renversment* is an IDEOLOGICAL policy by-product rather than a more or less continuously available DIPLOMATIC tactic, which is closer to its original meaning.

### Reparations

Compensation demanded by victors from the vanquished. It usually takes two forms: (a) as a punishment imposed on defeated STATES designed to cripple their future ability to make WAR; (b) as an indemnity for losses incurred during the war. It was exacted in both forms from Germany after the First World War, the French in particular, demanding large amounts to cover war damage and individual claims for loss. The Allied reparation policy was heavily criticized in the inter-war period by economists (J. M. Keynes) and political scientists (E. H. Carr) as a major contributory factor in the collapse of the German domestic economy and its aggrieved and unbending FOREIGN POLICY posture. After the Second World War, both the Soviet Union and Israel claimed the right to exact reparations from Germany.

### Repatriation

Policy of returning people to their country of origin or legal home. Repatriation can be voluntary or involuntary; in the case of the former some form of 'inducement' is usually resorted to, although where this does not succeed mandatory deportation usually follows. Inducement was mooted, though not undertaken, by sections of the UK Conservative Party in relation to immigrants from the Caribbean during the late 1950s and early 1960s. In relation to the VIETNAMESE 'boat people' the United Kingdom, in 1989, pursued policies both of inducement and enforcement. It often involves BILATERAL or MULTILATERAL international agreements as was the case in the aftermath of the two World Wars when thousands of eastern and central Europeans were sent back to their countries of origin, often against their express wishes and even under cover of some form of subterfuge. The cases of the forcible repatriation of Cossacks to the Soviet Union and of the Vietnamese seeking refuge in Hong Kong demonstrate that this policy is invariably a risky one which flirts dangerously near to infringements of HUMAN RIGHTS. This was clearly the case with President Amin's expulsion in 1972–3 of 50,000 Ugandan Asians to various COMMONWEALTH countries. In attempting to minimize domestic and international criticism of such policies, the UK government, in particular, has tended to distingush between 'genuine' REFUGEES and what it terms 'economic migrants'. The issue of the rights of illegal immigrants will continue to bedevil WORLD POLITICS since there is no universally agreed solution to the problem.

*See also:* ORBITERS; PRISONERS OF WAR

## Reprisal

A form of retaliation falling short of WAR, in which states engage to punish a wrongdoer or to obtain redress for some injurious act. Fear of reprisals is an important sanction underlying the effectiveness of international norms of behaviour. Reprisals include any measure which does not actually constitute an act of war, BOYCOTTS, seizure of assets or property, peaceful BLOCKADES or simply 'showing the FLAG' as a threatening gesture. Although not overtly an AGGRESSIVE act, it is often seen as such by target STATES. Reprisal must be distinguished from RETORTION

since reprisals are technically illegal. They must also be preceded by a demand that the offender make amends and the act of reprisal itself must not be excessive – the punishment must fit the crime. Reprisals involving the use of armed FORCE must comply with the SELF-DEFENCE and COLLECTIVE SECURITY provisions of the CHARTER OF THE UN. Reprisals can also be used in wartime, usually to force the enemy to comply with the laws of warfare.

*See also:* SELF-HELP

## Res publica Christiana

Term used mainly by diplomatic historians to delineate what is now more commonly called 'Western Christendom'. Before the establishment of the Westphalian system in the seventeenth century, which affirmed that Europe consisted of a largely secular multiplicity of states, post-Roman Europeans continued to regard themselves as part of a distinctive whole. Even as the rival IMPERIAL and papal claims to the government of Europe were being undermined in the fourteenth and fifteenth centuries, the emerging monarchical states interpreted their mutual relations not in terms of relations between totally separate and isolated units, but rather in terms of politically distinct parts of what was once a unified whole. As M. Keens-Soper (1978) puts it 'the implications of political fragmentation did not call in question the continued spiritual and legal unity of Christendom'. The net result of the process was that the modern European STATES-SYSTEM which was supposedly created at Wesphalia in 1648 was not particulary new and was in any case superimposed on an established sense of unity and common purpose. This enabled 'Christian' or 'European' states (the terms became interchangeable) to distinguish between relations among themselves, where certain conventions and rules were to be followed, and relations with outsiders where no such constraints operated. Thus, outsiders such as the Turks, the

Aztecs or the Indians were deemed incapable of belonging to the Christian COMMONWEALTH of states. They were therefore legitimate targets for IMPERIALISM conquest, subjection and subversion.

This sense of Europe as a self-conscious association of states, politically fragmented but culturally INTERDEPENDENT, had profound consequences for the development of a truly global states-system in the twentieth century. In particular, the persistence of its peculiar institutions (DIPLOMACY, the law of nations, the rules of WAR, BALANCE OF POWER and INTERNATIONAL ORGANIZATIONS) can be directly attributed to this conception of belonging to a common civilization. And although the last public occasion where the term was officially used was in the preamble to the Treaty of Utrecht in 1714, there can be little doubt that the practice of shared assumptions and common rules of conduct that it signifies persists to this day. Despite secularization and a widening of its geographical limits, the important ground rules of modern INTERNATIONAL RELATIONS are rooted in the notion of *res publica Christiana*.

## Retortion

A legal measure designed to punish an unfriendly act. For example, denial of economic AID after acts of NATIONALIZATION would be retortion. In US FOREIGN POLICY, the 'Hickenlooper Amendment' required the President to forego economic assistance to STATES which have expropriated US property without compensation. Thus, retortion was invoked against Ceylon in 1963–5 and was only withdrawn when a new government decided to pay compensation. This has now been repealed by the American Foreign Assistance Act of 1973.

## Revisionism

Most often used to denote challenges to the STATUS QUO. The term is especially associ-

ated with REALISTS who view INTERNATIONAL POLITICS in terms of a more-or-less permanent structural tension between defenders of the prevailing order and opponents of it. Thus, 'satisfied/dissatisfied', 'satiated/unsatiated', 'have/have not' and 'STATUS QUO/revisionist', are dichotomies commonly employed by theorists to describe this process. 'Revisionist' is especially associated with E. H. Carr's (1946) *Twenty Years' Crisis 1919–1939* and refers to types of FOREIGN POLICIES practised by certain states (Germany, Italy and Japan) in the inter-WAR period whereby they attempted to alter the existing international power and territorial distribution to their own advantage. Instead of accepting the inferior position accorded to them by the prevailing order (in this case the VERSAILLES system), revisionist states attempt, by means of DIPLOMATIC pressure, threats, FORCE, disregard for INTERNATIONAL LAW and existing TREATY obligations, to alter the situation in their favour. It is bound up with the POWER model and as such encourages the formation of ALLIANCES, coalitions and BLOCS in accordance with the principles of balance. Conflicts that result from this process are usually ZERO SUM. H. J. Morgenthau (1948), the doyen of the post-war school of US realists, substituted the term IMPERIALIST to indicate similar challenges, but this was less helpful since it carried moral and/or ideological overtones: the status quo then appears positive, normal and proper, the imperialist negative, abnormal and improper. Indeed, the idea of revisionism has suffered in the West because it has so often been linked with the policies of Hitler and Stalin, and the tendency of historiography to label pro-Soviet, anti-US analyses of the COLD WAR revisionist reinforces this prejudice.

Barry Buzan (1983), attempting to obliterate this ethnocentric distortion and to clarify the term, identifies a three-tier classification of revisionist objectives – 'orthodox', REVOLUTIONARY and 'radical'. Orthodox challenges operate within the prevailing framework of ideas and relations and are geared towards giving the challenger a better pecking order position within the hierarchical system (e.g. Imperial Germany and Imperial Japan prior to the First World War). Revolutionary revisionism involves a challenge to the organizing principles of the system itself (France after 1789, the Soviet Union after 1917 and perhaps Libya and Iran today). Radical revisionists fall between the other two groupings; they aim both for self-advantage and reform of the system. The Group of '77 and the quest for a NEW INTERNATIONAL ECONOMIC ORDER (NIEO) typifies this approach. Buzan's classification, while in general confirming the insights of the realist model, indicates a much more complex pattern and variety of challenges than the simple, zero sum HIGH POLITICS model presented earlier. Revisionism is now seen to be multi-faceted and is applicable to GREAT, MIDDLE and SMALL POWER politics and need not be tied to a particular ideological stance.

Other senses in which the term is used are as a description of reinterpretations of MARXIST/LENINIST dogma, where it usually implies a deviation from the orthodox view (e.g. PEACEFUL COEXISTENCE), or to indicate a fundamental reappraisal of the causes of the COLD WAR, especially in US historiography.

## Revolution

In WORLD POLITICS this is usually used in the following senses: (a) referring to a radical and sudden change in a system of government, often accompanied by violence; (b) referring to *any* fundamental change or transition in the institutions and values of a society, STATE or system. The first sense is clearly restrictive since it does not distinguish between changes of government which are not accompanied by radical social change (e.g. coups d'état or 'palace revolutions') and those which are. The second sense is restrictive in the opposite way, since it allows the term to be used in any context which has undergone radical transformation, to the extent that we can speak of an 'industrial revolution', a 'strategic' revolution, an 'intellectual' revolution and so on. For the MARXIST/LENINISTS who have dominated modern discussions of the phenomena, revolutions properly so-called involve not just a change of political REGIME; they also involve a fundamental change in the social and economic organization of society. Using this criterion, genuine revolutions in world politics, although enormously influential in terms of its structure and process, are comparatively rare. The French Revolution of 1789, the Bolshevik Revolution of 1917, the Chinese Revolution of 1949 and the Cuban Revolution of 1959 all clearly qualify, whereas the English 'Glorious Revolution' of 1688 and the American Revolution of 1776 equally clearly do not.

Apart from disagreements about its nature and cause and despite a general consensus about its overall importance in setting the agenda of modern world politics, most non-Marxist and non-sociological commentators have tended to ignore or marginalize the phenomena. Political REALISTS, for example, given the STATE-CENTRIC bias of the approach, have considered revolutions primarily in the context of non-conformity with the prevailing system, rather than *sui generis*. Thus, for example, it is a common generalization that after the initial heat and light of the revolutionary period, the affected state soon settles into, or is socialized by, the constraints imposed by the STATE-SYSTEM itself. Even realists who have devoted considerable time and energy investigating revolutions, e.g. E. H. Carr (1946) and Martin Wight (1978), have tended to assume that revolutions lead to instability and therefore are not conducive to the maintenance of order in INTERNATIONAL POLITICS. The FOREIGN POLICIES of revolutionary states are thus classified as 'revisionist' or 'dissatisfied' and must be responded to either through the process of ACCOMMODATION (often called APPEASEMENT) or through counterrevolutionary methods involving direct or indirect INTER-VENTION. Behaviouralists (who often regard themselves as 'revolutionaries' within the discipline) are also prone to treat revolutions as just a variant of violent group behaviour. J. N. Rosenau (1964), for example, preferred the term 'internal WAR' to revolution implying that it is a particular form of a general social phenomenon.

Reasons for this apparent neglect are not difficult to find. For most analysts of international affairs, the 'domestic' variables are held constant. Revolutions therefore, when they have been considered at all, have been viewed primarily in terms of the effect that they have had on FOREIGN POLICY style or behaviour. Despite Martin Wight's assertion that between 1492 and 1960 INTERNATIONAL RELATIONS has been more 're-volutionary' than 'unrevolutionary' (1978, p. 92), there is a prevailing assumption that it is somehow 'abnormal' or an 'aberration'. Outside COMMUNIST literature, where the distinction between domestic and international politics is unknown and where the concepts of permanent revolution and WARS OF NATIONAL LIBERATION are central, very little theoretical attention has been given to it as a formative influence on the development of world politics. The relationship between revolution and WAR is usually subsumed under studies of the general conditions of permissible intervention or else on the role and methods of the 'revolutionary liberator state'. In INTERNATIONAL LAW consideration of the concept is marginal. The presumption in favour of SOVEREIGNTY and DOMESTIC JURISDICTION means that apart from such metalegal ideas as LEGITIMACY or RECOGNITION and rules relating to compensation, revolution is treated as a temporary deviation from the norm. The assumption of the UN CHARTER, especially Article 2, paragraph 7 (NON-INTERVENTION) is that internal upheavals are essentially domestic matters and as such are beyond the range and SCOPE of the international legal REGIME. All this is in spite of the fact that twentieth century international politics in the FIRST, second and THIRD WORLDS has largely been about the realization of, or responses to, revolutions.
*See also*: INSURGENCY, J–CURVE

## Rush–Bagot treaty

An agreement between Britain and the United States concluded in 1818 to demilitarize the US–Canadian border and to prevent the Great Lakes becoming a zone of naval competition. It is still in force and can therefore be described as the longest lasting and most successful DISARMAMENT TREATY in international history. In addition to fostering good neighbourliness between the United States and Canada and making WAR unthinkable, it has also been an important factor in the SPECIAL RELATIONSHIP between the United States and the United Kingdom. This treaty was part of the general settlement of the war of 1812 and since then all disagreements between these two states have been settled without resort to the use of FORCE.

# S

## SAC

SAC is Strategic Air Command. It was created in March 1946 as part of the US Air Force (which at the time was actually the Army Air Force – USAAF). SAC comprises the strategic bombing CAPABILITY of American AIR POWER. In this role it is required to conduct offensive operations at both the nuclear and CONVENTIONAL levels in any hostilities. SAC was used in its conventional mode in both the KOREAN and the VIETNAM WARS.

With the advent of BALLISTIC MISSILES SAC assumed a new role; from 1959 onwards all land-based strategic MISSILE systems being under SAC's control. This accretion meant that two-thirds of the TRIAD was within the remit of the Command. Notwithstanding these changes, the heyday of SAC must remain the 1950s. The manned bomber was still pre-eminent within the US arsenal, while the concept of MASSIVE RETALIATION enabled SAC to figure prominently in the strategic planning of the period. The mystique and kudos of the organization with the motto 'peace is our profession' encapsulates the spirit of the time.

## Saddle point

A term used in GAME THEORY. A saddle point is that point on the matrix in a ZERO–SUM game which is the smallest in its row and the largest in its column. The saddle point represents a stable solution to the zero–sum game. Stability in game terms means that neither player can improve his position by moving independently away from the saddle point. This reasoning assumes that both players will act rationally throughout the exercise.

## SALT

An acronym for the Strategic Arms Limitation Talks. These were BILATERAL ARMS CONTROL talks held between the United States and the Soviet Union between 1967 and 1979. Two conventions were produced: SALT I and SALT II. SALT I was ratified by both parties and ran as an Interim Agreement for five years from 1972. SALT II was never ratified. Recently the SALT process has been replaced by the potentially more radical START negotiations.

### SALT I

It seems clear from all the available DIPLOMATIC evidence that initial enthusiasm for SALT came from the United States during the Johnson Presidency. In particular Robert McNamara, the US Secretary of Defense, was concerned that the burgeoning technology of anti-ballistic missiles (ABM) systems would lead to a new ARMS RACE between the SUPERPOWERS. The development of ABM TECHNOLOGIES during the 1960s threatened to undermine the stability of the offensive context of ASSURED DESTRUCTION by giving a new impetus to defensive systems and strategies.

For the Soviet Union the order of priorities at the start of SALT I was the reverse of the US perception. Facing at that time an adversary that had been superior to themselves throughout the period of the arms race, the Soviet DECISION-MAKERS were anxious to discuss limits upon offensive systems as well as, or in preference to, ABM restraints. US acceptance of this view meant that the negotiations that followed were of a dual-purpose nature. Diplomatically the SALT I Interim Agreement represented the attainment and RECOGNITION of their PARITY with the United States. Henceforth the Soviet Union would expect to be treated on the basis of full equality and all future NEGOTIATIONS would be predicated upon that basis.

Given the Soviet PERCEPTIONS, it was not surprising that the United States found them ready to negotiate a comprehensive TREATY on ABM systems once bargaining began in earnest in 1969. The Interim Agreement was more difficult. In particular the issue of defining what constituted a 'strategic' system proved to be contentious. The Soviet side wanted to include the so-called forward based systems (fbs) of the United States because these weapons could be used to launch attacks directly upon Soviet territory. From the US perception fbs were 'theatre' not 'strategic', being based in Europe as part of the US NUCLEAR UMBRELLA.

SALT I and the ABM treaty were signed in Moscow in 1972. The five-year Interim Agreement limited the Soviet Union to 1618 intercontinental ballistic missiles (ICBMs) and the United States to 1054. The Soviet Union would be allowed to deploy 950 submarine-launched ballistic missiles (SLBMs) on 62 submarines while the United States could deploy 710 SLBMs on 44 submarines. No restrictions were placed upon the fbs, bombers or mobile ICBMs. No restrictions were placed upon multiple independently targeted re-entry vehicles (MIRVs). The United States had begun to MIRV their missiles in the autumn of 1970 – while the SALT I Agreement was being negotiated – and the Soviet Union subsequently followed. The failure to address the MIRV issue is now generally regarded as the major specific omission of SALT I. This led to an acceleration in the qualitative arms race – or VERTICAL PROLIFERATION – and to a general air of cynicism about the Moscow Agreement. Verification was to be by so-called 'national technical means' – a diplomatic way of talking about INTELLIGENCE gathering. SALT I also established a Standing Consultative Committee between the two STATES to handle complaints and allegations. SALT I substituted mutual restraint for self-restraint, it may be concluded.

*SALT II*

The basic parameters of SALT II were agreed to at Vladivostok in November 1974. Negotiations had already been under way for two years when Ford and Brezhnev reached their understanding. As with the SALT I Interim Agreement, SALT II concentrated upon the central area of strategic weapons to the exclusion of US fbs, Soviet medium range ballistic missiles (MRBMs) and intermediate range ballistic missiles (IRBMs) and the deterrent forces of the United Kingdom and France. By concentrating upon this 'core' the two SUPERPOWER leaders agreed to a quantitative limit of 2,400 launchers which was to be reduced to 2,250 by 1982 under the subsequent treaty.

The treaty itself was not signed until June 1979. By this time relations between the two parties had deteriorated significantly from the kind of DETENTE responsiveness engendered in the early 1970s, and following the Soviet INTERVENTION in AFGHANISTAN, the draft treaty was withdrawn from the US Senate without forcing the issue to a vote. As already stated the unratified treaty consisted of broad quantitative limits under which sub-limits stipulated figures for various categories. In particular the sub-limits device tried to address the issue of MIRVs – which SALT I had failed to address – by limiting the number of launchers that could be MIRVd. As with SALT I, the mark II version was an Interim convention up to 1985. VERIFICATION would again be by national technical means and to assist this the signatories agreed to assist in verification by, for example, not encrypting the missile tele-metry during testing. Within the broadly permissive limits MODERNIZATION or improvements in weapon systems could continue. SALT accordingly had little im-pact upon the technical aspects of the arms race.

The whole SALT process ran like a con-stant theme throughout US–Soviet rela-tions between 1967 and 1979. During that time the United States went through four Presidents – Johnson, Nixon, Ford and Carter – whereas the Soviet LEADERSHIP showed considerable stability (if not gerontocracy). In the end it was not pos-sible to isolate the SALT process from the general drift in superpower relations. SALT was the product of bargaining and negotiation *within* as well as *between* these two states. This is evident from the more available US record, where interests within the military establishment and civilian political leaderships combined in opposition to defeat or weaken the SALT negotiations. Thus at various times issues such as the so-called 'heavy' missiles and latterly the WINDOW OF VULNERABILITY idea were raised to suggest that perhaps the United States was being disadvan-taged. Viewed from the contemporary position with significant arms control agreements concluded or in the process of negotiation, SALT looks very modest and somewhat conservative.

## Salus populi suprema lex

The supreme law is the health/security of the people. A classic metalegal doctrine of necessity associated with RAISON D'ÉTAT and the right of self-preservation. Its essen-tial character is that it gives virtually unre-stricted freedom to a state to take any action it deems necessary to protect its own self-defined interests. INTERNATIONAL LAW has attempted to restrict the sway of the doctrine but in the final analysis states can, and do, appeal to 'necessity' as a legitimate ground for action.

## Scenario

An imagined, hypothetical future state of affairs. The term is particularly popular within the STRATEGIC STUDIES tradition where 'WAR gaming' has been used for de-cades by senior military officers both for training purposes and for actual contin-gency planning before hostilities. The ad-vent of civilian strategists as the dominant intellectual influence after 1945 led to the scenario replacing the war game as the primary vehicle for such speculation. Whereas war games were rather narrowly confined to what were perceived to be pure-ly military matters, constructing scenarios required the author(s) to have regard to a much greater range of variables, including economic, legal and DIPLOMATIC.

The late Herman Kahn (1960) probably represents the best individual example of how thinking through the possibilities on NUCLEAR WAR or escalation can produce a series of colourful – or disturbing – scenarios. Probably his most famous in-stance was that of the so-called DOOMSDAY MACHINE. It is no accident that Kahn moved on to FUTUROLOGY in later life, because in the process of thinking through the next decades/centuries, use must necessarily be made of scenarios. If reference is made to Malthus (1826) and the theory of population growth, such speculation is – like war gam-ing – not new. Malthus established an early inclination towards pessimism in scenario building about the future and this tradition has been continued into the present context by groups such as the Club of Rome.

Trend analysis is a well established metho-dology and in general terms POLICY-MAKERS and their advisers often have to take account of future trends and tendencies in making pol-icy in the present context. In this sense scenario construction is simply prudential and it should not be condemned as a fad or a fetish of a particular individual, school or approach.

## Schuman plan

The Schuman plan for a Coal and Steel

Community in Western Europe, linking specifically France and West Germany, was initiated in May 1950. Schuman was the Foreign Secretary of France at the time and his intentions were clearly stated as being 'a first step in the direction of European federation'. Central to the Plan was the proposal that a genuinely SUPRANATIONAL body – the High Authority – would occupy a key position at the DECISION-MAKING centre of the new intergovernmental organization (IGO). A Council of Ministers would represent the interests of the member STATES, while a Judiciary would be the superordinate law-determining agency. Coal and steel were regarded as a vital sector for such INTEGRATION because their removal from state-based politics would eliminate a significant 'WAR potential' from purely national decision-making. In Schuman's own words, war as an instrument of policy in Franco–German relations was 'not merely unthinkable but materially impossible' once his Plan was implemented.

The Consultative Assembly of the COUNCIL OF EUROPE recommended the Plan to its members in August 1950 and the BENELUX states and Italy agreed to join with France and the Federal Republic of Germany as a result. Crucially for their future position in Europe, the Labour Government of the United Kingdom felt unable to join – the loss of SOVEREIGNTY was unacceptable. Negotiations between the six states culminated in the TREATY of Paris of April 1951 which established the European Coal and Steel Community (ECSC). RATIFICATION by the state legislatures took a further year to effect thereafter.

The ideas behind the Plan had been discussed within the Council of Europe in the summer of 1949. A possible Council convention recommending the HARMONIZATION of basic industrial production was being considered by the membership later in the year. At the same time the structural weaknesses of the Council of Europe precluded its use as an effective vehicle for integration. The significance of the Plan in the history of post-war western Europe is that it synthesized the perceived need for HARMONIZATION of industrial production with the desire of some ELITES and interest groups for genuine supranationalism.

## Scope

An ACTOR'S scope is a measure of the ISSUE AREAS on which it can effectively INFLUENCE WORLD POLITICS. The concept is used in the analysis of power relations and is usually used in conjunction with the concept of DOMAIN. As intervening variables in the explanation of how POWER – as a possession – is converted into power – as a relationship – the two ideas are crucial.

## SDI

An acronym for the Strategic Defense Initiative. This is a US ballistic missile defence (BMD) research programme initiated during the Presidency of Ronald Reagan. In March 1983, during an address to the US NATION, President Reagan challenged the US scientific and strategic community to develop means of intercepting and destroying BALLISTIC MISSILES before they reached the territory of the United States, or its allies. This 'Star Wars' speech, as it became known, was the proximate initiator for increased funding over a five-year period (commencing in 1985) to investigate whether new TECHNOLOGIES could be harnessed to this role.

US interest in the anti-ballistic missile (ABM) as a form of BMD dates from the late 1950s. Eventually after considerable debate and discussion within the policy ELITE in the United States it was decided to commit the United States to the 1972 ABM TREATY as part of the SALT I process. Enthusiasm for even the modest deployment permitted under the 1972 convention waned and by 1975 it seemed clear that the offensive concept of DETERRENCE was inviolate. A number of developments in the late 1970s appeared to challenge this fundamental assumption. First, unease increased regarding the so-called WINDOW OF VULNERABILITY of the US land-based missile force. This COUNTERFORCE gap, if it existed, could be closed in a number of ways. A BMD certainly would be one, although by no means the cheapest. Secondly, technology had moved on apace since the earlier period. In particular new battle management computers and exotic directed energy weapons seemed to answer some of the technological problems of the earlier period. Thirdly, there was concern that the Soviet Union might attempt to 'break out' of the 1972 ABM treaty and that, in these circumstances, the United States would need to revise its own WAR plans (see SIOP) and have the option of its own BMD. This classic ACTION–REACTION pattern of thinking is not untypical of the ARMS RACE dynamic. Fourthly, the SDI was a response to domestic pressures. Interest groups such as the HIGH FRONTIER lobby, strategists committed to COUNTERVAILING and opposed to ASSURED DESTRUCTION and PEACE MOVEMENTS uneasy about the unintended effects of NUCLEAR WAR as contained in the NUCLEAR WINTER thesis would all, for admittedly different reasons, welcome a move away from strategies that appeared to offer no alternative to holocaust and global destruction. A BMD offered a further insurance against 'cheating' on ARMS CONTROL agreements by the other side. If the United States was protected by its own defences rather than the word of its adversary then it had less to fear from being 'suckered' into arms control agreements that might turn out to be 'fatally flawed'.

The SDI decision was, therefore, an amalgam of factors which culminated in the March declaration. Any BMD system that subsequently emerges from the SDI decision is envisaged as a triple-layer system. The first two layers consist of exo-atmospheric interceptions involving the aforementioned exotic weapons, the aim being to intercept missiles initially as they lift off their launch pads before they can release their buses carrying the multiple independently targeted re-entry vehicles (MIRVS). This boost phase interception is essential if the missile attack is to be thinned out enough for the third layer – the point defence interception – to have any chance of defending the missiles and RADARS of the United States.

Conceptually SDI is a complete break with the tradition of offensive deterrence sometimes referred to as punishment deterrence. By enhancing defence rather that deterrence it is more in keeping with the ideas about contervailing developed in the United States from James Schlesinger (Bobbitt, 1989) onwards. SDI also has implications for the ABM treaty. If SDI was ever deployed, either in whole or in part, it would certainly be answered by measures to increase the ability of intercontinental ballistic missiles (ICBMS) to overcome such defences. In any event it would not deal with the challenge from air-breathing systems or depressed trajectory missiles.

## Second strike

A term used in strategic analysis. It refers to the CAPABILITY of an ACTOR to retaliate violently against an adversary having sustained in the meantime a FIRST STRIKE. Second strike capabilities are therefore those residual forces available for use against an opponent after his initial move has been made. As defined here, the idea of second strike is highly relative and contingent. The contingencies will depend upon two crucial variables: the state of TECHNOLOGY at any given moment and the capabilities and intentions of the adversary.

The major post-1945 TECHNOLOGICAL change that increased the plausibility and viability of second strike capabilities was the BALLISTIC MISSILE. The advent of the 'missile age' in the late 1950s, and particularly the second generation developments therein, placed a new emphasis upon DEFENCE, or at least counter-attack. The acquisition, first by the United States, of reliable solid fuel missiles meant that vulnerability to attack could be considerably reduced by basing these weapons on mobile platforms – the ultimate being the submarine – or by burying them in silos. The probability of being able to ride out an attack and still respond with ASSURED DESTRUCTION could now be contemplated by US DECISION-MAKERS and their advisers. At the same time these new weapons lacked the ACCURACY to make a first strike sufficiently viable. For what in retrospect was a transient period, DETERRENCE rested upon invulnerable second strike systems, COUNTER-CITY targets and mutual assured destruction (MAD).

It is now clear, a quarter of a century later, that this was a transient phase in the ARMS RACE. New technologies – in particular multiple independently targeted re-entry vehicles (MIRVs) – and increases in accuracy over greater distances have meant that missiles have dual characteristics: they still need to be invulnerable to a disarming first strike but, in addition, they are sufficiently accurate and numerous to offer the possibility of first strike facilities themselves. Thus part of the rationale for the US TRIAD was to enhance second strike but within that inventory are weapons systems which are clearly capable of carrying out COUNTERFORCE, damage limitation missions.

It is thus with the intentions and capabilities of the adversary, the second crucial variable, that the viability of second strike ultimately rests. Given that the overall relationship with the opponent is one of deterrence, presumably mutual from his perspective, then a second strike capability will have two immediate advantages. It enhances credibility and it reduces the incentive for a surprise or pre-emptive strike. Credibility is improved by second strike because one's forces are able to survive and respond, thus the conditional threat – which is the basis of all deterrent relationships – looks more sensible. Secondly, the premium often thought to be gained by surprise or pre-emption is denied by second strike capacity. In a situation of mutual deterrence both sides would benefit from the other's acquisition of a second strike capability and *ex hypothesi* stability is improved. Finally, because second strike reduces these provocative incentives, it is held to improve the chances of successful CRISIS MANAGEMENT.

Informed discussion of these ideas and issues began in the United States during the closing years of President Eisenhower's second term. In particular in a seminal article in *Foreign Affairs* (1959) Wohlstetter argued for the centrality of the notion of second strike to a full understanding of deterrence or the 'delicate balance of terror'. Wohlstetter states quite categorically that deterrence means 'a capability to strike second'.

## Secretary-General

The establishment of the first modern international governmental organizations in the nineteenth century led to the consequential development of international secretariats, and with them the office of Secretary-General. The first proposal for a neutral body of international civil servants was made in 1694 by William Penn in his *Essay towards the Present and Future Peace of Europe*. The nineteenth century secretariats, however, were composed mainly of 'national' civil servants or politicians whose primary loyalty was to their own member governments. The breakthrough in the development of a genuine international secretariat and Secretary-General, whose primary loyalty and responsibility was to the organization itself rather than to individual governments, came with the establishment of the LEAGUE OF NATIONS and SPECIALIZED AGENCIES after 1919. It has been argued since that in the careers of Sir Eric Drummond, the first Secretary-General of the League, and Albert Thomas, the first Secretary-General of the International Labour Organization (ILO) are the paradigm examples of the two modern traditions: the administrator/

civil servant and the DIPLOMAT/politician.

The starting point for the analysis of the role and function of any Secretary-General is an examination of the constitutional position of that office as stated in the documentation establishing the organization. This documentation will seek to address itself to the issue of whether the office of Secretary-General is to be primarily that of an administrator or that of a diplomat – or some combination of both roles. The administrator is seen as faithfully implementing the decisions and directives of the member STATES, as conveyed through their national delegations. The diplomat/politician tends to have a much greater degree of AUTONOMY to initiate policies, at least for discussion, among the member states. Indeed in this latter tradition the Secretary-General might pursue an independent line in public by making speeches, giving lectures and interviews and writing articles on questions actually or potentially within the remit of their organization. Recent instances of Secretaries-General taking this approach to their office might include Dag Hammarskjöld (UN) Raul Prebisch, United Nations Conference on Trade and Development (UNCTAD), and Diallo Telli, Organization of African Unity (OAU).

When the UN was established in 1945 the duality of the role of Secretary-General was recognized. Thus in Article 99 of its CHARTER, the incumbent is given certain powers of initiative: 'the Secretary-General may bring to the attention of the Security Council any matter which in his opinion may threaten the maintenance of international peace and security'. If this can be seen as creating greater SCOPE for the incumbent to act independently in voicing his views and concerns, the actual nominating procedure gives AUTHORITY to member states to refrain from supporting a contender for office, or an incumbent for a further term, if they are unhappy with his performance. In the instance of the UN, the Secretary-General is nominated by the SECURITY COUNCIL and confirmed by the Assembly for a five-year period of office. Incumbents such as Lie (UN) and Telli (OAU) were denied further terms in office because they fell foul of important states in their respective organizations.

The Secretary-General of any organization will be expected to fulfil the role of head of the secretariat in the appropriate organization. An important constraint upon any Secretary-General will be the extent to which he has a free hand to choose those who staff the secretariat. Normally member states will expect allocations to reflect various ideas about 'balance' between geographic areas and political divisions, This can result in GEOPOLITICAL differences being imported into the secretariat with divisive results. 'Promotion by favour' rather than 'promotion by merit' is the likely outcome from these intrusions.

Personality, skill and reputation, although difficult to stipulate objectively, must be included as factors in any assessment of the role and relevance of the office of Secretary-General in any organization. Two career patterns appear to be particularly productive of putative Secretaries-General: the world of politics and diplomacy is one, and the world of the academic and the public administrator is the other. Appropriately Albert Thomas and Eric Drummond represent these two backgrounds, while Hammarskjöld is perhaps the nearest to a synthesis of the two. His background was in the Drummond role but he saw the need to develop the office into directions more akin to Thomas-typologies. Hammarskjold was fortunate that his period in office coincided with fundamental changes in the character and composition of the UN as the log-jam on membership was broken and the organization moved towards universality. He was thus able to build a consensus of support amongst the emerging majority of non-aligned states from 1955 onwards until the Congo crisis of 1960 and the subsequent power struggle in that state (now Zaïre) led to the Soviet attack upon the man and the office of Secretary-General. The Soviet proposal that the office should become a troika of three Secretaries-General, representing the FIRST, second and THIRD WORLDS was the result of this attack. Although this troika proposal failed to win enough support, it was based upon plausible analysis, whatever the motivations of the Soviet Union for proposing it. The troika recognized that the UN was polarized into a number of factions. When this occurs in an intergovernmental organization (IGO) the Secretary-General is faced with two equally damaging choices, either to be impartial – and ineffective – or committed – and controversial. The paradigm instance of such organizational polarization is surely UNCTAD, which has had this characteristic since its inception. The various Secretaries-General of this IGO have tended to opt for the committed/controversial role.

The office of Secretary-General of any IGO is one of the most varied and vexatious positions available to international diplomats. It seems to be the case that once states have gone beyond a certain point in their relations they perceive the need to establish permanent institutions, including a Secretariat and a Secretary-General, the COMMONWEALTH being a case in point. At the same time the role and function of the Secretary-General will depend upon the three variables discussed above: (a) what stipulations the constitution of the IGO makes for the office; (b) the personality, training and background of the incumbent; and (c) the kind of global or regional system the IGO is envisaged as operating in. The systemic factor will provide constraints or opportunities working for or against task expansion in this regard.

## Security community

This concept was developed by Karl Deutsch in the 1950s after extensive empirical study of the North Atlantic area. Deutsch (Rosenau, 1961) maintained that the security community idea – and there were two versions of it – was a form of international cooperation which, under certain circumstances, could lead to INTEGRATION. Deutsch argued that a security community was formed among participating ACTORS when their peoples, and particularly their political ELITES, held stable expectations of PEACE between themselves in the present and for the future. Thus for Deutsch the United Kingdom and Eire, Norway and Sweden, the United States and Canada are all instances of security communities. The idea of what he called the 'no WAR community' would spill over into the absence of significant organized preparations for war or large scale violence. Deutsch argued that empirical evidence of this lack of preparation would tend to validate the 'no war' idea. The corollary of the idea that a security community is distinguished in this way was that when conflicts did occur between the participants, CONFLICT MANAGEMENT and CONFLICT RESOLUTION would be attempted.

Deutsch actually distinguishes two types of security community: the pluralistic from the amalgamated. The difference is the presence – or absence – of institutions. Thus in the amalgamated version the constituent members actually create a political community between themselves by institution-building. For Deutsch (1968) 'any reasonably well-integrated nation state' is an example of 'an amalgamated security community'. The examples cited above are, therefore, of pluralistic security communities. These are easier to establish and maintain. They require three antecedent conditions: compatibility of values, responsiveness to each other's needs and predictability of policy goals by political elites.

The argument that a number of states now conduct their relationships according to the 'no war' principle is an important insight. If validated it would certainly suggest that in at least those instances the traditional STATE-CENTRIC idea that war was the final arbiter between states needs to be dropped. It also leads to the conclusion that traditionally conceived conceptions of HIGH POLITICS are not the defining characteristics of these relationships. As such Deutsch's work represents an important break with previous perspectives on MACROPOLITICS. Along with other academics he points towards a greater emphasis in teaching and research upon a viewpoint that favours COMPLEX INTERDEPENDENCE as a growing characteristic of the study.

## Security Council

The Security Council is that organ of the UNITED NATIONS system given primary responsibility (see Article 24 of the Charter) for the maintenance of international peace and security. In one respect the establishment of the Council as the centrepiece of this arrangement was an intentional step predicated upon the perception that the LEAGUE OF NATIONS had lacked 'bite' and that its successor should be better equipped to take decisive action. Thus whereas the Council of the League had been hidebound and hamstrung by the UNANIMITY principle, no such blocking mechanisms were built into the Security Council – with one exception. The five permanent members of the Council: the United States, the Soviet Union, the United Kingdom, China and France, through the exercise of the VETO, retain the unanimity rule. In other respects, though, it is possible for the council to override any other STATE members and still make binding decisions. Moreover by allowing permanent members to abstain on a resolution without regarding such a move as an exercise of the veto, the Council has expanded its competence to make decisions on the key ISSUE AREA of PEACE and security.

Analytically the Council was seen as the hub of the COLLECTIVE SECURITY system of the UN CHARTER. By stipulating that five of the most significant states in the international HIERARCHY should concur with all Council decisions (other than procedural ones), the founders of the UN sought to ensure that whenever the Council decided to act the preponderance of available POWER and INFLUENCE in the system would be committed in support of the decision. Under Chapter VII of the Charter the Council is given binding DECISION-MAKING authority and in support of such commitments the same Chapter made a wide range of DIPLOMATIC, economic and military sanctions available for use against recalcitrant state(s). In this way it is possible to see the veto provisions of the charter as an essentially realistic and judicious recognition of the power configurations in WORLD POLITICS in 1945.

The outbreak of the COLD WAR after 1945 seriously damaged the ability of the Security Council to work as envisaged by the Charter. Article 43 on the establishment of a permanent UN force became inoperable. The veto became a means of paralysing decision-making and neutralizing the Council as an effective deliberating body. The veto was even used to restrict the entry of new members into the Organization, until the log-jam was broken in 1955. Cold War antagonisms prevented the People's Republic of China from occupying that seat designated for China on the Council until 1971. When the Security Council did work as intended in these early years – as in the case of the KOREAN WAR – it was a fluke made possible by the absence of the Soviet Union from the Council. The low point in the post-war decline was reached in 1955 when the Council held only twenty-two meetings. Many of the key issue areas of the early post-1945 period were simply not brought before the Council.

The influx of new members from the THIRD WORLD did much to revive the fortunes of the UN in general and the Council in particular. The second SECRETARY-GENERAL Dag Hammarskjold was responsible for developing the concept of PEACEKEEPING or preventive diplomacy after 1956. The Council played a major decision making role in these developments, in particular during the Congo (Zaïre) and Cyprus operations of the early 1960s. In December 1963 the ASSEMBLY agreed to expand the size of the Council from eleven to fifteen member states in order to increase THIRD WORLD representation. In resolving upon this expansion it was decided that half the non-permanent seats should go to Afro–Asian states (the remaining five are divided on a regional basis between Latin America, 2; Eastern Europe, 1; and Western Europe and other states, 2).

The Council played a central role in the Rhodesian ECONOMIC SANCTIONS issue, instructing all member states to implement mandatory measures against the illegal REGIME in December 1966. These selective sanctions were followed by comprehensive ones in May 1968. Although the sanctions policy was deliberately evaded by key multinational corporations (MNCs) and governments friendly towards the illegal regime in Rhodesia, the willingness of the Council to resort to such measures was indicative of its resuscitation.

The development of the PEACEKEEPING competence of the Council following the intrusion of Cold War considerations in the early years must be seen as the major development in the issue area of peace and security since 1945. Of course, the COLLECTIVE SECURITY provisions of the Charter remain available for use in any future contingency. Moreover, the possibility appears to be emerging that the Soviet Union intends to take a higher diplomatic profile in the UNO in the future. Such changes could encourage the permanent members to work closer in the future than they have sometimes in the past. The General Assembly has become increasingly unwieldy as its membership has expanded and this development alone might encourage the permanent members to keep key issues within the Council. In CRISIS situations certainly it will be the Council rather than the Assembly that member states, and the world in general, will look towards for a position on an issue. Its representative character could be further improved by increasing the number of permanent members to include perhaps India, Nigeria and Brazil. France and the United Kingdom

might collapse their representation if the EUROPEAN COMMUNITY becomes a federal ACTOR or this could be shared with a united Germany. Finally, the Council should seek to continue to develop policy positions on key ISSUE AREAS. The examples of Resolutions 242 and 338 on the Middle East are instructive here. By such initiatives the Council establishes a point of reference to which parties to conflicts may refer in seeking to reach a resolution or settlement of their differences.

## Security dilemma

A central tenet of REALISM and the realist paradigm, the security dilemma arises from the situation of ANARCHY that STATES find themselves in. By striving to increase their own security – by following policies that enhance their military CAPABILITIES – states inadvertently make others feel less secure. As a result of this behaviour a vicious circle or spiral of security–insecurity arises to which there is no permanent and lasting solution. John H. Herz (1950) was among the first to develop these ideas. Herz rested the dilemma not on any innate anti-social attributes of man *per se* but rather upon the social nexus – and the idea of anarchy – within which men, and groups, operate. The security dilemma may therefore be regarded as a structural attribute rather than a psychological one. It is to nurture, rather than nature, that one should look for explanations of why the dilemma occurs.

Herz returned to the subject in Chapter 10 of his 1959 book. The 'power and security dilemma', as it had now become, is still seen as immutable. Herz argued that the emerging BIPOLAR configuration of the COLD WAR period had exacerbated the dilemma. Comparing the bipolar system unfavourably with the BALANCE OF POWER, Herz concluded that 'bipolarity has given the security dilemma its utmost poignancy' (p. 241). Buzan (1983) seems to reflect similar views; again in his seventh chapter referring to the power-security dilemma,

Buzan argues for what he terms a 'mature anarchy' (p. 208) as the most stable outcome of the constant ACTION–REACTION pattern.

The most original contribution to the security dilemma idea since its inception has come from Robert Jervis in his book on PERCEPTION and MISPERCEPTION (1976) and then in his *World Politics* article (1978). In both publications Jervis analyses the dilemma in terms of GAME THEORY, and particularly the variable sum Prisoner's Dilemma – which balances its players between CONFLICT and cooperation strategies. Jervis argues that if WAR is costly and cooperation beneficial there will be strong incentives to overcome the dilemma by following policies that ameliorate rather than exacerbate relations between putative adversaries. If military TECHNOLOGY favours the DEFENCE, and if the opportunity costs of defence policy are high, incentives to manage the dilemma will correspondingly be high. Moreover if defensive postures can be easily distinguished from offensive postures – so that the risks of misperception are reduced – the dilemma will be reduced. Like Herz and Buzan, Jervis believes that a STATUS QUO orientation by the leading players in the system helps the management process.

There is no antidote to the dilemma within realism, of course. Realists are perforce committed to its principles. REGIME analysis offers a possible way out analytically. Philosophically the IDEALISTS believed that systems such as their COLLECTIVE SECURITY idea offered more permanent solutions, but this requires the importation of assumptions which realism cannot tolerate.

ity. As such, the dilemmas of politics are clearly reflected in the ambiguities of international law. Consequently, the right is fraught with uncertainties. International law is by no means clear as to what the 'self' refers to. Does it refer only to the use of FORCE for the protection of a STATE'S territorial integrity or can it be broadened to include other interests that states deem essential to their security? Is it limited to the employment of force in response to a prior attack or is there a right of anticipatory or pre-emptive self-defence? How are the requirements of immediacy, necessity and proportionality defined? Is it possible to distinguish operationally between matters of 'security' and matters of 'survival'? The traditional metalegal doctrine of *SALUS POPULI SUPREMA LEX* cuts across these difficulties and asserts that the state has a right to interpret the notion of self-defence expansively; that is, that it is permissible to undertake any action it considers necessary to protect itself against any actual or threatened injury to its self-defined interests. However, contemporary international law attempts to restrict the use of force to circumstances of a prior use of force. But this does not resolve the issue of the nature of 'self' or whether it is legitimate to use force against acts that may not involve force but are nevertheless considered to imperil the interests of a state.

Article 2, paragraph 4 and Article 51 of the UN CHARTER are ambiguous on this and may indeed be contradictory. As with other quasi-legal rights asserted by states the matter of limits and SCOPE will always be compromised by the claims of SOVEREIGNTY and the overriding duty of self preservation from which these rights derive (*see*: Osgood and Tucker, 1967).

## Self-defence

A legal sub-species of the more general political right of SELF-HELP. The evolution of the right of self-defence in customary and contemporary INTERNATIONAL LAW is a legal acknowledgement of political real-

## Self-determination

The right or aspiration of a group, which considers itself to have a separate and distinct identity, to govern itself and to determine the political and legal status of the territory it occupies. Thus, in the political sense it refers both to a process and to an idea. Closely identified with NATIONALISM and LIBERALISM it is probably best understood as a theory of the relationship between NATION and STATE which finds its fullest expression in the concept of the democratic NATION-STATE. However, there is nothing in the term itself that indicates preference for a particular form of political organization and it can mean the right of an established state to determine its own form of government free from external interference. In a general sense, then, political self-determination refers to the right of peoples to determine their own destiny in their own way.

The concept was implicit in the US Declaration of Independence of 1776 ('the consent of the governed') and in the French revolutionary Declaration of the Rights of Man in 1789 ('the divine right of the people'). Its influence was especially felt in the nineteenth century European STATES-SYSTEM and apart from France, it played an important part in the unification of Germany and of Italy and the independence of Belgium and Greece. Outside Europe it was the prime mover in the process of the liberation of South America from colonial rule. But it was not until the First World War that, under the impact of President Wilson's FOURTEEN POINTS, the idea of national INDEPENDENCE came to be known as national self-determination. Thereafter it has become one of the 'absolutes' of contemporary international thought and it featured prominently in the Covenant of the LEAGUE OF NATIONS and in the CHARTER OF THE UNITED NATIONS.

Despite its ubiquity the concept has never carried a clear legal connotation. The problem of determining which groups of people may legitimately claim this right has bedevilled its application in the twentieth century world. This is further complicated by the legal restrictions against INTERVENTION in another state's internal affairs. Consequently, in practice the emphasis has been placed on the notion of 'self' rather than on any external application of a known rule. Even so, the UNITED NATIONS has attempted on a number of occasions to link the concept to the process of DECOLONIZATION and thereby make it a positive duty and a legal right rather than an aspiration. The Declaration on the Granting of Independence of Colonial Countries and Peoples in 1960, for example, stated that 'all people have the right to self-determination; by virtue of that right they freely determine their political status and freely pursue their economic, social and cultural development'. The right of self-determination was again reaffirmed in the 1970 Declaration of Principles of INTERNATIONAL LAW which further emphasized that all states were under a positive duty to promote it. This all-embracing linkage with anti-colonialism, equal rights, economic, social and cultural development has in effect robbed the term of any practical meaning. Questions of definition remain. Who are the 'peoples' to whom it applies? Does it justify rebellion, REVOLUTION or secession? Must it result in full independence or can it be partial or fulfilled by means of ASSOCIATION? Answers to these questions are by no means clear-cut and the international community, both inside and outside the GENERAL ASSEMBLY, has tended to react to them in an *ad hoc*, interest-based fashion rather than in accordance with the guidelines of the 1970 Declaration, which in any case are much too vague for practical application.

## Self-fulfilling prophecy

Originally developed by the sociologist R. K. Merton in 1949, this theory refers to the way in which social behaviour is conditioned by the expectations that individuals and groups have of each other. Its basic premise is that these expectations will produce an erroneous DEFINITION OF THE SITUATION which will feed back into a pattern of behaviour that will seem to confirm the initial position. For instance, STATE

A perceives State B as having aggressive intentions towards it and, accordingly, in a SHOW OF FORCE moves its troops to the border. State B responds with some equally determined move and State A feels that its original position has been vindicated. This clearly oversimplified example nonetheless shows the principle of the theory.

The self-fulfilling prophecy has been widely applied by educational sociologists to such issues as the way tutors grade students and then seek confirmation of this grading subsequently. Economists are agreed that it is a contributory factor in 'panic buying' and banking and stock market crashes. Application to politics has been more popular among psychologists than sociologists, with Stagner probably the most influential.

## Self-help

For the REALIST the notion of self-help is a logical consequence of the anarchical structure of the international STATES-SYSTEM. For the IDEALIST it is the cause of it. Either way, self-help is endemic in INTERNATIONAL POLITICS. Given that STATES are INDEPENDENT political units that are primarily concerned with their own survival and advancement but are not subordinate to a central AUTHORITY, the idea of self-reliance is a compelling one. The search for security in a system of politics without government means that self-help is a necessary function of self-preservation. It is a natural response to the SECURITY DILEMMA as traditionally conceived. However, the right to self-help is not an absolute one. States might not be expected to surrender the general right of self-help but the INTERNATIONAL SYSTEM does attempt to restrict its SCOPE. Both INTERNATIONAL LAW and the UNITED NATIONS CHARTER are founded on the premise that there is no unrestricted right of self-help. Indeed, in this context the primary purpose of law and of SUPRANATIONAL institutions is to map out areas of consensus on permissible limits of the private use of force by SOVEREIGN states. Thus, SELF-DEFENCE is regarded as the most basic manifestation and requirement of the institution of self-help. Other characteristic forms of it are RETORTION and REPRISALS. Historically, states have been reluctant to allow encroachments on the rights of self-preservation but the nineteenth and twentieth centuries in particular have witnessed considerable, though frequently ambiguous, inroads into this entrenched doctrine. To date, there have been no viable or effective replacements, BALANCE OF POWER and COLLECTIVE SECURITY are variants of it, not alternatives. Accordingly, to some the persistence of the notion is an impediment to progress towards the establishment of a centralized executive world authority possessing a monopoly of the legitimate use of FORCE. But since self-help is a consequence of political independence, so long as the world is organized on a decentralized multi-state basis, it is unlikely to be replaced. Clearly, the absence of self-help as a fundamental behavioural principle would mean a radical transformation of the system. This eventuality is, at present, extremely unlikely.

## Self-sufficiency

A form of economic FOREIGN POLICY which seeks to reduce the dependence of a state ACTOR for external goods and services to a minimum. Since the TRADE system is based upon RECIPROCITY – one actor's IMPORTS are another's EXPORTS – widespread pursuit of self-sufficiency as a long-term goal will have deleterious effects upon the whole system. Self-sufficiency may also be pursued as a short-term expedient during times of acute CRISIS and violence – such as WAR. In this instance the aim is to conduct a kind of 'siege economy' system. Instruments such as rationing and substitution will be used to reduce dependence, but in the final analysis abstinence and denial may be necessary.

Self-sufficiency was rejected by classical economic theory and has always been attacked by ECONOMIC LIBERALISM. It does have its advocates amongst MERCANTILISM, however. The welfare implications of self-sufficiency in the twentieth century are dire and few political leaderships could sustain such an arrangement over a long period without the robust use of instruments of social control. If INTERDEPENDENCE is regarded as a defining characteristic of MACROPOLITICS then self-sufficiency is bound to have a bad press.

## Show of force

The deliberate use of an ACTOR'S military CAPABILITY to coerce an opponent by implication. The show of force is thus a diplomatic gesture, but one carrying coercive and punitive connotations. The coercion may be aimed directly at the opposition, or indirectly at a third party whose ties with the putative opponent are sufficiently strong and unequivocal for the true intention of the imposer to be understood. Whatever target is chosen, the essence of the show of force is its ambiguity. While this can leave the party making such a move with considerable flexibility, without more precision being introduced into the relationship – such as a precise verbal statement of intent, i.e. an ULTIMATUM – the political leadership in the target actor may be unclear about what is required of them if they wish to seek redemption in the eyes of the imposer. The most intimidatory show of force is that which implies that the imposer's forces are being prepared for military action. Putting one's forces on an alert status, dispersing existing forces to more secure positions and calling up reserves all come in this category.

*See also*: GUNBOAT DIPLOMACY

## SIOP

An acronym for the Single Integrated Operational Plan, a US planning exercise begun in the last years of the Eisenhower Presidency (1953–61). The planning specifically concerned the projected use of US nuclear forces against Soviet, Chinese and WARSAW PACT targets should DETERRENCE break down and WAR ensue. The first SIOP was endorsed in December 1960. Reflecting ideas about MASSIVE RETALIATION which had been influential in the early 1950s, this first SIOP envisaged a single all-out spasm attack, with little target discrimination, at the outset of hostilities. During the Kennedy Administration Robert McNamara succeeded in incorporating greater flexibility into the plan and this led to a revised SIOP in June 1962. Unlike the first one, this revision enumerated five options which would be available to US DECISION-MAKERS in the event of a NUCLEAR WAR.

The idea of options and target selection has remained a fundamental principle of all SIOPs since McNamara's time at the Pentagon. Throughout the period conscious efforts have been made to avoid two kinds of targets: major population centres and $C^3I$ facilities. Attacking cities from the outset is regarded as too provocative, while inviolable $C^3I$ is necessary to allow for bargaining and NEGOTIATION to ensure war termination.

SIOP represents the operationalization of nuclear POLICY-MAKING. It is the clearest available declaration of intention about how a STATE possessing NUCLEAR WEAPONS intends to use them should the threshold be crossed. Or rather, dropping the reification, it is a statement of the options available to the political LEADERSHIP in such circumstances. The development of sequential SIOPs since 1960 has thrown into sharp relief the discrepancy between action policy and declaratory policy. The SIOP has increasingly reflected also a commitment to COUNTERFORCE targets. Declaratory statements notwithstanding, SIOP reveals how the decision to go to nuclear war might be implemented.

## SIPRI

The Stockholm International Peace Research Institute (SIPRI) was founded in

1966 to commemorate the fact that Sweden had enjoyed 150 years without WAR. It is an independent institute funded mainly by the Swedish Parliament, with an internationally recruited staff and governing body. The Institute publishes books, monographs, papers and reports on all aspects of CONFLICT and cooperation. Since its inception, SIPRI has developed particular expertise in the ISSUE AREAS of ARMS RACES, ARMS TRADE, ARMS CONTROL and DISARMAMENT, and evolving TECHNOLOGIES. Probably its best known publication is its *Yearbook* which is arguably the most authoritative source of information about contemporary developments in the above fields. Unlike some research institutes, SIPRI works entirely with published data and source materials and, accordingly, it is not constrained in its own publications by perceptions of confidentiality. Philosophically, SIPRI is part of the PEACE RESEARCH tradition. It may be appropriately contrasted with other institutes – such as the London-based International Institute for Strategic Studies – which approach the same subject matter from the STRATEGIC STUDIES perspective.

## SLBM

A Submarine-Launched BALLISTIC MISSILE. First developed by the United States during the Eisenhower Administration as the Polaris system, the submarine launching platform for ballistic missiles is inherently invulnerable, at least until the nuclear-powered ballistic missile submarine (SSBN) declares its location by firing its missiles. The original Polaris system was not truly intercontinental in terms of its range. Later systems such as the Poseidon and Trident on the US side and the Soviet Navy's 'Delta' class SSBNs have longer range and can credibly threaten the adversary's homeland from much greater distances. This gives the respective submarines the option of cruise patrols much closer to, or even within, their own territorial waters where they may en-joy the additional protection of land-based air cover. SLBMs, like ballistic missiles in general, have been improved in ACCURACY as well as range of late. Thus the newest Trident system is generally believed to have a 'hard-kill' CAPABILITY, that is to say, an accuracy that would enable the missile to be used in a COUNTERFORCE mode. This facility, combined with the SSBN's mobility and inherent invulnerability, makes these projectiles highly potent weapons indeed.

## SLCM

Sea-Launched Cruise Missile. The launching platform for the CRUISE MISSILE in this mode would be a submarine or surface ship. The TECHNOLOGY of the SLCM is essentially the same as that for the air-launched cruise missile (ALCM) and the ground-launched cruise missile (GLCM). Again, like these, the SLCM is in principle a dual-purpose system, that is to say it can carry either CONVENTIONAL or nuclear warheads. The range of the missile would be affected by this choice, however.

## Small powers

Some scholars allege that all STATES that are not GREAT POWERS are small powers. The distinction is usually made on the basis of a state's ability to provide for its own security needs. Thus, small powers are those states that have to rely on external assistance for their security needs. Clearly this definition is too general to be useful and most commentators and practitioners, while acknowledging the difficulties of precise categorization, assert that small powers are those which fall between MIDDLE POWERS and MICROSTATES. In this way, most states are small or 'minor' powers. Spiegel (1972) identifies three groups of states in this class. The largest class consists of states which seek to play an important regional role (e.g. Zimbabwe). The second group he terms 'the mavericks' – those states which seek INFLUENCE outside their region because they have been denied influence within it (e.g. Libya). The third group consists of states which are similar to middle powers in terms of FOREIGN POLICY style, material resources and development, but they usually have smaller populations, lower GNPs and tend to allocate less expenditure on armed forces and DEFENCE (e.g. Denmark, Norway, New Zealand). These are also termed 'miniature middle powers'. The question 'how small is small?' is thus a problematical one. Acknowledging the dangers of generalization, and bearing in mind the distinction between the older small DEVELOPED STATES (mainly Western European) and the newer small developing states (mainly African, Asian and Latin American), the following appear to be characteristic behaviour patterns; limited involvement in world affairs, strong attachment to intergovernmental organizations (IGOs), support for INTERNATIONAL LAW, avoidance of the use of FORCE and a limited geographical and functional range of foreign policy activities.

## Social science approach

The term 'social science' is here taken to refer to those studies such as sociology, psychology, economics, social psychology, anthropology and political science. Distinctive in terms of such factors as their LEVEL OF ANALYSIS, they are similar in terms of their most fundamental methodological assumptions. Thus the social science approach to WORLD POLITICS involves applying the same methods, concepts, models and theories from any one or group of the above disciplines to the subject matter at hand. DECISION-MAKING, GAME THEORY and SYSTEMS ANALYSIS are but three examples of this interdisciplinary borrowing. The social science approach is therefore consistently and intentionally eclectic.

Historically, this approach to the subject matter has been US-inspired and wholly post-1945 in its development. The ascend-

ancy of the United States as a SUPERPOWER in the system meant that the intellectual challenges presented by a global FOREIGN POLICY have a spillover effect upon the colleges and research institutes of the United States. In short, US PERCEPTION of its new role in MACROPOLITICS encouraged a new interest in the subject. In the years after 1945, moreover, funds for basic research were available in the United States. The US Government played an important, if controversial, role in some of this funding but private foundations like Ford, Carnegie and Rockefeller were also important.

Political science had already developed some significance before 1945 in the United States. Probably the most famous faculty was that located at the University of Chicago under the leadership of Charles Merriam. After 1945 political scientists such as Lasswell (1948) and Almond, nurtured in the Chicago tradition of social science, began to move into INTERNATIONAL/WORLD POLITICS, a field traditionally reserved for historians, lawyers, philosophers and strategists: the so-called 'classical' tradition. Publication of the influential journal, *World Politics*, by Princeton Center for International Studies began in 1948. Thereafter there was a mushrooming of talented scholarship as various campuses in the United States developed an interest in the new field. Publications soon followed. Rosenau's 1961 *Reader* stands as an exemplification of the contributions made in the previous decade. By the beginning of the 1960s indeed the social science approach was well represented in US colleges and institutes and was beginning to have an impact across the Atlantic. In Europe the classical tradition was more entrenched and less willing to welcome these changes, preferring to see them as challenges instead. Hedley Bull's (1966b) article was typical of the unfavourable reaction from many European-based scholars. Accordingly the impact of the growth of a social science of world politics was delayed and somewhat diffused in Europe. Earlier, Dahl (1961b) labelled 'behaviouralism' as a protest movement. TRADITIONAL analysis simply left a vacuum which was filled by borrowing the concepts theories and techniques of the mainstream social sciences identified above.

Seemingly no sooner was one chapter closed than another opened. In 1969, Easton, a leading exponent of the deductive mode of systems analysis, proclaimed a 'new revolution' in political science and characterized the epoch as 'post-behavioural'. Attacking what he called the 'empirical conservatism' (p. 1052) of the behavioural approach, Easton called for a new emphasis upon the study of values and, conversely, for the abandonment of the value-free approach. In calling for more value-oriented, politically relevant research at the end of the turbulent 1960s, Easton anticipated certain trends that have been evident in the study of world politics since. There has been a definite proliferation of broad-based perspectives and paradigms of late. REGIME analysis, HEGEMONIC STABILITY THEORY, the WORLD SOCIETY approach, the new interest in POWER, and DEPENDENCY theories are all examples. Following Kuhn (1962), new concern has been shown in the idea of paradigms. Broadly speaking the argument runs that under a prevailing paradigm research can proceed with modest confidence provided that the fundamental assumptions and implications of the paradigm itself are not ignored. In 1971 Allison applied the concept of paradigm to basic decision-making models. In 1983 Vasquez used it critically in his examination of REALISM. The recent revival of the realist approach, now labelled neo-realism, has itself been contingent upon a paradigm shift. At the time of writing the social science approach shows itself to be a buoyant, if somewhat unruly, flock of activities. Another round of methodological introspection is possibly about due. Like the behavioural movement post-1945 and the post-behavioural trends of the last two decades, any retrenchment will be caused as much by events outside the discipline as by uncertainties within.

## Sovereignty

Often regarded as the enabling concept of WORLD POLITICS whereby STATES assert not only ultimate AUTHORITY within a distinct territorial entity but also assert membership of the international community. Internal sovereignty thus refers to a supreme DECISION-MAKING and enforcement authority with regard to a particular territory and population. External sovereignty on the other hand refers to its antithesis: the absence of a supreme international authority and hence the independence of sovereign states. Paradoxically, therefore, the doctrine of state sovereignty necessarily leads to the concept of INTERNATIONAL ANARCHY: the idea of a supreme authority within the state logically leads to a denial of the existence of a supra-sovereign above the state.

Historically, in the development of the European STATES-SYSTEM, it is usually associated with the works of Bodin (1576) and Hobbes (1651) where it appeared to be synonymous with the right to exercise unrestricted power. Thus, the HOBBESIAN system of INTERNATIONAL RELATIONS was characterized as a near-permanent state of WAR where sovereign authorities are not restrained by a common POWER. On this view, INTERNATIONAL LAW, because its provenance must be doubtful, cannot circumscribe or set limits on state behaviour. Sovereign states are judges in their own cause, have an absolute right to go to WAR to pursue their conceived interests and can treat those who fall within their DOMESTIC JURISDICTION in their own way. However, in practice the denial of a supra-sovereign authority beyond the state has never meant that sovereign states are free to do as they please. The history of the modern states system (which is to say the history of state sovereignty) from the seventeenth century onwards has been a conscious attempt to move away from the apparent rigidity of the early formulation of the doctrine while retaining its more useful characteristics, especially the idea of formal equality which it implies. The notion of absolute unlimited sovereignty, while being a useful and indeed an indispensable instrument to employ against the claims of a pope or emperor, was never more than a convenient fiction in the development of the modern STATE-SYSTEM. Increasing INTERDEPENDENCE, the reciprocal nature of international law and membership of INTERNATIONAL ORGANIZATIONS have thus led to the acceptance of the doctrine of 'divided sovereignty' where supremacy is qualified either through consent or auto-limitation. The UN CHARTER, for example, is an implicit RECOGNITION of this (Article 2 para. 1 recognizes the 'sovereign equality' of member states yet exhorts them to settle their disputes by 'peaceful means').

Many scholars today regard the doctrine of sovereignty as not only dangerous (it can lead to unrestrained pursuit of the NATIONAL INTEREST and is inimical to the development of international law) but also as misleading (few, if any states are as impenetrable or as impermeable as it implies). They argue that integrative developments and COMPLEX INTERDEPENDENCE on all fronts have rendered it, and the STATE-CENTRIC bias it encourages, obsolete. However, the continued influence of the idea of sovereignty in world politics is testified by the fact that 'at the political level it is the one and only organizing principle in respect of the dry surface of the globe, all that surface now being divided among constitutionally independent entities' (James, 1984).

## Special Drawing Rights (SDR)

A reserve asset created by the IMF. The facility was formally approved by the Board of Directors of the Fund in September 1967 and the requisite amendments to the Articles of the IMF were made by March 1968. By July 1969 sufficient member STATES had ratified these arrangements for them to come into force. The Managing Director of the Fund proposed the creation of 9.5 billion dollars of SDRs over the following three years and the first allocation was made in January 1970. The SDR is now the principal reserve asset of the IMF.

The creation of this new facility in the period 1967–9 was a significant, if belated, recognition by the membership of the IMF and the Group of Ten that a reserve asset, in addition to the traditional GOLD EXCHANGE STANDARD, was needed. The SDR is a fiduciary issue, not backed by gold or indeed any national currency. Instead the value of the SDR is calculated against a basket of some sixteen currencies. Since it is both a store of value and a means of settling indebtedness it does have many of the characteristics of money. SDRs are, moreover, interest bearing assets, states in credit earning small interest while states in deficit on their allocation are charged interest.

The creation of the SDR coincided with the demise of the dollar as the basis of the post-1945 system. Had the politicians and bankers acted sooner when the first intimation of the dilemma inherent in the BRETTON WOODS system was being pointed out at the end of the 1950s, events twenty years later might have been different. As it was, the fact that the SDR was not a national currency was its strength. It meant that the total reserve figure of SDRs could be expanded without a country running a balance of payments deficit. In the past this had been the only way whereby a leading state actor, such as the United States, could pump-prime the system. The creation of the SDR made such dollar deficit financing unnecessary.

A major issue that arose from the creation of the SDR was how this new reserve asset should be distributed. THIRD WORLD interests and economic liberals seek in the SDR the opportunity to expand the reserve position of developing states on the basis of need rather than ability to pay. Various proposals have been made for a so-called 'link' to be made between the creation and distribution of SDRs and other activities, notably international and TRANSNATIONAL economic assistance – or AID. The difficulty with all these initiatives is that they imply introducing new, and probably controversial, criteria into the SDR mechansim and ultimately into the IMF. If implemented these proposals would take the Fund further away from the original intentions of its founders and closer to the activities of other intergovernmental organizations (IGOS), notably the WORLD BANK GROUP.

## Specialized agency

Associated with the UN framework but not strictly a part of it, these are autonomous functional organizations dealing on an international level with economic, social, cultural, educational, medical, agricultural and other diverse fields. Each has its own headquarters, staff and budget. Membership is independent of UN membership but since the aim is universality, there is considerable overlap. Each agency was established by multilateral TREATY and maintains a special and close relationship with the UN through the coordinating role adopted by its Economic and Social Council (ECOSOC). Their organizational structures are broadly similar: (a) an assembly or conference which is the basic POLICY-MAKING organ; (b) a council which is the executive agency; (c) a secretariat and director-general which provides the overall administration. There exist to date sixteen specialized agencies. These are as follows: International Labour Organization (ILO), Food and Agriculture Organization (FAO), United Nations Education, Scientific and Cultural Organization (UNESCO), WORLD HEALTH ORGANIZATION (WHO), International Bank for Reconstruction and Development (WORLD BANK or IBRD), International Finance Corporation (IFC), International Development Association (IDA), INTERNATIONAL MONETARY FUND (IMF), International Civil Aviation Organization (ICAO), Universal Postal Union (UPU), International Telecommunication Union (ITU), World Meteorological Organization (WMO), Intergovernmental Maritime Consultative Organization (IMCO), World Intellectual Property Organization (WIPO), International Fund for Agricultural Development (IFAO) and United Nations Industrial Development Organization (UNIDO). Two other organizations which share family resemblances with specialized agencies are the International Atomic Energy Agency (IAEA) and the General Agreement on Tariffs and Trade (GATT).

These specialized agencies can be seen as part of the FUNCTIONALIST approach to world peace which views the solving of common social and economic problems as a necessary step in the direction of the creation of an orderly and stable INTERNATIONAL SOCIETY. However, the present structure for controlling these operations and their budgets (altogether over eight billion dollars per year) is often a matter of bitter dispute. In addition, East–West and more especially NORTH–SOUTH issues have led to fundamental divisions among member STATES, so much so that the future of some of these agencies often seems in doubt.

## Special Relationship

Term commonly used to describe the relations between the United Kingdom and the United States since 1940. The phrase has become part of the rhetoric of UK FOREIGN POLICY in particular, and every Prime Minister from Churchill onwards has alluded to it in one form or another, to the extent that in popular mythology the 'Special Relationship' with the United States is regarded as a permanent, almost structural feature of contemporary WORLD POLITICS. A shared language, an overlapping culture, a similar commitment to the values of capitalism, representative democracy and the common law system have combined to produce, in the public mind at least, feelings of mutual affinity between the two STATES. However, this relationship has rarely, except for relatively brief periods during and after the Second World War and again sporadically in the 1950s and 1960s, been quite as affectionate or intimate as the phrase suggests.

In fact, some commentators suggest that the idea of the singularity of the relationship was a deliberate ploy of Winston Churchill. Churchill not only had family connections with the United States but also pressing strategic and economic reasons for propagating the uniqueness of the United Kingdom's relations with the United States. Both his short-term goals (defeating Hitler's Germany) and his long-term goals (ENCIRCLING the Soviet Union and preserving Empire) needed the active assistance of the US colossus. Churchill had a world view (the 'three circles' idea) in which the United Kingdom and the United States in equal measure would form an impenetrable axis which could dominate and stifle the growth of international COMMUNISM and at the same time prolong the active life of the British Empire. The practical symbols of this bonding of 'the English-speaking peoples' were LEND-LEASE, MARSHALL AID and NATO.

The myth of the special relationship was, on this view, created to paper over gaping CREDIBILITY gaps in the belief that the United Kingdom still had a major role to play in the post-war world. The US NUCLEAR UMBRELLA and dollar support for sterling appeared, temporarily, to do the trick. For its part, the United States, after initial ISOLATIONIST and almost virginal reluctance to get involved, came to embrace the idea realizing that military and economic support for the United Kingdom and Western Europe was essential to contain the spread of COMMUNIST influence. The Americans had read Marx and understood that the economic and social devastation in Europe after the WAR had created a potentially very fertile soil for the growth of socialist ideas. It was therefore in their own interests to create a compliant, receptive, pro-market capitalist system in Western Europe to stave off the classic REVOLUTIONARY symptoms that had begun to appear. The United Kingdom, in their eyes, was valuable both as Trojan Horse and as Airstrip One in the coming battle with the Soviet Union.

Clearly interest, not emotion, both created and sustained the special relationship. Above all, the fear of Soviet expansionism did much to shape its course, and without this common COLD WAR perception Anglo–American relations may well have taken a different turn. Most commentators agree that as the PERCEPTION of the Soviet threat diminished, so too did the sense of common purpose and affinity between the United States and the United Kingdom. That the myth lingers may be due more to personality factors than objective assessments of strategic or economic realities. Looking at post-war relationships between the respective national leaders it emerges that it was 'special' when there were mutual personal friendships both at the highest level and at the level of officials concerned with formulating and implementing policy. Thus the administrations of Churchill–Roosevelt, Atlee–Truman, Macmillan–Kennedy, Callaghan–Carter and Thatcher–Reagan all had at different levels, and for different reasons, unusual degrees of sentimental attachment to one another. At these times, the level of mutual trust and respect was high, and at least from the UK point of view, benefits accrued: Churchill secured LEND-LEASE, Atlee Marshall aid and NATO, Macmillan Polaris, Callaghan economic support for an ailing economy and Thatcher vital US backing in the FALKLANDS. When personal relations were non-existent or frosty, the relationship was anything but special and at times spilled over into tacit if not active hostility. Eisenhower scuppered Eden's career over Suez, Wilson refused Johnson's request for UK assistance in VIETNAM, and Heath made it clear that the United Kingdom's future lay in Europe and not across the Atlantic. All these issues were more than mere domestic tiffs within a basically happy union and clearly when interests diverged, as they began to in the 1970s and 1980s, sentiment took a back seat. Whether this special relationship can survive full UK participation in the EUROPEAN COMMUNITY is a matter for debate. What is clear is that the special relationship between the two states is an unusual, albeit temporary, phenomenon in world politics. Other special relationships, not necessarily expressed in ALLIANCE formation, have existed in international affairs (e.g. between Germany and Austria or Russia and France in the nineteenth century, or between South Africa and Rhodesia in the 1970s) but none of these have had quite the force or the vitality as that between the United Kingdom and the United States in the twenty years or so following the Second World War. Indeed, the term, especially expressed in capitals, is reserved almost exclusively for this.

## Sphere of Influence

Refers to a territory or REGION over which an outside STATE claims control, influence or preferential status. The preferred state does not claim SOVEREIGNTY but does claim military, political or economic exclusiveness and in so doing not only restricts the rights of other foreign powers but imposes limitations on the INDEPENDENCE and AUTONOMY of the targeted area. These claims may or may not be enshrined in TREATY form but in either case have usually been conceded on a *quid pro quo* basis with third parties. The legal status of a sphere of influence is thus ambiguous. The first international agreement specifically to employ this term was the agreement between Germany and the United Kingdom in 1885 regarding their respective claims to territories on the Gulf of Guinea. Under the terms of this agreement both sides recognized each others' paramouncy in the specified areas and contracted not to interfere therein with the other's pursuit of its NATIONAL INTEREST. This agreement set the pattern for others and in the two decades spanning the end of the nineteenth century and the beginning of the twentieth similar ones were concluded by the major IMPERIAL powers. The most notable (and indeed, notorious) example was in relation to China, which between 1896–8 was sub-

jected to various forms of monopolistic servitude by the United Kingdom, France, Germany, Japan and the Soviet Union and which incidentally, prompted the US OPEN DOOR notes of 1899. Other agreements related to North Africa (1904, France and the United Kingdom), Persia (1907, the Tsarist Russia and the United Kingdom) and North Africa (1907, the Tsarist Russia and the United Kingdom). In relation to Latin America the UNILATERAL declaration by the United States of the MONROE DOCTRINE in 1823 had the effect of establishing, with the tacit connivance of the United Kingdom, unrivalled US dominance in the Western Hemisphere. Since World War Two the term has carried a somewhat looser connotation and refers generally to hemispheric regions dominated by the SUPERPOWERS: the Soviet Union in Eastern Europe, China in Southeast Asia and the United States in the Western Hemisphere. However, the difference between 'spheres of influence' and 'spheres of control' is not always easy to delineate as territories or states may be so overwhelmed by the hegemonic power as to be little more than protectorates or satellite states.

## Spillover

A term used in the NEO-FUNCTIONALIST approach to INTEGRATION. Spillover is a dynamic process which occurs during sector integration. By integrating a particular activity certain goals are set but once integration has occurred the participants see that goal-attainment can only be guaranteed by further integration. Conceptually spillover is linked to ideas about FEEDBACK because both positive and negative feedback can create spillover tendencies. If things are going well, the participants will be encouraged to move towards further task expansion. If things are going badly, the participants may need to remove distortions or impediments in other sectors to give their original purpose the chance of success. Haas (1964), the leading exponent of the neo-functionalist logic in the 1950s, modified his ideas about spillover to include an important distinction between manifest and latent functions of integration. According to this later gloss on the process, spillover occurs as much because of the unanticipated consequences of integration as the anticipated.

The main laboratory for the validation of these ideas has been the integration process that commenced in Western Europe with the SCHUMAN PLAN. Throughout the 1950s progress seemed to confirm these ideas but the advent of GAULLISM provided a severe check. In the light of this experience it is clear that spillover cannot proceed without confronting issues of HIGH POLITICS. This confrontation may not be settled at all or, if settled, it may not be in favour of extending integration.

## Sputnik

The world's first artificial satellite was launched from the Soviet Union in October 1957 and promptly dubbed 'Sputnik'. Weighing approximately 180 lbs, its signals to earth (which were easily picked up in the West) symbolized the apparent primacy of Soviet space TECHNOLOGY. When, six weeks later, Sputnik II was launched, carrying a dog and weighing approximately half a ton, the demise of the United States seemed complete. Eventually in February 1958 the United States succeeded in placing an Explorer satellite in orbit. Although much smaller than Sputnik, it carried more instruments and thus provided much more scientific data than its Soviet rival. The fact remains that few outside the scientific community remember Explorer, while Sputnik has passed into the folklore of the period.

The advent of Sputnik in the autumn of 1957 caused consternation in the United States. It was clear that the Soviets possessed very powerful and reliable rockets which could perform these tasks and the implication that they might have a more than passing family likeness to intercontinental ballistic missiles (ICBMS) was accepted as part of the US DEFINITION OF THE SITUATION. At the time the informed public in the United States was becoming used to thinking in terms of an adverse MISSILE GAP with the Soviet Union, and these events served to increase that PERCEPTION.

## SSBN

A nuclear-powered ballistic missile submarine. SSBN is the accepted abbreviation for a weapons TECHNOLOGY that was first developed in the 1950s in the United States with the Polaris system of submarine-launched ballistic missiles (SLBMS). This technology has probably been developed furthest in the United States, where commitment to a TRIAD of forces has encouraged research and development into all aspects of submarine warfare. In principle, SSBNs are among the most invulnerable of delivery systems because of their inherent mobility.

## Stalemate

A term borrowed from the game of chess and used to describe and identify a situation of deadlock or impasse. Its usage is particularly prevalent in DIPLOMACY and NEGOTIATION where parties have taken positions which are mutually exclusive or incompatible. Failing UNILATERAL measures, a stalemate may only be resolved by third party INTERVENTION.

## State

Sometimes called the NATION-STATE this is the main ACTOR in WORLD POLITICS. It has a legal personality and as such in INTERNATIONAL LAW possesses certain rights and duties. According to the Montevideo Convention on Rights and Duties of States (1933), which is widely regarded as the classic legal definition, states must possess the following qualifications: a permanent population, a defined territory and a government capable of maintaining effective control over its territory and of conducting INTERNATIONAL RELATIONS with other states. In respect of the last qualification the role of RECOGNITION by other states can often be crucial since it implies acceptance into the international community. These qualifications are not absolute and permit variations. For example there is no necessity in international law for settled BOUNDARIES or FRONTIERS. Many international conflicts take the form of BOUNDARY disputes, but their existence does not rob the disputants of legal personality. Israel, for example, is generally accepted as a state even though the precise demarcation of its boundaries has never been settled. Although there is a general requirement that a state has some form of government or means of exercising control, a state does not cease to exist when this control is in dispute or when it is 'temporarily' deprived of effective control as in wartime, CIVIL WARS, or REVOLUTIONS. Indeed, the attribute of SOVEREIGNTY itself, which is widely regarded as the defining characteristic of statehood, is by no means absolute. Some states, such as those in post-war Eastern Europe, are regarded as 'penetrated' or 'satellite' states, since the control they exercise over their internal and external environments is circumscribed by a powerful neighbour or HEGEMON. In the real world, as opposed to the world of political or legal theory, sovereignty can differ in degree and intensity among states without deprivation of international personality status. In general the capacity to enter into international relations with others is a necessary requirement but not a sufficient one. Non-state actors, for example the African National Congress (ANC), may have diplomatic relations with some states, but because they do not possess the other defining qualifications cannot be considered states. Regarding secessionary movements or national liberation organizations, RECOGNITION is generally withheld until victory over the

mother state (or occupying power) is secured. Yet even in these cases, recognition as a gesture of support can be given though the legal status may be in abeyance or dispute. Thus, in 1968 some states recognized Biafra even though Nigeria continued to exercise effective control. As with other rights, the right to SELF-DETERMINATION depends to a great degree on SELF-HELP. In sum, although the state has legal personality and essential defining characteristics, these are not static or absolute.

Not only is the state the main agent in international law, politically too it is dominant and has been for over four hundred years. With the exception of ANTARCTICA no significant territorial area is exempt from state control (*terra nullis*). Recognition of 'new' states therefore is likely to be at the expense of existing ones (Bangladesh in 1971 for example, at the expense of Pakistan, or Namibia in 1989 at the expense of South Africa). To date, there are over one hundred and sixty states in the international system, an increasing number of them being categorized as MICROSTATES. Despite their number and despite the fact that many liberation movements are still actively seeking statehood, some commentators have argued that the state is declining as the primary ACTOR in world politics. Not only is it functionally obsolete (because of its military and economic penetrability) but it is no longer capable of adequately handling global problems. The challenge of INTERDEPENDENCE and the proliferation of non-state actors have questioned the traditional assumptions concerning the dynamics of world politics. Yet, on the evidence presented so far, it is difficult to escape the conclusion that reports of its death have been greatly exaggerated.

## State-centrism

The state-centred or state-centric approach to WORLD POLITICS is the traditional view that the most valid perspective that can be taken of the subject matter is based upon

375

the STATE as dominant ACTOR. This perspective is associated with the REALIST paradigm which sees world politics in terms of INDEPENDENT states engaged in an endless competitive existence to preserve their security and well being. State-centrism often depicts world politics in terms of the metaphor of the billiard table. In this view states are impermeable, self-contained units which can influence each other by external pressure, as a billiard ball is moved by external and surface contact with other balls on the table. The contact was restricted to this external dimension by the concept of SOVEREIGNTY. Accordingly there was no authority higher than the state and state-centrism concluded that state interaction was conducted under a system of ANARCHY.

If the first rule of state-centrism was that states must be regarded as cohesive AUTONOMOUS actors, then the second rule was the territorial basis of the state. Planet earth is parcelled out among the state units of the system, accordingly. The concept of territorial jurisdiction asserted that rights to control territory and rights to control peoples settled on those territories was a fundamental precept of state-centrism. This approach therefore lays great stress upon the spatial identity of the state and the belief that loyalty to the state and identity with it could be provided through the concept of NATIONALISM. While it was understood that individuals would have other claims on their loyalties – for example to their tribe – it was assumed that in the last analysis any conflict of loyalties would be resolved in favour of the state.

In the actual conduct of FOREIGN POLICY, the state-centred view assumed that HIGH POLITICS of military security issues would prevail over LOW POLITICS. In the last analysis a state's most vital interests were those derived from conceptions of security and these questions would always predominate. The SECURITY DILEMMA dictated that states must assume responsibility for their own existence. If they could not resolve the dilemma themselves they attempted to do so by forming ALLIANCES. However, ally seeking can be provocative and force others to seek allies in return. The BALANCE OF POWER which emerges from these collective efforts to achieve security represents one of the most persistent features of world politics.

State-centrism sees POWER as a possession or attribute as the single most important characteristic of world politics. Recognition of this trait in the system leads state-centrism towards the idea of a power HIERARCHY headed up by GREAT POWERS or SUPER-POWERS. Unfortunately the idea of power hierarchy weakens the BILLIARD BALL metaphor because the conclusion is inescapable that the balls on the table are not equal. State-centrism thus had to distinguish between formal legal sovereignty and actual political sovereignty. The one is prescriptive, the other empirical. Clearly a stable hierarchy is not anarchic, in any common sense use of that term. So state-centrism modified the idea of ANARCHY towards the idea of an 'anarchical society'.

## Statelessness

Usually refers to individuals (though it can encompass other entities, such as ships) who do not possess NATIONALITY of any STATE. This condition was defined by the UN Conference on the Status of Stateless Persons 1954 as 'a person who is not considered as a national by any state under the operation of its law'. This can come about as a consequence of WAR or REVOLUTION where people can lose the nationality of one state and are not able to acquire the nationality of another. It is also possible to be born without nationality; in this case neither the enabling principles of *jus sanguinis* or of *jus soli* (or a combination of the two) are deemed to apply and the individual is placed in a legal limbo. Expatriation can also result in statelessness if the individual cannot acquire another nationality. This status is clearly disadvantageous since without a passport or visa, no

DIPLOMATIC protection can be enjoyed, civil liberties may be denied and DEPORTATION is a constant threat.

This problem, along with that of REFUGEES, has been a growing one in the upheavals of twentieth century WORLD POLITICS, and both the LEAGUE OF NATIONS and the UNITED NATIONS have attempted to address it. The principle that everyone has a right to nationality was first formulated in Article 15 of the 1948 Universal Declaration of HUMAN RIGHTS, and thereafter a number of UN-sponsored conferences have considered ways of resolving the issue, so far without conspicuous success. In 1961 the Convention on the Elimination or Reduction of Statelessness adopted a resolution recommending DE JURE RECOGNITION of DE FACTO stateless persons to enable them to apply for national status, but this has not been universally adopted or ratified. Since INTERNATIONAL LAW recognizes the primacy of the state regarding the acquisition of nationality, and since states are notoriously parsimonious in this regard, the problem is likely to persist.
*See also*: ORBITERS

## State-system

A term used to describe the relationships that were developed after the STATE became the significant, and then dominant, ACTOR in MACROPOLITICS. The emergence of states as first order political actors followed the gradual withering away of the political and social nexus that was known in Western Europe as feudalism. Strong, centralizing monarchies emerged in England (the Tudors), in Sweden (the Vasas) in Spain (the Habsburgs) and in France (the Bourbons) to challenge such TRANSNATIONAL institutions as the Catholic Church and the Holy Roman Empire. Absolute monarchy – as this system was termed – had become the predominant form of government by the beginning of the sixteenth century and these developments were supported by the new bourgeoisie, in opposition to the feudal nobility. This new class saw the monarchs as natural allies and accordingly they supported the growth of strong central government. The Treaty of WESTPHALIA of 1648 confirmed and consolidated these developments.

Interstate politics, as an activity, was a reserved area on the agenda for these monarchs, their personal advisers and ambassadors. The most important activity was associated with the conduct of warfare: the making of ALLIANCES, the fighting of campaigns, and the conclusion of settlements and PEACE TREATIES. Alliances were typically secret and often offensive in character and spirit, in contrast to twentieth century ideas. Apart from the conduct of WAR, the main activities of the absolute monarchs were the courtly politics associated with arranged marriages and the fostering of economic growth via trading policies which broadly reflected state interests and have come to be known as MERCANTILISM.

The state-system underwent a fundamental, once-and-for-all change with the rise of NATIONALISM following the French and US REVOLUTIONS. The typical unit of the system was now thought to be the NATION-STATE, although multinational states such as the Austro–Hungarian Empire under the Hapsburgs continued until 1919. The concept of SOVEREIGNTY, which was a key characteristic of the state-system from its inception, was carried over from the absolutist state to the nation-state. However, the locus of sovereignty ceased to be the person of the monarch but was instead held to reside in more representative institutions such as assemblies and parliaments. Between themselves, the absolutist monarchs had recognized no superior – at least no earthly superior – so the idea of equality had been included in the concept of sovereignty. In substance, therefore, the claim to sovereign equality remained the same between the absolutist state and the nation-state. This inalienable principle of the state-system is reflected in the CHARTER OF THE UN which states in Article 2:1 that: 'The Organization is based upon the principle of the sovereign equality of all its members.'

The structural implications of the principle of sovereign equality were profound. In INTERNATIONAL LAW all states are formally equal. In the GENERAL ASSEMBLY of the UN all states have formal equality – one vote. The UNANIMITY rule in international institutions is derived from the same idea. The INTERNATIONAL SYSTEM took on a fundamentally decentralized characteristic as a result of these developments. POWER and INFLUENCE in the system was dispersed among the constituent state units rather than being centralized in some sort of superordinate structure. International law, therefore, was similarly decentralized. States are traditionally the enforcers of international law as well as the makers. If one party is deemed to have broken the law, then under traditional conceptions, other states may take REPRISAL action. Law enforcement, in the state-system, was horizontally effected.

Any system of relations, even one as decentralized as the state-system, still requires some means of regulation. For long periods, until the rise of INTERNATIONAL ORGANIZATIONS in the twentieth century, the principal means of regulation was the BALANCE OF POWER. This was a very informal arrangement and for a brief period after the Napoleonic Wars an attempt at a security REGIME was made under the Concert of Europe. The Concert began to weaken in the 1820s because the principal states managing the security regime could not agree about whether to intervene to prevent the emergence of LIBERAL nationalist systems in Greece and Spain.

In retrospect the period 1815–1914 looks to have been the peak of the state-system. Although there has been a massive growth in state numbers in the twentieth century – particularly following DECOLONIZATION after 1945 – at the same time the state is under seige. TECHNOLOGY and economics have increased the permeability of the state from within, while the rise of mixed ACTORS from without has complicated the structural simplicity of the classic period. There is now a lively debate between realist STATE-CENTRISM and PLURALISM as to how far these trends and tendencies have gone.

It should be noted that the rise of the state-system led to the growth of an intellectual tradition of speculation and scholarship about interstate relations. This intellectual analysis, which might be called the 'classical' tradition, stems from four mainsprings: international lawyers contributed ideas about sovereignty, DOMESTIC JURISDICTION and non-intervention; political philosophers added ideas about international ANARCHY; practitioners and diplomats, with ideas about RAISON D'ÉTAT and the NATIONAL INTEREST and strategists who stressed the importance of war completed the quartet.

## Status quo

It means 'the existing state of affairs' and refers to the prevailing pattern of relations in INTERNATIONAL POLITICS. Essentially a conservative notion it implies that change is likely to be destructive of social order and therefore often tends to be imbued with connotations of sanctity, which the term itself does not necessarily warrant. Defenders of the status quo regard stability and order as key values and INTERNATIONAL LAW, TREATIES and orthodox diplomatic procedures are portrayed as legitimizing or codifying the system. A disturbance of the status quo is often met with the demand that a precondition of settlement would be a return to the status quo ante – the previous state of affairs.

It is linked with the REALIST model and is most often juxtaposed with REVISIONISM. Morgenthau (1948) identifies three basic policy types in relation to the power struggle: to preserve the status quo, to achieve imperialistic expansion, or to gain prestige. Status quo policies are likely to be adopted by those states with most to gain from a preservation of the existing territorial, ideological and POWER distribution.

Although change is generally inimical, not all international change is opposed. The MONROE DOCTRINE of 1823 is cited as a case in point: on one hand it was designed to preserve and promote US hemispheric superiority and on the other it was meant to encourage anti-imperialist drives within Latin America. Status quo STATES are also likely to have domestic values and structures which support and in turn are reinforced by the prevailing INTERNATIONAL ORDER. Thus, states like Malawi, Chile and even South Africa might be classed as status quo because a preservation of the existing order serves the interests of the DECISION-MAKING ELITE, even though it may not be in the interest of the people as a whole.

Since the Second World War, the United States has been the dominant status quo POWER and it defines its security (and hence the stability of the system) in terms of CONTAINMENT of revisionism. As the HEGEMON it has collected a number of sympathetic states (more than forty) around it, all of whom to a greater or lesser degree define their diplomatic existence in relation to the preservation of the existing order. COALITIONS, MILITARY ALLIANCES and BLOCS are thus characteristic behaviour patterns although in general status quo powers tend to react to revisionists rather than initiate action themselves. In this sense, it appears to have a static rather than a dynamic quality, but as the history of the Monroe doctrine illustrates, this lack of dynamism must not be overstressed.

Given that the realist model is addicted to hierarchies of power, status quo states can be differentiated according to position. Buzan (1983) has identified three categories besides the hegemon itself: an 'associate state', a 'client' state and a 'vassal' state. In the contemporary world the Western European states and Japan would claim associate status, South Korea and Egypt would be clients and South Vietnam (before 1973) and Cuba (before Castro) would be vassals. It must be emphasized, however, that broad identity of interest in system maintenance does not preclude CONFLICT between and among those in the status quo camp. Japan and states in Western Europe have had a number of public disagreements with the United States, for example. What is does ensure is that conflicts of interest tend not to become conflicts of FORCE. In the case of Britain and Argentina in 1982, while both are broadly status quo states (one 'associate' the other 'client'), in relation to the specific issue of the FALKLANDS/MALVINAS one is overtly status quo and the other is revisionist.

## Strategic studies

Strategic studies is that branch of the field of inquiry that is concerned to examine the ways in which ACTORS use their military CAPABILITY to achieve POLITICAL GOALS, in particular, with the way in which the threat and the use of FORCE has served these ends. It is sometimes referred to as the CLAUSEWITZIAN tradition after the nineteenth century Prussian strategist who did so much to advance the symbiosis between WAR and state policy. Judged by its historical pedigree, therefore, strategic studies must be regarded as a STATE-CENTRIC perspective. Until recently this characterization was perfectly legitimate. More recently studies of GUERRILLA WARFARE and its fusion with REVOLUTIONARY INSURGENCY have shown how an essentially MIXED ACTOR activity can still conform to all the essentials of the Clausewitzian approach.

Strategic studies has been primarily concerned with MILITARY POWER as the key attribute which has to be converted into usable instruments. As a result this branch of inquiry is generically part of the REALIST paradigm. The values relevant to the realist are the same as those understood to operate with strategy. War is the inevitable result of actors pursuing mutually exclusive or incompatible goals in a system that lacks superordinate AUTHORITY structures and can accordingly be termed ANARCHY. Because of its realist background, strategic studies has a strong TRADITIONAL or 'classical' bias, particularly outside the United States. The growth of the SOCIAL SCIENCE APPROACH has accordingly made fewer inroads than elsewhere in WORLD POLITICS.

Strategic studies is often thought of as a 'policy science'. Accordingly, strategists have not been averse to seeking a closer relationship with the POLICY-MAKER than other branches of the field of inquiry. While this can certainly appear to make the study seem to be more 'relevant' and clearly enables the individual and institutes concerned to have closer access to the decision centres, it is not without its dangers. Objectivity and detachment can be sacrificed and access to confidential data may be bought at the promise of silence. Policy ELITES often evince the tendency to take those parts of a perspective that are consonant with their own and policy failure can damage the adviser as much as the principal.

## Sub-system

A sub-system or subordinate system is a term used in SYSTEMS ANALYSIS. Applied to WORLD POLITICS it is virtually coterminous with the idea of REGION. Binder (1958) and Brecher (1963) are generally credited with early promotion of this approach. In 1969 the International Studies Association advanced the concept further with a special issue of their Quarterly. The more traditional term 'region' and the systemic 'sub-system' are sometimes run together as in 'regional sub-system'.

As the term implies a sub-system is a means of categorizing a whole (or system) into discrete parts. SYSTEMS ANALYSIS would expect the sub-system to evince the same characteristics as the system, though at a different level. Thus the basic and essential search for characteristic *structures* and *processes* would proceed in sub-system analysis in the same way, although not necessarily with the same results. For example, whereas the structure of a WORLD SYSTEM may be loose

BIPOLAR, the structure of a sub-system might be TRIPOLAR. Whereas INTEGRATION might be a peripheral trend in a world system, it might be a dominant trend in a sub-system. Ideas about HIERARCHY, which have frequently been applied to the MACROPOLITICAL system of world politics, can with equal validity be applied to sub-systems analysis. In this way a state ACTOR that is only fairly modestly ranked at one level may be a significant actor at another. India is a case in point. Lastly, the two crucial systemic processes of CONFLICT and cooperation can, when manifest at the sub-system level, spill over into the macrosystem. Thus the ARAB–ISRAELI CONFLICT, one of the most chronic conflicts within the Middle Eastern subordinate system has spilled into the world political system drawing in the SUPERPOWERS and the UN.

## Summit conference

Sometimes referred to as 'personal diplomacy' these are meetings of heads of governments of the major powers to resolve outstanding issues. As such, they bypass, or are superimposed upon, DIPLOMACY at the ambassadorial or ministerial level. The term is often used loosely to denote any meeting between principals, whereas in fact the following conditions apply: they consist of bipartite or multipartite gatherings, heads of government must take part, the leading STATES must be involved and there must be an effort to reach agreement. It is often assumed that summits are a twentieth century diplomatic innovation but this is not so. The term may be a new one (from an election speech by Winston Churchill in 1950, 'to parley at the summit'), but the phenomenon is ancient. International history is replete with examples of personal diplomacy, especially during the period of absolute monarchies when the identification of the state with the ruler in person was near total. The practice fell out of favour in the seventeenth century when permanent diplomatic missions assumed responsibility for inter-state NEGOTIATIONS and until the twentieth century the only major international conference to involve heads of government was the Congress of Vienna in 1815. The practice was revived by President Woodrow Wilson at the Paris Peace Conference in 1919 and was inspired by a profound distrust of professional diplomats and the 'secret diplomacy' they were alleged to indulge in. Since then in times of PEACE and WAR, summits have been a major feature of the international diplomatic landscape. During the COLD WAR, especially after the ice-breaking Geneva Conference of 1955, it was widely believed that SUPERPOWER summits were indispensable for maintaining world peace. In fact, these conferences have rarely resolved matters of substance, and when they have (e.g. the ARMS CONTROL agreement at Moscow in 1972) it has been as a result of protracted negotiations at professional levels conducted long before the actual event. Generally, the achievements are minimal; their value lies in the realm of psychology rather than diplomacy. They are useful devices for establishing goodwill or reopening communication but unless the groundwork has been professionally prepared, and unless the issue at stake is negotiable, summits are inherently risky. Given that heads of government are always aware of their domestic constituencies, the pressure for a 'successful' outcome within a narrow time-limit could prove disastrous. Henry Kissinger (1974), an experienced practitioner, referred to the process as 'a parody of diplomacy' and argued that the proper place of summit meetings in diplomacy was 'to put the finishing touches on agreements reached previously'. Without doubt, the drawbacks of summitry are now well known and well guarded against but by virtue of the domestic impact as well as the stature they confer on national leaders, these meetings will continue to feature prominently in world affairs. Their symbolic and ceremonial value alone will ensure this.

## Superpower

A term first used extensively by Fox (1944) in his book of the same name (Fox hyphenated 'super' and 'power' to show the etymology). On page twenty-one he defined the superpower as 'great power plus great mobility of power' and identified three states: The United States, the Soviet Union and the United Kingdom in this new category. Fox recognized that the Second World War had propelled the first two to the rank and status of world powers, while the United Kingdom was a residual member. The defeat of the AXIS coalition was a demonstration of their great military CAPABILITY, while their wartime CONFERENCE DIPLOMACY presaged the world role that they were to assume after 1945. Two developments occurred to alter Fox's TRIPOLARITY thereafter: the United Kingdom rapidly dropped out of the ranking to take up a more modest position of regional rather than global significance, while the COLD WAR confrontation between the two remaining 'supers' led to a new PERCEPTION of their world role. In particular, the United States' assumption of a HEGEMONIAL position in the Western military–security and economic welfare systems after 1945 would not have been so pressing or significant without the added ISSUE AREA of the Cold War.

The development of NUCLEAR WEAPONS by the two superpowers after 1945 should be seen as an effect as much as a cause of these structural changes. The fission and fusion programmes confirmed a status that was already well established by the events referred to above. It would certainly be an unwarranted simplification to equate the superpower attribute to this development solely or exclusively. In any event nuclear weapons lack FUNGIBILITY as a capability.

In terms of the wealth/welfare area of political economy, the Soviet Union was never really a superpower. In its attempt to attain and then maintain PARITY with the United States in the military–security field great opportunity costs were incurred by the Soviet economy and a highly distorted developmental pattern resulted. US hegemony in the political economy ISSUE AREA began to wane in the 1960s as rival economic power centres in Japan and the EUROPEAN COMMUNITY emerged. The United States' VIETNAM INTERVENTION created significant short-term economic problems and assisted in the demise of the dollar as the principal international currency.

Superpower is an analytical distinction based upon structural power considerations. It assumes a HIERARCHY of actors with the superpower at the top. In comparison with earlier periods, therefore, the superpower category may be seen as a replacement for the more traditional GREAT POWER category. Both stipulations share one characteristic: removal of the superpower/great power from the system would fundamentally change the overall structure of WORLD POLITICS/INTERNATIONAL POLITICS. Conversely, additions to that category would equally change systemic structures. Thus a tripolar system becomes BIPOLAR if a superpower/great power drops out, or becomes MULTIPOLAR if additions occur. Because the idea of superpower is based upon structural rather than causal conceptions of POWER it is difficult to reconcile the concept with empirical instances. The student of WORLD POLITICS would do well to resist being too dazzled by the putative power of the 'supers' and to concentrate instead upon a policy oriented approach. It may be concluded that the superpower has great VETO power to stop undesirable things happening in world politics but considerably less behaviour control over other actors needed to achieve more positive outcomes.

## Supranational

Refers to laws or institutions that are above the state. The POWER and AUTHORITY they exercise is not confined to one state but to many. Thus, supranationalism refers to DECISON-MAKING bodies which supersede or override the SOVEREIGN authority of individual STATES who are constituent members of the organization involved. Usually this transfer of authority from the state is voluntary, limited and specific (e.g. to issues of TRADE, commerce or DEFENCE). The clearest example of a supranational institution is the EUROPEAN COMMUNITY which has a common political structure authorized to make decisions within prescribed areas for member states. The UNITED NATIONS is not strictly speaking a supranational institution although under Article 25 of the CHARTER the SECURITY COUNCIL is empowered to exercise executive powers in relation to PEACE and security matters. To date, this authority to compel all member states to act has been used only once, in relation to the imposition of ECONOMIC SANCTIONS on Rhodesia in 1966. (The action undertaken by the Council with respect of Korea in 1950 was, contrary to the popular view, a RECOMMENDATION to member states, not an enforcement decision under Article 25.) Supranationalism is thus part of the general integrative process of WORLD POLITICS whereby INTERDEPENDENCE is given institutional recognition. The process of whittling away at the traditional bastion of state sovereignty which supranationalism represents is likely to continue.

*See also*: WORLD GOVERNMENT

## Surrender

Literally means handing over POWER or control to another party. It generally refers to military units in the field or to governments themselves. All cases of surrender, even UNCONDITIONAL SURRENDER, involve the imposition of some obligations on the victor. Unlike Greek and Roman custom, modern practice does not permit annihilation as a consequence of surrender. The HAGUE CONFERENCES and subsequent rulings in INTERNATIONAL LAW have underlined the obligation of the victors to at least spare the lives of the vanquished. Unless specifically unconditional, most surrenders are conditional and will be accompanied by articles of capitulation – terms or concessions agreed between the parties before the final act. These of course vary but are often conditioned by the remaining strength, or latent power, of the defeated side.

## SWAPO

South West Africa People's Organization. Formed in 1960 it is the main indigenous NATIONALIST political movement in Namibia. It was recognized in 1973 by the GENERAL ASSEMBLY of the UNITED NATIONS as the 'authentic representative of the Namibian people'. From 1961 it committed itself to a joint political and military campaign against South African occupation. The armed struggle began properly in August 1966 as a direct consequence of the failure of the INTERNATIONAL COURT OF JUSTICE (ICJ) to declare South Africa's presence in Namibia illegal. The military wing came to be known in the 1970s as the People's Liberation Army of Namibia (PLAN) which is linked to the National Executive (headed by Sam Nujoma) by a political commissar. Until 1989 SWAPO operated from Luanda in Angola and despite some military successes, was effectively held in check by the South African Defence Force (SADF). Notwithstanding SWAPO's claim to be the 'liberator' of Namibia it is clear that without considerable external pressure, especially as a consequence of the GORBACHEV DOCTRINE, South Africa would have retained control of what is termed South West Africa/Namibia. UN Resolution 435, which called for Namibian SELF-DETERMINATION, was finally implemented in 1989 as a result of the LINKAGE of the independence issue with the phased withdrawal of Cuban forces from Angola. Elections to a Constitutional Assembly took place on 6 November 1989 and, at the time of writing, SWAPO appears poised to achieve the two-thirds majority necessary to assume full POWER.

## Systems analysis

Systems analysis is a holistic perspective on a defined field of study. Thus if the field happens to be that of WORLD POLITICS, the systems analyst would look for definable and regular patterns of interaction between the constituent ACTORS, in particular to see what structural characteristics and persistent and regular processes could be identified. Systems analysis is derived from General Systems Theory, which Young (1967) called 'a movement aimed at the unification of science and scientific analysis' (p. 14). General Systems Theory (GST) thus seeks to unify discrete scientific subjects by employing a common language of analysis and conceptualization. Ludwig von Bertalanffy, generally regarded as the inspiration of GST, sought thereby to integrate all the sciences, natural and social. The basis of von Bertalanffy's approach was towards what is called 'open' systems analysis, an open system being a set or field that interacts with an environment. If a system is seen as open in this way it will monitor its behaviour in relation to its environment via the process of FEEDBACK. The end result of this adaptive behaviour should be HOMEOSTASIS or a steady state.

As stated above, systems analysis is a perspective or paradigm. It is thus open to application at any or all of the levels of ANALYSIS that can be stipulated for the study of world politics. Young states that the notion of system can be 'applied freely to virtually any set of related behaviour patterns...' (p. 20). Provided that the object of study can be recognized as what Young calls a 'complete functioning entity' (p. 23) then systems analysis can be relevant.

The impact of systems analysis upon foreign POLICY-MAKING studies has been significant. According to this view FOREIGN POLICY-making becomes a boundary activity between the national system and the international. The balance between internal and external attributes must eventually be answered by empirical research but the technique is broadly derived from the systems approach. Foreign policy analysts tend to use the term 'environment' extensively to identify these internal/external factors. Thus a PENETRATED STATE is an actor for which the external environment or INTERNATIONAL SYSTEM has come to totally dominate and determine mainsprings of political, economic and social life. Conversely a SUPERPOWER actor can conduct a globally defined foreign policy on the basis of a secure and significant internal environment.

The most telling contribution of systems analysis has been at the MACROPOLITICAL level. Systems analysts were in the vanguard of the SOCIAL SCIENCE APPROACH of the 1950s/1960s and the main thrust of their interest has been upon the international system. A basic division is popularly made between the system *per se* and regionally based SUB-SYSTEMS. Thereafter the basic structures and processes can be described and identified. Kaplan's 1957 work is widely regarded as an early example of an attempt at systemic understanding of macropolitics. This work is highly deductive and in 1963 Rosecrance attempted to redress the balance in favour of a more inductive approach. Debate and dissension has raged on the basic structural question between those favouring a BIPOLAR view and those a MULTIPOLAR. Nogee (1975) pinpointed some of the ambiguities in this dispute. CONFLICT and cooperation are widely seen as fundamental processes by all systems analysts. The relative weight to be given to them in reaching systemic descriptions often accounts for subsequent differences between scholars in the field.

# T

## Tactical nuclear weapons

A broad classification that uses technical and functional criteria to distinguish these weapons from the strategic type. Technically, tactical nuclear weapons have a shorter range and a lower yield. Functionally, their envisaged purpose is to destroy specific targets, usually military or political command centres outside the territory of the major adversary. Since NUCLEAR WEAPONS have not been used in combat circumstances since 1945, the distinction is hypothetical and somewhat controversial. In the last analysis a NUCLEAR WEAPON is a nuclear weapon and a single shot, however 'tactical' the intention, might be perceived as crossing a significant and symbolic threshold. In addition, the victims of the blast and radiation could be forgiven for regarding the distinction as invalid, at least as far as it applies to them.

In the immediate aftermath of HIROSHIMA it was thought that nuclear weapons would be used in future WARS in a strategic context. This view prevailed for a number of years thereafter. In the early 1950s opinions changed and the possibility of a tactical weapon became technically feasible and functionally plausible. In the light of its NATO alliance commitments the United States saw the possibility for tactical weapons in the European theatre, particularly as an antidote to the perceived superiority of the WARSAW PACT in CONVENTIONAL WARFARE terms. Stockpiles of these weapons were established accordingly. NATO's declaratory policy sought to officially recognize the tactical/strategic distinction in 1967 with the adoption of the policy known as FLEXIBLE RESPONSE. Developments since have blurred rather than enhanced the dichotomy. Technically the range and yield of tactical weapons has expanded into what are grey areas of systems that are not envisaged for the battlefield but do not pose a threat to the homeland of the adversaries deploying them. Such a weapon would be the CRUISE MISSILE. The development of the neutron bomb as a particular type of tactical weapon was also contentious.

Because of their size, tactical nuclear weapons have made VERIFICATION of ARMS CONTROL agreements more difficult. They can be readily concealed and hidden. They have also placed more destructive capacity into the hands of subordinate military officers than ever before in the history of warfare. Whatever the merits of this in terms of DETERRENCE requirements, it has undoubtedly increased the risks that nuclear violence might occur against the wishes of statesmen and political leaders.

*See also*: THEATRE NUCLEAR WEAPONS

## Tariff

A tariff is a tax upon IMPORTS. Historically tariffs have been a favoured way of raising revenue. As such they can be extremely lucrative and viable, particularly if the goods and services subject to such charges are demand inelastic. More recently tariffs have been used as a means of PROTECTIONISM by the authorities of STATES. Historically the United States was among the first industrialized countries to eschew FREE TRADE for tariff protection. In the post-1945 system of economic relations tariffs have been an important instrument in the formation of COMMON MARKETS and FREE TRADE AREAS. A common external tariff (cet) is the principal means whereby the participating states can shelter behind a 'tariff wall' thereby instituting protectionism upon a regional basis. Tariffs may be used as a FOREIGN POLICY instrument, usually by a dominant state, either as a punitive retaliatory measure or to establish an economic SPHERE OF INFLUENCE. In the latter context, the institution of preferential arrangements is the usual method of creating such a sphere. The dominant state usually exchanges tariff preferences upon a BILATERAL basis with a number of target participants. The latter may exchange preferences with each other but that is not a requirement of the preferential system. The best known of these arrangements was the Imperial Preference system instituted in 1932 at Ottawa with the United Kingdom as the 'hub' of the scheme.

The existence of the General Agreement on Tariffs and Trade (GATT) in the contemporary system has concentrated minds upon the commitment of all contracting parties to freer trade and the implementation of the MOST FAVOURED NATION (mfn) principle. The General Agreement has established the parameters for a series of MULTILATERAL tariff reduction negotiations, THE KENNEDY and TOKYO ROUNDS being the most significant to date.

*See also*: NON-TARIFF BARRIERS; QUOTA

## Technology

Technology is the application of knowledge to practical problem-solving. Historically, such applications have been a continuous and persistent feature of all social systems, no matter how 'primitive' they may superficially appear to be. As a result a continual process of change may be identified as occurring via technology. Other factors being equal, therefore, the faster tech-

nology changes, the faster the FEEDBACK into the recipient systems. In passing, it should be noted that 'change' should not be confused with 'improvement', although many apologists for unrestrained technological change might like to argue otherwise.

In a series of changes made in the conduct of manufacturing industries during the late eighteenth and much of the nineteenth centuries available technology revolutionized economic activity and, via the feedback process, the societies wherein it took place. This industrial REVOLUTION initiated a process that has continued ever since. It is now accepted as an axiom of economic development that significant and lasting inputs of technology will be required to achieve and sustain economic growth. Since available technology is differentially distributed among ACTORS the issue of TECHNOLOGY TRANSFER raises difficult questions about the terms and conditions wherein this exchange should take place.

In the context of WORLD POLITICS, technology has had the most significant impact upon issues of a military security nature. Violence and threats of violence between actors have been constrained by the technologies available for making them. What one author has called the 'war potential' of actors is a function of the technology available. Very often the technology that has been applied to military–security issues is itself derived from civilian contexts. Thus, the development of heavier than air flight at the beginning of the twentieth century was soon applied to the battlefield and, thereafter, to other theatres. The relationship between civilian and military technologies is, indeed, a complex feedback loop, the development of FISSION weapons in the Second World War having civilian applications in the post-1945 period. One of the factors that makes the stopping or controlling of NUCLEAR WEAPONS PROLIFERATION so difficult to effect is this interconnectedness of civilian and military technologies.

There is increasing conjecture, intellectually, about the balance sheet of technology. The unanticipated and unplanned effects of technology are the major contentious issues in this regard. The critique of unrestrained technological change is increasingly informed by empirical evidence that points to some of the more deleterious outcomes. Thus continued application of nuclear technology to energy production raises acute questions about the safety of plants from breakdown and malfunction and the toxicity of waste products from the generation process. The work of FUTUR- OLOGISTS and environmentally sensitive interest groups has stimulated this critical climate. The inexorable onrush of technology is unlikely to be deflected or denied by the heightened awareness of its mixed blessings, however. Research and development (often referred to simply as R & D) will continue and, for as long as it does, there will be good grounds perceived by vested interests for moving from that stage to application whenever and wherever possible.

### Technology transfer

This refers to the relationship between producers and consumers of TECHNOLOGY as it can be identified to operate across STATE BOUNDARIES and to involve various international ACTORS. Since the original industrial REVOLUTION demonstrated the importance of technological inputs, the issue of the terms and conditions under which such knowledge should be made available to others has become crucial. In contemporary WORLD POLITICS the issue is exacerbated by the fact that the producers of technology are the advanced industrial countries (AICs) and the consumers are the least developed countries (LDCs). Moreover, the conduit for a considerable amount of this knowledge transfer is the multinational corporation (MNC). Technology transfer has thus become caught up in the POLARIZATION of political economy

issues between the rich states of the NORTH and the developing states of the South.

Technology transfer can occur in a number of ways: by education and training programmes, by exchanges of consultants and experts, by licensing agreements to make patented instruments available, by consulting published sources and by copying products and techniques, with or without permission. Since technological innovation is occurring simultaneously with transfer, the latter process is likely to be continuous for the future as well. Since research and development is also differentially distributed in favour of the AICs as well the perpetuation of this situation of technological dependence is very probable.

### Terms of trade

This is a means of expressing the ratio of EXPORTS to IMPORTS for a particular ACTOR. Thus, if the terms of trade deteriorate, it will be because imports (expressed in monetary values such as prices) have risen faster than exports (expressed in the same way) or because export prices have fallen faster than import prices. Both sets of circumstances will be detrimental. If an actor is a sole, or significant, supplier of goods and services, or if a number of suppliers can form a cartel such as OPEC then it/they may be able to manipulate the terms of trade to its/their advantage. Failing this, adverse shifts in the terms of trade can be highly damaging and, in the long term, even disastrous. It will lead to the slowing of growth of real income, or worse, to actual decline.

Since 1945 the terms of trade have, with some exceptions, moved against the THIRD WORLD STATES and this factor has enhanced other structural difficulties they already have in achieving self-sustained growth. Following the establishment of the United Nations Conference on Trade and Development (UNCTAD) on a permanent basis after 1964 demands for intervention on behalf of the least developed countries

(LDCs) were increasingly made. The New International Economic Order (NIEO) Programme and Charter of 1974 concentrated upon this as one of the key issue areas in global economic relations.

## Terrorism

The use or threatened use of violence on a systematic basis to achieve political objectives. While there is no agreed comprehensive definition as to its character, motive or mode of operation, (for example, Schmid, 1984, lists over one hundred different definitions of the term), most analysts agree that the element of fear-inducement both horizontally and vertically is crucial. In addition ruthlessness, a disregard for established humanitarian values and an unquenchable thirst for publicity are characteristic traits. By no means a recent phenomenon (it can be dated at least as far back as the seventh-century AD Muslim world of the 'assassins') it is in the post-WAR era of rapid technological development and heightened media-awareness that terrorism has achieved its greatest global impact. Methods commonly used include HIJACKING, hostage-taking, bombings, indiscriminate shootings, assassinations and mass murders.

It is usual to distinguish between 'state' and 'political' or 'factional' terrorism. The former has been the more lethal due mainly to the monopolistic nature of the coercive agencies at the STATE's disposal combined with IDEOLOGIES that rest on ends/means rationalizations. The latter is carried out by non-state ACTORS and its focus is usually internal. However, as a sustained campaign of terror requires financial support, a steady weapon supply and a place of sanctuary, most groups have an international dimension. Indeed, many commentators have identified significant recent developments not merely in state-sponsored terrorism (internal factional groups with outside governmental support) but also with regard to TRANSNATIONAL and even intercontinental terrorist infrastructures and mutual support groups. Terrorism is not a species of GUERRILLA WARFARE although it is often confused with it. Nor is it an IDEOLOGY or a political movement. It is a strategy or a method that is common to groups of widely different political, philosophical and religious beliefs. It is used by nationalists (the single most successful grouping), religious extremists, revolutionary MARXISTS, racists and FASCISTS – the common demoninator being the creation and spread of fear, unrest and instability in the targeted area. Yet despite its ubiquity as an instrument of DESTABILIZATION, its overall record of success is so far, a modest one. The collapse of French and British colonial rule in Algeria, Cyprus, Aden and Palestine are the most notable examples, though even in these instances factors other than terrorism may have been decisive.

To date, the international community has not responded in any concerted way to the growth of modern terrorism. There have been regional initiatives (e.g. within the EUROPEAN COMMUNITY and NATO) but generally the phenomenon has been addressed on a state-to-state basis. Apart from a few highly publicized events (e.g. the US bombing raid on Libya in 1986 or the Israeli raid on Entebbe airport ten years earlier) most states have regarded terrorism privately, if not publicly, as a minor irritant and have been content to deal with it through 'quiet' DIPLOMACY and various forms of APPEASEMENT. This can only serve to encourage more emphasis on this high-value, low risk strategy. W. Laqueur and P. Wilkinson among others have warned that notwithstanding the possible use by those groups of nuclear, chemical or BACTERIOLOGICAL WEAPONS, terrorism is likely to outgrow its nuisance stage and without international cooperation at the highest level will inevitably become a major threat to international PEACE and stability (*see* especially: Wilkinson, 1986).

## Test ban

*See:* COMPREHENSIVE TEST-BAN TREATY (CTB); PARTIAL TEST-BAN TREATY

## Theatre nuclear weapons

A term that originated in the wake of the SALT agreements of the 1970s. The 'theatre' refers to weapons with a range of less than 5,500 km – those not covered in SALT. Within this very broad family grouping the following subdivisions are used:

1. Long-range theatre NUCLEAR WEAPONS (LRTNW) from 1,000 km to the upper limit of 5,500 km.
2. Medium-range from 200 to 1,000 km.
3. Short-range up to 200 km.

It is generally agreed that the term short-range theatre nuclear weapons is coterminous with the idea of the TACTICAL NUCLEAR WEAPON. LRTNW can be either strategic or tactical, while medium-range systems occupy a 'grey area'.

The confusion over where theatre nuclear weapons end and strategic nuclear weapons start is exemplified by the fact that under the definitional category of an LRTNW are included the Polaris system of the United Kingdom and all of the existing French FORCE DE FRAPPE, although both the STATES concerned regard these systems as strategic weapons of last resort.

*See also:* INF

## Third World

A portmanteau term for those STATES in Central and South America, Africa, the Middle East, Asia (except Japan) and the Pacific islands (except Australia and New Zealand) which have experienced DECOLONIZATION over the last two centuries. Currently they are pursuing goals of economic development and social change, national SELF-DETERMINATION and unification, and NON-ALIGNMENT. The Third World stands in contradistinction to the FIRST WORLD (of capitalist LIBERAL democracy) and the Second World (of socialist central planning). At the margin of the Third World is China, which has many of the attributes of a typical Third World state but has ruled itself out of full identification on ideological grounds.

Also at the margin are South Africa and Israel, which geographically and historically should be included but remain *PERSONA NON GRATA*, again on ideological grounds.

Although the Third World has shaken off the formal political control of COLONIALISM legacies of the past remain. Thus the actual territorial dimensions of many Third World states, notably in Africa, are the results of colonialist cartographers and political geographers. As a result of this arbitrary demarcation many states in the Third World are ethnically heterogeneous. Ethnic NATIONALISM as a centrifugal tendency, working against the centripetal state nationalism, is a divisive factor in many Third World states as a result.

MARXIST-inclined analyses of WORLD POLITICS deny that the formal granting of INDEPENDENCE made any substantial difference to the relative positions of the Third World *vis-à-vis* the First World – wherein, according to Marxists, IMPERIALISM arose. In particular the considerable economic power of the advanced industrial countries (AICs) of the First World is a determining factor in these relations. Assisting First World domination are the TRANSNATIONAL corporations which function as conduits for this influence. Many of the examples that inform this view are taken from Latin American experience and it would appear that a *comprador* middle class has developed in the REGION to provide a linkage with the dominant economic interests in the First World. Latin America may not be typical, however, and in other parts of the Third World, notably in Asia, a more nationalist bourgeoisie has developed. In the most dynamic newly industrialized countries (NICs), indeed, countervailing corporative growth can counterbalance the economic domination of First World interests.

As far as intergovernmental relations are concerned, the Third World has responded to this domination through organizations such as OPEC and the United Nations Conference on Trade and Development (UNCTAD) and by calling for change through the raft of demands submitted under the NEW INTERNATIONAL ECONOMIC ORDER (NIEO) initiative. The Third World states have also used their majority membership of organizations such as the UN to call for closer control and supervision to be exercised over transnational corporations. They have campaigned through UNCTAD for the abandonment of the BRETTON WOODS system of non-discrimination in favour of TRADE preferences aimed at assisting their development goals.

In the military–security ISSUE AREA, the Third World states have often faced significant problems in managing national security. Both the FIRST and the Second WORLDS have emerged as important AID donors in this context. This military aid has been distributed on a very selective basis to those perceived as allies and clients. Additionally, these same supplier states have in some instances intervened more overtly in military–security issue areas. As a general rule overt intervention aids incumbent governments, while covert intervention aids INSURGENT movements in these situations.

INTERVENTIONIST policies are not confined to the First and Second Worlds. States situated within the Third World have intervened in each other's military–security problems, VIETNAM in its neighbours, Cuba in Central America, Libya in Chad and Tanzania in Uganda being instances. Even the pariah states of South Africa and Israel have pursued similar policies in such states as Angola, Mozambique and the Lebanon.

Given the growth of INTERGOVERNMENTAL ORGANIZATIONS (IGOS) since 1945, it is to be expected that the Third World would likewise reflect this trend. The most inclusive grouping is the Non-Aligned Movement but regionally based groupings like the Organization of African Unity (OAU), the ARAB LEAGUE and the Association of South East Asian Nations (ASEAN) should be noted. As noted above, the Third World states are in a voting majority in the United Nations. As a result the world organization has undergone a shift in its position on many global issues.

The field of political economy has already been exemplified, but in areas of vestigial colonialism – such as APARTHEID – the Third World states have made their influence felt in world politics.

## Throw-weight

A term which refers to the 'business end' of the BALLISTIC MISSILE and is used as a measure of how much of a payload the rocket can lift into the post-boost phase. Other factors being equal, the greater the throw-weight, the greater the number of warheads and/or decoys the booster can lift. Soviet missiles have historically had a superior throw-weight to US and this was recognized in the SALT processes when the term 'heavy' was used to identify certain missiles in the Soviet inventory with this facility.

Throw-weight has become one of the yard-sticks whereby the two senior adversaries in the mutual nuclear DETERRENT relationship assess each other's force levels and structures. Simply counting missiles is now regarded as too crude and simplistic. Accordingly other variables such as accuracy and throw-weight have to be brought into the reckoning if comparative estimation is to have any purpose beyond pure PROPAGANDA.

## Thucydides

Thucydides' *History of the Peloponnesian War* is widely regarded as one of the very few classic studies of international affairs and of the anatomy of war. The *History*, which recounts the fifth century BC struggle between Athens and Sparta for mastery of the Hellenic world, is the first recorded political and ethical analysis of interstate CONFLICT which is not a mere chronical of events. As Thucydides put it: '. . . I have written not for immediate applause but for posterity, and I shall be content if the future student of these events, or of other similar events which are likely in human nature to occur in after ages, finds my narrative of them useful'. Although the study does not, as is sometimes alleged, display any developed theory of BALANCE OF POWER, most commentators regard it as the first to show glimmerings of an equilibrium theory as well as being the first sustained REALIST attempt to explain the origins of international conflict. His emphasis on the structure and process of the Hellenic status-system as a causal factor in individual state behaviour was an important conceptual leap in thinking about external affairs (see: Fliess, 1966). The enduring quality of the work, apart from its literary merit, is that it penetrates beneath the superficial causes of a particular WAR and offers an analysis of the dynamics of POWER-POLITICS which is timeless with regard to the insights it offers. In many ways, Thucydides can be regarded as the starting point of modern doctrine and practices in WORLD POLITICS.

In this study of GREAT POWER rivalry most of the now familiar concepts appear in embryonic form, including POWER, DIPLO-MACY, ALLIANCES, NEUTRALISM, IMPERIAL-ISM, TOTAL WAR, IDEOLOGY, HEGEMONY and the perennial conflict between expediency and ethics in state policy (see: MELIAN DIALOGUE). In addition, it analyses domestic influences on FOREIGN POLICY formulation, siege warfare, the strategic requirements of land- and sea-based power, the economic costs of prolonged warfare as well as TREATY formulation and ARBITRATION. In sum, it is the earliest and one of the best accounts of the systematic use of FORCE to achieve political ends and the consequences of this for the stability of the system as a whole.

## Tokyo Round

The Tokyo Round of Multilateral Trade Negotiations (often abbreviated to MTN) was conducted under the aegis of the General Agreement on Tariffs and Trade (GATT) between September 1973 and April 1979. This round constituted the seventh of such negotiations since the inception of GATT. It was the first of these sessions to

specifically and explicitly confront the issue of NON-TARIFF BARRIERS (NTBS) TO TRADE as well as the traditional fields of TARIFFS and their reduction.

Significant and disturbing shifts occurred in the international economic system during the five-and-a-half years that Tokyo was under discussion. The era of cheap oil prices ended abruptly within weeks of the original Tokyo declaration, while in January 1976 the articles of agreement of the IMF were revised to allow for the new system of floating exchange rates. Trends towards the resurgence of PROTECTIONISM were being detected and the whole philosophical assumptions of the BRETTON WOODS system appeared to be under critical scrutiny. Additionally, large sections of the system – often subsumed under the term THIRD WORLD – were explicitly calling for changes in the ground rules of this system.

Tokyo may therefore be seen as either the last post for the old system or the reveille for the new. By addressing, once again, the problem of manufacturing tariffs and obtaining agreement to further reductions phased in over eight years, the negotiations were a continuation of standard GATT procedures. By seeking to stipulate codes of conduct for the NTBs, Tokyo was breaking new ground. By re-establishing the principle that disputes about the trade REGIME should be settled within the GATT structure, Tokyo maintained an important role for the institution within the system. (for details see: GATT (1979).

## Total war

Strategists and historians of warfare are agreed that over the last two hundred years the character of WAR has changed. Some have sought to encapsulate this trend by referring to 'absolute' or 'total' war. Perhaps the best aphorism that can be quoted to summarize these changes is the statement that 'NATIONS not ARMIES fight wars'. Certainly this points to one of the most persistent and pertinent causal factors in the development of total war

– the growth of NATIONALISM. Other causes include the impact of demographic and TECHNOLOGICAL change, generation of national wealth through economic development, growth of IDEOLOGICAL factors (other than nationalism), growth in the size of the military as a class or interest group and the growth of totalitarian political systems and leaderships.

Nationalism is important to the concept of total war because it enables appeals to be made to individuals to fight, not for gain or financial reward but to defend or advance the interests of the national group. This enables the leadership within the nation to mobilize large numbers of people both for active military service and for ancilliary and support functions. When nationalism becomes coterminous with the STATE, so that one might identify NATION-STATES as ACTORS, then the dynamic impact of national mobilization is more profound. If nationalism is combined with demographic growth then, in principle, large numbers of able-bodied citizens can be recruited into the war effort.

Technological change has placed in the hands of warring actors the means to conduct such violent relations on a more destructive basis than before; in particular, those changes generically referred to as the industrial REVOLUTION, increased the war potential of state actors. The FEEDBACK loop between technological change and economic growth is evident in the total war concept. Technology creates the opportunities for growth and income generation which then provide the investment capital for technological research and development. Recently this symbiosis has continued beyond warfare and a MILITARY–INDUSTRIAL COMPLEX has been identified in some states with an alleged interest in extending the total war economy into peacetime.

The growth of ideologies, particularly those that present violence and warfare as natural and desirable, have also contributed to the idea that war should be total. Often these ideologies are associated with demands for revolutionary change. Such belief systems show a tendency to look for external enemies even after they have gained political POWER. The mobilization of particular classes, and the creation thereafter of political demands, can provide the rationale for the initiation and continuation of total warfare.

## Trade

Trade, that is the exchange of goods and services between ACTORS, is probably the most prolific relationship within WORLD POLITICS at the present time. Since the series of innovations known as the Industrial REVOLUTION first occurred in Western Europe at the end of the eighteenth century, the rationale for such exchange relationships has been apparent. Indeed intellectual justification for the expansion of trade was provided by economists such as Smith (1776) and Ricardo (1817) at the time. Ricardo, in particular, using concepts about comparative advantage, demonstrated how a trading system could function to the benefit of all parties. The impact of these views upon POLICY-MAKERS and intellectuals has been immense. The principle of FREE TRADE as a policy goal, as well as an end state, has had its advocates ever since.

As trade is about exchange, there is an implied or putative element of POWER in such relationships. Further, the more an actor gains from trade, the more dependent that actor becomes upon the trading relationship. It is thus possible for one actor, in a BILATERAL relationship, or for a number of actors in a MULTILATERAL relationship, to manipulate the situation to achieve political goals. In this way trading relationships have been used to increase cooperation and even INTEGRATION among actors on one hand, or to increase COERCION and CONFLICT on the other. In short, trading relationships may serve positive or negative ends. Since economic power is differentially distributed the ability to use trade relationships in this way will vary.

*See also*: TRADE BLOCS; TRADE SANCTIONS; TRADE SYSTEM

## Trade bloc

A grouping of ACTORS with a common interest in better TRADE relations, possibly seen as leading to closer cooperation and even INTEGRATION in the long term. The simplest form of trade BLOC is the *preferential area*. In this arrangement all members extend TARIFF preferences to each other over certain stipulated goods that are, or will be, the subject of mutual trade. The significance of the preferential area depends upon its SCOPE and DOMAIN, scope being defined as the number of goods covered and domain being the number of actors included in the area. Such arrangements can be quite discriminatory if the members of the area maintain differentially high tariffs with third parties outside the arrangement. Probably the most famous example in the twentieth century of such a system was that created from British Dominion and Imperial interests known as Imperial Preference.

The FREE TRADE AREA is an elaboration of the preferential system. Herein the members abolish tariffs over a specified range of goods traded between themselves. The variables of scope and domain are indicators of the significance of the system. Similarly, the higher the differential between tariff policy within the area and with the rest of the world, the more discriminatory the arrangement will be.

A CUSTOMS UNION is the most complex trade bloc. Here the members have a common external tariff (cet) *vis-à-vis* the rest of the system. Within this cet the members will progressively reduce tariffs until a complete system of free trade obtains. Such arrangements as these involve a good deal of coordination of DECISION-MAKING and a complex administration, both in order to secure the establishment of the union and to supervise it thereafter. Customs unions are often taken to be indicators that the member STATES intend to pursue a policy of integration rather than mere cooperation. The logic of FUNCTIONALISM argues that beyond a certain point integration becomes difficult to halt.

It is a moot point as to how far trade blocs create trade and how far they diversify existing trade into new patterns. Under the General Agreement on Tariffs and Trade (GATT) rules trade blocs are not prohibited *per se*. This is perhaps surprising given the commitment to mfn principles in GATT. In the event GATT has presided over a system which has seen the growth of trade blocs over the last four decades, the most powerful and significant of these being the EUROPEAN COMMUNITY.

## Trade-off

A term used in negotiations between international ACTORS. Its use signifies that an exchange of preferences has taken place between the parties. This exchange may take place as part of an overall agreement or as part of the process leading towards agreement. The exchange may be made about similar things or different things. Thus, parties may trade off landing rights for their civil aircraft with each other, or they may trade off landing rights, on one hand, for fishing rights on the other. A trade-off may be seen as a form of concession, but clearly the concessions are made on both sides. Trade-offs are particularly appropriate to those negotiating situations where the positions of the parties can be quantified – for instance in TRADE negotiations – because herein it is much easier to enumerate the preferences.

## Trade sanctions

The use of a TRADE relationship for political ends will be said to involve trade sanctions if at least one ACTOR seeks to secure more compliant behaviour from at least one other actor by making threats. The more extensive the trading relationship between the actors, the better chance the sanctions threat has of securing the compliance sought. If the threat actually has to be carried through, then the actor imposing the sanctions (hereafter the Imposer) will

experience costs, both direct and opportunity from this move. Trade dependence is
thus a crude measure of necessary, if not
sufficient, grounds for the view that the
actor suffering the sanctions (hereafter the
Target) will in fact experience serious
deprivation.

Trade sanctions tend to be slow-acting.
Agencies feel inclined to honour existing
contracts and Targets can often anticipate
the impact of sanctions by stockpiling
goods. Successful stockpiling is to some extent a function of the market so it will be
easier in those circumstances where there
are a number of significant suppliers. The
existence of appropriate substitutes may
mean that a Target can mitigate the worst
effects of sanctions in this way.

The role of third parties will be crucial to
the outcome of trade sanctions. In the absence of third party support and cooperation, an Imposer may simply be gratuitously relinquishing its share of world trade
to its rivals by engaging in unsupported
trade sanctions. Because of their importance third parties are often restrained from
breaking sanctions by global or regional institutions which will seek to lay down the
terms and conditions under which trade
with the Target will take place. The limiting instance would be where the Target was
regarded as a complete pariah and effectively banished from the TRADING SYSTEM
altogether.

Trade sanctions are normally considered
part of the repertoire of instruments that
actors employ when they are involved in
such acts of violence as warfare. In such
circumstances trade sanctions are perceived
as assisting the overall war effort of compelling the adversary to submit to one's
will. Alternatively, they may be used as
measures short of WAR where the Imposer
either cannot or will not use FORCE; for example in the wake of Rhodesia's UDI in
1965 the United Kingdom sought to implement a policy of trade sanctions against the
recalcitrant REGIME. The United Kingdom
had initially renounced the use of force in
this case. Similarly, after 1949 the Arab

states that had been engaged in fighting the
state of Israel sought to implement a policy
of trade sanctions after the use of force had
failed to secure a favourable outcome to the
Palestine issue.

The main instruments that actors use to
implement a policy of trade sanctions are
EMBARGOES and BOYCOTTS. An embargo is
a properly constituted statement prohibiting trade in specified goods and services.
Usually an embargo is thought of as an en-
actment by a STATE legislature or international institution. A list of prohibited
items will be published and steps may be
taken to identify and 'blacklist' persons and
organizations which infringe the terms of
the embargo. A boycott is a more general
expression of a desire to abstain from relationships and need not have anything to do
with trade sanctions – as in a sporting boycott. In the present context however, a boycott, if it is officially sanctioned, will
include embargoes.

Trade sanctions are, according to much
conventional wisdom, instruments of IN-
FLUENCE which have an indifferent record,
given the declared goals of the Imposers.
Discounting special pleading by those who
wish to denigrate them for their own purposes, trade sanctions are certainly slow
working and prone to third party infringement. It is not always easy, moreover, to
isolate the impact of sanctions from other
punitive measures. Their unintended effects
are haphazard and inequitable. Paradoxically, they remain attractive in circumstances where an Imposer cannot or will
not use physical force as a means of expressing opposition.

## Trade system

The activity of engaging in TRADE between
international ACTORS has created a trade
system. The contemporary system is the
outgrowth of the nineteenth century. In the
period after the end of the European wars
against revolutionary France international
trade grew by, on average, 4 per cent per

year until 1914. The primary generating force for this was the rapid industrialization that took place, initially in Western Europe and then in the Americas and in Asia. The primary result of this was an increase in wealth in these STATES so that as foreign trade increased so did national income, sometimes faster. As a result the phenomenon known as 'export-led growth' became recognized by political economists and sought after by political leaders.

Under the monetary system known as the GOLD STANDARD what would now be called a highly INTERDEPENDENT set of relationships developed. Scholars such as Professor K. Waltz (1979) have argued that the nineteenth century trade and payments system was the height of INTER-DEPENDENCE, at least in terms of wealth/welfare ISSUE AREAS. Because the system was so interdependent, individual actors were highly vulnerable to adverse and unanticipated changes.

This system was irreparably damaged by the First World War and the economic depression thereafter. World trade did not begin to grow significantly after 1914 until the decade of the 1950s when a new but less open system was created under the aegis of the United States as the HEGE-MONIAL actor. Trade growth was spectacular during the years that followed, but very uneven in its impact. Unlike the nineteenth century, the post-1950s trade system has seen the benefits from this expansion going mainly to a small group of advanced industrial countries (AICs) and an even smaller group of newly industrialized countries (NICs) in the THIRD WORLD. This is quite different from the preceding century when many of the 'new' states in the Americas and Asia were fully and successfully integrated into the system. The polarization of the trading system since the 1950s has led some observers to speak of a POLARIZATION between the NORTH and the SOUTH as a result of these differential benefits.

The trade system since 1945 is also substantially more institutionalized than in the previous one hundred years. In the wake of the BRETTON WOODS agreements it was anticipated that a trading REGIME committed to the principle of non-discrimination would be established. The failure to ratify the International Trade Organization (ITO) left the General Agreement on Tariffs and Trade (GATT) by default as the principle organizational expression of this philosophy. In practice the non-discriminatory principle was not applied with sufficient determination and, in particular, when the United States positively encouraged the establishment of a major TRADING BLOC among Western European states in the 1950s a potentially fatal flaw was generated.

The establishment of the OECD and the United Nations Conference on Trade and Development (UNCTAD) in the 1960s when the growth of trade was fastest indicate the extent to which the unevenness of this growth was to be institutionalized. The principle of non-discrimination is now firmly rejected by the majority membership of UNCTAD which has pressed for a return to preferential TARIFFS rather than reciprocal MOST FAVOURED NATION (MFN) treatment as the functional expression of their approach to the trade system.


## Traditionalism

Sometimes called the 'classical' or 'non-scientific' approach, this term was popularized by Kaplan (1966) to describe the methodological position adopted by opponents of the behavioural revolution in the study of INTERNATIONAL POLITICS. According to this characterization, traditionalists rely overmuch on idiosyncratic, highly personalized insights from history, philosophy, political theory and law and consequently tend to employ intuitive, subjective judgements unsupported by empirical evidence to explain international phenomena. For their part, the traditionalists argue that scientific methods involving strict standards of proof and verification, quantification, measurement and the construction of hypothetical models are wholly inappropriate when dealing with a subject matter that involves human purpose (*see*: Hedley Bull, 1966b). This 'debate', which raged throughout the 1960s and early 1970s, was thus essentially about methodology. In this sense, it was not an offshoot of the earlier REALIST–IDEALIST controversy. It is generally agreed now that although at the time it generated much heat in academic circles, the argument about methods and approaches is somewhat sterile. Since the substantive issue of subject matter was never in dispute both 'tradition' and 'science' can, and do, coexist as complementary modes within the field (*see*: Knorr and Rosenau, 1969).

## Transgovernmental relations

This term is used to refer to what might be termed the 'unofficial FOREIGN POLICY' that is frequently conducted between government departments of one STATE and those of another. To be able and willing to behave in this way, the departments have to operate in a system that is relatively autonomous from the constitutionally defined DECISION-MAKERS. Again, such behaviour is incompatible with the idea that states are unitary ACTORS. Recognition that state-to-state relations are transgovernmental as well as intergovernmental thus represents a shift in the paradigm away from traditional STATE-CENTRIC ideas.

The developments in contemporary WORLD POLITICS would appear to have influenced the growth of these relations. First, increasing INTERDEPENDENCE among all actors has increased both the sensitivity and the vulnerability of state actors. Implementing and coordinating policy, particularly in ISSUE AREAS that are highly complex and specialized, means that bureaucracies take over from cabinets. Secondly, the growth of INTERGOVERNMENTAL ORGANIZATIONS (IGOS) means that the institutional framework for such inter-

action is already in place. As a result, POLICY-MAKING is more complex and more in need of continual adjustment. Formal office holders are unable to cope and transgovernmental relations become prevalent.

## Transnational

Literally implying 'across nations', the term is now widely used in WORLD POLITICS both with regard to relationships or transactions and with regard to organizations. In both instances the usage connotes activities that cross STATE, rather than national, BOUNDARIES in point of fact. Transnational relations are dependent upon three kinds of movements: (a) the movement of physical objects, including human populations; (b) the movement of information and ideas; and (c) the movement of money and credit. Such transactions are certainly not novel or peculiar to the contemporary system. Thus the GOLD STANDARD, the movement of European peoples to the United States and the contagious spread of ideas about NATIONALISM are all nineteenth century instances of what would now be called transnationalism. Notwithstanding this historical background, the growth of such transnational linkages has been a feature of world politics in the contemporary period. Two MACROPOLITICAL conditions seem to have been particularly important here: the growth of the TECHNOLOGIES of communication and transportation and the growth of INTERDEPENDENCE between ACTORS. The twentieth century communications revolution has enabled transnational actors to control their activities, while the growth of interdependence has created a permissive climate for transnationalism to expand.

Huntington (1973), in a seminal article in *World Politics*, defined a transnational organization according to three criteria: that they are complex organizations internally, that they are functionally specific and that they operate, intentionally, across state frontiers. Huntington notes that since 1945, these organizations have proliferated both in DOMAIN and SCOPE. The best example of a contemporary transnational organization is the multinational corporation (MNC). Incorporated in one state (the 'home'), with subsidiaries in others (the 'hosts'), these corporate actors are involved in all three types of transnational movements identified earlier. Other contemporary instances of transnational organizations would be the PLO and the Roman Catholic Church. Within a particular ISSUE AREA, such as civilian air transport, it is possible to identify a whole complex REGIME including states, intergovernmental organizations (IGOs) and transnational organizations – in this instance large civilian airline companies. It should be noted that international non-governmental organizations (INGOs) are, by definition, transnational organizations, although their scope and domain is relatively insignificant in comparison with some of the other examples cited earlier.

The growth of transnational relations and transnational organizations has been identified with approaches favouring a MIXED ACTOR view of macropolitics. The more traditional, STATE-CENTRIC approaches can no longer suffice to provide a relevant isomorphism. There is, accordingly, the need for greater PLURALISM if these changes are to be accommodated. Governments cannot control the contacts across state boundaries that are the essence of transnationalism and recognition of this empirical reality has led to a further loss of confidence in traditional models. All in all, the empirical evidence adduced to support the growth of transnationalism is matched by the analytical shift in the paradigm of macropolitics away from state-centred thinking.

## Treaty

A written contract or agreement between two or more parties which is considered binding in INTERNATIONAL LAW. Parties to treaties may be STATES, heads of states, governments or INTERNATIONAL ORGANIZATIONS. They are normally negotiated by plenipotentiaries on behalf of governments and are usually subject to RATIFICATION which is an executive act. Oral agreements are not treaties though verbal undertakings are sometimes claimed to have the same validity. The term is an elastic one but generally its use is confined to more formal agreements concerning fundamental relations. Other terms denoting agreement which bear a family resemblance to 'treaty' are PROTOCOL, agreement, arrangement, accord, act, general act, declaration, compromise and charter (see: Myers, 1957, p. 576). Treaty is the most formal and highest instrument of agreement on this list. It is a moot point whether 'exchanges of notes', a common DIPLOMATIC practice, actually constitutes a treaty (the RUSH–BAGOT AGREEMENT of 1817 is often referred to as a treaty whereas it began life as an exchange of notes between the United Kingdom and the United States). Treaties can be MULTILATERAL or BILATERAL, can involve a definite transaction or seek to establish general rules of conduct. Usually they are binding only on signatories but there are exceptions to this rule. Sometimes treaties establish REGIMES which are considered objectively valid (*erga omnes*), for non-signatory third parties. For example, multilateral agreements made under the auspices of the UN and its agencies dealing with matters of common interest such as DIPLOMATIC IMMUNITY or the LAW OF THE SEA create obligations and duties for non-members like Switzerland. In cases of this kind, the notion of 'consent' is implied thus safeguarding the rights of SOVEREIGNTY upon which the INTERNATIONAL SYSTEM is built. Besides multilateral and bilateral treaties (which are sometimes called 'treaty contracts' to distinguish them from the more general kind), treaties can be political (e.g. PEACE or DISARMAMENT), commercial (e.g. TARIFFS or fisheries), constitutional or administrative (e.g. UN CHARTER and agencies) or legal (e.g. EXTRADITION, laws of war). They are usually constructed to a set pattern involving a preamble, specific articles, a time-scale, ratification procedure, signatures and added articles (Kant wrote *Perpetual Peace* in treaty form – even adding a 'secret article' according to normal eighteenth century diplomatic practice.)

Treaties are considered binding (*PACTA SUNT SERVANDA*) but may lapse naturally, through WAR or by denunciation. Some international lawyers argue that all treaties are subject to the principle of *REBUS SIC STANTIBUS*; that is, that the treaty ceases to be binding when a fundamental change of circumstance has occurred. The doctrine of changed circumstance leading to termination, though is not generally applied to fundamental treaties of communal application such as the UN Charter, the GENEVA CONVENTION or the Vienna Conventions. A further point of legal dispute is whether the treaty itself constitutes the agreement or whether it is merely the instrument that records it. The latter appears more sensible and is in fact the common view. Treaties are an important and recognized source of INTERNATIONAL LAW, the others being custom, general principles and judicial decisions and teachings (*see*: Article 38, para. 1 of the *Statute of the International Court of Justice*).

## Treaty port

Term used to describe ports in Asia, mainly China and Japan, which were forcibly opened up for FOREIGN TRADE and residence in the nineteenth century by the United Kingdom, France, Germany and the United States. Treaty ports first occurred in China in 1842 following defeat in the Chinese–United Kingdom TRADE WAR (the Opium War, 1839–42). The system was introduced to Japan in 1854 when Commodore Mathew C. Perry forced the Japanese to open the door to US commerce. They were abolished in Japan in 1899 when Japanese industrial and military strength began to assert itself. They continued in China, which by 1911 had over fifty such ports, until after the Second World War. In these treaty ports, Western subjects enjoyed rights of EXTRA-TERRITORIALITY and were granted quasi-DIPLOMATIC privileges. Usually, the ports developed their own (i.e. the IMPERIAL states) legal, judicial, police and taxation systems, and in this sense can be considered to be a form of ANNEXATION.

## Triad

A term used in strategic analysis. It refers to the three classes of weapons systems possessed by nuclear-capable STATES such as the United States. The classification is obtained thus: BALLISTIC MISSILES are divided into land-based and sea-launched systems, while the triad is completed by air-breathing systems, such as bombers, fighter-bombers and CRUISE MISSILES.

Such diversification is held to give certain advantages. First, the deleterious effects of technical failure or malfunction are reduced. Secondly, such a mix reduces the incentives for the adversary to launch a disarming FIRST STRIKE. Thirdly, a triad of FORCE CAPABILITIES presents more offensive options to the state possessing them. Finally, such discrepant systems can be said to have different advantages: land-based ballistic missiles are the most accurate, sea-based the most invulnerable, while air-breathing systems are the most flexible.

The idea of a triad of force capabilities originated in the United States in the late 1950s when that state began to develop a significant ballistic missile capability to add to its traditional air-breathing systems. Under the rearmament programme of President J. F. Kennedy the triad became a reality and it has remained a benchmark ever since.

## Trilateral commission

Founded in March 1973 to promote the ideas of TRILATERALISM, the Commission can best be described as a TRANSNATIONAL interest group recruited on an individual basis from among the policy ELITES of the United States, Western Europe and Japan. The leading intellectual figure in the movement was Professor Z. Brzezinski and the group reached the height of its influence (to date) when Jimmy Carter, a founder member, became President of the United States. In the post-VIETNAM retrospective period, many influential Americans were susceptible to the argument that POWER was now more diffused among ACTORS in the system than had hitherto been assumed.

## Trilateralism

An analysis of WORLD POLITICS which sees TRIPOLARITY as the most significant structural characteristic. Trilateralism is thus a form of applied SYSTEMS ANALYSIS. Its influence can be dated from the early years of the 1970s and was particularly influential among US scholars, DIPLOMATS and politicians. Applying an essentially economic concept of POWER, the trilateralists saw the possibilities of HEGEMONIAL cooperation between the 'poles' of the United States, Japan and the EUROPEAN COMMUNITY. Given their emphasis upon INTERDEPENDENCE as a sytemic characteristic trilateralists, almost by definition, were committed to a cooperative rather than CONFLICT model of world politics. Trilateralism was not exclusively STATE-CENTRIC because the important role of non-state ACTORS such as the TRANS-NATIONAL corporations was recognized and included in their assumptions and prescriptions.

## Tripolarity

A variation of the MULTIPOLAR system structure which identifies three 'poles' or polar ACTORS. The ACTORS that dominate a tripolar system need not be STATES; BLOCS or COALITIONS may qualify. On the vexed issue of stability – often held to be one of the key benchmarks in this type of SYSTEMS ANALYSIS – tripolar systems tend to be unstable. Thus, if any two actors combine against the third, the system will become BIPOLAR. If any one of the three slips out of the dominant category, the system will again become bipolar. If further dominant actors emerge, the system will become MULTIPOLAR. In short tripolarity has the tendency to revert to a less ambiguous bipolarity, or to develop into a more complex multipolarity.

Central to the tripolar configuration is the concept of POLARITY. Having identified the determinants of polarity, it is possible to see what relevance tripolarity has for contemporary WORLD POLITICS. Herein, a favoured ISSUE AREA is that of political economy. Many would see the United States, Japan and the EUROPEAN COMMUNITY as the tripolar actors. In the military–security issue area, tripolarity is less discernible. At the ideational level, tripolar configurations have clearly influenced those who see a THIRD WORLD as separate from the FIRST and Second.

## Trip-wire

A term used in strategic analysis. A trip-wire is a small token force which has a DETERRENT function, out of all proportion to its size, because it symbolizes the commitment of the STATE(S) concerned to escalate their military response rapidly and significantly should the token force be attacked. In this way the token force 'trips' the escalatory response.

The term was popular in NATO circles in the 1950s after the United States became committed to the strategic doctrine known as MASSIVE RETALIATION. It was argued that if the United States was willing and able to launch massive thermo-nuclear responses onto the territory of the Soviet Union and its allies then the rationale for CONVENTIONAL forces, particularly of a significant size, was thereby reduced. In effect the trip-wire strategy was a means of keeping down the size and costs of conventional forces at a time when the states of Western Europe were enjoying significant economic growth in the wake of the MARSHALL PLAN.

Towards the end of the 1950s and the early years of the following decade a number of factors caused these ideas to be increasingly questioned. First, in the United States itself opinion in some military circles was reassessing the importance of limited conventional war in the light of the Korean experience. Under the Democratic Administration of President Kennedy this became known as the idea of FLEXIBLE RESPONSE. Secondly, the experience of the BERLIN CRISIS, which culminated in the building of the Wall in the summer of 1961, appeared to query the deterrent value of small token trip-wire forces. The growing VULNERABILITY of both Western Europe and the United States to Soviet offensive systems led some to query whether the two sides of the Atlantic could be effectively coupled together. Certainly, this particular instance of the trip-wire looked increasingly incredible in these changed circumstances.

Analytically the trip-wire idea remains an intriguing possibility in those circumstances where an ACTOR wishes to achieve a DETERRENT relationship via the use of token forces. As the instance of Western Europe shows, however, the trip wire idea is not immune from the usual limiting factors in any deterrent relationship.

## Truce

A temporary cessation of physical violence between ACTORS. It may be used to alleviate some immediate and pressing situation, such as the removal of sick and wounded, or the provision of essential food and medical services. Alternatively, or additionally, a truce may be seen as the preliminary stage in the IMPLEMENTATION of a permanent settlement to the CONFLICT situation.

Negotiating a truce may not be easy. For example, in the KOREAN WAR (1950–3) negotiations for a truce between the parties proved costly and contentious. While the truce talks were being conducted the hostilities continued and significant casualties resulted, both among the combatants and the civilian population of Korea. Indeed the United States lost more men during the period of the truce NEGOTIATIONS than in the initial period of the WAR, when both sides were seeking forcible reunification of the divided peninsula.

Parties seeking a truce will often turn to an appropriate third party for mediation purposes and to assist in implementation once an agreement has been reached. INTERGOVERNMENTAL ORGANIZATIONS (IGOS) such as the UNITED NATIONS have often been used both for mediation and implementation purposes. THE ARAB–ISRAELI CONFLICT would be an appropriate example in this regard.

## Truman doctrine

An all-embracing FOREIGN POLICY statement proclaimed by President Truman which provided the framework of US COLD WAR strategy for more than twenty years. It began with a speech to a joint session of Congress on 12 March 1947 in which Truman, while requesting 400 million dollars AID to Greece and Turkey, declared that 'it must be the policy of the United States to support free peoples who are resisting subjection by armed minorities or outside pressures'. Truman asked for, and got, the largest American BILATERAL government aid programme in peacetime history. In addition, provision was made for the dispatch of military personnel to Europe, the United States thus assuming chief responsibility for the active peacetime defence of the Eastern Mediterranean. This dramatic speech and the policy implications it contained amounted to a REVOLUTION in US peacetime policy. It marked a clear break with the long-standing ISOLATIONIST tradition and it established a precedent for US economic and military aid programmes throughout the world. Although the Soviet Union was not specifically mentioned it was widely and correctly assumed that 'free peoples' and 'anti-communist' were synonymous. Under the doctrine, the United States was committed on a global scale to oppose the spread of COMMUNISM and to intervene, by force of arms if necessary, in any 'threatened' area. Although Truman specifically mentioned Greece and Turkey, it soon became clear that the doctrine itself knew no general geographical limits. The economic dimension of this strategy of world-wide CONTAINMENT of communism was provided by the MARSHALL PLAN, both of which in Truman's words constituted 'two halves of the same walnut'.

Critics have argued that the sweeping ideological generalizations the doctrine contained, especially the simplistic division of the world into 'good' and 'evil' states, prevented US POLICY-MAKERS for at least a generation from identifying genuine mass-based NATIONALIST movements and resulted in US aid to regimes with appalling records on HUMAN RIGHTS merely because they publicly opposed communism. The tragedy of VIETNAM was thus directly attributable to the Truman doctrine. Domestically, the doctrine represents the first post-war assertion of the 'Imperial Presidency'; Congress was informed of the new policy direction, not consulted. As a result of this precedent, Congress became virtually a passive participant in the making of US FOREIGN POLICY until, in the wake of the Vietnam debacle, it reasserted its authority with the War Powers Act of 1973. For a quarter of a century the philosophical, ethical and ideological premises upon which US policy rested were not publicly or seriously questioned by the legislature. The doctrinal statements made by Truman became articles of faith which were almost universally accepted as authoritative and unquestioned. In the words of one commentator it amounted to 'the American Declaration of the COLD WAR' and in this respect it may have been a SELF-FULFILLING PROPHECY.

## Trusteeship

The notion of international supervision of COLONIAL territories was introduced by President Woodrow Wilson in Paris in 1919. The purpose was to prevent ANNEXATION of territories previously controlled by the defeated STATES. The system operated by the LEAGUE OF NATIONS was known as the MANDATE system. The trusteeship system is thus the newer version of the original, and has the same general purpose; former colonies of defeated states were to be administered by a 'trust' power under overall international supervision until such time as the inhabitants were able to determine their own future either as self-governing units or as independent states. However, it differs from the earlier system in that the supervisory body, the UN Trusteeship Council, has wider powers of overview than the more limited Mandates Commission. Chapters 12 and 13 of the UN CHARTER established an institution that is broader and more objective than its predecessor. The Council is one of the six principle organs of the UN yet is subject to GENERAL ASSEMBLY authority and review. Its role is to provide supervision of those non-self-governing territories that are designated as trust territories. Articles 87 and 88 set out the main methods for exercising this supervisory role. These are: (a) the preparation of detailed questionnaires on the political, economic, social and educational progress of the inhabitants of the territory; (b) the provision of an annual report by the administering authority; (c) an oral examination of agents of the administering authority; (d) the receipt and examination of petitions from individuals or groups within the trust territory; (e) periodic visits to each trust territory by delegates of the Trusteeship Council. These devices were meant to give more effective supervision of conditions within these territories. By 1950, eleven territories had been put under trusteeship and seven states acted as trustees. All, except for Somalia which was under Italian trusteeship, had been former mandates within the League. (South Africa continually refused to place its mandated territory, South West Africa/Namibia, under the trust system and until recently this remained the one unresolved legacy of the First World War. However, in 1989 in return for the supervised withdrawal of Cuban forces from Angola, South Africa agreed to set in motion the process of SELF-DETERMINATION.) Of the eleven territories, only one (the US-held Trust Territory of the Pacific Islands) has not achieved independence though some measures of self-government have been granted. This latter territory was designated a 'strategic territory' in order to accommodate the military–security interests of the United States in the Pacific. In this case supervisory powers are exercised by the Security Council, thus giving to the United States a potential VETO over any action considered prejudicial to its security interests.

# U

## UDI

Unilateral Declaration of Independence. In November 1965, in defiance of the COLONIAL power of the United Kingdom and of the international community at large, Rhodesia's White settler government declared itself INDEPENDENT. This amounted to a complete reversal of the post-war anti-colonial process in British Africa. The United Kingdom from the start was reluctant to use FORCE to ensure compliance and settled for policies of NEGOTIATION and ECONOMIC SANCTIONS. In 1966 the SECURITY COUNCIL called for manadatory sanctions to be imposed by all member STATES. France and the Soviet Union abstained, while Portugal and South Africa refused to impose an embargo. In 1970 Rhodesia unilaterally declared itself a republic. The issue is significant in WORLD POLITICS in that the period 1965–80 (the date of the creation of Zimbabwe) demonstrates the general ineffectiveness of economic sanctions as a means of ensuring compliance. Despite hardships the white REGIME was able to survive due mainly to overt assistance from South Africa and covert sanctions-breaking from, among others, the United Kingdom, the United States and France. The regime eventually collapsed as a direct consequence of the armed struggle waged by the Zimbabwean liberation armies.

## Ultimatum

Used in two senses in DIPLOMACY. The first and most common use is with reference to a formal communication (a note or memorandum) from one government to another requiring compliance on some issue – failure to do so carrying the threat of a penalty. Used in this way it takes the form of a final demand and signals the beginning of the end of the negotiating process. It involves a time-scale both for presentation and response. Thus, it is a critical instrument of diplomacy and its use is generally confined to conditions of extreme international CRISIS, involving as it does an implicit or explicit threat to use means other than normal diplomatic bargaining to achieve objectives. The second sense is more general and does not involve threats of compliance. Here it refers simply to the 'ultimate' or maximum amount of concessions one side is prepared to concede in negotiations in order to reach a settlement.

## Unanimity

The unanimity principle or rule is a fundamental tenet of the traditional STATE-CENTRED approach to WORLD POLITICS. It derives its significance from the legal concept of state SOVEREIGNTY, and in particular on the derivation known as sovereign equality. Given the principle that at least in law, if not in terms of political realities, all STATES are equal, it follows that whenever states are gathered together in DIPLOMATIC meetings and conferences, each participating state should have equality of treatment. Voting procedures should reflect this equality and, therefore, each state will have the same vote – as opposed to the system known as 'weighted voting' – and, moreover, no state can be committed to a course of action against its consent. Voting, therefore, is also an expression of consent in these circumstances. It can now be seen that following the strict application of these prescriptions every participating state has to vote in favour of a proposed course of action and/or statement of principles for that resolution to be carried by the meeting.

The unanimity rule was written into the Covenant of the LEAGUE OF NATIONS in the fifth Article, which specifically stipulated that voting in both of the main organs of the League would be on the unanimity rule. The UNITED NATIONS, on the other hand, has gone a long way towards modifying these norms in its Charter. The major exception to this is exemplified in the VETO provisions concerning voting in the Security Council. Article 27 of the UN CHARTER states that the concurrence of the five permanent members will be required on all questions other than those on procedural matters.

The effect of the unanimity requirement upon interstate organizations is to restrict DECISION-MAKING to the lowest common denominator of agreement and to stifle and stultify the efforts of those parties who might wish to expand and enhance the role of the institution. As such it is quite appropriate to regard the unanimity principle as a bastion of traditional state-centrism. Strict adherence to its letter and spirit considerably weakens the impact that these organizations can have on world politics.

## Unconditional surrender

The termination of armed CONFLICT without prior stipulation of conditions. In such a surrender, the victorious side may legally impose whatever terms seem appropriate. The defeated are entirely under the discretionary authority of the victors. As a consequence, ANNEXATION, division, occupation, REPARATIONS, WAR CRIMES TRIALS, as well as enforced changes in economic social and political institutions, are all possible policy implications. The doctrine of unconditional surrender, while by no means unknown before the twentieth century, is particularly associated with the concept of TOTAL WAR and as such is alien and inimical to the idea of LIMITED WAR which for the most part dominated nineteenth century INTERNATIONAL POLITICS. Unconditional surrender was demanded in both World Wars and at the Casablanca Conference in 1943 President Roosevelt justified it in this way: its aim was 'not the destruction of the populace but the destruction of a philosophy which is based on conquest and subjugation of other people'. In this sense, it is more likely to be an instrument of IDEALISM rather than of REALISM. The policy was criticized on the grounds that it prolonged the WAR, it led to the use of ATOMIC BOMBS, it postponed serious discussion on the nature of the post-war settlement and it prevented the re-entry of the defeated STATES into the full play of post-war WORLD POLITICS. In the context of nuclear DETERRENCE the avoidance of unconditional surrender is often advanced as a rational basis for possessing NUCLEAR WEAPONS and threatening NUCLEAR WAR.

## Unification
*See*: INTEGRATION

## Unilateralism

A policy of reliance on one's own resources in the pursuit of FOREIGN POLICY objectives. An important consequence of the WESTPHALIA system it was once the most sought-after ideal in INTERNATIONAL RELATIONS since it maximized a STATE's freedom to manoeuvre and it did not involve the compromises implicit in ALLIANCE politics. A commitment to unilateralism was expressed in a number of ways, the most common forms being ISOLATIONISM, NEUTRALISM and NON-ALIGNMENT, all of which involve some degree of non-participation in MULTILATERAL aspects of WORLD POLITICS. Traditionally, island states (e.g. The United Kingdom, Japan), or states logistically remote from the main arenas of diplomatic activity (e.g. The United States, China) have been the main beneficiaries but TECHNOLOGICAL developments in the nineteenth and twentieth centuries have now rendered unilateralism difficult, if not impossible for any state to achieve. Most states, willingly or unwillingly, now define their military–security issues in terms of BILATERAL or MULTILATERAL REGIONAL alliance systems. The term is most often used in contemporary literature in connection with DISARMAMENT particularly with regard to the possession of NUCLEAR WEAPONS. To date no nuclear state has adopted this posture but the idea does have a measure of popular appeal and is high on the agenda of activists within the PEACE MOVEMENT. The arguments advanced by its proponents have both ethical and political components. Renunciation of nuclear weapons by a single state would set a moral example to the rest of the system and encourage others to follow suit. In addition, since many states are hosts to foreign nuclear BASES and arsenals, the act of expulsion would re-establish their INDEPENDENCE and SOVEREIGNTY. These beliefs, particularly varieties of the latter, have had an effect on DEFENCE issues in Western Europe, and further afield have led the New Zealand government to refuse to allow US nuclear warships landing rights on their territory. While NATO and ANZUS appear to have been affected by unilateral impulses within the alliances, these have not structurally altered the ability of the alliances to survive. However, unilateralist tendencies in Eastern Europe in late 1989 have raised serious doubts about the future viability of the WARSAW PACT.

## Unipolarity

A type of system structure with one 'pole' or polar ACTOR being identified as predominant. In a unipolar system the dominant actor need not be a STATE and indeed historically where unipolar systems have existed they have usually been multinational empires. Hypothetically, the limiting case of a unipolar system would be a WORLD GOVERNMENT where, by definition, the SUB-SYSTEMS are subordinate to the overall system structure.

Central to the unipolar model is the concept of POLARITY. In the contemporary world system the essential conditions for unipolarity simply do not exist. Universal actors such as the UNITED NATIONS, are too sub-systems dominant. Conversely, no state or BLOC actor can be identified with sufficient of the indices of polarity to place it in an unambiguous position at the top. Some have argued that, albeit briefly, the United States was a unipolar actor from 1945 to 1949.

Unipolar systems can be said to show stability – remembering that it is a relative, not an absolute, term – if the dominant actor can establish ground rules which are widely accepted throughout the system. A unipolar system need not be thought of as exploitative, however. In setting and maintaining the ground rules, the dominant actor may have to bear considerable direct and opportunity costs. Indeed, in the process of bearing these costs, the dominant actor may contribute to its own demise.

*See also:* HEGEMONIC STABILITY THEORY

## United Nations Charter

The Charter is in effect the written constitution of the UN. It is also a MULTILATERAL TREATY which in respect of the agreements, rights and duties it confers on its signatories and members is an important source of INTERNATIONAL LAW. It was signed in San Francisco on 26 June 1945, was subsequently ratified by fifty-one states and came into being on 24 October 1945 (United Nations Day). The Charter, which runs to 111 articles, provides the

UN's organizational structure, principles, functions and powers. It designates six agencies as principal organs:

1. The GENERAL ASSEMBLY.
2. The SECURITY COUNCIL.
3. The Economic and Social Council.
4. The TRUSTEESHIP Council.
5. The Secretariat.
6. The INTERNATIONAL COURT OF JUSTICE.

The primary objectives stated in the Charter are the following: (a) to maintain international PEACE and security through peaceful settlement of disputes and COLLECTIVE SECURITY; (b) to promote international economic and social cooperation; (c) to promote respect for HUMAN RIGHTS for all. The fact that the Charter has survived and grown over the last forty years or so is testimony not just to the general and vague nature of the principles initially agreed upon but also to the flexibility and adaptability of the original document. In addition, although the Covenant of the LEAGUE OF NATIONS was its intellectual forerunner, the Charter itself displays a much more realistic grasp of the mechanics of world affairs. For example, the allocation of VETO powers to the five permanent members of the Security Council may on occasion have stultified the organization, but without it in all likelihood the UN would have fared no better than its predecessor. That it survived intact the austere political climate of the COLD WAR is ample evidence of the sagacity of its original framers.

### United Nations Organization

The UN is the world's second attempt at creating an intergovernmental organization (IGO) to ensure world PEACE and to establish the economic, social and political foundations through which this can be realized. The organization developed directly from discussions among the Allies during the Second World War (in fact the term 'United Nations' was originally used to de-note those STATES which were allied against the AXIS powers), and subsequently at DUMBARTON OAKS and San Francisco between 1944–5. Indeed, the San Francisco conference (April–June, 1945) was the first major international conference in the history of the STATES-SYSTEM which was not dominated by European states. (Of fifty-one signatories only nine were European.) The UN therefore marks the formal end of the European states-system and its replacement by a genuinely global one. Although it relied heavily on the experience of the LEAGUE OF NATIONS the founders of the UN were anxious from the outset to create a new international organization and not merely a revised, patched-up version of the League. To this end, stronger executive powers were assigned to the SECURITY COUNCIL, member states were required to make armed forces available as PEACE-KEEPERS and a range of SPECIALIZED AGENCIES was envisaged to foster and sustain a global economic and social order. However, the fundamental premises of the old organization remained virtually intact in the new; state SOVEREIGNTY persisted alongside the notion of voluntary COLLECTIVE SECURITY as the twin basic tenets of the UN CHARTER. Like the League, members' obligations are limited, the organization has no means of enforcing its decisions and determination of obligations is left to members themselves.

Structurally, the UN has six main organs. The Security Council is the most important executive agency and sits in permanent session. It has fifteen members, five of which, Britain, China, France, United States and the Soviet Union, have permanent membership and enjoy the privileges of VETO. The GENERAL ASSEMBLY, in which every member state has a vote, is central to the organization and is in effect a world forum. It also exercises supervisory and coordinating functions for all other agencies associated with the UN. The TRUSTEESHIP Council succeeded the MANDATES Commission of the League, the INTERNATIONAL COURT OF JUSTICE (ICJ) succeeded the PERMANENT

COURT OF INTERNATIONAL JUSTICE and the Economic and Social Council succeeded the Economic Consultative Committee. All these organs are served by a Secretariat and SECRETARY GENERAL who is chief officer.

The UN has been continuously active in WORLD POLITICS since 1945 and has been especially innovative in preventative DIPLOMACY, peacekeeping and fact-finding missions. However, on military–security issues the UN has, at best, a mixed record. After the KOREAN WAR (1950–3) the collective security principle on which the organization was founded gave way under pressure of SUPERPOWER rivalry to the watered-down security concept of peacekeeping. Collective international INTERVENTIONISM is all but a dead letter. The real achievement of the UN lies elsewhere. Paradoxically, whatever success the UN may claim to date appears to lie in its non-political, non-security aspects, in particular in the extensive welfare network that is associated with the SPECIALIZED AGENCIES. Commonly described as 'the UN development system' the services presided over by the General Assembly and the Economic and Social Council have brought far-reaching changes to the INTERNATIONAL SYSTEM. The FUNCTIONALIST view that cooperation in non-political matters will create an international constituency where parochial interests are minimal (and which incidentally would make the UN obsolete) may be idealistic but few doubt that it is in this area that the UN system has had most impact. Even so, questions are continually being asked, especially in the developed West, whether the 'politicization' of the welfare agencies (e.g. UNESCO) has undermined their original humanitarian functions. In addition to the relative success of the practical social service aspects of the organization, the dominant position of HUMAN RIGHTS and NORTH–SOUTH issues on the agenda of contemporary world politics owes much to the expansive interpretation of its powers by the General Assembly, especially during periods when the exercise of the VETO has paralysed the Security Council. In sum, the UN system has proved more effective in dealing with low-profile functional issues than with the larger question of the preservation of peace which was its original rationale.

### Unit veto

A hypothetical international system discussed in the second chapter of Kaplan's (1957) book. The defining characteristic of this system is held to be 'the possession by all ACTORS of weapons of such a character that any actor is capable of destroying any other actor that attacks it even though it cannot prevent its own destruction'. (p. 50). His elaboration that it is a 'stand-off' system gives it a family resemblance to DETERRENCE. In other respects, though, the unit VETO system is highly deductive. Thus his stipulation that the system contains no hierarchies or universal actors (such as the UN) are stringent, and rather limiting, conditions. His conclusion that the system will prove to be highly unstable is, in the event, not suprising.

Serious methodological objections can be raised about the value of such single factor analyses as that exemplified above. To be fair to Kaplan, however, his exposition of other systems in the same chapter has been far more influential than the unit veto case. Historically, the whole volume is a fascinating early example of what is often termed 'grand theory' and it remains a testament to the 'behavioural' or 'social science' revolution which assumed such significance in both teaching and research in the years that followed the publication of Kaplan's book.

### Uranium

The fissile substance that is the original basis for the development of nuclear fission for military purposes and nuclear energy for civilian purposes. Uranium 235 is the fissile element in the mineral but since less than 1 per cent of natural uranium is 235, considerable enrichment of the material is required to produce weapons-grade uranium. Natural supplies of uranium are distributed among the continents, with the United States having the largest share. The latest TECHNOLOGICAL innovations using fast-breeder reactors promises to overcome the limitations of what would otherwise be a finite asset. This CAPABILITY is of more significance for civilian nuclear energy programmes than in weapons production. In the latter context PLUTONIUM production is of great significance.

## Utopianism

Refers to a tradition of thought in INTERNATIONAL RELATIONS which argues that perpetual PEACE, equality and the full satisfaction of wants is both desirable and possible in WORLD POLITICS. The term was popularized by Carr (1939), whose book itself was a devastating critique of this mode of thinking. Carr used the term in two distinct but related senses.

1. Utopianism is the first or 'primitive stage in the development of a science of INTERNATIONAL POLITICS where 'the element of wish or purpose is overwhelmingly strong'. This was the case, he believed, in the period immediately following the First World War when the inclination to analyse facts was weak or non-existent and when visionary projects (e.g. WORLD GOVERNMENT, COLLECTIVE SECURITY) dominated

thinking about the subject. This stage was followed by political REALISM which is 'a stage of hard and ruthless analysis' of external reality. Only when international politics has passed through both these stages could it properly be called a science or discipline and even then, as a social science, elements of utopianism would remain.

2. Utopianism also refers to a specific school of thought whose proponents, arguing from first principles, construct schemes for the elimination of WAR and the establishment of eternal peace. In this sense the term is also used interchangeably with IDEALISM, LIBERALISM and rationalism. Central to this school, according to Carr, is the *laissez faire* doctrine of HARMONY OF INTERESTS, whereby each ACTOR in pursuing his own rationally perceived good, also pursues the good of the international community as a whole. Politically, this doctrine of the identity of interests took the form of 'an assumption that every nation has an identical interest in peace, and that any nation which desires to disturb the peace is therefore both irrational and immoral' (p. 51). Principle twentieth century proponents were Woodrow Wilson, Bertrand Russell, Norman Angell, A. E. Zimmern, G. Lowes-Dickinson and Gilbert Murray, but the tradition also embraced philosophers such as the Abbé Saint-Pierre, Rousseau and Kant.

Carr's critique of utopianism in 1939 set the stage for the somewhat sterile realist/idealist debate which dominated Anglo–American academic international politics for at least the next two decades.

# V

**Vatican City State**
Official name of the INDEPENDENT state created in 1929 by the treaty of the Lateran Pacts. It is the smallest STATE in the world occupying 108.7 acres and it forms an ENCLAVE in the city of Rome. Outside this area there are other buildings and land belonging to the Holy See which have the status of permanent EXTRATERRITORALITY; these include the papal palace at Castel Gandolfo and the transmitting centre of the Vatican radio station at Santa Maria di Galeria. Vatican City is a state in all the formal senses: it possesses territory, population and SOVEREIGNTY. It maintains four armed corps (two of which, the Noble Guard and the Palatine Guard of Honour, are ceremonial) and also the Swiss Guards (133 in all) and a Gendarmarie of 184 policemen. It does not maintain armed forces in the usual sense of the term. It is an accepted member of the international community and maintains permanent DIPLOMATIC relations with about fifty states. According to the Lateran Treaty its territory is inviolable and its political status is one of permanent NEUTRALITY. Thus it eschews alliances, associations and overtly political unions and avoids full participation in international affairs unless specifically appealed to. However, the role of the Vatican in world affairs has not been without controversy, especially concerning its alleged silence concerning Nazi treatment of the Jews, and its conservative position with regard to LIBERATION THEOLOGY. It is not a member of the UNITED NATIONS but maintains official observer status. Vatican City and the Holy See are in theory distinct entities, and both recognized as such by INTERNATIONAL LAW. The former represents the temporal POWER and the latter the spiritual but both are united in the person of the Pope who is simultaneously head of the sovereign state and head of the Catholic Church.

This close union between the Catholic Church and this mini- or miniscule state renders it politically as well as juridicially unique in WORLD POLITICS. The influence it wields is out of all proportion to its size. As the only religious institution recognized in international law as having full diplomatic status, the Holy See might be regarded as a historical anomaly, but given the origins of the European STATE-SYSTEM and the development of the institution of DIPLOMACY it is not difficult to see why.
*See also*: RELIGION

**Ver**
Voluntary Export Restraint. A ver is a SELF-IMPOSED QUOTA. A deliberate decision by an EXPORTER to exercise quantitative restraint *vis-à-vis* a particular market. As such a ver is a system of PROTECTIONISM because market access, although available, is not fully exploited. It may be difficult to see why any trading STATE would rationally agree to implement such a policy. Usually a ver decision is made because the exporter fears that otherwise the market will be closed altogether. In short a ver is an instance of the old adage that 'half a loaf is better than no bread'. In terms of POWER analysis ver IMPLEMENTATION may be

forced upon a trading ACTOR because the relative bargaining position favours the IMPORTER. Thus the EUROPEAN COMMUNITY is able to exercise this kind of bargaining leverage to force trading actors wanting access to its substantial internal market to observe vers.

## Verification

This is the process whereby ACTORS seek to confirm that others are complying with agreements, conventions and understandings. Verification is particularly important where parties to an agreement see that it is to their advantage to act UNILATERALLY to break or infringe the understanding. In these circumstances, the successful defector gains at the expense of those who abide by the terms. Eventually all parties will lose confidence and mass defections will occur. Alternatively, the defector will be brought to account and attempts will be made to reconstitute and redefine the understanding.

Verification is the inverse of trust. In a system based upon mutual trust and understanding, verification of compliance would be both unnecessary and contrary to the spirit of the relationship. Indeed, in such circumstances requiring verification would be a contradiction in terms. Equally, in a system of total CONFLICT and suspicion agreement would be impossible and verification unnecessary. In such a ZERO-SUM relationship WORST CASE ANALYSIS would be the prevailing perception. Verification is thus crucial in those relationships that GAME THEORY calls mixed-motive. Verification that compliance is being observed strengthens trust, reduces suspicion and increases the incentives for cooperation. The positive outcomes of this dynamic are well illustrated in the GRIT strategy of Osgood (1962).

VERIFICATION requires implementation and actors can either attempt to verify each other's compliance unilaterally, using their own instruments, or MULTILATERALLY, using INTERGOVERNMENTAL, TRANS-GOVERNMENTAL or TRANSNATIONAL ORGANIZATIONS. Since the verification agency may have to adjudicate competing claims, impartiality is an advantage. Since the verification agency requires the CAPABILITY to monitor what the parties are actually doing, as opposed to what they are saying, good INTELLIGENCE is an advantage. Since the verification agency may have to respond to non-compliance, a repertoire of sanctions is an advantage.

Monitoring activity by actors is a continuous and continuing process. Verification is only one aspect of this activity. It is perhaps the most overt and explicit. It is certainly crucial if collaboration and cooperation between actors in controversial areas such as ARMS CONTROL and DISARMAMENT are to be effectively implemented.

## Versailles Treaty (1919)

Signed on 28 June 1919 in the Hall of Mirrors at Versailles, this settlement formed part of the Paris Peace Conference (1919–20) that formally ended the First World War. The bulk of the TREATY concerned territorial transfers from Germany: Alsace Lorraine which was restored to France, Eupen-Malmedy to Belgium, the Saar which was placed under control of the LEAGUE OF NATIONS, the Rhineland was demilitarized and Poland was given a corridor of land affording access to the Baltic. Danzig was to be a 'free city' under a League of Nations commissioner. In addition, Germany's union with Austria (ANSCHLUSS) was forbidden. It has been estimated that as a result of this treaty Germany lost 13.5 per cent of its territory, 13 per cent of its economic productive capacity and 10 per cent of its population. All COLONIES of the German empire became MANDATES of the League, the German army was limited to 100,000 men, conscription was forbidden and the navy and air force were seriously reduced both in capacity and CAPABILITY. The most contentious of the 440 articles was Article 231 (the War Guilt Clause) which placed responsibility on Germany and its allies for all the loss and damage caused by the WAR. Costs of REPARATION exceeded 6,000 million pounds but these were subsequently reduced in the Dawes (1924) and Young (1929) plans in response to a growing awareness in the United Kingdom and the United States that the terms were unrealistic and punitive. The Covenant of the League of Nations was, on Woodrow Wilson's insistence, made part of the treaty.

This settlement is one of the best examples of a PEACE treaty creating the preconditions for a future war and many REALISTS accordingly regard the events of 1939–45 as the second instalment of the First World War. Not surprisingly most Germans resented this 'Diktat' of Versailles and the success of the Nazis in the later 1920s and 1930s depended in no small part on their manipulation of the real and imagined consequences of the settlement. Outside Germany, the economist J. M. Keynes (1919) denounced its socio-economic implications and the political and strategic aspects were condemned by Carr (1939). The accumulated feelings of guilt about an excessive and unreasonable settlement imposed on post-war Germany led directly in some circles to the promotion of policies of ACCOMMODATION and APPEASEMENT during the inter-war years.

## Vertical proliferation

This process refers to the spread of NUCLEAR WEAPONS CAPABILITIES within existing nuclear STATES. It may be contrasted immediately with HORIZONTAL PROLIFERATION which is the spread of such capabilities to states that previously did not possess them. Conventional usage of the term 'nuclear proliferation' tends to obscure this important difference. Basically vertical proliferation takes the following forms: (a) enhancement of existing technologies – for instance the development of the neutron bomb, which was a refinement of fission–fusion systems; (b) development

of new technologies – such as multiple independently targeted re-entry vehicles (MIRVs); and (c) deployment of nuclear weapons and delivery systems into areas and environments from which they have previously been excluded, such as stationing nuclear weapons in SPACE.

Since the signing of the Treaty on the Non-Proliferation of Nuclear Weapons (NPT) vertical proliferation has continued to be a controversial ISSUE AREA. In particular the development of multiple warheads – the deployment of MIRVs – in the 1970s, for example, seemed to show the extent to which the SUPERPOWERS would cynically ignore their commitments under the NPT regime. Debate centred around Article 6 of the Convention which required the existing nuclear states to end vertical proliferation and make significant progress towards DISARMAMENT.

Critics of Article 6 suggest that it is little more than a convenient smoke-screen behind which the so-called 'hold-out' states can continue to defy the majority of states which have signed the NPT. Others see the failure of the superpowers on Article 6 as evidence of 'double standards'. Practical steps that could currently enhance the goal of halting vertical proliferation would include a Comprehensive Test Ban (CTB) and further commitment towards NUCLEAR-FREE ZONES particularly in Europe.

## Veto

A veto is an attribute of POWER. It is an ability to stop undesirable outcomes. Moreover, it is an ability which exists UNILATERALLY, although ACTORS may cooperate to exercise a combined veto. As an attribute of POWER, exercising a veto requires skill and motivation as well as the necessary CAPABILITY. Veto power is usually thought of as legitimate power so the term has implications which are legal or quasi-legal. If such veto power is legitimized by international agreement and convention, it can be argued that the veto has thereby become an attribute of AUTHORITY. Such authorization of veto power in organizations containing state actors is an exemplification of the UNANIMITY rule which is itself derived from notions of SOVEREIGNTY, EQUALITY and consent.

The best example of legitimate veto power is to be found in the CHARTER OF THE UNITED NATIONS although it should be noted that the word itself does not appear in the document. In Chapter V, Article 2 on the voting arrangements in the SECURITY COUNCIL, the five permanent members (China, France, the Soviet Union, the United Kingdom and the United States) are given veto powers over all substantive, as opposed to procedural, questions. Moreover, through the DOUBLE VETO procedure they can decide whether a question is substantive or otherwise. Possession of veto power was regarded by the framers as a vital mechanism for maintaining international PEACE, since without the cooperation or aquiescence of the more powerful states (which abstention from the use of the veto power implied) international disputes would be that much more difficult to resolve. The veto states in the UN can be regarded as a self-created oligarchy. The move to create an oligarchy was strenuously resisted by a number of states that attended the Charter conference in 1945 and is still a matter of some resentment today. There have been some attempts to moderate or eliminate it altogether but to date the privileged position of the five permanent members is entrenched. Voluntary relinquishment of this power is extremely unlikely. It is certainly arguable that the window of opportunity that 1945 presented to the veto powers would have been closed to them decades later when the composition of the UN had began its quantum shift towards the THIRD WORLD states. By stipulating that the veto power should apply to revisions of the Charter as well, the veto powers ensured that their oligarchy should be self-perpetuating. DIPLOMATIC practice since 1945 has clarified the status of abstentions and absences from the Council. Neither of these situations is regarded as a legitimate instance of the veto power being activated.

**Vienna, Congress of (1815)**
*See*: CONCERT SYSTEM

**Vietnam**
Vietnam, a South East Asian state of approximately 330 thousand square kilometres with a population of some 55 million people (making it about the equivalent in physical and demographic size to Italy) has been the arena for two twentieth century WARS. The first was conducted by the Vietminh (a NATIONALIST/COMMUNIST REVOLUTIONARY movement) against French COLONIAL control of the territory. Beginning at the end of 1946, the war ended with the withdrawal of France in 1954 and INDEPENDENCE but division of Vietnam in the aftermath. The second war was fought to reunite the partitioned STATE. This goal was eventually achieved in 1975 after a long and bitter struggle into which the United States became increasingly drawn under Presidents Kennedy and Johnson. This second Vietnamese War is arguably one of the most traumatic and divisive violent conflicts of the twentieth century. It is certainly one of the best known and most keenly debated.

French colonial control of Vietnam was initiated in 1858 and completed in 1883. By 1887 France had effective control over the whole of Indo–China (Vietnam, Laos and Cambodia). France remained in this position until its defeat by Germany in the summer of 1940. The political vacuum created in Vietnam by the collapse of the metropolitan centre of French colonial power was immediately filled by Japan, assisted by local Vichy French interests. In May 1941 a united front organization, hereafter known by its abbreviation as the Vietminh, was formed with the Indo–Chinese Communist

Party under its leader Nguyen Tat Thanh (Ho Chi Minh) in the vanguard of this movement. It was at this time that the decision was made in principle to seek national liberation from all outside intervention through a revolutionary INSURGENCY which would, following the pattern set in China, be a PEOPLE'S WAR.

The period between the spring of 1941 and the commencement of full-scale GUERRILLA WAR in 1946 was one of great uncertainty but equally great opportunity for the Vietminh and its nationalist/communist leadership. In retrospect the key watershed occurred in the autumn of 1945 when, following the surrender of Japanese forces, UK intervention in the South and Chinese nationalist intervention in the North prevented the Vietminh from fully capitalizing upon the defeat of Japan to institute Vietnamese INDEPENDENCE. Attempts by the Vietnamese leaders to use DIPLOMACY to change the international status of Vietnam failed and instead French colonial control was reinstated. The United States, which could have acted as broker in these circumstances, preferred a policy characterized in the Pentagon Papers as 'ambivalent and indecisive'. The Vietminh regrouped their forces in the mountains close to the northern border with China and the first Vietnamese War had begun by 1946.

For the last half century Vietnam has been the target state for constant external INTERVENTION and involvement in its affairs. This tradition, established following the defeat of France in 1940, was continued during the 1950s when developments in the external environment began to intrude significantly into the Franco–Vietnamese violence. Following Chinese and Soviet RECOGNITION of Ho Chi Minh's Democratic Republic of Vietnam in January 1950, the French appealed to the United States for military and economic assistance in their war against the Vietminh. In May 1950 US intervention in the fighting began with the commencement of the AID programme. Within four years the United States would be paying three-quarters of the costs of the French side of the war.

The background to US involvement in Vietnam after 1950 was the policy of CONTAINMENT and the TRUMAN DOCTRINE. Following the PERCEPTION that China had been 'lost' in 1949 after the Maoist forces' victory, the decision to assist France in Vietnam was taken at the same time as the decision to intervene in KOREA. Both moves were conditioned by a perception of Asian communism which tended to see the United States' relation with communism (itself viewed at the time as a monolith) in BIPOLAR terms. As a result the issues to be found in Vietnam were perceived as being much greater than a mere colonial war. In rejecting its own historical tradition of anti-colonialism, the United States embarked upon a course of action that produced in the years that followed a broad commitment to the prevention of a united, communist-led state of Vietnam.

Militarily French defeat in Vietnam was partial rather than total. The collapse of French resistance was more a matter of will and loss of political confidence in Paris than total defeat on the battleground. This is not to gainsay the significance of the engagement at Dien Bien Phu in 1954 in any way. The Vietminh abandoned their guerrilla tactics for a set piece battle using artillery and trench warfare to lay seige to the French garrison. The latter's request for direct US intervention was rejected by a divided Eisenhower Administration.

The Geneva Conference of 1954 which addressed the issue of what were legally speaking the three Associated States of Indo–China produced an interim settlement which realized some goals and frustrated or ignored others. The conference reached a series of agreements which effectively ended French control over all of Indo–China. The GENEVA ACCORDS did not provide for the immediate unification of Vietnam, however. Under considerable pressure from China, the Vietminh agreed at Geneva to the partition of Vietnam at the 17th parallel with the understanding that elections would be held after two years on a nation-wide basis which would lead to the eventual reunification of Vietnam. A cease-fire agreement was also concluded at Geneva between the French and the Vietminh. In fact, in South Vietnam a Government was established under Ngo Dinh Diem, a Catholic and staunch anti-communist, which refused to recognize and implement those parts of the Geneva Accords regarding elections and reunification. In the United States, the Eisenhower Administration which came into office in January 1953 was equally committed to the policy of containment. Indeed it was President Eisenhower himself who did much to popularize the image of the 'falling dominoes' which, it was alleged, would be the fate of South Vietnam under the DOMINO THEORY. In September 1954 the United States obtained approval for a PROTOCOL to the SEATO TREATY which included the territory of South Vietnam in its SCOPE. During 1955 the United States assumed responsibility for large-scale economic and military assistance to the Diem government.

Between the Geneva cease-fire of 1954 and the formation of the National Liberation Front by Southerners opposed to Diem, South Vietnam became in effect a US DEPENDENCY. Consequently, when it became clear to the incoming Kennedy Administration in 1961 that Diem faced an insurgency which threatened the continuation of his rule, the decision was taken in the words of the Pentagon Papers to convert the 'limited-risk gamble' under Eisenhower to the 'broad commitment' under Kennedy.

In summary, therefore, the years between the inauguration of Kennedy in 1961 and the 'abdication' speech of Lyndon Johnson on 31 March 1968 saw the rise and demise of US intervention in South Vietnam. Johnson's address to the American people wherein he announced that he was no longer a candidate for the 1968 Presidential election marks the turning point from escalation to de-escalation. The Tet offensive of January 1968 and the request for substantially more US troops to restore the initiative thereafter was the precipitant cause. Only by placing the United States on a semi-war footing could these demands be met. Instead, in what was to be the outgoing Democratic Administration, the decision was taken to begin to scale down the war, to reduce US involvement in proportion to South Vietnamese (a policy known as 'vietnamization') and to look for a negotiated withdrawal.

Under Kennedy and his successor, the United States had first attempted to address the Second Vietnamese War as an example of counter-insurgency and, when that failed, had sought to 'conventionalize' the violence into a mode that was closer to the tradition of two World Wars and KOREA. The war of attrition which the United States conducted between 1965 and 1968 resulted in an unsatisfactory STALEMATE which was manifested sharply by the events of the Tet surprise attacks. Diplomatically the conventionalization of the war under Johnson meant that the United States was combatant and that, accordingly, any cease-fire or TRUCE would involve the United States as a party. The principal demands of the National Liberation Front and the Democratic Republic of Vietnam (DRV) were for a phased withdrawal of US forces and the cessation of US bombing of Vietnamese targets – particularly strategic bombing of the DRV. Politically the main goal was recognition of the objective of re-unification of the two halves and, implicitly, the establishment of a communist REGIME. Although the war was dragged out for a further period until 1972 under Richard Nixon, the agreement of January 1973 ending the war effectively met all the above demands. With the withdrawal of US support the Southern Republic of Vietnam (RVN) rapidly collapsed into chaos. The final denouement came in the spring of 1975.

In terms of WORLD POLITICS the Vietnam Wars remain the most prolonged and traumatic instances of the process of

DECOLONIZATION in the twentieth century. Vietnam emerged a united but impoverished state. In its pursuit of the goal of resisting first French and latterly US intervention the political LEADERSHIP was probably pushed further into the arms of China and the Soviet Union than it cared to go. Particularly in the field of international economic relations, membership of COMECON is difficult to justify on purely economic grounds and must instead be seen as an IDEOLOGICAL and political expression of alignment. For the French the Vietnam experience was less searing than for the United States. In the case of the latter it produced a period of introversion and resentment. It was a contributory factor in the loss of status as a SUPERPOWER and even led to a questioning of the institutions of government and the attempt to redress the institutional balance in POLICY-MAKING between the Executive and the Legislative branches of government. Analytically the second Vietnam War certainly demonstrates a number of paradoxes about POWER which writers on that subject have recently noted.

## Vulnerability

Vulnerability is a condition where an ACTOR, or a group of actors, is/are exposed to events and circumstances which are difficult to control, even in the long term. Vulnerability is a function of POWER relationships and it occurs in situations of INTERDEPENDENCE. Two significant instances of vulnerability are usually discussed whenever the condition is identified in MACROPOLITICS. First, in the field of political economy, scholars have suggested that vulnerability is a key characteristic of relationships of COMPLEX INTERDEPENDENCE. Secondly, STRATEGIC STUDIES has shown increased interest in vulnerability of late.

Within the first field, Keohane and Nye (1977) talk of 'vulnerability interdependence'. Vulnerability is here defined as the liability to suffer costs imposed by external events, even after adjustments have been made to reduce the impact of such events upon the actor. Vulnerability, in short, is a situation it is difficult to get out of even if you try. Keohane and Nye contrast vulnerability with sensitivity as the other dimension of interdependence. Underlying much of their discussion is the concept of costs which other power theorists, notably Baldwin (1979), have sought to stress. Reducing vulnerability may not be possible, even in the long term, but even if it is achieved such adjustments will be costly. In the meantime this vulnerability will give other actors leverage and may be used to secure a more compliant behaviour pattern accordingly. All in all, vulnerability is seen as an inevitable result of interdependence according to this view.

The growth of strategic studies as a policy science in the post-1945 period has increased the interest of both practitioners and theorists in questions of vulnerability. In strategic analysis vulnerability is again seen in terms of interdependence – in this case, the relativities between the defensive CAPABILITIES of an actor and the offensive capabilities of a putative attacker. After 1945 the advent of NUCLEAR WEAPONS and AIR POWER seemed to presage a new era of increased vulnerability. BALLISTIC MISSILE TECHNOLOGY confirmed this trend and the doctrine of ASSURED DESTRUCTION and its corollary, mutual assured destruction (MAD), seemed almost to make vulnerability into a virtue, or at least a necessity, with the so-called 'hostage cities' idea. The paradox was complete because the very idea of mutual vulnerability and assured destruction was dependent upon possession of SECOND STRIKE capabilities which, by definition, were invulnerable.

# W

## War

War is direct, somatic violence between state actors. Wars occur when states in a situation of social CONFLICT and opposition find that the pursuit of incompatible or exclusive goals cannot be confined to non-violent modes. As a form of direct violence war occurs in different forms within social systems. Thus gang war, range war, class war, civil or internal war are distinguishable typologies. Analytically separate, these levels can interact and produce complex FEEDBACK loops. Civil war can become internationalized through INTERVENTION into interstate war. The various levels at which violence occurs can influence the occurrence of violence at other levels.

The idea of levels intrudes into the study of war in a second way. Within academic disciplines it is possible to discern differences in the manner in which violence is explained and discussed. This is made clear in a work such as that of Waltz (1959). Waltz examines the phenomenon from the levels of individual theories, societal theories and structural theories. Academically, therefore, a psychologist might be interested in war as a function of PERCEPTION, an anthropologist in why certain cultures seem to foster AGGRESSION. Sociology has drawn attention to the positive functions that violence can play within and between systems. Economists have, for instance, applied GAME THEORY concepts to the analysis of conflict, while political scientists have sought through policy analysis and SYSTEMS ANALYSIS to examine both the micro and the macro aspects of War.

Taking up the point attributed above to

sociology, war should not necessarily be regarded as dysfunctional. War in the INTERNATIONAL SYSTEM is not necessarily like disease in the biological system. Conflict and the fear of war have often been used to integrate STATES. In such circumstances the search for enemies assists in maintaining or increasing group solidarity. The threat of war can be used by groups within states to extend their control over the political and economic life of the state. Violence can even be used to create states. In the nineteenth century German UNIFICATION was achieved via the defeat of such neighbouring states as Denmark, Austria and France. Marxist theories of the twentieth century regard WARS OF NATIONAL LIBERATION as serving specific functional purposes.

The idea that violence and war are intrinsic parts of the INTERNATIONAL SYSTEM is the distinctive hallmark of REALISM. The forms of violence may change – under the influence of TECHNOLOGY, for instance. The scope of violence may differ as the actors in the system change. Notwithstanding these parameters, violence and war remain fundamental. Recognition by realism that war was a systemic variable of some persistence led to the search for some amelioration. Realism has usually found this in the BALANCE OF POWER mechanism. As Claude (1962) pointed out the balance of power was not fundamentally a means of war prevention but rather a means of structural maintenance which, in certain circumstances, might involve the use of FORCE. The implausibility of war serving this function in the era of NUCLEAR WEAPONS forced realists to modify their structural models in keeping with ideas about POLARIZATION and BIPOLAR/MULTIPOLAR configurations. Bipolarity or multipolarity were now favoured because violence would be reduced under one or the other.

If violence and war have long been recognized as regular occurrences in the WORLD SYSTEM, it is still the case that their intensity has increased of late. Thus the two World Wars (1914–18 and 1939–45) killed over sixty million persons among the major participants. More than eight million soldiers and one million civilians were killed in the fist instance, while almost seventeen million soldiers and thirty-five million civilians were killed in the second. Significant advances in medical TECHNOLOGY notwithstanding, it would seem that the intensity of violence is considerable.

While intensity has increased, frequency has decreased – at least in Europe where the STATE-SYSTEM originated. European evidence seems to show that wars are more concentrated and destructive but less frequent. In his 1964 study on the subject of war, Wright noted that there had been a decline in frequency in Europe from the sixteenth and seventeenth centuries to the nineteenth and twentieth. Whereas in the earlier period European states were more often at war than not, by the twentieth they spent less than one-fifth of their time at war.

The characteristic of systemic violence within the state-system has affected other processes. Violence among states has given rise to the INTERNATIONAL LAWS of war. Traditional international law did little to outlaw war, but rather to reduce its worst excesses and, as far as possible limit the distruption and damage to third parties. Although the UNITED NATIONS system has introduced some further restrictions upon the use of FORCE, it is still permitted under the doctrine of SELF-DEFENCE. Under Article 51 of the UN CHARTER states can effect self-defence measures unless and until the SECURITY COUNCIL can agree upon a collective response to any breach of the PEACE.

ALLIANCE formation among states appears to be related generally to recognition of the intrinsically violent nature of the system. The First World War was preceeded by the formation of rival alliances in the Triple Alliance of 1882 and the Triple ENTENTE of 1907. The outbreak of hostilities further expanded these alliances with Turkey and Bulgaria joining one side and the United States the other. Following the establishment of the LEAGUE OF NATIONS, the alliances disintegrated but during the 1930s a new AXIS emerged between Germany, Italy and Japan. After the Second World War alliance formation resumed, with NATO and the WARSAW PACT being leading instances. During the nineteenth century states formed an alliance about every other year. In the twentieth the rate increased more than four-fold to more than two new alliances per year.

ARMS RACES have followed the same pattern as alliances, since the dynamic for the arms race is at least initially PERCEPTION of external threat and general instability in the system. States arm themselves to provide a margin of equivalent or superior CAPABILITY *vis-à-vis* an adversary, according to worst case thinking. While it would be invalid to suggest that arms races cause violence to occur, there is a strong correlation between the activity of arms racing and ally seeking by states and increases in international tension and hostility.

War, violence, ally seeking and arms racing increase the level of military expenditures within states. Within societies the military mobilizes enormous rescources and organizes such complex tasks as research, development, production and maintenance of the military capability of the state. The existence of what some have identified as MILITARY–INDUSTRIAL COMPLEXES implies a strong vested interest in the continuation of a perceived level of hostility and tension between states. More generally there is a tendency for societies frequently threatened with violent conflict to become militarized. The military may eventually take over political LEADERSHIP roles from civilians if this militarization persists.

Any attempt at ameliorating violence, CONFLICT MANAGEMENT and/or RESOLUTION must first identify who the parties are and what the issues dividing them consist of. This preliminary inquiry will preceed any type of third party intervention in the violence. There is often a tendency within DIPLOMACY to seek short-term palliatives through management techniques and instruments. Thus UN PEACEKEEPING has sometimes been held up as an example of this concentration on the short-term need to end direct violence without always addressing the underlying issues in conflict between the parties. It is well to remember that, as stated at the outset, war is the most fundamental manifestation of conflict as a systemic process in WORLD POLITICS.

### War Crimes trials

The right of a victor to put to trial individual members of enemy forces for violations of the INTERNATIONAL LAWS of WAR has long been a customary one in international affairs but the twentieth century has seen some refinements and developments. The TREATY OF VERSAILLES made provision for the trial of the German Emperor and individual members of the German armed forces, although this was not carried out. After the Second World War, though, the Nuremberg and Tokyo trials set a precendent by trying German and Japanese leaders not only for 'war crimes' but also for 'crimes against peace' and 'crimes against humanity' – the last two being regarded in some quarters as retrospective legislation. Crimes against PEACE were defined by the Nuremberg Tribunal as ' . . . planning, preparation, initiation or waging of a war of aggression, or a war in violation of international treaties'. In this respect only leaders of a STATE are liable. Crimes against humanity were defined as follows: ' . . . murder, extermination, enslavement, deportation and other inhumane acts committed against any civilian population before or during the war, or persecutions

on political, racial or religious grounds in execution of or in connection with any crime within the jurisdiction of the Tribunal, whether or not in violation of the domestic law of the country where perpetuated'. Thus, crimes against humanity are wider than war crimes; they can be committed on one's own population and they are not confined to wartime. These precedents set at Tokyo and Nuremberg were subsequently approved by the GENERAL ASSEMBLY OF THE UN and by the International Law Commission. They are now seen as part of international law and must therefore be regarded as a further nail in the coffin of the traditional rule that a state may treat its own nationals as it pleases.

### Warsaw Pact

Founded in May 1955 when the Soviet Union signed a MULTILATERAL TREATY of friendship, cooperation and mutual assistance with representatives of all the People's Republics of Eastern Europe, except Yugoslavia. The Pact was a direct response to the expansion of NATO with the inclusion of the Federal Republic of Germany. Its military significance at its inception was slight since the Soviet Union already had BILATERAL treaties in existence with all the STATES concerned. The Pact may, accordingly, be seen as a political statement of BLOC solidarity rather than a system of COLLECTIVE DEFENCE.

The cohesion of the new group was soon challenged when in the autumn of 1956 the Hungarian government attempted to change the ORIENTATION of that state by leaving the Pact. The subsequent INTERVENTION of Soviet military forces in Hungary established the principle that loyalty to the Pact was regarded by the HEGEMONIAL state as a touchstone of commitment to 'socialist solidarity'.

In the years that followed the Hungarian challenge centrifugal tendencies became increasingly evident in two respects. The rift between the Soviet Union and the People's

Republic of China demolished the idea of socialist solidarity at a stroke. Increasing evidence of POLYCENTRISM among the Eastern European states weakened the common front. First, the Albanians left the organization. Secondly, the Rumanians showed consistent signs of wanting to follow a more independent FOREIGN POLICY by establishing links with the Federal Republic of Germany and by taking a more detached position over the ARAB–ISRAELI CONFLICT. Finally, the reform movement in Czechoslovakia provoked the second 'fraternal' invasion since 1955 in the late summer of 1968.

In the wake of the Czech crisis, the Pact members agreed to a package of institutional reforms in March 1969. Two new structures were created thereby: the Committee of Defence Ministers and the Military Council. Both these new organs had the effect of increasing the authority of the Eastern European states against that of the Soviet Union. At least in principle the instruments were created for more genuine political control by state defence ministers – through their committee. The Political Consultative Committee (PCC) (which was established at the outset) remains the organ that provides a broader coordination of REGIONAL security policy and, more generally, of the FOREIGN POLICY of the Pact. Indeed at the March 1969 meeting, the PCC issued a call for a European Security Conference to discuss the post-war divisions of the continent. This latter initiative was to lead to the Conference on Security and Cooperation in Europe (CSCE) and the HELSINKI ACCORDS.

The Soviet Union has a complete monopoly within the Pact as a supplier of military equipment. This gives the Pact forces a high degree of inter-operability and means that competitive, but sometimes highly wasteful, procurement disputes are avoided. There is some evidence to suggest that the Soviet Union is slow to make the latest equipment available immediately to fraternal forces. It has been noted that states like Egypt and Syria have taken delivery of the latest weapon systems before Pact states on occasions.

The reliability of some of the Eastern European contingents has also been questioned by some observers in the West, although not usually by NATO. Clearly, if morale and reliability are relevant queries that can be made about Eastern European forces, then too much credence should not be given to dogged quantification of FORCE levels between the Pact and NATO.

The Warsaw Pact remains an ACTOR which its state members would willingly sacrifice in order to achieve the disappearance of NATO. The bilateral structure of Soviet treaties with the other states of Eastern Europe would remain in place thereafter. However, the momentous events of late 1989 throughout Eastern Europe, especially the demise of COMMUNISM, the likelihood of German reunification and the apparent willingness of the Soviet Union to withdraw or substantially reduce force levels throughout the REGION have led to serious doubts about the continued viability of the Pact in its present guise. It is clear that future CSCE summits will need to reconsider the consequences of these developments within the general framework of European military/security issues.

## Wars of national liberation

A doctrine developed by MARXIST/LENINISTS calling for armed uprisings against the established orders in the developing world. Primarily directed at COLONIAL territories the concept argues that these WARS are JUST WARS since their purpose is to liberate the masses from ALIEN rule and establish the right to SELF-DETERMINATION. Both Marx and Lenin advocated proletarian REVOLUTION to establish a just social order but the anti-Western, anti-colonial and anti-IMPERIAL elements of the doctrine were first elaborated by Khrushchev in 1961. In this case INTERVENTION by external forces on behalf of the insurgents is justified and may also be a moral duty.

The idea of liberation wars became an important practical instrument of international COMMUNISM, especially in post-war Asia, Africa and Latin America. The official Soviet position has been that Western capitalism either directly or by proxy has deliberately exploited and oppressed both its own and its dependent populations. Wars which seek to break this chain of DEPENDENCE and liberate the masses are therefore entirely justified. Since the Western capitalists are constantly engaged in exporting 'counter-revolution', AID must be given to those engaged in the process of liberation. The form that this aid takes could involve external intervention but as a matter of practical policy, the Soviet Union, and to a lesser extent China, has avoided direct physical intervention and instead concentrated on supplying military advisers, arms and other forms of economic assistance. While Western states regard wars of national liberation as civil wars communist states view them as international wars, and this has important consequences in INTERNATIONAL LAW. Since civil wars are not covered entirely by the laws of war (although the GENEVA CONVENTIONS of 1949 tried to remedy this), international wars are. The First PROTOCOL to the 1949 Conventions, signed in 1977, asserted that 'armed conflicts in which peoples are fighting against colonial domination and alien occupation and against racist regimes in the exercise of their right of self-determination' are to be considered 'international' wars for the purpose of applying the laws of war generally. Out of a total of 163 signatories to the 1949 Convention, only 59 accepted this definition, reflecting the deep divisions in the international community over its exact status. If wars of national liberation are classified as international and not civil wars, then under an extended version of SELF-DEFENCE, external INTERVENTION may be justified. As a general rule external intervention is forbidden in civil wars so that there is clear dis-

agreement between Western states and others as to the legality of active interference in wars of national liberation. As a rule the GENERAL ASSEMBLY has adopted a permissive stance in these matters and has consistently opposed the Western view.

### Westphalia, peace of (1648)

A series of TREATIES (principally Munster and Osnabruck) which collectively ended hostilities in the Thirty Years War (1618–48). It is commonly said to mark the beginning of the modern system of INTERNATIONAL RELATIONS. In relation to seventeenth century Europe it marked the culmination of the anti-HEGEMONIC struggle against the Habsburg aspirations for a SUPRANATIONAL empire. It signalled the collapse of Spanish POWER, the fragmentation of Germany (thus delaying German unity for over two hundred years) and the rise of France as the major European power. A number of important principles, which were subsequently to form the legal and political framework of modern interstate relations, were established at Westphalia. It explicitly recognized a society of STATES based on the principle of territorial SOVEREIGNTY, it established the INDEPENDENCE of states and emphasized that each had jural rights which all others were bound to respect. It recognized the legitimacy of all forms of government and established the notion of religious freedom and toleration (*cuius regio, eius religio*). In sum, it established a secular concept of international relations replacing for ever the medieval idea of a universal religious authority acting as final arbiter of Christendom. By destroying the notion of universalism, the 'Westphalia system' gave impetus to the notions of REASON OF STATE and BALANCE OF POWER as key concepts in FOREIGN POLICY conduct and formulation. From 1648 onwards, the particularist interests of states became paramount both politically and legally. It should be noted, though, that the STATE-SYSTEM established at Westphalia was primarily Christian and European. The codification of rules concerning non-INTER-VENTION did not apply to ISLAM or to the rest of the world. This double standard persisted in European DIPLOMACY into the nineteenth and twentieth centuries when the Westphalia system gradually and often reluctantly became a global one.

## Wilson doctrine

Refers to INTERVENTIONIST policies initiated by President Woodrow Wilson in relation to Central and Latin America in 1913. In his declaration Wilson stated: 'We do not sympathize with those who establish their government authority in order to satisfy their personal interests and ambitions. . . . We must teach the Latin Americans to select the right man.' In accordance with this doctrine, on 21 April 1914 Wilson ordered military intervention in Mexico and American Marines occupied the port of Veracruz. This doctrine was a logical consequence of the Roosevelt corollary to the MONROE DOCTRINE, which asserted that 'chronic wrongdoing, or an impotence which results in a general loosening of the ties of civil society' would result in US intervention in the form of a UNILATERAL 'exercise of an international police power'. As with most US presidential 'doctrines' this was directed specifically at developements in THIRD WORLD STATES and characteristically used high moral pretext to disguise basic NATIONAL INTERESTS.

## Window of vulnerability

A term used by some members of the United States' DEFENCE policy establishment during the 1970s when fears were being expressed that the land-based component of the strategic forces TRIAD was becoming increasingly vulnerable to a disarming FIRST STRIKE by the Soviet Union. Three factors were held to give the Soviet Union this enhanced CAPABILITY: the de-

velopment of multiple warheads, the increase in missile accuracy, and the substantial THROW-WEIGHT of Soviet missiles.

Probably the best known spokesperson for these views was the distinguished diplomat, Paul Nitze. Institutionally, the Committee on the Present Danger campaigned for the United States to take steps to redress this perceived imbalance against itself. Politically, these warnings informed the defence policy of the Reagan Administration (1981–9) particularly during its first term. Active measures were taken during these years to increase the available strategic weapons systems of the United States. The whole scenario upon which the window of vulnerablitiy was based can be plausibly called an instance of WORST-CASE ANALYSIS.

## World Bank group

This collectivity consists of three intergovernmental organizations (IGOs): the International Bank for Reconstruction and Development (IBRD), the International Development Association (IDA) and the International Finance Corporation. The first named, the IBRD, is popularly known as the WORLD BANK. As the title implies the twin purposes of setting up the World Bank, as part of the BRETTON WOODS system of international economic institutions, was to facilitate the rebuilding of those essentially developed economies which had been shattered by WAR and to assist in the more basic task of economic development of the least developed countries (LDCs). The Bank is the twin organization of the IMF and indeed membership of the Bank is restricted to STATES which are also members of the Fund. Like the Fund, the Bank has a system of weighted voting which gives POWER to effect outcomes to those states which make the greatest contributions. These contributions are, in fact, expressed as subscriptions to the Bank and these member state subscriptions are one of the main sources of Bank funds. In addition the

Bank goes into the private capital markets to raise funds and these borrowings now constitute the largest source of Bank liquidity. Being heavily infused with commercial banking principles it comes as no surprise that the Bank's lending policy follows fairly strict commercial criteria.

The need for an institution that would provide 'soft' loans led to the establishment of the IDA in 1960. Like the Bank the IDA makes loans rather than grants and, again as with the IBRD, the would-be recipients are vetted beforehand. Loans are made to recipients to encourage the development of their infrastructure. Unlike the Bank, the IDA is totally dependent upon member states' contributions for its source of funds.

The International Finance Corporation was established in 1956 to encourage the growth of private enterprise and entrepreneurial skills in the LDCs. It limits its participation in projects to a minority shareholding and has particularly concentrated on secondary or manufacturing sectors.

The World Bank group, like the IMF, broadly reflects the principles of ECONOMIC LIBERALISM that were, and indeed remain, the dominant IDEOLOGY among these institutions. Structurally the Group and the Fund are dominated by the advanced industrial countries (AICs) (plus Saudi Arabia) and the influence of commercial banking criteria upon the ethos and activities of these institutions is clearly apparent.

## World Government

The centralization of AUTHORITY in a unitary SUPRANATIONAL body which would possess legislative and executive powers as well as a monopoly of the use of FORCE. The SOVEREIGNTY of STATES would be surrendered and disputes would be settled by ADJUDICATION under a single system of WORLD LAW. The concentration of powers and the creation of a singular world authority would normally involve the DISARMAMENT of states and its primary purpose and rationale would be the maintenance of international PEACE and order. Most advocates envisage a FEDERAL system wherby the central authority is vested with specific functions (establishing the rule of law and maintaining order) while the constituent units (previously states) are non-sovereign members of the global community holding residual powers of local administration. Such schemes have generally been advanced as solutions to the problems of ANARCHY and power-management in WORLD POLITICS. Indeed, it could be argued that world government is the only theoretically correct solution to these problems since the traditional alternatives, BALANCE OF POWER and COLLECTIVE SECURITY, are at best only partial solutions and at worst mere institutional disguises for the unbridled exercise of national self-interest (*See*: Claude, 1962). It is not surprising, therefore, that the idea of a single world state has been a seductive and a pervasive one in the history of international thought. On a more practical level, its actualization is envisaged in two ways. It could be achieved either through military conquest in the form of a single world imperium or through consent and cooperation on the lines of the DOMESTIC ANALOGY. The Roman Empire is cited as the clearest historical example of the former while the LEAGUE OF NATIONS and the UNITED NATIONS are often presented as early prototypes of the latter. Critics of such schemes, whatever their genesis, argue that world government might lead to world tyranny; that WARS, in the sense of interstate violence, would merely be replaced by CIVIL WARS or regional insurrections; that constitutions do not create INTEGRATION but are themselves products of it and that the practical question of simultaneously obtaining a consensus on relinquishing sovereignty among more than one hundred and sixty states, has never been properly addressed. For these and other reasons, advocates of world government have generally been side-lined as well-intentioned but misguided IDEALISTS and UTOPIANS.

While most of the older approaches to the idea of supranational governance have been preoccupied with the creation of formal political organizations much of the recent literature in this vein has come from the WORLD ORDER perspective and is structural, systemic and functional in character rather than simply ACTOR and/or institution orientated. Although not advocating world government in the above sense, this school shares a family resemblance in that it seeks alternatives to the present STATE-SYSTEM and seeks an erosion of sovereignty. The approach represents a shift from the TRADITIONAL near-exclusive focus on war prevention to a more dynamic framework for future order which includes economic well-being, social JUSTICE and ecological balance as well as PEACE among its priorities.

*See also*: WORLD ORDER

## World Health Organization (WHO)

Health problems, especially TRANS-NATIONAL diseases, have been a matter for practical international concern since at least medieval times but rarely do they figure in academic considerations of WORLD POLITICS. The dominance of the STATE-CENTRIC approach and its consequent concern with the diplomatic–strategic milieu has relegated most issues of social welfare, including health, to the level of Any Other Business on the agenda of INTERNATIONAL RELATIONS. However, since the establishment of WHO as a SPECIALIZED AGENCY of the UNITED NATIONS in 1948 the issue of global health, like that of ECOLOGY, has become a high profile one both for practitioners anxious to control and eradicate disease and for theorists concerned to move beyond the state and develop a wider understanding of the scope of international activity.

In 1851 a series of international conferences met to discuss quarantine regulations; this resulted eventually in the adoption of the International Sanitary Convention in 1903 and the establishment of the International Office of Public Hygiene in Paris in 1909. The LEAGUE OF NATIONS established a Health Organization in 1920 to work in conjunction with the Paris office and both of these were absorbed by the WHO in 1948. Since then it has become the largest of the specialized agencies, its general purpose being 'the attainment by all peoples of the highest possible level of health'. Its headquarters is in Geneva and its operations are decentralized into six regional committees and offices. It has a DIRECTOR-GENERAL, a Secretariat and an Executive Board and it convenes an annual World Health Assembly as well as various international health conventions. Membership is open to all STATES; members of the UN join automatically and other states become members when the World Health Assembly approves their application by a simple majority vote. Territories which are not responsible for the conduct of their INTERNATIONAL RELATIONS may become associate members. In January 1985 the WHO had 162 member states and two associate members.

The general record of WHO is impressive not just in the control or eradication of epidemic diseases such as smallpox or malaria but also in the areas of promoting primary health care and in assisting developing states in the creation of health services and training facilities. It maintains an Epidemiological Intelligence Network which can rapidly and efficiently collate and disseminate information about the intensity and likely spread of life-threatening diseases including cholera, typhoid, plague, smallpox, yellow fever and AIDS. In 1967 the WHO began a global campaign to eradicate smallpox within ten years. That year 131,418 cases were reported in 43 countries. By 1984, according to the WHO, the smallpox plague had been totally eradicated. In addition to combating disease, WHO functions effectively in the area of prevention and has initiated numerous projects on air POLLUTION, water supply, sewage disposal and the use of insecticides.

The organization is at the forefront of global campaigns to popularize and highlight the importance of transnational cooperation in health care matters. In 1978 for example, it convened the Alma-Ata Conference on primary health care which formulated the campaign for 'Health for All' by the year 2000. Whether or not these goals will be achieved in the face of entrenched beliefs about the primacy of economic growth (most commentators think not) none can doubt that the WHO is one of the most successful of the UN's specialized agencies.


## World law

Term popularized by Corbett (1956) and others to indicate an apparent post-war shift away from traditional STATE-CENTRIC INTERNATIONAL LAW towards a much wider based 'law of the world community'. It is especially associated with the WORLD ORDER perspective and is designed to promote a conception of law which reflects the dynamism of contemporary social values rather than one which is locked in to the predominantly Eurocentric assumptions of the WESTPHALIA system. They assert that the transition from 'international' to 'world' law is revealed in four broad areas: subjects of law are increasingly individuals and groups rather than just STATES; the scope of law has moved from an almost exclusive concern with political and strategic matters to economic, social, environmental and communication matters; the sources of law are now regarded as being community based rather than narrowly national and the role of the international lawyer has changed from exposition and interpretation of existing rules to a more dynamic 'policy-orientated jurisprudence'. According to adherents of this school (mainly, though not exclusively, US) this transition not only reflects reality, it also represents progress. However, many TRADITIONALISTS regard this optimism as both premature and misplaced. They contend that the persistence of the older view of consent-based law defining basic principles of coexistence within a society of states should not be underestimated (Bull, 1977).

The term is also used loosely to describe the legal system envisaged in the event of the establishment of WORLD GOVERNMENT.


## World order politics

Term popularized by Harvard political scientist Stanley Hoffman and which came to be used specifically to describe the FOREIGN POLICY outlook of the Carter administration in the United States (1976–80). On a general level, the term refers to underlying assumptions about how the world should be organized. Thus, CONTAINMENT was seen as a means not just to hem in the Soviet Union, but also through the use of US moral and material power to create a peaceful and lawful international environment. Revisionists subsequently argued that this particular vision of 'world order' was preoccupied with MILITARISM and rigid anti-COMMUNISM and therefore should be replaced by a REALIST view, which while stressing the primacy of the NATIONAL INTEREST, included within its ambit the moderating values of balance, restraint, DETENTE and MULTILATERAL DIPLOMACY. This perspective in turn was criticized as being exploitive, self-seeking and lacking a genuine moral dimension. US foreign policy, therefore, needed to divest itself of the narrower confines of Kissinger-style European REALPOLITIK and in the words of President Carter, create 'a more stable and just world order', and a 'framework of peace within which our ideals gradually can become a global reality'. The underlying assumptions of this putative Carter doctrine questioned the continued utility of military force as the key foreign policy instrument. The 'lessons of VIETNAM' – essentially that global CONTAINMENT was counterproductive – meant that 'world order' should replace 'national security' as the guiding premise of US DIPLOMACY. In addition, since the Soviet Union was a STATUS QUO power the United States should look beyond East–West relations and create a policy framework which would allow it to address global problems such as the promotion of HUMAN RIGHTS and the elimination or amelioration of poverty, hunger, racial divisions, ARMS RACES and NUCLEAR PROLIFERATION. The United States should not view change as necessarily inimical to its interests and should adopt a more flexible non-IDEOLOGICAL attitude to developments in the THIRD WORLD.

Without doubt, Hoffman's *Primacy or World Order* (1978) mapped out the philosophical foundations of this approach. This work was a sensitive critique of the Kissinger years and suggested that the 'diplomatic–strategic chessboard' which had once characterized world politics had now given way to new, pressing non-security imperatives which could only be grasped within the framework of COMPLEX INTERDEPENDENCE. Foreign policy had thus become 'the external dimension of the universally dominant concern for economic development and social welfare' (p. 113). The new policy therefore called for 'moderation plus'; that is, an awareness of the multi-faceted requirements of complex interdependence plus the compromise and restraint inherent in the traditional realist approach. However, according to Melanson (1983) it should be noted that although in broad outline the Carter administration accepted this view of contemporary INTERNATIONAL RELATIONS, Hoffman himself was sceptical about the eradication of REGIMES of social injustice being the centrepiece of a world order policy. Hoffman wrote that 'to make their elimination an explicit goal of world order would be slightly suicidal; any attempt at world order must initially try to enlist them. Their elimination can be a desired effect, not an open objective' (p. 187). Notwithstanding the ambiguities in the term 'slightly suicidal', Hoffman's reservations were largely ignored by the administration. The 'world order' perspective was replaced after 1980 by the REAGAN DOCTRINE.

## World politics

Unlike INTERNATIONAL POLITICS or INTERNATIONAL RELATIONS this term does not stress the primacy of intergovernmental relations and transactions. Instead its use indicates reference to a much wider range of ACTORS and activities than the WAR/PEACE/security/order scenarios involved in the classical STATE-CENTRED paradigms. The 'world politics perspective' is closely identified with the work of Keohane and Nye (especially *Transnational Relations and World Politics*, 1972) who argued that the state-centric view and its obsession with the interstate system provides an inadequate analytical framework for comprehending the contemporary world. This was not merely a question of semantics (the word INTERNATIONAL has long been thought of as unsatisfactory); it denoted a profound change in the structure, procedure and substance of the subject in the 1960s and 1970s. As the authors point out, given that many business enterprises have annual turnovers larger than the GNP of many voting members of the UN, and given that large private financial corporations can frustrate the financial policies of even powerful sovereign states, substantial modifications are needed to the original state-oriented model of international politics if those developments are to be grasped. The term 'world politics' is thus intended to expand the boundaries of the subject of inquiry, away from the narrow confines of interstate relations towards a recognition of global developments which are in effect beyond the range of the traditional approach. In this way it is closely allied to the WORLD ORDER and WORLD SOCIETY approaches in that it seeks to draw attention to the increasingly complicated network of relationships that now exist between non-governmental actors. Whereas international politics is concerned primarily with relationships between governments that involve conflicts of interest, world politics is characterized by a multiplicity of actor types and issue areas.

*See also*: MIXED ACTOR MODEL; PLURALISM

425

## World public opinion

Refers to the supposed existence of a global consensus as to what constitutes legitimate moral, legal or social behaviour in WORLD POLITICS. Apart from obvious cases such as GENOCIDE or the unrestricted use of chemical or bacteriological warfare, it is difficult to establish a core of widely shared patterns of values, norms and beliefs in an INTERNATIONAL SYSTEM characterized more by diversity than unity. INTERNATIONAL LAW does provide a rudimentary framework for the expression of international social norms but this does not, as such, represent the embodiment of world public opinion. General international norms exist (e.g. about HUMAN RIGHTS, SELF-DETERMINATION or AGGRESSION) but formulations of them are hedged about with ambiguities and inconsistencies. The incompleteness of the international political system, which is to say its STATE-CENTRIC character, is a severe limitation on the development of anything other than a vague humanitarianism which is difficult to translate into practical POLICY-MAKING. However, difficult as it may be to codify, most governments are sensitive to outside opinion about their policies, although they are not equally sensitive to all sources of opinion. Gauging the likely response of the international community to a proposed action is part of the DECISION-MAKERS' function but if achieving or defending their declared objectives is regarded as vital, global opinion, however vociferously expressed, is likely to be ignored. National imperatives are prone to dominate as they clearly have in the policies of the Republic of South Africa since 1948. 'World public opinion', then, is at best an elusive concept and should be approached with caution in FOREIGN POLICY analysis.

## World society

A challenging, if controversial, body of literature has emerged over the last twenty years under the rubric of the World Society Perspective. The perspective is derived from the writings of the Australian diplomat/scholar John W. Burton. In a series of books and articles of which *Systems, States, Diplomacy and Rules* (1968) and *World Society* (1972) are the most important, Burton has sought to advance his ideas about WORLD POLITICS and his criticism of more traditionally conceived approaches. Probably the best single volume treatment of this perspective is the collection of essays dedicated to Burton, *Conflict in World Society* (Banks 1984).

With remarkable prescience, Burton arrived at a set of conclusions about the redundancy of the state-centred or STATE-CENTRIC approach at approximately the same time as the US PLURALISTS were beginning to emphasize the significance of TRANSNATIONAL and TRANSGOVERNMENTAL ACTORS and processes. Burton labelled the traditional paradigm the BILLIARD BALL MODEL and he contrasted it with a three-dimensional cobweb model which he argued should replace it. By using the analogy of the billiard table Burton emphasized the way in which concepts such as SOVEREIGNTY seemed to suggest a hard and fast division between domestic politics on the one hand and world politics on the other. The billiard ball also emphasized the idea of territoriality as an attribute of state-centred approaches, Burton argued. Emphasizing the importance of transactions amongst a complex of actors, Burton suggested that traditional 'maps' were irrelevant and that the three-dimensional cobweb idea was more isomorphic with an increasingly complex world politics. These ideas owed a great deal to the pioneering work of Karl Deutsch, although unlike Deutsch, Burton did not immediately seek rigorous empirical testing of his ideas.

In earlier works Burton had sought to repudiate the concept of POWER as a central organizing idea in world politics. He subsequently linked the billiard ball model and power together in these later works by suggesting that the latter is an attribute of the former. Moreover in the view of Burton, and many of those who have followed him, over-emphasis upon power leads to what are termed 'self-defeating' strategies based upon such coercive instruments as DETER-RENCE and ideas about power 'balances'. Burton has for this reason become associated with non-coercive, cooperative approaches to problems of CONFLICT and this has led some of his critics to dub him an IDEALIST or 'neo-idealist'. Certainly, by repudiating power so totally Burton and his followers have denied themselves access to a rich vein of modern scholarship which has attempted a new and better understanding of one of the most contested, but important, concepts in world politics.

The World Society literature remains a fascinating, if flawed, field of analysis. Burton is without question one of the most challenging social theorists writing in the field. His refusal to be bound by the conventional canons of academic scholarship has left him free to mix analysis and prescription, fact and value, theory and practice in a way which few others would have the inclination or imagination to attempt.

### Worst-case analysis

Sometimes rendered as Worst-case Assumptions, Worst-case forecasting or Worst-case thinking. Worst-case analysis is a DEFINITION OF THE SITUATION that is applied in military–security policy-making and, in particular in DEFENCE planning. It rests upon a SCENARIO that takes the most pessimistic assumptions and estimates, both of CAPABILITIES and intentions, of a putative adversary. Having taken such a pessimistic view the ANALYSIS proceeds to sitpulate a series of responses that are perceived to meet the intitial position. To this extent worst-case analysis can lead to the SELF-FULFILLING PROPHECY dynamic. In the sixth chapter of his 1979 study of ETHNO-CENTRISM, Ken Booth argues that what he calls the 'operating principle' of worst case analysis is: 'when in doubt, think the worst' (p. 126). For Booth the perceptual framework for the worst case analyst is the 'inherently bad faith model'. Less critically perhaps, worst case analysis can be seen as a development of the desire to insure prudentially for an uncertain future. As a result it stimulates the tendency to constantly allow a margin of error or safety in estimating adversaries' intentions and capabilities. Gwyn Prins (1983) argues that worst case analysts become preoccupied with capabilities rather than intentions in this regard. Capability analysis certainly produces what can be seen as 'hard data about the adversary, whereas intention analysis is much more prone to conjecture and speculation.

It should not be thought that worst-case analysis is only stimulated by the kind of psychological mind set discussed above. Politicians, strategists and senior military figures may use worst case analysis to manipulate public and ELITE support for greater and greater amounts of defence spending by constantly bidding up the size and magnitude of the adversaries' threat.

### WTO

An acronym for the Warsaw Treaty Organization, or WARSAW PACT.

# X

## X

*Nom de plume* of George F. Kennan, American diplomat credited with formulating the doctrine of CONTAINMENT. Kennan had been a high ranking envoy in the US embassy in Moscow and in his famous 'long telegram' had warned Washington of the fanaticism of Soviet IDEOLOGY and of its unswerving commitment to world REVOLUTION. In 1947, as head of the State Department's policy-planning staff he enlarged on this and published, under the pseudonym 'X', 'The Sources of Soviet Conduct', in the influential journal *Foreign Affairs* (pp. 566–82). The article contained an ominous appraisal of Soviet intentions written from a REALIST perspective and was clearly designed to alert US DECISION-MAKERS to the dangers posed by the Soviet doctrine of the inevitablity of CONFLICT with capitalist powers and the expansive nature of Soviet FOREIGN POLICY. He concluded that 'In these circumstances it is clear that the main element of any United States policy toward the Soviet Union must be that of a long-term, patient but firm and vigilant containment of Russian expansive tendencies.' It declares that what was needed was 'the adroit and vigilant application of COUNTERFORCE at a series of constantly shifting geographical and political points, corresponding to the shifts and manoevres of Soviet policy'. This assessment crystallized into the main intellectual foundation of post-war US policy towards the Soviet Union and was specifically incorporated into the TRUMAN DOCTRINE and the policy of CONTAINMENT.

Kennan (1984, p. 16) subsequently disavowed the policies which his article inspired and claimed that his advice was misinterpreted and taken out of context:

> . . . I did not believe . . . that there was the slightest danger of a Soviet military attack against the major western powers or Japan. This was, in other words, a political danger, not a military one. And the historical record bears out that conclusion. But for reasons I have never fully understood, by 1949 a great many people in Washington – in the Pentagon, the White House and even the Department of State – seemed to have come to the conclusion that there was a real danger of the Soviets unleashing, in the fairly near future, what would have been World War Three.

Nevertheless, the doctrine of containment and 'X''s role in it, has remained a controversial one in contemporary reviews of US COLD WAR policies. It seems clear in retrospect that the 'X' article served to capture the public imagination by providing an explanation for a policy already adopted. In this sense, 'X''s long telegram may have been the real genesis of containment.

## Xenophobia

Fear, dislike, distrust or intolerance of foreigners either as individuals or groups. It is closely associated with extreme forms of NATIONALISM and ETHNOCENTRISM and often manifests itself in expressions of hostility towards outsiders. This can take the form of condemning whole groups (anti-Semitism), NATIONS (anti-English) or even continents (anti-American, anti-

European). It is often linked with ISOLA-TIONISM and in this sense xenophobia was the underlying emotion which spawned the policies of China and Japan (with good reason; *see*: TREATY PORTS) towards Europeans prior to the twentieth century. To a certain extent all STATES are tinged with xenophobia but the degree to which it intrudes into POLICY-MAKING varies. During wartime it is deliberately encouraged and fostered by governments anxious to maintain social cohesion and direct all attention towards the WAR effort. In peacetime, xenophobic tendencies can be manipulated to provide scapegoats for policy failures, both internally and externally. In this connection the UNHC Round Table on Refugees, Victims of Xenophobia held in Geneva in 1984 warned that this was a growing, rather than a diminishing problem in WORLD POLITICS, especially in the advanced industrial countries (AIC's) ' . . . the phenomenon of xenophobia is on the upsurge, more visible in Western industrialised societies where xenophobic tendencies contrast with previously tolerant attitudes to foreigners and where liberal admission policies in the past have permitted the growth of sizeable populations'. This tendency has been especially noticable in the EC countries which collectively employ over 15 million *Gastarbeiter* (guest workers) mainly in agriculture, services and industry. Apart from legal disputes between employers and employees, immigrant workers often face hostility and abuse from indigenous inhabitants anxious to protect their own livelihoods and cultural values.

In its most extreme form, xenophobia often reflects a paranoid view of the outside world. Hitler and Stalin were both xenophobic, and this was clearly reflected in their policies. One of the most blatant recent examples of state directed paranoic xenophobia was General Amin's expulsion of 50,000 Ugandan Asians in 1972 to the obvious detriment of his domestic economy and his international standing.

# Y

## Yalta conference

An agreement reached in the Crimea in February in 1945 between Roosevelt, Stalin and Churchill concerning the future conduct of the WAR and the shape of the post-war INTERNATIONAL ORDER. In relation to the war it was agreed that Germany should SURRENDER unconditionally, REPARATIONS should be extracted, WAR CRIMES should be punished and that the Soviet Union would join the war against Japan within three months of German's defeat. Regarding the post-war order, the Polish and Soviet borders would move westwards to the Oder–Neisse and Curzon lines at the territorial expense of Germany, Germany itself was to be divided into four zones of occupation and an Inter-Allied Control Council was established for Berlin. In addition there was an agreement that the liberated STATES of Eastern Europe should hold free democratic elections. The Conference also made important decisions regarding the proposed UNITED NATIONS ORGANIZATION, in particular that the GREAT POWERS would be given the power of VETO. in the SECURITY COUNCIL, and that the Soviet Union would receive three memberships (the Soviet Union, Byleorussia and Ukraine).

Since no formal peace TREATY was signed at the end of the Second World War, the Yalta agreements formed the basis of the post-war European settlement, and ever after have been the subject of considerable dispute. It has been alleged that Roosevelt, in his anxiety to appease the Soviet Union, in effect sold out most of Eastern Europe to COMMUNIST domina-

tion; that Yalta gave Stalin a position of dominance which otherwise he may not have achieved. On the other hand, it could be said that the West conceded very little since the Soviet armies were already firmly emplaced and that the most that could be achieved was some form of MULTILATERAL agreement concerning how this POWER should be exercised. The Yalta agreement, especially provisions relating to the post-war frontiers in Europe, became a matter of bitter dispute during the early years of the COLD WAR and continued to beset German politics up to and beyond OST-POLITIK. The absence of a specific PEACE treaty in Europe in 1945 has led to a complex and somewhat ambiguous legal position with regard to the status of Germany. In effect, three Germanies are recognized in INTERNATIONAL LAW: the Federal Republic (West Germany), the Democratic Republic (East Germany) and the Germany that existed in 1937. At the Potsdam conference, six months after Yalta, the German/Polish frontier along the rivers Oder and Neisse were referred to as 'provisional' since 'the final delimitation of the western frontier of Poland should await the peace settlement'. The events of 1989 in East Germany, especially the call for German unification, have raised potentially explosive issues concerning the legitimacy of the Yalta agreement and more especially regarding the possible transfer of territories from Poland (and by implication, from the Soviet Union) to recreate the last internationally accepted definition of Germany, i.e. the 1937 territorial entity.

## Yaoundé

Yaoundé, Cameroun, gave its name to the 1963 agreement between the original six states of the EEC and seventeen associated African states plus the Malagasy Republic. At the inception of the EEC on 1 January 1958 a number of the member states still had colonial territories and dependencies. It was clearly necessary to redefine their relationship with the Community both in economic terms and in constitutional convention, given the gathering trend towards the granting of INDEPENDENCE to colonial peoples and territories. After a transition period it was decided to establish a legal framework, via the process known within the Community as association, wherein the dependencies could enjoy continued access to markets within the Six. For the purposes of the NEGOTIATIONS the two parties were therefore regarded as unified ACTORS and the term 'associated African and Malagasy states' were referred to by the acronym AASM.

Yaoundé protected the AASM from the common external TARIFF of the Community and enabled them to gain access to a large and dynamic market. Although the AASM states were supposed to grant reciprocal treatment to EEC EXPORTS, they were allowed to continue or institute protective TARIFFS to raise revenue, protect infant industries or otherwise further their economic development. Additionally they received concessionary AID, mainly in the form of grants, from the Community under Yaoundé. The convention established a number of institutions including a council, parliamentary conference and court of ARBITRATION.

Yaoundé was renewed in 1969 but the putative membership of the United Kingdom precipitated the need to redefine the relationship with the AASM since the United Kingdom was likely to take a large number of overseas territories into the Community in its wake. Even allowing for the agreed exclusion of Asia, the number of potential African associates exceeded the existing membership of Yaoundé. This arrangement was, accordingly, replaced by the LOMÉ CONVENTION in 1975 as the legal framework for this system of association. *See also*; ACP

## Yen power

A phrase indicating Japan's remarkable post-war rise to SUPERPOWER status founded on the dynamism of its economic power alone. Unlike the other superpowers Japan is not a first order military POWER. Under its constitution, imposed by the United States after the Second World War, Japan is forbidden to maintain a 'war potential'. In fact Japan does possess a military dimension and recently under US direction has been developing, in particular, its naval power; but its defence budget is even now less than 1 per cent of national income compared with 6 per cent in the United States and 15 per cent in the Soviet Union. Japan's influence in WORLD POLITICS (dramatically demonstrated at the funeral of Emperor Hirohito in February 1989 where a record 163 countries were represented) is based on sheer economic power alone. In 1989 it has been estimated that Japan will overtake the United States as the world's largest donor of overseas financial AID. In a five-year AID plan Japan intends to give nearly £28 billion to development projects on a global scale. Thus, during a period of financial retrenchment in the West, Tokyo seems poised to become the financial centre and major instigator of global economic development. In 1988 the Japanese announced an International Cooperation Initiative which was specifically designed to heighten Japan's global profile through increased financial support for UN peace projects, through more extensive cultural exchanges and through a general hike in overseas aid programmes. The overall financial dominance of Japan is viewed as mixed blessing by the West. In the United States, for example, Japan is seen to be its strongest ally and trading partner as well as its greatest creditor and its most feared economic competitor. The EC, too, is wary of increased Japanese economic penetration and is designing strategies to counter it. In the THIRD WORLD, on the other hand, especially in Africa and South America, the new donor role of Japan is generally welcomed as an alternative to the somewhat dubious benefits of close association with the other superpowers. Clearly, if the twenty-first century is to be the Pacific century then Japan, well placed as it is on its GEOPOLITICAL rim, is destined to be its most powerful, albeit non-military, component.

# Z

## Zero–sum

A term derived from GAME THEORY. It refers to the fact that the numerical value of the 'pay-offs' add up to zero. It is, therefore, held to represent in mathematical terms a situation of pure CONFLICT where a gain to one party is a loss to the other.

The term is also used outside the strict confines of game theory. Students of CONFLICT analysis will often use it to characterize a particular PERCEPTION held by participants of the nature of their conflict. CONFLICT RESOLUTION may be made more difficult if this type of perception appears to be influential and deeply held.

## Zimmern, A. E.

First holder of the first chair of INTERNATIONAL POLITICS in the world, the Woodrow Wilson chair at the University of Wales, Aberystwyth in 1919. As with other contemporaries who share the distinction of founding the academic study of INTERNATIONAL RELATIONS (notably Gilbert Murray and G. Lowes Dickinson) Zimmern was a classicist who steadfastly believed in the latent HARMONY OF INTERESTS of STATES and in the inevitability of progress. Best known for his belief in the application of the 'rule of law' to WORLD POLITICS through the principle of the 'hue and cry'. A fervent supporter of the LEAGUE OF NATIONS and a founder member of the Royal Institute of International Affairs, Zimmern's IDEALISM was brilliantly savaged by one of his successors at the University of Wales (Carr, 1946). Zimmern's importance in the study owes less to the enduring value of his ideas (which at this distance seem simplistic and hopelessly optimistic) than to his lifelong concern to establish a secure academic base for inquiry into world politics. At Oxford, where he became the first Montague Burton professor of international relations in 1930, he was responsible for introducing international politics (as distinct from diplomatic history) into the undergraduate curriculum. He also succeeded in popularizing the study in London, Geneva and in the United States, which he regarded as the world's first 'free' GREAT POWER and which he hoped fervently would pave the way to INTERNATIONALISM and the collective abolition of WAR as an instrument of state policy.

# SELECT BIBLIOGRAPHY

The purpose of the bibliography is two-fold: first to identify and acknowledge sources used in the text, and secondly to enable the reader to explore and expand both the scope and depth of the explanations given in the entries. It is 'select' in the sense that a more comprehensive bibliography would, we suspect, require a complete volume of its own.

## Bibliography

Abercrombie, N., Hill, S. and Turner, B.S. (1984), *Dictionary of Sociology* (Penguin, Harmondsworth).

Akehurst, M. (1984), *A Modern Introduction to International Law*, sixth edition (George Allen & Unwin).

Allison, G., Carnesale, A. and Nye, J. Jnr (eds) (1985), *Hawks, Doves and Owls* (W.W. Norton, New York).

Allison, G.T. (1971), *Essence of Decision: Explaining the Cuban Missile Crisis* (Little, Brown, Boston).

Almond, G. A. (1966), *The American People and Foreign Policy* (Secker & Warburg, London).

Alperovitz, G. (1985), *Atomic Diplomacy: Hiroshima and Potsdam* (Penguin, New York).

Ambrose, S. (1985), *Rise to Globalism*, fourth revised edition (Penguin, New York).

Andrew, C. and Dilks, D. (eds) (1984), *The Missing Dimension: Governments and Intelligence Communities in the Twentieth Century* (Macmillan, London).

Angell, N. (1910), *The Great Illusion* (Heinemann, London).

Archer, C. (1983), *International Organizations* (Allen & Unwin, London).

Armitage, M.J. and Mason, R.A. (1985), *Air Power in the Nuclear Age, 1945–84: Theory and Practice* (Macmillan, London).

Aron, R. (1975), *The Imperial Republic: The United States and the World, 1945–73*, tr. F. Jellinek (Weidenfeld & Nicolson, London).

Aron, R. (1966), *Peace and War: A Theory of International Relations* (Weidenfeld & Nicolson, London).

Ashley, R.K. (1984), 'The Poverty of Neorealism', *International Organization*, **38** (Spring).

Austin, J. (1954), *The Province of Jurisprudence Determined* (Weidenfeld & Nicolson, London, first published 1832).

Bailey, S.D. (1987), *War and Conscience in the Nuclear Age* (Macmillan, London).

Baldwin, D.A. (1971), 'Money and Power', *Journal of Politics*, **33** (August).

Baldwin, D.A. (1974), 'Power Analysis and World Politics: New Trends versus Old Tendencies', *World Politics*, **31**, pp. 161–94 (January).

Baldwin, D.A. (1979), *Power Analysis and World Politics: New Trends versus Old Tendencies*, **31** (2) (January), pp. 161–95.

Baldwin, D.A. (1985), *Economic Statecraft* (Princeton University, Princeton).

Banks, M. (ed.) (1984), *Conflict in World Society* (Harvester Wheatsheaf, Hemel Hempstead).

Barber, J. (1979), 'Economic Sanctions as a Policy Instrument', *International Affairs*, 55 (3).

Barber, J. (1985), *The Presidential Character*, third edition (Prentice Hall, Englewood Cliffs).

Barber, J. and Smith, M. (eds) (1974), *The Nature of Foreign Policy: A Reader* (Open University Press, Milton Keynes).

Barnet, R.J. and Müller, R.E. (1974), *Global Reach: The Power of the Multinational Corporations* (Simon & Schuster, New York).

Barry, Brian and Hardin, Russell (eds) (1982), *Rational Man and Irrational Society* (Sage Publications, Beverly Hills).

Barston, R.P. (1988), *Modern Diplomacy* (Longman, London).

Bartlett, C.J. (1972), *The Long Retreat: A Short History of British Defence Policy, 1945–70* (Macmillan, London).

Beales, A.C.F. (1931), *The History of Peace: A Short Account of the Organised Movements for International Peace* (Bell, London).

Beard, C.A. and Smith, G.H.E. (1934), *The Idea of the National Interest: An Analytical Study in American Foreign Policy* (Macmillan, New York).

Beaufre, A. (1965), *Deterrence and Strategy* (Faber, London).

Beitz, C.R. (1979), *Political Theory and International Relations* (Princeton University Press, Princeton).

Bell, C. (1971), *The Conventions of Crisis: A Study in Diplomatic Management* (RIIA, London).

Beloff, M. (1977), *Foreign Policy and the Democratic Process* (Greenwood Press, Westport, Conn).

Bennett, A. Leroy (1988), *International Organizations: Principles and Issues*, fourth edition (Prentice Hall, Englewood Cliffs).

Bentham, J. (1970), *Introduction to the Principles of Morals and Legislation*, J.H. Burns and H.L.A. Hart (eds) (Oxford University Press, London, first published 1780).

Berki, R.N. (1971), 'On Marxian thought and the problem of International Relations', *World Politics*, October.

Berridge, G.R. (1987), *International Politics: States, Power and Conflict Since 1945* (Harvester Wheatsheaf, Hemel Hempstead).

Bertalanffy, L. von (1967), 'General System Theory', in N.J. Demereth and R.A. Peterson (eds), *System, Change and Conflict* (Free Press, New York, pp. 115–29).

Best, G. (1980), *Humanity in Warfare: the Modern History of the International Law of Armed Conflicts* (Weidenfeld & Nicolson, London).

Betts, R. (1982), *Surprise Attack* (Brookings Institution, Washington DC).

Betts, R.K. (1987), *Nuclear Blackmail and Nuclear Balance* (Brookings Institution, Washington DC).

Binder, L. (1958), 'The Middle East as a Subordinate International System', *World Politics*, **10** (3), 408–29.

Bobbitt, P., Freedman, L. and Treverton G. (1989), *U.S. Nuclear Strategy: A Reader* (Macmillan).

Bodin, J. (1955), *Six Books of the Commonwealth* (abridged and tr. M.J. Tooley) (Blackwell, Oxford).

Booth, K. (1979), *Strategy and Ethnocentrism* (Croom Helm, London).

Booth, K. (1985), *Law, Force and Diplomacy at Sea* (Allen & Unwin, London).

Boulding, K.E. (1956), *The Image: Knowledge in Life and Society* (University of Michigan Press, Ann Arbor).

Boulding, K.E. (1962), *Conflict and Defense: A General Theory* (Harper & Row, New York).

# BIBLIOGRAPHY

Boulding, K. (1975), 'National Images and International Systems', in W.D. Copley and C.W. Kegley Jr (eds), *Analyzing International Relations* (Praeger, New York).

Boyd, A. (1971), *Fifteen Men on a Powder Keg: a History of the UN Security Council* (Methuen, London).

Bozeman, A.B. (1960), *Politics and Culture in International History* (Princeton University Press, Princeton).

Braybrooke, D. and Lindblom, C.E. (1963), *A Strategy of Decision* (Free Press, New York).

Brecher, M. (1963), 'International Relations and Asian Studies: the Subordinate State System of Southern Asia', *World Politics*, **15** (2), 213–35.

Brecher, M. (1972), *The Foreign Policy System of Israel* (Oxford University Press, London).

Brierly, J.L. (1958), *The Basis of Obligation in International Law and Other Papers*, H. Lauterpacht and C.H.M. Waldcock (eds) (Clarendon Press, Oxford).

Brierly, J.L. (1963), *The Law of Nations: An Introduction to the International Law of Peace* (Clarendon Press, Oxford).

Brodie, B. (1965), *Strategy in the Missile Age* (Princeton University Press, Princeton).

Bronfenbrenner, U. (1961), 'The Mirror-Image in Soviet–American Relations: A Psychologist's Report', *Journal of Social Issues*, **XVII** (3), 45–57.

Brown, L. *et al.* (1989), *State of the World 1989* (W.W. Norton, New York).

Brownlie, I. (1963), *International Law and the Use of Force by States* (Oxford University Press, London).

Brownlie, I. (1967), *Basic Documents in International Law* (Clarendon Press, London).

Brownlie, I. (1973), *Principles of Public International Law* (Clarendon Press, London).

Brownlie, I. (ed.) (1981), *Basic Documents on Human Rights* (Clarendon Press, Oxford).

Buchan, A. (1966), *War in Modern Society* (Watts, London).

Bull, H. (1961), *The Control of the Arms Race: Disarmament and Arms Control in the Missile Age* (Weidenfeld & Nicolson, London).

Bull, H. and Watson, A. (eds) (1984), *The Expansion of International Society* (Clarendon Press, Oxford).

Bull, H. (1966a), 'Grotian Conceptions of International Society', in Butterfield, H. and Wight, M. (eds) *Diplomatic Investigations* (Allen & Unwin, London).

Bull, H. (1966b), 'International Theory: The Case for a Classical Approach', *World Politics*, **18**, 361–77.

Bull, H. (1977), *The Anarchical Society: A Study of Order in World Politics* (Macmillan, London).

Bull, H. (1979a), 'Recapturing the Just War for Political Theory', *World Politics*, **31** (4) (July).

Bull, H. (1979b), 'Natural Law and International Relations', *British Journal of International Studies*, **5** (2) (July).

Bull, H. (ed.) (1984), *Intervention in World Politics* (Oxford University Press, London).

Bundy, McGeorge *et al.* (1984), 'Nuclear Weapons and the Atlantic Alliance', in F. Blackaby *et al.* (eds), *No-First-Use* (Taylor and Francis, London, pp. 29–43).

Burton, J.W. (1965), *International Relations: A General Theory* (Cambridge University Press, Cambridge).

Burton, J.W. (1968), *Systems, States, Diplomacy and Rules* (Cambridge University Press, Cambridge).

Burton, J.W. (1969), *Conflict and Communication* (Macmillan, London).

Burton, J.W. (1972), *World Society* (Cambridge University Press, Cambridge).

Butterfield H. (1953), *Christianity, Diplomacy and War* (Epworth Press, London).

Butterfield, H. and Wight, M. (eds) (1966), *Diplomatic Investigations: Essays in the Theory of International Politics* (Allen & Unwin, London).

Buzan, B. (1983), *People, States and Fear: The National Security Problem in International Relations* (Harvester Wheatsheaf, Hemel Hempstead).

Buzan, B. (1987), *An Introduction to Strategic Studies: Military Technology and International Relations* (Macmillan Press for the International Institute for Strategic Studies, London).

Calvert, P. (1984), *Revolution and International Politics* (Frances Pinter, London).

Calvert, P. (1986), *The Foreign Policy of New States* (St Martin's Press, New York).

Calvocoressi, P. (1987), *World Politics Since 1945*, fifth edition (Longman, London).

Calvocoressi, P. and Wint, G. (1974), *Total War* (Penguin, Harmondsworth).

Carr, E.H. (1946), *The Twenty Years' Crisis, 1919–1939* (Macmillan, London), originally published 1939.

Choucri, N. and North R. (1975), *Nations in Conflict* (W.H. Freeman & Co., San Francisco).

Clark, G. and Sohn, L.B. (1960), *World Peace Through World Law* (Harvard University Press, Cambridge MA).

Clark, I. (1980), *Reform and Resistance in the International Order* (Cambridge University Press, Cambridge).

Clark, I. (1988), 'Making Sense of Sovereignty', *Review of International Studies*, **14** (4) (October).

Claude, I.L. (1962), *Power and International Relations* (Random House, New York).

Claude, I.L. (1971), *Swords into Ploughshares: The Problems and Prospects of International Organization*, fourth edition (Random House, New York).

Claude, I.L. (1986a), *American Approaches to World Affairs* (University Press of America, Charlottesville).

Claude, I.L. (1986b), 'Myths About the State', *Review of International Studies* **12** (1) (January).

Clausewitz, C.M. von (1968), *On War* (Introduction A. Rapoport) (Penguin Classics, Harmondsworth).

Cobban, A. (1969), *The Nation State and National Self-Determination* (Collins, London).

Cohen, R. (1981), *International Politics: The Rules of the Game* (Longman, London).

Corbett, P.E. (1956), *Morals, Law and Power in International Relations* (J.R. and D. Hayes Foundation, Los Angeles).

Council on Environmental Quality and the US Department of State (1982), *The Global 2000 Report to the President: Entering the Twenty-first Century* (Penguin, Harmondsworth).

Cox, R. (1979), 'Ideologies of the New International Economic Order: reflections on some recent literature', *International Organization*, 33 (2), 257–302.

Crabb, C.V. (1965), *The Elephants and the Grass, A Study of Nonalignment* (Praeger, New York).

Dahl, R. (1961a), *Who Governs?* (Yale University Press, New Haven).

Dahl, R. (1961b), 'The Behavioural Approach in Political Science: Epitaph for a Monument to a Successful Protest'. *American Political Science Review*, 55 (4), pp. 763–72 (December).

Dahl, R. (1984), *Modern Political Analysis* fourth edition (Prentice Hall, Englewood Cliffs).

Davies, James C. (1969), 'The J curve of rising and declining satisfactions as a cause of some great revolutions and contained rebellion' in H.D. Graham and T.R. Gurr (eds), *The History of Violence in America* (New York).

De Conde, A. (ed.) (1978), *Encyclopedia of American Foreign Policy: Studies of the Principal Movements and Ideas* (Scribner, New York).

Deutsch, K. (1953), *Nationalism and Social Communications* (MIT Press, Cambridge).

Deutsch, K. (1963), *The Nerves of Government* (Free Press, New York).

Deutsch, K.W. (1968), *The Analysis of International Relations* (Prentice Hall, Englewood Cliffs).

Deutsch, K. and Singer, J.D. (1964), 'Multipolar Systems and International Stability', *World Politics*, **16** (April).

# BIBLIOGRAPHY

Dickinson, G.L. (1916), *The European Anarchy* (Allen & Unwin, London).

Dickinson, G.L. (1926), *The International Anarchy* (Allen & Unwin, London).

Donelan, M. (ed.) (1978), *The Reason of States: A Study in International Political Theory* (George Allen & Unwin, London).

Dougherty, J.E. and Pfaltzgraff, R.L. (1981), *Contending Theories of International Relations* (Harper and Row, New York).

Doxey, M. (1971), *Economic Sanctions and International Enforcement* (Oxford University Press, London).

Dunant, H. (1947), *A Memory of Solferino* (Cassell, London).

Easton, D. (1969), 'The New Revolution in Political Science', *American Political Science Review*, 58 (4), pp. 1051–61 (December).

Edwardes, M. (1962), *Asia in the Balance* (Penguin, Harmondsworth).

Evans, G. (1981), 'All States are Equal, but. . .', *Review of International Studies*, 7.

Eysenck, H.J. (1954), *The Psychology of Politics* (RKP, London).

Faber, M. (1984), 'Island Microstates: Problems of Viability', *The Round Table*, 292.

Falk, R.A. (1970), *The Status of Law in International Society* (Princeton University Press, Princeton).

Falk, R.A. (1971) *This Endangered Planet* (Randon House, New York).

Falk, R.A. (1975), *A Study of Future Worlds* (Free Press, New York).

Farrell, R.B. (1966), *Approaches to Comparative and International Politics* (Northwestern University Press, Evanston).

Fink, C.F. and Boulding, E. (eds) (1972), 'Peace Research in Transition: A Symposium', *Journal of Conflict Resolution*, Special Issue, XVI (4).

Fleiss, P.J. (1966), *Thucydides and the Politics of Bipolarity* (Louisiana State University Press, Baton Rouge).

Forsythe, D.P. (1977), *Humanitarian Politics: the International Committee of the Red Cross* (Johns Hopkins University Press, Baltimore).

Forsyth, M.G., Keens-Soper, M. and Savigear, P. (eds) (1970), *The Theory of International Relations: The State of War* (Allen & Unwin, London).

Forsyth, M. (1979), 'Thomas Hobbes and the External Relations of States', *British Journal of International Studies* 5 (3) (October).

Fox, W.T.R. (1944), *The Super-Powers: the United States, Britain and the Soviet Union – their Responsibility for the Peace* (Harcourt, Brace, New York).

Frankel, J. (1963), *The Making of Foreign Policy: An Analysis of Decision Making* (Oxford University Press, Oxford).

Frankel, J. (1970), *The National Interest* (Pall Mall and Macmillan, London).

Freedman, L. (1981), *The Evolution of Nuclear Strategy* (Macmillan, London).

Freedman, L. (1988), *Britain and the Falklands War* (Blackwell, London).

Freedman, L. *et al.* (1986), *Terrorism and International Order* (Routledge, London).

Gaddis, J.L. (1983), 'Containment: Its Past and Future', in C.W. Kegley, Jr and E.R. Wittkopf (eds), *Perspectives on American Foreign Policy* (St Martins Press, New York).

Gallie, W.B. (1978), *Philosophers of Peace and War: Kant, Clausewitz, Marx, Engels and Tolstoy* (Cambridge University Press, Cambridge).

Garnett, J.C. (1984), *Commonsense and the Theory of International Politics* (Macmillan, London).

GATT (1979), *The Tokyo Round of Multilateral Trade Negotiations* (GATT, Geneva).

Geldenhuys, D. (1984), *The Diplomacy of Isolation: South African Foreign Policy Making* (Macmillan, Johannesburg).

Gellner, E. (1983), *Nations and Nationalism* (Blackwell, Oxford).

George, A. and George, J. (1964), *Woodrow Wilson & Colonel House: A Personality Study* (Dover, New York).

George, S. (1988), *A Fate Worst than Debt* (Penguin, Harmondsworth).

Gilpin, R. (1975), *U.S. Power and the Multinational Corporation* (Basic Books, New York).

Gilpin, R. (1981), *War and Change in World Politics* (Cambridge University Press, Cambridge).

Gilpin, R. (1985), 'The Politics of Transnational Economic Relations', in R. Maghroori and B. Ramberg (eds) *Globalism Versus Realism: International Relations' Third Debate* (Westview Press, Boulder, Colorado).

Gilpin, R. (1987), *The Political Economy of International Relations* (Princeton University Press, Princeton).

Graham, General (1982), *High Frontier: A New National Strategy* (Heritage Foundation, Washington DC).

Grosser, A. (1980), *The Western Alliance: European–American Relations Since 1945* (foreword by Stanley Hoffman) (Macmillan, London).

Grotius, H. (1949), *The Law of War and Peace (De Jure Belli ac Pacis)* tr. L.R. Loomis, introduction P.E. Corbett (Walter J. Black, New York).

Guicciardini, F. (1567), *Storia d'Italia (1573)* (Torretino, Florence).

Gulick, E.V. (1967), *Europe's Classical Balance of Power* (Norton, New York, first published 1955).

Haas, E.B. (1953), 'The Balance of Power: Prescription, Concept, or Propaganda', *World Politics*, 5 (July).

Haas, E.B. (1958), *The Uniting of Europe* (Stevens, London; Stanford University Press, Stanford).

Haas, E.B. (1964), *Beyond the Nation State: Functionalism and International Organization* (Stanford University Press, Stanford).

Halperin, M. (1963), *Limited War in the Nuclear Age* (John Wiley, New York).

Halperin, M.H. (1974), *Bureaucratic Politics and Foreign Policy* (The Brookings Institution, Washington DC).

Hansen, R.D. (1979), *Beyond the North–South Stalemate* (McGraw Hill, New York).

Hardin, G. (1977), 'The Tragedy of the Commons', in G. Hardin and J. Baden (eds), *Managing the Commons* (Freeman, San Francisco).

Hayter, T. (1971), *Aid as Imperialism* (Penguin, Baltimore).

Hermann, C.F. (1969), 'International Crisis as a Situational Variable', in J.N. Rosenau (ed.), *International Politics and Foreign Policy* (Free Press, New York), pp. 409–21.

Hermann, C.F. (ed.) (1972), *International Crises: Insights from Behavioural Research* (Free Press, New York).

Herz, J.H. (1950), 'Idealist Internationalism and the Security Dilemma', *World Politics*, 2 (2) (January).

Herz, J.H. (1951), *Political Realism and Political Idealism* (Chicago University Press, Chicago).

Herz, J.H. (1959), *International Politics in the Atomic Age* (Columbia University Press, New York).

Herz, J.H. (1957), 'Rise and Demise of the Territorial State', *World Politics*, 9.

Higgins, R. (1978), 'Conceptual Thinking about the Individual in International Law', *British Journal of International Studies*, 3 (1) (April).

Hinsley, F.H. (1963), *Power and the Pursuit of Peace: Theory and Practice in the History of Relations between States* (Cambridge University Press, Cambridge).

Hinsley, F.H. (1973), *Nationalism and the International System* (Hodder & Stoughton, London).

Hinsley, F.H. (1982), 'The Rise and Fall of the Modern International System', *Review of International Studies*, 8 (1) (January).

Hinsley, F.H. (1986), *Sovereignty* (Cambridge University Press, Cambridge).

Hobbes, T. (1965), *Leviathan* (introduction A.D. Lindsay) (Everyman edition, Dent, London).

Hobson, J.A. (1938), *Imperialism: A Study* (third edition) (Allen & Unwin, London, first published 1902).

Hoffman, S. (1965), *The State of War* (Pall Mall, London).

Hoffman, S. (1968), *Gulliver's Troubles, or the Setting of American Foreign Policy* (McGraw Hill, New York).

Hoffman, S. (1978), *Primacy or World Order: American Foreign Policy Since the Cold War* (McGraw Hill, New York).

Holbraad, C. (1970), *The Concert of Europe: A Study in German and British International Thought, 1815–1914* (Longman, Harlow).

Holbraad, C. (ed.) (1971), *Superpowers and World Order* (Australian National University Press, Canberra).

Holbraad, C. (1984), *Middle Powers in International Politics* (Macmillan, London).

Holloway, D. (1988/89), 'Gorbachev's New Thinking', *Foreign Affairs*, 68 (1).

Holsti, D. (1983), *International Politics: A Framework for Analysis*, fourth edition (Prentice Hall, Englewood Cliffs).

Holsti, K.J. (1985), *The Dividing Discipline: Hegemony and Diversity in International Theory* (Allen & Unwin, Boston).

Holsti, O.R. and Rosenau, J.N. (1984), *American Leadership in World Affairs: Vietnam and the Breakdown of Consensus* (Allen & Unwin, Boston).

Hopkins, R.F. and Mansbach, R.W. (1973), *Structures and Process in International Politics* (Harper and Row, New York).

Horowitz, D. (1969), *Imperialism and Revolution* (Allen Lane, London).

Howard, M. (1976), 'The Strategic Approach to International Relations', *British Journal of International Studies*, 2 (1) (April).

Howard, M. (1978), *War and the Liberal Conscience* (Temple Smith, London).

Howard, M. (1984), *The Causes of Wars* (Unwin, London).

Hsü, I.C.Y. (1960), *China's Entrance into the Family of Nations* (Harvard University Press, Cambridge, MA).

Huntington, S.P. (1973), 'Transnational Organisation in World Politics', *World Politics*, 25 (3) (August).

Iklé, F.C. (1964), *How Nations Negotiate* (Harper and Row, New York).

Jackson, R.H. (1986), 'Negative Sovereignty in sub-Saharan Africa', *Review of International Studies*, 12 (4) (October).

James, A. (1964), 'Power Politics', *Political Studies*, 12 (3) (October).

James, A. (1969), *The Politics of Peace-keeping* (Chatto and Windus, London).

James, A. (1973), *The Bases of International Order: Essays in Honour of C.A.W. Manning* (Oxford University Press, London).

James, A. (1978), 'International Society', *British Journal of International Studies*, 4 (2) (July).

James, A. (1984), 'Sovereignty: Ground Rule or Gibberish?', *Review of International Studies*, 10.

James, A. (1986), *Sovereign Statehood: The Basis of International Society* (Allen & Unwin, London).

Janis, I. (1972), *Victims of Groupthink* (Houghton Mifflin, Boston).

Jervis, R. (1976), *Perception and Misperception in International Politics* (Princeton University Press, Princeton).

Jervis, R. (1978), 'Co-operation Under the Security Dilemma', *World Politics*, 30 (2) (January).

Jervis, R. (1984), *The Illogic of American Nuclear Strategy* (Cornell University Press, Ithaca).

Jervis, R. (1985), 'From Balance to Concert: A Study of International Security Co-operation', *World Politics*, 38 (1) (October).

Jones, R.E. (1981), 'The English School of International Relations: A Case for Closure', *Review of International Studies*, 7 (1) (January).

Kahn, H. (1960), *On Thermonuclear War* (Princeton University Press, Princeton).

Kaiser, K. (1968), *German Foreign Policy in Transition: Bonn between East and West* (Oxford University Press, London).

Kant, I. (1948), 'On Eternal Peace', tr. in Carl J. Friedrich, *Inevitable Peace* (Harvard University Press, Cambridge MA).

Kaplan, L.S. (1984), *The United States and NATO: The Formative Years* (Kentucky University Press, Lexington).

Kaplan, M.A. (1957), *System and Process in International Politics* (Wiley, New York).

Kaplan, M.A. and Katzenbach, N. de B. (1961), *The Political Foundations of International Law* (Wiley, New York).

Kaplan, M.A. (1966), 'The New Great Debate: Traditionalism vs. Science in International Relations', *World Politics*, October.

Kaufmann, W. (1989), 'The Requirements of Deterrence', in P. Bobbit *et al.*, *US Nuclear Strategy* (Macmillan, London), pp. 168–90.

Keens-Soper, M. (1978), 'The Practice of a States-System', in *The Reason of States*, M. Donelan (ed.) (Allen & Unwin, London), pp. 25–44.

Kegley, C.W. and Wittkopf, E.R. (1988), *The Global Agenda: Issues and Perspectives* (Random House, New York).

Kegley, C.W. and Wittkopf, E.R. (1989), *World Politics: Trend and Transformation*, third edition (St Martin's Press, New York).

Kelsen, H. (1967), *Principles of International Law* (revised and edited R.W. Tucker) (Rhinehart and Winston, New York).

Kennan, G.F. (1954a), *Realities of American Foreign Policy* (Princeton University Press, Princeton).

Kennan, G.F. (1954b), *American Diplomacy, 1900–1950* (New American Library, New York).

Kennan, G.F. (1984), *American Diplomacy*, expanded ed (University of Chicago Press, Chicago).

Keohane, R.O. (1984), *After Hegemony* (Princeton University Press, Princeton).

Keohane, R.O. (ed.) (1986), *Neorealism and Its Critics* (Columbia University Press, New York).

Keohane, R.O. and Nye, J.S. (eds) (1972), *Transnational Relations and World Politics* (Harvard University Press, Cambridge MA).

Keohane, R.O. and Nye, J.S. (1977), *Power and Interdependence: World Politics in Transition* (Little, Brown, Boston).

Keohane, R.O. and Nye, J.E. (1981), 'Realism and Complex Interdependence', in Smith, M., Little, R and Shackleton, M. (eds), *Perspectives on World Politics* (Croom Helm, London).

Keohane, R.O. and Nye, J.S. (1987), 'Power and Interdependence Revisited', *International Organization*, **41** (4), pp. 725–53.

Keylor, W.R. (1984), *The Twentieth Century World* (Oxford University Press, London).

Keynes, J.M. (1919), *The Economic Consequences of the Peace* (Macmillan, London).

Kindleberger, C.P. (1973), *The World in Depression 1929–1939* (University of California Press, Berkeley).

Kissinger H.A. (1957), *A World Restored: The Politics of Conservatism in a Revolutionary Era* (Houghton Mifflin, Boston).

Kissinger, H.A. (1960), *The Necessity for Choice: Prospects of American Foreign Policy* (Chatto & Windus, London).

Kissinger, H.A. (1969), *Nuclear Weapons and Foreign Policy* (Norton, New York).

Kissinger, H.A. (1974), *American Foreign Policy* (Norton, New York).

Kissinger, H.A. (1979), *The White House Years* (Little, Brown, Boston).

Knorr, K. (1973), *Power and Wealth: The Political Economy of International Power* (Basic Books, New York).

Knorr, K. (1975), *The Power of Nations: The Political Economy of International Relations* (Basic Books, New York).

Knorr, K. and Rosenau, J.N. (eds) (1969), *Contending Approaches to International Politics* (Princeton University Press, Princeton).

Knorr, K. and Verba, S. (eds) (1961), *The International System* (Princeton University Press, Princeton).

Krasner, S.D. (1976), 'State power and the structure of international trade', *World Politics*, **28** (3) (April), pp. 317–43.

Krasner, S.D. (1983), *International Regimes* (Cornell University Press, Ithaca, New York).

Kubalkova, V. and Cruickshank, A.A. (1980), *Marxism – Leninism and Theory of International Relations* (Routledge & Kegan Paul, London).

Kubalkova, V. and Cruickshank, A.A. (1986), *Marxism and International Relations* (Oxford University Press, Oxford).

Kuhn, T. (1962), *The Structure of Scientific Revolutions* (University of Chicago Press, Chicago).

Langhorne, R. (1986), 'The Significance of the Congress of Vienna', *Review of International Studies*, **12** (4) (October).

Lacqueur, W. (1977), *Terrorism* (Weidenfeld & Nicolson, London).

Lacqueur, W. (1986), 'Reflections on Terrorism', *Foreign Affairs*, **65** (Fall).

Lapping, B. (1987), *Apartheid: A History* (Paladin, London).

Lasswell, H.D. (1948), *The Analysis of Political Behaviour: An Empirical Approach* (Routledge and Kegan Paul, London).

Lasswell, H.D. and Kaplan, A. (1950), *Power and Society: A Framework for Political Enquiry* (Yale University Press, New Haven).

Lauterpacht, H. (1933), *The Function of Law in the International Community* (Clarendon Press, Oxford).

Lauterpacht, H. (1950), *International Law and Human Rights* (Stevens, London).

Lawrence, T.E. (1935), *Seven Pillars of Wisdom: a triumph* (Cape, London).

Lebow, R.N. (1981), *Between Peace and War* (Johns Hopkins University Press, Baltimore).

Lenin, V.I. (1970), *Imperialism. The Highest Stage of Capitalism (1916)* (Foreign Languages Press, Peking).

Levy, J. (1983), 'Misperception and the Causes of War', *World Politics*, **35** (October).

Lichtheim, G. (1971), *Imperialism* (Praeger, New York).

Light, M. and Groom, A.J.R. (eds) (1985), *International Relations: A Handbook of Current Theory* (Pinter, London).

Lindblom, C.E. (1965), *The Intelligence of Democracy* (Free Press, New York).

Lindblom, C.E. (1977), *Politics & Markets* (Basic Books, New York).

Linklater, A. (1986), 'Realism, Marxism and Critical International Theory', *Review of International Studies*, **12** (4) (October).

Liska, G. (1967), *Imperial America: The International Politics of Primacy* (Johns Hopkins Press, Baltimore).

Little, R. (1975), *Intervention: External Involvement in Civil Wars* (Robertson, London).

Little R. (1987), 'Revisiting Intervention: A Survey of Recent Developments', *Review of International Studies*, **13** (1) (January).

Lorenz, K. (1963), *On Aggression* (Harcourt, Brace and World, New York).

Louis, W.R. and Bull, H. (eds) (1986), *The Special Relationship: Anglo–American Relations Since 1945* (Clarendon Press, Oxford).

Luard, E. (1982), *A History of the United Nations* (Macmillan, London).

Lyon, P, (1963), *Neutralism* (Leicester University Press, Leicester).

Machiavelli, N. (1950), *The Prince and the Discourses*, introduction Max Leiner (Modern Library edition, Random House, New York).

Mack, A.J.R. (1975), 'Why Big Nations Lose Small Wars: the Politics of Asymmetric Conflict', *World Politics*, **27** (2), 175–201.

Mackinder, H.J. (1904), 'The Geographical Pivot of History', *Geographical Journal*, **23**.

Mackinder, H.J. (1919), *Democratic Ideals and Reality: A Study in the Politics of Reconstruction* (Constable, London).

Mahan, A.T. (1890), *The Influence of Sea Power upon History: 1660–1783* (Boston).

Malthus, T.R. (1826), *An Essay in the Principles of Population, or a view of its past and present effects on human happiness, with an enquiry into our prospecting the future removal or mitigation of the evils which it occasions*, 6th edn (Ward Lock, London).

Mandelbaum, M. (1988), *The Fate of Nations: The Search for National Security in the Nineteenth and Twentieth Centuries* (Cambridge University Press, Cambridge).

Manning, C.A.W. (1962), *The Nature of International Society* (Bell, London).

Mao Tse-Tung (1971), *Selected Readings* (Foreign Languages Press, Peking).

March, J.G. and Simon, H.A. (1958), *Organizations* (Wiley, New York).

Markwell, D.J. (1986), 'Sir Alfred Zimmern revisited: 50 years on', *Review of International Studies*, **12** (1) (October).

Marx, K. and Engels, F. (1968), *Selected Works* (Lawrence and Wishart, London).

Mattingly, G. (1955), *Renaissance Diplomacy* (Cape, London).

Mayall, J. (ed.) (1982), *The Community of States: A Study in International Political Theory* (Allen & Unwin, London).

Mayer, P. (ed.) (1966), *The Pacifist Conscience: An Anthology of Pacifist Writings* (Hart-Davies, London).

Mazrui, A. (1977), *Africa's International Relations: The Diplomacy of Dependency and Change* (Heinemann, London).

McClelland, C. (1966), *Theory and the International System* (Macmillan, New York).

McKinlay, R.D. and Little, R. (1986), *Global Problems and World Order* (Frances Pinter, London).

Meadows, D.H., Meadows, D.L., Randers, J. and Behrens, W. III (1974), *The Limits to Growth* (Pan, London).

Medvedev, Z. (1986), *Gorbachev* (Blackwell, Oxford).

Meinecke, F. (1957), *Machiavellism: The Doctrine of Raison d'Etat and Its Place in Modern History* (tr. D. Scott) (New Haven, Conn.).

Melanson, R.A. (1983), *Writing History and Making Policy: The Cold War, Vietnam and Revisionism* (University Press of America, Lanham).

Melman, S. (1985), *The Permanent War Economy* (Simon & Schuster, New York).

Merle, M. (1987), *The Sociology of International Relations* (tr. D. Parkin) (Berg, Leamington Spa).

Merton, R.K. (1949), 'The Self-Fulfilling Prophecy', in *Social Theory and Social Structure* (Free Press, New York, 1957).

Miller, J.D.B. (1981), *The World of States* (Croom Helm, London).

Miller, J.D.B. (1986), 'Sovereignty as a Source of Vitality for the State', *Review of International Studies*, **12** (2) (April).

Mills, C.W. (1956), *The Power Elite* (Oxford University Press, New York).

Mitchell, C. (1981), *The Structure of International Conflict* (Macmillan, London).

Mitrany, D. (1943), *A Working Peace System* (RIIA, London).

Mitrany, D. (1975), *The Functional Theory of Politics* (Robertson, London).

Modelski, G. (1972), *Principles of World Politics* (Collier, Macmillan, New York).

Modelski, G. (ed.) (1972), *Multinational Corporations and World Order* (Sage Publications, Beverly Hills).

# BIBLIOGRAPHY

Moore, B. (1967), *Social Origins of Dictatorship and Democracy* (Allen Lane, London).

Morgan, P.M. (1983), *Deterrence: A Conceptual Analysis* (Sage Publications, Beverly Hills).

Morgenthau, H.J. (1948), *Politics Among Nations: The Struggle for Power and Peace* (Knopf, New York).

Morgenthau, H.J. (1951), *In Defence of the National Interest* (Knopf, New York).

Morgenthau, H.J. and Thompson, K.W. (eds) (1950), *Principles and Problems of International Politics* (Knopf, New York).

Myers, D.P. (1957), 'The Names and Scope of Treaties' *American Journal of International Law*, **51**.

Nag, K. (n.d.) 'The Diplomatic Theories of Ancient India and the Arthastra', *Journal of Indian History*, **V**, 331–58.

Nardin, T. (1983), *Law, Morality and the Relations of Nations* (Princeton University Press, Princeton).

Navari, C. (1978), 'Knowledge, the State and the State of Nature', in *The Reason of States*, M. Donelan (ed.).

Nicolson, H. (1950), *Diplomacy* (Oxford University Press, London).

Nicolson, H. (1954), *The Evolution of Diplomatic Method* (Constable, London).

Niebuhr, R. (1936), *Moral Man and Immoral Society* (Scribners, New York).

Niebuhr, R. (1953), *Christian Realism and Political Problems* (Scribners, New York).

Niebuhr, R. (1959), *Nations and Empires* (Faber & Faber, London).

Nixon, R. (1976), 'Asia after Vietnam', *Foreign Affairs*, **46** (1).

Nkrumah, K. (1965), *Neocolonialism: The Last Stage of Capitalism* (Heinemann, London).

Nogee, J.L. (1975), 'Polarity: An Ambiguous Concept', *ORBIS*, **18** (4) (Winter), pp. 1193–225.

Northedge, F.S. (1976), *The International Political System* (Faber & Faber, London).

Northedge, F.S. (1976), 'Transnationalism: The American Illusion', *Millenium*, **5** (1) (Spring).

Northedge, F.S. (1986), *The League of Nations: Its Life and Times, 1920–46* (Leicester University Press, Leicester).

Nussbaum, A. (1961), *A Concise History of the Law of Nations* (Macmillan, New York).

Nye, J.S. (1986), *Nuclear Ethics* (Collier Macmillan, London).

O'Connell, D.P. (1970), *International Law* (2 volumes), second edition (Stevens, London).

O'Connell, D.P. (1975), 'The Law of the Sea: Some Reflections on Caracas', *British Journal of International Studies*, **1** (1) (April).

Osgood, C. (1962), *An Alternative to War or Surrender* (University of Illinois Press, Urbana).

Osgood, R.E. (1953), *Ideals and Self-Interest in America's Foreign Relations* (Chicago University Press, Chicago).

Osgood, R.E. and Tucker, R.W. (1967), *Force, Order and Justice* (Johns Hopkins Press, Baltimore).

Osmanczyk, E.J. (1985), *The Encyclopedia of the United Nations and International Agreements* (Taylor and Francis, Philadelphia).

Paige, G. (1968), *The Korean Decision* (Free Press, New York).

Paige, G. (1977), *The Scientific Study of Political Leadership* (Free Press, New York).

Parkinson, F. (1977), *The Philosophy of International Relations* (Sage Publications, Beverly Hills).

Penn, W. (1694), *An Essay Toward the Present and Future Peace of Europe* (American Peace Society, Washington DC, 1912).

Penrose, E. (1976), 'Oil and International Relations', *British Journal of International Studies* **2** (1) (April).

Pentland, C. (1973), *International Theory and European Integration* (Faber & Faber, London).

Pepper, D. and Jenkins, A. (1985), *The Geography of Peace and War* (Blackwell, Oxford).

Perkins, D. (1955), *A History of the Monroe Doctrine* (Boston, Toronto).

Pettman, R. (1979), *State and Class: A Sociology of International Affairs* (Croom Helm, London).

Pettman, R. (ed.) (1979), *Moral Claims in World Affairs* (Croom Helm, London).

Plano, J.C. and Olton, R. (1982), *The International Relations Dictionary* (third edition) (ABC-Clio, Santa Barbara).

Plischke, E. (1977), *Microstates in World Affairs: Policy Problems and Options* (AEI, Washington DC).

Poznanski, K.Z. (1984), 'Technology Transfer: West–South Perspective', *World Politics*, **37** (1) (October).

Prebisch, R. (1964), *Towards a New Trade Policy for Development*. Report by the Secretary-General of UNCTAD (UN, New York).

Prins, G. (ed.) (1983), *Defended to Death* (Penguin Books, London).

Pruit, D.G. (1966), 'Definition of the Situation as a Determinant of International Action', in H.C. Kelman (ed.), *International Behaviour* (Holt, Rinehart Winston, New York).

Puchala, D. (1972), 'Of Blind Men, Elephants and International Integration', *Journal of Common Market Studies*, **10**.

Purnell, R. (1973), *The Society of States: An Introduction to International Politics* (Weidenfeld & Nicolson, London).

Purnell, R. (1976), 'The Relevance of Ancient History to the Contemporary Study of International Politics'. *British Journal of International Studies* **2** (1) (April).

Ricardo, D. (1817), *Principles of Political Economy and Taxation*, reprinted in *The Works & Correspondence of David Ricardo*, Volume 1, P. Sraffa (ed.) (Cambridge University Press, Cambridge, 1970).

Rapoport, A. (1960), *Fights, Games and Debates* (Michigan University Press, Michigan).

Rapoport, A. (1964), *Strategy and Conscience* (Harper and Row, New York).

Rapoport, A. (1974), *Conflict in Man Made Environment* (Penguin, Harmondsworth).

Reynolds, C. (1973), *Theory and Explanation in International Politics* (Robertson, London).

Reynolds, C. (1981), *Modes of Imperialism* (Robertson, London).

Reynolds, P.A. (1971), An Introduction to International Relations (Longman, Harlow).

Reynolds, P.A. (1975), 'The Balance of Power. New Wine in an Old Bottle', *Political Studies*, **xxiii** (2) and (3) (June/September).

Roberts, A. (1976), *Nations in Arms: The Theory and Practice of Territorial Defence* (Chatto & Windus, London).

Roberts, A. and Guelff, R. (eds) (1982), *Documents on the Laws of War* (Clarendon Press, Oxford).

Robinson, D. (1985), *Dictionary of Politics* (Penguin, Harmondsworth).

Rosecrance, R.N. (1963), *Action and Reaction in World Politics* (Little, Brown, Boston).

Rosecrance, R.N. (1973), *International Relations: Peace or War?* (McGraw Hill, New York).

Rosenau, J.N. (1961), *International Politics and Foreign Policy: A Reader in Research and Theory* (The Free Press, New York).

Rosenau, J.N. (1961a), *Public Opinion and Foreign Policy* (Random House, New York).

Rosenau, J.N. (ed.) (1964), *International Aspects of Civil Strife* (Princeton University Press, Princeton).

Rosenau, J.N. (1966), 'Pre-theories and Theories of Foreign Policy' in *Approaches to Comparative and International Politics*, R. Barry Farrell (ed.) (Northwestern University Press, Evanston).

Rosenau, J.N. (1967a), 'Foreign Policy as an Issue Area', in *Domestic Sources of Foreign Policy* (The Free Press, New York).

Rosenau, J.N. (ed.) (1967b), *Domestic Sources of Foreign Policy* (The Free Press, New York).

# BIBLIOGRAPHY

Rosenau, J.N. (1968), 'The concept of intervention', *Journal of International Affairs*, **22** (2), pp. 165–77.

Rosenau, J.N. (ed.) (1969), *International Politics and Foreign Policy* (The Free Press, New York).

Rosenau, J.N. (1969a), 'Intervention as a scientific concept', *Journal of Conflict Resolution*, **13** (2), pp. 149–71.

Rosenau, J.N. (1969b), *Linkage Politics* (Free Press, New York).

Rosenau, J.N. (1971), *A Scientific Study of Foreign Policy* (The Free Press, New York).

Rosenau, J.N. (1980), *The Study of Global Interdependence* (Frances Pinter, London).

Rothstein, R.L. (1972), 'On the Costs of Realism', *Political Science Quarterly*, **83** (September).

Rummel, R.J. (1972), *The Dimensions of Nations* (Sage, Beverly Hills).

Russell, F.M. (1936), *Theories of International Relations* (Appleton Century Crofts, New York).

Said, A.A. and Simmons, L.R. (eds) (1975), *The New Sovereigns* (Prentice Hall, Englewood Cliffs, NJ).

Satow, E. (1957), A Guide to Diplomatic Practice (Longmans, London).

Schelling, T.C. (1960), *The Strategy of Conflict* (Harvard University Press, Cambridge).

Schelling, T.C. (1966), *Arms and Influence* (Yale University Press, New Haven).

Schelling, T.C. and Halperin, M.H. (1985), *Strategy and Arms Control* (Pergamon-Brassey Classic Reprint).

Schlesinger, A. (1967), *A Thousand Days: John F. Kennedy in the White House* (Mayflower Dell, London).

Schmid, A.P. (1983), *Political Terrorism: A Research Guide to Concepts, Theories, Data Bases and Literature* (North Holland Publishing Company, Amsterdam).

Schuman, F.L. (1933), *International Politics: Anarchy and Order in World Society* (McGraw Hill, New York, 1969 edition).

Schumpeter, J.A. (1951), 'Imperialism and Capitalism', in Sweezy, P.M. (ed.), *Imperialism and Social Classes* (Blackwell, Oxford).

Schwarzenberger, G. (1941), *Power Politics* (Stevens, London).

Scott, A. (1965), *The Revolution in Statecraft* (Random House, New York).

Scruton, R. (1982), *A Dictionary of Political Thought* (Macmillan, London).

Seabury, P. (1963), *Power, Freedom and Diplomacy* (Random House, New York).

Segal, G. (1988), *Guide to the World Today* (Simon & Schuster, London).

Shaw, M.N. (1977), *International Law* (Hodder & Stoughton, London).

Sills, D. (ed.) (1960), *International Encyclopedia of the Social Sciences* (Macmillan and Free Press, New York).

Simon, H.A. (1965), *Administrative Behaviour* (Free Press, New York).

Singer, J.D. (1969), 'The Level of Analysis Problem in International Relations', in J.N. Rosenau (ed.), *International Politics and Foreign Policy* (Free Press, New York).

SIPRI (annual) *Yearbook of World Armaments and Disarmament* (Almqvist & Wiksell, Stockholm).

Skocpol, T. (1979) *States and Revolutions: A Comparative Analysis of France, Russia and China* (Cambridge University Press, Cambridge).

Small, M. and Singer, J.D. (1966), 'The Diplomatic Importance of States, 1816–1940', *World Politics* **xviii** (January).

Smith, A. (1776), *An Inquiry into the Nature and Causes of the Wealth of Nations* (London, Dent, Everyman edition, 1977).

Smith, B.L.R. (1966), *The Rand Corporation* (Harvard University Press, Cambridge, MA).

Smith, M., Little, R. and Shackleton, M. (1981), *Perspectives on World Politics: A Reader* (Croom Helm, London).

Smith, M.J. (1986), *Realist Thought from Weber to Kissinger* (Louisiana State University Press, Baton Rouge).

Snyder, G.H. (1961), *Deterrence and Defense* (Princeton University Press, Princeton, NJ).

Snyder, G.H. (1984), 'The Security Dilemma in Alliance Politics', *World Politics*. **36** (4) (July).

Snyder, G.H. and Diesing, P. (1977), *Conflict Among Nations: Bargaining, Decision Making and System Structure in International Crises* (Princeton University Press, Princeton).

Snyder, R.C., Bruck, H.W. and Sapin, B. (eds) (1962), *Foreign Policy Decision-Making: An Approach to the Study of International Politics* (Free Press, New York).

Spence, J.E. (1988), *The Soviet Union, The Third World and Southern Africa*, South African Institute of International Affairs, Bradlow Series, no. 5. (November).

Spero, J.E. (1985), *The Politics of International Economic Relations*, (third edition) (St Martin's Press, New York).

Spiegel, S.L. (1972), *Dominance and Diversity: The International Hierarchy* (Little, Brown, Boston).

Spykman, N.J. (1938), 'Geography and Foreign Policy', *American Political Science Review*, **32**, pp. 28–50.

Spykman, N.J. (1942), *America's Strategy in World Politics* (Harcourt Brace, New York).

Sprout, H. (1963), 'Geopolitical Hypotheses in Technological Perspective', *World Politics*, **15**.

Sprout, H. and Sprout, M. (1956), *Man–Milieu Relationship in the Context of International Politics* (Princeton University Press, Princeton, NJ).

Sprout, H. and Sprout, M. (1957), 'Environmental Factors in the Study of International Politics', *Journal of Conflict Resolution*, **1**, pp. 309–28.

Sprout, H. and Sprout, M. (1965), *The Ecological Perspective on Human Affairs: with special reference to International Politics* (Princeton University Press, Princeton, NJ).

Sprout, H. and Sprout, M. (1971), *Towards A Politics of the Planet Earth* (Van Nostrand Reinhold, New York).

Sprout, H. and Sprout M. (1972), *The Politics of the Planet Earth* (Van Nostrand, New York).

Stagner, R. (1965), 'The psychology of human conflict' in E. McNeil (ed.), *The Nature of Human Conflict* (Prentice Hall, Englewood Cliffs, NJ).

Sterling, R.W. (1958), *Ethics in World of Power: The Political Ideas of Friedrich Meinecke* (Princeton University Press, Princeton).

Stoessinger, J.G. (1985), *Crusaders and Pragmatists of Modern American Foreign Policy* (New York, Norton).

Strange, S. (1976), 'The Study of Transnational Relations', *International Affairs*, **52** (2) (July).

Strange, S. (1988), *States and Markets* (Frances Pinter, London).

Suganami, H. (1978), 'A Note on the Origin of the Word "International" ', *British Journal of International Studies*, **4** (3) (October).

Suganami, H. (1986), 'Reflections on the Domestic Analogy: The Case of Bull, Beitz and Linklater', *Review of International Studies*, **12** (2) (April).

Tanter, R. and Stein J. (1980), *Rational Decision Making* (Ohio State University Press, Columbia).

Taylor, A.J.P. (1979), *How Wars Begin* (Hamilton, London).

Taylor, P. and Groom, A.J.R. (eds) (1978), *International Organisation: A Conceptual Approach* (Pinter, London).

Taylor, P.J. (1985), *Political Geography: World-Economy, Nation-State and Locality* (Longman, London).

Taylor, T. (ed.) (1978), *Approaches and Theory in International Relations* (Longman, London).

Thee, M. (ed.) (1986), *Arms and Disarmament: SIPRI Findings* (Oxford University Press, Oxford).

# BIBLIOGRAPHY

Thomas, W.I. and Znanieki, F. (1958), *The Polish Peasant in Europe and America*, Vol. I (Dover Publications, New York).

Thompson, K.W. (1960), *Political Realism and the Crisis of World Politics* (Princeton University Press, Princeton).

Thompson, K.W. (1977), 'Idealism and Realism: Beyond the Great Debate', *British Journal of International Studies*, 3 (2) (July).

Thucydides (1959), *The Peloponnesian War* (tr. R. Warner) (Penguin, Harmondsworth).

Tocqueville, A. de (1955), *Democracy in America* (tr. H. Reeve) (Oxford University Press, New York).

Tucker, R.W. (1977), *The Inequality of Nations* (Robertson, London).

Tucker, R.W. (1988/89), 'Reagan's Foreign Policy', *Foreign Affairs*, 68 (1).

Vasquez, J.A. (1983), *The Power of Power Politics: A Critique* (Pinter, London).

Vattel, E. de (1758), *The Law of Nations* (Carnegie Institute, Washington, 1916).

Vincent, R.J. (1974), *Nonintervention and International Order* (Princeton University Press, Princeton).

Vincent, R.J. (1978), 'Western Conceptions of a Universal Moral Order', *British Journal of International Studies*, 4 (1) (April).

Vincent, R.J. (1986), *Human Rights and International Relations* (Cambridge University Press, Cambridge).

Vital, D. (1967), *The Inequality of States: A Study of the Small Power in International Relations* (Clarendon Press, Oxford).

Wallace, W. (1971), *Foreign Policy and the Political Process* (Macmillan, London).

Wallerstein, I. (1974), *The Modern World System. Capitalist Agriculture and the Origins of the European World-Economy in the Sixteenth Century* (Academic Press, New York).

Wallerstein, I. (1979), *The Capitalist World Economy* (Cambridge University Press, Cambridge).

Waltz, K.N. (1959), *Man, The State and War* (Columbia University Press, New York).

Waltz, K.N. (1964), 'The Stability of a Bipolar World', *Daedelus* (Summer).

Waltz, K.N. (1979), *Theory of International Politics* (Addison-Wesley, Reading, MA).

Waltz, K. (1981), *The Spread of Nuclear Weapons: More May be Better*. Adelphi Paper No. 171 (International Institute for Strategic Studies, London).

Walzer, M. (1978), *Just and Unjust Wars* (Allen Lane, London).

Waste, R. (ed.) (1986), *Community Power* (Sage, Beverly Hills).

Watson, A. (1982), *Diplomacy: The Dialogue Between States* (Methuen, London).

Weber, M. (1947), *The Theory of Social and Economic Organisation*, tr. A.M. Henderson and Talcott Parsons (Oxford University Press, New York).

Whaley, B. (1973), *Codeword BARBAROSSA* (MIT, Cambridge, MA).

Wight, M. (1966), 'Western Values in International Relations', in H. Butterfield and M. Wight (eds) *Diplomatic Investigations: Essays in the Theory of International Politics* (Allen & Unwin, London).

Wight, M. (1977), *Systems of States*, Hedley Bull (ed.) (Leicester University Press, Leicester).

Wight, M. (1978), *Power Politics*, Hedley Bull and Carsten Holbraad (eds) (Leicester University Press, Leicester).

Wilkinson, P. (1974), *Political Terrorism* (Macmillan, London).

Wilkinson, P. (1986), *Terrorism and the Liberal State* (second edition) (Macmillan, London).

Willets, P. (1979), *The Non-Aligned Movement* (Nichols, New York).

Williams, P. (1976), *Crisis Management: Confrontation and Diplomacy in the Nuclear Age* (Wiley, New York).

Windsor, P. (1971), *Germany and the Management of Detente* (Chatto & Windus, London).

Wohlstetter, R. (1962), *Pearl Harbor: Warning and Decision* (Stanford University Press, Stanford).

Wolf, E. (1971), *Peasant Wars of the Twentieth Century* (Faber, London).

Wolfers, A. (1949), 'Statesmanship and Moral Choice', *World Politics*, 1, pp. 175–95.

Wolfers, A. (1962), *Discord and Collaboration* (John Hopkins University Press, Baltimore).

Wolfers, A. and Martin, L. (1956), *The Anglo–American Tradition in Foreign Affairs* (Yale, New Haven).

Wolff, C.F. von (1749), *Jus Gentium Methodo Scientifica Pertractatum*.

Worsley, P. (1964), *The Third World* (Weidenfeld & Nicolson, London).

Wright, Q. (1955), *The Study of International Relations* (Appleton Century Crofts, New York).

Wright, Q. (1964), *A Study of War* (Chicago University Press, Chicago, originally published 1942).

'X' (Kennan, G.F.) (1947), 'The Sources of Soviet Conduct', *Foreign Affairs*, 25 (July).

Yalem, R.J. (1972), 'Tripolarity and the International System', *Orbis*, 15 (Winter).

*Yearbook of International Organisations* (annual) (Union of International Associations, Brussels).

Young, O.R. (1967), *Systems of Political Science* (Prentice Hall, Englewood Cliffs).

Young, O.R. (1972) 'The actors in world politics' in J.N. Rosenau, V. Davis and M. East (eds), *The Analysis of International Politics* (Free Press, New York).

Young, O.R. (1986), 'International Regimes: Toward a New Theory of Institutions', *World Politics*, 39 (1) (October).

Zimmern, A. (1939), *The Prospects of Civilization* (Oxford University Press, London).

Zimmern, A. (1945), *The League of Nations and the Rule of Law, 1918–1935* (Macmillan, London).